PROFESSIONAL WEBSITE PEF

MW00710125

INTRODUCTION xxiii

▶ **PART I** **FRONT END**

CHAPTER 1 A Refresher on Web Browsers. 3

CHAPTER 2 Utilizing Client-Side Caching 23

CHAPTER 3 Content Compression. 39

CHAPTER 4 Keeping the Size Down with Minification 53

CHAPTER 5 Optimizing Web Graphics and CSS 71

CHAPTER 6 JavaScript, the Document Object Model, and Ajax. 111

▶ **PART II** **BACK END**

CHAPTER 7 Working with Web Servers. 141

CHAPTER 8 Tuning MySQL 193

CHAPTER 9 MySQL in the Network 255

CHAPTER 10 Utilizing NoSQL Solutions. 309

CHAPTER 11 Working with Secure Sockets Layer (SSL). 359

CHAPTER 12 Optimizing PHP. 375

▶ **PART III** **APPENDIXES**

APPENDIX A TCP Performance. 405

APPENDIX B Designing for Mobile Platforms. 409

APPENDIX C Compression. 417

INDEX. 427

PROFESSIONAL

Website Performance

OPTIMIZING THE FRONT END AND THE BACK END

Peter Smith

WILEY

John Wiley & Sons, Inc.

Professional Website Performance: Optimizing the Front End and the Back End

Published by
John Wiley & Sons, Inc.
10475 Crosspoint Boulevard
Indianapolis, IN 46256
www.wiley.com

Copyright © 2013 by John Wiley & Sons, Inc., Indianapolis, Indiana

Published simultaneously in Canada

ISBN: 978-1-118-48752-5
ISBN: 978-1-118-48751-8 (ebk)
ISBN: 978-1-118-55172-1 (ebk)
ISBN: 978-1-118-55171-4 (ebk)

Manufactured in the United States of America

10 9 8 7 6 5 4 3 2 1

For general information on our other products and services please contact our Customer Care Department within the United States at (877) 762-2974, outside the United States at (317) 572-3993 or fax (317) 572-4002.

Wiley publishes in a variety of print and electronic formats and by print-on-demand. Some material included with standard print versions of this book may not be included in e-books or in print-on-demand. If this book refers to media such as a CD or DVD that is not included in the version you purchased, you may download this material at http://booksupport .wiley.com. For more information about Wiley products, visit www.wiley.com.

Library of Congress Control Number: 2012949514

To my wife, Stef, and my parents

ABOUT THE AUTHOR

PETER G. SMITH has been a full-time Linux consultant, web developer, and system administrator, with a particular interest in performance for the past 13 years. Over the years, he has helped a wide range of clients in areas such as front-end performance, load balancing and scalability, and database optimization. Past open source projects include modules for Apache and OSCommerce, a cross-platform IRC client, and contributions to The Linux Documentation Project (TLDP).

ABOUT THE TECHNICAL EDITOR

JOHN PELOQUIN is a software engineer with back-end and front-end experience ranging across web applications of all sizes. Peloquin earned his B.A. in Mathematics from the University of California at Berkeley, and is currently a lead engineer for a healthcare technology startup, where he makes heavy use of MySQL, PHP, and JavaScript. He has edited *Professional JavaScript for Web Developers, 3rd Edition* by Nicholas Zakas (Indianapolis: Wiley, 2012) and *JavaScript 24-Hour Trainer* by Jeremy McPeak (Indianapolis: Wiley, 2010). When he is not coding or collecting errata, Peloquin is often found engaged in mathematics, philosophy, or juggling.

CREDITS

EXECUTIVE EDITOR
Carol Long

PROJECT EDITOR
Kevin Shafer

TECHNICAL EDITOR
John Peloquin

PRODUCTION EDITOR
Rosanna Volis

COPY EDITOR
San Dee Phillips

EDITORIAL MANAGER
Mary Beth Wakefield

FREELANCER EDITORIAL MANAGER
Rosemarie Graham

ASSOCIATE DIRECTOR OF MARKETING
David Mayhew

MARKETING MANAGER
Ashley Zurcher

BUSINESS MANAGER
Amy Knies

PRODUCTION MANAGER
Tim Tate

VICE PRESIDENT AND EXECUTIVE GROUP PUBLISHER
Richard Swadley

VICE PRESIDENT AND EXECUTIVE PUBLISHER
Neil Edde

ASSOCIATE PUBLISHER
Jim Minatel

PROJECT COORDINATOR, COVER
Katie Crocker

PROOFREADER
Nancy Carrasco

INDEXER
Robert Swanson

COVER DESIGNER
Ryan Sneed

COVER IMAGE
© Henry Price / iStockphoto

ACKNOWLEDGMENTS

A LOT OF PEOPLE HAVE BEEN INVOLVED in making this book happen. I'd like to thank everyone at Wiley for their hard work, especially Carol Long for having faith in my original idea and helping me to develop it, and Kevin Shafer, my Project Editor, who patiently helped turn my manuscript into a well-rounded book. Special thanks are also due to John Peloquin, whose technical review proved invaluable.

I'd also like to take the opportunity to thank my friends and family for being so supportive over the past few months.

CONTENTS

INTRODUCTION   *xxiii*

PART I: FRONT END

CHAPTER 1: A REFRESHER ON WEB BROWSERS   3

A Brief History of Web Browsers   3
  Netscape Loses Its Dominance   4
  The Growth of Firefox   4
  The Present   5
Inside HTTP   5
  The HyperText Transfer Protocol   5
  HTTP Versions   8
  Support for Virtual Hosting   9
  Caching   9
How Browsers Download and Render Content   10
  Rendering   11
  Persistent Connections and Keep-Alive   12
  Parallel Downloading   14
Summary   21

CHAPTER 2: UTILIZING CLIENT-SIDE CACHING   23

Understanding the Types of Caching   23
  Caching by Browsers   23
  Intermediate Caches   24
  Reverse Proxies   25
Controlling Caching   25
  Conditional GETs   25
  Utilizing Cache-Control and Expires Headers   28
  Choosing Expiration Policies   30
  Coping with Stale Content   30
  How Not to Cache   31
Dealing with Intermediate Caches   31
  Cache-Control Revisited   31
Caching HTTP Responses   32
  The Shift in Browser Behavior   32
  Using Alternative 3xx Codes   34

DNS Caching and Prefetching   **34**

The DNS Resolution Process   35

DNS Caching by the Browser   35

How DNS Lookups Affect Performance   36

DNS Prefetching   36

Controlling Prefetching   37

Summary   **37**

CHAPTER 3: CONTENT COMPRESSION   **39**

Who Uses Compression   **39**

Understanding How Compression Works   **41**

Compression Methods   42

Other Compression Methods   47

Transfer Encoding   48

Compression in PHP   **49**

Compressing PHP-Generated Pages   49

Compressing Other Resources   51

Summary   **51**

CHAPTER 4: KEEPING THE SIZE DOWN WITH MINIFICATION   **53**

JavaScript Minification   **54**

YUI Compressor   55

Google Closure   56

Comparison of JavaScript Minifiers   58

CSS Minification   **59**

Use Shorthand   59

Grouping Selectors   60

CSS Minifiers   60

Improving Compression   62

HTML Minification   **63**

HTML Minification Techniques   64

HTML Minification Tools   66

Summary   **69**

CHAPTER 5: OPTIMIZING WEB GRAPHICS AND CSS   **71**

Understanding Image Formats   **71**

JPEG   72

GIF   72

PNG   73

SVG   73

Optimizing Images	**74**
Image Editing Software	74
Choosing the Right Format	74
Interlacing and Progressive Rendering	75
PNG Optimization	77
GIF Optimization	80
JPEG Compression	80
Image Optimization Software	84
Data URIs	85
Favicons	85
Using Lazy Loading	87
Avoiding Empty src attributes	88
Using Image Maps	89
CSS Sprites	**91**
Sprite Strategies	94
Repeating Images	94
CSS Performance	**99**
CSS in the Document Head	100
Inline versus External	100
Link versus @import	100
Redundant Selectors	100
CSS Expressions	101
Selector Performance	102
Using Shorthand Properties	102
Inheritance and Default Values	104
Doing More with CSS	104
Looking Forward	**109**
MNG	109
APNG	109
JPEG 2000	110
Summary	**110**
CHAPTER 6: JAVASCRIPT, THE DOCUMENT OBJECT MODEL, AND AJAX	**111**
JavaScript, JScript, and ECMAScript	**112**
A Brief History of JavaScript	112
JavaScript Engines	112
The Document Object Model	**115**
Manipulating the DOM	117
Reflowing and Repainting	117
Browser Queuing	119

Event Delegation 119

Unobtrusive JavaScript 120

Memory Management 121

Getting the Most from JavaScript **122**

Language Constructs 122

Loading JavaScript 127

Nonblocking of JavaScript Downloads 128

Merging, Splitting, and Inlining 130

Web Workers 134

Ajax **136**

XMLHttpRequest 136

Using Ajax for Nonblocking of JavaScript 137

Server Responsiveness 137

Using Preemptive Loading 138

Ajax Frameworks 138

Summary **138**

PART II: BACK END

CHAPTER 7: WORKING WITH WEB SERVERS **141**

Apache **141**

Working with Modules 142

Deciding on Concurrency 145

Improving Logging 146

Miscellaneous Performance Considerations 148

Examining Caching Options 150

Using Content Compression 155

Looking Beyond Apache **158**

Nginx 158

Nginx, Apache, and PHP 164

The Best of the Rest 168

Multiserver Setups with Nginx and Apache **169**

Nginx as a Reverse Proxy to Apache 170

Proxy Options 171

Nginx and Apache Side by Side 172

Load Balancers **173**

Hardware versus Software 173

Load Balancer Features 174

Using Multiple Back-End Servers 176

HAProxy 181

Summary **191**

CHAPTER 8: TUNING MYSQL 193

Looking Inside MySQL	**194**
Understanding the Storage Engines	**195**
MyISAM	195
InnoDB	196
MEMORY	197
ARCHIVE	198
Tuning MySQL	**198**
Table Cache	198
Thread Caching	202
Per-Session Buffers	204
Tuning MyISAM	**205**
Key Cache	205
Miscellaneous Tuning Options	210
Tuning InnoDB	**211**
Monitoring InnoDB	211
Working with Buffers and Caches	212
Working with File Formats and Structures	217
Memory Allocation	218
Threading	219
Disk I/O	219
Mutexes	222
Compression	223
Working with the Query Cache	**225**
Understanding How the Query Cache Works	225
Configuring the Query Cache	227
Inspecting the Cache	228
The Downsides of Query Caching	232
Optimizing SQL	**234**
EXPLAIN Explained	234
The Slow Query Log	237
Indexing	239
Query Execution and Optimization	247
Query Cost	248
Tips for SQL Efficiency	249
Summary	**254**

CHAPTER 9: MYSQL IN THE NETWORK 255

Using Replication	**256**
The Basics	256

Advanced Topologies   264
Replication Performance   270
Miscellaneous Features of Replication   273
Partitioning   **273**
Creating Partitions   274
Deciding How to Partition   276
Partition Pruning   276
Physical Storage of Partitions   277
Partition Management   278
Pros and Cons of Partitioning   278
Sharding   **279**
Lookup Tables   280
Fixed Sharding   281
Shard Sizes and Distribution   281
Sharding Keys and Accessibility   281
Cross-Shard Joins   282
Application Modifications   283
Complementing MySQL   **283**
MySQL Proxy   283
MySQL Tools   286
Alternatives to MySQL   **294**
MySQL Forks and Branches   294
Full-Text Searching   296
Other RDBMSs   307
Summary   **308**

CHAPTER 10: UTILIZING NOSQL SOLUTIONS   **309**

NoSQL Flavors   **310**
Key-Value Stores   310
Multidimension Stores   310
Document Stores   311
memcache   **311**
Installing and Running   312
membase — memcache with Persistent Storage   321
MongoDB   **325**
Getting to Know MongoDB   325
MongoDB Performance   328
Replication   339
Sharding   343
Other NoSQL Technologies   **353**
Tokyo Cabinet and Tokyo Tyrant   354
CouchDB   354

Project Voldemort   355
Amazon Dynamo and Google BigTable   355
Riak   356
Cassandra   356
Redis   356
HBase   356
Summary   **356**

CHAPTER 11: WORKING WITH SECURE SOCKETS LAYER (SSL)   **359**

SSL Caching   **360**
Connections, Sessions, and Handshakes   360
Abbreviated Handshakes   360
SSL Termination and Endpoints   **364**
SSL Termination with Nginx   365
SSL Termination with Apache   366
SSL Termination with stunnel   367
SSL Termination with stud   368
Sending Intermediate Certificates   **368**
Determining Key Sizes   **369**
Selecting Cipher Suites   **369**
Investing in Hardware Acceleration   **371**
The Future of SSL   **371**
OCSP Stapling   371
False Start   372
Summary   **372**

CHAPTER 12: OPTIMIZING PHP   **375**

Extensions and Compiling   **376**
Removing Unneeded Extensions   376
Writing Your Own PHP Extensions   378
Compiling   379
Opcode Caching   **381**
Variations of Opcode Caches   381
Getting to Know APC   382
Memory Management   382
Optimization   382
Time-To-Live (TTL)   382
Locking   383
Sample apc.ini   384
APC Caching Strategies   384
Monitoring the Cache   386
Using APC as a Generic Cache   386

Warming the Cache   387
Using APC with FastCGI   387
Compiling PHP   **388**
phc   388
Phalanger   388
HipHop   388
Sessions   **389**
Storing Sessions   389
Storing Sessions in memcache/membase   390
Using Shared Memory or tmpfs   390
Session AutoStart   391
Sessions and Caching   391
Efficient PHP Programming   **392**
Minor Optimizations   392
Major Optimizations   392
Garbage Collection   395
Autoloading Classes   396
Persistent MySQL Connections   396
Profiling with xhprof   **398**
Installing   398
A Simple Example   399
Don't Use PHP   401
Summary   **401**

PART III: APPENDIXES

APPENDIX A: TCP PERFORMANCE   **405**

The Three-Way Handshake   **405**
TCP Performance   **408**
Nagle's Algorithm   408
TCP_NOPUSH and TCP_CORK   408

APPENDIX B: DESIGNING FOR MOBILE PLATFORMS   **409**

Understanding Mobile Platforms   **409**
Responsive Content   **410**
Getting Browser Display Capabilities with JavaScript   411
Server-Side Detection of Capabilities   411
A Combined Approach   412
CSS3 Media Queries   413
Determining Connection Speed   413

JavaScript and CSS Compatibility   414
Caching in Mobile Devices   414

APPENDIX C: COMPRESSION   417

The LZW Family   417
   LZ77   417
   LZ78   418
   LZW   419
   LZ Derivatives   420
Huffman Encoding   421
Compression Implementations   424

INDEX   *427*

INTRODUCTION

THE PAST DECADE has seen an increased interest in website performance, with businesses of all sizes realizing that even modest changes in page loading times can have a significant effect on their profits. The move toward a faster web has been driven largely by Yahoo! and Google, which have both carried out extensive research on the subject of website performance, and have worked hard to make web masters aware of the benefits.

This book provides valuable information that you must know about website performance optimization — from database replication and web server load balancing, to JavaScript profiling and the latest features of Cascading Style Sheets 3 (CSS3). You can discover (perhaps surprising) ways in which your website is under-performing, and learn how to scale out your system as the popularity of your site increases.

WHY SPEED IS IMPORTANT

At first glance, it may seem as if website loading speeds aren't terribly important. Of course, it puts off users if they must wait 30 seconds for your page to load. But if loading times are relatively low, isn't that enough? Does shaving off a couple of seconds from loading times actually make that much of a difference? Numerous pieces of research have been carried out on this subject, and the results are quite surprising.

In 2006, Google experimented with reducing the size of its Maps homepage (from 100 KB to 70–80 KB). Within a week, traffic had increased by 10 percent, according to ZDNet (`http://www .zdnet.com/blog/btl/googles-marissa-mayer-speed-wins/3925?p=3925`). Google also found that a half-second increase in loading times for search results had led to a 20 percent drop in sales. That same year, Amazon.com came to similar conclusions, after experiments showed that for each 100-millisecond increase in loading time, sales dropped by 1 percent (`http://ai.stanford .edu/~ronnyk/IEEEComputer2007OnlineExperiments.pdf`).

The fact that there is a correlation between speed and sales perhaps isn't too surprising, but the extent to which even a tiny difference in loading times can have such a noticeable impact on sales certainly is.

But that's not the only worry. Not only do slow websites lose traffic and sales, work at Stanford University suggests that slow websites are also considered less credible (`http://captology .stanford.edu/pdf/p61-fogg.pdf`). It seems that, as Internet connections have become faster, the willingness of users to wait has started to wane. If you want your site to be busy and well liked, it pays to be fast.

If all this weren't enough, there's now yet another reason to ensure that your site runs quickly. In 2010, Google announced that loading times would play a role in how it ranked sites — that is, faster sites will rank higher (`http://googlewebmastercentral.blogspot.com/2010/04/using-site-speed-in-web-search-ranking.html`). However, loading times carry a relatively low weight at the moment, and other factors (relevance, backlinks, and so on) are still much more important.

Hopefully you are now convinced of the need for speed. So, let's take a look at some of the reasons why sites are slow.

Why Sites Are Slow

The most common reason why websites run slowly is that they simply weren't designed with speed in mind. Typically, the first step in the creation of a site is for a graphics designer to create templates based on the ideas of the site owner (who is often not technically minded). The graphic designer's main goal is an attractive looking interface regardless of size, and the nontechnical site owner generally wants lots of bells and whistles, again without appreciating the performance impact.

The next step is for a programmer to make things work behind the scenes, which typically involves a server-side scripting language (such as PHP or Perl) and a back-end database. Sadly, performance is often low on the programmer's agenda, too, especially when his or her boss wants to see visible results fast. It simply isn't worth the programmer's time to compress the bloated graphics created by the designer, or to convert them to sprites.

Another often overlooked fact is that much of the development and testing of a new website will probably be carried out on a development server under low load. A database query that takes a couple of seconds to run may not be a problem when the site has only a couple of users. But when the site goes live, that same query could well slow down the site to a crawl. Tools such as Apache Benchmark can simulate heavy traffic.

There is also the issue of caching. Those involved in the creation and development of a site typically already have primed caches. (That is, images and external JavaScript/CSS used by the site will already be cached in their browsers.) This causes the site to load much faster than it would for first-time visitors.

Other factors affecting the speed of a website are connection speed and computer "power." Developers typically have powerful computers and a good Internet connection, and it's easy to forget that plenty of people (especially in rural locations) still use dial-up modems and computers that are 10 years old. Care must be taken to ensure that such users are accommodated for.

The Compromise between Functionality and Speed

The creation of a website is often a battle between the designers who want looks and functionality, and the programmers who want performance. (Sadly, "battle" tends to be a more apt description than "collaboration.") Inevitably, some compromises must be made. Both sides tend to be guilty of tunnel vision here, but it's worth trying to develop a rounded view of the situation. Although speed is important, it's not the "be all and end all." In your quest for more and more savings, be wary of stripping down your website too much.

Scaling Up versus Scaling Out

There are two basic approaches to scaling your website:

➤ *Scaling up* (sometimes referred to as *scaling vertical*) means keeping the same number of servers but upgrading the server hardware. For example, you may run your whole setup from a single server. As your site gets more traffic, you discover that the server is beginning to struggle, so you throw in another stick of RAM or upgrade the CPU — which is scaling up.

➤ With *scaling out* (also referred to as *scaling horizontally*), you increase the number of machines in your setup. For example, in the previous scenario, you could place your database on its own server, or use a load balancer to split web traffic across two web servers.

So, which method is best? You'll hear a lot of criticism of vertical scaling, but in reality, it is a viable solution for many. The majority of websites do not achieve overnight success. Rather, the user base steadily increases over the years. For these sites, vertical scaling is perfectly fine. Advances in hardware mean that each time you want to upgrade, a machine with more CPU cores, or more memory, or faster disks will be available.

Scaling up isn't without its problems, though. You pay a premium for top-of-the-range hardware. The latest monster server will usually cost more than two mid-range servers with the same overall power. Also, additional CPU cores and RAM don't tend to result in a linear increase in performance. For example, no matter how much RAM you have, access to it is still along a fixed-width bus, which can transfer only at a finite rate. Additional CPU cores aren't a great benefit if your bottleneck is with a single-threaded application. So, scaling up offers diminishing returns, and it also fails to cope when your site goes stratospheric. For that, you need a topology where you can easily add additional mid-range servers to cope with demand.

Scaling out is trickier, because it involves more planning. If you have a pool of web servers, you must think about how sessions are handled, user uploads, and so on. If you split your database over several machines, you must worry about keeping data in sync. Horizontal scaling is the best long-term solution, but it requires more thought as to how to make your setup scalable.

Finally, be wary of taking the idea of horizontal scaling to extremes. Some people take the idea too far, setting up clusters of Pentium I machines because "that's how Google does it." Actually, Google doesn't do this. Although Google scales out to a high degree, it still uses decent hardware on each node.

Scaling out isn't without its drawbacks either. Each additional node means extra hardware to monitor and replace, and time spent installing and deploying code. The most satisfactory arrangement tends to be through a combination of scaling up and scaling out.

The Dangers of Premature Optimization

There's a famous quote by Donald Knuth, author of the legendary *The Art of Computer Programming* (Reading, MA: Addison-Wesley Professional, 2011). "Premature optimization is the root of all evil," he said, and this is often re-quoted in online discussions as a means of dismissing another user's attempts at more marginal optimizations. For example, if one developer is contemplating writing his or her PHP script as a PHP extension in C, the Knuth quote will invariably be used to dispute that idea.

So, what exactly is wrong with premature optimization? The first danger is that it adds complexity to your code, and makes it more difficult to maintain and debug. For example, imagine that you decided to rewrite some of your C code in assembly for optimal performance. It's easy to fall into the trap of not seeing the forest for the trees — you become so focused on the performance of one small aspect of the system that you lose perspective on overall performance. You may be wasting valuable time on relatively unimportant areas — there may be much bigger and easier gains to be made elsewhere.

So, it's generally best to consider optimization only after you already have a good overview of how the whole infrastructure (hardware, operating system, databases, web servers, and so on) will fit together. At that point, you will be in a better position to judge where the greatest gains can be made.

That's not to say you should ignore efficiency when writing your code. The Knuth quote is often misused because it can be difficult to say what constitutes premature optimization, and what is simply good programming practice. For example, if your application will be reading a lot of information from the database, you may decide that you will write some basic caching to wrap around these calls, to cut down on load on the database.

Does this count as premature optimization? It's certainly premature in the sense that you don't even know if these database calls will be a significant bottleneck, and it is adding an extra degree of complexity to your code. But could it not also be classed as simply planning with scalability in mind? Building in this caching from the outset will be quicker (and probably better integrated) than hacking it in at a later date.

If you're tempted to optimize prematurely, stop and consider these two points:

➤ Will there definitely be a benefit — and will it be a significant one?

➤ Will it make the code significantly more difficult to maintain or debug?

If the answers are "yes" and "no," respectively, you should optimize.

Time Is Money

Optimizing is a satisfactory experience — so much so that you may find yourself attempting optimization for the sake of it, rather than because it is needed. That's not necessarily a bad thing. Research has shown that even tiny increases in page loading times can have an impact on revenue and user experience, so optimization doesn't have to be a case of passively responding to complaints about speed. But time is also money, and sometimes simply throwing extra hardware at the problem is the best solution. Is spending the best part of a week trying to perform further optimizations the right move, or would spending $100 on a RAM upgrade be just as effective? The latter option seems like a cop-out but is probably the most cost-effective route.

TOOLS OF THE TRADE

The bottlenecks in an application don't always occur where you might expect them to, and an important precursor to optimization is to spend time watching how the application runs.

Waterfall Views

Waterfall views are extremely useful when looking at the front end of a website. These are graphs showing the order in which the browser is requesting resources, and the time that it takes each resource to download. Most waterfall tools also show things like the time spent for domain name service (DNS) lookups, for establishing a TCP connection to the web server, for parsing and rendering data, and so on.

There are a lot of waterfall tools out there — some run in your browser; others are websites into which you enter the URL that you want to check. But many have subtle flaws. For example, one popular online tool will request any resources contained in commented-out Hypertext Markup Language (HTML) such as the following:

```
<!--
<img src="foo.png">
-->
```

Web browsers have the sense to ignore such links, so this tool will give a distorted view of the page loading process. Another well-known online tool will fetch all the resources (images and fonts) referenced in the style sheet, even if the selectors containing them are not used in the HTML document. Again, in practice, web browsers are smart enough not to make this mistake.

WebPageTest.org

By far, the best online waterfall tool is probably `WebPageTest.org` (commonly known as WPT), developed by Google, AOL, and others. It offers dozens of locations around the world from which to perform tests and has an impressive list of browsers to test in — from Internet Explorer 6 through to 10, to iPhone, Firefox, and Chrome. Figure I-1 shows WPT in action.

Figure I-1 shows the results page for `http://www.google.com`. The six images at the top right indicate how the site scored in what WPT determined to be the six key areas. Remember that this is just a summary for quick reference and should not be taken as an absolute. For instance, in the test, `google.com` scored an "F" for "Cache static content," yet it is still well optimized. Clicking any of these scores will give a breakdown of how the grade was determined.

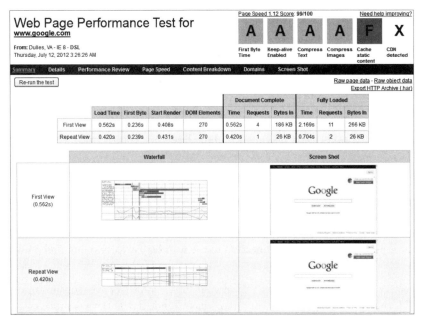

FIGURE I-1

The way in which a page loads can vary dramatically, depending on whether the user's cache is primed (that is, if the user has previously visited the site). Some static resources (such as CSS, JavaScript, images, and so on) may already be in the browser cache, significantly speeding things up. So, the default is for WPT to perform a First View test (that is, as the browser would see the target site if it had an unprimed cache), and a Repeat View test (that is, emulating the effect of visiting the site with an already primed cache). A preview image is shown for both these tests, and clicking one brings up the full waterfall graphic, as shown in Figure I-2.

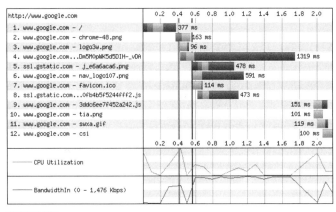

FIGURE I-2

The horizontal bar shows time elapsed (with resources listed vertically, in the order in which they were requested). So, the browser first fetched the index page (/), then chrome-48.png, then logo3w .png, and so on. Figure I-3 shows the first half second in more detail.

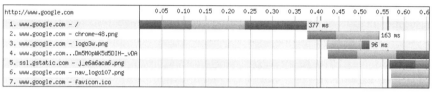

FIGURE I-3

The section at the beginning of the first request indicates a DNS lookup — the browser must resolve www.google.com to an IP address. This took approximately 50 milliseconds. The next section indicates the time taken to establish a connection to the web server. This includes setting up the TCP connection (if you're unfamiliar with the three-way handshake, see Appendix A, "TCP Performance"), and possibly waiting for the web server to spawn a new worker process to handle the request. In this example, that took approximately 70 milliseconds.

The next section shows the time to first byte (TTFB). At the beginning of this section, the client has issued the request and is waiting for the server to respond. There'll always be a slight pause here (approximately 120 milliseconds in this example), even for static files. However, high delays often indicate an overloaded server — perhaps high levels of disk contention, or back-end scripts that are taking a long time to generate the page.

Finally, the server returns a response to the client, which is shown by the final section of the bar. The size of this section is dependent on the size of the resource being returned and the available bandwidth. The number following the bar is the total time for the resource, from start to finish.

After the web browser fetches the HTML document, it can begin fetching resources linked to in it. Note that in request 2, there is no DNS lookup — the browser already has the response cached. For request 5, the resource resides on a subdomain, ssl.gstatic.com, so this does incur a DNS lookup.

Also notice two vertical lines at approximately the 40-millisecond and 55-millisecond marks. The first line indicates the point at which the browser began to render the page. The second line indicates the point at which the onLoad event fired — that is, the point at which the page had finished loading.

You'll learn more about these waterfall views later in this book — you'll learn how to optimize the downloading order, why some of the requests have a connection overhead and others don't, and why there are sometimes gaps where nothing seems to be happening.

Firebug

The downside to WPT is that it shows how the page loads on a remote machine, not your own. Usually, this isn't a problem, but occasionally you want to test a URL inside a members-only area, or see the page as it would look for someone in your country (or on your ISP). WPT does actually support some basic scripting, allowing it to log in to htpasswd-protected areas, but this isn't any help if you want to log in to something more complicated.

Firebug is a useful Firefox extension that (among other things) can show a waterfall view as a page loads in your browser. This is perhaps a more accurate portrayal of real-world performance if you're running on a modestly powered PC with home broadband because the WPT tests are presumably conducted from quite powerful and well-connected hardware.

The output of Firebug is similar to that of WPT, complete with the two vertical lines representing the start and end of rendering. Each resource can be clicked to expand a list of the headers sent and received with the request.

System Monitoring

This book is intended to be platform-neutral. Whether you run Berkeley Software Distribution (BSD), Linux, Solaris, Windows, OS X, or some other operating system, the advice given in this book should still be applicable.

Nevertheless, for system performance-monitoring tools, this will inevitably be quite platform-specific. Some tools such as netstat are implemented across most operating systems, but the likes of vmstat and iostat exist only in the UNIX world, and Windows users must use other tools. Let's briefly look at the most common choices to see how they work.

vmstat

vmstat is an essential tool on most flavors of UNIX and its derivatives (Linux, OS X, and so on). It provides information on memory usage, disk activity, and CPU utilization. With no arguments, vmstat simply displays a single-line summary of system activity. However, a numeric value is usually specified on the command line, causing vmstat to output data every *x* seconds. Here's vmstat in action with an interval of 5 seconds:

```
# vmstat 5
procs -----------memory---------- ---swap-- -----io---- -system-- ----cpu----
 r  b   swpd   free   buff  cache   si   so    bi    bo   in   cs us sy id wa
 4  0  28528 355120 160112 4283728    0    0     0     0    0    0 20  2 75  4
 4  0  28528 353624 160124 4283764    0    0     0   106  817 1303 28  1 71  0
 1  0  28528 358008 160128 4283808    0    0     0  1354  926 1511 28  1 71  0
 2  0  28528 351380 160132 4283828    0    0     0   167  757 1428 30  1 69  0
 2  0  28528 356360 160136 4283940    0    0     0  1309  864 1420 26  1 72  0
 3  0  28528 355552 160140 4284012    0    0    10   133  823 1573 37  1 61  0
 5  0  28528 349416 160144 4284092    0    0     5  1598  918 1746 30  1 68  0
 3  0  28528 353144 160152 4284116    0    0    14    82  791 1301 24  1 74  0
 1  0  28528 355076 160156 4284344    0    0    13  1242  839 1803 27  1 71  1
```

The first columns are as follows:

➤ r — This is the number of currently running processes.

➤ b — This is the number of blocking processes.

Blocking processes are those that cannot yet run because they are waiting on the hardware (most often the disks). Naturally, this is the least-desirable state for a process to be in, and a high number of blocking processes generally indicates a bottleneck somewhere (again, usually the disks). If the number of *running processes* exceeds the number of CPU cores on the system, this can also cause some degrading of performance, but blocking is the real killer.

The next four columns are similar to the information given by the free command, as shown here:

➤ swpd — This is how much swap memory is in use (expressed in bytes).

➤ free — This is idle memory.

➤ buff — This is memory used for buffers.

➤ cache — This is memory used for caching.

If you're coming to UNIX from the world of Windows, it's worth taking some time to ensure that you are absolutely clear on what these figures mean — in UNIX, things aren't as clear-cut as "free" and "used" memory.

The next two columns show swap usage:

➤ si — This is the bytes read in from swap.

➤ so — This is the bytes written out to swap.

Swapping is usually a bad thing, no matter what operating system you use. It indicates insufficient physical memory. If swapping occurs, expect to see high numbers of blocking processes as the CPUs wait on the disks.

Following are the next two columns:

➤ bi — This is the bytes read from block devices.

➤ bo — This is the bytes written to block devices.

Invariably, *block devices* means hard disks, so these two columns show how much data is being read from and written to disk. With disks so often being a bottleneck, it's worth studying these columns with the goal of trying to reduce disk activity. Often, you'll be surprised just how much writing is going on.

> **NOTE** *For a breakdown of which disks and partitions the activity occurs on, see the* iostat *command.*

Now, consider the next two columns:

➤ in — This is the number of CPU interrupts.

➤ cs — This is the number of context switches.

At the risk of digressing too much into CPU architecture, a *context switch* occurs when the CPU either switches from one process to another, or handles an interrupt. Context switching is an essential part of multitasking operating systems but also incurs some slight overhead. If your system performs a huge number of context switches, this can degrade performance.

The final four columns show CPU usage, measured as a percentage of the CPU time:

➤ us — This is the time spent running userland code.

➤ sy — This is the system time (that is, time spent running kernel code).

➤ id — This shows the idle time. (That is, the CPU is doing nothing.)

➤ wa — This shows the time that the CPU is waiting on I/O.

id (idle) is naturally the most preferable state to be in, whereas wa (waiting) is the least. wa indicates that the CPU has things to do but can't because it's waiting on other hardware. Usually, this is the disks, so check for high values in the io and swap columns.

Whether the CPU will mostly be running user code or kernel code depends on the nature of the applications running on the machine. Many of the applications discussed in this book spend a lot of time sending and receiving data over the network, and this is usually implemented at the kernel level.

The previous vmstat example was taken from a web server at a fairly quiet time of the day. Let's look at another example, taken from the same server, while the nightly backup process was running:

```
# vmstat 5
procs -----------memory---------- ---swap-- -----io---- -system-- ----cpu----
 r  b   swpd   free   buff   cache   si   so    bi     bo    in    cs us sy id wa
 1  1  26968 330260 161320 4328812    0    0     0      0     0     0 20  2 75  4
 4  0  26968 234492 160988 4370996    0    0  5329   6415  1041  3678 25  3 63  8
 1  1  26968 238424 158284 4377120    0    0  4729   5066  1035  2128 18  2 71  9
 0  2  27020 255812 150904 4386456    0    0  8339  14990  1169  1987 25  2 64  8
 1  6  27992 254028 142544 4366768    0   53 10026  13558  1194  3906 44  5 35 15
 4  0  27992 261516 138572 4384876    0    0  7706  17494  1081  2029 41  4 39 16
 1  1  31648 277228 131832 4374340    0    0 10300  17186  1127  2262 31  3 58  9
 1  2  31648 280524 130676 4385072    0    0  3330   5765   915  2059 23  2 68  6
 0  1  31648 282496 130220 4385120    0    0  2096   1918   934  1474 21  1 68 10
```

Although the machine is far from being overloaded, performance is not ideal. You see regular blocking processes, disk activity is higher, and the CPUs (this machine had six cores) are spending more of their time in the waiting (wa) state.

Depending on your operating system, there may be other data available from vmstat. For example, the Linux version can give a more detailed breakdown of disk activity (with the -d switch) and can show statistics on forking (with the -f switch). Check the man pages to see exactly what your system supports.

perfmon

On Windows, the Performance Monitor (perfmon) shown in Figure I-4 provides similar information.

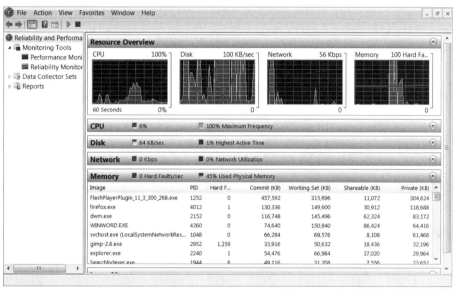

FIGURE I-4

Don't underestimate the power of perfmon. The default provides a wealth of information and can be extended to show all manner of additional data.

WHO THIS BOOK IS FOR

The information in this book is designed to appeal to a wide range of readers, from system administrators charged with managing busy websites, to web developers looking to write efficient, high-performance code.

This book makes no assumptions about your underlying operating system, and the information is (in most cases) equally applicable whether you run OS X, Linux, Windows, FreeBSD, or another flavor of UNIX. Situations are highlighted in which some of the information depends on the operating system used.

WHAT THIS BOOK COVERS

A wide range of technologies are in use on the web, and it would be futile to attempt to cover them all (or at least cover them in sufficient detail). Rather, the discussions in this book concentrate on the most popular open source technologies — PHP, MySQL, Apache, Nginx, `memcache`, and `mongodb`.

In this book, you'll discover many of the advanced features of these technologies, and the ways in which they can be utilized to provide scalable, high-performance websites. You'll learn current performance best practices, tips for improving your existing sites, and how to design with scalability in mind.

The browser market is wide and varied. The discussions in this book focus on the five main web browsers (which together make up the vast majority of web users) — Internet Explorer, Chrome, Firefox, Opera, and Safari. Behavior can vary in suitable (but important) ways between versions, and, in most cases, when particular aspects of browser behavior are examined, the discussion includes versions from the past 5 years or so. It's unfortunate (but inevitable) that a sizeable number of users will not be running the most current version.

HOW THIS BOOK IS STRUCTURED

The book is divided into two parts, covering aspects of website performance related to the front end (Part I) and the back end (Part II).

In the first part you'll meet topics such as the HTTP protocol, how web browsers work, browser caching, content compression, minification, JavaScript, CSS, and web graphics — all essential topics for web developers. Following are the chapters included in this part of the book:

➤ **Chapter 1, "A Refresher on Web Browsers"** — This chapter provides a look under the hood at how the web works. In this chapter, you will meet the HTTP protocol, and features such as caching, persistent connections, and `Keep-Alive`.

➤ **Chapter 2, "Utilizing Client-Side Caching"** — This chapter examines the ways in which web browsers cache content, and what you can do to control it.

➤ **Chapter 3, "Content Compression"** — Here you find everything you need to know about compressing content to speed up page loading times.

➤ **Chapter 4, "Keeping the Size Down with Minification"** — In this chapter, you discover the art of minifying HTML, CSS, and JavaScript to further reduce payload sizes.

➤ **Chapter 5, "Optimizing Web Graphics and CSS"** — Here you learn how to optimize the most common image formats, and discover ways in which CSS can be used to create lean, efficient markup.

➤ **Chapter 6, "JavaScript, the Document Object Model, and Ajax"** — JavaScript is an increasingly important part of the web. In this chapter, you learn about performance aspects of the language, with an emphasis on interaction with the document object model (DOM).

The second part of the book focuses on the technologies behind the scenes — databases, web servers, server-side scripting, and so on. Although many of these issues are of more interest to back-end developers and system administrators, they are vital for front-end developers to understand to appreciate the underlying system. Following are the chapters included in this part of the book:

➤ **Chapter 7, "Working with Web Servers"** — This chapter provides everything you need to know about tuning Apache and Nginx. The second half of the chapter looks at load balancing and related issues that arise (for example, session affinity).

➤ **Chapter 8, "Tuning MySQL"** — In this first of two chapters devoted to MySQL, you meet the myriad of tuning options and discover the differences between MyISAM and InnoDB.

➤ **Chapter 9, "MySQL in the Network"** — Here you learn how to scale out MySQL using such techniques as replication, sharding, and partitioning.

➤ **Chapter 10, "Utilizing NoSQL Solutions"** — NoSQL is a collective term for lightweight database alternatives. In this chapter, you learn about two of the most important players: memcache and mongodb.

➤ **Chapter 11, "Working with Secure Sockets Layer (SSL)"** — SSL can be a performance killer, but there are a surprising number of things that you can do to improve the situation.

➤ **Chapter 12, "Optimizing PHP"** — Perhaps the most popular back-end scripting language, PHP can have a significant impact on performance. In this chapter, you learn about opcode caching, and discover how to write lean, efficient PHP.

This book also includes three appendixes that provide additional information:

➤ **Appendix A, "TCP Performance"** — Transmission control protocol (TCP) and Internet Protocol (IP) are the protocols that drive in the Internet. In this appendix, you learn about some of the performance aspects of TCP, including the three-way handshake and Nagle's algorithm.

➤ **Appendix B, "Designing for Mobile Platforms"** — An increasing number of users now access the web via mobile devices such as cell phones and tablets. These bring about their own design considerations.

➤ **Appendix C, "Compression"** — This book makes numerous references to compression. Here you discover the inner workings of the LZW family, the algorithm behind HTTP compression, and many image formats.

WHAT YOU NEED TO USE THIS BOOK

To get the most out of this book, you should have a basic working knowledge of web development — HTML, JavaScript, CSS, and perhaps PHP. You should also be familiar with basic system management — editing files, installing applications, and so on.

CONVENTIONS

To help you get the most from the text and keep track of what's happening, we've used a number of conventions throughout the book.

> **NOTE** *Notes indicates notes, tips, hints, tricks, and/or asides to the current discussion.*

As for styles in the text:

➤ We *highlight* new terms and important words when we introduce them.

➤ We show keyboard strokes like this: Ctrl+A.

➤ We show filenames, URLs, and code within the text like so: `persistence.properties`.

➤ We present code in two different ways:

```
We use a monofont type with no highlighting for most code examples.
```

```
We use bold to emphasize code that is particularly important in the present
        context or to show changes from a previous code snippet.
```

ERRATA

We make every effort to ensure that there are no errors in the text or in the code. However, no one is perfect, and mistakes do occur. If you find an error in one of our books, like a spelling mistake or faulty piece of code, we would be grateful for your feedback. By sending in errata, you may save another reader hours of frustration, and, at the same time, you will be helping us provide even higher-quality information.

To find the errata page for this book, go to `http://www.wrox.com` and locate the title using the Search box or one of the title lists. Then, on the book details page, click the Book Errata link. On this page, you can view all errata that has been submitted for this book and posted by Wrox editors.

> **NOTE** *A complete book list, including links to each book's errata, is also available at* `www.wrox.com/misc-pages/booklist.shtml`.

If you don't spot "your" error on the Book Errata page, go to `www.wrox.com/contact/techsupport.shtml` and complete the form there to send us the error you have found. We'll check the information and, if appropriate, post a message to the book's errata page and fix the problem in subsequent editions of the book.

P2P.WROX.COM

For author and peer discussion, join the P2P forums at p2p.wrox.com. The forums are a web-based system for you to post messages relating to Wrox books and related technologies, and to interact with other readers and technology users. The forums offer a subscription feature to e-mail you topics of interest of your choosing when new posts are made to the forums. Wrox authors, editors, other industry experts, and your fellow readers are present on these forums.

At http://p2p.wrox.com, you will find a number of different forums that will help you, not only as you read this book, but also as you develop your own applications. To join the forums, just follow these steps:

1. Go to p2p.wrox.com and click the Register link.

2. Read the terms of use and click Agree.

3. Complete the required information to join, as well as any optional information you want to provide, and click Submit.

4. You will receive an e-mail with information describing how to verify your account and complete the joining process.

> **NOTE** *You can read messages in the forums without joining P2P, but to post your own messages, you must join.*

After you join, you can post new messages and respond to messages other users post. You can read messages at any time on the web. If you would like to have new messages from a particular forum e-mailed to you, click the Subscribe to this Forum icon by the forum name in the forum listing.

For more information about how to use the Wrox P2P, be sure to read the P2P FAQs for answers to questions about how the forum software works, as well as many common questions specific to P2P and Wrox books. To read the FAQs, click the FAQ link on any P2P page.

PART I
Front End

▶ **CHAPTER 1:** A Refresher on Web Browsers

▶ **CHAPTER 2:** Utilizing Client-Side Caching

▶ **CHAPTER 3:** Content Compression

▶ **CHAPTER 4:** Keeping the Size Down with Minification

▶ **CHAPTER 5:** Optimizing Web Graphics and CSS

▶ **CHAPTER 6:** JavaScript, the Document Object Model, and Ajax

1

A Refresher on Web Browsers

WHAT'S IN THIS CHAPTER?

➤ Reviewing web browsers and the HTTP protocol

➤ Understanding the steps involved in loading a web page

➤ Getting to know Keep Alive and parallel downloading

To access a website, you need a web browser — the piece of client-side software that requests resources from a web server and then displays them. Web browsers are one of the most important pieces of software in the modern Internet, and competition between vendors is fierce — so much so that many vendors have chosen to give their browsers away for free, knowing that an increased share of the browser market can indirectly reap profits in other areas.

Although such competition is good news for consumers, it can be a different story for web developers, who must strive to make their sites display correctly in the myriad of browsers, each of which has its own idiosyncrasies and nonstandard behavior. To understand how this situation has evolved, let's begin by returning to the early days of the World Wide Web.

A BRIEF HISTORY OF WEB BROWSERS

Although Mosaic is often thought of as the first web browser to hit the market, this isn't actually true — that honor falls on WorldWideWeb, a browser developed by Tim Berners-Lee in 1990 at the same time as he developed the HTTP 0.9 protocol. Other browsers soon followed, including Erwise, ViolaWWW, MidasWWW, and Cello — with Cello being, at this point, the only browser for Microsoft Windows. The year 1992 also saw the release of Lynx, the first text-based browser — the others all utilized graphical user interfaces (GUIs).

In 1993, Marc Andreessen and Eric Bina created Mosaic. Although Mosaic was not as sophisticated as its competitors, a lot of effort had gone into making it easy to install. And it had one other big advantage. Previous browsers had mostly been student projects, and as such, they often floundered after the students graduated. On the other hand, Mosaic had a team of full-time programmers developing it and offering technical support. Thanks to some clever marketing, Mosaic and the web were starting to become linked in the minds of the public.

In 1994, a dispute over the naming of Mosaic forced a rebranding, and Netscape Navigator was born. Unfortunately, regular changes to the licensing terms meant that, for the next few years, there was ongoing confusion over how free it actually was.

Microsoft entered the market in 1995 with Internet Explorer (IE) 1.0, which was also based on Mosaic, from whom Microsoft had licensed the code. IE 2.0 followed later that year, with IE 3.0 following in 1996. IE 3.0 was notable for introducing support for cascading style sheets (CSS), Java, and ActiveX, but Netscape continued to dominate the market, with IE making up only approximately 10 percent of the market.

Netscape Loses Its Dominance

Over the following years, the market swiftly turned in Microsoft's favor. By IE 4.0 (released in 1997), Microsoft's share of the market had increased to 20 percent, and, by the release of IE 5 in 1999, this had risen to 50 percent. Microsoft's dominance peaked in the first few years of the twenty-first century, with IE 6.0 (released in 2001) claiming more than 80 percent of the market.

Microsoft's aggressive marketing included a decision to bundle IE with Windows. But there's no denying that, at this point in the late 1990s, IE was simply the better browser. Netscape was prone to crashing, it was not as fast as IE, and it was beginning to look distinctly old-fashioned.

In an attempt to revive its fortunes, Netscape decided to release the source code for Navigator, and branded it as Mozilla (also known as Netscape 5), entrusting it to the newly formed Mozilla Foundation. Although this was an important turning point in the history of the web, it did little to help in the immediate future. AOL purchased Netscape, and released Netscape 6 in 2000 and Netscape 7 in 2002. This failed to halt the downturn, though, and AOL eventually announced the end of Netscape in 2008, a year after the release of both Netscape 8 and 9 (which, ironically, were now based on Firefox).

The Growth of Firefox

By 2000, it was clear that Microsoft had won the browser wars, and for the next few years, it enjoyed unchallenged dominance of the market. However, the Mozilla Foundation was still hard at work. Mozilla 1.0 was released in 2002 but failed to make much of an impact in the Windows environment.

Some Mozilla developers were becoming increasingly unhappy with the direction Mozilla was taking, feeling it was becoming increasingly bloated, and branched off their own port of the Mozilla code. After several changes to the name, this ultimately became Mozilla Firefox — usually referred to simply as Firefox.

Firefox 1.0 was released in 2004, but it wasn't until version 2.0, released 2 years later that things began to take off. Mozilla marketed Firefox heavily to the everyday user as a faster, more secure alternative to IE; while bloggers and techies were quick to praise the more advanced features. Finally, it was felt, there was a worthy rival to IE, and by the end of 2006, Firefox's share of the market had risen to 10 percent.

Firefox 3.0 was released in 2008, and by the end of 2010, had a market share of approximately 25 to 30 percent. It's ironic that just as IE's early growth was boosted by dissatisfaction among Netscape users, Firefox's growth was aided enormously by growing dissatisfaction among IE users. Indeed, it was felt that, having won the browser war, Microsoft had become somewhat complacent, with IE 6 and 7 being somewhat insipid.

The Present

Microsoft managed to get back on track with the release of IE 8 in 2008. As well as being compliant with CSS 2.1 and Acid 2, IE 8 finally included tabbed browsing — a feature that had been present in Opera and Firefox for some time.

In 2011, IE 9 was released, boasting CSS 3 support; improved graphics rendering; and a new JavaScript engine, Chakra, which was capable of better utilizing multicore CPUs. Also in 2011, Firefox 4 was released with its own new JavaScript engine (JagerMonkey) and hardware graphics accelerator.

INSIDE HTTP

Before beginning an examination of optimization techniques, it would be beneficial to understand how the web works. The remainder of this chapter recaps the basics of the HyperText Transfer Protocol (HTTP), discusses the differences between HTTP 1.0 and 1.1 (in particular, those relating to performance), and then follows the steps taken when a browser requests a page — from the initial domain name service (DNS) look-up through to the rendering. Later chapters revisit these steps in more detail, and you will learn ways to improve performance.

The HyperText Transfer Protocol

HTTP is the means by which web browsers (clients) communicate with web servers and vice versa. It's a text-based protocol operating at the application layer, and, as such, HTTP doesn't concern itself with issues such as routing or error checking: This is the job of the lower layers such as transmission control protocol (TCP) and Internet Protocol (IP).

THE OSI MODEL

The Open Systems Interconnection (OSI) model is a commonly used means of representing the various parts of network traffic in terms of layers, reflecting the way in which encapsulation of data works. The OSI model defines seven layers (the older TCP/IP model defines just four). The seven layers include the following:

- **Physical layer (layer one)** — This is the underlying means of transmitting the electrical signal across the network (for example, Ethernet, USB, or Bluetooth).

- **Data Link layer (layer two)** — This sits above the physical layer and provides transport across it. In the case of Ethernet, the data link layer handles the construction of Ethernet frames, and communicates with devices via their Media Access Control (MAC) addresses.

- **Network Layer (layer three)** — This deals with packet routing across more complicated networks. Internet Protocol (IP) is the most commonly used protocol at this level, and is capable of traveling across multiple networks, and through intermediate devices such as routers.

- **Transport Layer (layer four)** — This sits on top of the network layer and provides higher-level features such as flow control and the concept of connections. The most commonly seen protocols at this level are Transmission Control Protocol (TCP) and User Datagram Protocol (UDP).

- **Session Layer (layer five)** — This handles the management of sessions between the applications on either side of the network connection. Protocols used at this layer include NetBios, H.245, and SOCKS.

- **Presentation Layer (layer six)** — This handles the formatting of data. One of the most common examples is seen in telnet, where differences in the capabilities of terminals must be accounted for. Here, the presentation layer ensures that you see the same thing in your telnet session no matter what your terminal capabilities or character encodings are.

- **Application Layer (layer seven)** — At the top of the OSI model is the application layer, which contains some of the most well-known protocols, including Simple Message Transport Protocol (SMTP), HTTP, File Transfer Protocol (FTP), and Secure Shell (SSH). In many cases, these protocols are plain text (rather than binary), and are, by their nature, high level.

Instead, HTTP deals with the higher-level requests involved in navigating the web, such as, Fetch the Index Page from `http://www.google.com` or Post This Form Data to the CGI Script at Such-and-Such.

Navigating to a web page in your browser typically results in a series of HTTP requests being issued by the client to fetch the resources contained on the page. For each request, the server issues a response. Usually, the response contains the resource requested, but sometimes it indicates an error (such as the infamous 404 Not Found error) or some other message. Let's take a look at the HTTP protocol in action.

Using the Live HTTP Headers extension for Firefox, you can watch the HTTP headers that flow as you browse the web. This is an incredibly useful extension, and one that you will frequently use. If your knowledge of HTTP is a bit rusty, now would be a good time to install Live HTTP Headers and spend a bit of time watching traffic flowing.

Here is the traffic generated when you view a simple test page. (For brevity, some lines have been removed.)

```
GET /test.html HTTP/1.1
Host: 127.0.0.1
User-Agent: Mozilla/5.0 (X11; U; Linux x86_64; en-US; rv:1.9.1.8)
    Gecko/20100308 Iceweasel/3.5.8 (like Firefox/3.5.8) GTB7.1
Accept: text/html,application/xhtml+xml,application/xml;q=0.9,*/*;q=0.8
Accept-Language: en-us,en;q=0.5
Accept-Encoding: gzip,deflate
Keep-Alive: 300
Connection: keep-alive


HTTP/1.1 200 OK
Server: Apache/2.2.15 (Debian) PHP/5.3.2-1 with Suhosin-Patch mod_ssl/2.2.15
    OpenSSL/0.9.8m mod_perl/2.0.4 Perl/v5.10.1
Last-Modified: Thu, 29 Jul 2010 15:02:49 GMT
Etag: "31b8560-3e-48c8807137840"
Accept-Ranges: bytes
Vary: Accept-Encoding
Content-Encoding: gzip
Content-Length: 68
Keep-Alive: timeout=3, max=10000
Connection: Keep-Alive
Content-Type: text/html
---------------------------------------------------------
GET /logo.gif HTTP/1.1
Host: 127.0.0.1
User-Agent: Mozilla/5.0 (X11; U; Linux x86_64; en-US; rv:1.9.1.8)
    Gecko/20100308 Iceweasel/3.5.8 (like Firefox/3.5.8) GTB7.1
Accept: image/png,image/*;q=0.8,*/*;q=0.5
Accept-Language: en-us,en;q=0.5
Accept-Encoding: gzip,deflate
Accept-Charset: ISO-8859-1,utf-8;q=0.7,*;q=0.7
Keep-Alive: 300
Connection: keep-alive


HTTP/1.1 200 OK
   Server: Apache/2.2.15 (Debian) PHP/5.3.2-1 with Suhosin-Patch mod_ssl/2.2.15
       OpenSSL/0.9.8m mod_perl/2.0.4 Perl/v5.10.1
Last-Modified: Wed, 15 Apr 2009 21:54:25 GMT
Etag: "31bd982-224c-4679efda84640"
Accept-Ranges: bytes
Content-Length: 8780
```

```
Keep-Alive: timeout=3, max=9999
Connection: Keep-Alive
Content-Type: image/gif
---------------------------------------------------------
GET /take_tour.gif HTTP/1.1
Host: 127.0.0.1
User-Agent: Mozilla/5.0 (X11; U; Linux x86_64; en-US; rv:1.9.1.8)
     Gecko/20100308 Iceweasel/3.5.8 (like Firefox/3.5.8) GTB7.1
Accept: image/png,image/*;q=0.8,*/*;q=0.5
Accept-Language: en-us,en;q=0.5
Accept-Encoding: gzip,deflate
Accept-Charset: ISO-8859-1,utf-8;q=0.7,*;q=0.7
Keep-Alive: 300
Connection: keep-alive


HTTP/1.1 200 OK
   Server: Apache/2.2.15 (Debian) PHP/5.3.2-1 with Suhosin-Patch mod_ssl/2.2.15
       OpenSSL/0.9.8m  mod_perl/2.0.4 Perl/v5.10.1
Last-Modified: Wed, 15 Apr 2009 21:54:16 GMT
Etag: "31bd9bc-c9e-4679efd1ef200"
Accept-Ranges: bytes
Content-Length: 3230
Keep-Alive: timeout=3, max=10000
Connection: Keep-Alive
Content-Type: image/gif
---------------------------------------------------------
```

In this example, you first see the browser send a GET request for /test.html from the web server on 127.0.0.1. Notice that the wanted HTTP protocol version is also stated. The remaining lines of the request include some additional information: the browser user agent; the Multipurpose Internet Mail Extension (MIME) type, languages, and compression methods that the browser accepts; and Keep Alive/Connection options.

The server responds with HTTP/1.1 200 OK (indicating success) and returns test.html in the body of the response. (Remember, this discussion is about headers here, not bodies.) The server response indicates the MIME type of the resource returned (text/HTML), the size, and the compression type (gzip here). The last modified time is given, which will be important when you learn about caching.

After the browser has fetched test.html, it can parse the HTML and request any resources contained in it. The test page contains two images, and the browser now requests these. The responses are similar to the first, but there are a few subtle differences: The Content-Type in the response is now image/gif, and no Content-Encoding header is set. (This web server isn't configured to use compression when delivering images.)

A full discussion of HTTP could take up a whole book. Assuming you're broadly happy with HTTP, let's continue the discussion by looking at the areas that relate to performance.

HTTP Versions

The history of the HTTP protocol can be traced back to the first version, 0.9, defined in 1991. The web was a different place then, and although this crude protocol served the job, it wasn't long before refinements were made. These resulted in the creation of HTTP 1.0, defined in RFC 1945 in 1996.

Whereas HTTP 0.9 was limited to making simple GET requests with no additional headers, version 1.0 added most of the features now associated with the protocol: authentication, support for proxies and caches, the POST and HEAD methods, and an array of headers. HTTP 0.9 is pretty much obsolete now, but HTTP 1.0 is still occasionally seen in use and is still a usable protocol for navigating the modern web.

Although the move from HTTP 0.9 to 1.0 marked a major improvement to the protocol, the current version — HTTP 1.1 (laid out in RFC 2616 in 1999) — is essentially just a fine-tuning of HTTP 1.0, with particular improvements made to caching, reuse of connections, and support for virtual hosting. Let's look in more detail at the major improvements.

Support for Virtual Hosting

In the early days of the web, each domain had its own IP address, and there was never any need for an HTTP request to specify from which domain it was requesting a resource. It simply connected to the appropriate IP (obtained via DNS), and the web server knew which domain name this mapped to. As the Internet boomed, and concerns grew about the limited IPv4 address space, web servers began to support *virtual hosting* — a method to host multiple domain names on the same IP address. One of the changes in HTTP 1.1 was the introduction of the Host header, which enabled the client to specify for which domain it was requesting the resource.

A typical HTTP 1.0 request would have looked like this:

```
GET /index.html HTTP/1.0
```

In HTTP 1.1, this now appears as follows:

```
GET /index.html HTTP/1.1
Host: mydomain.com
```

Although this feature has little to do with performance, it had a big impact on the growth of the web and is one of the most compelling reasons to use HTTP 1.1 over 1.0.

Caching

Caching is an important topic that will be discussed numerous times in this book. In general, it consists of storing resources in a temporary location for faster retrieval in the future. In the case of client-side caching, this temporary location is an area of the user's hard disk, set aside by the web browser. In many situations, the browser can retrieve previously requested resources directly from the cache, without needing to query the web server.

Although the caching mechanisms of HTTP 1.0 provide fairly good caching support (albeit somewhat vaguely defined), HTTP 1.1 extends these and adds a host of new options, including the Cache-Control and Vary headers. These offer you much greater control over how browsers and intermediate proxies can cache your content.

> **NOTE** *You'll learn more about intermediate caches and proxies in Chapter 2, "Utilizing Client-Side Caching."*

HOW BROWSERS DOWNLOAD AND RENDER CONTENT

One of the most important building blocks for the budding web optimizer is an understanding of how browsers render websites. They don't always behave as you might expect, and there can be subtle differences from browser to browser. Only when you fully understand these can you be in a position to perform effective optimization.

"Waterfall" graphs are invaluable when trying to understand this. Let's dive in with an example, albeit for a fairly simple page — http://kernel.org, the home of the Linux kernel — shown in Figure 1-1.

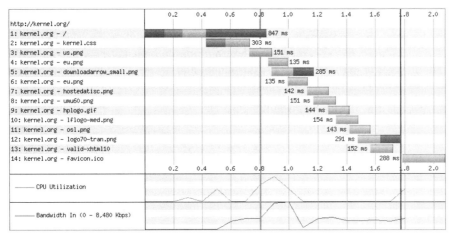

FIGURE 1-1

The first thing the browser does is resolve kernel.org to an IP address using DNS, as indicated by the first segment of the first request line. It then attempts to open an HTTP connection to kernel.org. The second segment shows the time taken to do this.

At the beginning of the third segment, the TCP connection has been created, and, at this point, the browser issues its request. However, it isn't until the start of the fourth segment that the web server starts to send back content. (This can be attributed to latency on the web server.) Finally, some 847 milliseconds (ms) after the start, the HTML document has been fully retrieved.

Of course, most web pages don't consist of simply an HTML document. (If they did, the lives of web masters would be less complicated.) Invariably, there are also links to style sheets, images, JavaScript, and so on, embedded in the page, which the browser must also retrieve.

The browser doesn't wait until it finishes retrieving the HTML document before it starts fetching these additional resources. Naturally, it can't start fetching them immediately, but as soon the HTML document starts to arrive, the browser begins parsing it and looks for links. The first of these is the style sheet (`kernel.css`) contained near the top of the page in the head, and it duly requests this. You now have two connections running in parallel — this is enormously faster than the requests made in a linear fashion, one by one.

This time, you don't have the delay of a DNS lookup (the response from the previous lookup has been cached by the browser), but you once again have a delay while the browser initiates a TCP connection to the server. The size of this particular CSS file is a mere 1.7 KB, and the download segment of the request is hence barely visible.

Given what you now know about the browser parsing the document as it comes in, why is there such a delay until `us.png` is requested? Perhaps this image isn't referenced until approximately three-quarters of the way through the document (because the download appears to begin approximately three quarters of the way through downloading the HTML). Actually, this image is first referenced on line 35 of the document (which is more than 600 lines in total).

The reason for the delay is that, historically, most browsers only download two resources in parallel from the same host. So, the request for `us.png` doesn't begin until the request for `kernel.css` finishes. Look carefully at the rest of the waterfall to see that at no point are there ever more than two requests running in parallel. (You'll learn more about this shortly.)

There's something else different about `us.png` (and the resources that follow it) — there is no TCP connection segment. The browser is reusing the existing TCP connection it has with the server, cutting out the time required to set up a new connection. This is an example of the persistent connections mentioned earlier in this chapter. In this example, the saving is approximately 0.1 second on each request — and more than 12 requests, which mounts up to sizeable savings.

It's also worth noting that, in this example, the overhead involved in making the request makes up a significant proportion of the overall time. With the first, fifth, and twelfth resources, the actual downloading of data accounts for approximately one-half the time needed to fetch the resource. With the other resources, the download time is virtually insignificant, dwarfed by the latency of issuing the request and waiting for a response from the server. Although this is only one example, the pattern of many small resources is common and illustrates that performance is not all about keeping the size of resources small.

Rendering

After the browser retrieves the HTML document, it can begin to parse the document and render it on the screen. Referring to the waterfall view in Figure 1-1, the first vertical line shows the point at which the browser begins rendering, whereas the second vertical line shows the point at which rendering is complete.

If the image dimensions are not known, the browser does not allocate any screen space to them during the initial rendering. As a result, the page flow must be recalculated after they have been downloaded, and the dimensions become known. This can lead to the rather ugly effect of text jumping around the page as the page loads.

Although the `kernel.org` example implies that the page takes approximately 1 second to render, this is a little misleading. Actually, the majority of the page renders in the blink of an eye. Then you must wait for the images to download. If no images were involved (or they were already in the browser's cache), how long would it take the browser to simply parse and render the HTML document? This is an area discussed again in Chapter 6, "JavaScript, the Document Object Model, and Ajax," when you learn about ways to reduce rendering times.

Persistent Connections and Keep-Alive

In HTTP 1.0, the default behavior is to close the connection after a resource has been retrieved. Thus, the following is the flow of events when the client needs to fetch multiple resources:

1. The client opens a TCP connection to the server.

2. The client requests the resource.

3. The server responds and closes the connections.

4. The client opens a new TCP connection.

5. The client requests another resource.

This is a rather wasteful approach, and the process to build up and tea down the TCP connections adds a significant amount of latency to requests (not to mention extra CPU and RAM usage on both client and server). This overhead is even more significant when requesting many small resources, which tends to be the nature of most websites.

Figure 1-2 shows this problem with a waterfall view showing a page containing 22 small images loading in IE 7. The effect has been exaggerated a bit by conducting the test from a dial-up connection to a web server located on the other side of the Atlantic. (So the latency is quite high.) The problem still exists for broadband users, just not to the same degree.

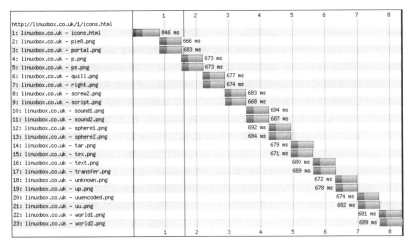

FIGURE 1-2

Clearly, this is not an ideal situation, which is one of the reasons that (as you have seen) browsers typically issue more requests in parallel when talking in HTTP 1.0.

Keep-Alive

This shortcoming was partially addressed by the introduction of `Keep-Alive`. Although it was never an official part of the HTTP 1.0 specifications, it is well supported by clients and servers.

With `Keep-Alive` enabled, a server will not automatically close the connection after sending a resource but will instead keep the socket open, enabling the client to issue additional requests. This greatly improves responsiveness and keeps network traffic down.

A client indicates it wants to use `Keep-Alive` by including the header `Connection: Keep-Alive` in its request. If the server supports `Keep-Alive`, it signals its acceptance by sending an identical header back in the response. The connection now remains open until either party decides to close it.

Unfortunately, browsers can't always be relied upon to behave themselves and close the connection when they finish issuing requests, a situation that could lead to server processes sitting idle and consuming memory. For this reason, most web servers implement a `Keep-Alive` timeout — if the client does not issue any further requests within this time period (usually approximately 5 to 10 seconds), the server closes the connection.

In addition, servers may also limit the number of resources that may be requested during the connection. The server communicates both these settings with a `Keep-Alive` header like this:

```
Keep-Alive: timeout=5, max=100
```

However, `Keep-Alive` is not an officially recognized header name and may not be supported by all clients.

Persistent Connections

HTTP 1.1 formalized the `Keep-Alive` extension and improved on it, the result being known as persistent. Persistent connections are the default in HTTP 1.1, so there's no need for the client or server to specifically request them. Rather, the client and server must advertise their *un*willingness to use them by sending a `Connection: close` header.

> **NOTE** *Just to clarify,* `Keep-Alive` *is the name of the unofficial extension to HTTP 1.0, and persistent connections are the name for the revised version in HTTP 1.1. It's not uncommon for these terms to be used interchangeably, despite the (admittedly small) differences between them. For example, the Apache* `KeepAlive` *directives (which you'll learn about in Chapter 7, "Working with Web Servers") also relate to persistent connections.*

Keep-Alive and Persistent Connections

Let's revisit an earlier example, again conducted from a dial-up connection but this time to a server that has `Keep-Alive` enabled. Figure 1-3 shows the waterfall view.

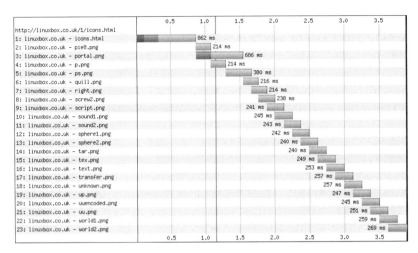

FIGURE 1-3

This time, the results are significantly better, with the page loading in less than half the time. Although the effect has been intentionally exaggerated, Keep-Alive is still a big asset in the majority of situations.

When Not to Use Keep-Alive

So, if Keep-Alive is only an asset in the *majority* of situations, under which circumstances might Keep-Alive not be beneficial?

Well, if your website mostly consists of HTML pages with no embedded resources (CSS, JavaScript, images, and so on), clients will need to request only one resource when they load a page, so there will be nothing to gain by enabling Keep-Alive. By turning it off, you allow the server to close the connection immediately after sending the resource, freeing up memory and server processes. Such pages are becoming rare, though, and even if you have some pages like that, it's unlikely that every page served up will be.

Parallel Downloading

Earlier in this chapter, you learned that most browsers fetch only a maximum of two resources in parallel from the same hostname and saw a waterfall view of IE 7 loading http://kernel.org to illustrate this point. Given that parallel downloading is so beneficial to performance, why stop at two?

The reason that browsers have (historically) set this limit probably stems from RFC 2616 (which details version 1.1 of HTTP; you can find it at http://www.ietf.org/rfc/rfc2616.txt). According to that RFC, "Clients that use persistent connections *should* limit the number of simultaneous connections that they maintain to a given server. A single-user client *should not* maintain more than 2 connections with any server or proxy.... These guidelines are intended to improve HTTP response times and avoid congestion."

However, the Internet has come a long way since 1999 when that RFC was written, and for some time, web developers have been more than happy to use tricks to get around this limit. You'll learn about some of these shortly.

More recently, browser vendors have started to flout this guideline, too, usually justifying it by pointing out that the RFC says "should not," not "must not." Of course, their main concern is with providing a faster browsing experience to users (especially if other vendors have already increased their maximum connections per domain) — any increase in network congestion or overloading of the web server isn't their problem.

The issue has caused fierce debate, with apocalyptic predictions of web servers being brought to their knees by this flood of parallel connections. This hasn't happened yet, though, and for good reason. While a browser making eight parallel requests rather than two can certainly increase server load, it stands to reason that these eight connections will be open for a shorter period of time. So, although it may cause a slight spike in load, it's only short-lived. It would be hypocritical for web developers to complain about this aspect of browser behavior because they often use tricks to increase parallel downloading.

The first major browser to break from this "rule" of two maximum connections per hostname was Safari, starting with version 3 in 2007. Firefox 3 and Opera followed in 2008, and IE 8 in 2009. Table 1-1 shows the current state of play.

TABLE 1-1 Maximum Parallel Connections Per Host

BROWSER	MAX PARALLEL CONNECTIONS PER HOST
IE 6 and 7	2
IE 8	6
IE 9	6
IE 10	8
Firefox 2	2
Firefox 3	6
Firefox 4 to 17	6
Opera 9.63	4
Opera 10	8
Opera 11 and 12	6
Chrome 1 and 2	6
Chrome 3	4
Chrome 4 to 23	6
Safari 3 and 4	4

It's worth noting that IE 8 automatically reduces this figure to two for users on dial-up connections and enables web developers to detect the current value in JavaScript via `window .maxConnectionsPerServer`.

Increasing Parallel Downloads

Earlier, you learned that web developers have traditionally often used tricks to increase the amount of parallelization. With the current generation of browsers all enabling more than two parallel connections, the need for this has greatly diminished. As of this writing, IE 7 still makes up a significant share of the market, though, so it's still a topic worth discussing.

Eagle-eyed readers will have noticed that this discussion has been quite pedantic in saying that browsers establish only x number of parallel connections *per hostname*. It's not globally (there's another limit for that), per server, per IP address, or even per domain. You can easily exploit this by forcing the browser to fetch more than two resources in parallel.

Consider the following HTML snippet:

```
<img src="images2/tar.png"><img src="images2/sound2.png">
<img src="images2/sound1.png"><img src="images2/screw1.gif">
<img src="images2/portal.gif"><img src="images2/world1.gif">
<img src="images2/pie1.gif"><img src="images2/pie2.gif">
<img src="images2/pie3.gif"><img src="images2/pie4.gif">
<img src="images2/pie5.gif"><img src="images2/pie6.gif">
<img src="images2/pie7.gif"><img src="images2/generic.png">
<img src="images2/folder.png"><img src="images2/link.png">
<img src="images2/layout.png"><img src="images2/dvi.png">
<img src="images2/broken.png"><img src="images2/bomb.png">
```

Let's look at how this loads in IE 7, a browser that sticks to the RFC guidelines, as shown in Figure 1-4.

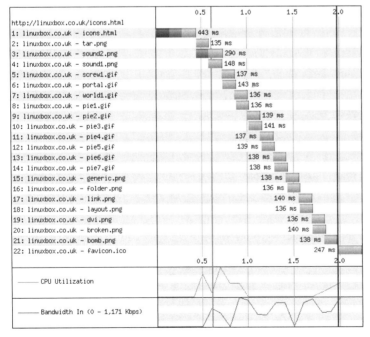

FIGURE 1-4

Increase the level of parallelization by splitting the images across two subdomains: `static.linuxbox`
`.co.uk` and `images.linuxbox.co.uk`, as shown here:

```
<img src="/images2/tar.png">
    <img src="http://images.linuxbox.co.uk/images2/sound2.png">
<img src="http://images.linuxbox.co.uk/images2/sound1.png">
    <img src="http://static.linuxbox.co.uk/images2/screw1.gif">
<img src="http://static.linuxbox.co.uk/images2/portal.gif">
    <img src="http://images.linuxbox.co.uk/images2/world1.gif">
<img src="http://images.linuxbox.co.uk/images2/pie1.gif">
    <img src="http://static.linuxbox.co.uk/images2/pie2.gif">
<img src="http://static.linuxbox.co.uk/images2/pie3.gif">
    <img src="http://images.linuxbox.co.uk/images2/pie4.gif">
<img src="http://images.linuxbox.co.uk/images2/pie5.gif">
    <img src="http://static.linuxbox.co.uk/images2/pie6.gif">
<img src="http://static.linuxbox.co.uk/images2/pie7.gif">
    <img src="http://images.linuxbox.co.uk/images2/generic.png">
<img src="http://images.linuxbox.co.uk/images2/folder.png">
    <img src="http://static.linuxbox.co.uk/images2/link.png">
<img src="http://static.linuxbox.co.uk/images2/layout.png">
    <img src="http://images.linuxbox.co.uk/images2/dvi.png">
<img src="http://images.linuxbox.co.uk/images2/broken.png">
    <img src="http://static.linuxbox.co.uk/images2/bomb.png">
```

As shown in Figure 1-5, using this simple technique has cut approximately 0.6 seconds off the page
loading time. (Keep in mind that the nature of the Internet makes it difficult to exactly replicate the
conditions between runs. The second run may have found the network a little quieter, or the web
server less busy.)

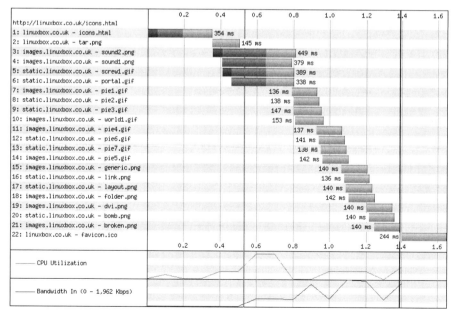

FIGURE 1-5

What if you take this to extremes and use enough hostnames to make all the images download in parallel?

```
<img src="/images2/tar.png">
    <img src="http://images.linuxbox.co.uk/images2/sound2.png">
<img src="http://images.linuxbox.co.uk/images2/sound1.png">
    <img src="http://static.linuxbox.co.uk/images2/screw1.gif">
<img src="http://static.linuxbox.co.uk/images2/portal.gif">
    <img src="http://content.linuxbox.co.uk/images2/world1.gif">
<img src="http://content.linuxbox.co.uk/images2/pie1.gif">
    <img src="http://resources.linuxbox.co.uk/images2/pie2.gif">
<img src="http://resources.linuxbox.co.uk/images2/pie3.gif">
    <img src="http://media.linuxbox.co.uk/images2/pie4.gif">
<img src="http://media.linuxbox.co.uk/images2/pie5.gif">
    <img src="http://bart.linuxbox.co.uk/images2/pie6.gif">
<img src="http://bart.linuxbox.co.uk/images2/pie7.gif">
    <img src="http://homer.linuxbox.co.uk/images2/generic.png">
<img src="http://homer.linuxbox.co.uk/images2/folder.png">
    <img src="http://marge.linuxbox.co.uk/images2/link.png">
<img src="http://marge.linuxbox.co.uk/images2/layout.png">
    <img src="http://lisa.linuxbox.co.uk/images2/dvi.png">
<img src="http://lisa.linuxbox.co.uk/images2/broken.png">
    <img src="http://maggie.linuxbox.co.uk/images2/bomb.png">
```

Figure 1-6 shows the result. It's not quite what you had hoped for — the page loading time has just doubled! Although the additional DNS lookups required haven't helped (but this could be eliminated by using IP addresses rather than hostnames), the main problem seems to be the web server (Apache, in this case), which was somewhat slow to answer the barrage of requests.

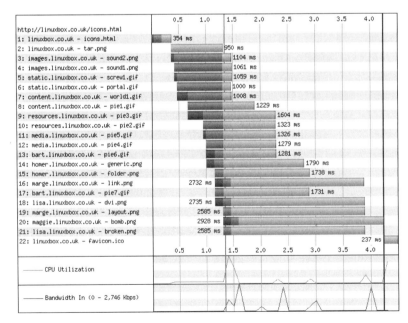

FIGURE 1-6

After a little Apache tuning (you'll learn exactly what was done in Chapter 7), if you rerun the test, the results are more promising, as shown in Figure 1-7.

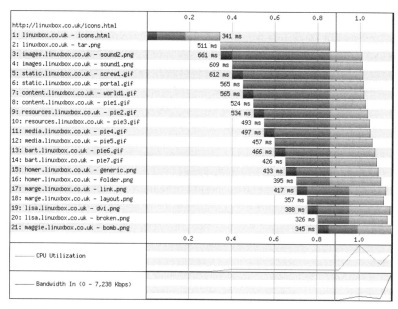

FIGURE 1-7

This time, the load time was 1.15 seconds, an improvement on the test using two subdomains. This illustrates that, unless the web server is geared toward such a flood of traffic, too much parallelization can dramatically reduce loading times.

So, where is the sweet spot? Research suggests that splitting content across two to four hostnames offers the best performance. With anything more than four hostnames, you risk flooding the server with requests, and (in the case of dial-up users) saturating the network connections.

It's a mistake to think that parallelization can solve the problem of pages being too heavy, too. It's a great way to reduce the latency involved with issuing many requests for small resources (which is how most sites are structured). However, if you have, for example, two large images, arranging for them to download in parallel will simply result in each downloading more slowly. Bandwidth is a finite resource.

Coping with Modern Browsers

Although splitting resources across hostnames used to be a great technique to reduce loading times, its days are numbered because the most recent generation of browsers moves away from the RFC guidelines. Catering for both older and newer browsers poses somewhat of a problem, though. It's quite easy to envision a scenario in which a site, carefully tuned to accommodate the two-connection limit of IE 7, results in a surge of connections in IE 8, driving up CPU usage on both the client and server, and killing performance.

One option is to compromise. Splitting resources across just two domains will still speed things up a little for older browsers but will lessen the risk of the more recent browsers creating a packet storm.

Another solution would be to use server-side scripting to determine the browser type and version, and rewrite the HTML document accordingly. Thus, a Firefox 2 user may see resources split across four domains, whereas a visitor on Safari would see them split across just two. Naturally, this causes some additional CPU usage on the server, but it need not be too intense if the server were simply returning different versions of a static document, rather than rewriting the page on-the-fly.

Coping with Proxies

This isn't quite the full story, though. When multiple users behind a proxy visit a site simultaneously, the web server sees a flood of connections all coming from the same IP address. With older browsers, the two-connection limit helped to lessen this effect. With newer browsers issuing perhaps four or six requests in parallel, the potential for a flood is much greater, and an Intrusion Detection System (IDS) could easily mistake this for a SYN flood or other form of denial-of-service (DoS) attack (perhaps leading to the IP address being blocked). For this reason, most newer browsers lower the number of parallel connections when the browser connects via a proxy, and, consequently, their behavior is more like that of older browsers.

Incidentally, most proxies don't support HTTP 1.1, so a client connecting through a proxy usually must downgrade to HTTP 1.0, which leads neatly into the next subject.

Parallel Downloads in HTTP 1.0

Although persistent connections (also known as Keep-Alive) are supported in many HTTP 1.0 implementations, they are not an official part of the specification. As such, clients connecting via a proxy — or to a server that does not support HTTP 1.1 — lose out on performance. Increasing the number of parallel connections is a way to mitigate some of this performance loss. As a result, many browsers use different levels of parallelization for HTTP 1.0 and 1.1. Thus, Table 1-1 can be refined to show the data in Table 1-2.

TABLE 1-2: Different Levels of Parallelization for HTTP 1.0 and HTTP 1.1

BROWSER	MAX PARALLEL CONNECTIONS	
	HTTP 1.1	HTTP 1.0
IE 6 and 7	2	4
IE 8	6	6
IE 9	6	6
IE 10	8	
Firefox 2	2	8

Firefox 3	6	6
Firefox 4 - 17	6	6
Opera 9.63	4	4
Opera 10	8	8
Opera 11 and 12	6	6
Chrome 1 and 2	6	4
Chrome 3	4	4
Chrome 4 - 23	6	6
Safari 3 and 4	4	4

The effect is most noticeable in the older browsers, with newer browsers generally having abandoned this strategy — perhaps because of the conflict with the proxy connection limitations previously discussed.

In the past, both aol.com and Wikipedia have intentionally downgraded to HTTP 1.0, presumably with the intention to speed up their loading times by tricking the browser into increasing parallelization. This seems to be a somewhat muddled logic. If you must increase parallelization, the techniques described in this chapter are a better path to follow.

SUMMARY

After a refresher on the history of the web, this chapter provided an inside look at the HTTP protocol, and some of the key concepts for performance — persistent connections, parallel downloading, and rendering. You also met caching, which is an essential part of any website — both for speeding up loading times for the user, and for reducing load on the server.

In Chapter 2, you'll learn about the various types of caching, how they work, and how to implement them to achieve blistering performance.

Utilizing Client-Side Caching

WHAT'S IN THIS CHAPTER?

➤ Discovering the different types of caches and proxies

➤ Learning how to encourage browsers to cache your contents

➤ Learning how browsers cache 301 redirects

➤ Understanding DNS caching and prefetching in the major browsers

Caching is an important part of the modern Internet, but it is also an issue surrounded by a lot of confusion and misunderstanding. The issue is so significant that many web masters see caching as their enemy and spend copious amounts of time trying to force content not to be cached. As you shall see, though, caching is a significant concept to ensure the smooth flow of the web, and web masters would do well to embrace it.

UNDERSTANDING THE TYPES OF CACHING

Caching is a somewhat broad term, but generally refers to the storage of web resources (HTML documents, images, and so on) in a temporary location to improve performance. Caches can be implemented by most web browsers, perimeter (intermediate) web proxies, and at the gateways of large internal networks. *Transparent proxies* (caches) are used by many Internet Service Providers (ISPs), *reverse proxies* sit in front of web servers, and the web server itself utilizes caching.

To understand caching, let's take a closer look at each of these scenarios.

Caching by Browsers

Most web browsers implement a cache (an area of disk on which previously retrieved resources can be temporarily stored) to hold recently and frequently accessed resources. This makes perfect sense — it's much faster to retrieve a resource from the cache than to request it again from the web server. When deciding what to cache, browsers are usually quite well behaved and respect the caching policy dictated by the server (which you learn more about in the "Controlling Caching" section of this chapter).

There are several problems with browser caching. First of all, the size of the cache tends to be quite small by default. Although the size of the average hard disk in a desktop PC has continued to grow at quite a rate, increases in the default browser cache size have been more modest. Given that web pages have become increasingly heavy, browsers would probably be more effective if they defaulted to much larger caches.

Table 2-1 shows a breakdown of the maximum cache sizes for common browsers.

TABLE 2-1: Maximum Cache Sizes for Common Browsers

BROWSER	MAXIMUM CACHE SIZE
Firefox 17	1024 MB
IE 6, 7, 8	1/32 of the drive space, capped at 50 MB
IE 9	1/256 of the drive space, capped at 250 MB
Safari	Unlimited
Opera 10+	400 MB
Chrome	300 MB

Also, when the cache becomes full, the algorithm to decide what to remove is crude. Commonly, the *Least Recently Used (LRU)* algorithm is used to purge old items. This may seem fine at first glance, but it fails to take into account the relative "cost" to request different types of resources. For example, the loading of JavaScript resources typically blocks loading of the rest of the page. (You will learn in Chapter 6, "JavaScript, the Document Object Model, and Ajax," why this doesn't need to be the case.) It makes more sense for these to be given preference in the cache over, say, images. Hopefully, this is something that future generations of browsers must take into consideration.

Finally, there is the human element. Many browsers offer an easy way for the user to remove temporary data (such as cached pages, sessions, and so on) for the sake of privacy. Users often feel that cleaning the browser cache is an important step in somehow stopping their PCs from running slowly. (Although, if you press them for the logic behind this, the most you'll get is a vague answer about giving things a spring cleaning.)

So, although the browser cache is a huge benefit, it's not without its faults.

Intermediate Caches

The intermediate cache/proxy (so called because so often it fulfills the purposes of both caching and proxying) is commonly used by ISPs and larger organizations.

When used by ISPs, it typically takes the form of a *transparent caching proxy* that silently intercepts HTTP traffic. When the client makes a request, the proxy intercepts it and checks its local cache for a copy of the resource. If none is found, it makes the request on the client's behalf and then relays this back to the client, caching a copy itself in the process. When another client on the same ISP requests the same resource, a cached copy is then already at hand.

Although this type of proxy can offer significant performance benefits (because the connection between the client and the proxy is generally low latency and high bandwidth), the downside is that there is some increased latency for resources that are not in the intermediate's cache.

Closely related to this type of cache are the *border-level caching proxies* implemented by many large organizations. Often, the primary reason for these is security (because they offer the capability to filter content), and clients inside the local area network (LAN) must configure their browsers to connect to the outside world via the proxy. However, they are often used for caching, too.

Reverse Proxies

Whereas browser caches and intermediate proxies are generally for the benefit of the client, *reverse proxies* are usually used for the benefit of the web server. These proxies sit in front of the web server and have two purposes (although sometimes they are used for just one of these reasons): caching and load balancing. For caching, they can be used to lighten load on the back-end web server by serving up cached versions of dynamically generated pages (thus cutting CPU usage). For load balancing, they can be used for load-balancing multiple back-end web servers.

CONTROLLING CACHING

Now that you have a grasp of the main types of caches and proxies available, let's look at methods that attempt to control them.

> **NOTE** *In most cases, all you can do is to suggest policies to caches and proxies, but most of them will respect these suggestions.*

Conditional GETs

Look again at the browser cache. How does it know if a local, cached copy of a resource is still valid? The standard way is to send a conditional GET request. This takes the form of an `If-Modified-Since` header in the request. If the server determines that the resource has been modified since the date given in this header (which will be set by the browser as the `Last-Modified` time returned with the original response), the resource is returned as normal. Otherwise, a `304 Not Modified` status is returned.

This can be neatly illustrated by requesting a resource in a browser, then re-requesting it a few seconds later. Unless the web server is overriding this default caching behavior, you see a `200 OK` the first time (assuming you don't already have a copy in the cache) and then a `304` the second time. Here's what you see when you request `http://www.debian.org/Pics/debian.png`:

```
http://www.debian.org/Pics/debian.png

GET /Pics/debian.png HTTP/1.1
Host: www.debian.org
User-Agent: Mozilla/5.0 (X11; U; Linux x86_64; en-US; rv:1.9.1.8)
     Gecko/20100308 Iceweasel/3.5.8 (like Firefox/3.5.8) GTB7.1
Keep-Alive: 300
Connection: keep-alive
Referer: http://www.debian.org/
Pragma: no-cache
Cache-Control: no-cache

HTTP/1.1 200 OK
Date: Sun, 01 Aug 2010 08:24:47 GMT
Server: Apache/2.2.9 (Debian) mod_perl/2.0.4 Perl/v5.10.0
Last-Modified: Sat, 30 Jun 2007 13:26:17 GMT
Accept-Ranges: bytes
Content-Length: 3895
Keep-Alive: timeout=15, max=99
Connection: Keep-Alive
Content-Type: image/png
-----------------------------------------------------------
http://www.debian.org/Pics/debian.png

GET /Pics/debian.png HTTP/1.1
Host: www.debian.org
User-Agent: Mozilla/5.0 (X11; U; Linux x86_64; en-US; rv:1.9.1.8)
     Gecko/20100308 Iceweasel/3.5.8 (like Firefox/3.5.8) GTB7.1
Keep-Alive: 300
Connection: keep-alive
Referer: http://www.debian.org/
If-Modified-Since: Sat, 30 Jun 2007 13:26:17 GMT
Cache-Control: max-age=0

HTTP/1.1 304 Not Modified
Date: Sun, 01 Aug 2010 08:24:50 GMT
Server: Apache/2.2.9 (Debian) mod_perl/2.0.4 Perl/v5.10.0
Connection: Keep-Alive
Keep-Alive: timeout=15, max=98
-----------------------------------------------------------
```

On the first request, a Last-Modified header of Sat, 30 Jun 2007 13:26:17 GMT is returned in the response. The browser caches the image, along with this date.

When you issue the second request, the header If-Modified-Since: Sat, 30 Jun 2007 13:26:17 GMT is sent to the server, saying "send me /Pics/debian.org if it has been modified since Sat, 30 Jun 2007 13:26:17 GMT." In this example, this isn't the case, and the server sends back a 304 Not Modified status.

The benefits of this should be obvious. Rather than spending time downloading the resource again, the browser can use its locally cached copy. However, there is also a significant drawback: The browser must still request the resource. In this example, in which the image was a mere 3.8 KB, the time in setting up the connection and issuing the request is likely to far outweigh the actual time that would be spent downloading the image.

Let's try another test, this time using an HTML document containing four small images. Figure 2-1 shows the waterfall view the first time the page is requested.

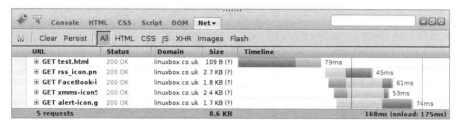

FIGURE 2-1

With none of the resources having previously been requested, the cache is empty, and all resources must be downloaded. When you repeat the test (as shown in Figure 2-2), all five resources are now in the browser cache. The server sends back 304 Not Modified in response to the conditional GETs, but this doesn't help much because the time spent actually downloading the resource was so small.

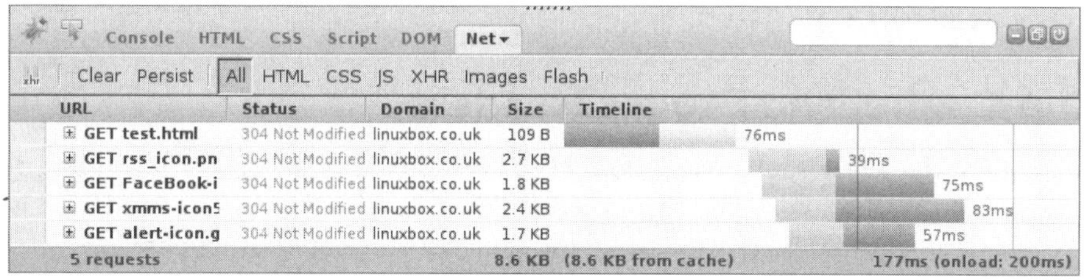

FIGURE 2-2

In this test, the second run was slightly slower than the first. This was a blip, perhaps because of network conditions or changes in load on the server. Even so, the improvement in performance is never going to be particularly big in this example.

That's not to say this method of caching is useless, but merely that, in cases in which the downloading of the resource forms only a small fraction of the request time, it doesn't have much benefit. Had you used larger images, the difference would be noticeable.

Figure 2-3 shows another test page containing a 3.7 MB JPEG image:

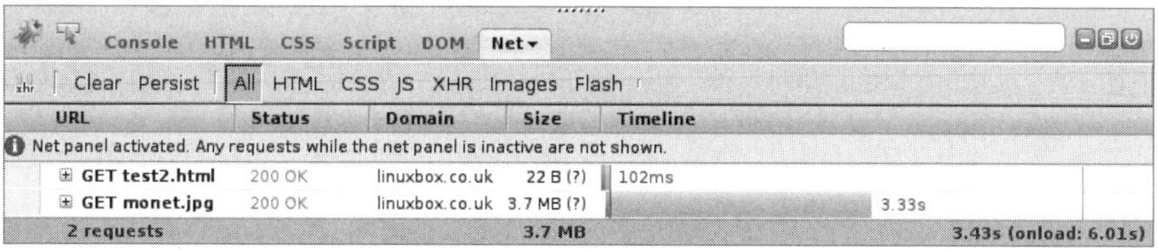

FIGURE 2-3

On the first run, the image takes a little more than 3 seconds to load, and the HTML page hasn't finished rendering until 6 seconds later.

On the second run (shown in Figure 2-4), with the cache primed, the overhead to send the conditional GET is almost insignificant to the size of the image, and the page loads in a mere 136 milliseconds (ms) — quite a saving.

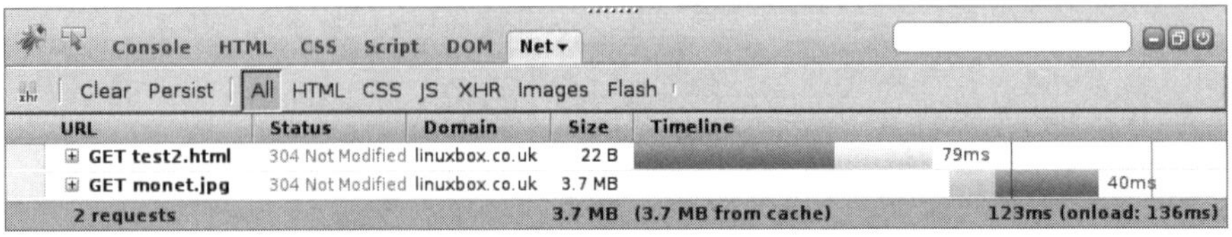

FIGURE 2-4

Of course, these two examples are extremes of the spectrum. But, in practice, pages do tend to be more like the first example (with many small resources) than the latter.

It would be great if there were a way to tell the browser not to issue these conditional GETs if it already had the resource in the cache. As it turns out, there is.

Utilizing Cache-Control and Expires Headers

In the previous examples, the server sent a Last-Modified header in responses, which contained the date that the resource was last modified. The client cached this date with the resource and used it to send an If-Modified-Since header when requesting the same resource at a future date.

There are two more headers that can control caching: Expires and Cache-Control: max-age. These headers effectively say to the client, "This resource expires on such-and-such a date. Until then, you can just use your locally cached copy (if you have one)." The result is that the client doesn't need to issue a conditional GET.

But why are there two different headers for doing this? What are the differences, and which is the best to use?

The main difference is that Expires was defined in HTTP 1.0, whereas the Cache-Control family is new to HTTP 1.1. So, in theory, Expires is safer because you occasionally still encounter clients that support only HTTP 1.0. Modern browsers understand both headers; although if both are present, preference is given to Cache-Control: max-age.

mod_expires

In Apache, the mod_expires modules can be used to set both Expires and Cache-Control headers at one time. The syntax is simple, but be sure that mod_expires is loaded first:

```
ExpiresByType image/gif "access plus 2 months"
```

This tells Apache to set `Expires` and `Cache-Control: max-age` headers with a date 2 months in the future (that is, 2 months from the date at which the request is made) for files of the `images/gif` Multipurpose Internet Mail Extension (MIME) type. Alternatively, you can set the values to a fixed date. (Most examples on the web seem to use a date of `Thu, 15 Apr 2010 20:00:00 GMT`, which suggests a lot of copy and pasting is going on.) However, this is recommended only for special circumstances — it's much better to use relative dates.

Let's set up some expiration rules in an `.htaccess`, and then run the example again. Set GIF, PNG, and JPEG files to expire in two months, as shown here:

```
ExpiresByType image/gif "access plus 2 months"
ExpiresByType image/png "access plus 2 months"
ExpiresByType image/jpeg "access plus 2 months"
```

First, you do a hard refresh of the page to force all resources to download again, as shown in Figure 2-5.

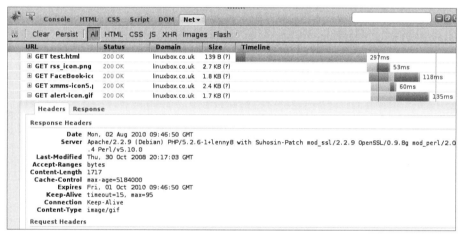

FIGURE 2-5

The header information has been expanded for the final request response to show the `Cache Control` and `Expires` headers that have now been set.

When you re-request the page, the difference is spectacular, as shown in Figure 2-6.

FIGURE 2-6

This time, only the HTML page is requested. The four images contained in it are simply loaded from the cache without bothering the server.

Choosing Expiration Policies

Armed with this powerful tool, you now must decide what to cache and for how long. Images are prime candidates, along with cascading style sheet (CSS), JavaScript, HTML, Flash movies, and so on. The only type of resources you don't usually want to cache (or at least not for long periods of time) is dynamically generated content created by server-side scripting languages such as PHP, Perl, Ruby, and so on. Implementation is then just creating a `ExpiresByType` directive for each MIME type. This can be done server-wide or on a per-directory basis, and, in the former case, you can always override it for specific directories.

How long should you cache for? One or two months seems like a good figure, although there's nothing to stop you from setting longer times. Clients re-requesting resources once every couple of months are unlikely to be a particular drain on the server, and for caching periods longer than this, the benefits become less and less.

What about nonstatic resources that change on a semi-regular basis? Although it might be tempting to not cache these, even a caching time of a couple of hours can make a significant difference in performance.

Coping with Stale Content

Although far-future `Expires`/`Cache-control` headers are great for performance, there will inevitably come a time when you need to roll out an updated version of your site's logo, CSS, or JavaScript. How do you deal with clients that already have these resources cached?

Fortunately, there are a few tricks you can use to make the client re-request the resource, all of which revolve around changing the URL to trick the browser into thinking the resource is not already cached. Following are some examples:

➤ Use a version/revision number or date in the filename (for example, `sitecode-1.0.1.js`).

➤ Use a version/revision number or date in the path (for example, `/javascript/2011-03-26/sitecode.js`).

➤ Switch the resource to a Canonical Name (CNAME) (for example, `http://rev101.mysite.com/javascript/sitecode.js`).

➤ Append a dummy query string (for example, `sitecode.js?v=1.0.1`).

The folks at `bbc.co.uk` go with the last method, as shown here:

```
<link rel="stylesheet" type="text/css"
  href="http://static.bbc.co.uk/homepage/css/bundles/domestic/main.css?553"
  media="screen,print" />
<link rel="stylesheet" type="text/css" href="http://static.bbc.co.uk/
    homepage/css/contentblock/promo/mediazone.css?553"
  media="screen,print" />
```

The folks at `eBay.co.uk` use a combination of the first and second examples, as shown here:

```
link rel="stylesheet" type="text/css" href="http://include.ebaystatic.com/
    v4css/en_GB/e679i/CCHP_HomepageV4_DLSR_e679i11667273_en_GB.css">
```

Few sites (if any) use the third method yet — probably because it involves additional work to set up the domain name service (DNS) and has no particular benefit over the other techniques.

It's also worth noting that some intermediate proxy-caches may not cache resources that contain a query string. So, the first two options are the safest bet.

With a bit of planning, none of these URL tricks should be difficult to implement, and rolling out new versions of resources should just entail changing global variables somewhere.

How Not to Cache

It's common to see meta tags used in the HTML of pages to control caching. This is a poor man's cache control technique, which isn't terribly effective. Although most browsers honor these meta tags when caching locally, most intermediate proxies do not — because they tend to look at only the headers of requests and not the body,. So, unless you're in a hosting environment in which you don't have control over HTTP headers (in which case, moving the host would be a much better bet), such meta tags should be avoided.

DEALING WITH INTERMEDIATE CACHES

Thus far, you have learned about controlling browser caching. What differences (if any) do you see with intermediate caching devices?

Cache-Control Revisited

The `Cache-Control` response header supports a lot more options than just `max-age`, and some of these options deal specifically with public caches. Following is a list of the most commonly seen `Cache-Control` options:

➤ `Cache-Control:max-age=<seconds>` — This is the maximum number of seconds for which the resource should be cached.

➤ `Cache-Control:s-maxage=<seconds>` — This is the maximum number of seconds for which the resource should be cached on shared (for example, public) caches.

➤ `Cache-Control:public` — This means that the response is cachable. This is used to override situations in which the response would usually be noncachable (for example, where HTTP authentication is used).

➤ `Cache-Control:private` — This means that shared caches should not cache this resource. Private caches (for example, those specific to a user, such as the browser cache) may cache this resource.

➤ `Cache-Control:no-store` — This means that the resource should not be cached in any situation, whether on shared or private caches.

➤ `Cache-Control:must-revalidate` — This requests that the cache must honor any `Expires/Cache-Control: max-age` headers set in the request. Without this, there are rare situations in which the cache may serve a stale copy of the resource.

➤ `Cache-Control:proxy-revalidate` — This is similar to `must-revalidate` but applies only to caching proxies.

➤ `Cache-Control:no-cache` — This means that the response must not be cached.

Recall from the earlier discussion about mod_expires that `Cache-Control:max-age` headers can be set using the `ExpiresByType` directive (which also sets `Expires` headers). To set other `Cache-Control` headers, you can use the `Headers` directive (part of mod_headers). Following is an example:

```
<FilesMatch "\.(php)$">
    Header set Cache-Control "private"
</FilesMatch>
```

Don't forget to ensure that mod_headers is loaded in your Apache configuration file.

`Cache-Control` options may also be combined, as shown here:

```
Cache-Control: max-age=7200, must-revalidate
Requests, not Orders
```

The guidance provided previously about `Expires` and `Cache-Control:max-age` should also apply to public proxies and intermediate caches. Just remember that all caching-related headers are requests, not orders. Although you can ask a cache to behave a certain way, you can't force it. Although browser caches are usually fairly well behaved, it's not uncommon to find intermediate caching proxies that stubbornly insist on doing things their own way. In these situations, sadly, nothing much can be done.

CACHING HTTP RESPONSES

Caching is usually associated with HTML documents and other resources, but there is also the opportunity for browsers to cache certain HTTP response codes, potentially saving a round trip to the web server. Unfortunately, this can cause problems for developers — especially if they are unaware of this behavior.

The Shift in Browser Behavior

A regular source of head-scratching for many web developers has been caused by a subtle shift in the way in which 3xx HTTP responses are cached by browsers.

Until a couple of years ago, none of the major browsers cached 301 redirect responses. So, if you set up a 301 redirect from, say, `http://mysite.com/a.html` to `http://mysite.com/b.html`, when a user entered `http://mysite.com/a.html` into the browser's address bar, the browser would always issue a request for `http://mysite.com/a.html` — even if it had previously seen this resource return a `301`.

Given that a `301` status means "Moved Permanently," it seems logical that browsers should cache (or have the option of caching) such responses, and the HTTP 1.1 RFC (RFC 2616 at `http://www.w3.org/Protocols/rfc2616`) says as much. According to that RFC, "This response is cacheable unless indicated otherwise."

Nevertheless, this doesn't mean that browsers *should* cache `301s`, and for more than 10 years (the RFC was published in 1999), none of the major ones did. Thus, web developers became quite used to the idea that `301` redirects could be modified server-side without any browser caching problems. .

Things changed in 2009 when the new browsers, such as Google Chrome and Firefox (perhaps driven by the increasing interest in performance), began caching `301` responses. The other major browsers followed suit soon afterward.

Technically, this is probably the right thing to do, and the RFC appears to encourage it. But for a generation of web developers used to the idea that `301s` would not be cached, it has caused a lot of controversy.

To compound the problem, many browser developers chose not to set a default expiration time on these cache entries (Firefox is a prime example). So, after they are in the browser's cache, they are in there forever. Even using the browser's option to empty the cache won't remove them because they are stored elsewhere. This creates no end to the problems if you have a `301` redirect in place and want to change it. Even though a `301` says, Moved Permanently, this probably will not apply for all eternity. In extreme situations, this caching can even result in infinite redirects, with the browser bouncing between two URLs that it believes redirect to each other.

It's not all bad news. Although many of the latest browsers can cache `301s` indefinitely by default, you can control this behavior (including disabling it) by setting an appropriate `Cache-control` or `Expires` header (or, for safety, both). In the past, the main problem has simply been that web developers did not realize they would need to do this.

On a more practical level, the issue arises of how to actually set `Cache-control` and `Expires` headers on a `301` redirect. In Apache, a standard `Redirect` doesn't offer this option and, at first glance, neither does `mod_rewrite`. If you've worked with `mod_rewrite` before, though, you know how powerful it can be. With a little bit of trickery, you can set additional headers on a `301`.

You must first abandon `Redirect` in favor of `mod_rewrite`, as shown here:

```
# Redirect 301 /a.html http://mysite.com/b.html
RewriteRule ^/a.html$ http://mysite.com/b.html [R=301,L]
```

The magic comes in when you also set an environmental variable at this stage. You can then create rules farther down that set headers if the `env` variable is set. The full code is as follows:

```
RewriteRule ^/a.html$ http://mysite.com/b.html [R=301,L,E=foo:1]
Header always set Expires "Thu, 01 Jan 1970 00:00:00 GMT" env=foo
Header always set Cache-Control "no-store, no-cache, must-revalidate" env=foo
```

In this example, the env variable is foo, and is given a value of 1 if the rewrite rule matches. You then set two headers to request that the client does not cache the result. Of course, you could just as easily set Expires headers in the near future to allow short-term caching of the redirect. Using mod_rewrite will always be more expensive than a simple redirect, but it's currently the only solution to set caching times on 301s.

Using Alternative 3xx Codes

Given that a 301 means Moved Permanently, it's worth rethinking the situations in which you use it. Web developers too often use a 301 for any form of redirect, no matter how transient it may be.

302 Found

A 302 Found response is one option. It indicates that the resource is temporarily located at another URL, and the RFC is quite clear that it should be cached only if appropriate Expires or Cache-control headers have been set to permit it. (Incidentally, the HTML meta refresh tag uses 302s.) This sounds promising but turns out to be something of a minefield for Search Engine Optimization (SEO).

Because many web masters may not appreciate the difference between 301 and 302, Google actually treats a 302 as a 301 if it decides the web master meant the latter. Bing and Yahoo don't appear to do this, but there is still concern over all three of the big search engines handling 302s in an unwanted way. Because a 302 is generally taken to mean a temporary redirect, it doesn't seem appropriate to use it for long-term redirects.

303 See Other

For redirects that you do not want to cache, a 303 See Other is perhaps the most suitable option. The RFC states that this response must not be cached, regardless of the presence or lack of caching-related headers. This makes it useful in situations in which you have limited control over headers or are worried about badly behaved browsers caching 302s.

In most cases, though, you probably do want redirects to be permanent (or at least semi-permanent), and a 301 is the most appropriate response. You just need to be aware that browsers will take this literally and set appropriate caching headers to prevent them from caching the 301s indefinitely.

DNS CACHING AND PREFETCHING

DNS is a prime example of effective, well-thought-out caching. Without caching, the whole system would fail under the load. DNS caching occurs at many levels, and although web developers or system administrators don't have a huge amount of control over how clients behave in this regard, it is important enough that it should be examined. Later, you'll learn about some specific measures introduced in web browsers, but to start let's review the DNS resolution process and the places in which caching can occur.

The DNS Resolution Process

When a user enters a URL into the browser's address bar, the first step is for the browser to resolve the hostname to an IP address, a task that it delegates to the operating system. At this stage, the operating system has a couple of choices. It can either resolve the address using a static `hosts` file (such as `/etc/hosts` on Linux), or it can query a DNS resolver. Most commonly, the resolving DNS server is hosted by the client's ISP, but some home users also run a resolver locally to increase performance. In larger corporate environments, it's common for a resolving DNS server to run inside the LAN.

If the queried resolver does not have the answer (to the DNS query), it attempts to establish which name servers are authoritative for the hostname the client wants to resolve. It then queries one of them and relays the answer back to the client that issued the request.

There's quite a lot going on here, with a single DNS query potentially resulting in a string of queries between multiple servers. Yet, despite this, DNS usually works efficiently, with a typical query taking less than 200 ms.

In practice, queries can be much faster than this because of the effects of caching. Whenever the client issues a request to an ISP's resolver, the resolver caches the response for a short period (the Time-To-Live, or TTL, set by the authoritative name server), and subsequent queries for this hostname can be answered directly from the cache. Because the latency between the client and the ISP's resolving name servers is generally low, responses are typically under 50 ms. (However, remember that wireless and dial-up connections have inherently higher latency.) Because this cache is shared among all customers of the ISP, the cache may well be primed already as a result of look-ups by other users.

The caching doesn't stop there, though. Even if end users aren't running their own caching (resolving) name server, the operating system typically caches DNS answers. Because this doesn't involve any network traffic, the latency is very low.

DNS Caching by the Browser

If that weren't enough, the major browsers now also implement their own DNS cache, which, in many cases, removes the need for the browser to ask the operating system to resolve. Because this isn't particularly faster than querying the operating system's cache, the primary motivation here is better control over what is cached and for how long.

For example, Opera caches DNS answers for 10 minutes, while Internet Explorer (IE) 4 and upward cache for 30 minutes. With Firefox 3.5 onward, the defaults are up to 400 cache entries with a 3-minute life, but this is configurable via `network.dnsCacheEntries` and `network` `.dnsCacheExpiration`. None of the big browsers offer a way to specifically clear the DNS cache; although using the option to clear general cached data will usually have the same effect.

How DNS Lookups Affect Performance

The result of all this caching is that DNS look-up times can vary dramatically — anything from a few milliseconds to perhaps one-half a second (longer look-ups aren't uncommon for users on high-latency links) if a remote name server must be queried. This manifests itself mostly as a slight delay when the user first loads the site. On subsequent views, the DNS query is answered from a cache. If you have a lot of resources spread across different hostnames (for example, to improve download concurrency, although this usually isn't necessary these days), these look-up times can mount up.

Using IP addresses rather than hostnames is one way to avoid the cost of the DNS look-up. But this doesn't tend to be practical given how extensively virtual hosting is used. (There's no one-to-one mapping between IP and hostname.) Instead, you should ensure that DNS queries on your domains are resolved quickly and used with a high TTL to encourage longer caching. If necessary, use your own name servers, where you have greater control over the TTL and network performance.

DNS Prefetching

Web browsers have another trick up their sleeves to help with DNS performance: DNS *prefetching*. Introduced in Chrome in 2008, prefetching involves performing DNS lookups on URLs linked to in the HTML document, in anticipation that the user may eventually click one of these links. All the major browsers now support DNS prefetching; although the implementations differ slightly.

Prefetching is slightly reminiscent of those annoying browsers and plug-ins that were popular a decade or so ago. They would prefetch all the links in an HTML document to improve responsiveness. Web masters hated these browsers because they drove up bandwidth and server load, made web stats meaningless, and end users often got a nasty shock if they were not on unmetered bandwidth. The difference with DNS prefetching is that the amount of data sent over the network is much lower. Typically, a single User Datagram Protocol (UDP) packet can carry the question, and a second UDP packet can carry the answer.

In Chrome, prefetching occurs in the background after the HTML document has been fetched — either while additional resources are retrieved, or the user is reading the page. Because a slow look-up on one query would cause a delay in resolving the others, Chrome uses multiple threads (up to a maximum of eight) on operating systems that don't support asynchronous DNS lookups (such as Windows). This ensures that a slow name server doesn't hold up any other queries.

It's interesting to note that when Chrome receives the responses to these DNS prefetch queries, it simply discards them, rather than storing them in its DNS cache. Although this may seem odd, it serves to prime the operating system's DNS cache, which can return a response immediately should the browser later request it.

Firefox 3.5 took Chrome's prefetching implementation one step further. Whereas the original Chrome implementation only prefetched hostnames used in anchor links, when Firefox downloads an HTML document, it immediately begins resolving hostnames used in other resources (such as images, CSS, and JavaScript). This is beyond the anticipatory prefetching used in other browsers and is more of a case of streamlining parallel downloading.

Controlling Prefetching

One situation in which prefetching fails to be effective is with links that redirect straight to another URL. A prime example would be the links in Google search results, which take the user to their intended destination after first passing through a tracking URL. Here, the tracking hostname would be prefetched but not the ultimate destination domain. To accommodate this, most browsers now support a `<link>` tag with the nonstandard `rel="dns-prefetch"` attribute. This causes the browser to prefetch the given hostname and can be used to precache such redirect links. Following is an example:

```
<link rel="dns-prefetch" href="http://www.example.com">
```

In addition, site owners can disable or enable prefetching through the use of a special HTTP header like this:

```
X-DNS-Prefetch-Control: off
```

Although introduced by Chrome, this header is recognized by all browsers that support prefetching.

SUMMARY

Caching is an essential part of website performance. Left to their own devices, browsers make a reasonable effort to cache through the use of conditional `GET`s. Although this cuts down on data transferred from the server to the client, it does nothing to reduce the number of HTTP requests. Instead, `Expires` or `Cache-Control` headers should be used because they are far more powerful and effective.

HTTP resources aren't the only things to be cached by browsers, however. All the major browsers perform some level of DNS caching, and within the last few years they have also begun to perform DNS prefetching. Again, the details vary from browser to browser.

The flip side to aggressive caching is that sometimes the client has stale content, and trickery is needed to force the browser to refresh. In recent years, this has become a particular problem with `301` redirects because of a shift in the way that browsers handle the caching of them.

Although you can set specific `Cache-Control` headers to discourage caching (for example, to stop intermediate proxies from caching private data), resources on which you have previously set a far-future expiration time are more problematic. The most common workaround is to use version numbers in either the filename or the query string (for example, changing your HTML source to reference `myscript-v2.js` rather than `myscript-v1.js`).

So far, you've seen only client-side aspects of caching. but in Chapter 7, "Working with Web Servers," you'll see caching from the opposite end, and learn how web servers can save themselves a lot of work by serving pre-generated content from a cache.

While caching is a very useful means of reducing loading times for repeated page views, it does nothing to speed up the initial loading of a page (where the user's cache is not primed). In Chapter 3, you'll see how compression can be used to reduce the amount of data that the client's browser needs to fetch.

3

Content Compression

WHAT'S IN THIS CHAPTER?

➤ Understanding how HTTP compression works

➤ Becoming familiar with browser quirks and how to handle clients that don't support compression

➤ Exploring alternatives to gzip and deflate compression

➤ Compressing directly in PHP

With bandwidth being a bottleneck for many users (and for dial-up users, easily the largest bottleneck), it's not surprising that web masters would want to compress their content. The benefits are obvious — faster loading times for users and reduced data transfer bills for web masters. This chapter examines the available methods of compression, which browsers support them, and situations in which compression is not appropriate.

WHO USES COMPRESSION

Armed with a list of the 1,000 most popular websites (courtesy of Alexa.com), a quick test of average page sizes and compression support revealed how the top 20 rate, as shown in Table 3-1.

TABLE 3-1: Average Page Sizes of the Top 20 Websites

DOMAIN	GZIP COMPRESSION SUPPORTED?	HOMEPAGE SIZE (UNCOMPRESSED) IN KB	HOMEPAGE SIZE (COMPRESSED) IN KB	PERCENT OF UNCOMPRESSED SIZE
Google.com	Yes	13.7	5.2	38
Facebook.com	Yes	30.9	9.6	31
Youtube.com	Yes	67.1	16.3	24
Yahoo.com	Yes	161.0	39.5	25
Live.com	No	35.0	—	—
Baidu.com	Yes	6.3	3.0	48
Wikipedia.org	Yes	46.9	11.7	25
Blogger.com	Yes	12.6	4.6	37
Msn.com	Yes	90.3	27.1	30
Twitter.com	Yes	44.1	9.4	21
qq.com	Yes	193.2	49.0	25
Yahoo.co.jp	Yes	29.0	7.0	24
Google.co.in	Yes	14.0	5.0	36
Taobao.com	Yes	166.2	31.3	19
Amazon.com	Yes	138.9	25.6	18
Sina.com.cn	Yes	172.4	11.7	67
Google.de	Yes	13.0	5.0	38
Google.com.hk	Yes	12.0	5.0	42
Wordpress.com	Yes	35.6	11.2	31
Ebay.com	Yes	356	11.5	32

As you can see, compression is well supported. Of the top 1,000 sites, 227 did not support compression, with only 1 in the top 20 (live.com) and 10 in the top 100 not supporting it.

There's also a fairly wide range in the amount of compression achieved in this Top 20 table, with the size of the compressed contents being anything between 15 percent and 60 percent of the original. In general, you should expect to see a compression ratio of approximately 1:3 or 1:4 for HTML, but it is highly dependent on the nature of the text (in particular, repeating patterns). Later in this chapter, you'll learn more about ways to improve this.

Although it's difficult to produce accurate empirical data about download times (because there are so many other factors), it would take a dial-up user approximately 14 seconds to retrieve the youtube.com homepage without compression. With compression, this figure drops to 2 seconds. For the painfully large sina.com.cn, without compression, dial-up users would need to wait more than a minute for the homepage HTML document to download, a figure that drops to an almost bearable 16 seconds with compression.

The picture isn't quite so bleak for broadband users. Uncompressed, the homepage HTML document of Sina.com.cn (which is, admittedly, unusually large) would take approximately 4 seconds to retrieve from a 1 megabit (mb) connection. Compressed, this figure drops to 1 second. For more reasonably sized HTML documents (such as those on the homepages of Wikipedia or Twitter), the benefits of compression for broadband users are fractions of a second. But this is still a saving worth making. As connection speeds have increased, so, too, have expectations of users.

UNDERSTANDING HOW COMPRESSION WORKS

Like many other features of HTTP (such as KeepAlive, as discussed in Chapter 1, "A Refresher on Web Browsers"), content compression occurs only when a client advertises, wants to use it, and a server indicates its willingness to enable it.

Clients indicate they want to use it by sending the Accept-Encoding header when making requests. The value of this header is a comma-separated list of compression methods that the client will accept. If the server supports content compression (or, more accurately, if it supports any of the compression methods that the client has advertised), it may deliver a compressed version of the resource. It indicates that the content has been compressed (and the compression method used) with the Content-Encoding header in the response, as shown here:

```
GET /1/icons.html HTTP/1.1
Host: linuxbox.co.uk
User-Agent: Mozilla/5.0 (X11; U; Linux x86_64; en-US; rv:1.9.1.8)
    Gecko/20100308 Iceweasel/3.5.8 (like Firefox/3.5.8) GTB7.1
Accept: text/html,application/xhtml+xml,application/xml;q=0.9,*/*;q=0.8
Accept-Language: en-us,en;q=0.5
Accept-Encoding: gzip,deflate
Accept-Charset: ISO-8859-1,utf-8;q=0.7,*;q=0.7
Keep-Alive: 300
Connection: keep-alive
Pragma: no-cache
Cache-Control: no-cache

HTTP/1.1 200 OK
Server: Apache/2.2.9 (Debian) PHP/5.2.6-1+lenny8 with Suhosin-Patch
    mod_ssl/2.2.9 OpenSSL/0.9.8g mod_perl/2.0.4 Perl/v5.10.0
Accept-Ranges: bytes
Vary: Accept-Encoding
Content-Encoding: gzip
```

```
Content-Length: 152
Keep-Alive: timeout=15, max=98
Connection: Keep-Alive
Content-Type: text/html
```

The `Content-Length` header in the response indicates the size of the compressed content, not the original, uncompressed contents.

If a client supports multiple compression methods, it may express a preference using so-called q-values. In the following example, the client expresses a preference for `deflate` by specifying a q-value of `1.0` for deflate and `0.5` for `gzip`.

```
Accept-Encoding: gzip;q=0.5, deflate; q=1.0
```

Compression Methods

The HTTP specifications define four possible compression values:

➤ `identity` — This indicates no compression. If a client advertises only this method in the `Accept-Encoding` header, the server should not compress the response contents. This value is used only in the `Accept-Encoding` header — a server sending uncompressed content should not send a `Content-Encoding: identity` header.

➤ `compress` — This method uses the UNIX `compress` method, which is based on the Lempel-Ziv Welch (LZW) algorithm. Use of `compress` is deprecated in favor of the next two methods.

➤ `gzip` — For a long time, `gzip` was the most popular compression format. It's based on LZ77, which, in turn, is based on LZW. As the name implies, it is the same algorithm used in the UNIX `gzip` tool.

➤ `deflate` — Essentially, this is just `gzip` without the checksum header. `deflate` tends to be a little faster but is also a little less efficient.

> **NOTE** *Rather than exploring the subtleties of these various compression formats here, you should look at Appendix A, "TCP Performance," which discusses them in more depth.*

Of these four methods (the first of which isn't actually a compression method), the latter two are the most important and are well supported by today's browsers. `deflate` is slightly superior, but any compression is better than nothing. So, if you are in the situation of using only `gzip`, don't worry too much.

What to Compress

Potentially any resource can be served up compressed, but compression is usually just applied to text-based content such as HTML, XML, CSS, and JavaScript. The reason is twofold:

➤ Text tends to compress much more than binary data.

➤ Many of the binary formats in use on the web already use compression. GIF, PNG, and JPEG are prime examples, and there is virtually nothing to be gained by applying content compression to these. That simply wastes CPU cycles and may even make the size slightly larger (because the compression method can add its own headers to the data).

In view of this latter point, there's usually nothing to be gained by compressing text resources smaller than a certain size either. The savings are minimal, and headers added by the compression method may well result in the compressed resource being larger than the original. When you learn about web servers in Chapter 7, "Working with Web Servers," you'll discover methods to compress only certain content.

Browser Support

Sadly, browser support for content compression hasn't always been great. Although the major browsers started to introduce support for this feature in the late 1990s, one browser in particular (no prizes for guessing which) has, until recently, suffered regular small glitches in its implementation. When a browser simply does not support content compression, that's fine. But when a browser claims to support compression, but does not do so correctly, this causes problems.

Table 3-2 summaries gzip and deflate support in the major browsers.

TABLE 3-2: gzip and deflate Support in Major Browsers

BROWSER	GZIP/DEFLATE SUPPORT?	NOTES
IE 4+	Yes	Support was added in Internet Explorer (IE) 4, but see the following for exceptions.
IE 4.5 and 5 (Mac)	No	
IE 5.5 and 6.0	Partial	A bug causes first 2,048 bytes of compressed content to be lost in some situations.
IE 6.0 SP1	Partial	A security update breaks gzip compression in some situations.
IE 6,7,8	Partial	These versions of IE implement deflate incorrectly, which may cause problems.
Netscape 4.06+	Partial	There were numerous bugs in versions 4.06 through 4.08.
Netscape 6+	Yes	
Firefox	Yes	

continues

TABLE 3-2 *(continued)*

BROWSER	GZIP/DEFLATE SUPPORT?	NOTES
Opera 5+	Yes	Opera 6 appears to be the only major browser that detects and automatically decodes compressed content if the server has not sent `Content-Encoding: gzip` (or `deflate`).
Lynx 2.6+	Yes	`deflate` support was added on version 2.8.6.
Safari	Yes	There have been problems in the past with compression of non-HTML data (for example, CSS).
Chrome	Yes	

The problems with IE's support for `deflate` stem from inconsistencies in the HTTP/1.1 RFC (2616). While the `deflate` compression algorithm is simply a stream of compressed data, RFC 2616 defines the `deflate` content encoding method as a `deflate` stream inside `zlib` wrappers (the wrappers provide error checking, among other things). Versions 6, 7, and 8 of IE expect to see just a `deflate` stream, and choke on the `zlib` headers.

Because of the confusion, many browsers choose to support both the HTTP/1.1 definition of `deflate` and the "raw" `deflate` stream. You can find a more detailed comparison at http://www.vervestudios.co/projects/compression-tests/results.

> **NOTE** *You can learn more about* `zlib` *and* `deflate` *in Appendix C,* *"Compression."*

In Chapter 7, when you learn about web servers, you can see how they can be configured not to compress content for browsers with known buggy implementations.

Dealing with Clients That Don't Support Compression

An analysis of log files shows that approximately 10 percent to 15 percent of clients don't advertise support for content compression (via the `Accept-Encoding` header). Can it actually be that 10 to 15 percent of the Internet still uses prehistoric browsers with no compression support?

It turns out that of this 10 to 15 percent, approximately one-half do actually support compression, even though they don't advertise it. The most common reasons for this discrepancy are intermediate proxies and antivirus software stripping the `Accept-Encoding` header from the requests.

Why would they do this? Proxies and antivirus software are often used to filter content, and it's easier for them if the content is uncompressed. Despite the fact that it should be relatively trivial for *them* to uncompress, they choose to penalize the client by stripping the `Accept-Encoding` header. Usually, the end user isn't aware that this is even happening. And, if you think this type of behavior would be restricted to uneducated two-bit software developers, think again. Big names such as McAfee, ZoneAlarm, Norton, and Squid have all been guilty of this practice in the past.

One strategy to deal with these problematic clients is to send some compressed content anyway to see how the clients handle it. If the client parses it correctly, it should be safe to use compression when delivering future content. The general logic of such checks would be as follows:

1. When the client issues a request, check for the presence of a cookie. (Call it gzip_ok.) If the cookie has a value of 1, you already know the client understands gzip compression and can deliver compressed content to it.

2. If the cookie is unset and the client is claiming not to support gzip, check to see if it can handle gzipped content. You do this by including a link to an external JavaScript file containing some simple script to set the gzip_ok cookie to 1. You configure the web server to always serve this script compressed. If the client can parse this JavaScript file, the gzip_ok will be set.

3. If the cookie has a value of zero, you know that you've already tested for gzip support, and it hasn't worked.

4. The next time a resource is requested, you can use the presence of the gzip_ok cookie to decide whether to serve compressed contents.

This seems like a somewhat long-winded technique and goes against the principals of keeping pages lean, reducing the number of external resources, and so on. But don't forget that this technique would be applied only on clients that claim not to support gzip compression, and even then it would be for only the first request. The major drawback to this method isn't its intricacy — it's that it relies on the client supporting JavaScript.

Another option is to compile a list of browsers that are known to support content compression, and then serve compressed content to them no matter what the Accept-Encoding headers says. This actually is not recommended, though. There may be legitimate reasons for the browser not advertising support for compression (such as the user having disabled it), and sending compressed content to a client that can't decode it can render your site inaccessible. Better to risk longer page loading times than no loading at all.

Even if you do concoct a mechanism such as one of these to deal with misbehaving clients, you'll still be left with perhaps 5 percent of clients that simply can't handle compressed content. As such, you should still strive to keep document sizes small. (Remember that a large document doesn't just mean larger download times; it also means larger parsing and rendering times.) Don't fall into the lazy trap to think that bloated HTML doesn't matter because it will shrink after it's compressed.

Disadvantages of Content Compression

Although content compression is almost always a good thing, there are a couple of small drawbacks.

First, there is additional CPU usage at both the server side and client side. The server must compress the document, and the client must decompress it. As you'll learn in Chapter 7, it's often possible for web servers to deliver precompressed versions of resources, rather than compressing resources on-the-fly each time a request is made.

Second, as already mentioned, there will always be a small percentage of clients that simply can't accept compressed content. Because of this, you can't use compression to excuse bloated HTML. In Chapter 4, "Keeping the Size Down with Minification,", you'll learn about techniques to reduce or improving compression ratios and minifying HTML.

gzip Performance

In Apache, `mod_gzip` and `mod_deflate` compress resources on-the-fly when a compression-aware client requests them. Apart from being rather wasteful of CPU cycles, just how good is the compression?

As you'll see in Chapter 7, with many web servers, you can compress the files and then have the web server deliver these precompressed versions when talking to compression-enabled clients. This allows you to break free from using the `gzip`/`deflate` implementation in the web server. But is there any real advantage in doing this?

Let's now revisit the list of the top 20 websites (refer to Table 3-1) — only this time, without the country-specific versions of Google and Yahoo, and `Live.com` (because it doesn't support compression). Can you improve on their compression ratios by using specialist compression tools? 7-Zip (`http://www.7-zip.org/`) has a reputation to pull out all the stops to deliver high levels of compression, and it can write files in the `gzip` format.

Table 3-3 compares this to the GNU `gzip` tool (running at its highest compression level).

TABLE 3-3: Average Page Sizes of the Top 20 Websites with gzip and 7-Zip

DOMAIN	UNCOMPRESSED SIZE IN BYTES	DEFAULT COMPRESSION SIZE IN BYTES	GZIP SIZE IN BYTES	7-ZIP SIZE IN BYTES	PERCENTAGE IMPROVEMENT IN 7-ZIP OVER DEFAULT
Google.com	13,725	5,220	5,346	5,288	−1.29
Facebook.com	30,923	9,586	9,261	9,124	4.82
Youtube.com	67,084	16,339	12,177	12,114	19.74
Yahoo.com	16,339	39,522	39,477	39,207	0.78
Baidu.com	62,969	2,993	3,003	2,978	0.5
Wikipedia.org	46,861	11,695	11,576	11,520	1.5
Blogger.com	12,584	4,647	4,653	4,603	0.95
Msn.com	90,329	27,126	25,030	24,817	8.51
Twitter.com	44,118	9,422	9,267	9,289	1.41
qq.com	193,192	48,984	48,996	48,471	1.05
Taobao.com	166,168	31,331	30,874	31,160	0.55
Amazon.com	138,941	25,526	27,944	27,676	−1.1
Sina.com.cn	172,398	116,726	36,486	36,267	68.93
Wordpress.com	35,591	11,177	9,927	9,821	12.13
Ebay.com	35,502	11,506	9,874	9,795	14.87

In each case, 7-Zip outperforms `gzip`; although the saving is so small as to be almost insignificant (averaging approximately 1 percent).

The results are made somewhat more confusing because you don't know the compression tools used by these sites. Some use the on-the-fly `gzip` modules shipped with their web server; others serve up pregenerated `gzipped` resources. However, the results do clearly show that many sites are not compressing as efficiently as they should be — WordPress, eBay, MSN, and YouTube are prime examples. As for `Sina.com.cn`, something is going seriously wrong.

> **NOTE** *Interestingly, Amazon's compression outperforms both* `gzip` *and 7-Zip, suggesting it uses a tailored* `gzip` *compression implementation geared toward higher levels of compression. Appendix C provides more information on the scope for performance improvements in the underlying algorithm used by* `gzip`.

In short, if you do need to compress on-the-fly, you should look at how efficient your compression routine is — in some situations, you may be surprised. Try compressing your data with GNU `gzip` and comparing the difference. If your setup allows you to serve pregenerated `gzip` data, you might as well use 7-Zip, but there probably won't be a huge difference over standard tools.

Other Compression Methods

Although `gzip` and `deflate` are widely used, a number of other compression methods are available. None of these are part of the HTTP specifications, however, and support for them across browsers is generally poor. Let's take a quick look at them here, in anticipation of them perhaps becoming more popular in the future.

bzip2

UNIX users have long been familiar with the `bzip2` format, which offers superior compression to `gzip` (at the expense of somewhat higher CPU usage). With HTTP supporting compression and `gzip`, it seems only natural that `bzip2` should also be supported. Despite this, none of the major browsers natively support `bzip2`. (Although some do by means of third-party extensions.)

SDCH

Apparently pronounced "sandwich," Shared Dictionary Compression for HTTP (SDCH) is a compression method developed by Google. It enables a high level of cross-request redundancy through the use of a domain-specific shared dictionary.

When a client first requests a resource from a domain, a link to download the shared dictionary is returned in the response header. This dictionary contains strings commonly used on the website. Subsequent responses may then have their content encoded by replacing such strings with a reference to their position in the dictionary.

This has the potential for huge savings. Elements common to many pages (such as the header, footer, navigation menu, and so on) — whole blocks of markup — can potentially be replaced with just a reference to the dictionary. Appendix C highlights the similarities with the dictionary-based encoding of formats such as LWZ.

SDCH also introduces problems for filtering proxies and personal antivirus software because malicious code could potentially be split across multiple requests, making it difficult to detect. The view among developers of such software already seems to be that it's easier just to strip SDCH-related headers from outgoing requests than to attempt to decode and parse SDCH-encoded content. After reading the earlier section in this chapter, "Dealing with Clients That Don't Support Compression," this attitude won't surprise you, but it's the end user who loses out.

At present, Chrome is the only browser that supports SDCH, and Google's web servers are the only servers that support it. Perhaps this will change in the future.

EXI

Intended for XML content, EXI encodes XML into a binary format, drastically reducing the file size. Although none of the major browsers support EXI natively yet, the W3C is acting favorably toward it, and it looks set to play an important part in the web in the future.

peerdist

Developed by Microsoft, `peerdist` applies the logic of peer-to-peer networks to the web by enabling a client to retrieve content from its peers, as well as the originating web server. In theory, this should enable faster retrieval and lighten the load on the originating server.

At the moment, support for `peerdist` is low, but with Microsoft being such a big player, it may change this in the future.

Transfer Encoding

To conclude this section, let's take a brief look at *Transfer Encoding (TE)*, which is often confused with *Content Encoding*. The two are similar. However, whereas Content Encoding is end-to-end, TE is hop-to-hop. Any intermediate devices that encounter messages with TE headers can uncompress the message and may not necessarily recompress before sending it on. As such, Content Encoding is to be preferred.

Dynamically generated content poses a problem for servers, which are expected to send a `Content-Length` header in responses. The server has the choice to either wait for the content to be fully generated (so that it may calculate the size), or omit the `Content-Length` header.

The latter method was fine under HTTP 1.0 where `Keep-Alive` was not the default. The server would simply close the connection after it had finished sending, and the client would infer that there was no more content to come.

With persistent connections in HTTP 1.1 (or `Keep-Alive` in HTTP 1.0), the problem is trickier. Because the connection will probably not be automatically closed, the client has no way to tell when the server has finished delivering the response content. The server *must* send a `Content-Length` header.

The disadvantage to this is that the server must wait until the back-end script has finished running before it can start sending the response. End users could easily be left twiddling their thumbs, waiting for a heavyweight PHP script to finishing running before seeing any content.

The solution is *Chunked Transfer Encoding (CTE)*, which enables an HTTP response (or, more rarely, a request) to be split into multiple smaller packets. After the server generates the first X number of bytes, it can send them off (with the appropriate `Content-Length` and a `Transfer-Encoding: Chunked` header), and the client knows that there is more to follow. The server indicates that it has finished by sending a zero-sized chunk. Each chunk can have content compression applied to it, too, which is the justification to include this discussion in this chapter.

By default, CTE is considered to be enabled in both client and server in HTTP 1.1, so no additional headers are needed to enable it, and there is no extra work for the web master or system administrator.

If CTE seems like a perfect solution, there is the small matter of increased packet flow across the network. Although the overall size of the response body stays the same, each chunk will have its own set of headers, which will increase the overall amount of data sent down the wire. Unless the client has severely restricted bandwidth or high latency, this shouldn't be a cause for concern, and the increase in speed perceived by the user will more than make up for it.

COMPRESSION IN PHP

A solution often used by web developers is to compress HTML output in a scripting language before sending it to the browser. This has the advantage of not requiring any modifications to the web server (for example, enabling or compiling in compression modules) and makes it well-suited for code that will be distributed. As you will see, though, this approach is ultimately less powerful than using the compression offered by many web servers.

Compressing PHP-Generated Pages

For compressing pages generated by PHP, there are a couple of options: output buffering and zlib. The latter is the preferred solution these days, but the first is still widely used, and you'll see examples of both here.

Using Output Buffering

Let's look at an example in PHP:

```php
<?php

ob_start("ob_gzhandler");
?>

<html>
 <head>
    ...
```

Here, output buffering is used with the `ob_gzhandler` callback function to compress the buffered output before sending it to the browser.

You can go one step further to create your own callback function to handle the compression. Although this doesn't mean you can use an alternative compression method such as `bzip` (you're still limited to what the client supports), it does provide the opportunity to deploy some minification. Consider the following:

```php
<?php
ob_start("myhandler");

    function myhandler($buffer) {
        $buffer = str_replace(
                array ("\r", "  ", "\n", "\t"),
                "");
        return $buffer;
    }
?>

<html>
 <head>
    ...
```

> **NOTE** *Chapter 4 discusses minification in more detail.*

There are two main drawbacks to this method. The first is that you must manually add the output buffering line to the top of all scripts. This can be mitigated by placing the code in an auto prepend file.

The second disadvantage is that, as a consequence of the buffering, no compression takes place until the script finishes executing. At that point, the data in the buffer will be compressed, and then drip-fed to the client. This contrasts with Apache's `mod_gzip`, which can perform streaming compression — as your code generates output and sends it to Apache, `mod_gzip` begins compressing it and sending it out to the client (which, in turn, can begin uncompressing the data immediately). Tricks like these can help to reduce the latency of requests, particularly for dynamic pages that take a long time to generate or are large.

Compressing with zlib

These days, the preferred method to compress with PHP is to enable the `output_compression` option of the `zlib` extension. (Although this may seem to suggest otherwise, `ob_gzhandler` uses the `zlib` extension, too.) This is a `php ini` option and can be set in either the code itself (via `ini_set()`), a `.htaccess` file, or, as shown here, `php.ini`:

```
zlib.output_compression = 1
```

Optionally, you can also set the compression level, as shown here:

```
zlib.output_compression_level = 9
```

The default value is -1, which causes PHP to pick a level.

The only disadvantage here is that the setting is global, so, unlike `ob_gzhandler`, you can't pick and choose to which scripts it will be applied. This usually isn't a problem, though, because you'll generally want to compress as much as possible.

Compressing Other Resources

What *is* a problem is that compression in PHP naturally applies only to the HTML document — style sheets, JavaScript, and so on, are not affected. You could argue that the benefits to compress these resources are lower because they are invariably being cached. But compression is generally a no-brainer and is worth using even in marginal cases.

Some web developers get around this by using a simple PHP script to serve up CSS and JavaScript like so:

```php
<?php

  header('Content-type: text/css');
  ob_start("ob_gzhandler");
  include('style.css');

?>
```

Then you link to it like so:

```
<link rel="stylesheet" type="text/css" href="myscript.php"/>
```

Evoking PHP to serve up static resources like this hurts performance, though, and actually isn't necessary when better alternatives (such as `mod_gzip`) exist. Although compression in PHP is certainly an option, it's usually faster, cleaner, and more efficient to use `mod_gzip` or similar.

SUMMARY

Compressing web content speeds up downloads and reduces your bandwidth bills. Although compression causes a slight increase in CPU usage on both the client and server, the benefits far outweigh this, and enabling compression is almost always the right thing to do. Any plain-text resource is a candidate for compression: HTML documents, style sheets, JavaScript, XML, and so on. But there is generally little to be gained from compressing binary resources. (Most images, for example, are already highly compressed.)

Browser support for compression has been buggy in the past, with some browsers incorrectly handling compressed CSS or JavaScript. Fortunately, those days have passed, and today you should generally compress as much as possible.

The standard compression methods are `gzip` or `deflate` — they are essentially the same thing — and, although other methods (offering better compression) have been proposed, none are yet widely supported.

The standard way to compress content is via a web server module such as `mod_gzip` (a topic that will be discussed in more detail in Chapter 7), but you can also generate compressed content directly via a scripting language. The examples provided in this chapter used PHP, but you can implement the same principals in ASP, Python, Ruby, Perl, and so on. Nevertheless, compression this way isn't as efficient, nor is it the preferred route.

While compression is an excellent way of improving page loading times, it is not being used to its full potential if the text being compressed is bloated. *Minification* refers to the process of stripping down the plain text (often prior to compression), and is the subject of Chapter 4.

Keeping the Size Down with Minification

WHAT'S IN THIS CHAPTER?

➤ Shrinking your CSS, JavaScript, and HTML

➤ Learning the tricks used by Google's Closure Compiler and Yahoo's YUI Compressor

➤ Comparing automatic minifiers

Minification is the act to strip out unnecessary characters from code to reduce the size, and a *minifier* is the tool that does it. Most often, the term is applied to JavaScript, but as you shall see, the technique can also be used on CSS and (to some extent) HTML.

For the web master, the aim of minification is, of course, to reduce file size and thus speed up transfer times for clients. Using gzip compression offers bigger reductions in file size, and it's often claimed that this makes minification redundant — a minified, gzipped page isn't much smaller than an unminified, gzipped page. Although there is some truth in this argument, minification is still a useful technique. And with approximately 10 percent of web traffic passing through browsers that don't support gzip compression (see http://developer.yahoo.com/performance/rules.html), there is a sizable minority of users for whom minification can help a lot.

The downside with minification is that code becomes difficult to read and modify. One solution is to store your code unminified and then minify it on-the-fly, as clients request it. This is a terribly inefficient way to handle what are usually fairly static resources, though, and definitely not something recommended. Instead, you should keep an unminified copy of the code in a separate directory and pass it through the minifier when you are ready for it to go live, possibly as part of your build process

> **NOTE** *For all but the most basic websites, it is common to automate the process of deploying a new version of the site via a basic shell script or batch file. This might consist of copying the code over from a development/staging area, setting the correct file permissions, pre-compressing resources, and so on. This is an ideal place in which to perform minification.*

What are "unnecessary characters"? In the languages discussed here, whitespace and comments are the main candidates for removal, and many simplistic minifiers remove only these. This is often just scraping the surface of what is possible though — especially with JavaScript, which is where the discussion in this chapter starts.

> **NOTE** *Be aware that minification shouldn't be used as an excuse to write sloppy code. Don't fall into the trap to think that it's okay to write bloated, badly structure code because a minifier will clean it up for you. Your first step should always be to manually clean up your code as much as possible; only then should you pass it through the minifier.*

JAVASCRIPT MINIFICATION

Of the three languages examined here (JavaScript, CSS, and HTML), JavaScript offers the most potential for minification. Aside from removing whitespaces and comments, Windows-style line breaks (CRLF) can be converted to UNIX-style breaks (LF), and variable names can be shortened.

Let's look at the typical minification process for a small block of code. In this case, the code handles a function to toggle the "visibility" (more accurately the display) of an element:

```
function toggle(elementID) {

    if ( document.getElementById(elementID).style.display != 'none' ) {
        document.getElementById(elementID).style.display  = 'none';
    }
    else {
        document.getElementById(elementID).style.display = '';
    }
}
```

As it stands, this function weighs in at 297 bytes.

Before you run it through a minifier, you should attempt some manual optimization. Using a variable holding a reference to the element's display would be a good start, as shown here:

```
function toggle(elementID) {
    var el = document.getElementById(elementID);
    if ( el.style.display != 'none' ) {
```

```
                        el.style.display = 'none';
                }
                else {
                        el.style.display = '';
                }
        }
```

This takes the weight down to 246 bytes.

You can simplify things a bit more by getting rid of the `if`/`else` block and using the ternary operator:

```
function toggle(elementID) {
        var el = document.getElementById(elementID);
        ( el.style.display != 'none' ) ? el.style.display = 'none' :
                el.style.display = '';
}
```

This takes it down to 193 bytes. So far, you have preserved whitespaces, and the code is still readable.

Now that you've seen how to clean up this code, you can pass it through a minifier.

YUI Compressor

One of the most popular minifiers is Yahoo's YUI Compressor. It's a command-line minifier, written in Java, that can process both JavaScript and CSS. You can download it from `http://developer.yahoo .com/yui/compressor/`. (Of course, you must have Java installed.) Running it is simple, as shown here:

```
$ java -jar /usr/local/bin//yuicompressor-2.3.5/build/yuicompressor-2.3.5.jar
    input.js > output.js
```

Now try it on the sample function introduced earlier:

```
$ java -jar /usr/local/bin/yuicompressor-2.3.5/build/yuicompressor-2.3.5.jar
    function.js > function_minified.js
$ cat function_minified.js
function toggle(a){var b=document.getElementById(a);if(b.style.display!="none")
    {b.style.display="none"}else{b.style.display=""}};
```

A few things have happened here. Unnecessary whitespaces have been removed, and the two variables have had their names shortened: `elementID` to `A`, and `el` to `B`. Because these variables exist only inside the function, it's safe to rename them without worrying about it impacting other code.

This takes the function's size down to 93 bytes — a significant improvement from the original 342.

Just to stress the importance of manually optimizing your code first, look at how the YUI Compressor copes with the original function before you made any changes to it:

```
function toggle(A){var B=document.getElementById(A);
    if(document.getElementById(A).style.display!="none")
    {document.getElementById(A).style.display="none"}
    else{document.getElementById(A).style.display=""}};
```

It has still renamed the local variables and removed whitespaces, but the long-winded `if/else` block with references to the element's display are still there, and the size is down to only 204 bytes. The YUI Compressor may be clever, but it's not a mind reader.

You may have wondered why, in the manual optimization examples, `var el = document` `.getElementById(elementID);` was not simply written to `el = document` `.getElementById(elementID);` to save a few more bytes.

Although it may seem that declaring a variable with `var` is unnecessary, there is a subtle impact on the variable's scope. Variables defined inside a function with `var` are local — that is, they exist only inside the function. Initializing a variable without `var` causes it to have a global scope, and it is available to code outside the function.

Aside from it making good programming sense to use local variables (because that lessens the potential for variable names to clash), the choice of a local versus global variable also has an impact on minification. For example, say that you run the following through the YUI Compressor:

```
function toggle(elementID) {
    el = document.getElementById(elementID);
    (el.style.display != 'none' ) ? el.style.display = 'none' : el.style.display = ";
```

Following is the output this time:

```
function toggle(A){el=document.getElementById(A).style.display;
    (el!="none")?el="none":el=""};
```

The YUI Compressor realizes that `el` is a global variable and shies away touching it in case it breaks another part of your code. In general, it's best to define your variables with `var`.

Google Closure

The YUI Compressor is not the only JavaScript minifier out there. The new kid on the block at the moment is Google's Closure Compiler (`http://code.google.com/closure/compiler/`), which is set to become the leader of the pack. Crude benchmarking suggests its standard mode offers levels of minification similar to the YUI Compressor, whereas the advanced (and less foolproof) option has the capability to make more savings.

Two of the most exciting features of this advanced mode are function inlining and the removal of unused code..

Inline expansion (or *inlining*) will be familiar to anyone who has studied C compilers. It's the act to insert the contents of a function into the place where the function would have been called. This can improve the execution speed (by cutting out the overhead involved in calling the function), and — in the case of small functions that are rarely called — reduce the overall file size.

Let's look at an example.

```
function showalert(message) {

        el = document.getElementById('alertbox');
        el.innerHTML = message;
        el.style.visibility = 'visible';

}

x = document.getElementById('formfield');

if (x.value == "no") {
        showalert("Did you really mean no?");
}
```

> **NOTE** innerHTML *is nonstandard but is well supported and a little faster than the alternatives.*

This is not a useful piece of code, but it serves nicely as an example. Look at the value of a domain object model (DOM) element named formfield. If the value is "no", you call a function to display an alert message.

Let's see what happens when you run this through Closure. For the sake of readability, let's use the PRETTY_PRINT formatting option to preserve whitespaces.

```
java -jar compiler.jar --compilation_level ADVANCED_OPTIMIZATIONS  --js
    example.js --formatting PRETTY_PRINT

x = document.getElementById("formfield");
if(x.value == "no") {
  el = document.getElementById("alertbox");
  el.innerHTML = "Did you really mean no?";
  el.style.visibility = "visible"
}
;
```

As you can see, the showalert function has been removed. Its content has been placed inline where the showalert() call previously was.

That's fine in this simplistic example, where the function is called only once. But what happens if your code makes multiple calls to the function, as shown here?

```
function showalert(message) {

        el = document.getElementById('alertbox');
        el.innerHTML = message;
        el.style.visibility = 'visible';

}

x = document.getElementById('formfield');
```

```
if (x.value == "no") {
        showalert("Did you really mean no?");
}

y = document.getElementById('formfield1');
if (y.value == "no") {
        showalert("Did you really mean no?");
}

z = document.getElementById('formfield2');
if (z.value == "no") {
        showalert("Did you really mean no?");
}
```

The result is as follows:

```
java -jar compiler.jar --compilation_level ADVANCED_OPTIMIZATIONS
     --js example.js --formatting PRETTY_PRINT

function a(b) {
  el = document.getElementById("alertbox");
  el.innerHTML = b;
  el.style.visibility = "visible"
}
x = document.getElementById("formfield");
x.value == "no" && a("Did you really mean no?");
y = document.getElementById("formfield1");
y.value == "no" && a("Did you really mean no?");
z = document.getElementById("formfield2");
z.value == "no" && a("Did you really mean no?");
```

This time, Closure had the sense not to inline the function.

The second cool feature of the advanced mode — removal of unused functions — is straightforward. If Closure deems that a function will never be called, it removes it.

The danger emerges when the function is called from elsewhere (for example, if you have a bunch of JavaScript files and are passing them through Closure one by one) or is called by means of an eval() statement. eval statements are a common stumbling block for minifiers, are slow to run, and are a potential security problem. So, whenever possible, you should avoid using them anyway. Google also recommends compiling all the code used on a page in one go (by passing multiple file-names to Closure at the command line) to lessen the problem of functions being removed.

Comparison of JavaScript Minifiers

So far, you've learned about the two big players, the YUI Compressor and Google Closure. But there are plenty of other JavaScript minifiers out there.

The examples presented in this chapter thus far have been small, hence the savings have been small, too. To illustrate how useful minification can be, a bigger example is needed.

Prototype (`http://www.prototypejs.org/`) is a popular JavaScript framework for AJAX developers. Version 1.6.0 consists of a single JavaScript file, weighing in at 122 KB.

Table 4-1 shows the results of passing `prototype.js` through five of the most popular JavaScript minifiers.

TABLE 4-1: JavaScript Minifier Comparison

MINIFIER	UNCOMPRESSED (KB)	GZIPPED (KB)
None	122	28
YUI Compressor	71	21
JSMin	91	23
Closure (simple)	70	21
Closure (advanced)	55	18
Packer (Perl port)	90	23

As you can see, the YUI Compressor and Closure are easily the leaders, and — in the case of the Closure's simple mode — offer similar levels of compression. If you're feeling brave, and are willing to debug any errors, Closure's advanced mode offers an even greater boost.

These results also address the criticism of minification given at the beginning of this chapter — that minification is largely redundant because of `gzip` compression. The difference in size between the `gzipped` unminified code and the `gzipped` YUI Compressor output is 7 KB, a reduction of 25 percent. With Closure's advanced mode, the decrease in size is more than 30 percent. Coupled with the fact that minified code tends to execute slightly faster, minification of JavaScript certainly should not be ignored.

CSS MINIFICATION

Many of the minification techniques outlined for JavaScript minification are also applicable to CSS — the removal of extra whitespaces, removal of comments, and conversion of CRLF to LF. And, as with JavaScript, this is where many simplistic minifiers end. At first glance, it may seem as if there isn't much more you can do to shrink the size of CSS, but as you shall see, this is certainly not the case.

Use Shorthand

Many properties have shorthand variations. Consider the following example:

```
.myclass {
        margin-left: 10px;
        margin-right: 10px;
        margin-bottom: 20px;
        margin-top: 20px;
}
```

You can write this simply as follows:

```
.myclass { margin: 20px 10px 20px 10px;}
```

Or, because in this case the top and bottom margins are equal to each other and so are the left and right, you could write this just as simply as follows:

```
.myclass { margin: 20px 10px;}
```

This shrinks the code to one-quarter of its original size (from 122 bytes to 31 bytes).

Similarly, consider the following:

```
p {
    font-size:12pt;
    font-family: verdana, helvetica, sans-serif;
    font-weigth:bold;
    font-variant: italic;
}
```

This can be more cleanly expressed as follows:

```
p { font: italic bold 12pt verdana, helvetica, sans-serif;}
```

Hex triple color codes may be written in shorthand, providing both characters of the triplet are the same. For example, #FFEEDD can be abbreviated as simply #FED, and #88DD22 as #8D2; conversely, #ABCDEF cannot be shortened.

Grouping Selectors

In some situations, selectors can be grouped together. Consider the following:

```
h1 { background-color:red;}
h2 { background-color:red;}
h3 { background-color:red;}
```

This can be shortened to the following:

```
h1, h2, h3 { background-color:red;}
```

CSS Minifiers

Earlier in this chapter, you learned about JavaScript minification, and that, although many minifiers could optimize certain aspects of the code (for example, shortening variable names, inlining functions, and so on), it still pays to do some manual optimization first. How true is this for CSS?

The following code has plenty of scope for optimization. Can you spot them all?

```
.myclass1 {
        margin-left: 10px;
        margin-right: 0px;
        margin-bottom: 20px;
        margin-top: 20px;
        background: #AABBCC;
        color:white;
}

.myclass2 {
        margin-left:10px;
        margin-right:0px;
        margin-bottom:20px;
        margin-top:20px;
        background:#AABBCC;
        color:white;
}
```

Aside from stripping whitespaces, you can group the two selectors together, shorten #AABBCC to #ABC, change 'white' to #FFF, and group the margin attributes together, ending with the following (with whitespace preserved for readability):

```
.myclass1, .myclass2 {
    margin:20px 0 20px 10px;
     background:#ABC;
     color:#FFF
}
```

Let's see how the YUI Compressor handles it:

```
java -jar /usr/local/bin/yuicompressor-2.3.5/build/yuicompressor-2.3.5.jar
    /tmp/test.css
.myclass1{margin-left:10x;margin-right:0;margin-bottom:20px;
    margin-top:20px;background:#ABC;color:white;}.myclass2
    {margin-left:10x;margin-right:0;margin-bottom:20px;
    margin-top:20px;background:#ABC;color:white;}
```

Although this has taken the size down from 334 bytes to 212, it's mostly because of whitespace being stripped out. The only other change has been to convert 0px to just 0. This is somewhat disappointing, considering how much else could be done.

Luckily, there are plenty of alternatives, and a personal favorite is CSSTidy (http://csstidy .sourceforge.net/), available for Windows, UNIX, and Linux. By default, CSSTidy preserves whitespace, but you can easily override this at the command line. Let's see how it copes with the sample style sheet.

```
$ wine csstidy.exe /tmp/test.css --template=highest output.css

Selectors: 2 | Properties: 12
Input size: 0.327KiB  Output size: 0.07KiB  Compression ratio: 78.51%
------------------------------------

3: Optimised number: Changed "0px" to "0"
```

```
6: Optimised color: Changed "#AABBCC" to "#ABC"
7: Optimised color: Changed "white" to "#FFF"
12: Optimised number: Changed "0px" to "0"
15: Optimised color: Changed "#AABBCC" to "#ABC"
16: Optimised color: Changed "white" to "#FFF"

------------------------------------
CSSTidy 1.3 by Florian Schmitz 2005, 2006
$ cat output.css
.myclass1,.myclass2{background:#ABC;color:#FFF;margin:20px 0 20px 10px;}
```

That's quite impressive, and the resulting file size is down to a respectable 73 bytes.

Is there anything more you can do? CSSTidy has an array of command-line options that control individual optimization tricks, but most are enabled by default. The option to remove the trailing semicolon from the end of the selector properties is not, however. Turning this on results in the following:

```
.myclass1,.myclass2{background:#ABC;color:#FFF;margin:20px 0 20px 10px}
```

There is a mere saving of 1 byte in this example, but you may as well still use it.

Improving Compression

Because you'll generally want to serve up CSS compressed (for example, using `mod_deflate` in Apache), anything that a minifier can do to improve the compression ratio is also welcome. As you will learn in Appendix C, "Compression," LWZ (the basis for `gzip` and `deflate`) compression likes repeating strings, so your aim should be to increase the frequency of these. Being consistent in your use of case and spacing helps to improve compression, as does listing properties in a consistent order. Consider the following:

```
.myClass {
    color:#FFF;
    background-color: #fff;
    border: solid 1px black;
}

.myOtherClass{
    border: solid black 2px;
    background-color:white;
    color:#fff;
}
```

This compresses poorly. The second rule uses lowercase for the hex color code and a color name for the background, lists the border attributes in a different order, is missing a space before the opening curly bracket, and lists the attributes in a different order than the first class rule. Now, rewrite the rules like so:

```
.myOtherClass {
    color:#FFF;
    background-color:#FFF;
    border: solid 2px black;
}
```

Here, the opportunity for greater compression is increased. Remember that LWZ uses a history window and searches only so far back when looking for repeating strings (how far depends on the implementation). So, although nearby rules may give matches, rules at the other end of the style sheet probably won't. As a result, you must think about the order in which rules (not just attributes) are defined, and you may find it beneficial to group together rules with similar attributes.

This is an aspect of minification that most minifiers ignore. But CSSMin (`https://github.com/barryvan/CSSMin/`) is different. Written in Java, CSSMin performs the ordering of properties, conversion to lowercase, and replacement of simple names with their hex or numeric equivalents. (For example, `font-weight:bold` is converted to `font-weight:600`, `color:black` to `color:#000`.) You get all this, plus the usual minification techniques.

> **NOTE** *Be aware, however, that re-ordering properties can cause problems. Occasionally, it is necessary to list properties in a specific order because of browser quirks.*

HTML MINIFICATION

Whereas minification of CSS and JavaScript are both popular techniques (as evidenced by the number of minifiers and blog posts on the subject), minification of HTML has so far failed to catch on.

Part of the reason for this is that it requires more thought to implement. Whereas CSS and JavaScript are usually static files, HTML is often generated on-the-fly by assembling fragments of markup using a back-end scripting language. Web masters are then faced with the choice to either minify each of these fragments, or perform the minification on-the-fly, prior to the HTML being sent to the client. In the latter case, the performance overheads may well outweigh the benefits (which can admittedly be quite low).

That said, minification of HTML is still a worthwhile endeavor. Although the benefits of CSS and JavaScript minification are often seen only once for the client (because these resources are generally cached by the browser, at least for the length of the session), the benefits of HTML minification are seen on each page load. So, although the percentage decrease in size may be lower for HTML documents, the cumulative effect over the length of the user's session is often greater than that for CSS and JavaScript.

HTML minification is also quite a controversial subject, partly because many of the minification techniques result in markup that is not valid XHTML. The whole HTML versus XHTML argument has been raging for years and isn't something to be examined here, except to say that using XHTML for your documents may not be as important as you think. (Most web servers still serve pages using the `text/html` content type, so, even if you use XHTML in your `doctype`, the browser still renders it as HTML. Part of the reason for the lack of uptake of XHTML — which would be served as `application/XHTML+XML` — is that Internet Explorer does not support it.)

HTML Minification Techniques

Let's look at some of the most popular HTML minification techniques. Some of these (such as removing comments and excess whitespace) are quick and painless. Others (such as the removal of attribute quotes or closing tags) can cause compatibility issues if you are not careful, and you should always be mindful of the Document Type Declaration (DTD, or doctype) that you are writing for.

Whitespace and Comments

Stripping comments and extra whitespace forms a large part of the minification process. (And, again, many basic minifiers stop here.) However, with HTML, even this can be problematic.

In most situations, consecutive whitespaces in (X)HTML documents are rendered as a single space. Consider the following example:

```
<p>This is a          space</p>
```

This is displayed identically to the following:

```
<p>This is a space</p>
```

This isn't the case for text wrapped inside `<pre>` tags, however. Text inside these tags is considered to be preformatted and is rendered as-is. It's easy for a minifier to spot `<pre>` tags and ignore the content between them, but the next problem is more challenging.

CSS supports the `white-space` property, which controls how whitespace in an element is handled. Consider the following:

```
<p style="white-space:pre">This is a          space</p>
```

This has an identical effect to the `<pre>` tag — that is, whitespace is preserved, rather than being collapsed down.

In practice, this property would most likely be defined in an external CSS file, rather than via the `style` tag in this example. So, for a minifier to determine which elements contain preformatted text, it would need to parse the CSS and calculate the properties associated with every element. Given the cascading nature of CSS and the powerful way in which selectors can be specified, this is no easy task.

So, perhaps it's not surprising that few (if any) of the HTML minifiers can cope with the `white-space` property. (Although, in fairness, some do acknowledge this problem.) The good news is that `white-space` isn't a widely used property. So, for the moment, the best approach is to check to see if your CSS rules make use of it; then either forgo whitespace compression, or manually repair your preformatted text afterward.

Attribute Quotes

According to the HTML 4.0 specifications (`http://www.w3.org/TR/REC-html40/intro/sgmltut .html#h-3.2.2`), it is acceptable to omit the quotes from attribute values, provided the value is limited to alphanumerics, hyphens, and periods. So, it is perfectly valid to say `<a href=index.php title=home>` rather than `<a href="index.php" title="home">`. Needless to say, removing attribute quotes will result in invalid XHTML.

Things get rather messy if you ignore the proviso about which characters are allowed in unquoted attribute values. In particular, using the forward slash in unquoted values can result in markup that still validates but fails to render correctly in browsers (according to `http://www.cs.tut .fi/~jkorpela/qattr.html`). If you use a minifier that supports this option, ensure that it understands the situations in which values must be quoted.

Inline CSS and JavaScript

It's usually good practice to keep as much of your CSS and JavaScript as possible in external resources, because this increases the potential for caching. Given the logistics of moving inline CSS/JavaScript out of the HTML document, this is almost certainly a task that you need to perform manually.

On the subject of JavaScript, it's worth noting that following frequently seen markup is deprecated (and has been for a long time):

```
<script language="JavaScript">
```

Instead, you can simply say the following:

```
<script>
```

Occasionally the `language=` property specifies a specific version of JavaScript to be used (for example, `language='JavaScript1.8"`), but this isn't particularly reliable and should be avoided whenever possible.

<strong> and <b>, <em> and <i>

Many web authors consider `<strong>` to be synonymous with `<b>`, and `<em>` to be synonymous with `<i>`. They tend to render identically in browsers, so it may be tempting to replace all occurrences of `<strong>` with `<b>` in a document, as a means to shrink the document size.

Unfortunately, this logic is flawed. Although `<strong>` and `<b>` may render the same in common browsers, their meaning is subtly different. `<b>` is purely a presentational tag, telling the browser to render the text in bold, but carrying no other meaning. In contrast, `<strong>` carries a semantic meaning — it indicates to the browser that the text is strongly emphasized. Most browsers render such text in bold, but this is purely a decision made by the browser — it is not a requirement.

Actually, the word "browser" probably isn't the right choice of words here. There is a wide range of user agents, of which desktop web browsers are only a handful. The real benefit to make a distinction between `<strong>` and `<b>` comes for agents such as audio readers, where there is a marked difference in meaning between bold text and strongly emphasized text.

In short, replacing `<strong>` with `<b>` (and `<em>` with `<i>`) generally isn't a good idea. This is worth mentioning because some HTML minifiers carry this option.

Removing title and alt Attributes

Another minification technique not recommended (but is offered by some minifiers) is the removal of `title` and `alt` attributes. An example might be transforming `<a href="/home .html" title="Home">Go Home</a><img src="link.png" alt="link icon" />` into `<a href="/home.html">Go Home</a><img src="link.png" />`. This certainly cuts down the size, but at the expense of accessibility and search engine optimization (SEO).

Boolean Attributes

In form elements, it's common to use attributes that simply have on/off values, such as `selected` and `checked`. The standard method to write these is like so:

```
<option value="red">Red</option>
<option value="blue" selected="selected">Blue</option>
<option value="green">Green</option>
```

However, it's perfectly valid in HTML 4 to omit the attribute value, as shown here:

```
<option value="red">Red</option>
<option value="blue" selected>Blue</option>
<option value="green">Green</option>
```

Again, this shortcut is not valid in XHTML documents.

Closing Tags

In many situations, it's also acceptable to omit closing tags in HTML (but not XHTML) documents, thus going against everything you were taught about clean markup. The previous example could, therefore, be condensed further to the following:

```
<option value="red">Red
<option value="blue" selected>Blue
<option value="green">Green
```

Or if you're happy with the `option` values being identical to their text labels, you could use the following:

```
<option>Red
<option selected>Blue
<option>Green
```

This results in 48 bytes of code, compared to the 104 bytes of the original.

If your conscience allows you to cut corners like this, the savings in size can be quite substantial.

HTML Minification Tools

As mentioned earlier, HTML minification hasn't yet taken off to the extent that CSS and JavaScript minification has. That said, there are plenty of tools available to perform it. As with CSS and

JavaScript minifiers, the quality varies a lot, with basic tools doing little more than stripping whitespace and comments (which is still a good start) — or even worse, replacing good markup with bad (such as removing `alt` attributes and replacing `strong` with `b`).

Two popular HTML minifiers are HTMLMinifier (`http://github.com/kangax/html-minifier`) and `htmlcompressor` (`http://code.google.com/p/htmlcompressor/`). The first is written in JavaScript and intended to be run via a web browser. The second is a command-line Java application.

HTMLMinifier is newer and is still experimental, but tests indicate that it does appear to offer slightly better levels of compression. It also has the option to include some riskier techniques, should you be feeling brave. Following are the available options:

➤   Remove comments.

➤   Remove comments from JavaScript and CSS blocks.

➤   Remove character data (CDATA) blocks from CSS and JavaScript.

➤   Collapse whitespace.

➤   Collapse boolean attributes (for example, `selected="selected"`).

➤   Remove attribute quotes (when it is safe to do so).

➤   Remove redundant attributes (for example, `language="JavaScript"`).

➤   Use short `doctype`.

➤   Remove empty attributes (for example, `title=""`).

➤   Remove optional closing tags.

➤   Remove empty elements such as `<p></p>`.

➤   Remove `type="text/javascript"` from inline script.

All these options are enabled by default, save for the last two, which are potentially dangerous.

HTMLMinifier also includes a Lint validator that reports on errors and deprecated code.

`htmlcompressor` is a little less adventurous but is still powerful; and being a command-line tool, it is easier to integrate into an automated build system. `htmlcompressor` can also compress XML documents and can integrate with the YUI Compressor to perform minification of any inline CSS and JavaScript.

Let's have a look at the available options:

```
$ java -jar htmlcompressor-0.9.1.jar -h
Usage: java -jar htmlcompressor.jar [options] [input file]

<input file>                    If not provided reads from stdin

Global Options:
  -o <output file>              If not provided outputs result to stdout
```

```
    --type <html|xml>            If not provided autodetects from file extension
    --charset <charset>          Read the input file using <charset>
    -h, --help                   Display this screen

XML Options:
    --preserve-comments          Preserve comments
    --preserve-intertag-spaces   Preserve intertag spaces

HTML Options:
    --preserve-comments          Preserve comments
    --preserve-multi-spaces      Preserve multiple spaces
    --remove-intertag-spaces     Remove intertag spaces
    --remove-quotes              Remove unneeded quotes
    --compress-js                Enable JavaScript compression using YUICompressor
    --compress-css               Enable CSS compression using YUICompressor

JavaScript Options (for YUI Compressor):
    --nomunge                    Minify only, do not obfuscate
    --preserve-semi              Preserve all semicolons
    --disable-optimizations      Disable all micro optimizations
    --line-break <column num>    Insert a line break after the specified column

CSS Options (for YUI Compressor):
    --line-break <column num>    Insert a line break after the specified column

Please note that if you enable JavaScript or Css compression parameters,
YUI Compressor jar file must be present at the same directory as this jar.
```

To get a rough idea of how HTMLMinifier and `htmlcompressor` compare, a test was performed by running the homepages of a couple of well-known sites through them. The level of minification is obviously heavily dependent on the content and will vary a lot from document to document. So, although sampling just two websites isn't enough to get any empirical evidence, it does provide a general idea of how efficient HTML minifiers are. Table 4-2 shows the results of the testing.

TABLE 4-2: Comparing HTMLMinifier and htmlcompressor

URL	UNCOMPRESSED (BYTES)	HTMLMINIFIER (BYTES)	HTMLMINIFIER PERCENTAGE IMPROVEMENT	HTMLCOMPRESSOR (BYTES)	HTMLCOMPRESSOR PERCENTAGE IMPROVEMENT
Kernel .org	29,143	25,655	11.93	26,604	8.71
Amazon .com	183,066	173,940	4.99	179,054	2.19

HTMLMinifier is the winner here, with a 3,478-byte reduction on `kernel.org` (approximately 12 percent) and a 9,127-byte reduction on `Amazon.com` (approximately 5 percent — although, after having looked at the markup on `amazon.com`, HTML minification should be the least of the priorities).

SUMMARY

Minification plays an important role to reduce the size of resources (which speeds up download times) and can often result in a slight increase in execution speed. The downside is that it reduces the readability of code. Although on-the-fly minification is possible, it's wasteful of resources, and minification is best carried out once, when the code is deployed.

In this chapter, you have learned about some popular minification tools: YUI Compressor (JavaScript and CSS), Google Closure Compiler (JavaScript), CSSTidy, HTMLMinifier, and `htmlcompressor`. Whichever tools you use, remember that they are not a magic bullet. Your first step in minification should always be to manually clean up the code, and, in the next two chapters, you will learn more about writing efficient and concise JavaScript and CSS.

In Chapter 5, you'll spend some time looking at the issues surrounding web graphics and image optimization.

5

Optimizing Web Graphics and CSS

WHAT'S IN THIS CHAPTER?

➤ Getting to know the three primary image formats

➤ Achieving high levels of compression

➤ Cutting down on HTTP requests by using CSS sprites

➤ Making your CSS leaner

The images used on a website are often created by a web designer or graphic designer, for whom quality is the primary concern (because this is the standard by which they are usually judged). So, it's not surprising that optimization is often ignored. You can frequently cut 10 KB or 20 KB off an image without any visible loss in quality.

If graphic designers are guilty of tunnel vision in this respect, you should be careful not to fall into the same trap. Although size is your primary concern, and some loss of quality is probably acceptable, you should resist the temptation to over-optimize — tacky looking graphics are just as likely to put off visitors as slow loading times.

UNDERSTANDING IMAGE FORMATS

For a long time, two main image formats were used on the web: JPEG and GIF. JPEG (which is an acronym for Joint Photographic Experts Group) were used for photographs, and GIF (which stands for Graphics Interchange Format) was used for computer-generated images such as icons.

In the mid-1990s, it came to light that the Lempel-Ziv Welch (LZW) compression method used by GIF was patented, and the search was on for an alternative. In 1996, the first specification for a new format, PNG (which stands for Portable Network Graphics), was released. Later that year, it had become a World Wide Web Consortium (W3C) recommendation, with most major browsers supporting it by the end of that decade. Although the LZW patent expired in 2003, PNG had shown itself to be a superior format, and GIF never fully recovered.

Although the roles of JPEG and GIF are well defined, PNG's purpose is vague. The PNG format can be used as a replacement for both JPEG and GIF. So, let's start with a review of these three formats. Because much of this is common knowledge to those with even a basic knowledge of web development, this examination is brief.

JPEG

JPEG is a lossy compression method (there is a lossless mode, but it's not widely supported), and is well-suited to photographic images, which typically have many different colors and gradients. With JPEG, there is a trade-off between file size and image quality, but even at the lowest compression level (that is, the largest file size), where artifacts are virtually nonexistent, JPEG images are still considerably smaller than nonlossy formats such as TIFF (which stands for Tagged Image File Format).

> **NOTE** *With lossy compression, some data is lost during the compression. With lossless compression, no data is lost during the compression.*

JPEG compression levels are usually specified as either a percentage (where 0 percent is the smallest file size, but lowest quality, and 100 percent is the best quality, but largest size) or a number in the range 0 to 1. A value of approximately 60 percent to 80 percent is generally considered a good middle ground for web images.

GIF

GIF has been around since 1987 and is commonly used for logos, sprites, and clip art.

GIF images use a color table (also known as a *palette*), which can hold up to 256 colors. Each pixel of the GIF image is then replaced by a number representing which of these colors it contains. The obvious limitation here is that a GIF can contain only 256 different colors at most. But, surprisingly, this is still often enough — especially because the color table is not preset but allocated from the colors actually used in the image. (So, for example, the image could contain 256 shades of red.)

It's also interesting to note that GIF compression is based around LWZ, a revised version of the LZ78 algorithm, which as you learned in Chapter 3, "Content Compression," is used in gzip and deflate.

Because compression occurs in horizontal rows (from left to right), images that contain a horizontal color gradient compress worse than those with a vertical gradient. Consider the images shown in Figure 5-1. The image on the left weighs in at 25 KB, whereas the one on the right is only 17 KB.

FIGURE 5-1

PNG

PNG is a lossless format that was designed as a replacement for GIF after the licensing issues with LWZ became apparent. PNG uses the `deflate` algorithm (which itself uses LZ77, which, as you learned in Chapter 3, is similar to LWZ).

PNG supports both paletted and non-paletted RGB and RGBA (RGB with an alpha channel) images. Paletted flavors are often referred to as PNG8 (for PNG), PNG24 (for RGB), and PNG32 (for RGBA), with the numbers reflecting the number of bits per pixel.

➤ PNG8 is the most similar to GIF, using an 8-bit (that is, 256) color table. In most cases, it outperforms GIF, making it an ideal drop-in replacement. It's worth noting that PNG8 supports both paletted and RGBA, making it a potential choice for image alpha transparency.

➤ The RGB mode (PNG24) is sometimes also used as a lossless alternative to JPEG; although the large file size means this is not commonly used on the web.

➤ PNG32 is similar to RGB mode but includes an alpha channel. Although this mode isn't used much, there are certain situations in which it is the only viable format. For an image with lots of color gradients that also require transparency, neither JPEG, GIF, nor PNG8 are ideal (because JPEG lacks support for transparency, whereas GIF and PNG8 have limited color depths). PNG32 handles such images well — but don't expect the file size to be small!

> **NOTE** *Although* PNG *has been around since the late 1990s, Internet Explorer (IE) has had numerous flaws in its support for the format, particularly* PNG32. *For example, IE 6.0 and earlier versions fail to handle alpha transparency correctly, whereas IE 7.0 struggles when transparency is used on top of semi-transparent HTML elements. (See* http://support.microsoft.com/kb/265221 *for more information.)*

SVG

The image formats examined thus far all work along similar principles, containing information on the color of each pixel in the image. What differs is the way in which this information is encoded.

Scalable Vector Graphics (SVG) takes a completely different approach by using XML to describe an image in terms of geometrical shapes. If you've ever drawn on a canvas in your favorite programming language, you'll be familiar with the idea of specifying the dimensions of polygons, setting a fill color, overlaying text, and so on. Following is the content of a simple SVG file:

```
<?xml version="1.0"?>
<!DOCTYPE svg PUBLIC "-//W3C//DTD SVG 1.1//EN"
  "http://www.w3.org/Graphics/SVG/1.1/DTD/svg11.dtd">
<svg xmlns="http://www.w3.org/2000/svg" version="1.1">
   <circle cx="100" cy="50" r="20" stroke="black" stroke-width="1"
        fill="blue" />
</svg>
```

This draws a circle on the canvas with radius 20 pixels at coordinates 100×50 pixels. The circle is filled with a blue color, and has a black border of radius 1 pixel. Aside from circles, ellipses, polygons, and text, SVG also supports color gradients, filters, blur effects, and drop shadows.

In many situations, SVG is an ideal alternative to traditional image formats. It can result in smaller file sizes (sometimes, but not always), and (as the name implies) is scalable, meaning that the image can be resized without affecting its quality.

One of the main reasons why the SVG format is not as widely used as it should be is because of poor support in IE. While most of the major browsers have had some level of SVG support since around 2005 (Konqueror in 2004, Firefox in 2005, Opera in 2005, Chrome and Safari in 2006), IE did not begin to offer native support for SVG until version 9 in 2011. Because a sizeable number of your visitors will still be using earlier versions of IE, the only practical solution if you wish to utilize SVG files is to use content negotiation and serve up a non-SVG version of the graphic to earlier versions of IE.

While SVG files are not affected by traditional image optimization considerations (that is, compression levels, color depths, interlacing, and so on), the fact that they must be parsed and rendered by the browser raises its own performance considerations. The larger the XML file, the more shapes must be drawn, and this has the potential to be slower than merely displaying an image in a format such as GIF or PNG (even taking into account that these formats require decoding). Particularly costly are advanced effects such as gradients, fillers, and opacity. However, provided that you use these sparingly, SVG files need not be particularly CPU-intensive to render.

OPTIMIZING IMAGES

Now that you have refreshed your memory about the three main image formats, let's look at some of the techniques to keep image sizes down.

Image Editing Software

A bewildering array of image-editing software is available, but one favorite is the GNU Image Manipulation Program (GIMP) (http://www.gimp.org). It's free, it works on UNIX, Windows, and Mac, and it does a good job to compress images. So much so that, although there are a large number of tools available specifically for optimizing images, they rarely result in any significant reduction in file size when run on images saved by GIMP.

Choosing the Right Format

The general rule for using the JPEG format for photography and GIF or PNG for everything else can serve you well most of the time. But occasionally you encounter images somewhere in between — often images generated digitally that contain more than 256 colors, or lots of gradients. In these situations, trial and error (and a good eye for detail) is the best approach. Experiment with different formats and different compression levels until you find the best trade-off between size and quality.

Interlacing and Progressive Rendering

So far, you have learned a bit of background on techniques to keep image file sizes low. However, user perception of how quickly a page loads is important, too, so now think the unthinkable. Let's look at a couple of techniques that actually often increase file size but can improve the user perception of loading times.

The default compression method for JPEG is called *baseline*, in which the data is compressed from top to bottom. This leads to the well-known effect where a large JPEG image starts rendering from the top downward, as shown in Figure 5-2.

FIGURE 5-2

JPEG also offers a second method of compression, known as *progressive*, in which multiple passes are made of the image, each producing higher detail. When loaded in a browser, such images start out blurry and gradually become more detailed, as shown in Figure 5-3.

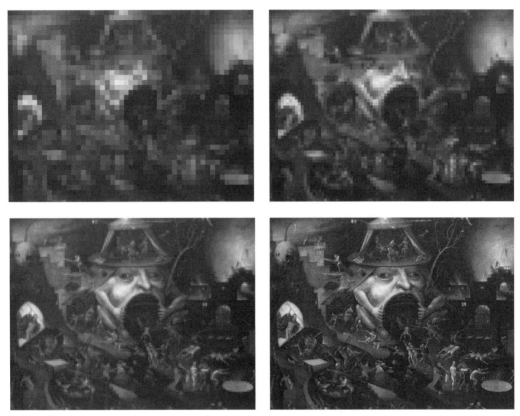

FIGURE 5-3

In terms of usability and user perception of speed, progressive JPEG files are generally considered to be a good thing, especially for those who use slow connections. Progressive JPEG files provide a rough overview of the image quickly, and the final stages of rendering are often unnoticed by the user. Not everyone feels this way, though. There is the danger that the user is never quite sure if the image has finished loading, or sees the early passes and assumes the image is of a poor quality.

How does progressive rendering affect file size? It actually tends to reduce the size slightly; although this isn't always the case. Research at Yahoo (http://yuiblog.com/blog/2008/12/05/imageopt-4/) suggests that approximately 10 KB is the sweet spot. For images larger than this, progressive rendering results in a decrease in file size. For images smaller than this, file size goes up a little.

GIF and PNG formats both support a similar technique (of which PNG's is far superior), which is known as *interlacing*. As with progressive JPEGs, the idea is to show the image in multiple passes, each pass adding more detail. With a GIF file, the first pass draws every eighth line, the second pass every fourth line, the third pass every second line, and the fourth (last) pass the remaining lines.

By contrast, PNG uses a two-dimensional interlacing scheme consisting of seven passes. The result is a much smoother transition with more clarity in the early stages of rendering.

The downside to interlacing is that it always increases the file size — more so for PNG than GIF. Interlacing is almost always unnecessary for small images, so the dilemma arises only for large PNG and GIF files, which themselves are not common. As always, it's difficult to make hard and fast rules. You should experiment with and without interlacing on an image to see which you prefer. A common opinion is that interlacing is unnecessary the majority of the time.

PNG Optimization

Optimization of PNG images can be divided into four steps:

1. Remove redundant headers.

2. Reduce the color depth. (For example, switch from RGB to paletted, or reduce the number of colors in the palette.)

3. Re-implement or use alternative filters.

4. Improve the performance of the LZ77 and `deflate` algorithms. Sometimes custom implementations are used.

Let's look at each of these steps in more detail.

Removing Redundant Headers

This step involves removing meta data that is not of the image itself. As such, there is no loss in image quality; although whether this step can truly be referred to as lossless is debatable because data is still being removed.

The PNG format supports more than a dozen additional headers, which are not required to be present, and many can be omitted without ill effect. Following are prime candidates for removal:

➤ bKGD — Specifies a default background color. This option is not used by web browsers.

➤ pHYs — Gives the intended aspect ratio or pixel size of the image.

➤ sBIT — Stores the number of significant bits, enabling a decoder (for example, a web browser) to reconstitute images converted from a lower sample depth.

➤ sPLT — Stores a suggested palette when the viewer lacks the capability to show the full intended color range.

➤ HIST — Contains a palette histrogram, charting how frequently each color appears in the image.

➤ tIME — The last modified time of the image.

➤ cHRM — Stores the X/Y coordinates of the primary colors used in the image.

In addition, there are three text fields (zTXT, tEXT, and iTXT) that may be used to store textual information relating to the image. Typically, this includes title, author, description, copyright information, comments, and so on.

Reducing the Color Depth

Hopefully, this step is not required because you should already have experimented with setting the lowest acceptable palette depth.

While it is common knowledge that PNG8 supports binary transparency (that is, a pixel is either transparent or it is not), less well-known is the fact that PNG8 also supports alpha transparency. If you have been using PNG32 simply because you needed alpha transparency, now is the time to experiment with PNG8. File sizes should be significantly smaller.

The most frequent problem with alpha transparency in PNG32 is the buggy support in earlier versions of IE. Versions 6 and earlier could not handle the alpha channel, and would render alpha pixels in grey, with less than pleasing results. While IE6 still does not support alpha transparency in PNG8, it chooses to display such pixels as fully transparent, which is usually more acceptable.

Re-Implementing (or Using Alternative) Filters

At the precompression stage, filters can transform the data into a form that can compress easier. (Note that, in this context, "filter" has nothing to do with visual aspects of the image such as alpha channels.) LZ77 looks for repeating sequences, and anything you can do to increase these can aid compression.

> **NOTE** *Appendix C, "Compression," provides more detail on LZ77.*

Consider the following sequence:

```
1,2,3,4,5,6,7,8,9
```

With no repeating sections, this sequence offers no scope of LZ77 compression. And yet, there is a definite pattern — each value is one more than the previous.

Let's apply a filter where each value in the sequence is replaced with the difference between itself and the previous value. (So, for example, the difference between 5 and 6 is 1, the difference between 6 and 7 is 1, and so on.) The sequence now looks like this:

```
1,1,1,1,1,1,1,1,1
```

This is the kind of data that LZ77 loves, and provided that you know the filter that was applied, you can easily reverse it to recover the original string.

Of course, this was a contrived example. Consider the following sequence:

```
2,3,4,5,2,3,4,5,2,3,4,5
```

Here, the filtered sequence would be as follows:

```
2,1,1,1,-3,1,1,1,-3,1,1,1
```

This actually compresses a little less. You might say that it compresses less *for this particular* filter — with a bit of thought you could no doubt come up with a more complicated filter for which this sequence did compress better.

PNG currently offers five different filters (although the first simply says "no transformation is made"), and (rather usefully) a different filter may be used on each row of the image. The four remaining filters are as follows:

➤ Sub — Each pixel is replaced with the difference between it and the pixel to its left (as in the earlier example).

➤ Up — Each pixel is replaced with the difference between it and the pixel above it (that is, in the previous row).

➤ Average — Each pixel is replaced with the difference between it and the *average* value of the pixels above and to the left of it.

➤ Paeth — This is a much more complex filter based around the Paeth Predictor and using pixels to the left, top, and top left. The details are outside the scope of this book, but if you want to learn the nitty gritty of Paeth, *PNG: The Definitive Guide* (Sebastopol, CA: O'Reilly Media, 1999) by Greg Roelofs is, well, the definitive guide.

Because these filters are preset, there's no scope to implement your own filter. The only scope for optimization at this stage is deciding which filter to use. Although a different filter may be used on each row of the image, it is mathematically impractical to try every possible combination, except on small images.

Improving Algorithm Performance

Having removed meta data and reduced the size of the raw image, the last possibility for optimization is in the compression.

As mentioned earlier, PNG uses the deflate algorithm. Just to refresh your memory, deflate uses a combination of LZ77 and Huffman encoding. LZ77 is a dictionary coder that looks for sequences of data that match sequences that have already been encoded. Such sequences are then replaced with a length-distance pair representing the size and offset of the earlier occurrence. Huffman uses a tree structure (usually referred to as a *table*) to encode frequently occurring symbols into shorter representations.

Recall that LZ77 uses a sliding window and searches back only a limited distance when looking for matches. Although this lowers memory and CPU usage, it does tend to result in matches being missed. In deflate tools (such as gzip) that enable the compression level to be set, the size of this window is typically one of the factors that can be changed.

The zlib implementation offers nine levels of compression, but if you're happy with trading slower compression for smaller file sizes, there's no reason why you cannot go beyond this. As such, custom deflate implementations tend to offer the capability to set larger window sizes.

Similarly, the efficiency of the Huffman encoding is effectively limited by memory. Output from LZ77 is piped to the Huffman encoder, and the buffer is flushed when it reaches a maximum size. Raising the size of this buffer allows a larger, more organized tree.

Lossless Compression

Which, if any, of these steps are lossless? That depends on how you define lossless. Generally, lossless means no loss in visible image quality, but, strictly speaking, step 1 involves the potential loss of meta data in the image headers, even if this has no effect on image quality.

Step 2 can be lossless or lossy, depending on the situation. Shrinking the palette to remove unused colors is lossless, but sometimes it may be acceptable to lose a few colors for the sake of size, in which case loss does occur.

The final two steps are always lossless. PNG optimization tools often contain their own implementation of `deflate`, which outperforms that found in image-editing software. It's worth noting that such images can still be viewed correctly by the client — no special decoding method is needed.

GIF Optimization

With PNG generally being a superior format to GIF, there's no need to spend too much time discussing optimization of GIFs. In fact, GIF offers less scope for optimization, and optimization techniques tend to be somewhat pedestrian — reducing the size of the palette to a visually acceptable level and removing unnecessary meta data.

GIF supports three sets of text-format meta data (usually referred to as *extensions*), and each may appear multiple times in the file. They are `Comment`, `Plain text`, and `Application`. All may safely be removed.

A discussion of GIF optimization would not be complete without a quick look at animated GIFs. (However, many developers are still scarred by their extensive misuse in the early days of the web.)

Reducing the number of frames is usually the first step — the less the better, although, of course, quality will suffer. When possible, you should also use frame differencing (also known as *inter-frame transparency*). Using this technique, each frame contains only the pixels that have changed from the previous frame.

JPEG Compression

JPEG compression is something new and quite different from the LZW family of encoding schemes. Whereas LZW and LZ77 perform lossless encoding, JPEG encoding is intentionally lossy — this is where most of the savings occur. Unfortunately, JPEG compression is a significantly more complicated technique than `deflate` or LZW, and a detailed explanation is outside the scope of this book. So, let's settle for a brief overview.

> **NOTE** *Appendix C, "Compression," provides more detail on LZ77.*

Compression Internals

The first step in compression is to convert the image from RGB to YCbCr (where "Y" is the brightness, "Cb" the blue chrominance, and "Cr" the red chrominance). Humans are much less sensitive to changes in chrominance than brightness, and the YCbCr color space takes this into account, allowing the image to be compressed more without a noticeable loss in quality.

To achieve this compression, down-sampling is then applied to reduce the resolution (and, thus, the level of detail, and the size) of the Cb and Cr components. The JPEG format supports numerous ratios of sampling, of which the three most common are: 4:4:4 (no resampling), 4:4:2 (resampling on the horizontal), and 4:4:0 (resampling on both the horizontal and vertical).

Next, the image is split into 8 × 8 pixel blocks, and a Discrete Cosine Transform (DCT) is applied to each pixel in the block, resulting in a frequency domain. While the math involved in this step is well beyond the scope of this book, the result is a two dimensional grid in which each frequency in the image is plotted against its magnitude — low frequencies appear at the top left of the grid, and high frequencies appear at the bottom right. Quantization (that is, compressing a range of values to a single quantum value) is then applied. Because the DCT tells you the relevance of each value, you can apply more quantization to lower-frequency values, and use less quantization for the higher frequencies. The result is that less significant data is compressed more than more significant data. It's at this stage that the compression level set by the user (typically offered as a percentage) comes into play, with a lower value resulting in more quantization.

> **NOTE** *The terminology here can be rather confusing. Some utilities such as GIMP refer to this setting as "quality" and use a percentage, whereas higher values mean higher quality. Other tools use a number between 0 and 1. Still others call the setting "compression level" and lower values mean higher quality. For consistency, the setting will be referred to here as "quality" or "quality level."*

The final stage is to pass the quantized data through a modified Huffman encoder.

Optimization

What does this all mean in terms of optimization? Well, in addition to the quality level, you also have the ability to choose which sampling method to use. Although 4:4:2 tends to be the default ratio, there are situations in which better overall compression can be achieved by using 4:4:4 in combination with a lower quality level. This is typically the case in images with small amounts of fine detail, such as images with text on them.

From this (albeit basic) understanding of JPEG compression, you can also draw some conclusions about the types of images that compress well, and methods to improve the compression ratio:

➤ JPEG files excel with gradual changes in color (the exact opposite of PNG and GIF files). As such, adding a small amount of blur to produce softer edges can aid the compression process.

➤ Similarly, reducing the color saturation produces smoother color transitions, leading to better compression.

➤ Decreasing the contrast lowers the range of brightness, which again allows better compression.

Admittedly, none of these techniques is hugely practical because they mean altering visible aspects of the original image. But they're still useful to know.

It's also important to remember that acceptable quality levels vary from image to image. One image may show no visible artifacts at, say, 60 percent quality, whereas another may look bad. This makes it difficult to do any sort of batch resampling of JPEG files, and for the best optimization, the human eye is still no match for a machine.

It should also be noted that because JPEG is a lossy format, resaving a JPEG — even if no changes to quality/compression are made — still results in loss of information. Ideally, the original image should be stored using a nonlossy format (such as some flavors of PNG or TIFF, or even an application's native format, such as GIMP's XCF) and converted to JPEG as the final stage in publishing.

Zonal Compression

Although having fine-grained control over the level of compression used for a JPEG file is useful, it can be somewhat inflexible because the same level of compression is applied to every part of the image. *Zone compression* (also referred to as *spatial, weighted,* or *regional compression*) is a technique whereby different parts of an image are compressed at different levels. This can lead to lower file sizes and better quality in the parts of the image that matter.

Zonal compression is ideally suited to JPEG photography where a main subject is set against a less important background — outdoor shots are a prime example.

In the photograph shown in Figure 5-4, the main focus is the black cat. Although it's nice to appreciate the clarity of the weeds in the background, these are of secondary importance. You can reduce the file size significantly by applying a higher level of compression to this region.

FIGURE 5-4

Although GIMP does not support zonal compression, both Adobe Photoshop and Fireworks do. In Fireworks, you first select the region you want to keep at a higher quality using the Lasso tool, and then save it as a JPEG mask (Modify ⇨ Selective JPEG). The masked area is highlighted in a different color, as shown in Figure 5-5.

FIGURE 5-5

Finally, you can use the Optimize dialog (as shown in Figure 5-6) to set the quality level of the highlighted region ("Selective quality") and the remainder of the image ("Quality").

Figure 5-7 shows the original image with a quality level of 70 for the cat's face and 20 for the background. (A low quality level has been used so that the differences in compression are more pronounced.)

FIGURE 5-6   **FIGURE 5-7**

Figure 5-8 shows a more realistic quality level of 70 for the face and 40 for the background. This results in a file size of 24 KB — a significant saving on the 42 KB size when the entire image is saved at a quality level of 70.

FIGURE 5-8

Image Optimization Software

Image-manipulation programs such as GIMP and Photoshop usually do a decent job to create lean images. (However, sometimes this isn't the default behavior, and you must hunt around for a "save for the web" option or something similar.) But there is usually at least some room for improvement. Sometimes, it is virtually insignificant; at other times, it can have a big impact.

There are a number of (usually command-line) tools for optimization PNG, GIF, and JPEG images. Each has its own fan base, and if you search the Internet, it's not hard to find "evidence" that any one tool is better than the others. The differences tend to be small, though, and given what Disraeli had to say about statistics (although Mark Twain attributed "lies, damn lies, and statistics" to Disraeli, the phrase doesn't appear in any of Disraeli's writings), no attempt has been made by the author to quantify the performance of each of these tools. You should just go with the one you feel most comfortable with.

Following is more information about a few of these tools:

➤ PNGOUT (http://advsys.net/ken/utils.htm#pngout) is a freeware tool, available for Windows and Linux. It uses a custom implementation of the deflate algorithm, which results in better compression, at the expense of speed.

➤ pngcrush (http://pmt.sourceforge.net/pngcrush/) is an open source tool for manipulating PNG images. One of its most useful features is a "brute force" mode in which it will attempt every possible combination of optimization options to find which give the best (smallest) file size.

➤ advpng (part of AdvanceCOMP, at http://advancemame.sourceforge.net/comp-readme.html) also uses a custom implementation of deflate, this time from the 7-Zip program. OptiPNG (http://optipng.sourceforge.net/) is an improved version of pngcrush, offering automatic reduction of bit depth and color palette. It also features a "brute force" mode, which outperforms pngcrush in many ways.

➤ RIOT (http://registry.gimp.org/node/20778) is a Windows-only plug-in for GIMP that offers a huge array of optimization techniques for PNG, GIF, and JPEG.

➤ GIFSicle (http://www.lcdf.org/gifsicle/) can be used on both animated and inanimate GIFs to remove comments, redundant colors, and so on.

➤ JPEGTran (http://jpegclub.org/) can strip comments and other meta data, and can perform lossless editing.

Data URIs

One of the most exciting recent developments (actually the idea has been around since 1998, but it's only in recent years that browsers have started to support it) is the data URI scheme. This scheme enables data (such as images) to be embedded inline in web pages, rather than from an external source. The syntax is as follows:

```
data:<mime type>;base64,<data>
```

Following is an example:

```
<img src="data:image/gif;base64,R0lGODlhDAAKAMQAAAS/A///
    zI7ccj7MMs7spRzKFlvMSavkid7ysgDMAKfihgjCBtjxrbvplmTRUEr
    NO+X2t0TSNh7HGADFAADYANbvpd7vrWXTUQAAAAAAAAAAAAAAAAAAAAAAAA
    AAAAACH5BAEHAAEALAAAAAAMAAoAAAUmYCCOZElChjlCRaGKw4K8AnW80PSYVa
    RcCYaJsJhMHK/GBCB8OUMAOw==" width=12 height=10>
```

Of course, the advantage is that by embedding the image data inline, you cut out a HTTP request. You can even use data URIs in CSS, rather than directly in the HTML, thus taking advantage of caching.

As you've probably guessed, though, there are downsides. Firstly, although all the major browsers do now support data URIs, IE 7 and earlier versions (which still make up a significant share of the market) do not. The workaround here is to load a different version of the CSS (not using inline images) for such users, either through the use of CSS conditional comments, or back-end PHP code.

Secondly, as you might have noticed from the previous example, the image data needs to be base 64 encoded, which typically increases the size by approximately one-third. There's also the matter to convert the data into base 64; although this is easily achieved with PHP or other scripting languages, as shown here:

```
<? php
  $contents = file_get_contents($file);
  $base64   = base64_encode($contents);
?>
```

It should also be noted that IE 8 imposes a 32-KB limit on the length of the URI string.

Favicons

Creating a high-performing website means looking at all aspects of page loading times, not just the low-hanging fruit. *Favicons* (the filename is actually `favicon.ico`) are a prime example. These small images are so often overlooked, yet there are a few things you can do to improve them.

The first thing to appreciate is that browsers will request them no matter what. So, even if you don't plan to use a favicon, it's better to return a 200 OK (or even a 204 No Content) than a 404 Not Found. The situation can be improved further by setting far-future Expires/Cache-Control headers on .ico files.

The standard way to specify the favicon is via a link tag in the document head:

```
<link id="favicon" rel="shortcut icon"    href="/favicon.ico">
```

But because browsers will just request /favicon.ico anyway, if you omit the tag, is there any real benefit to using it? Unless you want to use a different name for your favicon, the answer is "no" — quite the reverse, in fact. With no link to the favicon in the HTML document, most browsers will request /favicon.ico toward the end of the page loading process. However, if a favicon link is present, it will be requested near the beginning of the page loading process. So, although there is no net change in page loading time, leaving out the favicon link should cause a perceived increase in speed (and trim a few bytes off the size of your HTML document).

Supported File Formats

While the ICO file format is the standard way of storing favicons, many browsers support other formats too. PNG, GIF, and JPEG are supported by Firefox, Chrome, Opera, and Safari (but, note, not Internet Explorer); while Firefox, Chrome, and Opera also support animated GIFs. Because of IE's limitations, ICO is the most widely used format, and there is generally little to be gained from attempting to deliver, say, a PNG favicon for non-IE users and an ICO file for IE users. (Despite what many people think, ICO files do support alpha transparency — you are not stuck with PNG.)

If you do decide not to use the ICO format, the MIME type for the favicon can be explicitly set like so:

```
<link id="favicon" rel="shortcut icon"  type="image/png"
    href="/favicon.ico">
```

The official MIME type for ICO files is image/vnd.microsoft.ico, but it's interesting to note that this causes problems in IE, and is best omitted.

Keeping the Size Down

Keeping the size of the icon down is worth exploring, too. Favicons can be created at various sizes, but 16 × 16 pixels is the most common. (Anything up to 48 × 48 pixels is commonly seen.) You should prefer 16 × 16, partly because of the smaller file size, and partly because your icon should be understandable at these dimensions. There's no point to create a beautiful icon at 48 × 48 if no one can understand what it is meant to be when a browser resizes it to 16 × 16.

Icon images are paletted, so one of the points made in the earlier discussion on GIF and PNG8 holds true — try to keep the number of colors down. Also, try to keep the file size of the favicon low; anything more than 1 KB or so is too big.

Eliminating the HTTP Request

One of the reasons that favicons are so frustrating for those who care about performance (aside from the fact that they can't be disabled) is that they result in an additional HTTP request. Because the icon is usually small, the overhead to issue the request is relatively high.

To that end, there are a few techniques to eliminate the HTTP request. They all have their problems, though, and this is probably a case in which the simplest solution is the best — just use far-future `Expires` headers, and accept that there will still be a favicon request from clients without a primed cache. Still, for the sake of completeness, let's take a brief look at a couple of techniques.

The first is to use a data URI, like so:

```
<link id="favicon" rel="shortcut icon" type="image/png"
    href="data:image/png;base64,....==">
```

As you have already seen, support for data URIs is not universal, with Internet Explorer (IE) being the main problem. You could get around this by using IE conditional comments, such that a traditional `favicon.ico` is used for IE, and data URIs for other browsers — but, in some ways, this is a step backward. At least with a favicon you can ask the browser to cache it for future use. With a data URI, you have the overhead to contain the embedded icon in your HTML documents with every request.

Moving the data URI into an external style sheet is one way to increase the chances of it being cached. You could set it as the background image of the element with ID `favicon`. This is an even less supported method, though, and appears to be handled inconsistently between browsers.

Finally, if you're happy with not having a favicon, another option is to point the `href` to a resource that has already been loaded (or is in the process of being loaded). Because the resource is already being requested, this won't cause an additional HTTP request. Following is an example:

```
<link id="favicon" rel="shortcut icon" type="image/png"
    href="/style/style.css">
```

Intentionally feeding the browser a resource that you know it wouldn't parse as an icon seems the wrong thing to do, which could potentially cause unexpected behavior. But, in practice, this method seems to work well.

Using Lazy Loading

Lazy loading is a term generally applied to the loading of resources as they are needed, rather than in anticipation of them being needed at some point. In the context of images, this usually means not automatically loading images that fall below the page fold, and, thus, are not visible on the initial page load. As the user scrolls through the page, the missing images are loaded as needed. Lazy loading can be implemented in JavaScript.

The benefits are obvious. By loading only the images needed immediately, you can cut down significantly on the volume of data that must be sent to the client. To the user, it appears that the page has loaded quicker. Of course, if the user scrolls through the rest of the page, the images will still be loaded anyway, but lazy loading results in the browser's page loading feedback (for example, a turning wheel or loading bar) finishing earlier, and these feedback cues are an important part of a user's perception of speed.

Don't underestimate the effect on data transfer with this method, either. A large number of your visitors won't scroll past the page fold, and if you have a significant number of images lower down the page, the bandwidth savings will be considerable. Not only that, web server processes will be freed up quicker, resulting in a lighter load on the web server.

There is, of course, a downside. There's always latency involved in sending HTTP requests and receiving a response — more so when a connection must be established first. When lazy loading is used for images, there can be a noticeable flicker — the user scrolls the hidden part of the page into view, and it might be half a second or so before the image loads. This can have a negative effect on the user's perception of the site.

Still, lazy loading is an idea that is worth looking at — particularly if you have a large number of images below the fold. Both YUI and jQuery have lazy loading plug-ins, or you can write your own — but be careful to cover all situations in which additional content may come into view (for example, resizing of the browser window, removing/resizing dynamic elements on the page, scrolling, and so on).

Avoiding Empty src attributes

As back-end code has grown more and more complex, the opportunities for accidentally outputting `<img>` tags with empty `src` attributes have increased. Consider the following example,:

```
<img src="<?php echo $image ?>">
```

If the `$image` variable is not set, you end up generating an empty `src` attribute. It would seem logical that browsers should ignore image tags if no source URL is given, but the reality is surprising. Firefox 3.5 and later will not issue a request; Opera will not issue a request; but Safari, Chrome, and IE will.

In the case of IE, a request is made to the parent directory. Thus, if the current URL is `http://www.example.com/news/articles.html`, a request will be made to `http://www.example.com/news/`. Most likely, this URL will return an HTML document or a `404` error rather than an image, so the response will simply be ignored.

With Safari and Chrome, a request is made to the current URL — `http://www.example.com/news/articles.html` in the previous example.

While browsers have the sense not to attempt to parse HTML documents or error pages as images, this behavior still results in an additional HTTP request. Equally troublesome is the impact it could have on the server, because the number of requests on the URL is potentially being doubled. For a heavily scripted page, this could cause a significant increase in server load.

Setting Appropriate Width and Height Attributes

The dimensions of an image can be specified either via the `width` and `height` attributes of the `<img>` tag, or through the `width` and `height` CSS properties. But since the page will apparently load just fine without them, why not keep your code slim by leaving them out?

The problem is that, without these attributes, the browser has no way of knowing the image dimensions until it begins to load them. As each image is loaded, the browser must redraw the page to accommodate them. The result is the often seen effect where content jumps around on the page as it is loading.

By specifying the width and height of each image, the browser immediately knows how much screen space the images will occupy, and can allocate appropriate space for when they are finally loaded. The result is a much smoother page loading.

You should ensure that the width and height that you specify match the dimensions of the image. It's not uncommon for web masters to intentionally scale images by setting larger or smaller dimensions, but the results are not good. Scaling images up in this way results in a noticeable drop in quality, while scaling down is inefficient. The image file that is being requested will be larger than is necessary. For best results, always resize images with image-editing software (such as Gimp or Photoshop) first, and set the correct width and height in your mark-up.

Using Image Maps

As you learned in Chapter 1, "A Refresher on Web Browsers," cutting down the number of resources on a page is one of the main ways to boost performance. However, although you may have merged your CSS and JavaScript files, there will typically still be numerous images. Earlier in this chapter, you learned about reducing the size of images, and now it's time to look at reducing the number of images requested.

Image Maps

In a normal image link, the whole graphic becomes a clickable link to the destination. *Image maps* are a popular technique for mapping specific parts of the image to different destinations. (Actually, there are two forms of image maps — client-side and server-side — but the former is much more common. Because of this, a reference to just an "image map" actually means "client-side image map.")

A common use of image maps is for hyperlinking different parts of a map, as shown in the screenshot of `http://time.gov` in Figure 5-9.

Moving the mouse around different parts of the image causes the name of the time zone to be displayed at the bottom left, and the link URL to change to a location showing the time in this particular zone. (The HTML for creating this image map is somewhat tedious, with each region being a polygon described by a series of coordinates.)

In this situation, an image map was the obvious choice — it would have been impractical for the map to have been composed of multiple images, one for each time zone. However, there are situations in which the obvious choice is a series of adjacent images, and, in these cases, an image map can be used to reduce these images to one.

Consider the icons shown in Figure 5-10.

FIGURE 5-9

FIGURE 5-10

It's not too difficult to imagine these six icons forming part of a toolbar on, say, a social networking site. The HTML might look something like this. (Yes, `alt` and `title` attributes have been omitted — it's for clarity though, not laziness,)

```
<a href="/games.php"><img src="applications-games.png"></a>
<a href="/videos.php"><img src="applications-multimedia.png"></a>
<a href="/mail.php"><img src="internet-mail.png"></a>
<a href="/calendar.php"><img src="office-calendar.png"></a>
<a href="/search.php"><img src="system-search.png"></a>
<a href="/help.php"><img src="help-browser.png"></a>
```

Because they sit adjacent on the page, these icons are ideal candidates for an image map.

First, you combine them into a single image using GIMP, as shown in Figure 5-11, and then save it as a PNG8 file.

Next, you create the image map, as shown here:

FIGURE 5-11

```
<map name="navigation">
<area href="/games.php" shape="rect" coords="0,0,42,32">
<area href="/videos.php" shape="rect" coords="42,0,79,32">
<area href="/mail.php" shape="rect" coords="79,0,116,32">
<area href="/calendar.php" shape="rect" coords=117,0,154,32"">
<area href="/search.php" shape="rect" coords="155,0,190,32">
<area href="/help.php" shape="rect" coords="191,0,230,32">
</map>

<img border=0 src="imagemap_nav.png" usemap="#navigation">
```

As you can see, the image map consists of a series of `<area>` tags that define *hotspots* in the image — regions that will be clickable. Numerous shapes are possible, but a rectangle is the natural choice here, and the four coordinates specify the bottom-left X,Y and top-right X,Y coordinates of the hotspot (with the origin being the top left of the image).

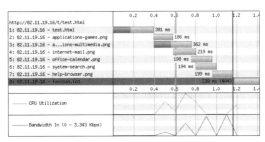

FIGURE 5-12

The end result is indistinguishable from the original, but you've reduced the number of images from six to one, and along the way saved a few kilobytes — the six individual images totaled 11,092 bytes, whereas the sprite weighs in at just 4,461 bytes.

Figure 5-12 shows a waterfall view of the original page loading (using IE 7 and a DSL connection).

Ignoring `favicon.ico`, you have seven requests in total and a loading time of 1.16 seconds. Now, take a look at Figure 5-13 to see the effect of using the image map.

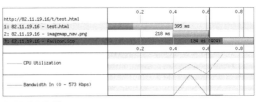

FIGURE 5-13

Here, the number of resources has dropped to two, and the loading time is down to 0.62 seconds — a saving of approximately one-half of a second.

If all this seems too good to be true, it might just be. There are a few problems with using image maps:

➤ Navigation breaks for users on text-based browsers (or those who have images turned off), and may cause accessibility issues for text-to-speech engines.

➤ Mouse-over effects become problematic.

➤ Images must be adjacent.

Of these, the first should be the biggest drawback. In practice, it tends to be the second and third that discourage web masters.

Luckily, there is a much more powerful technique for merging images.

CSS SPRITES

The CSS `background-image` property enables you to set an image to be used as the background of a given element. One of the neat things about CSS backgrounds is that an offset for the image may be given using the `background-position` property. Take a look at the example in Figure 5-14.

Figure 5-14 shows an image that measures 554 pixels wide and 394 pixels high. To display this as a background image, you can use the following code:

FIGURE 5-14

```
<style>
    .mybackground {
        background-image:url('/images/flowers.png');
        width: 554px;
        height: 394px;
    }
</style>

<div class="mybackground"></div>
```

However, using `background-position`, you can display only a section of the image. Now pick an arbitrary region inside the image, as shown in Figure 5-15.

The upper-left coordinates of the highlighted area are 193 pixels and 100 pixels, and the region is 95 pixels wide and 71 pixels deep. Thus, consider the following:

FIGURE 5-15

```
<style>
    .mybackground {
        background-image:url('/images/flowers.png');
        background-position: -193px -100px;
      width: 95px;
        height: 71px;
        border: solid 1px black;
    }
</style>

<div class="mybackground"></div>
```

For added clarity, a small border has been put around the div. As shown in Figure 5-16, when you load this in a browser, only the selected region of the background image is shown.

FIGURE 5-16

Perhaps you have already surmised how background-image and background-position could be used to great effect. You can join together multiple images into one larger montage, and then selectively show regions of this montage in the appropriate place. This slashes the number of image requests, and the montage — or *sprite,* as it is more commonly called — is usually significantly smaller than the sum of the images it contains.

Earlier in this chapter during the discussion on image maps, you saw how to combine six icons into a single file (as shown in Figure 5-17), with the intention of using a client-side image map.

FIGURE 5-17

Let's try this again; only this time, using CSS sprites.

In the previous example, you set the background for a div element, but things are trickier for links. If you set the background for the <a> element, like so, nothing is shown:

```
<a href="/games.php" class="sprites"></a>
```

With no content inside the anchor tags, the element takes up zero screen space, even if you use width/height attributes in CSS. You can get around this by setting the display: block, but that causes your icons to display on new lines.

One solution is to use an <img> element inside the anchor, and assign a CSS class to this. You can't leave the image blank, though, so instead, you use a holding image — a 1 × 1 pixel transparent gif (with an alt attribute for the benefit of those with images turned off), as shown here:

```
<a href="/games.php"><img class="sprites" alt="games" src="holder.gif"></a>
```

Thus, the full code looks like so:

```
<style>

    .sprite {
        background-image:url('imagemap_nav.png');
        width: 37px;
        height: 44px;
```

```
        }
    .sprite_games {      background-position: -4px -0px; }
    .sprite_videos {     background-position: -41px -0px; }
    .sprite_mail {       background-position: -78px -0px; }
    .sprite_calendar {   background-position: -115px -0px; }
    .sprite_search {     background-position: -152px -0px; }
    .sprite_help {       background-position: -189px -0px; }

    img {        border:0;      }

</style>


<a href="/games.php"><img alt="games" class="sprite sprite_games"
    src="holder.gif"></a>
<a href="/videos.php"><img  alt="videos" class="sprite sprite_videos"
    src="holder.gif"></a>

<a href="/mail.php"><img alt="mail"  class="sprite sprite_mail"
    src="holder.gif"></a>
<a href="/calendar.php"><img alt="calendar" class="sprite sprite_calendar"
    src="holder.gif"></a>

<a href="/search.php"><img alt="search" src="holder.gif" class="sprite
    sprite_search"></a>
<a href="/help.php"><img alt="help" src="holder.gif" class="sprite
    sprite_help"></a>
```

Two CSS `class` selectors have been used for each anchor tag — one containing "core" attributes of the sprite and the other containing specifics for the region in question. Although this isn't essential, it keeps your CSS rules slim and is the logical thing to do. (The advantages would not have been so clear-cut if the icons had not been of identical sizes.)

The downside to this approach is that the `<img>` elements are largely redundant. You can eliminate the need for a 1 × 1 pixel holding the image and remove the `<img>` element completely with a little extra thought — either by giving the anchor tags the `block` display property (`inline-block`), or by using `float` positioning (for example, `float:left`).

Alternatively, since it is common practice to hold navigation links inside a styled list (this approach degrades well in older browsers and has more semantic meaning), you can often just apply the background sprite to the `<li>` element, as shown in the following example:

```
<ul class="sprite">
    <li class="sprite_games"><a href="/games.php"></li>
    <li class="sprite_videos"><a href="/videos.php"></li>
. . . .
```

CSS sprites have a few obvious advantages over an image map:

➤ The images no longer must be adjacent. Although the six icons are side-by-side in this example, they could just as easily be scattered across the page.

➤ Each image can be used multiple times, in different places.

➤   You retain the ability to set an `alt` attribute for each image, thus improving accessibility.

Google is one of the biggest names to use CSS sprites and does so effectively. In fact, the majority of the images used on `google.com` are contained in a single sprite, as shown at `http://www.google .com/images/srpr/nav_logo13.png`.

No doubt you can recognize many of these images from the various parts of the Google site.

Sprite Strategies

The Google master image also raises an interesting implementation issue. With only a few of the sprites appearing on any one page, there's a performance hit when the master image is first retrieved. The master image is currently 28 KB, whereas an image containing just the sprites used on a particular page would be one-half that. Certainly, this is bad for performance in the short term — a user who visits `google.com`, does a basic web search, and then leaves, has downloaded an unnecessarily large image. But in the long term, the big master image does improve performance.

Deciding on which images to place in the master sprite is tricky and should be based on an analysis of client usage patterns. Although you certainly want to place core icons used on every page in your master image, it may make sense to place lesser-used images in a separate master image, or even not sprite them at all. Although a master file containing every image used on your site is beneficial for devoted visitors, the large file size will punish the casual visitor. Keeping first-time visitors on your site is almost as important as getting them to visit in the first place, and a bulky master image won't do much to help that cause.

Repeating Images

A common use of background images is to tile a much smaller image horizontally or vertically (or both). As shown in Figure 5-18, Microsoft's current homepage provides a neat example of this.

FIGURE 5-18

The actual image used for the red-yellow gradient is a single pixel wide, as shown in Figure 5-19.

However, the gradient is tiled horizontally using the `background-repeat` property, as shown here:

```
div.h15-header
{
    background-image: url('/global/en/us/publishingimages/
        office_canvas_bg_top.jpg') !important;
    background-repeat: repeat-x;
    background-color: transparent;
    border: none !important;
    color: #FFF !important;
}
```

How do you achieve a similar effect with sprites? Sprites may be repeated vertically or horizontally (but not both!). The key is their positioning in the master image.

For the Microsoft background image, which was 1 pixel wide and 556 pixels high, you can place additional sprites below this image, providing the width of the master image does not exceed 1 pixel (the width of the Microsoft background image). This somewhat limits what you can place there — another repeating background image is probably the only practical possibility. An alternative would be to widen the first image (as it repeats horizontally) to, say, 20 pixels, providing sufficient width to place some icons below it but sacrificing file size a little.

FIGURE 5-19

Horizontal or Vertical?

All this talk of horizontally and vertically aligned images raises a question. In situations in which you don't need to worry about repeating backgrounds — and can, hence, arrange your sprites vertically or horizontally — is there anything to be gained by choosing one direction over the other?

Because the LWZ compression method (used in GIF and PNG) scans horizontally, there should theoretically be an increase in compression (or rather the possibility for compression) if you stack your sprites horizontally.

Again, Figure 5-20 shows the sprites used earlier in this chapter.

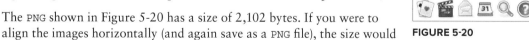

The PNG shown in Figure 5-20 has a size of 2,102 bytes. If you were to align the images horizontally (and again save as a PNG file), the size would be 2,297 bytes.

FIGURE 5-20

So, there certainly is some advantage to aligning vertically, albeit not a big one in this example. Except in the case of repeating background sprites, it generally doesn't matter which axis the sprites are aligned along. So, you may as well use vertical and save a few bytes.

Drawbacks to Using Sprites

Although CSS sprites may seem too good to be true, there are a number of drawbacks to using them.

The first is that they are somewhat fiddly to create and implement — merging images, calculating pixel offsets, creating appropriate CSS rules. If one sprite must be changed at a later date to an image of different dimensions, this can affect the offset of many of the other sprites. In the section, "Automating the Process," later in this chapter, you'll learn about some useful tools for automating this process.

A much less common problem (but still one worth noting) is that a GIF or PNG file is stored uncompressed in memory by the browser. Situations have occurred (albeit not often) in which a huge (in terms of dimensions) background image — mostly consisting of whitespace — is used. Although such an image compresses well, and, hence, has an apparently innocent file size, it's a different matter when the browser loads the image.

A disadvantage of background images in general is that when a page is printed, browsers tend not to include them. (However, the client usually has the capability to override this.) In many cases, this is actually wanted behavior. Printing unnecessary images slows down printing and wastes ink, but sometimes these "background" images are an integral part of the page. In such situations, a separate style sheet for printing (using the media="print" attribute when linked to) can alleviate the problem.

Finally, you should not lose sight of the big picture. The overall aim is to improve page loading times, and although reducing the number of HTTP requests is usually beneficial, this isn't always the case. Let's look at an example.

Say that you have a master image containing four sprites (Van Gogh paintings, actually) that are the sizes shown in Table 5-1.

TABLE 5-1: Sprites in Sample Master Image

IMAGE NAME	SIZE (BYTES)
Vg1.jpg	44318
Vg2.jpg	35172
Vg3.jpg	35067
Vg4.jpg	57824

The total size of these four images is 172,381 bytes, whereas the master image is an almost identical size at 173,354 bytes. (The images chosen were intentionally quite big, so no sort of optimization was attempted on any of them.) Figure 5-21 shows the waterfall view for the loading of this page.

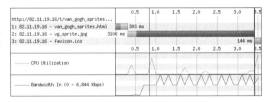

FIGURE 5-21

Clearly, this 173 KB image is the bottleneck in the loading of the page. (Although you didn't need a waterfall view to tell you that.) Would it be more efficient to keep the images separate and make use of parallel downloading? With most browsers downloading only two resources in parallel, you would need to split the four images across two domains.

Of course, this turns out to be false logic. Although the images would now download in parallel, they would be competing for finite bandwidth. Hence, each one would take longer to download. The overall loading time would almost be the same as when using sprites.

There is, however, one situation in which this technique would be beneficial. If the client has more bandwidth than the server, splitting the images across two separate servers prevents server bandwidth from being the bottleneck.

Figure 5-22 shows the result of using this technique, and the loading time has almost been cut in half. Admittedly, situations such as this are rare, but they do help to illustrate the potential danger of spriting everything in sight.

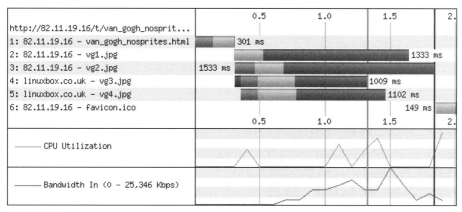

FIGURE 5-22

Palette Colors

An additional problem with sprites concerns the number of colors. Most likely, you'll want to create a paletted master image in GIF or PNG8 format, both of which limit the number of colors that can be used. And with an image containing a variety of sprites, you may find that there isn't enough space in the color table to hold all the unique colors. The result is that the sprites look ragged or crudely drawn.

This problem can be partly mitigated by grouping sprites with similar color palettes and using several master images rather than one. An alternative is to use a nonpaletted format, such as PNG24 or JPG — but you'll likely pay a big price in increased file size. If it's just one image that uses a dramatically different color palette than the rest, it may simply be best not to sprite it at all. Sprites are a powerful technique, and you can easily get carried away with it. Learning when *not* to use them is an important consideration.

Automating the Process

Creating sprites is a tedious process, but a number of tools are available to automate the process. These range from simply spriting a series of images supplied by the user, to automatically parsing a page and then generating sprites and CSS for all images found. Although tools in the latter category are certainly clever, you may find you prefer a more hands-on approach.

Following are a couple of favorites:

➤ CSS Sprite Generator (online at `http://spritegen.website-performance.org/`, or available to download from `https://launchpad.net/css-sprite-generator`) creates a master image from a list of user-supplied images. It offers the capability to resize images, align horizontally or vertically, and can output in JPG, PNG, or GIF format. Optionally, supporting CSS can be generated, too. This is a valuable tool because it is simple, yet powerful, with plenty of options.

➤ SpriteMe (`http://spriteme.org/`) uses the novel approach to run via a JavaScript book-mark. Simply visit the site you want to inspect, find SpriteMe in your bookmarks, and click it. The SpriteMe widget then loads on the page, as shown in Figure 5-23. The widget lists all the images found on the page and notes those that are possible candidates for spriting, and those that are not (for example, because they repeat both vertically and horizontally). With just a few clicks, you can generate a master image, and SpriteMe can show you the changes you need to make to your CSS.

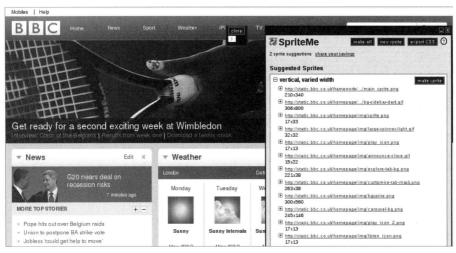

FIGURE 5-23

> **NOTE** *Although SpriteMe is sleek and has many useful features, it doesn't offer any control over the automatically generated master image, so you still need to optimize it manually. As always, you should exercise caution before blindly accepting the SpriteMe suggestions.*

Although interactive tools are all okay, in some situations, you may need to create sprites programmatically.

For example, consider a dating site on which photos of the ten most recent members are shown on the homepage. The obvious way would be to select the ten newest members from the database, then select the primary photos associated with each member, and dynamically generate the appropriate HTML to display them. A better way (that is, better in terms of performance anyway) would be to use a `cron` job to generate this HTML fragment every hour or so, thus cutting down on database queries. What if you wanted to go a step further and convert these ten images into sprites? Clearly a scriptable, command-line solution is needed.

> **NOTE** *On UNIX and its derivatives (Linux, OS X, and so on), the widely used* cron *utility lets you schedule commands to be executed at specified times.* cron *is used for everything from periodically cleaning up temporary files, to updating spam and anti-virus definitions, to generating stats on system load.* cron *is ideal for periodically compiling HTML fragments to cut down on the server-side scripting and database queries. Under Windows, the Task Scheduler performs a similar role, and can also be used for such web automation.*

With a little bit of magic (ImageMagick, that is), this is actually quite an easy task. ImageMagick (`http://www.imagemagick.org/`) is a suite of command-line tools used for manipulating images, one of which — `convert` — can be used to join images together. The syntax can be as simple as the following:

```
convert image1.png image2.png image3.png -append output.png
```

This creates a vertically aligned master image named `output.png` from the three specified files. For a horizontally aligned master image, just use +append instead of -append.

`convert` accepts a whole host of other options, too, including the capability to set the image type (for example, paletted versus RGB), color depth, and transparency. Following is an improved version of the previous command:

```
convert -type Palette -colors 256 -background Transparent
        image1.png image2.png image3.png -append PNG8:output.png.
```

This specifies a paletted PNG file with a transparent background, and a color depth of 256, which is probably closer to what you want. Although `convert` does a decent job to keep the file size down, you may still want to pass the resulting image through something like pngcrush.

Of course, there's nothing to stop you from using something like the command-line version of CSS Sprite Generator. However, you may prefer the power and flexibility to roll your own solution.

CSS PERFORMANCE

In contrast to the other areas examined thus far in this chapter, there isn't a great deal to say about CSS performance. Still, there are a few small areas of interest, and a couple of popular performance "rules" that deserve some clarification.

CSS in the Document Head

With JavaScript, it is advantageous to load external scripts as late as possible. With CSS, the opposite is true. Most browsers delay rendering a page until the CSS has been downloaded to avoid a repaint/redraw, so it's usually best to place links to external style sheets in the `<head>` of the document. Unlike JavaScript, these links do not block, and the browser can happily continue with downloading other content.

Inline versus External

The decision on whether to include CSS inline or as an external file boils down to the trade-off between the number of HTTP requests and cachability. If you include the CSS inline, you eliminate an HTTP request but increase the size of the HTML document. If you use an external style sheet, you have an additional HTTP request, but the resource can be more readily cached. (Most of the time, you don't want to cache the HTML document because it has been dynamically generated.)

Link versus @import

Most of the time, you want your style sheet to be external, but you then have the choice of whether to use `<link>` or `@import` to load the resource. This is an easy decision. Stick with `<link>` because it is nonblocking, and can enable other resources to download in parallel.

Steve Souders has written an excellent article (although note that it is a few years old) on the subject at `http://www.stevesouders.com/blog/2009/04/09/dont-use-import/`, showing how different browsers implement `@import`, and what happens when you mix `@import` with `<link>`. All cause blocking behavior to some extent, and because there isn't a valid reason for favoring `@import` over `<link>` in the first place (old browsers don't support `@import`, so it can be used as a hack to stop them from loading the CSS), the solution is simply not to use it.

Redundant Selectors

Over time, your style sheets can become rather messy and out of sync — duplicate rules are added, elements are removed from the HTML document, but the developers forget to remove the CSS selectors, and so on. The result is redundant selectors adding unnecessary weight to your style sheet. Of course, in theory, this shouldn't happen. Your development and deployment process should be rigorous enough to ensure that the CSS is kept in sync. But, in practice, it does happen.

Dust-Me Selectors is a popular Firefox extension that can be used to find unused CSS selectors. However, development of the product seems to have stopped, and it will not work in the latest versions of Firefox.

Instead, check out CSS Usage (`https://addons.mozilla.org/en-US/firefox/addon/css-usage/`), which is an extension for the always useful Firebug. Figure 5-24 shows CSS Usage in action on `kernel.org`. Toward the bottom is a link enabling you to export the cleaned-up CSS if you are happy with the scan.

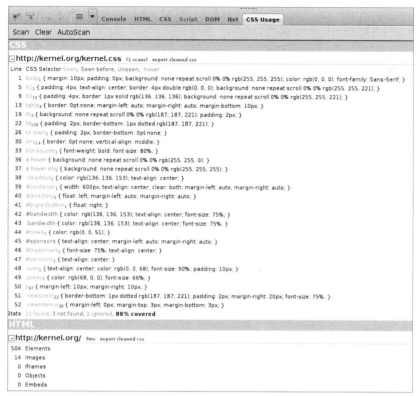

FIGURE 5-24

The big danger with any automated tool like this is that it might miss rules that actually *are* being used. For a global style sheet, you should scan every page of the site to be sure you haven't missed a rule that is used on only one page, buried deep inside the site. Even then, you risk missing DOM elements added by JavaScript, or content that varies based on the user's country, logged-in status, and so on. At best, these tools should just be used to find *possible* candidates for removal, which you can then check over manually.

CSS Expressions

Avoiding the use of CSS expressions was once one of the most important rules for CSS performance. But the use of these beasties has been deprecated for a while now (since IE 8, and they were supported only in IE anyway), so there's no point wasting too much time covering them here.

CSS expressions were a way to set CSS attributes dynamically using JavaScript embedded in the style sheet. Unfortunately, the rules are re-evaluated every time the browser window is resized or scrolled, or the mouse is moved. The result is that an expression can easily be re-evaluated thousands of times during a page view. Although the expressions are generally fairly light, with this number of executions, performance can suffer.

You can use expressions that will be evaluated only once, but almost always the same end result can be achieved using pure JavaScript — which isn't IE-specific and isn't deprecated.

Selector Performance

The performance of CSS selectors themselves has received a lot of attention in the past few years, mainly because of some well-publicized benchmarks showing a dramatic drop in performance under certain conditions.

Selectors are parsed from right to left. Consider the following example:

```
#body div div p {
    background:red;
}
```

When the browser hits this rule, it goes through every `<p>` element in the page and checks whether it is the child of a `<div>` tag. Then it checks if this `div` is the child of another `div`, and if this other `div` is the child of an element with ID `body`. This seems like quite a lot of work, and the obvious conclusion is that you should keep your chain of selectors short to minimize all this backtracking.

The problem often isn't as bad as you might expect in practice. Consider the following:

```
#body div div p .highlight {
    background:red;
}
```

This time, you match elements only with `class="highlight"`, so, although you have the same level of nesting, the more specific selector means that less elements are going to match. Wildcard selectors are the most dangerous to use, but, in general, there isn't a significant performance impact, and it's not worth your while to try to optimize your selectors.

What about the benchmarks? Many of these were rather artificial examples using deeply nested selectors with lots of wildcards on a huge DOM. Although it might seem reasonable to assume that the effect would still be there (albeit to a lesser degree) on a normal page, it turns out things are not quite that simple.

It seems that many browsers will hit a threshold at which performance drops off significantly. As you add DOM elements, the time taken to parse the CSS gradually increases in a linear fashion. But after you get into the tens of thousands of DOM elements, you hit a point in which CSS parsing suddenly starts to tail off dramatically. So, although these benchmarks are correct in showing that selectors do affect performance, the magnitude of the effect isn't quite so significant on real-life sites.

Using Shorthand Properties

Many CSS properties support a shorthand notation that is much quicker to write, which can make a big impact on the size of the style sheet.

One example is when specifying colors. Generally, a hex triplet is used, with two digits for each RGB part (for example, #F368C4, where F3 is the red component, 68 the green, and C4 the blue). When the two digits in each part are the same, you can omit one of them; thus, #FF99CC becomes #F9C.

With the `margin` and `padding` properties, the longhand way is to write them like so:

```
margin-top:5px;
margin-bottom:4px
margin-left:3px;
margin-right:2px
```

However, this can be simplified to the following:

```
margin:5px 2px 4px 3px
```

Notice the order of the values. You start at the top and go around clockwise — so the top margin first, then the right margin, then bottom, and then left.

If the top and bottom values are the same, and so, too, are the left and right, you can simplify things further, as shown here:

```
margin: 10px 5px
```

With only two values passed, browsers assume that the first refers to the top and bottom margins, and the second to the left and right margins.

There are many other shorthand notations. Table 5-2 shows some CSS properties along with their shorthand equivalents.

TABLE 5-2: CSS Properties and Shorthand Equivalent

LONGHAND	SHORTHAND
`border-width:1px;` `border-color:#000;` `border-style:solid;`	`border: 1px solid #000;`
`background-color:red;` `background-image:url(foo.png);` `background-repeat:no-repeat;` `background-attachment:fixed;` `background-position:0 0;`	`background: red url(foo.png) no-repeat fixed 0 0;`
`font-family: Helvetica;` `font-size:1em;` `font-style:italic;` `font-weight:normal;`	`font: italic normal 1em Helvetica;`

Inheritance and Default Values

Some of the biggest savings in CSS come from knowing when properties can safely be omitted — either because they have been inherited from a parent element, or because the default value is appropriate. In many cases, the default value for a property is inherited. Check the online CSS documentation if you're unsure.

Doing More with CSS

In many situations, it makes sense to use CSS more rather than less because it's the most efficient option. Certainly, placing style rules in an external style sheet (cacheable by the browser) is generally a better option than embedding the rules in the HTML document. (The exception is when there are a large number of rules used only on one page — here, inlining is sometimes better.)

CSS versus Data URIs

With CSS sprites being a better supported way to achieve a similar effect, is there a need for data URIs? You'll recall from the earlier discussion of CSS sprites that it isn't always practical to convert images to sprites sometimes because of the color table, and sometimes because of horizontal and vertical repetition. In these situations, data URIs are an excellent solution.

Mouse-Over Techniques

Using CSS, rather than JavaScript, for mouse-over effects (for example, in menus) is a popular option. Previously, this was the preserve of JavaScript (or even worse, Java or Flash applets). But for basic effects, CSS is better suited, and can do a surprisingly lot — pop-over windows, image switching, pull-down menus, and so on. For example, to swap an image with another one when the mouse is moved over it, the HTML and CSS is simply as follows:

```
<span class="swap">
    <img src="image1.png" />
</span>

span.swap {
    background-image: image2.png;
    background-repeat:no-repeat;
    display:block;
}
span.swap:hover img{
    visibility:hidden;
}
```

Aside from being more elegant, this method works even if the client does not support JavaScript (or has it disabled). Unfortunately, CSS solutions lack many of the keyboard navigation shortcuts, and JavaScript still has the edge here.

Creating Rounded Corners

Rectangular boxes are so 1990s. These days, site owners want aesthetically pleasing boxes with rounded corners. There are a number of ways to achieve these, but most are rather ugly, rely on creating images for each corner, and possibly the use of HTML tables.

Again, CSS comes to the rescue by defining the `border-radius` property, which can be used to round the corners of a rectangular box. `border-radius` first appeared in CSS 3 but had been under discussion for several years previous. As a result, many browsers had already started to implement support for it but had used their own naming.

Creating rounded corners in CSS is currently best achieved using rules such as the following:

```
.roundedcorner {
    -moz-border-radius: 5px;
    -webkit-border-radius: 5px;
    -khtml-border-radius: 5px;
    border-radius: 5px;
}
```

`-moz-border-radius` is Mozilla's name for the property and is supported by most Gecko-based browsers (Firefox, Konqueror, and so on). `-webkit-border-radius` is used by WebKit-based browsers such as Chrome and Safari, whereas `-khtml-border-radius` is for older versions of Konqueror. `border-radius` is the accepted CSS 3 name, and you should include it for future-proofing — for a time when all the major browsers support this and begin to deprecate their own naming conventions.

What about IE and Opera? IE began to support only border radii from version 9 onward but did so using the correct CSS3 property name — so there are no browser-specific hacks for IE. It's an identical story for Opera, which began supporting `border-radius` from version 10.5 onward.

In fact, most of the other major browsers now support `-border-radius`, too, so the browser-specific properties are becoming less necessary. For the next few years, it will still be important to continue to use these hacks, however, to ensure compatibility with older browsers.

What about older versions of IE and Opera? Various hacks are available for these browsers (mostly involving falling back on images or JavaScript), but another option is simply to ignore them. One of the beauties of `border-radius` is that it degrades gracefully — if a browser doesn't support it, it simply falls back on displaying the border without nonrounded corners.

CSS3

Rounded corners are just one of the many new cool features offered by CSS3 and are a prime example of how advances in CSS can solve problems that previously required JavaScript. CSS3 is modular in nature, and with each module being at a different stage of development, it isn't simply a case of asking, "Does browser X support CSS3?" All of the major browsers do now support CSS3, but to varying degrees. The main browsers to watch out for are IE 7 and 8, which have limited CSS3 support. With IE 9, Firefox, Chrome, Safari, and Opera, support is much more comprehensive.

Let's look at some of the ways in which CSS3 can improve performance.

Multiple Background Images

With CSS3, the `background` property now supports multiple images, which will be displayed on top of each other (the first image listed will appear at the top), like so:

```
background:
    url("/images/image1.png") 800px 40px no-repeat,
    url("/images/image2.png") ,
    url("/images/image3.png")
;
```

In some situations this can be a very efficient way to reduce the size of complex images. Too often, it seems, you encounter images for which neither palette nor RGB color schemes are wholly suitable — for example, a company name in a stylized font on top of a photographic image. If you save as a JPEG, the text will become jagged; if you save in a paletted format, the file size will be huge.

One way to solve this is by storing the two parts of the image separately, and using CSS3 to superimpose them. In this way, you can apply the most appropriate compression method to each. Even though this does result in an extra HTTP request, the overall saving may be worth it.

Text Shadows

On the subject of text inside images, the preferred method is to place a text element on top of an image using CSS, rather than having the text embedded in the image. Aside from reducing the image size, this is better for both accessibility and search engines.

If you have highly styled text, this isn't always possible, but the introduction of text shadows takes you one step closer (in fact, they were proposed in CSS2, but Safari was the only browser to implement them), and can be used to create surprisingly advanced images.

Figure 5-25 shows an example using the following styling for the text element:

```
.selector{
color:white;
text-shadow:2px 2px 4px #000000;
}
```

The first two parameters specify the horizontal and vertical offset of the shadow, while the third parameter sets the level of blurring, and the fourth the color of the shadow.

CSS Text Shadows

FIGURE 5-25

Box Shadows

Shadows around boxes are aesthetically pleasing, but have historically been rather messy to implement, often relying on tables or a mess of nested `divs`, coupled with a handful of small graphics. CSS3 has changed all this, and box shadows are one of the most popular

FIGURE 5-26

and frequently used new features — especially since they degrade well in browsers that do not support them. Figure 5-26 shows an example box shadow, and here's the CSS for the box element:

```
#shadow {
box-shadow: 8px 8px 5px #666;
}
```

IE has supported box shadows since version 9, while Firefox has supported the `box-shadow` property since version 4.0. Prior to that, the Firefox-specific `-moz-box-shadow` was needed, and it's still a good idea to include it for backward compatibility. With WebKit-based browsers (Chrome, Konqueror, and Safari), the `-webkit-box-shadow` property is still required. Thus, a more robust example would be the following:

```
#example1 {
-moz-box-shadow: 8px 8px 5px #666;
-webkit-box-shadow: 8px 8px 5px #666;
box-shadow: 8px 8px 5px #666;
}
```

Custom Fonts

The `@font-face` selector first appeared in CSS 2, was dropped in 2.1, and finally re-appeared in CSS 3 as part of the CSS Fonts Level 3 module. Firefox 3.5 supports it, as do Opera 10, Safari 3.1, and Chrome 4. Surprisingly, IE has supported `@font-face` since version 5 back in the late 1990s, albeit using a proprietary font format (ironically called Embedded OpenType, or EOT). The other major browsers support TrueType (TT) and FreeType (FT),

In light of these cross-compatibility issues, it's wise to store two copies of the font on your server, in both EOT and TT/FT format. (Be sure to check first that the licensing on the font allows you to redistribute it, because this is essentially what you are doing.) In addition, it can be helpful to provide the font in SVG format for older browsers. The CSS then looks like this:

```
@font-face {
  font-family: "myfontname";
  src: url(/media/fonts/MyFont.eot);
  src: url(/media/fonts/MyFont.ttf) format("truetype");
  src: url(/media/fonts/MyFont.svg) format("svg");
}

.customFont {
  font-family: "myfontname", sans-serif;
}
```

You start by giving the font a name for internal use (`myfontname`). The next two `src` lines then specify the location of the font file for IE and non-IE browsers, respectively. At a later point in your CSS, you can then use the font name defined as you would any other font.

> **NOTE** *Although font files are generally small, remember that they also incur the overhead of an extra HTTP request. Use a custom font only if you really need it, not for the "wow" factor.*

Linear Gradients

Another situation in which images are commonly used for styling is with background gradients on buttons and text boxes. Typically, a single pixel-wide gradient image is repeated horizontally using CSS (you saw an example of this in Figure 5-19, earlier in this chapter). Although such images are usually tiny, they still result in an additional HTTP request.

CSS3 introduces support for linear color gradients, with the option for the browser to fall back on using an image if it does not support gradients. Unfortunately, the major browsers all use their own specific versions of this property at the moment, so the CSS is rather long-winded. Let's look at an example:

```
.gradient {
    background-color: #00F;
    background-image: url(images/gradient.png);
    background-image: -webkit-gradient(linear, 0% 0%, 0% 100%, from(#F00),
        to(#00F));
    background-image: -webkit-linear-gradient(top, #F00, #00F);
    background-image: -moz-linear-gradient(top, #F00, #00F);
    background-image: -ms-linear-gradient(top, #F00, #00F);
    background-image: -o-linear-gradient(top, #F00, #00F);
}
```

This creates a linear, vertical gradient, starting with red at the top, and ending with blue at the bottom.

You start by setting the background color, followed by a fallback image. Versions of Safari prior to 5.1, and Chrome prior to 6, would annoyingly still load the fallback image anyway (even though they did support gradients). This bug has now been fixed.

Next come the browser-specific rules. -webkit-gradient is for Safari 4 onward and Chrome 1 through Chrome 9. However, this syntax is now deprecated (hence, there's no need to explain each property). For more recent versions of these two browsers, -webkit-linear-gradient is preferred.

Gradient support was added in Firefox 3.6, in the form of -moz-linea-gradient. IE introduced gradients in version 10, via -ms-linear-gradient, while Opera introduced -o-linear-gradient in version 11.10. Eventually, there should be an official, cross-browser property, but in order to maintain backward compatibility, these browser-specific solutions will be around for several years to come.

Transformations

CSS3 introduces both two-dimensional (2D) and three-dimensional (3D) transformations, although the latter are not yet supported in IE or Opera. Two-dimensional transformations are probably the most useful (although IE has only supported them since version 9), offering the capability for you to scale, rotate, stretch, and move elements.

As with many new CSS3 features, transformations are currently implemented using browser-specific prefixes. Thus, to rotate an element by 90 degrees, the following code is needed:

```
.myrule {
transform: rotate(90deg);
-ms-transform: rotate(90deg); /* IE 9 */
-moz-transform: rotate(90deg); /* Firefox */
-webkit-transform: rotate(90deg); /* Safari and Chrome */
-o-transform: rotate(90deg); /* Opera */
}
```

Like rounded corners, shadows, and gradients, transformations are exciting because they raise the possibility of eliminating images (and, in this case, possibly JavaScript), resulting in a lighter page.

LOOKING FORWARD

There are many exciting developments in the field of web graphics on the horizon, and over the next few years, these should enter the mainstream. In fact, some are already supported to some degree; although lack of complete cross-browser support (you can guess which browser is behind all the others) means that none are actually suitable for production use yet.

To conclude this discussion of all things graphics-related, let's take a look at what the future has in store.

MNG

One of the main reasons that the GIF format hasn't died out on the web (aside from inertia) is that its replacement, PNG, doesn't support animation. Although this may seem like an oversight by the creators of PNG, it was intentional — because they were also developing the lesser known Multiple-Image Network Graphics (MNG) format specifically for animation.

Although the idea of the MNG format began at approximately the same time as PNG, its development has slowed down, and the format hasn't caught on. As of 2012, only Konqueror supported the format natively, although plug-ins are available for IE, Firefox, and Opera.

Perhaps part of the reason for the slow uptake is that, thankfully, animated GIFs have fallen out of fashion. With alternative formats under development, however, it may be that MNG may never enjoy widespread support.

APNG

Animated Portable Network Graphics (APNG) is an extension to PNG, and offers features similar to MNG. Its chief advantages over MNG are better browser support and a less-complicated format.

Because the first frame of an APNG file looks like a regular PNG file, browsers with no APNG support can still display the first frame — thus, there is some degree of backward compatibility. Currently, Opera and the Gecko-based browsers are the only ones that support APNG natively, although Chrome supports it via a plug-in.

JPEG 2000

JPEG 2000 is intended to replace JPEG. But despite it having been around since 2000, only Konqueror and Safari currently support it natively (IE and Firefox both support it via plug-ins). It looks as if things will stay this way for a while.

The main advantage of JPEG 2000 will be better compression, offering smaller file sizes and higher image quality. Other goodies include error checking, multiple resolution representations, and support for alpha channels.

SUMMARY

Choosing the right file format is an essential first step to optimize your images, and an understanding of the underlying compression algorithms used by the three main image formats (PNG, JPEG, GIF) can help you to make further reductions in file size.

Each image used in a page results in an extra HTTP request, so cutting down on the number of images is a worthwhile goal. The two main techniques are image maps and CSS sprites. Sprites are the best general-purpose solution, but they are somewhat fiddly to implement.

It's worth being aware of the way in which selectors are parsed (right to left) and the effect of this on CSS performance — especially when wildcards are used. Also, ensure that you become familiar with the shorthand notations available for many CSS properties because these can make your style sheets significantly smaller in size.

While advances in CSS can be utilized to cut down on the use of JavaScript, there are still many situations where JavaScript is the only viable solution. Love it or hate it, JavaScript is an essential part of the modern web (especially so since the birth of Web 2.0), and an understanding of how to optimize it is essential. In Chapter 6, you learn all about JavaScript, the Document Object Model, and Ajax.

JavaScript, the Document Object Model, and Ajax

➤ Looking at the JavaScript engines used by the major browsers

➤ Understanding the impact that the Document Object Model has on performance

➤ Looking at performance considerations of the JavaScript language

➤ Understanding how browsers download and execute JavaScript

➤ Getting some tips for efficient Ajax programming

In the late 1990s, JavaScript suffered from a poor reputation among professional web developers. Too often it was used for flashy (but pointless) special effects and was a nightmare for cross-browser compatibility. Even visiting a particular vendor's website using its own browser might have resulted in JavaScript error messages.

The situation has improved dramatically in the last decade, with browser-specific quirks having decreased, along with the need for ugly hacks to get around them. In a testament to how much things have changed, Ajax (which is built around JavaScript) is now such a big part of the modern web and works surprisingly smoothly most of the time. There's also been a shift in how JavaScript is used, with less emphasis on gimmicks and more on usability. These days, the majority of big sites (and most Web 2.0 sites) use JavaScript to some degree, often without it being particularly apparent.

This chapter looks at the performance considerations for using JavaScript and the ways in which browsers download and execute it. JavaScript is closely related to the Document Object Model (DOM), and you'll also learn how the DOM affects page rendering times, as well as how JavaScript interacts with it. Finally, this chapter looks at Ajax, and ways in which it can be sped up.

JAVASCRIPT, JSCRIPT, AND ECMASCRIPT

Before getting into the intricacies of JavaScript performance, it's worth looking at the history of the language, including the competing implementations, the official standards, and the engines used by each browser. Toward the end of this section, you learn about the different approaches offered by the engines, and the ways in which they aim to boost performance.

A Brief History of JavaScript

The first release of JavaScript was in Netscape Navigator 2.0, in 1995. Originally, it was called LiveScript, but within a few months, it had been rebranded to JavaScript. (Many commentators have suggested that this was simply a marketing ploy to cash in on the success of Java, which had become something of a buzzword.)

Naturally, Microsoft was not going to be left behind, and by the following year, the newly released Internet Explorer 3.0 contained Microsoft's implementation of JavaScript. To avoid any trademark disputes, it named its scripting language JScript.

At around the same time, Netscape passed the language to the European Computer Manufacturers Association (ECMA) standards organization, the international standards organization for Information Communication Technology (ICT) and Consumer Electronics (CE), which began formalizing and standardizing the language. The result was ECMAScript, which continues to undergo regular refinements and enhancements.

So, ECMAScript is the blueprint for the language. JavaScript and JScript are vendor-specific names for their particular implementations of the language. Although it's probably more accurate to say ECMAScript, most people still refer to the language as JavaScript, and they aren't necessarily talking specifically about Netscape's implementation but the language in general. (In this book, this implementation will be specifically referred to as Netscape's JavaScript.)

Surprisingly, the differences between JScript and Netscape's JavaScript have never been huge, even in the ugly days of the browser wars. This was no doubt partly because of the neutral role played by ECMA. Still, there were enough small niggles that writing cross-browser JavaScript was tricky. (However, many of these problems were because of differences in the DOM, rather than JavaScript.)

The situation has improved since then. Although differences still exist, they are well known and can be worked around. With the increased interest in JavaScript, there are plenty of libraries and frameworks that can accommodate the differences. For the most part, the differences these days tend to be in vendor-specific extensions, rather than incompatibilities in core features.

JavaScript Engines

The major browser vendors have all developed their own engines for interpreting and executing JavaScript, and this is where most of the exciting development is happening these days. With the increase in the use of JavaScript at the professional level (as already noted, in the late 1990s, it was often viewed as a toy for amateur web developers), performance has become an important factor, and vendors are currently falling over themselves to offer the best speeds.

Firefox

Versions of Firefox prior to 3.5 used the SpiderMonkey interpreter, which had been in use since the early Netscape Navigator days. Recent versions of Firefox have benefited from the addition of several JIT compilers running alongside SpiderMonkey, which itself has seen numerous enhancements.

TraceMonkey

The first of these JIT compilers was TraceMonkey, which debuted in Firefox 3.5 in 2009, and used the innovative technique of tracing to produce the majority of the performance gains. One of the reasons that executing JavaScript is slow is that the language is weakly typed — a variable could happily contain a string, integer, or floating-point number, and it's difficult to predict in advance which will be used. As a result, compiled code must handle them in a generic way. Contrast this with C, where variable types are declared in advance, and the compiler can optimize accordingly.

> **NOTE** Tracing *is a relatively new method for improving the performance of JIT compilers. It works by observing the code as it executes, and from this, it determines variable types, allowing further optimizations to take place.*

In TraceMonkey, the first time the script runs, it does so through the relatively slow SpiderMonkey interpreter. TraceMonkey watches, determines the variable types, and compiles type-specific code. Execution then switches to this compiled version.

Of course, just because a variable contained an integer value on the first run, it doesn't mean that this will always be the case. So, TraceMonkey also inserts type checks into the code. If any of these fail, execution switches back to the interpreter, and another branch of the code is compiled using the new variable type.

TraceMonkey has a few shortcomings:

➤ Only loops are traced. They have the biggest potential for gain, and compiling and running code that executes only once is often slower than simply interpreting it.

➤ Code with lots of branches or type changes tends to run more slowly in TraceMonkey because of the extra time needed to compile these different branches.

➤ Because tracing is primarily used to distinguish between strings, floats, and integers, TraceMonkey doesn't offer a significant performance increase for objects.

JägerMonkey

It wasn't long before Mozilla began refining TraceMonkey in an attempt to reduce some of its shortcomings, and the result was JägerMonkey, released in Firefox 4.

As you have just seen, in many cases with TraceMonkey, control must switch back from execution of native code to the interpreter because of changing variable types. In practice, this happened a lot more than had been expected. Therefore, JägerMonkey adopts the more traditional "method JIT compilation" approach used by most other JavaScript engines. Onto this, it then adds tracing to further optimize loops.

IonMonkey

Looking toward the future, Mozilla is already working on a new JavaScript engine named IonMonkey. It will essentially be a refined and updated version of JägerMonkey, with an emphasis on adding additional optimization techniques. Initially, IonMonkey was planned for release toward the end of 2011. This proved to be rather optimistic, but a release should not be far away.

Google Chrome

The impetus for change in Firefox and IE was in part because of the arrival of Google Chrome, which boasted particularly fast JavaScript execution in the form of the V8 engine. V8 uses a JIT compiler and compiles directly into native code (rather than a bytecode intermediate, as was the common strategy in other browsers at the time).

CrankShaft is the name for V8's current compilation infrastructure, and consists of two distinct compilers. The first is a quick-and-dirty compiler that does very little in the way of optimization, but compiles very quickly in order to reduce start-up latency. When a page is first loaded, this base compiler is used to enable the JavaScript to start executing quickly.

While code from the first compiler is being executed, the second compiler kicks into action. This compiler is slower, but produces faster code, thanks to numerous optimization techniques. By watching execution of the code generated by the first compiler, it is also able to determine variable types, and makes use of this knowledge when compiling.

Internet Explorer

As with Opera, Internet Explorer (IE) has seen a move away from the traditional runtime interpreter introduced in IE 3, to a just in time (JIT) compiler for performance reasons. The new engine, Chakra, was introduced in IE 9, and has done a lot to improve the image of IE. (At the time, IE 8's JavaScript performance was particularly poor in comparison to that of other browsers.)

Chakra introduces a number of innovative features and is particularly suited for today's multicore processors. The most significant change is the introduction of a JIT compiler, but because this can be slow to start up (although the code produced runs faster), IE 9 continues to use an interpreter for the first run of the script. At the same time, the JIT compiler is started up in the background in another thread to compile the script. This compiled version is then used for subsequent runs of the script.

This approach makes better utilization of multicore processors (the JIT compiler can run on a different core) and gets around the dilemma over whether JIT is a better solution than interpreting.

Opera

Until 2009, Opera used an engine named Futhark for JavaScript execution. At the time of its introduction (1996), it was the fastest engine available, which was built with the intention of being small and having a low-memory footprint.

In Opera 10.5, a new engine, Carakan, was unveiled. The new engine reflects the way in which JavaScript usage has grown, and this time the primary focus is on speed. For example, whereas Futhark first compiled scripts into platform-neutral bytecode, Carakan compiles some or all the script directly into native machine code. This enables it to avoid operations such as loops that are costly in bytecode. In addition, caching of compiled code is performed, further increasing performance.

The second significant change in Carakan is a move away from the stack-based model of Futhark (in which instructions are pushed and popped from the stack) to a register-based approach. Instead of a dynamically sized stack, fixed-size registers are used, and these can be accessed directly without the need to move data back and forth from the stack. Tests (by Opera) show Carakan to be about twice as fast as Futhark.

Safari

As with the other main browsers, Safari has seen a shift away from a relatively slow JavaScript interpreter to a bytecode interpreter and compiler.

Prior to 2008, the interpreter used was named JavaScriptCore (part of WebKit, on which Safari is built). The new SquirrelFish (also called Nitro and SF) engine was introduced with Safari 4. As with other engines of this period, SquirrelFish generates intermediate bytecode and performs most of its optimizations at this level. It uses registers rather than stacks and supports some degree of type inference.

Within a few months, there was already talk of an improved version of SquirrelFish, and SquirrelFish Extreme (also known as SFX or Nitro Extreme) was released the following year in beta versions of Safari 4. SFX expands on the new approach introduced in SquirrelFish and uses a JIT compiler to generate native code for faster execution. Other changes include a significantly faster regular expression (regex) engine (WebKit claims a five-fold speed increase), inline caching, and better type prediction.

> **NOTE** *You'll learn more about regexes in the section, "Regular Expressions," later in this chapter.*

In the last five years, the major browser vendors have invested a great deal of effort into improving their JavaScript engines. Partly as a result of this, the major bottleneck nowadays in JavaScript-heavy sites tends not to be in the compilation and execution of the language, but rather in the way that JavaScript interacts with the browser's Document Object Model.

THE DOCUMENT OBJECT MODEL

The Document Object Model (DOM) is a tree-like structure that describes the relationship between every element in the HTML document. When a web browser has finished retrieving a document, the HTML is parsed and the DOM constructed, and from this the page is rendered.

After the DOM has been constructed, it is accessible through JavaScript. You can traverse the tree, enumerate an element's parent or children, get and set an element's properties, and even add and remove sections of the tree. DOM manipulation is at the core of most JavaScript.

A large DOM affects performance in a number of ways. It generally means a large HTML document, which takes longer to download, parse, and render by the browser. But the biggest impact is on JavaScript. Manipulating the DOM becomes increasingly expensive, and some operations cause a reflow or repaint (more on these later), which can take longer with a heavy DOM.

So, keeping the size of the DOM down makes for an overall increase in responsiveness. But how big is too big? As ever, there's no right or wrong answer, but you can get an idea of what's acceptable by seeing how the big names compare. They've generally spent a lot of time looking into performance.

> **NOTE** *It would seem that* `sina.com.cn` *is an exception, however, because it has more than 150 KB of CSS and JavaScript embedded in the index page.*

An easy way to count the number of elements in the DOM is with JavaScript using the Firebug extension for Firefox. Simply open up the Firebug console and enter the following:

```
document.getElementsByTagName('*').length
```

Table 6-1 shows the results for the top 20 websites at the beginning of 2012.

TABLE 6-1: Number of DOM Nodes in Top 20 Websites

DOMAIN	NUMBER OF DOM NODES
Google.com	244
Facebook.com	430
Youtube.com	1,279
Yahoo.com	884
Live.com	251
Baidu.com	70
Wikipedia.org	638
Blogger.com	621
Msn.com	1,431
Twitter.com	242
qq.com	2,370
Yahoo.co.jp	860
Google.co.in	252

Taobao.com	1,404
Amazon.com	1,861
Sina.com.cn	3,710
Google.de	241
Google.com.hk	240
Wordpress.com	317
Ebay.com	1,073

There's quite a lot of variation here, but perhaps that shouldn't be surprising. The home page of Amazon.com is a lot busier than Google's, and it's inevitable that a richer page will have a larger DOM. It's well known that both Amazon.com and Google have invested a lot of resources into studying performance. Clearly, for Amazon.com, the benefits of a rich page outweigh the cost of a heavier DOM.

So, it's impossible to give guidelines on what an acceptable DOM size is. In some cases, a heavy page is justified because it contains plenty of contents to catch the user's attention, but you should be particularly cautious of heavy pages that also perform a lot of DOM manipulation in JavaScript.

No matter how big or small, it's worth reviewing your HTML and seeing if you can simplify the structure without affecting the visible layout. Although tables are often criticized for creating bloated layouts, many web developers are also guilty of excessive use of <div> elements, and use multiple levels of nested divs where one will do. Content Management Systems (CMSs) are some of the worst offenders for this.

Manipulating the DOM

In JavaScript, a common way to access the DOM is in this fashion:

```
document.getElementById('id_of_element')
```

This forces the entire DOM to be traversed until the matching element is found. So, if you intend to access the element multiple times, it makes sense to cache a reference to the element and use this:

```
var foo = document.getElementById('id_of_element');
foo.style.display = 'none';
foo.style.display = 'block';
```

Reflowing and Repainting

Earlier in this chapter, you learned that after the DOM has been constructed, the browser then renders the page. But actually there's a little more to it than that. The DOM is concerned with structure, not physical appearance, and after the DOM has been constructed, a *render tree* is then generated. The render tree is similar in structure to the DOM but contains the computed styles for each element (based on the parsed CSS). After the render tree has been constructed, the output is then drawn (painted) to the browser.

In many situations, modifying the DOM with JavaScript causes a change on the layout of the page (for example, if you resize a visible element). This triggers a *reflow* — the browser must regenerate the render tree (or at least all parts of the tree that have been affected by the change) and draw it to the screen. By contrast, a *repaint* occurs when the DOM is modified in a way that does not affect the page geometry (for example, if you change the background color of an element). This also causes the render tree to be updated and the screen repainted.

So, both reflow and repaint are expensive and take longer as the number of DOM elements in the page increases. They adversely affect the user experience and give the impression of the page being sluggish. What can you do to minimize them?

First, let's look at common actions that cause a reflow/repaint. Reading the properties of DOM elements (for example, capturing the text entered into a form field) generally aren't a problem (although see the discussion in the later section, "Browser Queueing"). It's writes that you must be wary of. Anything that changes the visible layout of the page can cause a reflow/repaint. This includes changing the *display* or *visibility* of an element, changing its position, color, and so on — basically any action that changes style properties of an element.

Some of these actions are more visually disruptive than others. Resizing an element at the top of the page causes a more noticeable effect than changing the color of some text. But all involve repainting some (or all) of the screen and recalculating the render tree. Because the browser reconstructs only parts of the render tree that have been invalidated (rather than rebuilding it from scratch), changes to nodes toward the end of the tree (or with fewer children) can help to minimize disruption.

Modifying the DOM is particularly expensive because this results in both the DOM *and* the render tree being updated. Thus, adding and removing nodes from the DOM should be avoided where possible.

It's not all doom and gloom though. In situations in which you need to perform several modifications to the same DOM element, you can reduce the number of reflow/repaints that occur. Consider the following:

```
var el = document.getElementById('mydiv');
el.style.background = '#EEE';
el.style.border = '2px';
el.style.color = 'red';
```

Normally, this would result in three reflow/repaints. You can get around this by temporarily setting the element's display property to none, making your changes, and then making the element visible again. Having two reflow/repaints instead of three is not a huge change, but is increasingly useful as the number of changes you're making increases.

Another option here is to define all these style changes in a separate CSS class, and then just change the className property of the element. This time, there would be only one reflow/repaint.

Yet another option is to use the `cssText` property to set (or get) the style declarations on an element, as shown here:

```
document.getElementById('mydiv').style.cssText =
    'background:#EEE; border-width:2px; color: red'
```

Again, this only causes one reflow/repaint, and, in some situations, is simpler than declaring a separate CSS class.

Browser Queuing

Most modern browsers are smart enough to queue changes that would cause a reflow/repaint, and execute them in a batch. In the example just presented, browsers wouldn't, in practice, execute three reflow/repaints. Instead, the operations would be queued and executed as a batch a fraction of a second later.

There is a catch, though. If you attempt to retrieve layout information about an element, this forces the browser to execute any queued actions (because it wants to be sure that it is not returning stale data), and you lose the benefit of queuing. So, setting a style property on an element that affects its layout, and then immediately retrieving layout properties of the same element, should be avoided. In fact, querying layout information on any element that may have been affected by the change will cause the queue to be flushed.

Event Delegation

Often, JavaScript interacts with the DOM through event handlers. You add, say, an `onClick` attribute to an element's HTML mark-up and execute some code when the element is clicked. These event handlers can quickly add up. Imagine if you need to add a handler to every item in a list, or every cell in a table. This increases the size of your mark-up, takes the browser longer to initialize, and consumes more memory.

The solution is *event delegation*, which makes use of the *event bubbling* feature of JavaScript. With event bubbling, when an event is triggered on an element, it bubbles up through each of the element's ancestors until it reaches a handler, or the top of the DOM. For example, here's the traditional approach:

```
<ul>
  <li id="item1" onClick="foo('item1')">Item 1</li>
  <li id="item2" onClick="foo('item2')">Item 2</li>
  . . .
</ul>
```

With event delegation, you add the handler to the `<ul>` element instead:

```
<ul onClick="foo(event)">
  <li id="item1">Item 1</li>
  <li id="item2">Item 2</li>
  . . .
</ul>
```

With no event handlers assigned to the `<li>` elements, clicking these causes the event to bubble up to the `<ul>` element, where it reaches your handler and stops. In your JavaScript, you can easily tell which `<li>` element triggered the event like so:

```
function foo(e) {
    // This is the IE way var target = e.srcElement;     // Other browsers var
        target = e.target;
    var target = e.target || e.srcElement
    if (target.nodeName.toLowerCase() === 'li') {
        alert("Click li element with ID " + target.id);
    }
    e.stopPropagation(); // stops the even from propagating further for IE9 and
onward only
}
```

IE uses a different method to access the target element than other browsers, but most JavaScript frameworks accommodate this.

Unobtrusive JavaScript

Just as you use CSS to separate style from content, you can also (to some degree) separate JavaScript from your document. This is known as *unobtrusive JavaScript*. Revisiting the event delegation example, rather than adding the event handler to the `<ul>` element in the markup, you can use `addEventListener` and an anonymous function for a more aesthetically pleasing solution:

```
<ul id='ourlist'>
  <li id="item1">Item 1</li>
  <li id="item2">Item 2</li>
  . . .
</ul>

document.getElementById('ourlist').addEventListener("click",
        function (e) {
        var target = e.srcElement; // The IE way
        var target = e.target; // Other browsers

            if (target.nodeName.toLowerCase() === 'li') {
                alert("Click li element with ID " + target.id);
            }
        , false
    );
```

Note that `addEventListener()` was only introduced in IE in version 9 (other browsers have supported it for much longer). For earlier versions of IE, `attachEvent()` is needed:

```
document.getElementById('ourlist').attachEvent("onclick",
        function (e) {
        var target = e.srcElement; // The IE way

            if (target.nodeName.toLowerCase() === 'li') {
                alert("Click li element with ID " + target.id);
            }
        }
    );
```

There's a lot to be said for this approach. It improves maintainability if you have different developers working on the markup and the JavaScript, and it shifts the weight from the HTML document into a (presumably) external resource where it has a better chance of being cached. You're much more likely to be setting far-future expiration headers on your JavaScript files than on your HTML documents.

Memory Management

In the old days, memory management wasn't a big issue for JavaScript developers. That's not to say that browsers didn't have memory leaks (and lots of them), but these were mostly problems that the vendors needed to deal with, and there was little that web developers could do. The potential certainly exists for JavaScript to be wasteful of memory, but the short lifetime of web pages tended to stop this from being a problem. As soon as the user clicked to another page, the memory was freed up again (although note that this wasn't the case with IE 6).

With the rise of JavaScript-heavy web applications, things have changed. It's quite feasible that the user may spend his or her entire session just on one page, with Ajax being used to communicate with the server. As a result, inefficient memory usage has the opportunity to mount up into something more significant.

Generally, the most common problem is circular reference — specifically, when a JavaScript reference still exists to a DOM node (either directly, or indirectly through closure) when the DOM node is removed from the DOM, preventing its memory from being reclaimed. If a DOM node is removed and there are no circular references keeping it or its descendant nodes in memory, there generally should not be an issue.

JavaScript uses the garbage collection methodology for managing memory. Memory is allocated to objects, and reclaimed by the garbage-collection process when the object is no longer being used. To determine if an object is in use, browsers keep a count of how many references there are to each object. If the number of references drops to zero, the object can be removed (and the memory reclaimed).

Circular references occur when two objects reference each other, meaning that their reference counts will never be less than 1 (hence, they are not candidates for garbage collection). Although most JavaScript implementations are intelligent enough to spot circular references between two JavaScript objects, things get tricky when the reference is between a DOM node and a JavaScript object, because both use their own separate garbage collectors.

Let's look at an example using one of the most common sources of such circular references: referencing a DOM element from inside an anonymous function attached to the element via an event handler.

```
<script>
function addHandler() {
    var mydiv = document.getElementById("myid");
    mydiv.onclick = function() {
        alert(this.innerHTML);
    }
</script>
```

```
. . .
<body onload="start()">
<div id="mydiv"></div>
. . .
```

In this example, the global variable `myobject` refers to the DOM element `mydiv`, which refers back to `myobject` (via `expandoProperty`).The result is a circular dependency between the DOM and JavaScript. The solution, of course, is to nullify `myobject` once you are finished with it.

By now, you should have a good understanding of the importance of the DOM, and how interacting with it via JavaScript can be surprisingly expensive. As noted at the beginning of this section, DOM interaction tends to be one of the main areas where performance can suffer. But as you will see in the following section, there is often plenty of scope for improving the performance of purely JavaScript code.

GETTING THE MOST FROM JAVASCRIPT

Advances in the JavaScript engines of the big browsers have gone a long way toward improving JavaScript performance. But this is not an excuse for laziness. As a JavaScript programmer, you should still strive to write optimal code for your website's visitors. In this section, you discover some of the most common causes of performance problems in the JavaScript language, along with ways to efficiently load JavaScript resources into your documents.

Language Constructs

As the previous section has hinted, it's generally DOM manipulation that is slow, rather than JavaScript itself. Nevertheless, there are situations in which JavaScript can perform poorly. Let's look at the common cases.

Loops

As with most other languages, loops are a potential source of severe performance degradation because tiny inefficiencies are magnified each time the loop runs. Consider the following example:

```
for (var x=0; x < myarray.length; x++) {
    . . .
}
```

The problem here is that the number of items in the array is calculated for each iteration of the loop, which is unnecessary. You can improve the situation dramatically by fetching the size of the array outside of the loop, as shown here:

```
var count = myarray.length;
for (var x=0; x < count; x++) {
    . . .
}
```

If you don't mind traversing the array in reverse order, you can remove an extra condition from the loop and write it as simply the following:

```
var count = myarray.length;
for (var x=count; x--;) {
    . . .
}
```

These differences are small when dealing with a modest number of iterations but can reduce time significantly for large numbers of iterations. Incidentally, if you wonder whether `for` is faster than `while` or `do`, the answer is that it doesn't actually matter.

In the previous example, it was fairly obvious that `myarray.length` would cause the length of the array to be calculated. But sometimes it's not so obvious, and, in general, you should be wary of any loop conditions — they may not behave quite as you expect.

A prime example is if you want to act on all the elements of a particular type in the document. Your loop might look something like this:

```
for (var x=0; x < document.getElementsByTagName("span").length; x++) {
. . .
}
```

This also causes the number of span elements in the document to be recalculated for each iteration. Surprisingly, the following code is also affected:

```
for (var varx=0, elements = document.getElementsByTagName("spans"); x <
    elements.length; x++) {
. . .
}
```

Again, the solution is to calculate the length outside of the loop.

A commonly used optimization technique by C/C++ compilers is function inlining, where the body of a function is inlined directly at the point where the function would have been called. Although this increases the size of the code, it also eliminates the overhead involved in calling the function (passing arguments to the function, jumping to execution of another part of the program, and so on).

Inlining is most useful for functions called inside loops, especially if the loop is iterated through many times. Knowing that calls to functions carry some overhead, you can perform inlining yourself where it is appropriate. Consider the following example, which converts between the Celsius and Fahrenheit temperature scales:

```
for (x=0; x <1000; x++) {
    var Fahrenheit = convertCF(x);
    // now do something with Fahrenheit
}
function convertCF(x) {
    return x*1.8+32;
}
```

Admittedly, this a rather trivial example, but it illustrates the logic used in many scripts. To cut the overhead of calling `convertCF`, you can rewrite the loop like so:

```
for (x=0; x <1000; x++) {
    var Fahrenheit = x*1.8+32;
    // now do something with Fahrenheit
}
```

In the real world, candidates for inlining aren't always this clear-cut. If the `convertCF` function were less trivial and were used in other places in the code, maintainability would suffer — after all, the whole point of functions is to reduce code duplication. Still, when it comes to loops, inlining can be a very attractive option.

Variable Scope

JavaScript uses the concept of local and global variables. *Local variables* exist only inside the function in which they are defined; *global variables* are accessible from anywhere. Although local variables are generally preferred because of their limited scope (which limits the chances of accidentally clobbering another variable with the same name), they need a little more thought to deploy, and many web developers lazily use global variables. Consider the following example:

```
var x = 1;
function foo() {
    var y = 2;
    alert (x); // x has global scope, so this displays "1"
    alert(y); // displays "2"
}
```

Using global variables inside functions comes at a cost, though. JavaScript uses *lexical scoping*. At the top is the global scope, and beneath that are any variables defined in top-level functions. If any of these functions contain functions of their own, then variables in these nested functions are stored in a second level of scope, and so on. Consider the following code:

```
var a = 1;
function bar() {
    var b = 2;
    function baz() {
        var c = 3;
    }
}
```

Here you have three levels of scope. What happens if, inside function baz, you decide to use the global variable a? To determine the value for a, JavaScript must climb up the chain until it finds a. So, first it checks the local scope, then it looks in its parent chain, and then finally it checks the global scope and finds a. Backtracking through the scope chain incurs a slight cost, which can be eliminated (or at least reduced) by prudent use of local variables. Aside from that, local variables are generally a cleaner way to code.

One way to get around the use of globals inside of a function is to pass the variables that you need as function parameters:

```
var x = 1;
function foo(z) {
    alert(z); // local variable, with value of 1
}
foo(x);
```

Or if you must access a global multiple times inside the function, copy it to a local variable first. The following example causes the global x to be looked up twice:

```
var x = 1;
function foo() {
    var y,z;
    y = x * 2;
    z = x * 3;
}
foo();
```

The following example results in only one global lookup of x:

```
var x = 1;
function foo() {
    var y,z;
    var tmp = x;
    y = tmp * 2;
    z = tmp * 3;
}
foo();
```

Of course, the downside here is an increase in memory usage, since the data is being stored twice: once globally, and once in the local scope. Unless the variable is very large, this is usually an acceptable trade-off.

eval()

eval() suffers from a bad reputation in JavaScript for a number of reasons. It can be slow (although this situation is changing); it can introduce security issues; and it has a tendency to be wildly misused. There are situations in which eval() is the right choice, but care must be taken, and too often there are better ways to do things. That's not to say you should never use eval(). Just think carefully beforehand.

The reason for the poor performance of eval() is that browsers typically did not cache the compiled code. So, every time the eval() was executed, the browser would be forced to recompile the code. The situation has changed in the last few years, though, and most browsers now actually do cache the code, assuming that it is static. If the contents of the eval() statement are dynamic, there is no opportunity for caching.

Regular Expressions

Regular expressions (regexes) are an important part of most high-level programming languages. JavaScript is no different, and the tips presented here are mostly equally valid for other languages, too.

> **NOTE** *Regular expressions are found in most high-level languages (Perl, Python, PHP, Ruby, and so on) and many UNIX tools (such as* grep, sed, *and* awk*). They also provide advanced pattern matching for strings. The power of regular expressions (or regexes, as they are often known) goes well beyond standard string searching, offering support for wildcards, character classes (for example, any lowercase letter), and back-tracking. For many people, regular expressions are mysterious and daunting, but it's well worth learning at least the basics — they are incredibly useful and powerful when used correctly.*

However, think before you use a regex. Is it actually needed? If you simply want to test whether one string is contained in another, or occurs at the beginning or end of the string, use one of JavaScript's string functions, which will be a lot faster.

Generally speaking, the longer the string that you match against, the more JavaScript has to do when applying the regex. So, keep the target string as short as possible (trim it first, if possible), and try to use ^ or $ to anchor the pattern being matched — that enables the regex parser to quickly eliminate many impossible matches.

Modifiers

Regex modifiers are used to alter the meaning of the pattern being matched. In JavaScript, the two most common modifiers are i (match case insensitive) and g (global, don't stop after the first match found). If you don't need these modifiers, don't use them. If you do think you need them, consider if it is possible to rewrite the regex with them, because, although they are not a serious problem, they do cause extra work for JavaScript.

Reusing Expressions

The following example shows one of the most common ways of using regexes in JavaScript:

```
for (var x = 0; x < array.length; x++) {
    var matches array[x].match(/patterntomatch/)
    if (matches.length > 0) {
        // we've got a match
    }
}
```

Here, the pattern is passed directly to the match method, which returns true if there is a match.

The problem here is that JavaScript must internally parse and compile the regex, and this happens for each iteration of the loop. In these situations, using the RegExp construct is a better option, because it allows you to build the pattern once, outside of the loop, and then reuse it.

```
var myregex = /patterntomatch/
for (var x = 0; x < array.length; x++) {
    if (myregex.test(...)(array[x]) {
        // we've got a match
    }
}
```

This time, the regex is compiled by JavaScript and stored in the `myregex` object. You can then call the `test()` method (or `exec()` if you want to return the string matched) on the object without incurring the performance hit of having to recompile the regex. This change can result in a substantial speed increase, but note that if you are not planning to reuse a regex, it's cheaper simply to pass the pattern directly, rather than creating a `RegExp` object.

Loading JavaScript

Let's return to the examination of how JavaScript interacts with the browser. During the initial page loading, browsers usually download resources in parallel. With JavaScript, the situation is a little different. If the browser encounters a link to an external JavaScript file, it begins to download it in the usual way but blocks any other downloads from starting until the JavaScript is retrieved, parsed, and executed.

An example should help to clarify this. Consider the following code:

```
<img src="paypalcards.jpg">
<script type="text/javascript" src="test.js"></script>
<img src="forum.jpg">
```

Figure 6-1 shows the waterfall view when this page loads in IE 8.

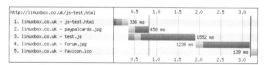

FIGURE 6-1

The browser first encounters the link to `paypalcards.jpg` and begins to retrieve this. Next comes the external JavaScript, and because you haven't reached the maximum number of parallel requests, this begins to download, too. Notice, however, that the second image does not begin to download until `test.js` has been fully retrieved.

One reason for this blocking behavior is to guard against race conditions when downloading multiple JavaScript files because you have no guarantee of the order in which they would finish downloading and be executed. A script sourced further down in the HTML document could easily be executed before an earlier script, even if there were a dependency between them. Serialization of script execution is essential for avoiding nasty surprises.

Other resources are blocking from download in parallel with scripts for similar reasons. The script may modify the DOM, which may cause unpredictable behavior if other resources have already been downloaded.

This blocking behavior is one of the reasons why it is suggested to load any scripts at the end of the page. (Another reason might be that many scripts simply don't need to be loaded until the end.) By loading visual elements first, you create a site that seems faster.

Let's rewrite the test page a little to see what happens:

```
<img src="paypalcards.jpg">
<img src="forum.jpg">
<script type="test/javascript" src="test.js"></script>
```

Figure 6-2 shows the waterfall view.

With the JavaScript pushed to the end, there's an increase in the amount of parallelization, and the overall loading time of the page is reduced.

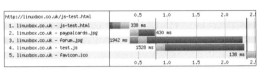

FIGURE 6-2

This works great if there is only one external script to load, and if you can happily place it at the end of the document. But what happens if you must source several external scripts? You can't execute them in parallel (for reasons already given), but there's no reason why you shouldn't *download* them in parallel.

Nonblocking of JavaScript Downloads

There are a few methods to create the nonblocking of the download of JavaScript. Let's take a closer look.

defer Attribute

The defer attribute is an IE extension that has found its way into Firefox (starting with v3.5), Safari (v5), and Google Chrome (v7). The syntax is as follows:

```
<script type="text/javascript" defer src="test.js"></script>
```

In supporting browsers, parsing this causes the script to be retrieved immediately, in a nonblocking fashion, but it will not be executed until the page has finished loading. Order is preserved, so scripts appearing earlier in the document will be executed first.

The drawback with this method is a lack of browser support. For a long time, it was an IE-only extension, and it has been only recently that other browsers have started to support it.

async

In HTML 5, you can use the async attribute to ask the browser to download the script without blocking other downloads:

```
<script type="text/javascript" async src="test.js"></script>
```

This time, the script will be executed as soon as it has downloaded. So, when multiple scripts are used on the page, the order of execution cannot be predicted.

iframes

Another method is to load the script inside an `iframe` like so:

```
<iframe src="loader.html"></iframe>
```

Here, `loader.html` is a simple HTML document containing the appropriate `<script>` tag. This method results in the script downloading and executing immediately.

There are two main reasons why this method isn't favored:

➤ `iframes` are relatively expensive to load — many times slower than other DOM elements — although for a single `iframe`, this probably isn't significant.

➤ For JavaScript loaded in an `iframe` to access the parent page DOM, changes must be made to the code.

Dynamically Writing Script Tags

Probably the most popular method to invoke the nonblocking of the download of JavaScript is to dynamically write the `script` tag with JavaScript. This method has traditionally been the best supported (although note the earlier comments about the increase in support for `defer`), and does not have the performance penalty associated with the `iframe` method.

```
var newjs = document.createElement('script');
newjs.src = 'test.js';
var head = document.getElementsByTagName('head')[0];
head.appendChild(newjs);
```

When the external script is included in this way, it is downloaded without blocking, and executes immediately after the download has finished. Despite its popularity, this method has the drawback that execution order is not guaranteed. So, again, you may end up with scripts executed in the "wrong" order.

User Feedback

When a web page is busy loading, the user typically gets some form of feedback — often an animated turning wheel near the top and information in the status bar (assuming it has not been hidden). Usability research has shown that these are important parts of the user experience. Users like to feel that a page has finished loading before they start to interact with it.

How do the nonblocking JavaScript methods affect this behavior? Not surprisingly, the answer isn't consistent from browser to browser, but, in general, all the methods cause loading feedback, with the exception of Ajax techniques. (However, this still causes feedback in Chrome and Safari.) This can be a good thing or a bad thing.

> **NOTE** *You'll learn more about Ajax techniques in the "Ajax" section later in this chapter.*

With code that forms an essential part of the page, displaying loading feedback discourages users from interacting until the code has fully loaded. On the other hand, if the code is not essential, there is no harm in the user browsing the site before it has finished loading. Showing a busy indicator simply makes the site look sluggish.

Picking the Right Method

At the moment, dynamically inserting the `script` tag into the DOM is probably the best method; although the `defer` attribute is becoming increasingly well supported and may be the way to go in the future. If you want to avoid browser feedback, use one of the Ajax methods discussed in the "Ajax" section of this chapter.

Some newer browsers do actually support nonblocking JavaScript by default, and, in the not too distance future, the techniques just described will hopefully become increasingly unnecessary. For example, IE8 onward downloads multiple scripts in parallel (and will execute them in the correct order), as does Firefox 3.5 onward. With the two market leaders having adopted this, it's likely that other vendors will eventually follow suit.

Merging, Splitting, and Inlining

Web designers are often particular about their code, and enjoy nothing more than separating different JavaScript functionality into different files. Thus, inside the <head> of a document, it's common to see half a dozen or more <script> tags loading external files, some with only a small amount of code in them.

Merging

There's no question that storing scripts separately is the best way to maintain a big project. But for a production website, it has an adverse effect on performance. For each request, there's the additional latency to send the request to the server and wait for a response. So, merging everything into one file (then minifying it, of course) is often the way forward. If necessary, you can keep the scripts separate in your source tree and write a simple shell script to "publish" them for the live site.

Figure 6-3 shows the waterfall for a page with five small scripts in the document head.

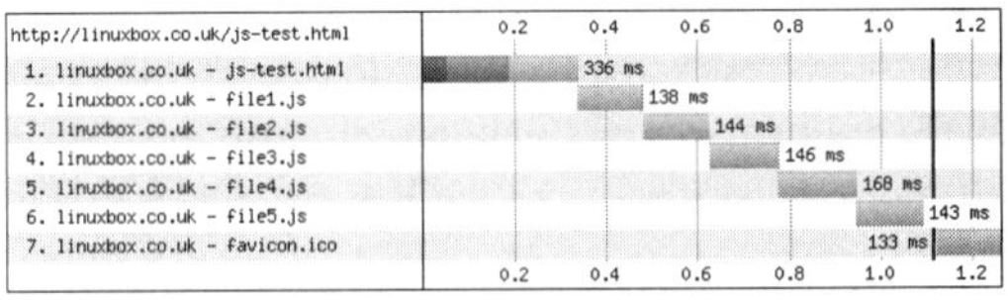

Each script is 1,447 bytes, so the time spent downloading the scripts is tiny and is not visible in this waterfall. Instead, the browser spends most of its time waiting for the web server to respond.

FIGURE 6-3

Figure 6-4 shows a waterfall after merging the five scripts into a single file (`combined.js`). As you can see, you save about 0.4 second by merging.

FIGURE 6-4

In the previous section, you learned that recent browsers now download JavaScript in parallel. The example shown in Figure 6-4 was for IE 7. Figure 6-5 shows that the results are quite different for IE 8.

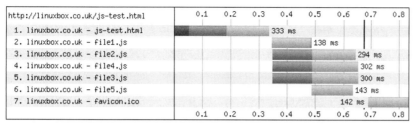

FIGURE 6-5

IE 8 can download up to four resources in parallel (including JavaScript), so, although the waterfall diagram shows a lot of time being spent creating the connection and waiting on the web server, the overall page loading time isn't dramatically different from when the five scripts were merged together. This test shows a slight improvement — although such small fluctuations should be taken with a pinch of salt when benchmarking against a live server over an unreliable medium (such as the Internet).

The relevance of this test has also suffered from short-sightedness. It fails to consider how the overall page loading time is affected. If you add four images to the page, the waterfall view (again with IE8) looks as shown in Figure 6-6.

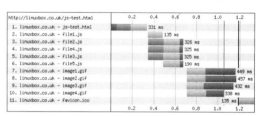

FIGURE 6-6

As before, four JavaScript resources are loaded in parallel. Once the JavaScript has been loaded and executed, the image resources are then fetched over the already-open connections.

In Figure 6-7, the combined JavaScript file is used. Resource 3 is fetched over the existing connection, but resources 4 and 5 each require a new connection to be opened.

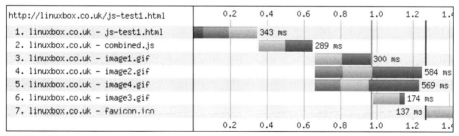

FIGURE 6-7

This time, the overall page loading time is approximately one-half a second lower, and there are a few interesting things happening here.

In both waterfalls, JavaScript finishes loading at roughly the same time. But, in Figure 6-6, the four parallel connections have already been established at this point, and the image requests do not suffer the penalty of waiting for a connection to be established. In Figure 6-7 two of the images are retrieved over new connections, increasing the request latency.

> **NOTE** *Incidentally, you may have noticed a slight gap in some of the waterfall figures, between the JavaScript download finishing and the next request starting. Figure 6-6 shows a good example of this, at approximately the 0.7 seconds mark. The reason is, after downloading the script, the browser must next execute it. It does this before it issues any more requests. Usually, the delay is minimal, but large gaps here can indicate inefficient JavaScript — or just lots of it.*

To some extent, though, this penalty is offset by better utilization of bandwidth. In the waterfall shown in Figure 6-6, there is a period (from approximately 0.7 to 0.9 seconds) when the browser is not downloading anything, but simply waiting for the web server to respond. After the four images begin to download, they do so in parallel, resulting in bandwidth being split across them. In the waterfall shown in Figure 6-7, image1.gif begins downloading first, and benefits from having the whole bandwidth (well near enough — packets are still flowing as the browser sets up the other two connections) to itself.

In browsers that support parallel downloading of JavaScript, keeping scripts separate actually improves loading times in many cases. But you must keep in mind that not all browsers do this, and the overall gain is dependent on resources in the rest of the page.

The results also depend on the degree of parallelization offered by the browser. As you've already seen, older browsers generally supported two requests in parallel, whereas newer browsers usually perform four, six, or eight. With IE 8, this value is six, so there's nothing to be gained on IE 8 from having more than six external scripts (six external scripts next to each other in the document, anyway). If the six scripts were scattered through the page, the situation would be different. So, merging your JavaScript into a maximum of two or four scripts is probably the best trade-off for performance versus cross-browser compatibility.

One thing not yet touched upon is how blocking affects all this. In the waterfall images so far, nothing else happened until the JavaScript had been downloaded. Clearly, IE 8 will download other JavaScript files in parallel, but not other resources. (This is more noticeable in the tests using the combined JavaScript file.) Let's try again in IE8 using the defer attribute.

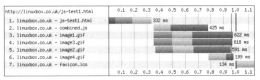

FIGURE 6-8

Figure 6-8 shows the defer attribute being used to load the combined JavaScript file. No blocking occurs, and three of the images are requested immediately.

In Figure 6-9, the defer attribute is used on each of the four JavaScript resources. This leads to an increase in the amount of parallelization, but the effect is still an increase in loading time. The combined version is approximately 1 second faster to complete.

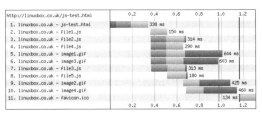

FIGURE 6-9

So, sometimes it pays to merge your JavaScript into a single file, and sometimes it doesn't. Too much depends on the nature of your code and other resources on the page. There is no hard-and-fast rule on whether to merge the JavaScript on your site, but at least you now know about the tools for you to make your own decision.

Splitting

Some websites use a set of one or more external JavaScript files that need to be loaded on every page, but for many sites, the script needed varies from page to page. For example, you might have some form-checking code that needs to be loaded only on a contact page.

If you opt to merge all the JavaScript into a single file, you have a dilemma. If you include the code that is specific to certain pages, you increase the size of your global, combined file. If you leave it out, you increase the number of resources to be downloaded. So, where do you draw the line? If one of your JavaScript libraries is used on half the pages on your site, should you merge it into the global script? What if the script is used only on a few pages, but is only a few hundred bytes?

One solution seen in many CMSs (where the JavaScript and CSS used tend to be large and can vary greatly depending on admin settings) is to pass a list of required files to a dynamic script that builds the JavaScript or CSS on-the-fly. A call to such a script might look like this:

```
<script type="text/javascript"
    src="/rollup.php?files=main.js,forms.js,ajax.js,toolbar.js"> </script>
```

The back-end PHP script fetches these four files, merges them together, and spits out the result (with an appropriate `content-type` header).

The advantage here is that you can load only the code you need for this particular page, and you have only one browser request. The downsides are that it makes caching difficult, increases latency (running some PHP code and opening multiple files is always going to be slower than serving a single static file), and puts extra work on the server, (Usually you'd want to serve static resources from something like Nginx without evoking PHP.) So, although this is sort of okay for people who don't want to get their hands dirty, for websites where performance ranks high, it's not good enough.

Although merging is often the right thing to do, generally it also makes sense to keep code separate if it is used only on a few pages (to avoid the overhead of loading where it is not needed). In some cases, that can even mean that splitting an existing script is the right thing to do.

In the case of sites with a members area, one possible way of bundling is to group your code into two files: one for logged-in users and one for guests. Typically, guests wouldn't have access to what-you-see-is-what-you-get (WYSIWYG) editors for making posts, instant messaging chat widgets, and so on. Here's a simple example of how such logic might work:

```
<script type="text/javascript" src="/resources/guest.js">
<?php
if ($_SESSION['userid'] > 0) {
    print '<script type="text/javascript" src="/resources/member.js">';
    }
</script>
```

guest.js is loaded no matter what. But if the user is logged in (in this example, the session variable userid holds a numeric ID if the user is logged in), a second resource, member.js, is also loaded.

Usually, the goal is to minimize loading times as much as possible for the first page that visitors hit. Web users can be impatient, and you don't want slow loading times to scare them away. If you have a page that receives a clear majority of incoming traffic (such as the homepage), it can make sense to keep the scripting on this to a bare minimum — don't load code used on the majority of the rest of the site because visitors may not even get that far.

Inlining

Usually, you store JavaScript in external files because it is cacheable and reduces overall page loading times; although web developers do it because it increases maintainability and ease of development. However, for small files, the cost to fetch an additional resource outweighs the decrease in the size of your HTML document. If you load other scripts, you can simply append a small script to one of these. Failing that, putting your JavaScript inline (directly inside the HTML document) can be the best option.

It's difficult to say at which exact point this becomes the more attractive option, but it's roughly at the 1 KB or 2 KB upward mark that issuing an additional request for external code becomes faster overall than inlining.

Web Workers

The last few years have seen great advances in the performance of many JavaScript engines for many browsers, but they are still held back by JavaScript's inherently single-threaded nature. In many situations, this isn't a problem. Typically, JavaScript is used to execute short blocks of code based on user interaction — for example, the user submits a form, and some field checking takes place. As such, responsiveness tends not to be too sluggish.

Things are different, though, if you must execute particularly intensive or long-running code (as has become increasingly common with today's JavaScript-rich sites, which often behave almost like desktop applications). Because there is only one thread, nothing else can execute until the long-running block of code has finished.

For example, consider a script for drawing the Mandelbrot set. After the user has clicked a button to start the script running, all other scripts on the page will be unresponsive until it has finished — that includes unrelated scripting such as form checking or JavaScript navigation menus. Of course, plotting the Mandelbrot set is something of an extreme example, but there are plenty of situations in which this single-threaded behavior causes the interface to appear slightly sluggish.

One option is to use timers (specifically, the setTimeout() function) to periodically pause execution of a long-running block of code, allowing other code to be handled. This gives the impression of multi-tasking, but is rather hacky, and still not as smooth as you would wish.

The solution comes in the form of *web workers* — background threads running separate scripts, and communicating with the parent thread via messages. All the major browsers now support web workers, and Table 6-2 shows when support was introduced.

TABLE 6-2: Introduction of Web Workers

BROWSER	WEB WORKERS INTRODUCED
Firefox	Version 3.5
IE	Version 10.0
Opera	Version 10.6
Chrome	Version 4.0
Safari	Version 4.0

Because web workers run in their own thread, there is some work to do in initializing the thread and communicating with the parent. Web workers are only intended for heavy, long-running scripts (such as the Mandelbrot example). For anything smaller, the overhead of initializing the worker thread cancels out any performance gains.

The first step is to create a new worker thread, passing it the name of the script to load:

```
var worker = new Worker('code.js');
```

A new worker thread is created, and the code is downloaded in this thread. But execution does not start until specifically instructed, as shown here:

```
worker.postMessage();
```

As well as starting the worker code running, `postMessage` is also used for communicating with the worker:

```
worker.postMessage("hello");
```

The worker can capture these messages by setting up an event listener:

```
self.addEventListener('message',
    function(e) {
        // e.data contains the string "hello"
    }
, false);
```

Data can also be passed as JavaScript Object Notation (JSON) and is automatically parsed by the receiver. In the following example, the message object is automatically serialized to JSON by the `postMessage` method:

```
// in main script
worker.postMessage({'action': 'execute', 'order': '66'});

// in worker script
self.addEventListener('message',
```

```
        function(e) {
            if (e.data.order == 66) {
                ...
            }
        }
    , false);
```

Usually, you want to communicate both ways, and catching messages sent from the worker to the parent works in a similar fashion via an event handler — this time, a property of the worker object, as shown here:

```
worker. addEventListener('message',
    function(e) {
        // again, e.data holds the received message
    }
    , false);
```

If you've written threaded applications before, you'll be aware of how messy things can get. For this reason, web worker threads have limited access to the DOM (because they could potentially write to the DOM at the same time as other threads are reading or writing). This is the main reason why an elaborate messaging system is used between threads and parents.

In addition to restrictions on accessing the DOM, web workers have no access to the window, parent, or document objects. They can, however, use XMLHttpRequest, access the navigator and location objects, and load external JavaScript files. Worker threads also have the capability to spawn subworkers, but situations in which these are needed are rare. Remember that there is an overhead associated with spawning a new worker.

AJAX

In recent years, Ajax has become a buzzword and is one of the driving forces behind the annoyingly titled Web 2.0. Yet, Ajax is quite a loose term and refers to technologies that have been around for some time — JavaScript, DOM manipulation, and XML/JSON.

It's misleading to think of Ajax performance as a separate concern because it is just a question of performance in these areas. There are no magic tricks specifically for Ajax. Rather, benefits come from optimized JavaScript, careful use of the DOM, and a responsive back-end web server.

XMLHttpRequest

At the heart of Ajax is the XMLHttpRequest (XHR) function used in JavaScript to load a resource in the background. This function allows for both synchronous and asynchronous calls. The latter (asynchronous calls) are preferable because they do not cause the calling script to block. Instead, you write an event listener to trigger when the request has completed.

XHR also offers the choice of GET or POST requests. Surprisingly, it turns out that, even when POSTing tiny amounts of data, the request is split into two packets — the first containing the HTTP header and the second containing the POST data. All the major browsers (with the exception of Firefox) behave like this. With GET, the data is contained in a single packet. So, if all other things are equal, GET is the preferred method.

All other things aren't always equal, though. Caching and privacy are the other major factors, and there are sometimes cases where POST is preferred because the response will not be cached.

Using Ajax for Nonblocking of JavaScript

You can also use Ajax as a means to invoke the nonblocking of the download of JavaScript. You can fetch the script via XHR and then execute it by passing the response through eval(). Some libraries such as Prototype even have an option to automatically use eval() on the response.

Alternatively, you could use XHR to fetch the script, and then insert it into the DOM inside a <script> tag.

These methods don't offer any advantages over the other techniques examined earlier in this chapter. They cause the script to be downloaded without blocking; it executes immediately, and there is no guarantee of the order of execution. In addition, with this being Ajax, you can fetch scripts hosted only on the same domain name. These methods also mean loading an Ajax library; although you can write a simple cross-browser XHR library in 20 or 30 lines of code.

Server Responsiveness

The responsiveness of the web server is crucial to create an Ajax application that does not feel sluggish — even more so than with standard HTTP requests — and you want to minimize latency as much as possible. Using a lightweight server such as Nginx usually helps, and you should keep the use of back-end scripting and database lookups to a minimum. Serving cached contents where possible is an even better idea.

If you do use preforked Apache, keeping a high number of idle servers free cuts out the possible overhead of spawning a new child process to handle incoming XHR requests. Unfortunately, there may also be situations in which Apache is up to its MaxClients limit and is queuing requests. Although this may add "only" a second or two to the response time, this can be noticeable on Ajax-driven sites.

> **NOTE** *The Apache web server (which you will learn about in much more detail in Chapter 7, "Working with Web Servers") supports several modes of process management, of which* prefork *is the most common. In this mode, each request is handled by a separate child process. This contrasts with the* worker *module, which is built around threading. To avoid overloading the server, Apache is configured to handle a maximum number of requests simultaneously (*MaxClients*). If this limit is reached, requests are queued up, leading to a delay in the request being served.*

Apache's mod_qos can be used to shape traffic, giving priority to requests on a particular directory. In this way, you could ensure that all requests for Ajax scripts go to the top of the queue, should there be a backlog. In practice though, connection queuing indicates a server straining to cope, and you should be looking at scaling up or out, rather than taping up the cracks.

Using Preemptive Loading

Ajax can take advantage of *preemptive loading*. With Ajax, you have the capability to load scripts in a manner that (with the exception of Safari and Chrome) will not generate any loading feedback in the browser. Thus, one option is to load what you need for the landing page, wait until the page has rendered, and send an Ajax request for the remaining JavaScript. Although you don't need it yet, it will be cached in the browser in anticipation.

Ajax Frameworks

Many developers use a framework such as Prototype or JQuery to develop Ajax websites. These libraries have a lot of features that can make Ajax a breeze, but they can also be rather heavy. If all you need is XHR, a full-blown framework isn't necessary. Instead, a lightweight solution is microajax (`http://code.google.com/p/microajax/`), which provides a cross-browser XHR wrapper in 841 bytes.

SUMMARY

Developers of the major browsers have made significant improvements to their JavaScript engines, and manipulation of the DOM tends to be the most expensive part of JavaScript-rich sites. Knowing this, you can minimize your use of the DOM and employ tricks such as storing references in variables to lessen this.

Browsers have historically loaded JavaScript in a blocking manner, which can make pages appear slow to load. This is gradually changing, but there are also a number of tricks to get around this. You must also think carefully about how JavaScript is arranged. Should it be inline, external, or a combination of the two? A lot depends on what it is used for, and how users access the site.

Ajax is popular, and although most of this chapter's discussion on JavaScript and the DOM applies here, there are a number of small tips specifically for Ajax development.

So far, you have learned about a variety of front-end aspects of website performance — from JavaScript and CSS to minification and compression. The second part of this book is devoted to the back end — the applications and code that run behind the scenes to make the web work. You'll be learning how to tune the most commonly used tools (PHP, MySQL, Apache, and Nginx) for optimal performance, discovering what all the hype over NoSQL is about, and seeing how load balancing and other multi-server setups work. Chapter 7 begins with a review of web servers.

PART II
Back End

▶ **CHAPTER 7:** Working with Web Servers

▶ **CHAPTER 8:** Tuning MySQL

▶ **CHAPTER 9:** MySQL in the Network

▶ **CHAPTER 10:** Utilizing NoSQL Solutions

▶ **CHAPTER 11:** Working with Secure Sockets Layer (SSL)

▶ **CHAPTER 12:** Optimizing PHP

7

Working with Web Servers

WHAT'S IN THIS CHAPTER?

➤ Tuning Apache for optimal performance

➤ Using Nginx for both static and dynamic content

➤ Setting up load balancing across multiple servers using Nginx and HAProxy

For the majority of system administrators and web developers, Apache is the automatic choice for a web server. It's (fairly) fast, powerful, widely used, and available precompiled for most operating systems. Apache is so popular in the Linux world that it's easy to forget that alternatives exist. Yet, Apache is not perfect, and as web growth has accelerated (and as Ajax has changed the nature of some of this traffic), the need to serve huge numbers of requests has given birth to several lightweight web servers specifically designed with performance in mind.

This chapter examines performance considerations for Apache, before taking a look at the most prominent of the competitors that have emerged in the last decade. This chapter also discusses the challenges that can arise when moving away from Apache, and takes a brief look at caching, front-end proxies, and load-balanced server pools.

APACHE

The Apache HTTP Server is such an important part of the Internet's history (and the history of Linux, for that matter, too, since Apache + Linux + x86 quickly became a viable alternative to commercial web servers running on UNIX mainframes in the 1990s). Because of that, this discussion assumes that you have at least a basic knowledge of Apache management and configuration, even if you have never compiled it from source (because so many operating systems offer precompiled Apache binaries in their package systems).

Numerous aspects of Apache have the potential to affect performance, and, in this section, you'll learn how modules impact memory usage, the differences between the various Multi-Process Models (MPMs), how to choose an optimal level of concurrency, the various caching modules available, and much more.

Working with Modules

Part of the reason for Apache's popularity is its modular system, enabling third-party developers to extend the core functionality. The number and variety of modules are a testament to Apache's success. There are modules that provide both forward and reverse proxying, enhanced security, all manners of alternative authentication systems, and even passive operating system fingerprinting.

But these modules come at a price. Each additional module loaded increases the memory footprint of Apache, and sometimes increases the CPU overhead when handling a request. Thus, one of the first steps in tuning Apache should be to remove any unnecessary modules from the configuration files.

This isn't quite as easy a task as it might seem. A typical default Apache installation can have dozens of modules enabled, and some are useful enough to be considered almost essential (for example, the handling of MIME types with `mod_mime`). Before blindly removing modules, it's worth checking precisely what they do.

You can find a good overview in the Apache 2.2 docs at `http://httpd.apache.org/docs/2.2/mod/`. In addition, Linux distribution vendors configure their Apache packages in slightly different ways. On Red Hat-derived distributions (such as CentOS or Fedora), `LoadModule` statements are typically contained in the main `httpd.conf` file (under `/etc/httpd/conf/`), whereas Debian-derived systems use a separate file for each module, contained under `/etc/apache2/mods-available`. In most situations, it's enough to comment out the `LoadModule` directive. Any directives specific to the module are typically wrapped in `<IfModule>` blocks to prevent them from being executed if the module has not been loaded.

Of course, this assumes that Apache has been compiled with support for dynamically loadable modules. Most distribution vendors do this, but if you compile Apache from a source, you have the choice.

The alternative is to compile the modules that you need directly into Apache and disable dynamic shared object (DSO) support. Removing DSO support lowers Apache's footprint a little (and can be useful for security, too, because it prevents an attacker inserting malicious modules). But it can also be greatly inconvenient — if you ever want to add or remove a module, you need to recompile Apache. For this reason, removing DSO support should be left until the list of modules that are required has been decided and tested.

Multi-Process Modules (MPMs)

Apache 2 introduced the concept of *Multi-Process Modules* (MPMs), which control how Apache handles concurrent requests. Only one MPM can be loaded at a time. (A recompile is required to change MPMs.) For Linux, there are two MPMs to choose from (special MPMs that are specific to the operating system exist for OS2, Netware, and Windows): prefork and worker. *Prefork* is generally the default and is the most stable, whereas *worker* is more experimental but promises better performance.

Prefork MPM

The *prefork MPM* is a nonthreaded model in which multiple child processes each run as a single thread, and each child handles a single connection at a time. The following configuration snippet shows the available prefork options:

```
StartServers           10
MinSpareServers        5
MaxSpareServers        10
ServerLimit            100
MaxClients             100
MaxRequestsPerChild    1000
```

StartServers is the initial number of child processes to start, whereas MinSpareServers and MaxSpareServers control the minimum and maximum number of spare processes to keep in the pool. MaxClients controls the maximum number of child processes that may run at any one time — and, therefore, the maximum number of clients that Apache can serve concurrently — but this is also governed by ServerLimit.

Why have two directives that appear to do the same thing? Changes to the value for MaxClients can be affected by sending Apache a SIGHUP (that is, a reload), whereas any change to ServerLimit requires a full stop/start of Apache. This is because ServerLimit also helps Apache to judge the amount of shared memory to allocate when starting up. Therefore, ServerLimit should always be equal to (or higher than) MaxClients. In practice, it's useful to keep it slightly higher, allowing MaxClients to be raised slightly without a full restart.

Finally, MaxRequestsPerChild governs how many requests a single child process can handle in its lifetime. The reason this is not unlimited (although you can set this value to zero for unlimited if you want) is that memory leaks can (and do) occur. By setting a reasonably high value, you prevent memory leaks from accumulating too much while lessening the overhead involved in spawning new children too often.

This, then, is what happens when a preforking Apache server receives a request. The parent process receives the request and attempts to assign it to a child. Parent and child communicate with each other through a scoreboard, which is implemented in shared memory. (This is the default under Linux, anyway.) If a spare child exists in the pool, it handles the request. If no spare child processes exist (and MaxClients has not been reached), a new child is spawned to handle the process. If the maximum number of child processes is already running, the request is queued until a child becomes available.

After the request has been served, a number of things may happen. If MaxRequestsPerChild has been reached, or there are already MaxSpareServers in the pool, the child is destroyed. Otherwise, the child is kept alive so that it may serve future requests.

The reason to maintain a pool of spare servers is that the act to spawn a new child is somewhat CPU-intensive and adds to the latency of responses. By keeping a handful of children spare, you reduce the likelihood that a new process needs to be spawned — unless, of course, a sudden flood of requests requires more than MaxSpareServers number of processes.

The downside to having a large number of spare children in the pool is that they all add to memory usage — and memory is a precious resource. The overhead from spawning a new child is not so great that it should be avoided at all costs, and it is generally not worth setting the maximum and minimum number of servers high in the hope that Apache will rarely need to spawn extra children. The memory could be put to better use.

Still, if the machine runs as a dedicated web server, or request latency is of high importance (such as in an AJAX application), it's generally a good idea to raise these two values significantly. Remember, too, that with modern web browsers requesting up to eight resources in parallel from the same host, a single client could take up to eight child processes.

Worker MPM

The *worker MPM* uses a multithreaded model in which each child process runs many threads, with each thread handling a single request. This makes the worker MPM ideally suited for multiprocessor machines, and it offers the promise of being faster, having a lower memory footprint, and scaling better than the prefork MPM.

The configuration options for a worker MPM are similar to those for prefork:

```
StartServers           2
MaxClients             150
MinSpareThreads        25
MaxSpareThreads        75
ThreadsPerChild        25
MaxRequestsPerChild    1000
```

Again, StartServers specifies how many child processes to start when Apache is launched. MaxClients controls the maximum number of concurrent requests, and MaxRequestsPerChild governs how many requests a single child processes before terminating.

The worker MPM has three different settings, however. ThreadsPerChild sets the number of threads that each child process will run, whereas MinSpareThreads and MaxSpareThreads control the number of threads that are kept spare. These are analogous to the maximum and minimum spare servers in the prefork MPM, only this time, these options deal with threads, not child processes.

This promise of a slimmer, more efficient model may sound too good to be true. There is a significant downside to the worker MPM. All Apache modules must be thread-safe. For trivial modules, this usually isn't a problem. But for the likes of mod_php, this is a big problem. Not only must the programming language (covered in more detail in Chapter 12, Optimizing PHP) be thread-safe, but any libraries that it depends on must also be. In practice, this makes it extremely difficult to ensure that PHP is thread-safe. Unless you are brave, PHP combined with a worker MPM is simply not a viable option at the moment.

There's also the question of just how efficient the worker MPM is. Although benchmarking figures are sometimes unreliable, they do tend to vary a lot for the worker MPM. Some users report a performance increase of a few hundred percent, others see little difference, whereas still some actually see a drop in performance. This suggests that it is far from being a magic bullet, but it is suited to particular workloads.

If thread safety is not a problem, you should try the worker MPM. Most likely, it can improve performance. But be aware that, in some situations, it might make things worse. For the remainder of this chapter, let's assume that the prefork MPM is used.

Deciding on Concurrency

No matter which MPM you choose to use, you must decide on the maximum number of concurrent clients that Apache should handle. If you decide to use too few, the hardware will be under-utilized. If you decide to use too many, you risk sending the server into a downward spiral of swapping.

Setting MaxClients

It's best to start with a conservative figure and gradually raise MaxClients after you are sure that the system can handle it. Although there's the temptation to set MaxClients as high as the server can tolerate, this doesn't usually lead to the best overall throughput. At this level of concurrency, each request will doubtlessly take longer for Apache to process, so the overall throughput may well remain the same (or lessen, because of increased context switching). Rather than aiming for the highest possible concurrency, aim for the fastest overall handling of a client's request.

You can attempt to calculate an approximate limit for MaxClients based on the memory usage of a single child. This relies on the principle that MaxClients times memory per child should never exceed the amount of RAM you have set aside for Apache. On a dedicated web server, this would be a little less than the overall installed memory because some would be needed for the rest of the operating system. On a dual-purpose Apache/MySQL box, this might be approximately one-half the available RAM.

When looking at the memory usage of multiple instances of the same application, the resident set size (RSS) usage is the most appropriate because it excludes the footprint of shared libraries. Under Linux and other flavors of UNIX, you can see the RSS in the output of ps:

```
# ps -ylC apache2 --sort:rss
S   UID   PID  PPID  C PRI  NI   RSS     SZ WCHAN   TTY          TIME CMD
S    33  1955   585  0  80   0  9048  18462 -       ?        00:00:00 apache2
S     0   585     1  0  80   0 16604  18347 -       ?        00:00:06 apache2
S    33  1863   585  1  80   0 24216  20075 -       ?        00:00:01 apache2
 . . .
S    33 32077   585  1  80   0 36356  21004 -       ?        00:00:08 apache2
S    33 26948   585  1  80   0 36504  21131 -       ?        00:00:37 apache2
R    33  1166   585  1  80   0 38832  23345 -       ?        00:00:02 apache2
```

So, the hungriest Apache process currently running uses approximately 38 MB. On a dedicated web server with 6 GB of RAM, you could run approximately 150 of these processes, still leaving a few hundred megabytes free for the rest of the operating system.

There are so many assumptions and over-simplifications here, however, that this figure must be treated with a pinch of salt, and only used as a rough ballpark figure. For starters, not every child will use 38 MB of memory — as the ps output showed (or would have shown had it not been truncated), most were using less. Conversely, because these figures show only a single point in time, it might be that Apache children are regularly using more than 38 MB.

Secondly, it has been assumed that RAM is only bottleneck. It may well be that your server hits CPU and I/O bottlenecks before the 150-client limit is reached.

Finally, memory usage in many operating systems can be rather complicated, and asking how much memory an individual process "uses" is ambiguous. Still, it provides a rough figure from which to start and helps to illustrate the importance of removing unneeded modules. A small change in the memory footprint of a single child can become significant when multiplied by a few hundred children.

ListenBacklog

One thing not yet mentioned is what happens when `MaxClients` is reached. The answer is that Apache queues requests up to a maximum defined by the `ListenBacklog` directive. (The default for this option is 511; although it depends on the operating system.)

In most web browsers, this results in a blank, white page with the progress bar stalled at zero, with only the browser's animated loading icon showing that something is still happening. When the request reaches the front of the queue, it is passed to a child process and is handled as usual. If the backlog queue becomes full, Apache returns a `503` status code, and the browser displays a message along the lines of The Server Is Too Busy. It's almost always fine to leave `ListenBacklog` at its default value.

Improving Logging

A busy web server can generate a significant number of log entries. Naturally, Linux buffers these writes, but with disk I/O being one of the most common bottlenecks, it makes sense to look closely at logging. In addition, because it is common to use separate log files for each virtual host, Linux may regularly seek not just one, but dozens of different files.

Apache offers two types of log files: access logs and error logs.

An *error log* contains error messages and has an associated logging level — one of the standard eight logging levels used by `syslog` and others, including `debug`, `info`, `notice`, `warn`, `error`, `crit`, `alert`, and `emerg`. Thus, a log level of `warn` would log error messages of a *warning* level or higher (`error`, `crit`, `alert`, and `emerg`).

Some modules (in particular PHP) can be rather verbose in their error logging, and it pays to set the log level to a reasonably high value — certainly debugging events are unlikely to be of any interest on a production server. The default level is `warn`, but `error` is generally a better value for use on production servers:

```
ErrorLog logs/error_log
LogLevel error
```

An *access log* is a log of all requests sent to the server, and access logs pose more of a challenge. To start with, they tend to be much bigger, and turning off logging is not an option for most sites. They rely on statistics generated from the access logs to monitor access patterns, incoming links, search engine search terms, and so on.

Log Formatting

The good news is that Apache is extremely flexible when it comes to logging. Not only can you control what is logged, but also where it is logged to, as shown here:

```
LogFormat "%h %l %u %t \"%r\" %>s %b \"%{Referer}i\" \"%{User-Agent}i\""
    mylogformat
CustomLog logs/access_log mylogformat
```

In this example, you create your own log format named `mylogformat` and write it to `logs/access_log`. A complete list of available format strings is available at `http://httpd.apache.org/docs/current/mod/mod_log_config.html#formats`. This example produces log entries like so:

```
1.2.3.4 - - [22/Nov/2012:11:49:01 +0000] "GET /favicon.ico HTTP/1.1" 200 3638
    "-" "Mozilla/5.0 (Windows NT 6.1; WOW64) AppleWebKit/535.2 (KHTML,
    like Gecko) Chrome/15.0.874.121 Safari/535.2"
```

One approach to keeping the size of the logs down is to be more selective about which fields you log. For example, if you decide you can live without the browser's user agent, you halve the size of each log entry. The result should be more log entries that are buffered in memory before Linux needs to write them out to disk. Similarly, you might decide you can live without the HTTP status returned (`%s`) and the number of bytes transferred (`%b`). The savings here are rather modest, though, and if this data has any use for monitoring or statistics, just leave it in.

Conditional Logging

Another option is to attempt to reduce the number of log entries that each visitor generates. When a user visits your website (especially if it's with an empty cache), there will typically be a flood of requests — for example, images, external CSS and JavaScript, favorite icon, and so on — with a log entry for each request. In practice, though, you probably want to know the name of only the page that the user requested.

You can filter out the noise using conditional logging and environmental variables (so ensure that the `SetEnvIf` module is loaded), as shown here:

```
SetEnvIf Request_URI "\.(PNG|png|gif|GIF|jpg|JPG|css|CSS|js|JS|ico|ICO)$""
    ignorethese
LogFormat "%h %l %u %t \"%r\" %>s %b \"%{Referer}i\" \"%{User-Agent}i\"" mylogformat
CustomLog logs/access_log mylogformat env=!ignorethese
```

This example sets an `env` variable, `ignorethese`, if the request URI is for any of the file extensions listed. If the `env` variable has been set, `CustomLog ignores` does not log the entry.

This should have a dramatic effect on the size of your log files. But remember that sometimes this extra information does have its uses. For example, you can get an idea of how effective your caching strategies are by looking at the number of clients who request a page, but not the associated media.

Similarly, you can restrict logging based on a handful of other conditions — for example, ignore requests from `localhost`, or on a resource in a particular directory.

Piping Logs

As well as writing logs to a file, Apache also supports the piping of log events to an external application. This can be an incredibly useful feature, which opens up several new possibilities.

For example, you could feed your logs directly to a stats-generation application, which, in turn, would need to only write a summary of events to disk. Or you could send the events to a logging daemon on a remote host, removing the need to write anything to the local disk. Of these two ideas, the latter is the most practical because any local log parser application inevitably takes away resources from Apache.

Rather than reinventing the wheel, it makes sense to use `syslog`/`syslog-ng` for this because it already supports remote logging over the network. For the `ErrorLog` directive, you can simply specify `syslog` as the destination, optionally including the `syslog` facility, as shown here:

```
ErrorLog syslog:remoteapache
```

For the access log, you must pipe to the `logger` binary, which can be used for sending log events to `syslog`:

```
CustomLog "|/usr/bin/logger -t 'apache 192.168.0.1'" -p remoteapache combined
```

Both of these examples assume that the `remoteapache` log facility has been appropriately defined in `syslog.conf`.

Miscellaneous Performance Considerations

Let's take a look at a somewhat random collection of performance tips for Apache, which don't fit cleanly into any of the previous sections, and which don't warrant detailed discussion.

Reducing DNS Lookups

Hostnames are generally easier to work with than IP addresses, and many administrators would prefer that Apache's access logs use hostnames rather than IP addresses. This option is controlled by the `HostnameLookups` directive, but unless you have a compelling reason to enable this, it is best left turned off (the default). Not only does it increase network traffic (because Apache queries the nameserver), it also increases request latency.

If you need to resolve IP addresses to hostnames in the Apache logs, there are a couple of options. You can run a caching, resolving `nameserver` on the local web server, eliminating network latency. Or you can simply perform the lookups at a later time — for example, as part of the log rotation script. Apache includes a tool, `logresolve`, specifically designed for this.

Even with `HostnameLookups` turned off, there are still some situations in which Apache performs DNS lookups. For example, if you use hostnames in access clauses such as `Allow From` and `Deny From`, a two-way lookup will be performed on the client — first to resolve the IP address to a hostname, and then to resolve the hostname back to an IP address (to ensure you get back to the same IP). Generally, such access rules are used only on restricted areas, though, so the impact on (nonmischievous) users should be minimal. However, if you're in the habit of blocking sitewide access based on hostname (for example, blocking a whole ISP or country), you should be aware of this performance hit. Again, using a local caching, resolving nameserver can help.

Disabling .htaccess Files

When Apache receives a request, it must backtrack up the directory tree checking for the existence of any .htaccess files. For example, if a request is made for http://www.example.com/news/2012/July/stories.html, it would check for the existence of /var/www/example.com/news/2012/July/.htaccess, /var/www/example.com/news/2012/.htaccess, /var/www/example.com/news/.htaccess, and /var/www/example.com/.htaccess (assuming the document root is /var/www/example.com, of course).

Although this isn't a huge performance issue, you can eliminate it nevertheless by setting AllowOverride None (disabling .htaccess files) and putting your .htaccess rules directly in the Apache configuration files. This makes it a little inconvenient to edit your rules because you must restart Apache after making any changes. But on a production server, such changes should be rare anyway.

Dealing with symlinks

For the sake of security, Apache can be configured not to follow symlinks, or to follow them only if they have the correct ownerships. As with .htaccess files, this involves backtracking up the directory tree and checking if any component of the path is a symlink. If you're willing to forgo these security checks, you can improve performance a little by telling Apache not to care about symlinks like so:

```
Options +FollowSymLinks -SymLinksIfOwnerMatch
```

DirectoryIndex Wildcards

It's standard to specify a list of directory index files, in order of preference:

```
DirectoryIndex index.php index.html index.htm index.pl
```

But there is a lazier option, as shown here:

```
DirectoryIndex index
```

This causes any filename beginning with the string index to match. Needless to say, this method doesn't result in great performance, and the former way should be used.

Setting SendBufferSize

This SendBufferSize directive controls how much data Apache writes out to a socket before blocking (that is, waiting for a response, or acknowledgment, from the client). Raising this value means that Apache can send more data without blocking, which can be useful on high-latency links.

An ideal size for the buffer would be slightly larger than the biggest web page you have, allowing you to send the whole document in one chunk without needing to wait for acknowledgments from the client. But, in practice, it may be that you have one or two unusually large documents, and you should simply aim for SendBufferSize to be large enough for the *majority* of web pages.

> **NOTE** *Incidentally, setting this value to zero causes Apache to use the buffer sizes set by the operating system. Also, setting* SendBufferSize *to a value higher than the kernel's TCP send buffer won't have any effect.*

Examining Caching Options

Caching is a vital part of high-traffic websites. In addition to operating system-level disk buffering, PHP opcode caches, client-side caching, caching proxies, and the MySQL query cache, Apache also provides its own caching support. This section looks at Apache's caching options and discusses their advantages and disadvantages.

Apache actually offers several server-level caching modules (not to be confused with the likes of mod_expires and mod_headers, which can be used to encourage client-side caching). Some of these are interconnected, and because they all have similar names, things can get a little confusing.

mod_cache

The primary caching module is mod_cache, which provides a flexible and powerful caching solution. In turn, mod_cache relies on a storage module, and the current choices are mod_disk_cache and mod_mem_cache (nothing to do with memcache). So, if you use mod_cache, you must also enable either mod_disk_cache or mod_mem_cache.

> **NOTE** *You learn more about* memcache *in Chapter 10, "Utilizing NoSQL Solutions."*

mod_disk_cache

As the name implies, mod_disk_cache provides disk-based storage of cached files and provides directives controlling the cache root, file size limits, and directory structures.

For each cached HTML document, two files are created: one containing the headers and the other containing the document. The filename is based on a 22-character hash of the resource (including the protocol, path, query string, port, and hostname), and files can optionally be stored in a hierarchy by setting the CacheDirLevels directive.

For example, with three levels of depth, a cache file named abcdefghijklmnopqrstuv would be stored as a/b/c/defghijklmnopqrstuv. With 64 possible characters (case-sensitive, alphanumeric), this gives you a maximum of 64 directories at any one level. Setting CacheDirLevels gives you a way to limit the number of files in a given directory because a large number of files in a single directory can cause performance problems with many filesystems.

The real power of caching comes on dynamically generated code. But even static documents can benefit from disk caching. This may seem surprising because you're still reading from disk, but files served from the cache bypass many of Apache's filters and handlers — .htaccess rules, for example. Figure 7-1 shows the flow of events when a client make requests to a server using mod_disk_cache.

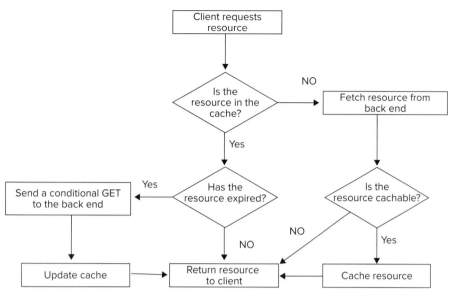

FIGURE 7-1

When Apache receives a request, it first checks if the resource exists in the cache. If it doesn't, mod_cache fetches it from the back-end server and returns it to the client, caching it in the process (if it is deemed cacheable). If the resource is in the cache but has expired, mod_cache sends a conditional GET request to the back-end server, asking for a fresh copy only if the resource has been modified. The cache is then updated — either with a fresh copy of the document or with fresh expiration headers.

By default, mod_disk_cache caches items for 1 hour; although this can easily be changed using CacheDefaultExpire. However, if the resource contains its own expiration times, these take precedence. It's worth noting, though, that even expired resources are often served faster from the cache than noncached resources because mod_cache needs to perform only a conditional GET on the back-end server. Typically, this simply involves using a stat() call to check to see if the file's size or last modified time has changed..

It should also be remembered that not all resources are deemed cachable — for example, if they contain Authorization headers or are in response to requests with POSTed data. In addition, resources with query strings won't be cached unless they contain suitable Expires or Cache-Control headers.

This brings up the subject of cache performance and efficiency. If you do decide to cache resources with query strings, resources with differing query strings will be stored as separate entries in the cache. (As you have already seen, the cache entry key is composed of the full URL.) In some cases, this is the right thing to do — news.php?page=1 will clearly contain different contents from news .php?page=2. But other times, this is undesirable.

For example, news.php?sessionid=12345 could well be the same as news.php?sessionid=23456 if you simply use the query string to track session data. (But, on the other hand, the pages might show slightly different content based on the user's session.) You can ignore all query string components with `CacheIgnoreQueryString On`, but it makes more sense to ignore only some keys, which you can achieve like so:

```
CacheIgnoreURLSessionIdentifiers sessionid id
```

In these examples, query string keys named `sessionid` or `id` will be stripped from the URL before it is hashed into a cache filename.

It's also worth turning on `UseCanonicalNames` in `httpd.conf` so that `http://www.example.com/foo.html` and `http://example.com/foo.html` are not stored as two separate cache entries, which is probably not what you want.

`mod_disk_cache` provides basic maintenance of files stored in the cache, removing entries if they are no longer valid. However, it has no controls on the overall size of the cache, and regular maintenance is usually needed to stop the cache from becoming too large. (Although, if disk space permits, there's certainly nothing wrong with this.)

`Htcacheclean` is a tool shipped with Apache that you can use to keep the cache size in check. In can be run either as a daemon (in which case it actively monitors cache entries being added/removed) or as a standalone application that can be run via `cron`. You simply pass the maximum cache size to `htcacheclean`, which then ensures that the cache does not grow larger than this.

Alternatively, you can roll your own solution, allowing more intelligence over purging. For example, less frequently accessed entries could be removed in preference to more frequently used entries, or static resources could be purged in preference to cached dynamic content (because the latter is typically more expensive to generate).

mod_mem_cache

The second storage module for `mod_cache` is `mod_mem_cache`, which provides in-memory caching. It offers two different caching modes: caching of documents and caching of open file descriptors. Although the caching of documents is the preferable mode, memory is a scarce resource, and caching of open file descriptors provides a good trade-off between memory usage and performance gain.

It may seem automatic to choose `mod_mem_cache` over `mod_disk_cache` — after all, you know that memory-based caches are several orders of magnitude faster than disk-based caches. However, `mod_mem_cache` has one subtle (but significant) drawback that limits its effectiveness. It operates on a per-process basis.

If you set a 10 MB maximum cache size and have 20 Apache processes running, each process will have its own private memory cache up to 10 MB in size. Entries cannot be shared across these caches, and the cache will be destroyed when the process is destroyed (for example, when `MaxRequestsPerChild` is reached). Not only does this cause this method of caching to be inefficient, it also significantly increases the potential memory usage.

You can alleviate this to some degree by setting a higher value for `MaxRequestsPerChild`. But unless you have a small set of resources that are accessed heavily, `mod_mem_cache` is rarely as useful as you might have hoped. In addition because Linux caches disk I/O, it's likely that many of the resources cached by `mod_disk_cache` can actually reside in memory already, lessening the potential advantage of memory-based caching.

mod_file_cache

An alternative to mod_cache is mod_file_cache, which implements a more basic form of caching without many of the features offered by mod_cache. As with mod_mem_cache, mod_file_cache offers both the caching of file handles and the contents of files in memory, and it is aimed firmly at static content that rarely changes.

To use the module, you specify in httpd.conf a list of files/handles to be loaded at startup, as shown here:

```
CacheFile /var/www/html/index.html    ## Cache file handle
CacheFile /var/www/html/contact.html
MmapFile /var/www/html/about.html    ## Map file into memory
```

As with mod_mem_cache, there are memory-scaling issues here. Each child process receives its own private copy of the cache, so you must be careful not to over-allocate memory.

There are a few drawbacks to this module. There is nothing in the way of cache management (such as expiring or revalidation of stale resources). If a file/file handle is in the cache, it is used. If not, the cache is ignored. If you want to add new entries to the cache or expire old ones, you must restart Apache (and possibly edit httpd.conf). And all cache entries are held in memory. In the case of large caches, it is usually best to opt for disk-based caching and let the operating system buffer the more frequently accessed entries in memory.

mod_memcache_cache

One of the strengths of Apache is that anyone can write a module. Although the previously covered caching modules form part of the standard Apache distribution, third-party solutions do exist.

One such module is mod_memcache_cache (http://code.google.com/p/modmemcachecache/), which is a storage module for mod_cache (like mod_mem_cache or mod_disk_cache) that uses memcached as the back end. Using a network-aware back end opens up new possibilities. Your cache is no longer confined to the available RAM on the web server, and you can balance the cache among multiple memcached nodes. If you run a pool of web servers, each can access a common cache, which is hugely more efficient (in terms of cache size and duplication) than each web server having its own private cache.

> **NOTE** *You learn more about* memcache *in Chapter 10.*

Although activity on mod_memcache_cache is low, it hopefully illustrates the potential for building new caching structures.

Monitoring with mod_status

Aside from a highly useful logging module that enables you to compile all manner of usage statistics, Apache also provides a real-time monitoring module in the form of mod_status. When enabled, this module provides a URL that you can visit to view a scoreboard containing a breakdown of all the requests currently handled.

Enabling is as simple as loading the module, setting a URL through which the status page can be accessible, and configuring a list of hosts allowed to view the page. The following example also turns ExtendedStatus on, which gives a more detailed report:

```
LoadModule status_module mod_status.so
<Location /my-server-status>
SetHandler server-status
ExtendedStatus On

Order Deny,Allow
Deny from all
Allow from 1.2.3.4
</Location>
```

With these rules in place, you can head over to http://example.com/my-server-status to view the breakdown. The first part of the output shows some overall server statistics — uptime, number of resources served, CPU usage, and average requests per second:

```
Server uptime: 13 hours 23 minutes 18 seconds
Total accesses: 771875 - Total Traffic: 6.5 GB
CPU Usage: u442.53 s10 cu.02 cs0 - .939% CPU load
16 requests/sec - 140.4 kB/second - 8.8 kB/request
30 requests currently being processed, 21 idle workers
```

Next is the scoreboard showing what each Apache child process is currently doing:

```
K_CKKK_CK__.WW_K_K__KK__.K_K___KW.W..KKK_C.K.CK..K.......C.....
..._...._._K.KK_...._.............................................
.....................
Scoreboard Key:
"_" Waiting for Connection, "S" Starting up, "R" Reading Request,
"W" Sending Reply, "K" Keepalive (read), "D" DNS Lookup,
"C" Closing connection, "L" Logging, "G" Gracefully finishing,
"I" Idle cleanup of worker, "." Open slot with no current process
```

In this example, the majority of children are idle (as denoted by a period). The rest are in varying stages of handling requests. Some are sending a reply to the client, others are initiating the connection, but the majority are in the Keep Alive status. They've already handled one request and are listening for others. This gives you a useful at-a-glance overview of what Apache is up to.

The remainder of the status page provides a breakdown of what each Apache child process is currently doing: the request being handled (if any), the vhost, client IP, and various stats on CPU/memory usage and processing time. Following is an example:

```
Srv PID  Acc        M  CPU SS Req Conn Child Slot  Client  Vhost     Request
4-0 6110 0/142/10263 _ 10.47 0 0  0.0  1.30  83.25 x.x.x.x xxx.com GET
     /favicon.ico HTTP/1.1

SrvChild Server number - generation
PID OS process ID
Acc Number of accesses this connection / this child / this slot
```

```
M Mode of operation
CPU CPU usage, number of seconds
SS Seconds since beginning of most recent request
Req Milliseconds required to process most recent request
Conn Kilobytes transferred this connection
Child Megabytes transferred this child
Slot Total megabytes transferred this slot
```

If Secure Sockets Layer (SSL) support is enabled in Apache, a final section of the page shows some SSL-related statistics.

> **NOTE** *You can learn more about SSL in Chapter 11, "Working with Secure Sockets Layer (SSL)."*

mod_status is useful (and many monitoring tools like munin generate graphs based on its output), but there is a performance hit to enabling it with ExtendedStatus On. Each time Apache handles a request, it makes two calls to gettimeofday(). This isn't a killer, but it's a needless expense if you have no intention to use mod_status. So, as always, if you don't need it, disable it.

Using Content Compression

Content compression is one of the most important things you can do to improve performance, and you first met it in Chapter 3, "Content Compression." The focus then was client-side support, and the practicalities of implementing compression on specific web servers was left open for this discussion. This section looks at how to set up content compression in Apache, potential gotchas, and how to deliver precompressed content.

mod_deflate

In the Apache 1.x series, mod_gzip was the stock compression module. Version 2 of Apache introduces mod_deflate as its replacement, and although the two are similar, they are not identical. (You may want to refer back to the discussion of deflate versus gzip in Chapter 3.) The performance differences between gzip and deflate are minor, and because Apache 2 supports only mod_deflate, the differences are academic.

Assuming mod_deflate has been compiled, the following example can cause some of the most common plain-text resources to be compressed:

```
LoadModule deflate_module /usr/lib/apache2/modules/mod_deflate.so

<IfModule mod_deflate.c>
        AddOutputFilterByType DEFLATE text/html text/plain text/xml text/css
            application/x-javascript application/javascript
        DeflateCompressionLevel 9
</IfModule>
```

You specify the resource by its MIME type (rather than, say, file extension). These can vary a little from platform to platform. For example, sometimes JavaScript is application/javascript, application/x-javascript, or even text/javascript, and you may want to verify the

Content-Type header being set on such resources (for example, using HTTP Live Headers for Firefox) before you add the deflate filters.

Some older browsers (most notably Netscape 4.x) have trouble handling deflated contents; either all deflated resources, or resources other than the HTML document. The following (somewhat old) rules are often seen on the Internet for working around this:

```
# Netscape 4.x has some problems...
BrowserMatch ^Mozilla/4 gzip-only-text/html

# Netscape 4.06-4.08 have some more problems
BrowserMatch ^Mozilla/4\.0[678] no-gzip

# MSIE masquerades as Netscape, but it is fine
# BrowserMatch \bMSIE !no-gzip !gzip-only-text/html

# NOTE: Due to a bug in mod_setenvif up to Apache 2.0.48
# the above regex won't work. You can use the following
# workaround to get the desired effect:
BrowserMatch \bMSI[E] !no-gzip !gzip-only-text/html
```

In reality, though, these rules probably aren't necessary. Netscape 4.08 dates back to 1998, and the latest release in the 4.x series was version 4.8 in 2002. Stats from statcounter.com show Netscape had a mere 0.07 percent of the market in 2008. These days, its market share is so low (0.01 percent for August 2012, according to statcounter.com) that it is generally just lumped in to the "other browsers" category in stats reports. Aside from that, Netscape 4's CSS support was so messed up that there's a good chance your site won't render correctly in it anyway.

As its name suggests, the DeflateCompressionLevel controls the level of compression — 1 is the lowest and 9 the highest. As usual, this is a trade-off between better compression and high CPU usage. The differences are modest. Setting a compression level of 9 won't cause a big increase in CPU usage but won't cause a big decrease in content size either. Feel free to experiment with different values for DeflateCompressionLevel, but in the section, "Precompressing Content," later in this chapter, you'll learn about a more powerful method that eliminates this trade-off.

Aside from setting the compression level, mod_deflate offers a few other options:

➤ DeflateBufferSize <bytes> — This is the size of the buffer to use. When the buffer is full, mod_deflate compresses it and flushes it to the client, so this is effectively the block size.

➤ DeflateMemLevel <int> — This is how much memory is available for mod_deflate to use when compressing. Rather than specifying the number of bytes, a value in the range 1 to 9 is given.

➤ DeflateWindowSize <int> — Accepting a value between 1 and 15, this controls the window size used during compression.

Recall that zlib (the underlying compression method used by mod_deflate) uses a history window when searching for multiple occurrences of a string. Thus, a larger window and buffer size give greater opportunity for compression, at the expense of slightly higher memory and CPU usage.

Again, it's a case of experimenting to see what works best in practice. But setting these values to the maximum shouldn't cause any serious problems, and will give the best levels of compression (albeit possibly only a slight increase).

Precompressing Content

The big drawback to `mod_deflate` is that it offers no way to serve up precompressed content. Although the memory and CPU usage from deflating content on-the-fly isn't huge, it's incredibly wasteful to compress a relatively static HTML document each time it is requested. It is better to compress the resource in advance and then serve this up. The old `mod_gzip` in Apache 1 offered this, as does Nginx (as you'll see soon). But if you want to precompress with `mod_deflate`, a few ugly hacks are needed.

Things become complicated because not all clients support compression. So, you can't just `zip` up your files and serve this. You must keep two copies of each: one compressed and one uncompressed. You then need a bit of magic to ensure that the correct content is served to the client, based on whether the client advertises `gzip` compression support.

Using mod_rewrite

Assume that you have an external script named `init.js`. The first step is to create a compressed copy (using `gzip`, or compatible) named `init.js.gz`. Because this is one-off compression, you can afford to set the highest compression level available, as shown here:

```
$ gzip -9 init.js
$ ls -1
init.js
init.js.gz
```

Next, you use some rules in `.htaccess` (or `httpd.conf`) to set the MIME type on all `.js.gz` files to `text/javascript` and to send the `Content-Encoding: gzip` header:

```
<FilesMatch "\.js.gz$">
ForceType text/javascript
Header set Content-Encoding: gzip
</FilesMatch>
```

Finally, you redirect the client to the `.gz` version of the file, if it advertises compression support via the `Accept-Encoding: gzip` header:

```
RewriteCond %{HTTP:Accept-Encoding} gzip
RewriteCond %{REQUEST_URI} \.(js|css)$
RewriteRule ^/(.*)$ /$1.gz [L,QSA]
```

Thus, if the client requests `init.js` and supports compression, `init.js.gz` will be served up to it.

Using Content Negotiation

The downside to use the `mod_rewrite` method is the extra load on the server. `mod_rewrite` isn't the leanest of modules, and regular expressions are relatively expensive. An alternative technique makes use of type-map files and content negotiation.

Again, you start with two copies of the resource: a compressed version and a plain version. You then create a type-map file (traditionally the `.var` extension is added, so `init.js.var`) containing the following:

```
URI: init.js
Content-Type: text/javascript; charset=UTF-8

URI: index.js.gz
Content-Type: text/javascript; charset=UTF-8
Content-Encoding: gzip
```

The type-map file is divided into blocks (each separated by a blank line) that define different content types, depending on what the client is willing to accept. The first block is the default (the uncompressed JavaScript), whereas the second (the compressed script) is delivered if the client advertises `gzip` support.

Finally, you must tell Apache to treat files with the `.var` extension as type-maps and set the appropriate content-type headers on `.js.gz` files. These rules can be in either the main `httpd.conf` or a `.htaccess` file:

```
AddHandler type-map .var
AddType text/javascript js.gz
AddEncoding x-gzip .gz
```

Now, if the client requests `init.js.var`, the appropriate resource will be returned.

This is certainly funky to set up, but it does avoid the need for `mod_rewrite`. In this example, the link to the resource changed as well (from `.js` to `.js.var`). If you're careful, you could define `.js` as the type-map file and use, say, `.js.uncompressed` for the uncompressed version of the file to avoid having to rename files in your HTML code.

While Apache is a very powerful and popular web server, it is by no means the only option, and in the next section you'll learn about some of the most popular alternatives.

LOOKING BEYOND APACHE

Although you have seen lots of ways in which Apache performance can be tuned, many would argue that Apache is built on a model that is fundamentally unable to deliver high performance (more on this in a minute) — no matter how much tuning you do. Coupled with the fact that Apache is a general-purpose web server, the search is on for a mean, lean alternative.

In this section, you discover one of Apache's main competitors, Nginx, and learn how it can be used to complement Apache, or even replace it. This will then lead to a look at how web servers can be clustered and load-balanced.

Nginx

Nginx (pronounced "engine X") appeared on the scene in the mid-2000s, and although initial uptake was slow because of lack of documentation, it has quickly gained in popularity. Many surveys now show it to be the third most used web server (behind Apache and IIS), and it is particularly popular for high-traffic sites.

Nginx's structure is notably different from Apache's. As you have seen, Apache uses processes or threads (depending on the MPM used), each of which use significant resources (not to mention the overhead involved in creating and destroying child processes). By contrast, Nginx uses an asynchronous, event-driven model, which removes the need for each request to be handled as a separate child/thread. Instead there is a single master process with one or more worker processes.

The performance impact of this change is huge. Whereas each additional Apache process consumes an extra 4 MB or 5 MB (if the likes of mod_php have been loaded, this figure will be more like 15+ MB) of memory, the impact of additional concurrent requests on Nginx is tiny. The result is that Nginx can handle a huge number of concurrent requests — much more than Apache, even with the newer threaded MPM.

Configuration

The discussions earlier in this chapter skipped the basics of Apache configuration because it was assumed you had some knowledge of this already (because of Apache's ubiquitous nature). The same isn't necessarily true for Nginx, though, and many administrators are cautious about straying away from the safety of Apache. So, let's look at various Nginx configuration options, including a complete minimum configuration.

The configuration of Nginx has changed a little over the years, and the structure of configuration files tends to vary from system to system. For example, installing Nginx from under Debian results in the sites-enabled and sites-available directories, familiar to Debian Apache users. In general, though, configuration files for Nginx on UNIX or Linux live under /etc/nginx, with the master file being /etc/nginx/nginx.conf.

As with Apache, this may, in turn, reference other configuration files using the include syntax. As of this writing, the default config file shipped with the Nginx Debian package looks like this:

```
user www-data;
worker_processes  1;

error_log  /var/log/nginx/error.log;
pid        /var/run/nginx.pid;

events {
    worker_connections  1024;
    # multi_accept on;
}

http {
    include       /etc/nginx/mime.types;
    access_log  /var/log/nginx/access.log;

    sendfile        on;
    #tcp_nopush     on;

    keepalive_timeout  65;
```

```
    tcp_nodelay        on;

    gzip  on;
    gzip_disable "MSIE [1-6]\.(?!.*SV1)";

    include /etc/nginx/conf.d/*.conf;
    include /etc/nginx/sites-enabled/*;
}
```

Let's spend some time looking through a few of these options. This isn't intended to be an exhaustive guide to configuring Nginx (you can find plenty of documentation on http://wiki.nginx .org), so let's just concentrate on performance-related options.

Worker Processes and CPU Affinity

As previously mentioned, Nginx does not use the process-per-request model of traditional web servers, so why would it need multiple worker processes? Certainly, Nginx can run just fine with this option left to the default value of 1, but on machines with multiple processing cores, increasing the number of workers can be advantageous.

A lot depends on workload. When using SSL or gzip compression (both of which are CPU-intensive), CPU bottlenecks can occur. Remember that a single process can be executed only on one core, so with worker_processes set to 1, Nginx can max out only a single CPU core, leaving the others idle. A good starting point, therefore, is to set worker_processes to the number of CPU cores on the system. Raising it above this level is unlikely to produce any benefit — if anything, performance will degrade a little from an increase in context switching.

Disk I/O also causes bottlenecks, and although there is no advantage to having multiple workers all reading from the same disk at once (overall throughput will still be the same), when content is spread over multiple disks, you can raise the amount of parallel reading by increasing worker_ processes to equal the number of disks on which web content is stored. (Don't forget any writes to access/error logs, too.)

With *processor affinity*, Linux might schedule all worker processes to run on the same CPU, which is almost certainly not what you want. The worker_cpu_affinity directive enables you to control this.

Each option to worker_cpu_affinity is a bit mask specifying on which CPU a worker should run. Thus, on a quad-core machine, you'd probably set worker_processes to 4 and would need to specify four bit masks to worker_cpu_affinity, as shown here:

```
    worker_cpu_affinity 1000 0100 0010 0001
```

This can be particularly useful for processors that support hyper-threading because you can assign a worker to multiple logical processors. For example, a mask for 0101 assigns a worker to both the first and third processors.

Concurrency

Nginx has no MaxClients directive, but the worker_connections option in the events block serves a similar purpose. This limit is per-worker. So, with worker_connections set to 1024, and worker_processes set to 8, you allow a maximum of 8,192 simultaneous connections.

With Apache's prefork MPM, you could estimate an approximate value for MaxClients by looking at the typical memory usage of a child process. But this doesn't work for a worker model such as Nginx (or Apache's worker MPM, for that matter). The good news is that setting too high of a limit on concurrency doesn't tend to risk sending the system into a downward spiral, the way it does with Apache, so you can afford to be fairly liberal.

Watching CPU/RAM use of Nginx workers and monitoring disk I/O and CPU blocking (for example, with vmstat) can be useful to identify bottlenecks if you are too optimistic with worker_connections. But, in reality, most bottlenecks occur in things like the PHP subsystem (which you'll learn about in Chapter 12, "Optimizing PHP").

tcp_nodelay and tcp_nopush

In the earlier discussion about Apache's SendBufferSize directive, you learned about the potential usefulness of sending the entire HTTP response in a single chunk, without waiting for a response from the client.

In Nginx, tcp_nodelay serves a similar purpose, instructing the server to use the TCP_NODELAY option when creating a socket. tcp_nopush (which passes the TCP_NOPUSH option to the socket) has a similar effect and can cause Nginx to attempt to send out HTTP headers inside a single packet. It's generally worth enabling both of these options.

> **NOTE** tcp_nodelay *and* tcp_nopush *are discussed in more detail in Appendix A,* "*TCP Performance.*"

sendfile

As with Apache, you can use sendfile to provide faster serving of static files. Rather than reading the contents of a file into userspace (that is, the web server), sendfile enables the web server to simply copy the data from one file descriptor to another (the latter being a socket). This is all done inside the kernel, making it more efficient. Naturally, this works only on static files that don't contain any dynamic code.

Disk I/O

In theory, you can improve performance substantially by using Asynchronous I/O (AIO) to perform nonblocking disk reads and writes. Rather than sitting and waiting for data to be read from disk, Nginx can continue execution and be alerted when the data becomes available.

This sounds great in theory, but there are a number of drawbacks under Linux. (Note that some operating systems such as FreeBSD don't have these limitations.)

For starters, you can't use sendfile and must use direct I/O (O_DIRECT). This causes the file to bypass Linux's disk caches, so you don't benefit from having the file potentially cached in memory. Usually, you want this caching, but in a few situations, not caching is better. For example, if the file is large (say a video), you probably don't want to fill your disk buffers with it. Similarly, if you have a large working set (too large to all fit in memory) being accessed in a fairly distributed manner, the disk cache may not help much. In these two cases, the benefits of AIO can outweigh the drawbacks.

The Nginx documentation gives the following example of AIO usage:

```
location /video {
    aio on;
    directio 512;
    output_buffers 1 128k;
}
```

You need to explicitly enable direct I/O and have the option of also setting a minimum size. Only files larger than this size will be read using direct I/O. It makes a lot of sense to use only AIO on directories containing large files — at least until the Linux implementation improves. For direct I/O, it's worth experimenting with using it globally with a high value to prevent large files from polluting your disk caches. But remember that enabling direct I/O causes sendfile to be disabled.

sendfile isn't always the ideal method for reading from disk. Because the operating system reads the data in fairly small chunks, there may be a lot of seeking back and forth on busy systems, as the operating system attempts to read multiple files at once. When sendfile is disabled (or isn't being used because you're serving dynamic content), you can control the size of the chunks of data that are read from disk using output_buffers, as shown here:

```
output_buffers 2 512k;
```

This causes Nginx to create two buffers in memory, each of 512 KB. When handling requests, it then attempts to read 512 KB of data from disk in one chunk, before processing it. The 512 KB should be big enough to hold even a large HTML document.

Compression

As you'd expect, Nginx supports gzip compression, and the options are mostly similar to Apache's. You can set the compression level (1 through to 9), a list of MIME types to compress, the capability to disable compression for certain user agents, and a minimum document length. (It's generally not worth compressing small documents because the additional gzip headers cancel out any saving.)

Nginx also has the capability to serve up precompressed contents via the Gzip Precompression module (--with-http_gzip_static_module). However, this module is not compiled in by default. With this module enabled — and gzip_static set to on — Nginx can check for the existence of a precompressed version of the requested file, and return this in preference to the original if it has a newer timestamp. Thus, if a client requests http://www.example.com/news/archive.html, Nginx checks for the existence of archive.html.gz in the news directory of the document root.

If Nginx doesn't find a precompressed version of the requested document, the standard gzip module kicks in (if it is turned on) and compresses the document on-the-fly. It won't save a compressed copy for future use, though. Creating the precompressed files is an exercise for the system administrator. A small shell script can be used to recursively compress the documents under the web root.

Another benefit of precompressing is that you can use the highest compression level because you will presumably compress only occasionally, when static pages have been edited. Usually, the lowest compression level gives the best compromise between size and compression speed. You don't have to use gzip because there are alternatives that offer slightly better compression levels.

With Nginx, you also have control over the size of the `gzip` buffer(s). Actually, that's not entirely true. The buffer is a fixed size of 4 KB (one page of memory), but you can increase the number of buffers. Under Linux, the current defaults are as follows:

```
gzip_buffers 16 k
```

Note that, since the individual buffer size is fixed, the second argument here has no effect.

> **NOTE** *Most operating systems handle memory in fixed size blocks known as pages. On x86 and x64 architectures, the most common page size is 4 KB, with Linux, FreeBSD, and Windows all using this default. On the SPARC architecture (mostly used for Solaris), 8 KB pages are the default.*

So, with 16 buffers, each at 84KB, you would have 64 KB. Thus, the maximum size for your *compressed* contents is 64 KB. That's enough for most purposes because the uncompressed contents would likely be approximately 5 to 10 times this size. But if you plan to compress large documents, the number of buffers can be increased as necessary.

Modules

Development of Nginx is currently moving at quite a rapid pace, often with several releases per month. As such, precompiled Windows binaries and the package repositories of most Linux/UNIX distributions will be quite behind (especially for those distributions that favor stability over bleeding edge), and Nginx is one of those applications where it's definitely a good idea to compile from source.

Unlike Apache, Nginx does not support dynamically loadable modules — everything needs to be compiled in. And, as usual, package maintainers tend to favor more rather than less. The result is a packaged binary that probably contains more modules than you need (and maybe lacks some that you do need) — although the performance penalty of extra modules is much lower than in Apache because you aren't running hundreds of child processes.

The full list of configuration options for Nginx is available by running `./configure --help` (from inside the Nginx source directory). The defaults are quite sensible with support for Common Gateway Interface (CGI), logging, basic authentication, `gzip`, URL rewriting, and so on, all being included. A few of these standard modules may not be needed, though, and they must be explicitly disabled. These include the following:

➤ Support for server-side includes (SSIs)

➤ Load balancing (via the Upstream module)

➤ FastCGI, Simple CGI (SCGI), and uWSGI

> **NOTE** *CGI isn't just for Perl. If you want to use PHP under Nginx, you need some form of CGI support.*

Of the modules *not* enabled by default in Nginx, the most likely ones that you'll need include the following:

➤ SSL support

➤ Stub Status (server stats)

➤ Real IP for correct logging of IP addresses in `X-Forwarded-For` headers (for example, behind load balancers/proxies)

Aside from the official modules, a healthy collection of third-party modules must be downloaded separately and then compiled in. These include an enhanced FastCGI module (AFCGI), etags, a filter for on-the-fly stripping of excess whitespace from contents, and alternative load-balancing techniques.

Nginx, Apache, and PHP

One of the biggest issues for users moving away from Apache is the lack of a PHP module in Nginx. Whereas with Apache you can just load `mod_php` and happily run PHP scripts, with Nginx, you must use CGI. This isn't anywhere near as bad a performance issue as you might imagine, though, and with a bit of work, you can equal the performance of Apache plus `mod_php`, and get a more flexible setup in the process.

FastCGI (fcgi)

The main reason that CGI tends to be so slow is because a new process (be it Perl, Python, PHP, and so on) must be forked to handle the request. FastCGI solves this by maintaining a pool of persistent processes to handle CGI requests. When the web server needs to process a CGI script, it connects to the FastCGI daemon over a socket and sends the request. FastCGI then delegates the request to a free worker process and returns the response to the web server over the same socket. Figure 7-2 shows the topology of an Nginx-FastCGI setup.

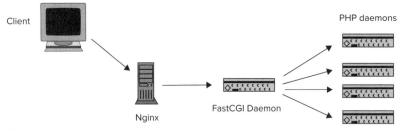

FIGURE 7-2

There's nothing Nginx-specific about FastCGI. It's a technique used for other web servers that don't natively support PHP (or similar), too. There's even a FastCGI module for Apache. But why would you want to go to the trouble to use FastCGI with Apache when `mod_php`, `mod_perl`, `mod_python`, and so on, make life so much easier?

Separating the processing of your dynamic code from the web server actually has two significant benefits. First, you avoid the overhead of loading the scripting module for requests that might not even contain dynamic code (for example, static HTML, images, and so on). Earlier in this chapter, you learned how the likes of `mod_php` dramatically increase the memory footprint of each Apache child. Second, it gives you the flexibility to execute the PHP on a different server — or even spread the load across a pool of servers.

FastCGI is by no means a poor man's alternative to `mod_php`.

Setting Up FastCGI for PHP

Providing that PHP has been compiled with CGI support (or the appropriate `php-cgi` package installed), you can use PHP 5's built-in FastCGI support to launch the FastCGI daemon from the command prompt like so:

```
export PHP_FCGI_CHILDREN=5
php-cgi -b 127.0.0.1:9000
```

In this example, the daemon can listen for incoming connections on 9000/TCP of the localhost. The number of worker daemons to spawn is governed by the `PHP_FCGI_CHILDREN` environmental variable. Alternatively, a simple `init` script can be used — the Nginx FastCGI documentation at `http://wiki.nginx.org/FcgiExample` provides a suitable example.

With FastCGI running, all that is left is to tell Nginx to use it:

```
location ~ \.php$ {
  include /etc/nginx/fcgi_params.conf;
  fastcgi_pass  127.0.0.1:9000;
}
```

In this example, any request ending with `.php` is passed to FastCGI. Note the inclusion of an external file containing FastCGI configuration options. The example given on the Nginx wiki is as follows:

```
fastcgi_param  GATEWAY_INTERFACE  CGI/1.1;
fastcgi_param  SERVER_SOFTWARE    nginx;
fastcgi_param  QUERY_STRING       $query_string;
fastcgi_param  REQUEST_METHOD     $request_method;
fastcgi_param  CONTENT_TYPE       $content_type;
fastcgi_param  CONTENT_LENGTH     $content_length;
fastcgi_param  SCRIPT_FILENAME    $document_root$fastcgi_script_name;
fastcgi_param  SCRIPT_NAME        $fastcgi_script_name;
fastcgi_param  REQUEST_URI        $request_uri;
fastcgi_param  DOCUMENT_URI       $document_uri;
fastcgi_param  DOCUMENT_ROOT      $document_root;
fastcgi_param  SERVER_PROTOCOL    $server_protocol;
fastcgi_param  REMOTE_ADDR        $remote_addr;
fastcgi_param  REMOTE_PORT        $remote_port;
fastcgi_param  SERVER_ADDR        $server_addr;
fastcgi_param  SERVER_PORT        $server_port;
fastcgi_param  SERVER_NAME        $server_name;
```

Aside from `fastcgi_param`, there are a few other `fastcgi_*` directives of interest from a performance perspective. `fastcgi_buffers` controls the number of buffers (as before, under Linux IA64, each is 4 KB) used for reading in the response from the FastCGI daemon. Just to complicate matters, Nginx also maintains a second buffer (controlled by `fastcgi_buffer_size`) used for the FastCGI response header, and the first part of the response. After this buffer has been filled, the buffers controlled by `fastcgi_buffers` are used to hold the remainder of the response. Again, the default is one page, or probably 4 KB.

For `fastcgi_buffers`, the default is eight buffers, giving 32 KB (8 × 4 + `fastcgi_buffer_size`) plus however big `fastcgi_buffer_size` is in total, but it's worth raising this to approximately 256 to give just more than 1 MB of buffer space. Any response larger than the total buffer space is written to a temporary file on disk, so it makes sense to raise `fastcgi_buffers` to a value large enough to hold the majority of responses. (Of course, the response contains the full HTML document, after the PHP in it has been parsed.)

You can disable the writing of oversized responses to disk by setting `fastcgi_max_temp_file_size` to 0, but this isn't recommended. Although it might seem tempting, with this option turned off, FastCGI returns its response as fast as the client can read it (via Nginx, of course), which probably is a lot slower than writing to disk. FastCGI is still relatively resource hungry, and you should aim to minimize for how long each PHP worker runs. Nginx is much more suited for drip-feeding the response to the client.

FastCGI Caching

Nginx supports the capability to cache responses from FastCGI, which has the potential to dramatically cut down on work load for the PHP workers. Caching dynamic pages is always tricky, though, and you must take care not to cache (or make allowances for) user-specific copies of pages. (You don't want regular users to see admin-specific versions, for example.)

Caching is enabled by setting a value for `fastcgi_cache`. This option takes an arbitrary string as the name for the cache, as shown here:

```
fastcgi_cache  mycache;
```

As you'd expect, you can set the caching period, and Nginx offers the neat capability to specify different values for different HTTP return codes. Thus, you might cache 200 OKs for a few hours, but 404s for a shorter period. By default, only 200, 301, and 302 codes are cached, but you can easily override this, as shown here:

```
fastcgi_cache_valid    200 302 1d;
fastcgi_cache_valid    301 7d;
fastcgi_cache_valid    404 5m;
fastcgi_cache_valid    any     10m;
```

> **NOTE** *The* any *keyword serves as a catch-all, acting on any return code.*

You also have the capability to set the key used for the cache entry. This requires a bit of thought, however. If you use the script name as the key, you risk duplicates. (Imagine Nginx serving a dozen virtual hosts, each with an `index.php`.) If you get around this by using the domain name plus the script name, you hit issues when `http://example.com/foo.php` and `https://example.com/foo.php` contain different content. So, you must also include the protocol in the key, as shown here:

```
fastcgi_cache_key        $scheme$host$request_uri;
```

This results in keys such as `http://www.example.com/foo.php?bar=baz`, and also solves the potential problem of different query strings resulting in different content being shown.

This still isn't the end of the matter, though. Different HTTP methods can result in different responses. For starters, you probably don't want to cache POST requests — luckily, these are disabled by default in Nginx. HEAD requests are more of an issue because these generate a blank response (save for the headers). If a client issues a HEAD request and the result is cached, subsequent GET requests on the resource cause a blank page to be returned.

The best thing you can do is include the request method in the key name, as shown here:

```
fastcgi_cache_key        $scheme$host$request_uri$request_method;
```

This is not perfect because you are potentially cluttering the cache with cached HEAD responses. But because they are small (and relatively uncommon), you needn't worry too much about cache space.

A final issue is how to deal with the caching of pages for logged-in users (or users who see specific content for whatever reason). If you store authentication information (such as a session ID) in the query string, all is well — you already know about including the query string in your cache key. Passing a session ID in the query string isn't great for security, though, and the usual method would be to store authentication information in a cookie.

Again, the solution is to modify the cache key string, this time to add the value of a given cookie to it. In Ngnix, you can access cookie data using the syntax `$cookie_COOKIENAME`. For example, if you use `$cookie_Userid`, the cache key now looks something like this:

```
fastcgi_cache_key
        $scheme$host$request_uri$request_method$cookie_userid$server_port;
```

FastCGI under Apache

Although `mod_php` is the most popular way of running PHP scripts under Apache, there is something to be said for using FastCGI instead. First of all, it eliminates the overhead of loading the PHP interpreter for every request, which is particularly useful if you are using Apache to serve static resources, too (although, as noted, the likes of Nginx generally make better static file servers than Apache). Secondly, it provides a scaling option, since the PHP FastCGI back ends can be distributed across multiple servers. Perhaps more importantly, it also means that you can run Apache with the worker MPM. As you saw earlier in this chapter in the section, "Multi-Processing Modules," the worker MPM is more efficient, but does not sit well with `mod_php`.

From a non-performance perspective, it can also be used as a way of executing PHP code under the user ID of the owner, rather than as the Apache user.

Installation

Under Apache, `mod_fcgid` is currently the recommended module for providing FastCGI support. Its licensing is less restrictive than the older alternative, `mod_fastcgi`. If you've compiled Apache from source, you'll need to manually download and build the `mod_fcgid` module (download from `http://httpd.apache.org/mod_fcgid/`). On systems that use packages/ports (for example, FreeBSD, Ubuntu, or CentOS), it will probably be available from there. (On Debian, the package is `libapache2-mod-fcgid`.)

Configuration

Configuration is a simple case of loading the module, and then instructing Apache to use it for PHP files (don't forget to disable `mod_php`):

```
LoadModule fcgid_module modules/mod_fcgid.so
AddHandler fcgid-script .fcgi .php
MaxRequestsPerProcess      1000
MaxProcessCount            10
FCGIWrapper /usr/bin/php-cgi .php
IdleTimeout                240
```

Also, remember to ensure that `+ExecCGI` is listed in the `Options` directive for each vhost for which you want to enable `mod_fcgid`.

The Best of the Rest

Although Apache might dominate the Linux and UNIX web server world, there is plenty of competition. In the past, the competition has tended to be heavyweight alternatives such as Apache Tomcat, NCSA, Oracle, or (under Windows) IIS. But the past decade has seen increasing demand for lightweight servers, such that the most interesting (and actively developed) web servers tend to be in this area. You've already learned about one of these, Nginx, but there are numerous other alternatives. Let's take a closer look at a couple of alternatives.

lighttpd

Usually pronounced "lighty," lighttpd offers a similar set of features to Nginx. A threaded model enables for high concurrency and low resource usage, along with all the usual extras — FastCGI, SSL, virtual hosting, URL rewriting, and SSI. Actually, lighttpd's FastCGI implementation is more integrated that that of Nginx and will spawn processes as (and when) needed without the need for you to maintain a separate FastCGI daemon. lighttpd also has native support for standard CGI — something missing in Nginx.

lighttpd's other historical advantage over Nginx is that the documentation has been much better, and configuration has been simpler. Unfortunately, lighttpd was also bugged by reports of memory leaks and benchmarks that showed higher CPU usage than Nginx. A lot of these factors are outdated now. Documentation for Nginx has improved significantly, and many of the alleged memory leaks in lighttpd have either been fixed or turned out to be false alarms.

Speaking of benchmarking, lighttpd versus Nginx is one of those subjects that provides as much heated debate as vi versus emacs, or Linux versus BSD, and each side can invariably provide benchmarks that show Nginx is "better" than lighttpd, or vice versa. It's worth remembering that these benchmarks are often narrow, and often the tester will have more experience with one server than the other, potentially leading to one having been configured better than the other.

The benchmarking results are narrow because all they show is how the two servers cope with a specific workload. For example, you might bombard Nginx and lighttpd with 10,000 requests for a static 1 KB HTML document, and plot the average time taken to handle the request. Most likely, the results will be close, but whichever server wins, benchmarking with say a 50 KB HTML document could produce different results. (Think of how `sendfile` or `output_buffers` could affect Nginx performance here.)

It's also important to remember that performance isn't just about how long it takes to serve a client's request. If a particular web server uses significantly more CPU and memory than the other, a small decrease in response time is often missing the point.

Overall, Nginx might be preferred over lighttpd because Nginx uses less resources in production environments. It's a close call, though, and when making your decision, just remember that a lot of the pros and cons are outdated now.

thttpd

thttpd stands for Tiny HTTPD or Turbo HTTPD (or various other things). thttpd is a small and basic web server, which makes Nginx and lighttpd look feature-rich in comparison. Performance doesn't tend to be significantly better than either Nginx or lighttpd, so thttpd's main use is for specialist situations — for example, embedded applications because it is so small. However, it does support CGI, so it is sometimes used alongside Nginx. (Although CGI modules are now available for Nginx.)

Development of thttpd seems to have ground to a halt, too, with the last stable release in 2003. For these reasons, thttpd isn't a suitable general-purpose, light web server these days.

Node.js

`Node.js` is a JavaScript framework that can be used to create high-performance web servers (among other things). It is built around Chrome's V8 JavaScript engine, and uses an event-driven I/O model to provide high levels of concurrency.

Although relatively new (the first release was in 2009), `Node.js` has gained increasing popularity. Its capability to provide PUSH services makes it a useful alternative to Comet technologies.

So far, you've seen how Apache and Nginx can work in single-server setups. Eventually, there will (hopefully) come a time when your website outgrows a single web server, and you must split tasks across several servers. In the next section, you discover various ways in which Apache and Nginx can run together.

MULTISERVER SETUPS WITH NGINX AND APACHE

You've now learned about some of the core performance-related features of Apache and looked at one of its main lightweight competitors, Nginx. Although in many situations there's a strong case of abandoning Apache in favor of Nginx, a lot of system administrators are wary about leaving the familiarity and safety of Apache completely (or still want to retain some of the advanced features offered by Apache). Certainly it's true that there's a learning curve involved. You must learn a new syntax of rewrite rules, probably set up some form of FastCGI scripting, and so on.

As a result, many administrators choose a dual-server setup, with Nginx handling static resources (where it excels) and Apache continuing to serve dynamic content such as PHP or Perl CGI scripts (where the advantages of Nginx are less clear cut).

There are two main ways to do this:

➤ Running Apache and Nginx side by side (on different IP addresses)

➤ Using Nginx's proxying abilities to forward requests for dynamic resources to an Apache back-end server

Let's look at the latter method first.

Nginx as a Reverse Proxy to Apache

You can easily use Nginx as a reverse proxy to Apache using Nginx's proxying support, as shown in Figure 7-3. As shown in the following code snippet, Nginx is set up on 80/TCP of the public-facing IP address, and then Apache is configured to listen on a different port — say, 8080. If Nginx receives a request for a static resource, it handles it itself; otherwise, it proxies the result on to the back-end Apache server.

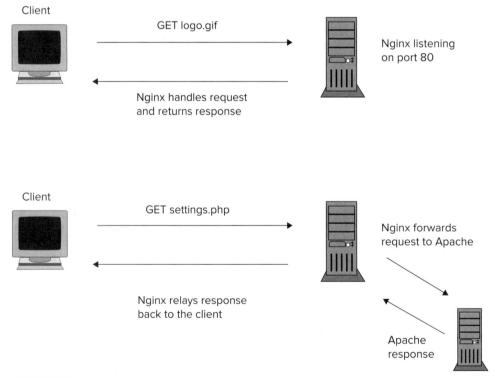

FIGURE 7-3

```
location ~ ^/(images|javascript|js|css|media|static)/ {
root /var/www/html/;
expires 30d;
}

location / {
proxy_pass http://127.0.0.1:8080;
include /etc/nginx/proxy.conf;
}
```

In other words, any URL under /images, /javascript, /js, and so on, is served directly.
Everything else is proxied to Apache listening on 8080 of the loopback interface.

Proxy Options

As you might expect, Nginx offers a wealth of proxy-related configuration options, and it makes sense to store them in an external file (/etc/nginx/proxy.conf in the previous example) for reuse. Let's spend a few moments looking at these options.

proxy_redirect is needed only when the back end (for example, Apache) generates Location headers that must be rewritten — for example, to the URL of the front-end server. In most cases, you can leave this turned off.

Nginx uses a similar approach to buffering proxy traffic as it does for gzip and regular output. Each buffer is a fixed size (equal to one page of memory — usually 4 KB), but you can increase the number of buffers to increase the overall size, as shown here:

```
proxy_buffers 20 4k
```

(Again, note that the second parameter has no effect, because it is fixed.)

This gives a total of 80 KB. When buffering is enabled, Nginx reads the response from the back-end server straight into the buffer and then feeds this back to the client as fast as the client can receive it. With proxy buffering turned off, the rate at which Nginx reads from the back-end server is dependent on the rate at which the client can read the response from Nginx (because there is no temporary buffer to hold the data). Because the back-end server is generally a lot heavier than Nginx, it makes sense to minimize the time it spends handling requests, and proxy buffering should generally be turned on (and the buffer size set large enough to handle the majority of responses).

One frequent problem is that, with a proxy in place, you lose the ability to track client IP addresses in the back end (because all requests now appear to come from Nginx). The solution is to set the following custom headers via Nginx:

```
proxy_set_header X-Real-IP $remote_addr;
proxy_set_header X-Forwarded-For $proxy_add_x_forwarded_for;
```

The back-end code (say, PHP running under Apache) can now access the X-Real-IP variable to get the client's true IP address (for example, $_SERVER['X-Real-IP']). This isn't much use if you need to rewrite your application, though, and there's a handy Apache module called `mod_rpaf` that solves this problem:

```
LoadModule rpaf_module /usr/lib/apache2/modules/mod_rpaf.so
<IfModule mod_rpaf.c>
RPAFenable On
RPAFsethostname On
RPAFproxy_ips 127.0.0.1
</IfModule>
```

With `rpaf` in place (note `RPAFproxy_ips` has been set to the IP address of the Nginx server), the proxy is effectively hidden, and you can access the client's IP address in the usual way (for example, `$_SERVER['REMOTE_ADDR"]`). This also eliminates the need to rewrite the Apache logging directives to log the true IP address.

Nginx also offers a handful of options for controlling timeouts when talking to the back-end server. You'll learn more about these in the section, "Load Balancers," later in this chapter.

Nginx and Apache Side by Side

Proxying requests for dynamic content through Nginx adds a small amount of latency to each request/response and also adds another point of failure. If Nginx goes down, both static and dynamic content is affected. If you have only one Apache server and want to use Nginx for serving static resources, a better solution is to run them both side by side on different IP addresses (but both on the same machine). This ensures the least latency and means that if one web server daemon goes down, the other isn't affected.

To save on the use of an additional IP address (which, given the current IPv4 address space situation, is a growing concern), you could run both web servers on the same IP address, but on different ports — Apache on port 80, and Nginx on, say, 8080 — ensuring that the links to static resources in your HTML documents contain the port number. Unfortunately, corporate and personal firewalls are too varied to make this a reliable method. There are simply too many users whose browsers cannot access resources on anything other than ports 80 and 443.

Aside from these issues, an additional downside is that this model doesn't scale so well. After you reach the stage of needing multiple Apache servers, you're going to need middleware in front of them anyway (to handle load balancing). Nginx fills this role nicely, so you might as well just use it in front of Apache from the start.

So far, you've seen how Nginx and Apache can co-exist, with Nginx proxying requests to Apache, or sitting alongside it. Once you start proxying requests to multiple back-end servers, extra considerations arise. How does the system cope if one of the back-end servers goes down? In fact, how do you even decide if a server is down — does it have to be completely unresponsive, or should it be pulled out of the pool if the system load gets higher than a certain level? Should each server receive an equal share of traffic, or do some of the servers have better hardware than others?

Devices that proxy to multiple back-end servers are known as load balancers, and the questions raised in the previous paragraph show just how involved the subject can be. In the following section, you discover how to handle these issues and much more.

LOAD BALANCERS

Using Nginx to distribute requests across a pool of back-end servers is an example of the more generic class of devices known as *load balancers*. Load balancers are often divided into software (typically open source applications running on generic PC hardware) and hardware.

But the distinction isn't so clear-cut — after all, even hardware load balancers invariably run some sort of software. There's also a great range in load-balancer intelligence, from simple round-robin handling of requests to more complex algorithms based on the health of individual back-end servers. Many load balancers also include complementary features such as SSL acceleration, traffic shaping, and firewalling — more on these shortly, in the section, "Load Balancer Features."

In this section, you'll learn some of the advanced features offered by load balancers, and how Nginx and HAProxy can be used to provide highly configurable software-based balancing. But let's start by looking at the differences between hardware and software load balancers.

Hardware versus Software

Although the distinction is blurred (and the nomenclature somewhat inaccurate), it's still useful to think in terms of software and hardware load balancers.

Hardware load balancers often run on special hardware and contain any software pre-installed and configured by the vendor. Management is usually performed through a web interface. This makes them a black box in many ways, which can be a blessing or a curse. You can't hack in new features or changes, but you are also relieved from having to set up and maintain the system. Hardware load balancers also have the potential to offer the lowest latency (although, in practice, the difference in latency compared to a well-tuned software load balancer is relatively small).

By contrast, *software load balancers* usually just run on standard PC hardware, using applications like Nginx and HAProxy. This provides a huge amount of control over the balancing but can take longer to set up and monitor.

Hardware load balancers generally operate on Layers 3 and 4 of the OSI model (see Chapter 1, "A Refresher on Web Browsers," for more information about the OSI model) and simply work in terms of TCP/IP packets — routing traffic to back-end servers and possibly handling Network Address Translation (NAT). Software load balancers have the capability of operating on Layer 7 (the OSI application layer) and, as such, can "talk" HTTP. They can perform the compression of resources passing through, and perform routing based on the presence of cookies (based on the request URL and so on).

Balancers that operate solely on Layers 3 and 4 tend to be a little faster and have high capacity (because there isn't the need to analyze the Layer 7 contents). However, they are also less intelligent and flexible. In practice, many hardware load balancers also support Layer 7.

So which is best? There's no concrete answer to that question. Both are perfectly viable solutions. However, the following discussion concentrates on software load balancing.

Load Balancer Features

Load balancing might seem like quite a straightforward task — spread a series of requests evenly over a bunch of back-end servers. But deciding what "evenly" means can actually be rather complicated. Let's consider the basics of a simple balancing algorithm to see how it rapidly becomes complex.

Using a round-robin algorithm is the simplest method of balancing. The round-robin just cycles through a list of servers and sends each new request to the next server. When it reaches the end of the list, it starts over at the beginning.

This method assumes that all requests have an equal performance cost on the server, and that each server has identical processing power. In reality, the power of each back-end server might vary, so you add weighting to allow some back-end servers to receive more requests than others.

This still leaves you with the problem that not all requests are equal. A request for a static resource will be several orders of magnitude less resource-intensive than a request for a dynamic resource. You can adjust for this by comparing the number of requests forwarded on to a server with the number of responses received. If a particular server starts to build up a backlog, you can automatically lower its weighting and forward subsequent requests on to a quieter server.

This still isn't perfect, though, because a request taking a long time to be answered is not necessarily an indication of an overloaded back-end server. For example, a PHP script that generates reports from a database might take a long time to return — but most of the load would be on the database server, not the back-end server.

To deal with this, you need monitoring that is more sophisticated than simply watching requests going back and forth. You need to query the back-end server to discover memory and CPU usage, server load, and perhaps even network latency. Many load balancers do, indeed, do this, either using Simple Network Management Protocol (SNMP), or a dedicated communications channel (for example, a daemon running on each back-end server that talks to the load balancer over a long-running TCP connection). Even this isn't perfect, though, because load on a back-end server can change dramatically in a short period of time. (For example, think of a request that uses a lot of CPU but runs only for one-tenth of a second.)

Load-balancing intelligence doesn't need to stop there. As you will soon see, sending requests from the same client to the same back-end server each time can be useful to ensure *sticky sessions* (that is, ensuring the session data is not lost). But this can defeat the purpose of trying to spread load evenly over each back-end server. When you try to factor in both *session affinity* (sticky sessions) and balancing of the load, things get even more complicated.

Hashing based on an IP address ensures that, if the client has a fixed IP address, subsequent requests will all go to the same back-end server. This is great for session affinity and produces a fairly even balance across servers with a large enough sample. Unfortunately, there'll always be a small percentage of users behind proxy farms, whose IP addresses change from request to request. Often, it's just the last octet that changes, and hashing on the first three octets solves this. But you can't always guarantee this, and you usually can't afford to alienate these users. Conversely, some users will be behind NAT devices, making them all appear to originate from the same IP address (the address of the NAT device).This behavior is mostly seen on corporate LANs that only have one public-facing IP address.

A solution to the problem of a client's IP address changing between requests is cookies, of which there are two possible options:

➤ The load balancer sets a cookie when the client first issues a request. This cookie contains the ID of the back-end server that was assigned to handle the request. The balancer checks for the cookie on subsequent requests from the client and routes them to the same back-end server.

➤ The balancer utilizes a cookie already set by the application (for example, a session ID).

Both methods rely on the client accepting cookies, of course. But with the latter option, your application probably won't work if the client doesn't. So, this isn't penalizing clients any more than they already have been. The latter method does require that the load balancer maintain a lookup table mapping session ID to back-end server, though, and this table can grow rather large. In practice, you must keep the table to a reasonable size by expiring entries after a certain time, and this can cause session affinity to be lost.

Ultimately, the best solution to session affinity is simply not to store session data on individual back-end servers. memcache is the ideal alternative.

> **NOTE** *You learn more about* memcache *in Chapter 10.*

SSL Acceleration and Termination

SSL communications can cause a significant amount of CPU overhead, both during the initial handshake (when keys are exchanged) and the encryption/decryption of packets sent over the connection. This can have an impact on the performance of back-end servers, and many load balancers offer features to take over some of the work.

> **NOTE** *Advances in hardware over the past decade mean this is much less of a problem than it was. See* http://www.imperialviolet.org/2010/06/25/overclocking-ssl.html *for a discussion of Gmail's experiences.*

With SSL termination, the load balancer becomes one endpoint of the SSL connection, rather than the back-end web server. (The other endpoint is the client, of course.) This relieves the back-end servers of the overhead of managing the SSL connection. Whether this is beneficial is debatable because all you've done is to shift the processing from the back end to the load balancer. If the load balancer runs specialist hardware, it's probably more economical to place the extra load on relatively inexpensive back-end servers, rather than risk causing a bottleneck on an expensive load balancer.

Still, there are a couple of advantages to making the load balancer the termination point. For starters, it means that the load balancer can inspect the contents of the HTTPS packets (because they have been decrypted). This allows enhanced firewalling and means that you can balance requests based on the contents of the packets — for example, the request URI, virtual host, the content (or presence of) cookies, and so on. With encrypted HTTPS content, many of the advanced balancing methods previously discussed simply aren't possible.

Another advantage is that some hardware load balancers (in particular, the high-end ones) include an additional processor specifically for SSL encryption/decryption. These dedicated cryptography processors can offer a huge boost in performance (hence, they are often referred to as *SSL accelerators*), but this is reflected in the cost — it may be cheaper just to invest in more powerful back-end servers.

SSL acceleration isn't just available on custom hardware, though. A number of manufacturers produce PCI cards containing SSL processors. Using these is as simple as plugging them in and loading the appropriate driver module into the kernel. These cards aren't cheap, though, and, again, there's the suspicion that it may be just as economical to invest in a faster motherboard CPU. Still, for a PC acting as a load balancer and SSL endpoint, these cards are certainly worth looking into.

Security

Although security isn't a primary concern in this book, it's worth noting that software load balancers add an additional layer of security to the network by hiding the back-end web servers from the Internet. Because all requests to back-end servers must first go past the balancer, they also provide the capability to filter out unwanted requests (for example, /phpmyadmin/, /admin/) or limit them to authenticated users only. Load balancers can also help to protect against SYN floods (DoS attacks) because they pass traffic only on to a back-end server after a full TCP connection has been set up with the client.

Traffic Shaping

One interesting possibility with a load balancer is to prioritize certain types of traffic. You can attempt to improve caching by hashing to ensure that the same request goes to the same back-end server each time. With traffic/rate shaping, you could give priority treatment to certain IP blocks or requests.

For example, you could send all requests for a reports-generating script to a particular server. Requests may end up being queued on this server (because of the intensive, long-running nature of the report-generating script), but end users will probably be okay with waiting longer for this kind of request, and it stops spikes on the rest of your back-end servers.

Using Multiple Back-End Servers

One advantage of using Nginx and Apache side by side is that it paves the way for a multiserver setup with more than one back end, and even includes its own load-balancing proxy (Nginx), as shown in Figure 7-4.

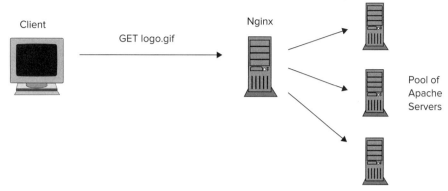

FIGURE 7-4

Nginx can serve the following three roles here:

➤ Nginx acts solely as a load-balancing proxy, forwarding all requests to an Apache back end.

➤ Nginx forwards requests for dynamic content to Apache and serves static resources.

➤ Nginx forwards all requests to Apache (including static resources) but also acts as a cache for static and/or dynamic content.

Having Nginx forward requests for dynamic content to Apache (and serving static content) is generally the most optimal. You could even combine it with elements of the third option so that FastCGI responses are cached. You then end up with Nginx acting as a reverse proxying, load-balancing, static file serving, dynamic request cache — quite a mouthful.

Nginx as a Load-Balancing Proxy

The key to load balancing with Nginx is the upstream module compiled in by default. Rather than passing an IP:port to proxy_pass, use the upstream directive to define a pool of back-end servers; then pass the name that you've assigned to this pool to proxy_pass, as shown here:

```
upstream apachepool  {
  server 192.168.0.100 weight=5;
  server 192.168.0.101 weight=10;
  server 192.168.0.102 weight=10;
}

server {
  location / {
    proxy_pass  http://apachepool;
  }
}
```

This code example creates an upstream named apachepool and assigns three servers to it. (Port 80 is assumed by default.) The first server is given a lower weight to illustrate how a mixture of hardware power can be used.

Nginx can balance requests across these three servers using the weighting given. (If none is given, each server is considered equal.) If a back-end server is down, Nginx moves on to the next one.

It's usual to want more control over this process, and, as always, Nginx does not disappoint. The `server` directive accepts the following additional parameters that can be used to fine-tune behavior:

➤ `max_fails` — This is the number of times a back-end server can fail before Nginx considers it to be "down." By default, a timeout or connection error is considered a failure. The default for `max_fails` is 1.

➤ `fail_timeout` — This is the time frame for `max_fails`. If more than the specified `max_fails` occur during this time, the server is considered "down," and Nginx moves on to the next one. The default is 10 seconds.

When a server is marked as "down" by Nginx, how long does it stay "down"? This value is also defined by `fail_timeout`. So, with `max_fails=3` and `fail_timeout=15`, a server will be considered "down" if more than 3 requests fail within the space of 15 seconds. When this happens, the server will be temporarily removed from the pool for a further 15 seconds.

`Proxy_next_upstream` can be used to control exactly what it means for a server to be "down." The default is for just transmission errors (timeouts, errors sending requests/reading responses) to trigger a fail, but you can extend this to include specific HTTP status codes. In the following example, this is specified, for example, if the back-end server returns a `500 Internal Server Error`:

```
proxy_next_upstream error timeout http_500
```

Nginx's default load-balancing logic is far from perfect, though. It uses a round-robin approach, so, if all servers have the same weight, it simply cycles through them. This approach fails to take into account the cost of serving each request.

For example, generating a report might take 10 seconds, whereas generating the index page might take only 0.2 second. Consider what happens with a pool of three servers if a hit on the report-generating page is received, followed by five hits on the index page:

1. Nginx passes the report-generating page request to the first server in the pool.

2. The first index page request is passed to the second server.

3. The second index page request is passed to the third server.

4. The fourth index page request is passed to the first server again, even though it is still struggling with generating the report.

5. The fifth index page request is passed to the second server.

Clearly, step 4 is not optimal — it's preferable for the first server to be skipped because the other two are sitting idle. The third-party module (so you need to compile it in) `upstream_fair` solves this problem. It keeps tracks of how many requests are currently served by each back-end server and routes requests to the server with the least load.

Actually, `upstream_fair` uses a "weighted least-connection round-robin" algorithm. So, although the load on each back-end server is the major factor, it also takes into account the weighting of each server and uses the round-robin approach when two servers are otherwise equal. In addition, `upstream_fair` has a number of options for specialist situations (such as the capability to disable the round robin). The module is available from `http://nginx.localdomain.pl/wiki/UpstreamFair`.

It's likely that you'll be using some form of PHP opcode cache on each FastCGI back-end server. This is a topic discussed in a lot more depth in Chapter 12. But if you're unfamiliar with such caches, all you need to know for now is that they can improve performance by providing partial caching of PHP code. Naturally, it's rather inefficient if each cache is duplicating data stored in the caches of other FastCGI nodes, and it's equally poor if a given FastCGI server does not have in its cache elements the request it is currently handling while its neighbor does.

Clearly, neither of the load-balancing options examined thus far help here, but there are a couple of possible solutions.

The `upstream_fair` supports an option to load balance based on a hash of the client's IP address. (Actually, it uses the first three octets from the IP, such as 192.168.5.x.) So, a client will always be served by the same back-end server (unless the server is "down," in which case the next available server is used).

This isn't a great help for efficient opcode caching, but it can be used for *session affinity* (also known as *sticky sessions*) to ensure that session data (which is often stored in a file on the back-end server) isn't lost between requests.

> **NOTE** *There are lots of other ways to deal with the problem of session affinity, such as storing in a database (which can be a performance bottleneck), storing all client-side data in cookies (which can be insecure), or using a network filesystem (for example, an NFS partition) to hold the session files. One favorite is* memcache, *though. You learn more about* memcache *in Chapter 10.*
>
> *HTML5 also introduced* sessionStorage *and* localStorage, *which are features that allow the client to store data locally. As with cookies, however, there is the potential for the user to tamper with this data, and you should treat it accordingly.*

You can enable IP hashing like so:

```
upstream apachepool  {
  ip_hash;
  server 192.168.0.100 weight=5;
  server 192.168.0.101 weight=10;
  server 192.168.0.102 weight=10;
}
```

Another solution is the third-party Upstream Hash module (`ngx_http_upstream_hash_module`), which performs hashing based on environmental variables. The possibilities here are endless. If you hash based on the request URI, you can ensure that requests for the same dynamic content always go to the same server, which is the most efficient in terms of utilizing opcode caches.

```
upstream apachepool  {
  hash $request_uri;
  server 192.168.0.100;
  server 192.168.0.101;
  server 192.168.0.102;
}
```

> **NOTE** *You can't use weighting when using Upstream Hash.*

You can even hash a combination of the request URI and client IP address to ensure a high hit rate on your opcode caches while preserving session affinity, as shown here:

```
hash $request_uri$http_remote_addr;
```

Just how useful is balancing based on a URL, though? It certainly increases the efficiency of your PHP opcode caches, but this may offer only a minor performance gain, and you lose out on the capability to distribute requests based on the load on each back-end server. Session affinity is probably an issue that can be left out of the equation for the moment because there are better solutions (for example, storing session data globally in memcache). Ultimately, you should be aware of both possibilities, but balancing based on load is probably the superior solution overall.

Nginx as a Load Balancer and Static File Server

An improvement on this model is to have Nginx handle static files, taking weight off the back-end servers (which are more suited for handling dynamic content than serving static files). Adding this is simple. You just define a location before your `location /` catch-all, as shown here:

```
location ~ ^/(images|javascript|js|css|media|static)/ {
    root /var/www/html/;
    expires 30d;
}
location / {
    proxy_pass  http://apachepool;
}
```

Nginx as a Load Balancer and Cache

A third option is to let Apache continue to serve static resources but implement caching of them in Nginx to reduce (or even eliminate) the need to bother Apache. The end result isn't much different from the previously discussed model (Nginx as a load balancer and static file server), but it may be more appropriate in certain situations. Most of the time, though, having the static resources on a centralized server (the Nginx load balancer) rather than distributed across each back-end server is the more sensible solution.

Nginx as a Load Balancer, Static File Server, and Dynamic Content Cache

With this final option, Nginx serves static files locally and load balances requests for dynamic content across a pool of back-end servers. But it also caches the (dynamic) responses from the back-end servers, further cutting down on traffic to them. The caching of FastCGI has been previously discussed.

Eliminating Apache

The topologies examined thus far have clung on to Apache as a back-end server for dynamic content. But as you've already seen, Nginx plus FastCGI can be just as good of a replacement — and when it comes to multiserver setups, it can even be a better option because FastCGI can load balance across multiple back-end servers.

Figure 7-5 shows a simple layout in which a single Nginx server handles dynamic content via FastCGI, balancing the load across a pool of FastCGI back-end servers.

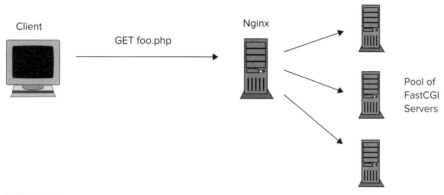

FIGURE 7-5

You've already seen how to use FastCGI for handling dynamic content. Implementing load balancing into this is actually rather simple. You use the `upstream` module, as shown here:

```
upstream phppool  {
  server 192.168.0.100:9000 weight=5;
  server 192.168.0.101:9000 weight=10;
  server 192.168.0.102:9000 weight=10;
}

location ~ \.php$ {
  include /etc/nginx/fcgi_params.conf;
  fastcgi_pass  phppool;
}
```

Now, you just need to ensure that your FastCGI daemon is listening on the appropriate interface and port on each host. As before, you can use weighting, `max_fails`, `fail_timeout`, and `proxy_next_upstream` to control how load is spread across these back-end servers, and what happens when a node goes down.

HAProxy

Nginx already seems to work quite well as a load balancer (and optionally a cache, too), but there are plenty of alternatives. One of the most popular is HAProxy, a fast balancer that also implements high-availability features. Although HAProxy does not offer caching, benchmarks usually show it to be a little faster than Nginx (in terms of the number of connections per second it can handle), and it has a wealth of extra features. Let's take a look at HAProxy configuration options before looking at topologies involving `HAProxy` and Nginx.

> **NOTE** *HAProxy is known to run on Linux (this being the favored), Solaris, FreeBSD, and OpenBSD, but other platforms are not supported.*

Configuration

The HAProxy configuration (usually `/etc/haproxy/haproxy.cfg`) file generally consists of three sections:

> ➤ `global` — This is where global parameters (mostly relating to HAProxy) are defined.

> ➤ `defaults` — This contains options specific to the proxying method (for example, connection timeouts).

> ➤ `listen` — This is a block defining the interface/ports on which to listen and the back-end servers to proxy to.

You can dispense with the `defaults` block and place its directives directly inside a `listen` block, and you can write the `listen` blocks in a more verbose form. But the three-section approach is preferred. A simple configuration file might be as brief as the following:

```
global
    daemon
    maxconn 256

defaults
    mode http
    timeout connect 5000ms

listen mybackends
    bind *:80
    server server1 192.0.0.101:80 maxconn 16
    server server2 192.0.0.102:80 maxconn 16
```

This tells HAProxy to run as a daemon allowing a maximum of 256 connections. The `defaults` section defines the protocol as HTTP (HAProxy can be used to balance many protocols), and a connection timeout of 5 seconds. Finally, this instructs the proxy to listen on port 80/TCP on all interfaces and to load balance across two back-end servers (192.168.0.101 and 192.168.0.102). Let's take a more detailed look at the global configuration options.

> **NOTE** *Incidentally, most of the work carried out by HAProxy goes on in kernel space, rather than user space. (By its author's observations, approximately 95 percent of the time is spent in the kernel.) As such, tuning the operating system/ kernel has a much greater impact on performance than application-level settings.*

Global

The `global` section contains the majority of the performance-related options for HAProxy. But remember that it runs on many platforms, and some of these options (for example, event polling on BSD systems) may not be relevant. You can find a full list of options in the documentation at `http://haproxy.1wt.eu/download/1.4/doc/configuration.txt`.

> **NOTE** *Speaking of event polling, on Linux, HAProxy defaults to speculative event polling, and there isn't usually a good reason to stray from this default.*

One potential gotcha is the `nbproc` option, which controls how many processes to spawn. It's tempting to see this as analogous to `worker_processes` for Nginx, and set it to equal the number of CPU cores on the system. This isn't recommended, though.

As you've already seen, the vast majority of the processing carried out by HAProxy is at the kernel level — and the kernel is multithreaded, so it makes good use of multiple cores. Increasing the number of userland processes isn't going to help here. If anything, performance will be reduced because there is now the additional overhead of the worker processes communicating with each other over shared memory.

`nbproc` was introduced to only work around limits on the number of file descriptors an individual process could create on some operating systems. This isn't (or at least, doesn't have to be) an issue on Linux. Thus, `nbcproc` can be left to the default of `1`.

TCP splicing is a relatively new feature of the Linux kernel, which can reduce CPU overhead on systems that are acting as a proxy. Some versions of the 2.6 kernel have bugs in their implementation, though, and HAProxy offers the capability to disable splicing via the `nosplice` option. Buggy splicing can be difficult to diagnose, so unless you are sure that the kernel you are running is not affected (or cannot afford to sacrifice the reduction in CPU usage), or are not using Linux, it's probably safest to turn splicing off.

`maxconn` sets the maximum number of concurrent connections that HAProxy will accept. You can afford to set this relatively high because HAProxy can queue connections to the back-end servers — this is governed by the `maxconn` setting in the `listen` section(s).

The remaining global performance options all take the form `tune.xxx <number>` and shouldn't need changing from their defaults. In brief, they are as follows:

➤ `tune.bufsize` — This is the per-request buffer size. Lowering this value will allow more sessions to co-exist in memory but will break requests with large amounts of data in the HTTP header.

➤ `tune.chksize` — This is the size of the buffer to use when performing string matching on HTTP headers. Setting this too low may cause matches to be missed; setting it too high wastes memory. It's best for performance not to be in the situation of needing to parse potentially large HTTP headers anyway.

➤ `tune.maxaccept` — This option is mostly for use in multiprocess mode (that is, when `nbproc` is greater than 1) to ensure a fair distribution of requests across each process. It sets the maximum number of requests that a single process will accept in one batch.

➤ `tune.maxpollevents` — This controls the number of events that will be processed in each call to the polling system. The HAProxy documentation notes that lowering this value tends to cause a small reduction in latency (at the expense of extra bandwidth), whereas increasing it has the opposite effect. Either way, this option is usually set automatically, and there shouldn't be a need to change it.

➤ `tune.maxrewrite` — Related to `bufsize`, this is the size of the buffer used when rewriting headers (for example, inserting cookies). If this value is too low, any particularly large request won't fit fully. If it is too high, you waste memory. The suggested starting point is `1024`.

➤ `tune.rcvbuf.client`, `tune.rcvbuf.server`, `tune.sndbuf.client`, and `tune`
`.sndbuf.server` — These final four options tune the kernel socket buffer size for sending and receiving on both the client and server sides. Normally, these will be set automatically by HAProxy, based on the amount of system memory. But it can occasionally be useful to lower these to save memory (at the expense of an increase in CPU usage).

> **NOTE** *Unless you are absolutely sure that there is a need to change any of these values, it is strongly recommended to leave them alone.*

defaults

Whereas the `global` section lets you configure global options for HAProxy, the `defaults` section specifically deals with options for the chosen proxy mode. Because you're dealing only with HTTP, this distinction may seem unimportant. But it makes perfect sense if HAProxy is used as a load balancer for several protocols at once.

Currently, three proxy modes are supported: `tcp`, `http`, and `health`. The latter is for performing health checks on servers, so let's concentrate on the first two for the moment.

With `tcp` mode, HAProxy operates at the TCP level (OSI Layer 4 — see Chapter 1 for an overview of the OSI model) only. It forwards traffic between client and server without caring (or even understanding) the higher-level HTTP protocol. This offers the lowest latency but is the least flexible because it cannot balance based on HTTP content.

In `http` mode, HAProxy acts on OSI Layer 4 (TCP) and Layer 7 (HTTP). This gives HAProxy the power to inspect and rewrite HTTP packets, allowing for more advanced load balancing. But it also means more work, so there is an increase in latency, as well as CPU and memory usage. Usually, these overheads aren't significant, and the advantages of having a Layer 7-aware proxy more than make up for them.

Timeouts

The `default` section is also the home for setting the various timeout options. All these options accept a numeric value and can optionally include a `units` suffix (for example, `10s`). If no units are given, milliseconds are assumed. Following are the timeout options:

➤ `timeout check` — When performing health checks on servers, this option determines how long HAProxy should wait until it decides a back-end server is timing out. Health checks should be a lot faster to run than normal HTTP queries, so you can set this quite low, unless the back-end servers are on a high-latency link.

➤ `timeout client` — This is the timeout period when communicating with clients.

➤ `timeout connect` — This is the timeout when HAProxy is attempting to establish a connection to a back-end server. Although you'd usually expect back-end servers on a local area network (LAN) to respond within, say, 100 milliseconds, it's advisable to set this option to a few seconds to accommodate the occasional dropped packet or server spike. The default is no timeout, but this should be avoided because it has the potential to cause a buildup of half-open connections.

➤ `timeout http-keep-alive` — When the back-end servers use `Keep Alive`, HAProxy must keep the connection open following the first request and response, in case the client wants to send further requests. This option defines for how long the connection will be allowed to remain open without the client issuing any requests. If unset, the `timeout http-request` is used.

➤ `timeout http-request` — It's often quite easy to perform denial-of-service (DoS) attacks on heavy web servers like Apache by opening hundreds of connections, but not sending any data (or sending data at a slow rate — say, one character per minute). This option requires that the HTTP request headers have been fully sent by the client within this period of time. It doesn't apply to the request body, unfortunately, because `POST` data could potentially take much longer to send. Generally, a value of a few seconds is best, and if not set, the value of `timeout client` will be used.

➤ `timeout queue` — HAProxy can be configured to limit the maximum number of concurrent requests it sends to a back-end server (to avoid overloading it). When this limit is reached, requests are queued in HAProxy, and this option defines how long an item may remain in the queue before HAProxy throws a `503 Service Unavailable` error. If no value is set, `timeout connect` is used.

➤ `timeout server` — Whereas `timeout client` deals with timeouts when communicating with the clients, this option governs the timeout period when waiting for a back-end server to acknowledge a request or send a response. Obviously, the time taken for the back-end server to process the request is the major delay here, so this value should be set sufficiently large.

Cookies and Session Affinity

As mentioned earlier, cookies can be used to ensure session affinity, and (unlike IP address hashing) these work even if the client is behind a proxy farm that causes the IP address to change from one request to the next.

In HAProxy, the `appsession` option can be used to set session affinity based on the presence of a particular cookie (for example, `PHPSESSID`). When HAProxy sees a server set the cookie, it stores the cookie's contents and the server ID in a lookup table. If HAProxy subsequently sees a client issue a request with the cookie in the headers, it checks the lookup table and directs the request to the appropriate server.

The full syntax for `appsession` is as follows:

```
appsession <cookie name> len <length> timeout <lifetime> [request-learn]
```

Following are the options used:

➤ `Len` is the number of characters (starting at the beginning) of the cookie to store in the lookup table. Using this option helps to keep the size of the table down but is only practical if the cookie can be uniquely identified by these characters.

➤ The `timeout` value specifies how long before unused cookie entries are removed from the table, again helping to reduce memory usage.

➤ When `request-learn` is set, HAProxy attempts to learn client-server associations if it spots the cookie in a client request, but does not have an entry for it in the lookup table. This improves reliability in situations in which the cookie entry has been expired from the lookup table.

Although this sticky behavior is desirable for requests for dynamic content, it's usually unnecessary if the client is requesting a static resource. But the cookie would usually be sent with these static requests as well (unless the cookie path or domain had been carefully set to exclude them), and, hence, they would all go to the same back-end server. To stop such behavior, HAProxy offers the `ignore_persist` option, which enables the cookie to be ignored in certain user-defined situations — for example on requests for files in a particular directory or with a particular extension.

Access Control Lists

These user-defined situations are implemented as Access Control Lists (ACLs), and a thorough examination could easily fill the next dozen pages exploring the intricacies of HAProxy's implementation of them. Briefly, though, you would define an ACL using the `acl` keyword, like so:

```
acl static_resources path_end .gif .png .jpg .css .js .ico .txt
```

It should be apparent that this defines an ACL named `static_resources`, which applies when the path of the request ends in any of the extensions listed. You can subsequently use this ACL with `ignore-persist`, as shown here:

```
Ignore-persist if static_resources
```

This only scrapes the surface of what is possible with ACLs, though. For example, you could balance dynamic requests across a pool of heavy back-end servers such as Apache plus mod_xxx, while static requests are sent to a lightweight Nginx instance. The HAProxy documentation contains more information, along with plenty of useful examples.

Connection Handling and Keep Alive

Another significant part of the HAProxy `defaults` configuration is the handling of connections, particularly for `Keep Alive`. You can use these options to override the behavior of back-end web servers and correct bad protocol implementations. Hopefully, you won't need any of these, but in brief they are as follows:

➤ `option httpclose` — This adds a `'Connection: close'` header to the request and response, if one does not already exist. This effectively prevents `Keep Alive`, even if the back-end servers support it.

➤ `option forceclose` — This closes the connection as soon as the server has responded. This is a faster (but less graceful) way to close the connection than `option httpclose`, and, naturally, it also prevents the use of `Keep Alive`.

➤ `option http-pretend-keepalive` — If either of the previous two options are set, HAProxy ends up adding a `'Connection: close'` header to the request sent to the back-end server. With some web servers, this causes them not to use chunked encoding in responses. With `http-pretend-keepalive`, the server will think that a persistent connection is used, eliminating this behavior.

listen

Let's now take a look at the heart of the configuration — the `listen` section — the part that specifies your back-end servers and how to balance across them. An example shows that the syntax isn't a million miles away from that of Nginx, and is easy to pick up.

Let's start by defining the IP(s) and port(s) on which the proxy should listen:

```
bind 192.168.0.10:80
```

The `balance` keyword is used to specify the load-balancing method to use; although, this applies only to nonpersistent connections — session affinity takes precedence where applicable. Currently, the following balancing methods are available:

➤ `static-rr` — This uses a weighted round-robin approach — something you've already learned about in detail.

➤ `roundrobin` — This offers an improvement over static round-robin in that weightings are dynamic and can be adjusted in real time by HAProxy. One use for this is so-called *slow starts*, in which a server that had previously been marked as offline is brought back slowly into the pool, rather than bombarding it with connections when it comes back online. This method uses slightly more CPU than the `static-rr` method.

➤ `leastconn` — Here, HAProxy balances based on the number of existing connections to each back end server and falls back to a round-robin if several servers have the same number of connections. Because the HTTP requests are generally short-lived, the number of connections to a back-end server can vary dramatically in a short period of time. As such, this isn't a good balancing method for web traffic; although it is excellent for long-running requests such as a POP3 session.

➤ `source` — This uses hashing of the client's IP address, resulting in stickiness — a given client will always be directed to the same back-end server provided the number of back-end servers remains the same. Cookies are usually a better way to achieve session affinity, but this method can be used if HAProxy runs in TCP mode (rather than HTTP mode) or, for other reasons such as to stop cookies from being used (for example, when clients refuse cookies).

➤ `uri` — This balances based on the request URI (excluding any query string). As previously discussed, this improves cache hits and efficiency (if caching is used) because requests for the same resource always go to the same back-end server. But it doesn't give a particularly even spread of requests across the back-end servers.

➤ `url_param` — Similar to the `uri` method, this time HAProxy searches the query string for a particular parameter (hashes) and balances on this. This can be used for session affinity in situations in which a unique identifier is passed from page to page in the query string. (Although it can also be set to search `POST` data.)

➤ `hdr(name)` — This method balances based on the content of the header given (or falls back on round-robin if the header is not present). This is more of a specialist method, but possible uses would be for balancing based on vhost, the client's country of origin, or even if the client supports `Keep Alive` or `gzip` compression.

➤ `rdp-cookie` — Remote Desktop Protocol (RDP) is used for ensuring that RDP sessions are correctly routed to the back-end servers when HAProxy runs in TCP mode, which is not a concern for this discussion.

Following are a few examples:

```
balance static round-robin
balance url_param uid
balance hdr(Accept-Encoding) gzip
```

It's interesting to note that cookie-based balancing doesn't appear in this list. In fact, you enable this separately (if wanted), using the `cookie` option. You still set a balance method, though, which will be used if the cookie isn't present.

Aside from the name of the cookie to use, you must also tell HAProxy whether it will be using an existing cookie (that is, one generated by the web application), or adding a cookie of its own by using either `rewrite` (using existing cookie) or `insert` (add cookie). In most situations, it is preferable to insert a cookie to cause minimal interference to the web application, as shown here:

```
cookie SERVERID insert
```

This is closely related (but not identical) to the `appsession` option discussed earlier. With `appsession`, HAProxy maps `cookie` to the back-end server using an internal lookup table. With `cookie`, HAProxy actually creates or modifies cookies.

Finally, your list of back-end servers is specified as a name followed by an address/port, and optional additional arguments. Thus, your whole `listen` block can be as simple as this:

```
bind 192.168.0.10:80
balance round-robin
server server1 192.168.0.100:80
server server2 192.168.0.101:80
server server3 192.168.0.102:80
```

This balances across three back-end servers using the round-robin method.

The real fun comes with the extra options available because these enable you to set up weighting, connection queuing, health-checking, and slow starts. Let's take a look at the most interesting options.

weight <integer>

This option takes an integer value between zero and 256 specifying the relative weight of the server. Following is an example:

```
server server1 192.168.0.100:80 weight 50
server server2 192.168.0.101:80 weight 50
server server3 192.168.0.102:80 weight 100
```

In this situation, `server3` should receive approximately one-half of the total traffic, and `server1` and `server2` approximately one-quarter each.

maxconn <integer>

This defines the maximum number of concurrent connections that HAProxy allows the server to receive. Any further connections to this server will be queued. This can be useful to prevent a server from being overloaded with connections; although `MaxClients` (or equivalent) should already have been prudently set on the server to prevent overloading. Still, you can use this option as an additional safety check, or for some non-HTTP services that may not offer the capability to limit concurrency.

maxqueue <integer>

If `maxconn` is reached, connections will be queued, and this option defines the maximum size of the queue. The default is zero (unlimited), but there is a case for setting it to a finite value. If the queue fills up, requests will be sent to another server in the pool, and although this will break any session affinity, it will probably offer the best response time for the client.

It's worth thinking about situations in which `maxconn` and `maxqueue` might be high when deciding on suitable values. If the server pool is under high load, in general, it's inevitable that connection queuing needs to take place, and you need to set the queue high enough that clients won't be turned away too quickly.

However, if queuing starts to happen on an individual server, it could be that the server is locked in a downward spiral. (Perhaps the requests that it handles are particularly intensive, or an unrelated process is hogging resources.) In this case, there's a good chance that queued requests will never be processed. Hence, it may be better to keep the queue small, forcing the requests to go to other servers. You'll lose your session affinity, but at least the request will get a response.

> **NOTE** *HAProxy can still take servers out of the pool if they are completely unresponsive. This is just to guard against situations in which a server enters into a downward spiral.*

check

At its most basic level, health checking consists of HAProxy attempting to establish a TCP connection to a back-end server on the IP address and port that it is balanced to. Thus, on web servers, the check would (probably) be on TCP/80, as shown here:

```
server server1 192.168.0.100:80 weight 50 check
```

Checking is set on a per-server basis, giving you the option to disable it on certain back-end servers if necessary.

Of course, simply attempting to create a TCP connection to the back-end service is no guarantee that things are running perfectly, and HAProxy offers enhanced checking for a number of protocols: HTTP, SMTP, MySQL, and SSL. The syntax is as follows:

```
option httpchk
option httpchk <uri>
option httpchk <method> <uri>
```

The default is to send an OPTIONS request, which is low on overhead and should be a good indication of the web server's sanity. HAProxy treats a 2xx or 3xx response as success, and anything else as a fail.

inter

The time period between health checks is governed by the inter parameter to server, and defaults to 2,000 milliseconds. To not flood the network with packets, checks are automatically staggered a little. But you can increase this further (if wanted) using spread-checks. This global parameter takes a percentage value between 0 and 50 that specifies the degree of randomness in the checking time. Thus, with a check interval of 2,000 milliseconds on a server and a spread-checks value of 10 percent, health checks would take place at intervals between 1,800 and 2,200 milliseconds. Following is an example:

```
spread-checks 20
server server1 192.168.0.100:80 weight 50 check inter 2000
```

fall <integer>

By default, a health check must fail three times in a row before HAProxy flags the server as "down," but this can be overridden using the fall option, as shown here:

```
server server1 192.168.0.100:80 weight 50 check inter 2000 fall 5
```

Be wary of setting this too low. Taking a server out of the pool puts additional strain on the remaining machines, which, in turn, could cause them to fail. So, you must avoid being too trigger-happy here. Certainly, a value of 1 would introduce the possibility of too many false positives.

rise <integer>

Even when a server has been marked as "down," HAProxy still sends health checks, and this option defines how many consecutive successful checks are needed for the server to be deemed "alive" again. The default is 2.

slowstart <integer>

When HAProxy does detect that a back-end server has come back to life, it can be advantageous not to immediately start bombarding it with connections. For web servers like Apache, a gradual increase in the number of requests gives time for additional processes to be forked without causing spikes in CPU and disk I/O. Even for web servers that don't operate on a process-per-request model, slow starts can be used if there's a danger of the server immediately falling down as soon as it has come back up.

This option takes a time period (by default, in milliseconds) during which the weight of the back-end server will move from 0 percent to 100 percent of its configured value. In addition, maxconn moves from 0 percent to 100 percent during this time, too.

In most situations, slowstart isn't essential; although a smallish value (say a couple of seconds) can reduce latency in handling requests if the back-end server must spawn new children to handle each request. Following is an example:

```
server server1 192.168.0.100:80 weight 50 check inter 2000 slowstart 2000
```

observe <mode>

As an alternative to proactively sending out health checks, HAProxy can assess server health by monitoring the traffic already flowing from the server. For example, if a back-end server starts generating 5xx error codes in response to client requests, HAPRoxy can spot this and act on it.

Two observation modes are support: layer4 and layer7. In layer4 mode, HAProxy simply looks at the TCP packet level — are TCP connections to the back-end failing? In layer7 mode, HAProxy has the power to analyze HTTP responses and detect HTTP error codes, too.

There are dangers to relying on passive health checking. For example, an HTTP error code may not mean the whole server is "down." It may even be down because of a badly behaved client. As a result, you should use dedicated health checking, but if you'd like to try passive checking, there are more details in the HAProxy documentation.

SUMMARY

Although Apache is a great multipurpose web server, it doesn't cope well with high levels of concurrency, especially when the prefork MPM is used. Nginx provides an excellent high-performance alternative, and although using PHP with Nginx is a little trickier, the end result is a more powerful and flexible setup. When you have outgrown a single-server setup, Nginx makes it easy to balance traffic across multiple back-end servers.

Despite that, HAProxy has the edge over Nginx when it comes to load balancing. It offers health monitoring of the back-end servers and provides greater control over how traffic is balanced across them. Using HAProxy as a load balancer with several Nginx and FastCGI back-end servers results in a powerful and robust setup.

Web servers are naturally at the heart of a website's back-end setup, but database systems also play a highly important part in many infrastructures. MySQL is one of the most popular database solutions in the open source world, and will be covered in detail over the next two chapters. In Chapter 9, you discover the intricacies of MySQL replication and load balancing. But before that, let's see how single-server MySQL setups can be tuned for blistering performance, which is the focus of the discussion in Chapter 8.

8

Tuning MySQL

WHAT'S IN THIS CHAPTER?

➤ Getting to know the myriad of performance tuning options available in MySQL

➤ Writing efficient SQL queries, and spotting bottlenecks in existing queries

➤ Getting the most out of the MySQL query cache

➤ Discovering the latest advances in MyISAM and InnoDB

As a relative newcomer on the scene (with the first release in 1995), MySQL has quickly become the *de facto* relational database management system (RDBMS) for Linux, and one of the most popular for Windows and UNIX. Despite lacking some of the more advanced features found in other RDBMSs (this is gradually changing, but things like stored procedures and transactions are still relatively new additions), MySQL is lightweight, and has a good reputation for speed, making it an excellent choice for general-purpose web development.

Despite this reputation for speed, there is typically still a huge scope for optimization, both in the configuration of the MySQL server, and in queries themselves. This chapter familiarizes you with the performance aspects of MySQL.

This chapter begins by examining how the main storage engines differ, and the impact that this has on performance. After looking at general MySQL tuning issues, this chapter discusses tuning of the two most popular engines: MyISAM and InnoDB. After a discussion of MySQL's query caching capabilities, this chapter concludes with tips on how to write more efficient SQL queries, and how to debug slow-running queries.

> **NOTE** *The terms* cache *and* buffer, *and* index *and* key *are often used interchangeably throughout the MySQL community. Thus,* index buffer *means the same as* index cache, key cache, *or* key buffer. *The discussions in this book also use the terms interchangeably — partly for variety, and partly because they reflect real-world usage.*

LOOKING INSIDE MYSQL

MySQL's internal structure can be divided into several logical sections, and, in most cases, each of them can be tuned. Figure 8-1 shows the major components of MySQL.

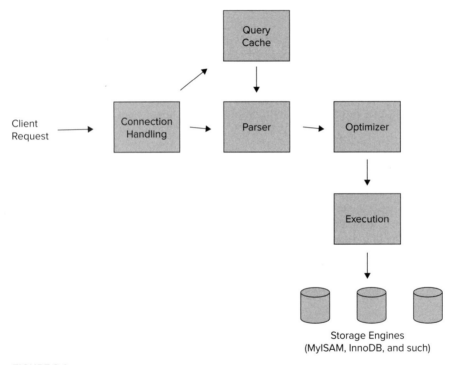

FIGURE 8-1

At the core is the *parser*, whose job it is to parse the SQL statement issued by the client, and check the syntax. At this point, the parser may pass the query to the *query cache* in an attempt to find an already cached response to the query, or send it straight to the optimizer. The *optimizer* decides on the best (most efficient) way to execute the query and then passes it to the *execution engine*. Before a request gets this far, though, the *connection handling layer* deals with matters such as authentication and threading.

Storage engines are a separate logical entity and are modular in nature. The rest of the internal structure of MySQL doesn't need to know the internal details of how the storage engines store the data, only a set of standard methods for interacting with them. As a result, storage engines can be radically different in how they manage things like the physical storage of data, indexing, and locking.

Most tuning is performed through the MySQL configuration file, `my.cnf`, which usually resides in `/etc` or `/etc/mysql/` on Linux and UNIX. Unfortunately, MySQL doesn't have a reload option, so if any changes are made in `my.cnf`, you must perform a restart to force MySQL to re-read the configuration.

> **NOTE** *Many MySQL* `init` *scripts offer a reload option, which, in turn, runs* `mysqladmin reload`. *However, this reloads only the* `grants` *table. Be sure to perform a full stop and start after making changes to* `my.cnf`.

As an alternative, global variables (those appearing in `my.cnf`) can also be set at the MySQL command-line interface (CLI) by users with privileged rights. The syntax is as follows:

```
SET variable-name=value;
```

Global variables set in this way are reset (to the values in `my.cnf`) upon a server restart, so permanent changes should go in the configuration file. However, as a means to make a quick change without having to restart MySQL, global variables used in this manner are ideal.

UNDERSTANDING THE STORAGE ENGINES

As previously mentioned, the storage engine is a distinct part of MySQL, and you are free to use any one of a number of built-in engines (or even write your own!). Some are general-purpose engines, whereas others are designed for a specific purpose. Each engine has its own strengths and weaknesses. This section looks at performance aspects associated with the two main engines (`MyISAM` and `InnoDB`), and covers some of the less common engines that are of particular interest when considering performance.

MyISAM

Up until MySQL version 5.5, `MyISAM` was the default engine and is probably still the most widely used. Conventional wisdom has it that `MyISAM` is faster (whatever you choose that to mean) than its main rival, `InnoDB`, but this isn't always the case. `MyISAM` does have a reputation for speed, however, particularly with `SELECT` queriesl

The main disadvantage of `MyISAM` from a performance point of view is that it uses table-level locking for write queries. That is, if a `DELETE`, `INSERT`, or `UPDATE` query is being executed, the whole table is locked for the duration of the query. During this time, all other queries on the table (including `SELECT`s) must wait.

This can be a particular problem on interactive sites such as forums or social networking where there is a higher ratio of writing to reading. (The traditional maxim was that databases used for websites spend approximately 90 percent of their time handling read queries, and 10 percent handling write queries. But, as the web has become more interactive, this gap has lessened a little, and it can vary a lot from site to site.). As you'll see later in this chapter in the section, "Tuning MyISAM," this problem can be mitigated by using concurrent inserts, a `MyISAM` feature that allows `INSERT` queries to run without blocking `SELECT` queries.

Although it's obvious that slow-running write queries can cause problems when table-level locking is in force, slow-running `SELECT` statements can also affect performance because any write queries need to wait for these to finish before they can acquire a write lock.

The `MyISAM` engine also enables tables to be packed using the `myisampack` tool. Packed tables are compressed on a row-by-row basis and are typically half the size of uncompressed `MyISAM` tables. This makes accessing data a little faster (even when the cost of uncompressing is factored in because there is less data to be read from disk), but such tables are read-only, which limits their usefulness somewhat. Still, if you have a table with data that is rarely changed, the performance gain from packing it may make up for the manual intervention involved in unpacking, updating, repacking, and re-indexing.

Another popular reason for using MyISAM is its support for full-text searching — a feature not offered by any of the other stock storage engines. As you'll see in the next chapter, however, full-text searches can cause a significant performance hit, and busy sites tend to opt for alternative solutions.

InnoDB

`InnoDB`'s support for transactions is often the main reason why developers move away from `MyISAM` (which has no support for them). But for a long time, it suffered a reputation for being slower than `MyISAM` (a reputation that was not always deserved) and was generally thought of as something of a specialist engine.

THE CONCEPT OF TRANSACTIONS

Transactions are a database concept in which several queries can be run atomically — that is, either they all run or none run. This is vital in some situations, the most commonly cited example being banking. Imagine transferring money from one user's account to another. This might consist of the following two queries:

```
UPDATE user1 SET balance=balance-100
UPDATE user2 SET balance=balance+100
```

It simply isn't acceptable for the second query to fail (perhaps because the server crashes, or the disk becomes full). Transactions guard against this by keeping a log of all actions performed, and rolling back if the entire transaction does not complete successfully.

In the last few years, things have changed. Although development of MyISAM has slowed down, there has been a lot of focus on InnoDB. Oracle's decision to make InnoDB the default engine in MySQL version 5.5 onward sent a clear signal that it is now the favored engine.

A lot has happened over the past few years. Performance issues that had dogged InnoDB on multicore machines have been resolved, support for compressed tables has been added (through the addition of a new file format), and a whole host of additional tuning options have been added. InnoDB is rapidly making MyISAM seem rather primitive. If you've looked at InnoDB in the past and discounted it, now might be the time to re-evaluate it.

Despite its reputation for being slower on lookups than MyISAM, InnoDB has always offered particularly fast lookups on primary keys. The situation with secondary keys is more complicated and is a subject that will be addressed later in this chapter in the section, "Tuning InnoDB." But by no means is it an inevitable performance killer.

InnoDB also offers significant advantages over MyISAM when it comes to locking. Whereas MyISAM must lock a whole table when issuing an UPDATE or DELETE query, InnoDB implements row-level locking. On write-heavy tables, this alone can be enough reason to use InnoDB.

Finally, it should be noted that, although InnoDB offers a lot of features, it lacks full-text support. If you require this, you'll either have to stick with MyISAM, or implement search routines outside of MySQL.

MEMORY

The MEMORY engine (also sometimes referred to by its earlier name, HEAP) is unique in that it stores the entire table in memory. This makes for fast access. Like MyISAM, it lacks support for transactions, foreign keys, and row-level locking. There are also a number of specific drawbacks that limit it from general use.

The contents of MEMORY tables do not persist across server restarts, meaning that they are only useful for holding temporary data. (Session data is the classic example.) There is also a limitation on column types, with neither blob nor text columns allowed.

The indexing method can also be problematic in some situations. The MEMORY engine supports both B-tree and hash indexes, with the latter being the default. B-trees are generally quite a bit slower than hashes, but in situations in which there are many duplicate index values, performance of hash indexes can (not will) deteriorate rapidly, and B-trees can be a better option.

The maximum size of MEMORY tables is limited by the max_heap_table_size variable, which defaults to 16 MB.

Finally, the MEMORY engine uses fixed-size rows, with the memory allocated for each row being determined by the size of the largest row. This is somewhat inefficient, and can result in a lot of wasted memory.

B-TREES AND HASH INDEXES

The MEMORY engine is the only major storage engine to offer the choice of B-tree or hashing for indexes — MyISAM and InnoDB both use B-tree only. So, which is better?

B-trees are particularly suited for large indexes where it is impractical to keep the entire structure in memory. They take into account that the majority of the tree will be held in secondary storage (that is, a hard disk), and they are designed to minimize the number of disk reads required. Because of their tree structure, B-trees make it easy to perform range searches (for example, =>, =<, BETWEEN) and prefix matching (for example, LIKE 'foo%').

Hash indexes are less flexible but are also much faster. Rather than traversing a tree structure, MySQL can go directly to the value in the table. The table structure also means that range searches aren't particularly efficient. With a B-tree, a whole branch may be returned, whereas with hash tables, the whole table must be scanned.

So, B-trees are usually a better choice for large indexes (which won't fit fully into RAM). Hash tables are faster but only for smaller indexes (they don't scale as well as B-tree), and only when performing equality tests.

ARCHIVE

In many ways, the ARCHIVE engine is similar to packed MyISAM tables, although it does support INSERTs. Both use compression to save disk space and speed up reading, and both are read-only. ARCHIVE uses zlib, and generally offers slightly better compression that packed MyISAM. However, ARCHIVE doesn't support indexing. Locking occurs at the row-level (like InnoDB), thus improving concurrency.

TUNING MYSQL

Having looked at various aspects of the MySQL internal structure, let's now concentrate on performance tuning. MySQL provides a whole host of configuration options that can impact performance. Some are specific to individual storage engines, whereas others affect MySQL as a whole. Let's start with the latter.

Table Cache

The table cache is perhaps the single most important aspect of nonengine-specific tuning but is a little more complicated than some of the other caches/buffers. Also, some minor improvements and changes to variable names were introduced in MySQL version 5.5, so be careful of online documentation written for earlier versions of the software.

The table cache improves performance by holding open tables (that is, tables that are being read/ written by a MySQL process via a file handle) in memory, eliminating the overhead involved in opening them. (This also involves a write because the table header must be modified each time the table is opened. The header of the table contains a counter that keeps track of how many open file handles there are for the table.) Generally, it's a good idea to strive for all tables being held in the cache, but in some situations, this is not possible.

If the cache becomes full, and a client attempts to access a table not in the cache, a Least Recently Used (LRU) algorithm is used to remove (that is, close and write back to disk) an old cache entry. Running FLUSH TABLES causes all tables in the cache to be removed.

table_open_cache

The primary configuration option for the table cache is table_open_cache (previously known as just table_cache), which controls the maximum number of tables the cache can hold.

Simply setting this variable to the total number of tables in your databases is unlikely to yield good results, however. To avoid locking problems when multiple clients simultaneously attempt to access the same table, MySQL actually keeps a separate copy of the table open for each client accessing it. Although this results in higher memory usage, it greatly improves performance. Therefore, the most desirable size for the table cache is proportional to the max_connections — the more clients simultaneously connected, the higher the number of open tables.

The last thing you want to happen is for tables to be opened and closed mid-query. Therefore, you should aim for a cache size at least large enough to cope with a worst-case scenario in which the maximum number of allowed clients is connected, each issuing queries across multiple tables. To calculate this value, look through your web code for the most tables ever used in a single query, and multiply by your max_connections. At a minimum, table_open_cache should be set to this value.

Of course, this ensures that tables won't be opened and closed mid-query. Ideally, you want the table cache to be large enough to minimize the number of tables being opened — period. You could modify the previous equation and set a value for the table cache equal to max_connections multiplied by the total number of tables in your databases. But in many situations, this is overkill and would use an unacceptably large amount of memory. (There are also some performance issues with large table caches, which will be discussed shortly.) Instead, you should start with a reasonable minimum value (given by the first equation), then observe MySQL running, and tune the cache size up based on how well the table cache is utilized.

The main variable of interest is opened_tables, which counts the number of times MySQL has opened a table (that is, not served it from the table cache) since it was last restarted. By observing the rate at which this increases, you can judge whether table_open_cache should be increased.

> **NOTE** *Don't forget that because the table cache starts out empty,* opened_tables *will initially increase rapidly before gradually tailing off. Therefore, you should avoid sampling these figures until MySQL has been running for some time. (Twenty-four hours is generally considered the minimum.)*

The following results were taken from a dedicated MySQL server with 6 GB of RAM. max_connections was set to 1000 and table_open_cache to 3000. (The biggest JOIN query ran on three tables.) MySQL had been running for more than one week.

```
mysql> SHOW GLOBAL STATUS LIKE 'Opened_tables';
+---------------+-------+
| Variable_name | Value |
+---------------+-------+
| Opened_tables | 19915 |
+---------------+-------+
```

After a few minutes, the query was rerun and produced the following results:

```
mysql> SHOW GLOBAL STATUS LIKE 'Opened_tables';
+---------------+-------+
| Variable_name | Value |
+---------------+-------+
| Opened_tables | 19978 |
+---------------+-------+
```

With 63 tables having been opened in this period, you should definitely look at increasing table_open_cache.

An additional way to analyze the effectiveness of table caching is to look at the number of currently open tables, as shown here:

```
mysql> SHOW GLOBAL STATUS LIKE 'Open_tables';
+---------------+-------+
| Variable_name | Value |
+---------------+-------+
| Open_tables   | 3002  |
+---------------+-------+
```

In other words, the table cache is full. Increasing the size should be your priority here (memory permitting).

> **NOTE** *Incidentally, if you wonder how you can have 3,002 open tables when the table cache size is only 3,000, MySQL enables the cache size to be temporarily increased if none of the existing cached tables can be removed (because they are all in use by other clients).*

table_definition_cache

New to MySQL version 5.1 was table_definition_cache, a lightweight partner to the table cache. One drawback of the table cache (aside from memory usage) is that it requires a lot of file descriptors (which you'll learn more about shortly), and the table definition cache offers an alternative strategy in which only the table definitions (describing the structure of the table, column types, indexing, and so on) are held in memory. Because these are not open tables, entries in this cache aren't using file descriptors, and the memory footprint of each entry is a lot lower than table_cache.

Despite these advantages, `table_definition_cache` doesn't offer as great a performance increase as the standard `table_cache`. The recommended way to utilize it is as a secondary caching mechanism when the table cache becomes full. (In some situations, memory constraints, `max_connections`, or the sheer number of tables that exist mean that it is impractical to set `table_open_cache` large enough to hold all tables.) The default value in MySQL version 5.5 upward is 400, and any value from 256 to 524,288 is permitted.

File Descriptors and open_files_limit

File descriptors (sometimes referred to as *file handles*) are created by the operating system when a file is opened, and the kernel imposes limits on both the number of descriptors a particular process can create, and the maximum number of descriptors globally. A large table cache means lots of open files. In the case of `MyISAM` tables, two descriptors are needed per table, and, in some situations, this can cause the operating system to run out of file descriptors.

In Linux, you can view the current global limit via `proc`, as shown here:

```
$ cat /proc/sys/fs/file-max
205094
```

But, for more details, inspect via `file-nr`, as shown here:

```
$ cat /proc/sys/fs/file-nr
6688    184       205094
```

These three columns show the following:

➤ The number of descriptors currently in use

➤ The number of allocated descriptors available

➤ The maximum number of descriptors that can be allocated

As files are opened, and descriptors are allocated, this second field decreases. When it gets to zero (or close to zero), Linux simply makes more descriptors available, up to the maximum.

It's unlikely that MySQL alone can exhaust the global maximum number of descriptors. (But if it is sharing a server with other busy services, it may be worth keeping an eye on usage.) Rather, the problem for MySQL is usually the per-process descriptor limit imposed by Linux, which typically defaults to 1,024 — too small in many cases. You can inspect and set this limit in the bash shell using `ulimit`, as shown here:

```
# ulimit -n
1024
```

The root user also has the power to change this limit, as shown here:

```
# ulimit -n 2048
# ulimit -n
2048
```

You can inspect the limit imposed on any running process by inspecting /proc/_PID_/limits, as shown here:

```
# cat /proc/'pidof /usr/local/mysql/bin/mysqld'/limits|grep "Max open files"
Max open files              3310                3310                   files
```

> **NOTE** *The first figure is the soft limit, and second is the hard limit.*

It's not uncommon for init scripts to use ulimit to raise the file descriptor limit for the daemons they launch, and this is one way to solve the problem with MySQL. However, MySQL provides an easier solution, the open_files_limit configuration option, which essentially does this same thing. (The value is actually just passed to mysqld_safe, which calls ulimit.)

If you find MySQL complaining about Too Many Open Files, raising open_files_limit should be your first avenue. You can estimate a suitable minimum value based on the earlier observations that MyISAM tables need two descriptors per table, and the maximum number of open tables is determined by the table_open_cache size. (However, this limit can be temporarily exceeded.) However, don't forget that MySQL still needs file descriptors for other things, too.

For InnoDB, the number of file descriptors needed depends on the storage method being used. (You'll learn about these shortly in the section, "Tuning InnoDB.") Traditionally, all InnoDB tables were held in a single file (hence the "too many open files" problem rarely appeared), but there is now also the option to store each table in its own file. Unlike MyISAM, only one file per table is used.

> **NOTE** *Under Windows, MySQL version 5.1 and earlier had a hard limit of 2,048 file descriptors. The problem has been fixed in version 5.5 and later.*

Table Cache Scaling

A recurring theme with MySQL cache tuning (and sometimes caching in general) is that bigger is better — but often only up to a point. Throughout this chapter, you'll see examples of situations in which setting a cache too large can actually be detrimental to performance.

The table cache is one such case. As the size of the table cache increases, the speed at which tables can be closed (which is triggered if the table cache is full) actually decreases. Thus, if you are in a situation where you have lots of frequently used tables, and you know that the table cache can never be big enough to hold them all, a lot of table opening and closing will be inevitable. It may make sense to keep the table cache small to speed up this activity. Admittedly, this is a somewhat extreme scenario, but it does illustrate the dangers of blindly following the "bigger is better" mantra.

Thread Caching

MySQL is a multithreaded service. As such, a new thread must be created each time a client connects. On busy servers, this can result in a significant amount of time spent simply creating and destroying threads.

To combat this, MySQL provides a thread cache to allow existing threads to be reused. When a client connects, MySQL first checks the thread cache. If there is a spare thread, it is used; otherwise, a new thread is created. When the client disconnects, the thread is placed in the cache for future use.

The size of the thread cache is controlled by `thread_cache_size`, which accepts values between 0 at 16,384. Note that the default size is zero, effectively disabling this feature.

How big should the cache be? Although there is a performance hit associated with creating and destroying threads, it may not be particularly noticeable unless the server receives many connections per second. So, in some situations, the thread cache may have an impact on performance. In other situations, the effect will be marginal.

Let's start by looking at the counters available for inspecting thread activity:

```
> SHOW GLOBAL STATUS LIKE 'thread%';
+-------------------+--------+
| Variable_name     | Value  |
+-------------------+--------+
| Threads_cached    | 2      |
| Threads_connected | 10     |
| Threads_created   | 158703 |
| Threads_running   | 2      |
+-------------------+--------+
```

`Threads_cached` shows the number of threads currently in the cache, naturally enough, whereas `Threads_connected` gives the number of currently open connections. Because some of these open connections may be sleeping, waiting for further queries, `Threads_running` displays how many of these are actually running.

Of particular interest is `Threads_created`, which shows the number of times a thread has been created (that is, not served from the cache) since MySQL was last restarted. Because this value is dependent on MySQL's uptime, the absolute value is largely irrelevant. Instead, you are interested in the rate of change — that is, how fast the counter is increasing. If the number of threads created is increasingly rapidly, you should look at increasing the `thread_cache` size. If the rate of increase is modest, there will probably be little to gain from upping the cache size.

Another statistic you can look at is the connections counter. By dividing the number of threads created by this (shown previously as 158,703), you can calculate the cache miss ratio.

```
> SHOW GLOBAL STATUS LIKE 'Connections';

+---------------+---------+
| Variable_name | Value   |
+---------------+---------+
| Connections   | 9201962 |
+---------------+---------+
```

In this example, you would arrive at a miss ratio of 0.0173 (158,703/9,201,962) — in other words, the vast majority of connections use threads from the cache. Be wary of attaching too much significance to this ratio, though, because it doesn't tell you the actual number of threads created. On a relatively quiet server, a high miss ratio might translate to only one or two new threads per minute. Conversely, on a busy server, an apparently healthy miss ratio may hide that hundreds of new threads are created each minute. This is an important point, and one that will be repeated when looking at other caches.

Per-Session Buffers

Although the table cache and thread cache are important enough to warrant detailed study, there are also a number of other lesser buffers worth a brief examination. None of these is specific to a particular storage engine, and, in most cases, none offer potential performance gains anywhere near the table and thread caches. But there are always exceptions to the rule.

sort_buffer_size

The sort buffer is allocated on a per-client basis for any query that needs to perform a sort operation (that is, `ORDER BY` and `GROUP BY` operations). The whole buffer is allocated in one go, so setting `sort_buffer_size` too high can quickly use up a lot of memory if `max_connections` is high, aside from the performance penalty of allocating overly large chunks of memory.

On Linux, MySQL uses `mmap()` rather than `malloc()` for allocating sort buffer sizes larger than 256 KB, and this is somewhat slower. So, ideally you should keep the sort buffer at 256 KB or less. There is a similar threshold at 2 MB. If you do require a value higher than 256 KB, you should also aim to keep it under 2 MB.

If you have only a few queries that would benefit from a large sort buffer, you can set a modest global default and then increase it on a per-session basis by issuing a `SET SESSION` query after connecting.

read_buffer_size

The read buffer is used for queries that perform sequential scans of tables. As with the sort buffer, the full buffer size is allocated for queries that need it (by using `read_buffer_size`), and so similar caveats apply. Again, there are also thresholds at 256 KB and 2 MB, above which performance can drop, and you are advised not to blindly raise this value too high (unless you have a good reason).

In particular, `LIMIT` queries on large tables can cause some unexpected detrimental behavior when `read_buffer_size` is set too high. In these situations, the whole table is read into the buffer; although only the number of rows specified by `LIMIT` is returned — the rest are simply discarded.

read_rnd_buffer_size

The `read_rnd` cache is the counterpart to `read_buffer` used when reading sorted rows (rather than sequential rows) and helps to cut down on disk seeks. However, as with the sort and read buffers, this cache is allocated per client, and you should be careful not to raise it too high globally. Instead, set it on a per-session basis with `SET SESSION`.

join_buffer_size

`join` buffers are allocated per-session, with one buffer for each non-indexed join between two tables. Thus, with complex queries, multiple `join` buffers may be created. They are used for only non-indexed joins, and, in most cases, better column indexing produces a greater performance increase than raising this buffer. As with the other per-session buffers discussed here, care should be taken not to make the join buffer too big.

Having looked at tuning aspects of MySQL itself, let's take a look at performance aspects of the main storage engines (MyISAM and InnoDB). While many of the MyISAM options are well known, InnoDB is evolving rapidly, and new features are regularly being added. As such, even if you are an old hand at configuring MySQL, you may learn something new.

TUNING MYISAM

There is a distinct difference between tuning options of MySQL (which you just learned about) and tuning of individual engines. So, let's now look at MyISAM-specific settings, and, later in this chapter, tuning for the InnoDB engine will be examined.

Key Cache

The MyISAM key cache is a memory buffer used to hold frequently accessed index (key) blocks. The size of the cache can be one of the most important MyISAM-specific tuning options, yet there is also a lot of misinformation about picking an appropriate size. Unfortunately, a large amount of guessing is often involved.

The key_buffer_size ini directive is used to control the size of the cache, with a value of zero disabling it. Disabling the cache isn't quite as bad as it may seem because the operating system's disk buffering should help to reduce the frequency of index reads from disk. But it is still advisable to turn the key cache on and set it to a reasonable size.

For a dedicated MySQL server, the general rule of thumb is to allocate between 25 percent and 50 percent of the total memory to the key cache. However, as always, this is only a rough figure.

If you have a particularly small dataset (or a huge amount of memory), this figure may be too large. Conversely, you should be careful not to set this figure too high. The key cache is used only for buffering indexes, and MySQL still needs memory for the tables' contents.

If the key cache is too large, the system may run out of physical memory and start swapping — a situation that can cause a huge deterioration in performance. Remember that the key cache is for MyISAM tables only. InnoDB tables have their own buffer, and the size of the MyISAM key cache needs to be reduced.

So, how do you determine a suitable size for the cache? Looking at MySQL's counters is a good start, as shown here:

```
mysql> SHOW STATUS LIKE '%key_read%';
+-------------------+----------+
| Variable_name     | Value    |
+-------------------+----------+
| Key_read_requests | 14052595 |
| Key_reads         | 96504    |
+-------------------+----------+
```

Key_read_requests shows the total number of requests to read a key block, whereas Key_reads shows the number of times a key block was read from disk (because it was not in the cache). You can calculate the ratio of cache misses by dividing Key_reads by Key_read_requests. In the previous example, you would end up with a figure of 0.0069 (96,504/1,405,295).

Because you know that reading from disk is several orders of magnitude slower than reading from memory, it follows that you should probably experiment with increasing the key buffer size in an attempt to reduce the number of Key_reads. Unfortunately, things aren't quite that simple. You'll often hear figures bandied about — the most popular seems to be that the cache miss ratio shouldn't exceed approximately 0.01 — but, by now, you should know to treat such statements with a pinch of salt.

For starters, a ratio is just that. It contains no information on the actual number of misses, nor the period of time over which these misses occurred.

Consider the situation of a MySQL server that has been running for the past 24 hours. During this time, there have been 1,000 key read requests and 48 key reads. This yields a miss ratio of 0.048 (almost five times higher than many sources recommend), and yet this translates only as two disk-based key reads per hour (on average). Conversely, on a server that handled 288,000 key read requests during the past 24 hours, of which 1,440 had been from disk, the healthy looking miss ratio of 0.005 fails to tell the full story — that disk-based key reads have been averaging one per second [$1440/(24 \times 60)$].

The second problem with this ratio is the assumption that cache misses will actually be several orders of magnitude slower. Because many operating systems use free memory for caching disk I/O, you can't be sure that these key reads will actually be from disk at all.

Finally, you must also be careful not to sample these counters too soon after a server restart. As you know, the key buffer starts out empty — hence, the miss ratio starts out high and gradually decreases over time.

Perhaps a more useful metric would be to look at the *rate of* change of the key read counters because this would tell you how many potential disk reads were occurring per unit interval. To do this, you can simply execute SHOW STATUS LIKE '%key_read%', as shown here:

```
mysql> SHOW STATUS LIKE '%key_read%';
+-------------------+------------+
| Variable_name     | Value      |
+-------------------+------------+
| Key_read_requests | 14092559640 |
| Key_reads         | 889876     |
+-------------------+------------+
```

Then, wait about 30 seconds, and run it again:

```
mysql> SHOW STATUS LIKE '%key_read%';
+-------------------+------------+
| Variable_name     | Value      |
+-------------------+------------+
| Key_read_requests | 14092701815 |
| Key_reads         | 889877     |
+-------------------+------------+
```

Here you see 142,175 read requests (14,092,701,815 − 1,4092,559,640), of which only 1 resulted in a (possible) disk read.

You can take this one step further and use `mysqladmin` to generate stats at regular intervals (in this example, every 60 seconds):

```
# mysqladmin ext -ri60 | grep Key_reads
| Key_reads                       | 889918 |
| Key_reads                       | 6      |
| Key_reads                       | 4      |
| Key_reads                       | 6      |
| Key_reads                       | 4      |
| Key_reads                       | 5      |
| Key_reads                       | 3      |
| Key_reads                       | 1      |
| Key_reads                       | 4      |
```

Discounting the first field (which shows the total number of key reads so far), you can see that MySQL averages approximately four key reads — which may or may not result in disk reads — every minute. You can now ask two questions. Is this level of potential disk activity liable to cause a deterioration in performance for other aspects of MySQL (or other services running on the system)? Is disk activity high enough (or the disks slow enough) that reading these blocks from disk will cause a significant performance penalty? (Note that `iostat` can shed further light on both these questions.) In many cases, the answers to both of these questions will be "no," and a small level of cache misses is quite acceptable.

Index Preloading

When MySQL is first started, the key cache is naturally empty, and blocks are gradually added to it as they are accessed from disk. This adds a little overhead, and also results in index blocks existing in the cache in a somewhat scattered fashion.

Assuming the key cache is big enough to hold them, you can preload entire indexes into the buffer by using the `LOAD INDEX INTO CACHE <table name>` statement. This has the advantage of sequential blocks being faster to access, and cuts down on possible disk reads at a later stage. Optionally, you can append `IGNORE LEAVES` to not preload leaf nodes. This helps to counter the main disadvantage of this technique — that loading an entire index into the cache will be wasting valuable space if many blocks are never accessed.

The `preload_buffer_size` variable can be used to control the size of the cache used when preloading indexes. The default value is 32,768, with accepted values in the range 1,024 to 1,073,741,824 bytes (1 GB).

Optimum Block Sizes

MySQL enables you to control the size of the blocks of memory used in the cache with the `key_cache_block_size` configuration option. In addition to this, you can also tune the size of blocks in the physical index files using the `–myisam_block_size` startup option. Accepted values for both range from 512 to 1,6384 bytes, with the defaults being 1,024 bytes.

Your motivation for changing these is to match the block size used by Linux for disk I/O (not to be confused with the filesystem's block size). On x86 Linux, use a value of 4 KB.

> **NOTE** *On most flavors of UNIX (including Linux), the following Perl one-liner can be used to show the disk I/O block size:*
>
>   perl -e '$a=(stat ".")[11]; print $a'
>
> *Other flavors of UNIX support adding the* -g *flag to the* df *command to show block sizes.*
>
> *On Windows, the* fsutil *command can be used (look for the* Bytes Per Cluster *value in the output).*

Using Multiple Key Caches

Prior to MySQL version 4.1, access to the key caches was linear, with only one request allowed at a time. Fortunately, this situation has now changed, but there are still a couple of caveats:

➤ If the buffer is being updated, clients must still wait for the update to complete before they can access it.

➤ If the buffer is full, concurrent accesses are permitted only if they do not cause keys being used by another client to be purged from the cache.

To reduce these problems, MySQL enables you to create multiple key caches of user-defined sizes. After allocating a name and size to these caches, you can then assign individual table indexes to them. (Any indexes not assigned will continue to use the default key cache.) Following is an example:

```
mysql> SET GLOBAL mycache1.key_buffer_size=1024*1024*16;
```

Here, a cache named 'mycache1' has been created, and 16 MB of memory has been allocated to it.

The syntax for querying the size of the cache, or the size of each block, is a little different and requires you to use the @@GLOBAL syntax, as shown here:

```
mysql> select @@GLOBAL.mycache1.key_buffer_size;
+-------------------------------+
| @@GLOBAL.mycache1.key_buffer_size |
+-------------------------------+
|                      16777216 |
+-------------------------------+

mysql> select @@GLOBAL.mycache1.key_cache_block_size;
+------------------------------------+
| @@GLOBAL.mycache1.key_cache_block_size |
+------------------------------------+
|                               1024 |
+------------------------------------+
```

The CACHE INDEX statement is used to assign the indexes on a table to a given key cache, as shown here:

```
mysql> CACHE INDEX categories, comments IN mycache1;
+-----------------+---------------------+----------+----------+
| Table           | Op                  | Msg_type | Msg_text |
+-----------------+---------------------+----------+----------+
| live.categories | assign_to_keycache  | status   | OK       |
| live.comments   | assign_to_keycache  | status   | OK       |
+-----------------+---------------------+----------+----------+
```

Aside from the benefits of reduced contention, you attain more control over block retention through careful selection of which indexes to cache where. For example, if you have an index that you never want to be flushed from the cache (by the LRU or MIS implementations), you can assign it to its own key cache (making sure that the cache is large enough to fit the index).

Hot, Cold, and Warm Caches

The MySQL documentation also outlines a suggested three-tier setup, in which indexes are assigned to a cache based on how static or dynamic they are likely to be. Let's take a broad look at this.

You assign 60 percent of your key cache memory to the default cache and then create two additional caches, each of 20 percent. The first of these new caches, referred to as the *hot cache*, is used for the indexes of tables that are searched heavily, but rarely updated. The second custom cache, the *cold cache*, is used for tables that are frequently being modified. All other indexes go in the default cache, which is referred to as the *warm cache*, and contains tables that fall in the middle ground (that is, neither hot nor cold).

Because index blocks in the hot cache never (or rarely) change, if you reach the stage where the cache is full and blocks must be removed to make way for new ones, the purged blocks won't need to be written back to disk.

The use of a cold cache improves the chances that the frequently modified (but not necessarily searched) indexes remain in memory. This makes updating of the index much faster.

Configuring Multiple Key Caches

So far, you've learned how to create custom key caches at the MySQL prompt. To conclude this section, let's briefly look at the configuration file syntax.

For creating a cache, you simply prepend your wanted cache name to the beginning of the variable, as shown here:

```
mycache1.key_buffer_size = 512M
mycache2.key_buffer_size = 1G
```

Things are a little tricky if you want to automate the CACHE INDEX statement to assign table indexes to these caches. For this, you need an init file, which you simply populate with the queries to execute, as shown here:

```
CACHE INDEX categories, comments IN mycache1
CACHE INDEX userprofiles IN mycache2
```

You then source this file (you can imagine that it has been saved as `/var/lib/mysql/custom.sql`) from `my.cnf` like so:

```
init_file=/var/lib/mysql/custom.sql
```

Caching Algorithms

When the key cache becomes full, an LRU retention policy is used by default — that is, frequently used blocks are more likely to remain in the cache than less frequently used ones. If a block set for removal is dirty (that is, it has been modified since it was read in from disk), it is written back to disk first.

If the LRU policy seems a little crude, `MyISAM` also supports a Midpoint Insertion Strategy (MIS).

If you choose to use MIS for the key cache, there are a couple of configuration options to set:

➤ `key_cache_division_limit` — This specifies the percentage of the key cache to allocate to the warm list. The default value, 100, effectively causes MIS to be disabled (because the hot list will be of zero size). When lowering this value, remember that the warm list will be used more than the hot list, and the sizes of each should reflect this. Broadly speaking, a division limit of approximately 60 percent to 90 percent should be right in most cases.

➤ `key_cache_age_threshold` — This controls how long an unused entry should stay in the hot list before being moved back into the warm list. The default is 300 seconds, and permitted values range from 100 seconds upward.

Miscellaneous Tuning Options

Although the key cache is the cornerstone of tuning performance of `MyISAM` tables, there are a number of other `MyISAM`-specific configuration options that can help, so let's take a brief look at some of them.

concurrent_insert

Enabled by default, the `concurrent_insert` option enables `INSERT` statements to be executed on a table at the same time as `SELECT` queries are reading from it. This partly alleviates the table-level locking previously described. (Although it does nothing to help the table-level locking that occurs on `UPDATE` and `DELETE` queries.)

Things aren't quite that simple, though. The `concurrent_insert` variable actually supports three settings:

➤ A setting of `0` turns this option off.

➤ A setting of `1` (the default) enables concurrent inserts only when there are no deleted rows in the middle of the table.

➤ A setting of `2` enables concurrent inserts even if such deleted rows exist. If any `SELECT` queries are running, the data will be inserted at the end of the table. Otherwise, it will be inserted in the gap left by the deleted row (the default behavior).

low_priority_updates

Despite its name, `low_priority_updates` doesn't just lower the priority of UPDATES — it also applies to DELETES and INSERTS. As you might have guessed, it causes queries that modify a table to have a lower priority than those that read from it. So, if multiple queries are waiting to be run against a table, write queries are pushed to the bottom of the queue.

If you choose not to enable this option globally, it can still be set on a per-query basis using the following syntax:

```
update low_priority into …
```

delay_key_write

When a MyISAM index/key is updated, the default behavior is to write the changes back to disk. For frequently modified tables, this can result in a lot of disk writes. By enabling `delay_key_write` (either on a per table basis, or globally by specifying a value of ALL), changes to the indexes are buffered in memory, and not written out to disk until the table is closed. This greatly speeds up index updates.

The downside is that if MySQL is not shut down cleanly, there's a good chance of index corruption (because the buffer will not have been flushed to disk). You can fix this with `myisamchk`, but for big tables, it will take a while to run.

As you have seen, MyISAM provides a wealth of tunable configuration options, and careful use of these can have a huge impact on how well MySQL is able to handle heavy usage.

For many years, MyISAM was the *de facto* storage engine, and InnoDB was seen as something of a specialist engine, mainly used in situations where transactions were needed. This is emphatically no longer the case, and InnoDB has evolved (and continues to do so) into a very powerful storage engine. Let's take a closer look at it.

TUNING INNODB

InnoDB has come a long way over the last few years, and provides an impressive set of configurable parameters. Since InnoDB has become the default storage engine for MySQL, this situation can only improve. Certainly, as you'll see in this section, InnoDB is where all the exciting developments are taking place.

Monitoring InnoDB

The primary means of monitoring the status of InnoDB is via the InnoDB monitor, accessible via the following command:

```
show engine innodb status\G
```

This provides detailed information on the health of various aspects of InnoDB, including threads, buffers, and semaphores. Although the majority of this information probably doesn't mean much at this stage, each of these areas will be covered in the following sections.

Figure 8-2 shows the first page of the monitor's output taken from a busy database server.

```
mysql> show engine innodb status\G
*************************** 1. row ***************************
  Type: InnoDB
  Name:
Status:
=====================================
120905 15:01:22 INNODB MONITOR OUTPUT
=====================================
Per second averages calculated from the last 11 seconds
-----------------
BACKGROUND THREAD
-----------------
srv_master_thread loops: 17017844 1_second, 16766673 sleeps, 1697685 10_second, 43035 background, 43035 flush
srv_master_thread log flush and writes: 19438924
----------
SEMAPHORES
----------
OS WAIT ARRAY INFO: reservation count 3048501, signal count 5082931
Mutex spin waits 40781379, rounds 43905374, OS waits 917985
RW-shared spins 3216781, rounds 60468862, OS waits 1872812
RW-excl spins 277838, rounds 11712061, OS waits 237546
Spin rounds per wait: 1.08 mutex, 18.80 RW-shared, 42.15 RW-excl
--------
FILE I/O
--------
I/O thread 0 state: waiting for completed aio requests (insert buffer thread)
I/O thread 1 state: waiting for completed aio requests (log thread)
I/O thread 2 state: waiting for completed aio requests (read thread)
I/O thread 3 state: waiting for completed aio requests (read thread)
I/O thread 4 state: waiting for completed aio requests (read thread)
I/O thread 5 state: waiting for completed aio requests (read thread)
I/O thread 6 state: waiting for completed aio requests (write thread)
I/O thread 7 state: waiting for completed aio requests (write thread)
I/O thread 8 state: waiting for completed aio requests (write thread)
I/O thread 9 state: waiting for completed aio requests (write thread)
Pending normal aio reads: 0 [0, 0, 0, 0] , aio writes: 0 [0, 0, 0, 0] ,
 ibuf aio reads: 0, log i/o's: 0, sync i/o's: 0
Pending flushes (fsync) log: 0; buffer pool: 0
16541911 OS file reads, 230963809 OS file writes, 25446993 OS fsyncs
0.00 reads/s, 0 avg bytes/read, 12.54 writes/s, 1.45 fsyncs/s
-------------------------------------
INSERT BUFFER AND ADAPTIVE HASH INDEX
-------------------------------------
Ibuf: size 1, free list len 5, seg size 7, 26756 merges
```

FIGURE 8-2

Working with Buffers and Caches

The InnoDB buffer pool (innodb_buffer_pool_size in my.cnf) is the most important cache provided by InnoDB, holding a similar importance to the key buffer in MyISAM. But whereas the MyISAM key buffer caches only indexes, leaving caching of data to the underlying operating system, InnoDB caches both indexes and data in its buffer pool. Taking this task away from the operating system gives extra responsibility to InnoDB, and, as you'll see shortly, a more advanced LRU algorithm is used.

In an ideal world, you'd make the buffer pool large enough to hold all your data, thus drastically reducing disk I/O access times. This largely depends on the size of your data, but in many situations, it is feasible, albeit with several potential hurdles along the way.

On 32-bit hardware, a process won't access more than 4 GB of memory. However, 32-bit architectures are becoming increasingly uncommon, especially on high-end servers, and, in most situations, this won't be an issue.

Even if the entire data set won't fit into memory, you should still strive to make the buffer pool as big as possible. The buffer pool itself has some overhead, as does the rest of MySQL, and you must ensure that you leave enough memory for these and other applications running on the server.

One issue that may get in the way is the disk buffering implemented by the operating system. As you have already seen, many operating systems reduce disk I/O by caching reads and writes in free memory, and this largely duplicates the caching done in the buffer pool by InnoDB. This can potentially lead to double-buffering situations, with data cached in both places. Usually, you might prefer operating system-level caching, but in this situation, the InnoDB buffer pool is much better suited for the job. Thus, you want to prevent the operating system from also caching the data.

As luck would have it, MySQL provides a cnf setting for this, innodb_flush_method. By setting this to O_DIRECT, you can eliminate operating system-level caching for InnoDB. In case you wonder, double buffering is an issue with MyISAM, too. It's just that MyISAM doesn't provide a way to bypass it.

> **NOTE** O_DIRECT *is only available on Linux, FreeBSD, and Solaris. On Windows, the flush method is always unbuffered.*

NUMA AND SWAPPING

Linux will swap out pages of memory to disk if it starts to run out of physical memory. But a significant number of MySQL users on high-end servers have observed behavior where Linux starts to swap heavily, despite there being plenty of free memory. Naturally, this is a performance killer and seems bizarre.

The explanation turns out to center on low-level kernel memory management on newer multiprocessor machines. In traditional symmetric multiprocessing (SMP) — also known as Uniform Memory Access (UMA) — architectures consisting of a single processor with multiple cores, each core has equal access to the available memory. By contrast, Non-Uniform Memory Access (NUMA) architectures (of which the AMD Opteron was one of the first) divide the memory between each processor (processor, not core). Each processor can still access the entire range of system memory, but some regions of memory will be closer — and hence lower latency — than others.

To quantify this, on a NUMA machine with two processors and 32 GB of RAM, each processor has 16 GB of local RAM. Processes prefer to use this local RAM because of the lower latency, but, of course, they may still use the nonlocal RAM if necessary. (However, this does not mean that each processor is limited to accessing 16 GB of memory!)

The problems start when a single process requires more memory than what is local to the processor on which it is running. In these situations, some version of the Linux 2.6 kernel decides it would be better to swap out to disk than suffer the slight performance hit of accessing this nonlocal memory. The result is swapping, despite there being lots of free memory.

continues

continued

Some administrators have attempted to solve this problem by simply turning off swap space, but this is certainly not recommended. Although you generally want to strive to avoid significant swapping at all costs, swap spaces provide a useful safeguard if there is a temporary spike in memory usage. Without that swap space, the kernel OOM (out of memory) killer would simply kick on and start killing processes to free up memory. In this situation, swapping is probably the lesser evil.

A better solution is to launch MySQL with the –memlock option, which uses the underlying kernel function mlockall to lock a process in memory, preventing it from being swapped. Numerous bugs have been reported in mlockall, however, which may cause stability problems — a lot depends on your distribution and kernel.

Another partial solution is to change the swappiness of the system with the following:

```
echo 0 > /proc/sys/vm/swappiness
```

Remember, though, that this doesn't prevent swapping. It merely discourages it.

Finally, you can also use the numactl tool to configure how Linux treats memory on NUMA architectures. Adding the following entry to mysqld_safe causes MySQL to launch with interleaved memory (that is, the memory used for MySQL will be spread out evenly, reducing the likelihood that the memory local to a particular processor will become full):

```
cmd="/usr/bin/numactl --interleave all $cmd"
```

Managing the Buffer Pool

InnoDB uses a modified LRU for the buffer pool, based on an MIS.

With the InnoDB buffer pool, the default division is for the cold list (containing less frequently accessed items) to occupy 37 percent of the pool size, with the hot list (frequently accessed items) taking the remaining space. Should you want, though, you can change this value with the innodb_old_blocks_pct configuration option, which accepts values in the range 5 to 95.

For applications that occasionally access large tables, it often make sense to reduce innodb_old_blocks_pct, to prevent this less commonly accessed data from being cached so heavily. Conversely, for small, frequently accessed tables, raising innodb_old_blocks_pct increases the likelihood that this data will be kept in memory for future use.

As with other MIS algorithms, new pages are inserted at the top of the cold list, making them prime candidates for promotion to the hot list. Occasionally, though, this behavior is not wanted because it may cause a page that is accessed a couple of times in short succession, and then never again to be promoted. In fact, during a table scan, blocks are accessed several times in short succession, so even one SQL query may be enough to promote the data to the hot list.

InnoDB provides a way to control this behavior via `innodb_old_blocks_time`. This configuration option controls the number of milliseconds that must elapse before a newly added page can be promoted to the hot list. The default value is zero, but raising this to a relatively small value (such as 500 milliseconds) can go a long way to preventing this "problem." (However, this MIS insertion strategy isn't always undesirable behavior.)

Inspecting the Buffer Pool

The primary means to monitor the buffer pool is via the InnoDB monitor (`show engine innodb status`), and the following snippet shows some sample output:

```
----------------------
BUFFER POOL AND MEMORY
----------------------
Total memory allocated 160972800; in additional pool allocated 0
Dictionary memory allocated 99761
Buffer pool size   9599
Free buffers        0
Database pages      15549
Old database pages 5720
Modified db pages  0
Pending reads 0
Pending writes: LRU 0, flush list 0, single page 0
Pages made young 7042, not young 263971
0.12 youngs/s, 5.02 non-youngs/s
Pages read 49210, created 10, written 1538
0.93 reads/s, 0.00 creates/s, 0.00 writes/s
Buffer pool hit rate 984 / 1000, young-making rate 2 / 1000 not 88 / 1000
Pages read ahead 0.00/s, evicted without access 0.00/s
LRU len: 15549, unzip_LRU len: 1556
I/O sum[44]:cur[0], unzip sum[29]:cur[0]
```

Of particular interest are the following fields:

➤ `Database pages` — This is the number of pages (by default 16,000) in the buffer pool.

➤ `Old database pages` — This is the number of pages in the cold list. Subtracting this value from `Database pages` gives the number of pages in the hot list.

➤ `Pages made young` — This is the number of pages that have been promoted from the cold list to the hot list.

➤ `Pages made not young` — This is the number of pages that have stayed in the cold list without being promoted.

➤ `youngs (not-youngs)/s` — This shows the rate (in seconds) at which pages in the cold list have or have not been promoted to the hot list.

As you have seen, the promotion of pages from the cold to hot list is sometimes undesirable, especially in situations where the promoted pages are unlikely to be accessed regularly. This information can give you an insight into this. As always, though, it's generally the rate of change (`youngs/s` and `non-youngs/s`) that you should be most interested in, rather than absolute figures. A low number of `youngs/s` shows that few pages are promoted to the hot list. In an application that regularly accesses the same data, this would suggest that `innodb_old_blocks_time` be lowered. Conversely, a high number of `youngs/s` on applications that perform frequent large scans would suggest that `innodb_old_blocks_time` be raised.

In addition to taking into consideration the general behavior of your application (for example, is there any benefit to modifying the behavior of a hot list promotion?), it can be beneficial to look at these statistics during any regular irregular activity, such as the daily generation of reports. (In such situations, you probably don't want a high `youngs/s` rate.)

Using Multiple Buffer Pools

On busy systems with large buffer pools, there will typically be many threads accessing data simultaneously from the buffer pool, and this contention can be a bottleneck. Starting with MySQL version 5.5, InnoDB enables multiple buffer pools to be created. Each is managed independently and maintains its own LRU and mutual exclusion (mutex). Cached data is randomly assigned to the pools, however, so the database administrator has no control over how the data is divided.

> **NOTE** *You'll learn more about mutexes later in this chapter.*

The `innodb_buffer_pool_instances` configuration option is used to control this and takes a value between 1 (the default) and 64. Because the use of multiple pools is intended only for high-end systems, this option has no effect when `innodb_buffer_pool_size` is lower than 1 GB.

Insert Buffering

A subset of the buffer pool, the *insert buffer* is used to cache changes made to secondary indexes. Write queries on a table often result in secondary indexes becoming unordered, and re-ordering them can be I/O-intensive (unless the affected pages are already in the buffer pool). By caching these changes, they can be grouped together and executed when the affected pages are next loaded into the buffer pool.

This buffer can dramatically reduce disk I/O in applications that perform many write queries on tables. However, because it is part of the buffer pool, it also reduces the amount of memory available for data page caching. For this reason, if memory is in short supply, it may make sense to disable insert buffering — especially for data that has few secondary indexes.

The `innodb_change_buffering` configuration option controls whether such changes are buffered. Starting with MySQL version 5.5, this option also enables you to control what will be buffered. Following are accepted values for `innodb_change_buffering`:

➤   `All` — Caches inserts, deletes, and purges (physical deletion). This is the default value.

➤   `None` — Disables the insert buffer.

➤   `Inserts` — Caches insert operations only.

➤ `Deletes` — Caches delete operations.

➤ `Changes` — Caches both inserts and deletes.

➤ `Purges` — Caches purges only.

Adaptive Hashing

Adaptive hashing is a feature of `InnoDB` designed to improve performance on machines with large amounts of physical memory.

For tables that almost fit fully into memory, hash indexes provide a faster means of lookup than the default B-tree indexes. With adaptive hashing enabled, MySQL monitors index-based queries and built in-memory hash tables on those indexes that are frequently accessed.

In many cases, this does improve performance. But it's worth remembering that these hashes require maintenance, just like any other index. This results in locking when the hashes are written to, and on multiprocessor machines (where `innodb_thread_concurrency` is higher), deadlock can occur. If you do choose to enable adaptive hashing, look out for frequent Holds Adaptive Hash Latch messages in the `transactions` section of the `InnoDB` monitor.

Adaptive hashing can be enabled/disabled via the `ini` setting `innodb_adaptive_hash_index`.

Working with File Formats and Structures

As with most other storage engines (`MEMORY` being the most notable exception), data in `InnoDB` databases is held on disk, and this underlying storage can have an effect on performance. In this section, you learn how `InnoDB` arranges files on disk, and how the structure of these files impacts the speed of searching on primary and secondary indexes.

Mutliple Tablespaces

`InnoDB` has traditionally used a single file to hold all data in all databases. This is in contrast to `MyISAM`'s use of a directory for each database, containing three files for each table (`format`, `index`, `data`). However, multiple tablespaces are now also supported, allowing each table to occupy its own file. The `innodb_file_per_table` directive can be used in `my.cnf` to control this.

The primary advantage here is flexibility over where table files are stored. For example, you may want to split them across disks for performance, or simply because of their size. The performance gain is often over-estimated, though, and the most likely reason that you'd want to enable multiple tablespaces is to allow table compression (which you'll learn more about shortly).

Multiple tablespaces can actually be detrimental to performance because of increased disk I/O and an increase in the number of file descriptors used. `InnoDB` uses `fsync()` to flush data files after writes. Unlike the preferred `fdatasync()`, `fsync()` also causes meta data such as the last modification time to be updated, increasing (albeit only slightly) the amount of data written. In addition, `InnoDB` cannot group writes occurring across multiple tablespaces, leading to an increase in `fsync()` calls. Coupled with the increased disk activity caused by using `fsync()` over `fdatasync()`, this can cause a noticeable performance drop. For this reason, you should generally avoid multiple tablespaces unless they are required (for example, for compression).

File Formats

InnoDB version 1.0 introduced an alternative file format named `Barracuda`. (The existing format has since been named `Antelope`.) Although there are a handful of small changes behind the scenes, the primary concern here, of course, is with possible performance improvements. Mostly, there is little difference between `Antelope` and `Barracuda`, but there are two new features to InnoDB for which the `Barracuda` format must be used: compression and variable-length columns. Both of these topics will be covered in detail shortly. The `innodb_file_format ini` directive is used to control the format used when creating or altering a table.

Data Structure

InnoDB stores data in a B-tree, using the primary index as the key. This results in excellent performance for lookups on a table's primary key, but weaker performance when searching against secondary keys. For fixed-length columns, the data is stored directly under the node. But variable-length columns (such as `varchar`) — which may be too large to fit in a B-tree page — pose a problem. With the `Antelope` format, the first 768 bytes of variable-length columns are stored in the B-tree, and any remaining data is stored in a separate overflow page.

By storing the first 768 bytes in the B-tree, you remove the need for overflow pages to be used (and, hence, cut disk I/O, too) for data smaller than this size. However, too many variable-length columns can cause the B-tree to fill more heavily with data than indexes, reducing its efficiency.

The `Barracuda` format offers some improvement on this situation. When `ROW_FORMAT=DYNAMIC` (or `ROW_FORMAT=COMPRESSED`) is used, variable-length columns more than 768 bytes are stored fully off-page, which is naturally more efficient that splitting the data across two locations.

Memory Allocation

InnoDB was initially developed at a time when multicore processors were starting to enter the mainstream market. The default memory allocation libraries of many operating systems were not tuned for multiple cores, and the InnoDB developers made the decision to implement their own memory allocation routines.

The situation has changed since then, and a handful of high-performance memory allocation libraries are now available that surpass the performance of InnoDB's own library. As such, you will probably want to use one of these, rather than InnoDB's.

The `ini` setting `innodb_use_sys_malloc` controls whether InnoDB uses its own library, or the underlying operating system's library. Setting this value to 1 (the default) causes the library of the operating system to be used. Note that enabling this limits InnoDB's built-in memory-tracking statistics, which decreases the verbosity of the `memory` section of the InnoDB monitor's output.

MEMORY ALLOCATION IMPLEMENTATIONS

In Linux, the default C library is `glibc`, which uses `ptmalloc2` (itself an enhancement of `dlmalloc` — the `pt` stands for per-thread) for memory allocation. Numerous alternatives exist, and although they were often written with Linux in mind, they mostly work across Windows and UNIX, too.

➤ `TCMalloc` (thread-cache `malloc`) is Google's implementation. It claims to be much faster than `ptmalloc`, while also reducing lock contention (a problem under multicore machines) via the use of spin locks. Despite this, it tends to use more memory than the likes of `ptmalloc2`.

➤ `JEMalloc` (named after Jason Evans, the author) is used on Facebook and in Firefox. It is also the default `malloc` under FreeBSD. Implementations are available for OS X, Solaris, and Windows; and performance is considered similar to that of `TCMalloc`.

➤ `Nedmalloc` claims to be faster than any other `malloc` implementation and is primarily targeted at Windows; although it will happily run on most UNIX derivatives, too.

Memory allocation isn't just about `InnoDB`, or even `MySQL`, and is one of the most under-appreciated aspects of system performance in general. Switching to an alternative `malloc` implementation is painless, can be done on a per-application basis, and usually results in a significant performance improvement.

Threading

`InnoDB` makes extensive use of the threading capabilities of the underlying operating system, allowing it to scale well on multicore systems. Some threads are used to service user requests, whereas others run in the background to perform housekeeping. The maximum number of threads used can be raised and lowered, and there are both advantages and disadvantages to this.

In the past, it was often necessary to limit the number of concurrent threads because the high levels of context switching would eat away at performance. However, increases in the scalability of both operating systems and `InnoDB` on multicore architectures have decreased this need, and `InnoDB` generally runs fine with no limit on the number of concurrent threads. Should you want to set a limit, however, it is controlled by `innodb_thread_concurrency`, the default being zero (no limit).

Disk I/O

Given that disk IO is the major bottleneck in many systems, it's not surprising that the `InnoDB` developers have devoted considerable time to optimizing performance in this area. When you learn more about threading in the later section, "Background Threads," you'll see how flushing dirty pages (that is, pages of memory that have been modified and must be written back to disk) can cause spikes in disk activity, and you'll discover the ways in which `InnoDB` attempts to solve this. But, for the moment let's concentrate on the most significant feature of disk I/O handling — the `read-ahead` mechanism.

read-ahead Requests

read-ahead requests involve prefetching data from disk if usage patterns suggest that it may soon be needed. In InnoDB, memory pages are grouped in *extents*, where an extent consists of 64 consecutive pages. If more than a certain number of pages from an extent exists in the buffer cache, MySQL preloads the remaining pages in the extent.

In the past, InnoDB supported two methods of read-ahead:

➤ **Random** read-ahead — Here, the decision of whether to prefetch remaining pages was based solely on the number of pages from the extent already in the buffer.

➤ **Linear** read-ahead — Here, the decision is based on the number of sequential pages that have been read.

In many cases however, random read-aheads actually reduced performance, and they were dropped in InnoDB version 1.0.4.

So, that leaves linear read-aheads, which can be controlled via the innodb_read_ahead_ threshold ini directive. This variable controls the number of sequential pages in an extent that must be accessed (and be in the buffer cache) to trigger a read-ahead for the remaining pages. (The default is 56.) When the last page of a sequence falls at the end of an extent, InnoDB will also read in the whole of the next extent.

Although it may be tempting to set a low threshold, this, of course, increases disk activity, and could prove counter-productive, because there will likely be a high level of "waste." One useful metric to look at is the number of pages prefetched and the number of pages that were subsequently evicted from the buffer pool without having been accessed. You can do this like so:

```
mysql>  show status like '%ahead%';
+-------------------------------------+-------+
| Variable_name                       | Value |
+-------------------------------------+-------+
| Innodb_buffer_pool_read_ahead       | 4602  |
| Innodb_buffer_pool_read_ahead_evicted | 682 |
+-------------------------------------+-------+
```

Here, out of 4,602 pages prefetched, 682 were later evicted from the buffer cache without having been used — so, approximately 15 percent. Trying to dictate rules over what constitutes an acceptable eviction rate is misguided, but because the general aim is to keep this figure lower, it gives you a basis for monitoring any changes made to innodb_read_ahead_threshold. Also, any changes to the operation of the buffer cache (such as changing the size or innodb_old_blocks_time) have an impact on the eviction rate.

Similar metrics can be obtained from the InnoDB monitor, this time in the form of read-aheads and evictions per second (since the monitor was last queried):

```
Pages read ahead 15.08/s, evicted without access 2.66/s
```

Background Threads

Previous versions of InnoDB used a single background thread for reading and writing to disk, but starting with InnoDB version 1.0.4, this number is now configurable. Each thread can handle up to 256 pending requests, and a maximum of 64 threads may be configured. Two ini settings are provided, each of which accept values in the range 1 to 64, and default to 4. They are innodb_read_io_threads (maximum number of read threads) and innodb_write_io_threads (maximum number of write threads).

Before rushing to increase these limits, remember that they will not increase bandwidth on individual disks; although they will potentially help to alleviate bottlenecks in high-load environments, where data is spread across multiple disks.

Then Pending reads and Pending writes columns of the InnoDB monitor's output can help you judge if the thread concurrency would benefit from being raised. Recalling that each thread can queue up to 256 requests, if you see more than *256 × number of threads* pending reads or writes, this will clearly cause a bottleneck, and a gradual increase in the number of read/write threads would be beneficial.

Adaptive Flushing

In earlier versions of InnoDB, the flushing of dirty pages from the buffer occurred when the percentage of dirty pages exceeded a preconfigured value (innodb_max_dirty_pages_pct). This had the tendency to cause spikes in disk I/O, and an adaptive flushing mechanism was introduced in InnoDB version 1.0.4.

With adaptive flushing, InnoDB attempts to calculate the rate at which flushing needs to occur, based on the number of dirty pages and the rate at which they have historically been flushed. This allows the master thread to perform flushing at a much more constant rate, eliminating these spikes in disk usage. Adaptive flushing — which is enabled by default — can be controlled using the boolean innodb_adaptive_flushing ini directive.

Disk Bandwidth

Although adaptive hashing will indirectly attempt to calculate the disk I/O throughput, it can occasionally be useful to override this. innodb_io_capacity enables you to specify the number of I/O operations per second that the disk subsystem can handle. The default is 200, and accepted values are from 100 (the previous default) upward.

> **NOTE** *Setting this parameter incorrectly can cause significant problems. In most cases, it should be left at the default, allowing InnoDB to calculate the available bandwidth itself and adapt to varying workloads.*

Purging

The purging of data back to disk has traditionally been performed by the master thread in InnoDB. From InnoDB version 1.1 (MySQL version 5.5) onward, the option now exists for this to be carried out by a separate thread: innodb_purge_threads. The default of 0 disables the use of a separate thread, whereas a value of 1 enables it. Note that this setting applies only to garbage collection (in particular, removing unneeded entries from the undo log — innodb_write_io_threads still controls threading when writing dirty pages out to disk).

In theory, a separate thread should improve performance. But in many situations, it simply shifts the bottleneck from one place (queue in the thread) to another (disk contention). Still, this option is worth knowing about, particularly for high-end systems.

Mutexes

In a multithread environment, care must be taken when threads try to simultaneously access the same resource. In general, concurrent reading of a resource isn't a problem. But when writing to a resource, care must be taken to ensure that multiple threads don't attempt to write at the same time. In many cases, you also want to prevent read requests when writing is taking place.

InnoDB (and MySQL, in general) implements this through extensive use of *mutual exclusion* (*mutex*) locks, and, not surprisingly, write locks are often the source of bottlenecks (because they generally also prevent other threads from reading the resource). In addition to this, the process of initializing and destroying locks introduces some overhead, which, in some cases, can be significant.

This section focuses on the technique of spin locking and how this relates to mutexes.

Inspecting Mutexes

Mutexes in use by InnoDB can be viewed using SHOW ENGINE INNODB MUTEX to produce output similar to the following snippet:

```
+--------+----------------------------------------------+----------------+
| Type   | Name                                         | Status         |
+--------+----------------------------------------------+----------------+
| InnoDB | ../../../storage/innobase/fil/fil0fil.c:1313 | os_waits=111   |
| InnoDB | ../../../storage/innobase/srv/srv0srv.c:886  | os_waits=12183 |
| InnoDB | ../../../storage/innobase/thr/thr0loc.c:227  | os_waits=1     |
| InnoDB | ../../../storage/innobase/mem/mem0pool.c:206 | os_waits=10    |
+--------+----------------------------------------------+----------------+
```

Previous versions of MySQL displayed more verbose output, including counts on spin locks and the number of times a mutex had been requested. From MySQL version 5.0.33 onward, this extra information is displayed only if MySQL is compiled with UNIV_DEBUG enabled. You'll learn more about the os_waits column in a minute.

MySQL version 5.0.33 also hides entries relating to the buffer pool, or where os_waits is zero. The intention here is to clean up the output, which would often run to many thousands of lines. Removal of buffer pool mutexes is a prime candidate in this effort because they are unlikely to be the cause of bottlenecks. (Each 16 KB block of the buffer pool has its own mutex.)

Spin Locks

If a thread fails to acquire a lock, the usual procedure would be for it to sleep for a short period before trying again. However, mutexes in InnoDB are often short-lived, and it can be more efficient for the thread to repeatedly poll the mutex in the hope that it will soon become free. If the lock is not freed within a short time, the thread sleeps.

The name *spin lock* (also referred to as a *spin loop*) comes from the polling technique. When an InnoDB thread enters this state, the code loops through a tight set of instructions. This prevents the operating system's task manager from rescheduling the task (that is, causing it to sleep). The downside, of course, is that this loop can eat away at system resources, especially if the loop delay is too low. Modern CPUs tend to implement a PAUSE instruction, however, and InnoDB will use this where possible to reduce resource usage.

The period between polling is controlled by innodb_spin_wait_delay, which takes a value between zero and $2^{32}-1$. The default is 6, while a value of zero disables polling.

The os_waits column of the SHOW ENGINE INNODB MUTEX output shows the number of times that InnoDB failed to acquire a lock through polling, and fell back on the operating system's thread sleeping. Rapidly increasing values here (remember that you're usually interested in the rate of increase, rather than the absolute figure) could signify that the mutex is causing a bottleneck, and it may be worth experimenting with raising innodb_spin_wait_delay in the hope that less threads need to be sent to sleep.

Compression

Earlier in this chapter, you learned that the ARCHIVE and MyISAM engines support table compression. Although compression increases CPU usage (because pages must be compressed and decompressed as they are written or read from disk), it cuts down on the amount of data that must be transferred to and from disk. This is generally a good compromise (because disk I/O is so often the bottleneck) — especially for read-heavy applications. Unfortunately, MyISAM's compression support can be used only for read-only tables, whereas ARCHIVE is something of a specialist engine, making it unsuitable for general-purpose use.

The good news is that InnoDB also supports compression (of both tables and indexes), and for the most part, it is transparent, not limiting the functionality of the database. In fact, the only real restriction on compression is that you must configure InnoDB to use the Barracuda file format (the default), rather than the newer Antelope format.

The compression algorithm is based on zlib (LZ77) and is applied to both table data and indexes — a significant measure, given that table indexes can often be large. It's also worth noting that, where possible, MySQL keeps a copy of a compressed page in the InnoDB buffer pool in both compressed and uncompressed form. When the pool becomes full, an LRU algorithm is once again used to decide what to evict.

The twist is that the decision to evict compressed versus uncompressed pages is based on the status of the server. If the server appears to be I/O-bound, uncompressed pages will be the first to go (freeing up more space in which to cache pages, thus reducing disk I/O). Conversely, if the server appears to be CPU-bound, MySQL favors the eviction of compressed pages in an attempt to reduce CPU usage. In general, this means that compression is particularly suited to machines that have adequate CPU and plenty of memory, but relatively poor disk I/O.

Enabling Compression

Compression is enabled on a per-table basis, by passing additional attributes to the CREATE/ALTER TABLE statements. But first, you must enable support for compression in my.cnf, as shown here:

```
innodb_file_per_table = ON
innodb_file_format = Barracuda
```

The KEY_BLOCK_SIZE attribute is used to control the size of compressed blocks, and, therefore, the amount of compression to apply. Permitted values are 1, 2, 4, 8, and 16 (KB), but because the default size for uncompressed InnoDB blocks is 16 KB anyway, setting a KEY_BLOCK_SIZE of 16 offers little compression. Generally, smaller values are preferred because they result in greater compression. However, if the compressed page size is too small to hold a complete record, errors occur (42000: Row size too large). For that reason, KEY_BLOCK_SIZEs of 1 and 2 KB are rarely used. Because the maximum size of an InnoDB record is 8 KB, a KEY_BLOCK_SIZE of 8 KB is a safe compromise and is the value most commonly used.

```
ALTER TABLE test KEY_BLOCK_SIZE=8 ROW_FORMAT=COMPRESSED;
```

When the KEY_BLOCK_SIZE is specified, ROW_FORMAT=COMPRESSED is assumed and can be omitted. If no KEY_BLOCK_SIZE is given, it defaults to 8 KB.

Monitoring Compression

The primary means for inspecting compression statistics is via the INNODB_CMP table in the information_schema database. This table holds counters for the number of compression/decompression operations, and the time spent on each, as shown here:

```
mysql> select * from information_schema.INNODB_CMP;
+------+----------+----------+----------+------------+-----------+
| page | compress | compress | compress | uncompress | uncompress|
|_size | _ops     | _ops_ok  | _time    | _ops       | _time     |
+------+----------+----------+----------+------------+-----------+
| 1024 |        0 |        0 |        0 |          0 |         0 |
| 2048 |        0 |        0 |        0 |          0 |         0 |
| 4096 |        0 |        0 |        0 |          0 |         0 |
| 8192 |   891744 |   887177 |      531 |     232865 |        79 |
|16384 |        0 |        0 |        0 |          0 |         0 |
+------+----------+----------+----------+------------+-----------+
```

In this example, all compressed tables are using a KEY_BLOCK_SIZE of 8, so there is no data to show other page sizes. The remaining columns are as follows:

- ➤ compression_ops — This is the number of page compressions attempted.

- ➤ compression_ops_ok — This is the number of successful page compressions.

- ➤ compress_time — This is the total time spent on compression (in seconds).

- ➤ uncompress_ops — This is the number of page uncompressions performed.

- ➤ uncompress_time — This is the total time spent uncompressing pages (in seconds).

Because compression and uncompression are mostly CPU-based operations, relatively high values here suggest additional CPU cores would benefit performance. However, a high number of compress/uncompress operations could also indicate a shortage of memory in the buffer pool, causing pages to be written back to disk.

What about the ratio of `compress_ops` to `compress_ops_ok`, and why would these two values not be identical? With a `KEY_BLOCK_SIZE` of 8 KB, MySQL will attempt to compress each 16 KB block (the size of uncompressed blocks in `InnoDB`) into 8 KB blocks. If this cannot be achieved, the data must be reorganized and recompressed, resulting in multiple compression operations. The result is an increase in `compress_ops` but not `compress_ops_ok`.

Ideally, `compress_ops` and `compress_ops_ok` should be identical, but a small difference is quite common and not a cause for undue alarm. However, reorganization of the data wastes CPU cycles, and you should generally strive for a successful percentage in the high 90s (`compress_ops_ok/ compress_ops` × 100). If the ratio is lower than this, switching block sizes may help. Or you may want to be more selective about which tables are compressed.

As always, comparing ratios does not tell the full story, and you can also learn something by comparing the absolute values of the columns in the `INNODB_CMP` table. A large number of compression operations indicates that tables are updated frequently, forcing content to be recompressed and written out. In these situations, disabling compression on the affected table may improve overall performance. Or you can experiment with a higher compression block size. In general, compression is much more effective when the compressed tables are light on writes and heavy on reads.

So far, you've seen how the two major storage engines compare, along with general tuning tips for MySQL. In the next section, you'll meet the query cache, MySQL's built-in caching mechanism. When used correctly, the query cache can be a huge benefit, cutting load on the server and lowering query times. But to get the most from it, you'll first need to understand how it works.

WORKING WITH THE QUERY CACHE

One of the most important features of MySQL (from a performance perspective) is the *query cache*. First introduced in version 4.0.1, this is a built-in feature that can be used to cache `SELECT` queries and their responses, resulting in significant performance boosts for frequently run queries. It's not without its problems, though, and this section looks at advantages and disadvantages of using the cache, along with ways to monitor and manage it.

Understanding How the Query Cache Works

The query cache intercepts incoming `SELECT` queries and compares them against the list of queries in its cache. If it finds a match, the cached response is returned. If not, the query is executed as normal, and the response is stored in the cache (usually, but there are exceptions). The result is that previously seen queries can be fetched directly from the cache, saving MySQL considerable work. Let's look at an example:

```
mysql> SELECT username FROM user GROUP BY usergroupid LIMIT 0,3;
+-----------+
| username  |
+-----------+
| Unknown   |
| ian       |
| dave      |
+-----------+
3 rows in set (2.25 sec)

mysql> SELECT username FROM user GROUP BY usergroupid LIMIT 0,3;
+-----------+
| username  |
+-----------+
| Unknown   |
| ian       |
| dave      |
+-----------+
3 rows in set (0.00 sec)
```

The first time this query was run, the cache was unprimed, and MySQL took 2.25 seconds to return the result. The second time around, the query cache delivered the response, and execution time was virtual insignificant.

As mentioned, MySQL will cache only SELECT queries. Specifically, it checks (in a case-insensitive manner) if the query begins with the string "SELECT". It used to be that any leading spaces or comments in SELECT queries would fool MySQL into not caching, but this is now (as of MySQL version 5.0) no longer an issue. It's still worth remembering, though, in case you find yourself using an older version of MySQL.

A closely related gotcha is that the query cache will return a result from the cache only if the SELECT query is identical to a previously cached SELECT. Using the earlier example, let's see what happens if FROM is changed to from:

```
mysql> SELECT username from user GROUP BY usergroupid LIMIT 0,3;
+-----------+
| username  |
+-----------+
| Unknown   |
| ian       |
| dave      |
+-----------+
3 rows in set (1.43 sec)
```

Although the execution time is less than the original 2.25 seconds, this can be attributed to other factors (such as table caching, disk contention, and so on), and isn't the result of query caching.

This behavior isn't surprising. With any other language, you wouldn't expect the two strings that differed like this to be considered identical, and MySQL is no different. It's worth remembering, though, especially in dynamically constructed queries, where variations in the amount of whitespace often occur and aren't usually considered an issue.

Configuring the Query Cache

The first step in configuring the query cache is to check if MySQL has been compiled with query cache support, as shown here:

```
mysql> SHOW VARIABLES LIKE 'have_query_cache';
+------------------+-------+
| Variable_name    | Value |
+------------------+-------+
| have_query_cache | YES   |
+------------------+-------+
1 row in set (0.00 sec)
```

This says nothing about whether the cache is enabled, but simply that your copy of MySQL has query cache support built in. To check if the cache is enabled and running, you must check for nonzero settings for both query_cache_type (which governs the type of caching used) and query_cache_size (which controls the size). A zero-sized cache means the cache is effectively disabled. Following is an example:

```
mysql> SHOW VARIABLES LIKE 'query_cache_type';
+------------------+-------+
| Variable_name    | Value |
+------------------+-------+
| query_cache_type | ON    |
+------------------+-------+

mysql> SHOW VARIABLES LIKE 'query_cache_size';
+------------------+----------+
| Variable_name    | Value    |
+------------------+----------+
| query_cache_size | 33554432 |
+------------------+----------+
```

In this example, you can see that the cache is ON and has a maximum size of 32 MB. Both of these can be configured via my.cnf, along with a number of other options. Let's take a look at some of these options.

query_cache_size

Given how useful the query cache can be, it seems logical to set query_cache_size as large as memory permits. Unfortunately, this can actually be counterproductive. With a large cache, MySQL ends up spending a significant amount of time simply sorting and maintaining the cache.

How large is too large? There's no simple answer. The average size of cached queries is one factor (a handful of large queries are easier to manage than many smaller ones), as is how well utilized the query cache is. If your web application can make extensive use of the query cache, you'll be willing for MySQL to spend more time on cache management than on an application that can seldom utilize the query cache.

query_cache_type

Using `query_cache_type`, you can set one of two types of query cache. The most common (equivalent to setting this variable to 1) is a cache-by-default approach, where all `SELECT` queries will be cached, unless you specifically ask MySQL not to cache them by starting the query `SELECT SQL_NO_CACHE`. A value of 2 causes an on-demand method of caching, with queries being considered only as candidates for caching if they begin with `SELECT SQL_CACHE`.

This poses the question, "Why would you *not* want to cache?" As you shall see soon, there are actually several good reasons.

query_cache_limit

You use `query_cache_limit` to set the maximum size for cached queries, with results over this size not being cached. The justification here is that you probably don't want a single, huge query filling up the cache. However, if you find that your query cache is under-performing, it may be that you have a lot of large queries that are too large to be cached. In that case, raising this value (the default is 1 MB) should help.

query_cache_wlock_invalidate

The `query_cache_wlock_invalidate` option causes the locking of a table used for writing to invalidate all query cache entries relating to the table. You'll learn more about this in a minute.

query_cache_min_res_unit

MySQL allocates memory to the query cache on demand, in small chunks. Because the size of a result set is not known in advance (because the results of a query are fed into the cache), MySQL keeps allocating chunks of memory as needed. Allocating memory is somewhat expensive, and you can use `query_cache_min_res_unit` to increase performance a little by increasing the size of these chunks (hence, reducing the number of calls).

You needn't worry about the tail end of the query resulting in the waste of an entire block of memory because MySQL prunes the last block down to the required size after the response is complete. However, there is the related problem of fragmentation — something you would be all too familiar with if you were a Microsoft Windows user in the 1990s when disk fragmentation was a regular issue.

With the query cache, this results in small regions of memory that are effectively wasted because they are not big enough to hold a cached result. Although this can be a problem on any MySQL server, it is a particular concern when memory is allocated in large chunks (that is, when `query_cache_min_res_unit` is increased). For this reason, blindly raising this value isn't a good idea. Shortly, you'll see how to measure the amount of fragmentation, and how to decide on a suitable size for `query_cache_min_res_unit`.

Inspecting the Cache

Your best hope to set suitable values for the cache size, limit, and memory units is to inspect the cache during normal day-to-day running. It goes without saying that this is site-specific and should be done in conditions as close to the real world as possible.

A handful of cache stats can be obtained from MySQL using the SHOW STATUS command, as shown here:

```
mysql> SHOW STATUS LIKE 'Qcache%';
+-------------------------+-----------+
| Variable_name           | Value     |
+-------------------------+-----------+
| Qcache_free_blocks      | 1991      |
| Qcache_free_memory      | 6847496   |
| Qcache_hits             | 726951573 |
| Qcache_inserts          | 68370986  |
| Qcache_lowmem_prunes    | 11224754  |
| Qcache_not_cached       | 2995801   |
| Qcache_queries_in_cache | 3665      |
| Qcache_total_blocks     | 12205     |
+-------------------------+-----------+
```

The names of these variables should be self-explanatory but following are some brief descriptions:

➤ Qcache_free_blocks — This shows the number of free memory blocks in the cache.

➤ Qcache_free_memory — This shows the amount of free memory.

➤ Qcache_hits — This shows how many hits there have been on the cache.

➤ Qcache_inserts — This shows the number of queries inserted into the cache.

➤ Qcache_lowmem_prunes — This lists the number of entries that were removed from the cache because of a lack of memory.

➤ Qcache_not_cached — This lists the number of queries that were not cached, perhaps because of a lack of memory, or because they simply weren't cacheable.

➤ Qcache_queries_in_cache — This is the number of queries in the cache.

➤ Qcache_total_blocks — This is the total number of memory blocks in the cache.

In addition, the following counters are helpful:

```
mysql> SHOW GLOBAL STATUS LIKE 'com_select';
+---------------+----------+
| Variable_name | Value    |
+---------------+----------+
| Com_select    | 71940007 |
+---------------+----------+

mysql> SHOW GLOBAL STATUS LIKE 'com_insert';
+---------------+---------+
| Variable_name | Value   |
+---------------+---------+
| Com_insert    | 8619823 |
+---------------+---------+
```

```
mysql> SHOW GLOBAL STATUS LIKE 'com_update';
+---------------+----------+
| Variable_name | Value    |
+---------------+----------+
| Com_update    | 10598217 |
+---------------+----------+

mysql> SHOW GLOBAL STATUS LIKE 'com_delete';
+---------------+--------+
| Variable_name | Value  |
+---------------+--------+
| Com_delete    | 524326 |
+---------------+--------+
```

These show the number of SELECTs, INSERTs, UPDATEs, and DELETEs performed.

All variables are reset when MySQL is started, so they may not provide an accurate summary until MySQL has been running for some time (anywhere between a few hours to a couple of days, depending on how busy your sites are).

Armed with this data, you can begin to analyze how your cache is performing.

Cache Size

The most obvious thing to check first is how full your cache is, as shown by Qcache_free_memory blocks. If the cache is full, you can consider increasing its size (via query_cache_size, but see the earlier warning about making the cache too big). Conversely, if little is cached, you can save some memory by decreasing the size. (It would be worth exploring why the cache is under-utilized, too. Is it because your highly efficient client-side code is taking the strain off MySQL, or are too many of your queries noncacheable?)

Cache Hit Rate

com_select is incremented only when a SELECT query is actually performed — not when a SELECT query is answered by the cache. Thus, you can compare com_select to Qcache_hits to determine the extent to which the cache is utilized. The following equation gives you the percentage of SELECT queries that were handled by the cache:

```
(qcache_hits /(qcache_hits + com_select)) * 100
```

The figures here yield a healthy hit rate of 91 percent.

There's no pat answer for what sort of hit rate you should be striving for because this equation doesn't take into consideration the level of saving. Even a 25 percent hit rate may offer substantial performance gains, if the queries that are cached are particularly intensive ones. Again, ratios (in this case, the ratio of cache hits over com_selects) can be a somewhat over-simplification, and you should think carefully before attaching too much significance to them.

Invalidation

What happens if the data in your tables changes? Will MySQL continue to serve the now stale data from the query cache?

Although this is how some caches operate, it's not the case with MySQL. Any actions that cause the structure or contents of a table to be altered (for example, UPDATE, DELETE, and so on) cause all entries in the cache that reference that table to be immediately invalidated. Often, this is overkill, but that's the way MySQL does it.

Invalidation is one of the main causes of poor cache performance. Consider a busy web forum where posts are held in a single database table. MySQL will be receiving many SELECT queries on this table as users browse the forum and read posts. It may seem advantageous to cache as many of these queries possible, but as soon as someone submits an individual post, MySQL receives an INSERT query on the table, and suddenly every cache entry referencing that table has become invalid.

If the post table contains a counter field to indicate how many times a particular post has been viewed, the situation is even worse. This time, merely viewing the post is enough to send an UPDATE query, invalidating the cache. Most likely, the web code will perform a SELECT to retrieve the post, immediately followed by an UPDATE to increment the counter, and the query will be in the cache for only a fraction of a second. When you take into account the cost of cache management, this scenario actually ends up worse than no caching at all!

One way to diagnose high levels of invalidation is to look at Qcache_inserts (the number of queries inserted into the cache) — in particular, comparing this to Qcache_queries_in_cache, Qcache_lowmem_prune and com_select. In the earlier example (which, incidentally, was taken from a live server that had been running for approximately 3 months), 68,370,986 queries had been inserted into the cache. Of these, 11,224,754 had been removed because of lack of memory. At the time, an inspection of the counters revealed that there were 3,665 queries in the cache. That leaves 57,142,567 (68,370,986 – 11,224,754 – 3,665) queries that were removed from the cache because of invalidation.

Although these figures look bleak, they don't tell the full story. In situations in which many queries spend only a short amount of time in the cache before being invalidated, performance can suffer. But if the same percentage of queries is invalidated after, say, 12 hours in the cache, you'd probably be quite happy with this. It all depends on how long the query stays in the cache.

At the beginning of this section, you learned that the query_cache_wlock_invalidate setting has the power to cause cache invalidation when a table is locked for writing. Does this mean you can prevent invalidation altogether by turning this setting off? Sadly, the answer is "no" because write-lock invalidation is somewhat more subtle than this. Invalidation always occurs when a table is written to. query_cache_write_lock simply offers some control over the point at which the invalidation occurs.

With the option turned off, cache entries will be invalidated after the INSERT or UPDATE has completed. With the option turned on, they become invalid as soon as the table is locked for writing. It's generally best to leave this option disabled. Table locking is enough of a nuisance as it is, without compounding it.

Fragmentation and query_cache_min_res_unit

As previously mentioned, increasing the query_cache_min_res_unit size is something of a double-edged sword — speeding up the process of memory allocation but increasing the risk of fragmentation. Using the Qcache_* statistics, though, you can make a reasonably well-informed estimate as to a suitable size.

Subtracting `Qcache_free_memory` from the `query_cache_size` (as set in `my.cnf`) gives you the amount of memory in use by the query cache. If you then divide this figure by the number of queries in the cache (`Qcache_queries_in_cache`), you have an average size for each query. Let's try it on some sample data:

```
SHOW GLOBAL VARIABLES LIKE 'query_cache_size';
+------------------+----------+
| Variable_name    | Value    |
+------------------+----------+
| query_cache_size | 33554432 |
+------------------+----------+
(33554432 - 6847496) , 3665  = 8968
```

So, on average, each query takes up just more than 8 KB of space in the cache. Perhaps you should be increasing your value of `query_cache_min_res_unit` from the 4 KB default.

The problem here is that this figure is only an average. It could be the case that the vast majority of queries fit nicely into the default 4 KB block size, and that a handful of large queries are skewing the average up. If this were the case, raising `min_res_unit` would be a mistake. Perhaps, instead, you should be lowering `query_cache_limit` to prevent these huge queries from being cached — not because of concern over the performance penalty of allocating memory in small blocks, but because you may not want them taking up precious cache space. It depends on how often you expect a cache hit on these large queries.

Despite these caveats, the calculations suggest that raising `query_cache_min_res_unit` to a little more than 8 KB would certainly be worth trying. However, only with knowledge of the queries being executed can you make an educated decision.

The reason for being cautious about raising `query_cache_min_res_unit` is that it will likely cause an increase in fragmentation. You can gauge the level of fragmentation by looking at the ratio of free blocks to total blocks:

```
(Qcache_free_blocks / Qcache_total_blocks) * 100
```

This example data gives a fairly respectable figure of 16 percent. Values of approximately 10 percent to 20 percent are common and are not a cause for undue alarm.

When high levels of fragmentation exist, the `FLUSH query cache` command can be used to defragment the cache. Despite the slightly misleading name, this does not remove entries from the cache — if you ever want to do that, use `RESET query cache`.

The Downsides of Query Caching

As already hinted, the query cache is far from perfect, and there may be situations in which best performance can be achieved by turning it off.

One source of problems is the additional overhead imposed by enabling the cache. For each incoming `SELECT` query, MySQL must first check the cache for a match. If none is found, the query is executed as normal, and, if the query is cachable, the result is then inserted into the cache. Although this overhead is fairly low, and, in most cases, an acceptable penalty for using the cache, it is wasteful in situations in which cache hits are low.

This leads to the next big problem: invalidation. You've already learned that writing to a table causes cache entries that reference the table to be invalidated. When this happens, the cache is temporarily locked, and nothing can read from it. So, not only does MySQL waste time with housekeeping, it makes every other query wait until it has finished.

Caching Modes

An ideal situation would be one in which you simply didn't cache queries that you knew (or suspected) would be quickly invalidated. If you have the `query_cache_type` set at 1 (cache everything by default), you can disable caching on a per-query basis by adding `SQL_NO_CACHE` to the query:

```
SELECT SQL_NO_CACHE foo FROM bar
```

Or if you choose to disable caching by default (by setting `query_cache_type` to 2), caching can be enabled on a per-query basis with the following:

```
SELECT SQL_CACHE foo FROM bar
```

Armed with this, you can now sift through your web code, deciding on a case-by-case basis whether to cache. Remember, though, the aim is not to prevent invalidations completely but merely to prevent situations in which invalidation occurs so quickly that caching is pointless — and this is somewhat subjective.

Nondeterministic Queries

Another shortcoming of the query cache (actually, it's not a shortcoming — it makes perfect sense) is that nondeterministic queries cannot be cached. Prime examples of these are the `RAND()`, `NOW()`, and `CURRENT_DATE()` functions — any query using these will not be cached.

You can often get around this by performing the function in your scripting language instead. For example, consider the following PHP snippet:

```
$r1 = mysql_query("SELECT * FROM users WHERE registered = CURRENT_DATE()");
```

This query won't be cached, but if you rewrite it to the following, it *will* be cached by MySQL:

```
$r1 = mysql_query("SELECT * FROM users WHERE registered = '" . date("Y-m-d") . "'");
```

For queries that use `RAND()`, there probably isn't much you can do. You could fetch the entire data set and then choose entries from it at random. But this is unlikely to give an overall performance boost, unless your query is particularly complex. (In which case, the savings from caching might just outweigh the cost of fetching the entire data set and selecting random entries from it.) Even then, the data set might exceed `query_cache_limit`.

On the subject of time and date stamps, can you spot the reason why it would probably be pointless to change a query such as the following (again, with PHP as the scripting language)?

```
$r1 = mysql_query("SELECT  username FROM users WHERE
    account_expires < NOW()");
```

You could change this query to the following:

```
$rl = mysql_query("SELECT  username FROM users WHERE
    account_expires < '" . date("Y-m-d H:i:s") . "'");
```

Although MySQL will cache the latter, the precision of the date stamp means that if you execute the query again, a second later, the date stamp will have changed, and the query won't match the previously cached one. You end up filling the cache with queries that you know will never be executed again.

Sometimes situations like these can be avoided by rethinking the WHERE clause a little. (In this example, lower the precision of the date stamp so that if the code is run a short while later, the data stamp is still the same.) Failing that, you can use SQL_NO_CACHE or SQL_CACHE to avoid pointless caching.

You've seen how powerful the query cache can be when used properly, but there is also a lot to discover about SQL itself (or at least the MySQL implementation of SQL). In the next section, you'll learn how indexing can be used to speed up queries by several orders of magnitude, and how tools such as EXPLAIN and the slow query log can be used to find bottlenecks in your database queries.

OPTIMIZING SQL

So far, this discussion has focused on tuning the MySQL application. You've learned how MySQL and individual storage engines interact with the underlying operating system, and how system administrators can ensure harmony between the operating system and MySQL.

Let's now focus on the second key area of MySQL performance tuning: the queries. Again, there is often a huge scope for improvement, but as a system administrator, the changes aren't always so easy to implement. Rather than simply tweaking a few buffer sizes in my.cnf, you may edit or rewrite large portions of badly written applications to change the way in which they interact with MySQL.

EXPLAIN Explained

MySQL's EXPLAIN command offers insight into how MySQL executes queries, and is invaluable when trying to diagnose why a query runs slowly, or not as expected. To use it, simply prepend EXPLAIN to the beginning of a SELECT query, as shown here:

```
mysql> EXPLAIN SELECT * FROM wp_users WHERE user_login LIKE 'pete%'\G
*************************** 1. row ***************************
           id: 1
  select_type: SIMPLE
        table: wp_users
         type: range
possible_keys: user_login_key
          key: user_login_key
      key_len: 180
```

```
       ref: NULL
      rows: 1
     Extra: Using where
```

The output columns are as follows:

- ➤ id — This is the ID of the SELECT query. If the query contains subqueries, each will have a unique ID.

- ➤ select_type — For simple select queries (that is, those not using UNION or subqueries), this will always be SIMPLE.

- ➤ table — This is the table being operated on.

- ➤ type — This is the join type.

- ➤ possible_keys — This is a list of indexes that MySQL has found to choose from.

- ➤ key — This is the actual index that MySQL decided to use.

- ➤ key_len — This is the length of the key being used.

- ➤ ref — This is either the name of the columns that MySQL compares to the index given in key, or to denote that a constant is being searched for.

- ➤ rows — This is the number of rows retrieved for examination.

- ➤ Extra — This provides additional information about how MySQL handles the query.

Some of these columns are important enough to warrant a more detailed discussion. Let's start with select_type.

select_type

Aside from SIMPLE, there are eight other possible values for this column:

- ➤ PRIMARY — This is the main SELECT query in statements containing subqueries.

- ➤ UNION — This shows SELECT queries in a UNION other than the first SELECT.

- ➤ DEPENDENT UNION — In UNIONs, this shows SELECT statements (other than the first) that are dependent on the main query.

- ➤ UNION RESULT   This is the result of a UNION.

- ➤ SUBQUERY — This shows any SELECT statements that are part of a subquery.

- ➤ DEPENDENT SUBQUERY — This shows SELECT statements in a subquery that are dependent on the main query.

- ➤ DERIVED — This shows that the table is derived from a subquery.

- ➤ UNCACHEABLE SUBQUERY — This shows that the results of the subquery cannot be cached and, hence, must be re-evaluated each time (for each row of the main query).

SIMPLE select_types are the most common, but the others do crop up regularly in more complicated queries.

type

The next column of special note is the `type` (of join), of which there are a dozen possible values. The `type` (of join) used can have a big effect on performance, and when debugging a slow query, it's always worth checking that MySQL uses the type of join you would expect. Use of the word "join" is a little confusing here and refers to MySQL's method of executing queries — it doesn't imply that multiple tables are joined together in the SQL sense.

Following are the join types (listed in order from best performance to worst performance):

➤ `system` — The table is an in-memory system table containing just one row, so there is little work to be done.

➤ `const` — This is used when a `PRIMARY` or `UNIQUE` is compared to a constant value, resulting on only one row (or no rows) being returned. Following is an example:

```
SELECT * FROM users WHERE ID=3
```

This assumes that the ID column is unique.

➤ `eq_ref` — This occurs in join queries when a unique non-null index (or primary index) matches a single row of the second table, for each result row of the first table. Consider the following example:

```
SELECT * FROM t1, t2 WHERE t1.indexed_column = t2.column
```

In this situation, `eq_ref` can (and will) be used for `t1`. `eq_ref` only when using the equality operator (=).

➤ `ref` — Almost identical to `eq_ref`, a `ref` access type occurs when multiple matches occur on the table. This usually occurs because the index is not unique (and does not contain `null` values). Because multiple rows are returned, this join type isn't as desirable as `eq_ref`.

➤ `ref_or_null` — This is identical to `ref`, except `null` values occur in the index.

➤ `full_text` — The join occurs on a full text index (`MyISAM` only).

➤ `index_merge` — Multiple indexes can be merged and used. (You'll learn more about this later in the "Indexing" section.)

➤ `unique_subquery` — This is similar to `ref` but for unique indexes in subqueries.

➤ `index_subquery` — This is identical to `unique_subquery` but for nonunique indexes in subqueries.

➤ `range` — This indicates that a range of rows will be returned, such as the following:

```
SELECT * FROM products WHERE price > 100;
```

This is still an improvement on a plain index join because the number of rows is limited.

➤ `index` — A full scan of the index is required. This is the default when none of the previously listed join types are suitable.

➤ ALL — This requires a full scan of the data in the table and happens when searching against an unindexed column. In these situations, performance is usually poor (worsening dramatically as the size of the table increases).

That's a lot of different join types, but the majority of the time, you'll encounter only eq_ref, ref, range, and index. All join types are particularly poor performers but are usually easily fixed through appropriate indexing.

Extra

As previously mentioned, the Extra column provides additional information about the query. As of this writing, 25 different values can appear in this column. Rather than provide an exhaustive list of these, let's concentrate on the most important ones. You can find the complete list in the online MySQL documentation (http://dev.mysql.com/doc/refman/5.6/en/explain-output.html).

➤ Using where — The presence of a WHERE clause is limiting the number of rows matched. Usually, this is what you want, rather than MySQL scanning all rows in the table.

➤ Using filesort — This is something of a misnomer because it doesn't imply the use of files. Rather, it occurs when a sort on a nonindexed column is performed. You'll learn more about ORDER BY and GROUP BY optimization in the upcoming section, "Indexing."

➤ Using index — This occurs when only the data from indexed columns is required. In these situations, the query can be answered solely by searching the index, with no need to search the row (or for MyISAM, the data file).

➤ Using temporary — A temporary table is used to hold the results. Typically, this is needed when performing a GROUP BY and ORDER BY. Temporary tables aren't a problem by themselves, but if a temporary table is written to disk (for example, because it is too big for memory), performance will suffer.

As you can see, the EXPLAIN command can be an incredibly useful tool.

The Slow Query Log

MySQL offers the capability to log all queries that take longer than a user-defined number of seconds to run, and this log can be invaluable when debugging slow applications. Even when you're not aware of any particular slowdown, it can be useful to leave the slow query log enabled, and periodically review it — you just might be surprised.

Enabling the Log

The my.cnf configuration options are as follows:

```
long_query_time = 5
slow_query_log = 1
slow_query_log_file = /var/log/mysql/slow-queries.log
```

This logs any query taking more than 5 seconds to execute to `/var/log/mysql/slow-queries`
`.log`. (Note that you may first need to create and set appropriate ownerships on this file.) It's worth
noting that query execution time does not include the time taken to acquire table locks. If a query
regularly runs slowly because of a high level of locking, it will not be logged.

Optionally, you can also restrict the slow query log to those queries that cause more than a certain
number of rows to be examined, as shown here:

```
min_examined_row_limit = 500
```

> **NOTE** *This feature was introduced in MySQL version 5.5.*

Inspecting the Slow Query Log

An example entry for a real-world slow query log follows. In addition to the query, you see information on the user that executed it, the date-time stamp, the time taken for the query to run, and the
number of rows examined.

```
# Time: 110422  4:56:28
# User@Host: forums[forums] @ localhost []
# Query_time: 10.119974  Lock_time: 0.000065 Rows_sent: 1   Rows_examined: 1191
SET timestamp=1303444588;
SELECT COUNT(*) AS posts
                FROM post AS post
                WHERE threadid = 83035 AND visible = 1
                AND dateline <= 1194968540;
```

It's worth remembering that an entry in the slow query log does not mean that the query is inherently
slow, merely that it executed slowly on this particular occasion. This could be caused by other factors,
such as the number of concurrent clients running queries against the database, another client running a
particularly CPU-intensive query, high load on the server caused by the generation of backups, or even
because MySQL's caches have not been primed (for example, because MySQL hasn't been running long).

Whenever you spot a slow query, you should generally repeat the query at the MySQL CLI — having
first inspected the operating system and MySQL's process lists (SHOW PROCESSLIST) — before deciding if it is a cause for concern.

mysqldumpslow

For all but the smallest slow query logs, manually reviewing the log file can be tedious. Fortunately,
MySQL ships with a useful tool that can analyze such logs. mysqldumpslow counts the number of
occurrences of each query in the log, allowing you to see at a glance the worst offenders.

Queries Not Using Indexes

Indexes (as you'll soon see) play such an important part in MySQL, that an option exists to cause
any queries that don't use indexes to be written to the slow query log.

```
log-queries-not-using-indexes = 1
```

Actually, that's not entirely true. With this option enabled, MySQL actually logs any queries that cause all rows in the table to be retrieved. Mostly, this is a result of no suitable index being found, but occasionally it is because the query actually returns all rows of the table. This is a subtle point, but worth remembering.

Indexing

Probably the single biggest way to improve the performance of SELECT queries is through the use of appropriate indexing. (Note the use of the word "appropriate." As you'll see later, in the section, "When Not to Index," indexing everything in sight is counter-productive.) Much like a book, where an index saves you from looking through every page of the book, indexes on columns saves MySQL from examining every record in a table. Just as the index of a book tells you the page to go to, a database index tells MySQL the position of the data on the disk to jump to.

The simplest way to create an index on an existing table is through the alter command, as shown here:

```
alter table regions add index(country);
```

This adds an index on the country column of the regions table. You can view the existing indexes with describe, as shown here:

```
mysql> describe regions;
+-----------+------------------+------+-----+---------+----------------+
| Field     | Type             | Null | Key | Default | Extra          |
+-----------+------------------+------+-----+---------+----------------+
| regionId  | int(10) unsigned | NO   | PRI | NULL    | auto_increment |
| country   | char(2)          | NO   | MUL |         |                |
| name      | varchar(64)      | NO   |     |         |                |
| district  | varchar(64)      | NO   |     |         |                |
+-----------+------------------+------+-----+---------+----------------+
```

The Key field of the output shows the index type (if any). For the country index, it's MUL (multiple), meaning that multiple occurrences of the same value are permitted — that is, the index does not require that values in this column be unique. By contrast, the existing index on regionID is PRI (primary), a special type that enforces uniqueness on data in the column. You'll learn more about primary indexes in a minute.

Following are other possible index types:

➤ UNI (unique) — This requires that all values in the column be unique. For columns that always hold unique values (such as the Social Security number of an employee), using UNI over MUL offers a performance increase.

➤ FUL (full-text) — This is a MyISAM-specific index type, allowing for fast string matching using MATCH or AGAINST.

Specifying the index type is as simple as adding it to the previous alter query:

```
alter table regions add index uni (country);
```

Primary Indexes

The *primary index* is special. Only one primary index may exist in a table, and the column indexed must contain unique values. The most common technique is to create an auto-incrementing integer column (`regionId` in the example) and assign a primary key to that, or use a Universal Unique Identifier (UUID). But you're free to not create a primary key at all if you want.

In `MyISAM`, indexes are stored in a B-tree structure in a separate file (with the `.MYI` extension in MySQL's data directory). This causes a slight performance overhead because MySQL must first scan the index and then scan the data to the offset given in the index. This is minor overhead, though, and is usually easily compensated for by the improvement in performance provided by using indexes.

With `InnoDB`, the primary key is stored alongside secondary keys. So, if the table contains secondary keys, it pays to keep the primary index small — preferably an integer.

Clustered Indexes

`InnoDB` internally uses *clustered indexes*, which exist in the same page as the data they reference. This makes lookups on the clustered index fast because the disk heads are already in the correct location. (Compare this with `MyISAM`, where the disk must first seek to the entry in the index file, and then to the entry in the data file.)

Only one clustered index is permitted for a table, and `InnoDB` defaults to using the primary key. If no primary key is set on the table, the first unique index is used. If there are no unique indexes, `InnoDB` creates a hidden, auto-incrementing numeric column and assigns a primary key to this.

All other indexes in `InnoDB` tables are nonclustered, secondary indexes. These indexes contain the primary index column for the row, allowing `InnoDB` to then look up this primary index. This two-step process is similar to how `MyISAM` handles indexes but is slightly slower. This is the reason why there is a gap in performance between primary and secondary lookups in `InnoDB` (and why the primary key is of special importance). In `MyISAM`, there is no difference in performance between different index types, and the primary key holds no particular importance.

Which Columns to Index?

In general, you want to place indexes on columns that are frequently used for SELECT, GROUP, ORDER, and `join`. Specifically, MySQL uses indexes (where they exist) in the following situations:

➤ Comparison operators (=, >, <, >=, <=, IF NULL, and BETWEEN)

➤ LIKE clauses that do not begin with a wildcard

➤ Table joins

➤ ORDER BY and GROUP BY

➤ MAX() and MIN()

Thus, all the following queries would make use of any index that exists on the `mycolumn` column:

```
SELECT * FROM mytable WHERE mycolumn=5
SELECT * FROM mytable WHERE mycolumn >5 AND mycolumn < 10
SELECT * FROM mytable WHERE mycolumn LIKE 'something%';
```

```
SELECT * FROM mytable, myothertable WHERE mytable.mycolumn = myothertable.userID
SELECT * FROM mytable ORDER BY mycolumn DESC
SELECT MIN(mycolumn) FROM mytable
```

If MySQL decides that using an index will probably result in more than a certain percentage of the table being returned (currently approximately 30 percent, but the exact value has varied between releases), it will ignore the index and perform a full table scan because this linear disk access will be faster than repeatedly seeking to different points of the data.

HEAP tables are also handled slightly differently, and indexes won't be used for ORDER BY clauses, or comparisons that don't use the equality operator.

Let's return to the regions table of the earlier example. This was actually part of a real estate search portal and mapped various locations around the world to the country they belonged to. The table listing each property included a regionId column, corresponding to an entry in the regions table.

Given that joining the two tables on the regionId will likely be such a common task, it makes perfect sense that the regionID column of region be indexed. But what about the other three columns in this table? If the application enables the end user to view all properties in a particular country or region, it makes sense to index these columns, too. Let's use EXPLAIN to show how MySQL would handle a SELECT against one of these columns, both with and without indexes.

```
mysql> explain select regionId from regions where country="UK"\G
*************************** 1. row ***************************
           id: 1
  select_type: SIMPLE
        table: regions
         type: ALL
possible_keys: NULL
          key: NULL
      key_len: NULL
          ref: NULL
         rows: 170
        Extra: Using where
```

Without an index on country, MySQL must scan all 170 rows of the table. Now, add an index and rerun the query:

```
mysql> alter table regions add index(country);
mysql> explain select regionId from regions where country="UK"\G
*************************** 1. row ***************************
           id: 1
  select_type: SIMPLE
        table: regions
         type: ref
possible_keys: country
          key: country
      key_len: 67
          ref: const
         rows: 19
        Extra: Using where
```

This time, MySQL can immediately ignore the 151 rows where the country is not "UK".

One slightly lesser-known feature of indexes is that MySQL uses only a maximum of one per table in most cases. Consider the following example:

```
mysql> alter table regions add index (region);
mysql> explain SELECT regionId FROM regions WHERE country="UK" AND
    region="North East"\G
*************************** 1. row ***************************
           id: 1
  select_type: SIMPLE
        table: regions
         type: ref
possible_keys: region,country
          key: region
      key_len: 67
          ref: const
         rows: 4
        Extra: Using where
```

The `possible_keys` column shows that MySQL has correctly identified that both the `region` and `country` columns contain indexes, but that it ultimately chose to use the index on `region`. The reason lies in the number of rows left to examine. MySQL calculated that using the `region` index would result in 4 rows to scan, and using the `country` index would have resulted in 19. As you would expect, only one row of the table matches both `country="UK"` and `region="North East"`, and scanning 4 rows to find this match is a lot faster than scanning 19.

MySQL version 5 introduced changes that enable multiple keys to be used in some circumstances. When range scans are used on multiple indexed columns, MySQL scans using the indexes of each and then merge the results. This is the `index_merge` method mentioned previously:

```
mysql> explain SELECT regionId FROM regions WHERE country="UK"
    or region="North East"\G
*************************** 1. row ***************************
           id: 1
  select_type: SIMPLE
        table: regions
         type: index_merge
possible_keys: region,country
          key: country,region
      key_len: 67,67
          ref: NULL
         rows: 13
        Extra: Using union(country,region); Using where
```

> **NOTE** *Both indexes are listed in the* key *column, and the* Extra *information shows that a* union *was used.*

Composite Indexes

The solution to the problem of searching on multiple indexes in a table can be solved through the use of *composite indexes* (also referred to as *multiple column indexes*). As the name suggests, these are indexes that span two or more columns, or column prefixes.

Composite indexes are ideally suited for situations in which SELECT queries will regularly be performed against a particular combination of columns. Going back to the real estate example, you can see that most queries will either specify country, or country and region in the WHERE clause. So, a composite index on country and region seems obvious. The syntax is simply as follows:

```
ALTER TABLE regions ADD INDEX countryregion (country, region);
```

(Of course, you can call the index whatever you like.)

Rerunning the earlier query, you can see that MySQL now finds three possible indexes to use and chooses the newly created composite index:

```
mysql> explain select regionId FROM regions WHERE country="UK"
    and region="North East"\G
*************************** 1. row ***************************
           id: 1
  select_type: SIMPLE
        table: regions
         type: ref
possible_keys: region,country,countryregion
          key: countryregion
      key_len: 134
          ref: const,const
         rows: 3
        Extra: Using where
```

Does this mean you can now remove the indexes on region and country because both exist in the composite index? Let's try the following:

```
mysql> ALTER TABLE regions DROP INDEX country;
mysql> ALTER TABLE regions DROP INDEX region;
mysql> explain SELECT regionId FROM regions WHERE country="UK"\G
*************************** 1. row ***************************
           id: 1
  select_type: SIMPLE
        table: regions
         type: ref
possible_keys: countryregion
          key: countryregion
      key_len: 67
          ref: const
         rows: 9
        Extra: Using where
```

```
mysql> explain SELECT regionId FROM regions WHERE region="North East"\G
*************************** 1. row ***************************
           id: 1
  select_type: SIMPLE
        table: regions
         type: ALL
possible_keys: NULL
          key: NULL
      key_len: NULL
          ref: NULL
         rows: 17
        Extra: Using where
```

Unfortunately, things didn't go as hoped. Selecting on country still ran as expected, but selecting on region failed to utilize the countryregion index.

The reason centers on the order of the columns in the index. In this example, country was put first, followed by region. This allows MySQL to utilize the index when searching on country, or country *and* region, but not just on region. In this example, this actually makes perfect sense. Sometimes you'll want to search on just country; other times, you'll want to search on country and region. But you are unlikely to want to search on just region.

Sometimes things aren't this clear-cut. Don't be afraid to duplicate columns across composite and noncomposite indexes if the situation warrants it. But remember to think carefully about the order of columns in a composite index, and remember that indexes create overhead.

Prefix Indexes

Indexes take up disk space, and it is preferable to keep index sizes as small as possible because it reduces disk seek times and I/O, and allows more of the index to fit in the key buffer. MySQL supports *prefix indexes* (not to be confused with *partial indexes* — a feature not supported by MySQL), in which only the beginning or end of a column's value is indexed (with the former being the most common). Prefix indexes can greatly reduce the size of an index but can also limit their effectiveness, and care must often be taken to find a happy middle ground.

The ideal length for a prefix is one that keeps the index size low but still maintains enough uniqueness to limit the number of rows matched. For a column with a UNIQUE index on it, it isn't always possible (or preferable) to maintain that uniqueness in the prefix, and the index type may need to be changed to MULTIPLE.

Consider a table containing information on books. There are columns for the book's title, author, publisher, and publication date. Say, you will often be searching on title, so you add an index on this column. But rather than indexing the whole column (which could take up a lot of space, given the number of characters in many book titles), what if you just index the first *x* number of characters? This will almost certainly decrease the level of uniqueness but will also reduce the index size considerably.

For this example, load in a list of 31,416 book titles from Project Gutenberg (www.gutenberg.org).

```
mysql> select count(*) from books;
+----------+
| count(*) |
+----------+
|    31416 |
+----------+
```

Now, count the number of distinct titles to get an idea of the current level of uniqueness.

```
mysql> SELECT COUNT(DISTINCT (title)) FROM books;
+------------------------+
| COUNT(DISTINCT (title)) |
+------------------------+
|                  30510 |
+------------------------+
```

You can calculate the cardinality by dividing the total number of unique entries by the total number of rows. In this case, you get a value of 0.97 (the maximum value, of course, will be 1), indicating a high level of uniqueness.

What if you index just the first five characters of the title?

```
mysql> SELECT COUNT(DISTINCT (left(title,5))) FROM books;
+---------------------------------+
| COUNT(DISTINCT (left(title,5))) |
+---------------------------------+
|                            8376 |
+---------------------------------+
```

This causes the cardinality to drop to 0.266 (8,376/3,1416), indicating a significant drop in uniqueness. This isn't too surprising. After all, lots of books will start with the same five characters. Table 8-1 shows the results with other key lengths.

TABLE 8-1: Results with Varying Key Lengths

KEY LENGTH	DISTINCT VALUES	CARDINALITY
1	41	0.001
5	8,376	0.266
10	19,555	0.622
15	25,660	0.817
20	27,582	0.878
25	28,436	0.905
30	29,010	0.923

From this, the optimal prefix length looks to be approximately 10 to 15 characters. Values more than 15 give only a modest increase in uniqueness, whereas for key sizes less than 10, there is a sharp drop-off in cardinality, causing more rows to match — which means more work for MySQL in examining those rows and more disk I/O as they are read in.

The best index length is clearly highly dependent on the nature of the data, and may even change as the data itself changes, requiring you to regularly monitor the health of the index.

Covering Indexes

Earlier in this chapter, you learned about the two steps involved when performing a SELECT against an indexed column in MyISAM. First, MySQL scans the index to obtain the row pointer, and then it scans the data file to the position given in the pointer. (Of course, much of this data will hopefully already be in memory.) However, if you've asked for only columns that exist in the index, this second step can be avoided, giving a significant boost in performance.

Covering indexes are just a special case of a composite index, in which the index contains all the columns that you need. Rather than creating a composite index to include columns you'll be searching on, you create it with the specific aim to eliminate scans of the data file — even if this means including columns that you have no need to search on. So, although covering indexes and composite indexes are ultimately the same thing, the motivation behind creating them is what creates the distinction.

Now, return to the real estate example. Most of the time, you want to SELECT the regionId for a particular combination of region and country, as shown here:

```
SELECT regionId FROM regions WHERE country="UK" or region="North East"
```

By creating a composite index on regionId, country, and region, all the data that MySQL needs is in the index file, and there is no need to query the data file.

The use of covering indexes can cause a dramatic increase in performance, but, of course, there are downsides. The most notable is an increase in the size of the index file, and larger index files mean more disk I/O and less caching in memory. Depending on the columns being indexed, the use of a covering index could easily double or triple the size of the index file. Naturally, large covering indexes take longer to update, too, which can slow down UPDATE, DELETE, and INSERT queries.

Finally, covering indexes are less of an advantage in InnoDB, where primary indexes are stored on the same page as the data, and the two-step approach of MyISAM is not needed.

When Not to Index

At first glance, it seems as if indexes are a win-win situation. Certainly there are plenty of situations in which an index on a column will never be used, but is an unused index doing any harm?

The first problem with indexes is that they slow down INSERT and UPDATE queries. Each time the data in an indexed column is modified, the index must be updated. For the majority of web applications, where tables are read from much more than they are written to, this isn't a problem. But for write-heavy tables containing large amounts of data, it can cause a noticeable slowdown.

In addition to this, indexes take up disk space, and although the cost of storage is low, larger numbers of indexes take longer to scan through.

There are also some situations in which indexes aren't used — for example, in MySQL versions prior to 5.0, only one index would ever be used per table.

None of these problems are reasons not to use indexing where appropriate, because the benefits far outweigh the drawbacks — but they are enough to make over-indexing something to be avoided.

Index and Table Management

MySQL maintains statistics on various properties of tables and indexes, such as the number of rows and sizes of indexes. These figures are used for (among other things) estimating the optimal query executing path, but they can become quite distorted after heavy writes.

The ANALYZE TABLE table_name statement can be used to regenerate these statistics, and it makes sense to regularly run this on tables that are write-heavy. On MyISAM, this causes the whole table to be locked. With InnoDB, only row-level locking is used, but it's also less important because InnoDB's table stats are never 100 percent accurate anyway — and MySQL knows this.

Closely related to the ANALYZE TABLE statement is OPTIMIZE TABLE table_name, which is used to defragment tables. Table fragmentation is most common after deleting large numbers of rows. Although MySQL will attempt to gradually plug these holes with subsequent INSERTs, the gappy nature of the data in the meantime will result in increased disk reads, thus reducing performance. Defragmenting the table causes the data to be repacked tightly, eliminating these gaps.

In addition, running OPTIMIZE TABLE on MyISAM tables causes all indexes to be sorted and rebuilt, which can enhance performance when querying them. Unfortunately, InnoDB indexes can't yet be re-sorted because of their structure (something that was discussed earlier in this chapter).

As with ANALYZE TABLE, optimizing causes table-level locking in MyISAM and row-level locking in InnoDB. But it's still worthwhile optimizing on a regular basis, especially for tables that are written to frequently (or after performing batch deletions).

With MyISAM tables, rows are physically ordered chronologically (InnoDB always orders by primary key), but by using ALTER TABLE, you can ask MySQL to re-order a table by a different column. This can improve performance in situations in which you will regularly be searching or sorting on that column. The syntax is simply as follows:

```
ALTER TABLE table_name ORDER BY column_name
```

> **NOTE** *Remember that, on large tables, this could take some time.*

Query Execution and Optimization

For a query to be executed by MySQL, numerous steps, such as syntax checks and permissions' checks, must be performed. The two steps that are of particular interest to use are optimization and generation of the parse tree. It is at this latter stage that MySQL attempts to determine the most efficient method to execute the query before ultimately generating a Query Execution Path (QEP).

MySQL tokenizes the query and builds from these tokens a tree-like structure (the *parse tree*) detailing all the possible execution paths that may be taken. It is then the job of the optimizer to determine the most efficient path to take.

The size of the parse tree increases exponentially as the number of tables in the query increases, and it could potentially take hours for MySQL to calculate the cost of each potential path. Thus, the first step of the optimizer is to apply a number of heuristics to eliminate obviously slow paths. These hard-coded rules are general techniques that MySQL knows can improve performance in the vast majority of cases (but occasionally it does get things wrong), and includes re-ordering joins, using covering indexes, and early termination (for example, when a LIMIT clause is used).

Query Cost

At this stage, the parse tree will hopefully have been pruned substantially. For the remaining branches, MySQL will attempt to determine the cost of each path before settling on the cheapest. Terms like "best" and "cheapest" can be a little ambiguous. In this situation, MySQL defines them by the number of 4 KB data pages (and by extension, therefore roughly the number of rows) that it estimates must be read to fulfill the query. Thus, a path that causes fewer pages to be read is "cheaper."

Of course, this logic isn't always true. It doesn't take into account that sequential page reads will generally be a lot faster than random page reads (thus, it would probably be faster to read four sequential pages than three nonsequential pages), and it assumes that all page reads are from disk. In practice, some pages will likely be cached in memory.

To estimate the cost of the various paths, MySQL looks at statistics for the tables, such as the number of rows, the length and number of keys, and key distributions. Based on these, a numeric query cost is calculated for each path. You can see the calculated query cost for a given query by examining the last_query_cost variable immediately after executing a query:

```
mysql> SELECT SQL_NO_CACHE * FROM regions WHERE region="North East";
....
mysql> SHOW STATUS LIKE  'last_query_cost';
+-----------------+----------+
| Variable_name   | Value    |
+-----------------+----------+
| Last_query_cost | 2.799000 |
+-----------------+----------+
```

This provides a useful metric to use when creating indexes or rewriting queries. For example, if you remove the region index from the table and rerun the query, you get a query cost of 5.832594 — twice as expensive as when the index was in place. Despite this, the cost is still relatively low — for joins across large tables, it's not uncommon to see costs in the tens or hundreds of thousands.

```
mysql> select SQL_NO_CACHE propref, addr FROM property JOIN regions ON
    property.regionId=regions.regionId WHERE regions.region="North East";
...
```

```
mysql> show status like 'last_query_cost';
+-----------------+--------------+
| Variable_name   | Value        |
+-----------------+--------------+
| Last_query_cost | 25073.649391 |
+-----------------+--------------+
```

A second problem with estimating the query cost is that the statistics aren't always that accurate. For example, although MyISAM keeps an exact count of the number of rows in a table, InnoDB has only a rough idea (unless, of course, you perform a COUNT query). Key distributions are rarely perfectly uniform either. Consider an index of employee surnames — in most English language countries, there will be a lot more beginning with "S" than "Z."

Tips for SQL Efficiency

The remainder of this section focuses on tips for writing better (or, perhaps, more efficient) SQL.

Bulk Writes

In some situations, it's common to perform bulk UPDATE/DELETE/INSERTs on a periodic basis — for example, pruning log entries on a nightly basis, or loading in data from a comma-separated value (CSV) file. The presence of indexed columns can make this process painfully slow because the indexes will be updated after every query. And as the indexes grow bigger, they take longer to update — especially if they are too large to fit in memory.

Ideally, you'd like to tell MySQL to delay updating the indexes until you finish the batch operation. You can do this by temporarily disabling indexes on the table like so:

```
ALTER TABLE table_name DISABLE KEYS;
```

After you finish writing, indexes can be re-enabled using the following:

```
ALTER TABLE table_name ENABLE KEYS;
```

The cost to update the indexes following a bulk query should not be significantly higher than following a single write query.

The disadvantage to this technique is that unique indexes can't be disabled because checks must be performed after each write to ensure the data in the indexed column is unique. Despite this, temporarily disabling keys can still be useful in reducing the number of indexes updated after each write.

With InnoDB, an additional trick you can use is to temporarily disable autocommit mode. With autocommit enabled (the default), each write to a table causes a log entry to be written to disk, immediately followed by a flush — so you don't even benefit from I/O buffering at the OS level. Use the following to turn autocommit off:

```
SET autocommit=0;
```

After performing the batch write, you then issue the COMMIT statement to flush the log entries to disk.

In a similar vein, if foreign key constraints are used on an InnoDB table, these can temporarily be disabled while performing batch operations. The syntax is simply as follows:

```
SET foreign_key_checks=0;
*perform batch writes *
SET foreign_key_checks=1;
```

Again, this can speed up batch INSERTs significantly by stopping MySQL from checking foreign keys after each INSERT.

Usually, INSERT queries have the same priority as other queries in MySQL. When a client issues an INSERT, MySQL queues it up and returns a response to the client after it has been processed. In the case of batch INSERTs, priority generally isn't an issue — you usually aren't in a particular hurry for the INSERTs to complete. If anything, you'd probably prefer these queries to have a lower priority, to minimize disruption to other clients.

You can achieve this by using a modified form of the INSERT syntax including the DELAYED keyword:

```
INSERT DELAYED INTO table .....
```

This causes two things to happen. First, control is immediately returned to the client, allowing it to execute further queries (presumably more INSERTs). Second, MySQL queues up the INSERTs in memory with a lower priority and executes them only when the table is not in use by any other clients. In practice, this tends to result in the INSERTs being grouped together and written in clumps, further improving performance.

In addition, you may also want to tune the bulk_insert_buffer_size variable (the default is 8 MB), which controls the size of this buffer for MyISAM tables. It is allocated per client, so care must be taken not to exhaust system memory.

The downside to delayed INSERTs is that you cannot be sure when the queries will eventually be executed. On a busy table, it could take some time. During the time that the queries are in memory waiting to be executed, they are somewhat volatile, too. If MySQL is restarted or the structure of the table altered, these queries will be lost. Delayed INSERTs are also a little slower than regular INSERTs, making the latter preferable if activity on the table is low enough not to warrant delayed INSERTs.

Yet another trick to improve INSERT performance is through the use of multiple-row INSERT statements, as shown here:

```
INSERT INTO table VALUES ("Smith", " Peter") , (" Roberts", "Stefanie");
```

Although this is no faster to execute for MySQL, it does reduce the amount of data transmitted.

Normalization

Normalization is a staple of computer science books, especially when dealing with relational database systems such as MySQL. The main goal is to eliminate (or at least reduce) data redundancy, thereby reducing the possibility of inconsistencies. (If data is duplicated in multiple places, care must be taken to update each copy.)

Although normalization leads to elegant data structures, you aren't taking an exam in computer science, and consideration must be given to performance. In some situations, duplicating data or merging columns into a single table (the so called *Spreadsheet Syndrome*) is the right thing to do, and you shouldn't be afraid to go against what the textbooks say if it leads to better performance. The general rule is to normalize as much as possible and then denormalize as performance dictates — sound advice.

Joins

Badly written joins have the potential to be painfully slow, and when analyzing a slow query log, you often find that joins are the most common (and expensive) entries.

Unless there is a compelling reason not to, it's almost always a good idea to index columns used in joins. The benefit can be exponential.

In the following example, the two tables both have approximately 26,000 rows, and neither of the two joined columns have indexes on them. You can use the query cost metric to gauge relative performance. (You could instead have looked at the number of rows examined or the execution time, but the query cost is the most accurate.)

```
mysql> select SQL_NO_CACHE count(*) from vacancies,vacancy2industry WHERE
    vacancy2industry.VAC_VacancyID=vacancies.VAC_ID;
+----------+
| count(*) |
+----------+
|    26207 |
+----------+
1 row in set (41.43 sec)

mysql> show status like 'last_query_cost';
+-----------------+-------------------+
| Variable_name   | Value             |
+-----------------+-------------------+
| Last_query_cost | 143290315.390895  |
+-----------------+-------------------+
```

A query cost of more than 143 million is a far cry from the value of 2.79 seen for the simple SELECT earlier in this chapter, and a 41-second execution time is unacceptable for a web application. Let's try the query again having added an index on vacancy2industry.VAC_VacancyID:

```
mysql> show status like 'last_query_cost';
+-----------------+-----------------+
| Variable_name   | Value           |
+-----------------+-----------------+
| Last_query_cost | 1672048.503979  |
+-----------------+-----------------+
```

Better, but now add an index on `vacancies.VAC_ID`, too:

```
mysql> show status like 'last_query_cost';
+-----------------+--------------+
| Variable_name   | Value        |
+-----------------+--------------+
| Last_query_cost | 32862.859059 |
+-----------------+--------------+
```

That's much better. Although the numbers are still fairly high, this is a huge difference — the indexed version of the query is 1,000 times faster. It's not difficult to see why optimizing one join query can do more for performance than optimizing a dozen `SELECT`s.

It also helps MySQL if the columns joined are of the same type and length. Thus, joining a `varchar(32)` with a `varchar(16)` is better than a `varchar(32)` with an `int`. But `varchar(32)` with `varchar(32)` is even better. This is one situation in which it makes sense to go against the rule to keep column lengths as short as possible. Don't be afraid to experiment with increasing the size of a frequently joined column to match that of the second column.

> **NOTE** *Incidentally, joins on integers are more efficient than on text columns. Unless you need negative values, go for unsigned integers.*

Only SELECT What You Need

`SELECT *` is the lazy way to read data from MySQL, and there are a couple of good reasons to explicitly list column names instead.

First, there's the danger than any changes to the number of columns in the table will break web code — especially if the code is structured to expect columns in a particular order.

Second, in many cases, you don't need all the columns. Requesting them simply means more data being transferred between the server and client, more memory used for send buffers, and more memory used by the web code to hold the results. Carefully selecting which columns are actually needed also increases the opportunity for covering indexes to be used, which can be a huge boost to read performance.

DELETE versus TRUNCATE

When you want to delete all the rows from a table, `TRUNCATE table_name` is generally a better (much faster) choice than `DELETE`, but there are a few other subtle differences. For example, `TRUNCATE` also causes `auto_increment` counters to be reset, and, in many ways, `TRUNCATE` can be thought of as a shortcut for `DROP table`/`CREATE table`.

DNS Lookups

Remote connections to a MySQL server typically involve DNS lookups because MySQL attempts to establish whether the hostname of the client matches any of the access masks in the grants table.

Naturally, the latency that this introduces is largely dependent on the responsiveness of the resolving DNS server being queries.

You can cut out this step by adding `skip-name-resolve` to `my.cnf`, which causes MySQL not to perform a `PTR` record lookup on the IP address of the connecting client. But be aware that access masks in the grants table now need to use IP addresses rather than hostnames.

Actually, this isn't as big an advantage as it may first seem. MySQL has a built-in cache for DNS lookups, capable (by default) of holding 128 entries. (If you want to increase it further, you need to recompile MySQL.) Typical MySQL usage patterns involve a relatively small number of clients making frequent connections (for example, a pool of web servers). So, the vast majority of the time, DNS responses will be cached in memory anyway.

SQL_SMALL_RESULT and SQL_BIG_RESULT

These two `SELECT` options provide hints to MySQL on how to handle the data returned by the query, and are particularly suited for use with `GROUP BY` or `DISTINCT`.

For queries that return a large amount of data, `SQL_BIG_RESULT` tells MySQL not to bother trying to hold the result in memory (which it normally would), and instead use a disk-based temporary table. Conversely `SQL_SMALL_RESULT` asks MySQL to hold the results in memory, which is a lot faster than disk-based tables.

In most situations, `SQL_SMALL_RESULT` isn't necessary because in-memory temporary tables are what MySQL will use by default anyway, only falling back on disk-based tables if the result set is too large. By specifying `SQL_BIG_RESULT`, you save MySQL the effort of fitting a large result set in memory, failing, and using a disk-based table. The savings here are only modest, though.

More worrisome is the incorrect use of these options. If you specify `SQL_BIG_RESULT` on a query that actually returns a modest amount of data, you lose the performance boost of having the results returned directly from memory. Similarly, if `SQL_SMALL_RESULT` is used on a query that returns lots of data, you confuse MySQL into attempting to store the results in memory.

Given the modest savings offered by these options, and the potential for them to be used incorrectly, a lot of care must be taken. Only use `SQL_BIG_RESULT` when you're sure the result will be big — and don't bother with `SQL_SMALL_RESULT`.

Prepared Statements

In MySQL and many other database management systems (DBMSs), *prepared statements* offer a more efficient way to execute similar statements repeatedly. Unlike standard queries, in which the complete statement to execute is sent to the server in one go, prepared statements consist of two steps.

In the first step, a template statement is sent in which placeholders (question marks) are used in place of one or more values. MySQL parses, compiles, and optimizes the query, but without actually executing it.

The template can be executed at a later date by passing values for the placeholder variables to the server. This step may be repeated as many times as necessary.

From a performance perspective, the main advantage here is that the parsing, compiling, and optimizing need only be performed once, reducing MySQL's workload. Prepared statements are also popular because they reduce the possibilities of SQL injection attacks.

In PHP, both the `mysqli` and PDO MySQL extensions support prepared statements (the `mysql` extension does not). Here's an example using `mysqli`:

```
$statement = $mysqli->prepare("INSERT INTO preferences(option, value) VALUES (?,?)");
# Now bind and execute. The first paramter to bind_param is the
#  bind type; in this case two strings.
$statment->bind_param("ss","favorite color", "orange");
$statement->execute();
$statment->bind_param("ss","cats or dogs?", "dogs");
$statement->execute();
```

Because prepared statements involve an extra round trip to the server, using them to execute a single query is more costly than the traditional method, and there is little to be gained when you are only executing a handful of queries. As the number of queries executed increases, the benefits of prepared statements become more apparent.

With write queries, the method outlined earlier in the section, "Bulk Writes," is often a better solution.

SUMMARY

MySQL performance tuning covers a vast area. As well as tuning MySQL, there is a huge range of options available for individual storage engines. It's worth being clear on which tuning options are properties of MySQL, and which are properties of engines.

The two main storage engines are MyISAM and InnoDB. MyISAM was the default for many years and offers fast lookups on indexed columns. In recent years, though, InnoDB has overtaken MyISAM and is now the default engine in MySQL. InnoDB offers fast lookups on primary keys (but less so on secondaries because of the way keys are stored in file), and handles high levels of concurrency better. It also supports transactions, something missing in MyISAM.

Indexing is an important aspect of tuning, and careful indexing can offer a huge speed boost to queries. A good understanding of how MySQL parses and executes queries is needed first, though, and tools such as EXPLAIN and the MySQL query profiler are invaluable here.

MySQL also offers its own built-in query cache, which can drastically reduce CPU usage. The query cache is not without its drawbacks, though, and you must understand both the situations in which invalidations occur, and the impact of nondeterministic functions (such as RAND) in queries.

So far you've seen how to tune MySQL and the two major storage engines (MyISAM and InnoDB) for a single-server setup. As your network grows, and a single MySQL instance is no longer enough, issues of scaling and load balancing arise. In Chapter 9, you'll see how MySQL can scale horizontally using concepts such as replication, partitioning, and sharding.

MySQL in the Network

WHAT'S IN THIS CHAPTER?

➤ Setting up and managing MySQL replication

➤ Discovering advanced features of replication

➤ Partitioning data in MySQL

➤ Setting up sharding

➤ Discovering alternatives to MySQL

Many websites start with the web server and MySQL sharing a single server. This works for a while, but (hopefully) there comes a time when a single server just isn't powerful enough. The next step (particularly on database-heavy sites) is usually to put MySQL on its own server. Separating these two distinct functional areas is easy, and often requires little more than changing the MySQL connection string in the web code. As the site continues to grow, more CPU and RAM are thrown at the database server.

This "monolithic monster" approach to MySQL actually works surprisingly well and is a long-term solution for many websites. Continuing advances in CPU and RAM capabilities mean that even if a high-end server is reaching saturation point now, something bigger and better will soon be available.

Simply throwing CPU and memory at a single machine has diminishing returns, however. You aren't increasing the data transfer rates from disk or from memory, or decreasing disk seek times, and so on. Sure, you can update these parts of the system, too (although the rate of advance in memory speed and disk speed is not nearly so fast), but you still end up with a system where the bottlenecks are more pronounced than ever.

> **NOTE** *It's also worth remembering that core speeds can be just as important as the number of cores. A nonthreaded process (that runs on a single CPU core) is no faster on a 16-core machine than a 1-core machine — although it may need to wait longer to be executed.*

So, although a single MySQL beast can go a long way, eventually there will be the need to move away to a multiserver setup. This chapter looks at the options available after you outgrow a monolithic monster.

The first topic examined in this chapter is replication, which is a built-in feature of MySQL that is commonly used to scale across multiple servers. Replication isn't without its drawbacks, though, and you'll also see how partitioning and sharding can be used to achieve better effects. Sharding is a particularly important and powerful concept, and is a topic you'll meet again in Chapter 10, "Utilizing NoSQL Solutions."

Finally, in this chapter, you'll also discover MySQL Proxy, a highly scriptable application that can be used to load balance and create other advanced topologies. The chapter concludes with a look at some of the most popular alternatives to MySQL, including the various forks and branches that are available.

USING REPLICATION

Although creating a pool of web servers is a relatively straightforward procedure (even though sessions can be a nuisance), multiserver MySQL setups require a little more, though, because of their read-write nature. How do you ensure that each server is in sync with the others? What happens if two servers modify data simultaneously?

For a long time, the only practical option was MySQL's built-in replication. There are other options now (such as clustering), but replication is still one of the most popular methods, which works reasonably well. This section discusses the pros and cons of replication, the possible uses (it's not just for load balancing), and the myriad of possible topologies.

The Basics

Replication uses a master-slave configuration. In the most basic setups, a single server acts as the *master*, with one or more *slaves* syncing their content from this master. Both master and slaves can perform read queries, but because of the one-way nature of the replication, write queries must be performed only on the master. If a write is performed on a slave, it never propagates to the master (or to any other slaves). Figure 9-1 illustrates this basic setup.

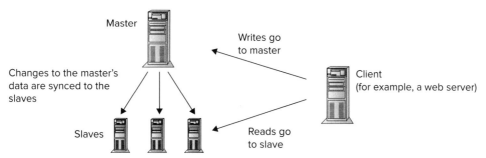

FIGURE 9-1

The most obvious drawback to this topology is that writes are still centralized on a single server. You'll see ways to work around this (to some extent) in the upcoming section, "Advanced Topologies," but because most Linux, Apache, MySQL, and PHP (LAMP) applications are read-heavy (80 percent reads and 20 percent writes is an often quoted figure — but this ratio can vary hugely depending on the application), this often isn't a huge problem — at least not under moderate loads.

> **NOTE** *In MySQL, the* binary log *is a log of events that result in changes to the dataset — for example, changes to table structures, adding/deleting rows, and so on. This log can be used to recover corrupt tables, or for the purposes of replication. The* relay log *is created by replication slaves to hold binary log events that have been received from the master.*

How does the mechanism of replication actually work? You can think of it in terms of the following three steps:

1. The master writes events to its binary log (which must first be enabled).

2. An I/O slave thread on the slave copies events from the master's binary log to the slave's relay log.

3. A SQL slave thread replays events from the relay log.

If the slave also has binary logging enabled, a fourth step involves the slave writing the replayed events to its own binary log.

Setting Up Replication

Setting up replication won't be examined in great detail here because the web is already awash with tutorials on setting up replication. But, briefly, the process is as follows.

The following three options must be added to the `my.cnf` file on the master:

```
log-bin = /var/log/mysql/mysql-bin.log
binlog-do-db=my_database
server-id=1
```

The first line specifies the location of the binary log, whereas the second contains a comma-separated list of databases to replicate. It's generally preferable to select individual databases to replicate, rather than to have MySQL replicate everything because you usually want to keep the access permissions stored in the MySQL database private. The third line specifies an arbitrary numeric ID for the server, which must be unique (that is, not used by any other slaves or masters in the setup).

At the master MySQL's command-line interface (CLI), you create a user with the replication privilege. The slave connects as this user to sync from the master's binary log.

```
GRANT REPLICATION SLAVE ON my_database.* TO 'slave_user'@'slave.example.com'
    IDENTIFIED BY 'my_password';
FLUSH PRIVILEGES;
```

Next, you flush and lock the tables in the database, and make a note of the master's current position in the binary log.

```
USE my_database;
FLUSH TABLES WITH READ LOCK;
SHOW MASTER STATUS;
+------------------+----------+--------------+------------------+
| File             | Position | Binlog_Do_DB | Binlog_Ignore_DB |
+------------------+----------+--------------+------------------+
| mysql-bin.001026 | 1031     | my_database  |                  |
+------------------+----------+--------------+------------------+
1 row in set (0.08 sec)
```

Locking the tables prevents any write operations that would cause the position in the binary log to change.

On the slave, you add the following to the `my.cnf` file, adjusting as appropriate:

```
server-id=2
```

After restarting the slave, you must copy data across from the master so that both servers are in sync and ready to start replication. There are two choices here:

➤   Take a dump of the data from the master (using `mysqldump`), and then copy it across and import into the slave.

➤   Use the LOAD DATA FROM MASTER command at the slave's CLI.

The latter choice is deprecated, however, and causes long periods of locking on the master (as well as not supporting `InnoDB`). So, you should instead use `mysqldump` (or `mysqlhotcopy`).

For large tables, it's generally faster to pipe the output of `mysqldump` directly to the slave server, as shown here:

```
mysqldump my_database| mysql -h slave_ip_address -u username -ppassword my_database
```

After the slave is up-to-date with the master, you can tell it the position and name of the master's binary log, at which point it should start replicating, and then start up the `slave` thread, as shown here:

```
SLAVE STOP;
CHANGE MASTER TO MASTER_HOST='192.168.1.10', MASTER_USER='slave_user',
    MASTER_PASSWORD='my_password', MASTER_LOG_FILE='mysql-bin.001025',
    MASTER_LOG_POS=1031;
SLAVE START;
```

Any write operations performed on the master should now replicate across to the slave. You can repeat this process to create additional slaves, if necessary, but remember to give each slave a unique `server-id`.

Understanding Replication Lag

One drawback of replication is that it offers no guarantees that slaves will be up-to-date with the master. In perfect conditions, a query executed on the master will be replicated to the slaves in a fraction of a second. But it's not uncommon to see a lag of a few seconds on even moderately busy servers. In more extreme situations, slaves can be hours, or even days, behind their master.

Replication lag can occur for a number of reasons. Occasional spikes can be the result of other processes (such as a backup script) running on the slave, or a particularly heavy burst of write activity (perhaps caused by a `cron` script) on the master, or even network congestion. These spikes tend to sort themselves out. But if you notice that slaves are taking a long time to recover from such spikes, it's likely an indication that the slave is close to saturation. Don't ignore this early warning sign.

For more persistent lag, it's likely that the slave simply isn't powerful enough. Remember that the slave replays every write query performed on the master, as well as answering queries for clients — so it needs to be of similar power to the master. The only way around this is to upgrade the hardware or use filtering to reduce the amount of data replicated.

Assuming that your hardware *is* powerful enough, your web application still must appreciate and cater to the fact that lag may occur. For example, if users edit their profile (causing a write to the master), it may be a few moments before the changes are visible (that is, available to be read from a slave). Most of the time, this delay is less than a couple of seconds. But, occasionally, it could be longer. Better to warn users that changes are not instantaneous, rather than leaving them unsure of whether the changes were actually saved.

Monitoring and Maintenance

Unfortunately, setting up replication isn't the end of the story. It requires frequent monitoring to ensure that everything runs smoothly. MySQL provides a couple of useful commands for this.

Executing SHOW SLAVE STATUS on each slave provides a lot of information on the status of the replication, as shown here:

```
mysql> SHOW SLAVE STATUS\G
*************************** 1. row ***************************
                Slave_IO_State: Waiting for master to send event
                   Master_Host: 192.168.1.10
                   Master_User: root
                   Master_Port: 3306
                 Connect_Retry: 60
               Master_Log_File: mysql-bin.000012
```

```
                Read_Master_Log_Pos: 438
                     Relay_Log_File: slave1-relay-bin.000143
                      Relay_Log_Pos: 47
              Relay_Master_Log_File: mysql-bin.000012
                   Slave_IO_Running: Yes
                  Slave_SQL_Running: Yes
                    Replicate_Do_DB:
                Replicate_Ignore_DB:
                 Replicate_Do_Table:
             Replicate_Ignore_Table:
            Replicate_Wild_Do_Table:
        Replicate_Wild_Ignore_Table:
                         Last_Errno: 0
                         Last_Error:
                       Skip_Counter: 0
                Exec_Master_Log_Pos: 438
                    Relay_Log_Space: 1875
                    Until_Condition: None
                    Until_Log_File:
                     Until_Log_Pos: 0
                 Master_SSL_Allowed: No
                 Master_SSL_CA_File:
                 Master_SSL_CA_Path:
                    Master_SSL_Cert:
                  Master_SSL_Cipher:
                     Master_SSL_Key:
              Seconds_Behind_Master: 0
    Master_SSL_Verify_Server_Cert: No
                      Last_IO_Errno: 0
                      Last_IO_Error:
                     Last_SQL_Errno: 0
                     Last_SQL_Error:
          Replicate_Ignore_Server_Ids: 0
```

Slave_IO_State gives details of the status of the slave thread. The most common status, Waiting for master to send event, indicates that the slave's relay log is up-to-date with the master, which is the preferable state to be in. There are more than a dozen other possible states though, some of which indicate an error.

Particularly useful is Seconds_Behind_Master, which shows by how much replication is lagging. This might not be zero, even if Slave_IO_State reports Waiting for master to send event because this indicates only that the relay log is up-to-date. Events from the relay log still must be replayed. This would be a clear indication that the slave is struggling to cope with the volume of writes sent by the master.

SQL Errors

Also worth watching are Last_SQL_Errno and Last_SQL_Error. If the slave chokes on any SQL queries, the most recent error will be stored in these fields. These types of errors cause replication to halt, requiring manual intervention to fix, so they are a serious problem. But how do they happen? Surely, if a SQL query has executed fine on the master, it will execute okay on the slave, right?

The most common reasons for SQL errors are because of writes carried out on the slave, or because the master and slave run different versions of MySQL. But there are numerous other situations in which replication can break, including corruption of binary or relay logs, or crashes on the master or slave. It's a sad fact that most database administrators will battle with replication errors at least once in their careers.

When errors do occur, you have a few options. If you're confident that the error can safely be ignored, you can skip the problem query by stopping the slave thread, instructing MySQL to skip the query, and then restarting the slave thread. Following is an example:

```
SLAVE STOP;
SET GLOBAL SQL_SLAVE_SKIP_COUNTER = 1;
SLAVE START;
```

Errors like these have a habit of snowballing, though. So, unless you are sure that the error can safely be ignored, skipping it may simply lead to more errors in the future as the slave's data becomes even more out-of-sync with the master's data.

Usually, though, the only way to recover from an error (and be satisfied that the problem is completely solved) is to resync from the master. This isn't an attractive prospect, but it's a better long-term solution than battling with an out-of-sync slave. Resyncing involves copying over a dump from the master and setting the slave to the correct position of the master's binary log — much like setting up replication from scratch. But because of table locking and the possible size of the database, it can still be a problem on live servers.

You can do a few things to lessen the likelihood of SQL errors — or at least limit the damage caused. For starters,, you can set the slaves to read-only using the read_only option in my.cnf. Users with the SUPER privilege can still carry out write operations, and replication can still run correctly, but standard users will be prevented from writing to tables.

Because many errors are caused by the master crashing (with the most recent binary log events not yet having been flushed to disk), you can use sync_binlog=1 in my.cnf on the master to force MySQL to flush events to disk after a transaction. This isn't ideal because you lose the performance benefit from caching these writes. But, in many cases, the extra degree of safety makes this a must.

Finally, you can also use skip-slave-start (again in my.cnf) on slaves to prevent them from automatically starting replication when MySQL is started. This is particularly useful after a crash, when you may want to manually repair tables first. If replication starts automatically, any table corruption may not be immediately apparent, and may manifest itself only further down the line — by which stage the slave is so out-of-sync that you have no option but to resync from the master.

Monitoring Lag

As previously discussed, lag is an unfortunate consequence of replication, and web applications that connect to a replicating MySQL server pool must sometimes accommodate for at least a small amount of lag. When replication is lagging by more than a few seconds, or for long periods, this generally calls for attention, though, because it can be a sign that the slave is close to its maximum capacity.

You've already seen that the output of SHOW SLAVE STATUS gives you the number of seconds by which the slave is lagging, but this isn't entirely accurate, and will be zero if replication isn't even running. Instead, the preferred method to monitor lag is to write a simple monitoring script that writes data to a temporary table on the master, and then checks the slave for this data. If it takes more than x number of seconds for the data to propagate across, a warning generates. Such a script could easily be incorporated into a monitoring/stats tool like munin or nagios to plot trends in the lag, and raise varying levels of alarm, depending on the extent of the lag.

You can even use a script like this as the basis for a routine to turn away read requests to a heavily lagged slave, preventing clients from seeing stale data, and giving the slave a chance to catch up. The danger here is that this would result in more traffic to the other slaves, which could, in turn, cause them to lag and be temporarily removed from the pool. This effect would snowball until there was just one slave left (presumably the script would be intelligent enough not to remove a lagging slave if it were the only slave left in the pool), attempting to handle the work of many slaves. In the section, "Complementing MySQL," later in this chapter, you learn how to use MySQL Proxy to balance requests across a pool of MySQL slaves, even taking into account the load on each.

The Single Master, Multiple Slave Model in Practice

So far, this discussion has focused on one replication topology (although it is by far the most common) — a single master replicating to multiple slaves, with each slave holding an identical copy of the data to the master. How would you go about using this topology in practice?

If your web code uses a database abstraction class for connecting, it should be possible to modify the class so that all write queries go to the master (just look for strings like 'UPDATE', 'INSERT', and so on, in the SQL before sending it off for execution), and some or all read queries go through a slave. (Depending on the nature of the application and your hardware, you may have the luxury of sending the most important read requests to the master, eliminating the possibility of lag.)

There are a few methods of selecting which slave to use, assuming all carry identical data, but the most common is round-robin DNS. Create a DNS entry such as slave.example.com and have it resolve to multiple IP addresses. Clients (for example, web servers) can pick a random IP address from the list returned.

Unfortunately, this kind of load balancing is quite crude and fails to take into account that some slaves may be more powerful than others, or under more load than the others. In the upcoming section, "Complementing MySQL," you learn how MySQL Proxy can be used for more advanced load balancing.

Types of Replication

MySQL offers two types of replication. *Statement-based replication* (SBR) has existed since MySQL version 3 and is usually what people mean when they refer to replication. *Row-based replication* (RBR) was added in MySQL version 5.1 and deals with some of the shortcomings of SBR. Let's look at the differences between them.

SBR revolves around SQL statements. Each write statement executed on the master is stored in the master's binary log and eventually re-executed on each slave. This works well in most cases and has the advantage of generating low volumes of data — so, log files are small, and network transfer is low.

Unfortunately, there are some types of queries that don't replicate well with SBR. For example, the nondeterministic nature of a query, such as the following, means that the 10 rows deleted on the slave may not be the same 10 rows deleted on the master:

```
DELETE FROM test LIMIT 0,10
```

The outcome of this query cannot be predicted in advance, and will likely return different results each time it is executed.

Examples of other functions that are unsafe include LOAD_FILE(), SLEEP(), UUID(), and USER(). To confuse matters a little more, RAND() and NOW() *are* SBR-safe.

RBR solves these problems; although it introduces problems of its own. With RBR, it is the changes to the data itself that are recorded and replicated, not the SQL query. This is much safer than SBR but comes at the cost of increased network traffic and log sizes.

If deciding between these two alternative methods seems like a tough choice, the good news is that MySQL also supports a mixed-format replication, in which both modes are used. With mixed logging, MySQL switches between the two formats as the situation demands. This pretty much means that SBR will be used the majority of the time, but MySQL will switch to RBR if it encounters a query that would be unsafe with SBR.

The replication mode can be set in my.cnf using the binlog-format directive. Accepted values are STATEMENT, ROW, or MIXED, and the default is STATEMENT. Following is an example:

```
binlog-format = "STATEMENT"
```

More on Filtering

You've learned that MySQL enables you to replicate on a per-database basis, but there's more to it than that. For starters, you have the option of whether to carry out the filtering at the master or at the slave. You can filter at the master by using the following. (To filter multiple databases, repeat these statements.)

```
binlog-do-db=mydatabase
binlog-ignore-db=anotherdatabase
```

These rules control whether the event is logged to the master's binary log, so filtering in this fashion has a direct result on the amount of traffic flowing from the master to the slaves. However, this method of filtering is also the most dangerous because it breaks on queries that don't use the currently selected database. As an example, what happens if the following queries are executed on the master?

```
USE testdb;
UPDATE anotherdatabase.anothertable SET x=1;
```

Surprisingly, MySQL considers the second query to be acting on the currently selected database — `testdb` — and, as a result, may or may not log it, depending on the `binlog*db` settings. Such unexpected behavior could easily lead to data becoming out-of-sync on the slave. So, unless you can be sure that situations like this won't arise, it's best not to use filtering at the master, despite its benefits.

The alternative to filtering at the master is, naturally, to filter at the slave. Filtering rules at the slave all take the form `replicate*`. Earlier in this chapter, you saw how to incorporate `replicate-do-db` in the `my.cnf` file of the slave to initially set up replication, and this is complemented by `replicate-ignore-db`. Because database names may legally contain commas, neither of these options allows you to give a comma-separated list of databases. Instead, the configuration statements must be duplicated, one for each database.

Filtering at the slave also gives you more control over exactly what is replicated. Whereas filtering at the master limits you to listing which databases can and cannot be logged, filtering at the slave lets you specify individual tables to replicate or ignore (for example, `replicate-do-table=mydatabase.mytable` and `replicate-ignore-table=mydatabase.mytable`) and even lets you use wildcards (for example, `replicate-wild-do-table=mydatabase.my%` and `replicate-wild-ignore-table=mydatabase.my%`). Filtering at the slave also gets around the current database quirk that you encountered with `binlog*db`.

Advanced Topologies

There are a number of problems with the single-master, multiple-slave topology that has been discussed thus far:

> ➤ Because each slave must replay every write query executed on the master, each slave already has significant overhead.

> ➤ Adding extra slaves slightly increases work for the master. If slaves are at different points in the master's binary log, this increases the chances that the data will already have been flushed from memory, increasing disk I/O on the master.

> ➤ Each additional slave increases network traffic.

> ➤ Although this setup helps to scale read requests, it does nothing to improve writes.

> ➤ Each slave maintains its own private query cache, resulting in inefficient caching — the same query might be cached across multiple servers.

Future versions of MySQL may well implement the query cache as a plug-in, capable of spanning multiple nodes to create a single, centralized cache. Until then, you can either accept that query caching will be inefficient, or implement your own global cache using something like `memcache`.

> **NOTE** *You learn more about* `memcache` *in Chapter 10.*

Functional Separation

You can solve some of the shortcomings of the previous model by assigning different functions to each slave.

Consider an online dating site. Rather than having a pool of identical (in terms of content) slaves for the web servers to choose from, you could use one slave for searching profiles, another for sending and retrieving messages, and another for viewing member profiles.

As shown in Figure 9-2, this layout has a number of benefits. It makes better use of the query cache on each slave and avoids queries potentially being cached across multiple nodes. (It also provides the capability to disable the query cache on slaves where you know it will be of little use.) It enables you to be selective over which tables are replicated to each slave, potentially cutting down on network congestion (actually, as discussed earlier, only master-side filtering cuts down on network traffic, but, in the upcoming section, "Replication Performance," you learn how you can achieve slave-side replication without the additional traffic) and easing load on the slaves.

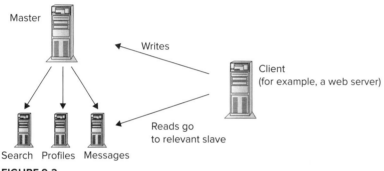

FIGURE 9-2

Unfortunately, the distinction between tables isn't usually clear-cut. For example, retrieving and listing a user's message box probably won't rely solely on the Messages table. Most likely, messages are stored with the sender's numeric membership number, and you'd need to join against the Profile table to retrieve the sender's name (and possible age, location, and photo, too — the latter may involve joining to an additional Photos table). There are a few work-arounds for this:

➤ Rather than replicating single tables, replicate as many tables as might be used to satisfy the query. For the message box, this would mean also replicating the tables containing basic user information (username and the like), primary photo, profile, and so on.

➤ Denormalize the data so that joins are not required. For example, add extra columns to the Messages table to hold the username, age, location, and photo.

➤ Use federated tables to span multiple servers. (This isn't recommended because it introduces further interserver dependencies.)

➤ Perform the parts of the join query at the application level. For example, retrieve the sender's numeric ID from the Messages table, and then query the Profiles slave for the user's profile information.

If the tables lend themselves to fairly clear distinctions in functionality, the first method (replicating many tables) is the preferred solution. But if you must duplicate a significant number of tables across each server, the advantages of this method start to diminish.

The denormalization technique might seem to go against everything you've learned about database design, but it can be a practical solution. It can increase the number of writes, however, because some data must be updated in multiple places — and writes are usually the main problem because they are more difficult to scale.

Finally, decomposing the join and running each query separately at the application level has the drawback of being linear in nature, and, hence, slower. You must run one query, wait for the result, issue another query, wait for the result, and repeat the process.

Figure 9-3 shows an improvement on this model. This time, the Messages server is separate from the rest of the replication setup, and handles both reads and writes to the Messages table.

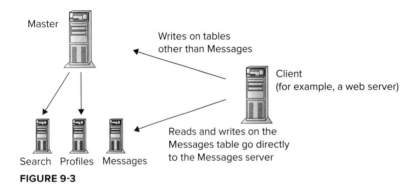

FIGURE 9-3

> **NOTE** *This discussion focuses on the private messaging feature of the fictitious site, but these principles could easily apply to other areas, too*

This topology helps to lessen write activity on the master — always a good thing, with this being the main source of bottlenecks — but it makes things awkward if you must join against other tables when querying the Messages server. You can denormalize or decompose the join in the web application, but there's another option, too.

Figure 9-4 shows a modification to the setup in which the Messages server replicates the Profiles table from the master, enabling you to perform joins across the Messages and Profiles tables. The Messages slave is still the authority for the Messages table, and the Messages table doesn't need to exist on the master.

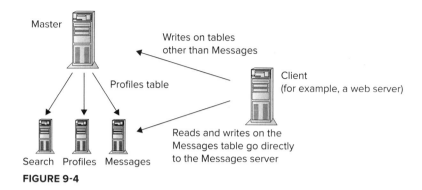

FIGURE 9-4

Pyramid/Tree Structure

As the number of slaves directly attached to the master increases, so does the load on the master — something you want to avoid, given that resources on the master are precious. One way around this is to use a pyramid structure, as shown in Figure 9-5. Here, you connect a small number of slaves to the master, and each of these slaves, in turn, acts as a master for other slaves.

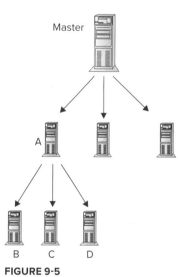

FIGURE 9-5

Server A is both a slave to the main master and a master to servers B, C, and D (refer to Figure 9-5). Only one branch of the pyramid is shown, but, in practice, the other primary slaves could all have secondary slaves attached to them. In theory, a third level of slaves could also be introduced (B, C, and D each have a number of slaves attached to them), but it would be a large application that needed this number of slaves.

Configuring a node as both a master and a slave is actually fairly straightforward, and uses nothing more than the configuration options and methodology provided earlier. The node copies events from its master's binary log into its own relay log. These events are then replayed, and — because binary logging is enabled — are then written to the node's binary log. This binary log is, in turn, read by each slave that copies it into its relay log.

There are two main disadvantages to this model, both coming as a result of the additional chain(s) in the replication. First, there is the danger of one of the intermediate servers crashing, breaking the replication chain. Second, there is a great opportunity for replication lag because events must propagate down the tree before they reach the bottom level. The chances of lag increase as the number of intermediates (or the load on the intermediates) increases.

> **NOTE** *Most likely, you would use only the bottom level of slaves for client queries (for example, B, C, and D) because the intermediate levels would have their work cut out acting as both slaves and masters.*

Blackhole and Intermediate Masters

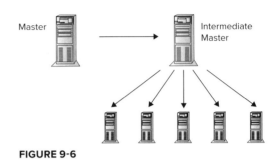

One of MySQL's more esoteric storage engines is the `Blackhole` engine, a sort of glorified /dev/ null. Any data written to a table using this engine is simply discarded silently, whereas any read queries against the table return no results.

The `Blackhole` engine is useful in replication setups because, although SQL statements will be logged (in the binary log), there is no work associ-

FIGURE 9-6

ated with executing the query. This makes the `Blackhole` engine perfectly suited for intermediate masters (such as in the pyramid topology just discussed) because it greatly cuts down on overhead. Chances are that with an intermediate master such as this (sometimes also called a *distribution master*), you can connect all your slaves directly to it, as shown in Figure 9-6.

This proves to be a good topology for several reasons:

➤ The master needs to replicate only to the intermediate master, cutting down load on the master.

➤ Because the intermediate master uses the `Blackhole` engine, there is less load on it. Thus, the hardware demands aren't so high, and more slaves can connect directly to the intermediate.

➤ By using slave-side replication filtering on the intermediate master, you can cut traffic between the intermediate master and the slaves.

This last point is worth reading again and is the solution hinted at over the last few pages. Although this won't reduce traffic between the master and the intermediate master, it means that the binary log on to the intermediate feels the effect of the slave-side replication filters, and, thus, traffic between the intermediate and its slaves is reduced.

Setting an intermediate master to use the `Blackhole` engines is as simple as running ALTER TABLE on each table, and changing the engine to `Blackhole`. Remember, though, that any new tables created on the master do not automatically use the `Blackhole` engine when they propagate to the intermediate. You can get around this to some extent by specifying the following in `my.cnf`:

```
default-storage-engine = blackhole
```

This causes the newly created table to use the `Blackhole` engine, unless the engine is specifically given in the CREATE TABLE command. In this situation, there isn't much you can do other than being vigilant.

Master-Master Replication

So far, all the discussed topologies have used a single master with multiple slaves. Although a slave may have only one master, there are still numerous possible topologies in which multiple masters exist. In such setups, each server acts as both a master and a slave, syncing its contents to the other server(s). Figure 9-7 illustrates a basic setup.

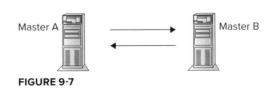

FIGURE 9-7

Any writes to Master A are replicated across to Master B, whereas any writes on Master B are replicated over to Master A. MySQL has the intelligence not to then replicate the query back to the originating server.

Many administrators are attracted to this model by its apparent advantages. Because write queries are usually the big bottleneck in master-slave setups, it seems to make sense that you can distribute the load by having two active masters. Unfortunately, this isn't the case. Each master still must execute the same number of write queries, regardless of which node they were sent to. If Master A receives a write query, it executes it directly, whereas if the query executes on Master B, it replays on Master A a few moments later anyway.

Master-master replication is also quite error-prone, and can be extremely difficult to fix, should the two servers become out-of-sync. As an example, consider what happens if both masters execute an update on the same table simultaneously. This could lead to a situation in which each master holds a different view of the table, yet no replication errors are generated.

When replication errors do occur in a master-master setup, they make resyncing the two servers a nightmarish task. In standard master-slave replication, you'd simply discard the slave's data and take a fresh copy from the master. But in master-master replication, both servers may have data that has yet to be replicated to the other. There's no easy solution to this, other than manually inspecting the data and attempting to merge changes by hand.

For these reasons, the master-master structure is generally best avoided unless you have special requirements. But there is a variation on this structure that *is* rather useful.

Active-Passive Master-Master Replication

The active-passive master-master replication topology is almost identical to the master-master topology but with one crucial difference. You direct writes only to one of the servers. The other server takes on a passive role, replaying events from the active master but generating no events.

The advantage of this model (and what distinguishes it from a simple master-slave setup) is that you can swap which server is the active one whenever you want. For example, if you want to take Master A down for a hardware upgrade, you simply divert all write traffic to Master B, and then shut Master A down (having first checked, of course, that it has no events waiting to be replicated to Master B). When Master A comes back online, it can catch up with Master B. You can then either switch writes back to Master A or leave them at Master B. The ease with which you can swap the roles of each master makes this an excellent model for high availability — if one server crashes, you can simply fail over to the other.

Of course, it's not quite that straightforward. Even if downtime on the currently active master was scheduled, it would still be inconvenient to change your web code (and probably various `cron` jobs, too) to point to the other master.

Using DNS records is one possibility. You could create `writes.examples.com` and have it resolve to whichever server is currently the active master. A monitoring script could even automatically update the DNS record if one server went down. The problem here is that DNS changes can be slow to propagate. Even if you set a very low Time-to-Live (TTL) on the DNS records, not all intermediate caches will honor these times (more so if the times are very low).

Rather, a better solution is to use a virtual IP address, which can be swapped between the two servers. Each server will have one IP address that is always bound to it. But a third IP address will also be present, and will be bound to whichever server is the current master.

It may seem wasteful to have a second master in a passive role, essentially doing nothing the majority of the time other than replicating events from the active master. If you have trouble financially justifying a passive master, remember that it also offers an excellent way to generate MySQL dumps without locking the master. The passive master could also double up as a slave, handling some of the read queries on the setup.

Just make sure your code can cope with situations in which the passive master is down, or takes on the role of active master. (In which case, it may not handle the additional read queries.) Given these extra complications, it's preferable to keep the passive master essentially idle if possible.

Speaking of slaves, how do they fit into a master-master replication system? Because a slave can have only one master, this slave subsystem (be it a single slave, group of slaves, or intermediate master) can be connected to only one of the two masters. In the case of a distribution master, you could just manually re-point it at whichever master was currently the active one.

Apart from requiring manual intervention (which you'd like to avoid), this would also be cumbersome if many slaves were connected directly to the master. Again, the answer is virtual IP addresses. The same solution that you can use for directing write web traffic to the active master can also be used to direct the slaves to the correct master.

Replication Performance

Despite being intended to improve performance, many replication setups introduce their own performance issues. Let's look at some of the most common areas in which bottlenecks occur, and what (if anything) you can do about them.

Network Performance

The amount of network traffic generated by a replication setup is largely dependent on the number of slaves, the type of replication (RBR or SBR), and the volume of writes. With SBR, the size and number of queries is the controlling factor, whereas with RBR it's the number of rows affected. Naturally, SBR tends to use more bandwidth than RBR.

It's generally preferable to connect masters and slaves together over a private, switched network. This eliminates the possibility of spikes in nonreplication traffic slowing down replication traffic and vice versa.

In cases in which a low number of slaves exists, you can even connect each to the master directly with an Ethernet crossover cable, further reducing latency by removing the need for a network switch. As the number of slaves increases, this quickly becomes impractical, though, because each will require its own network interface card (NIC) on the master.

Bandwidth and latency are rarely an issue when nodes of a replication setup connect over a local private network, but it's a different story if they connect over the Internet. Network conditions can be variable, and there isn't usually much you can do about it. For situations like these, MySQL provides the `slave_compressed_protocol` configuration option for use on the slave. When enabled (default is disabled), this boolean variable causes the data stream to be compressed, generally cutting bandwidth usage by at least half. Of course, this compression doesn't come for free and causes a small increase in CPU usage on both the master and slave. It's for that reason that you should not use compression on local network setups.

If you feel adventurous, you could shun MySQL's compression option and set up a secure shell (SSH) tunnel. Expect similar levels of savings but with the added benefit of encryption — always a good thing for data passing through a public network.

Slave Performance

Earlier in this chapter, you learned that slaves generally need to be of similar hardware specifications to the master because they must be powerful enough to replay all the write queries executed on the master. There's actually a bit more to it than that.

On a master with multiple CPU cores, several queries could run simultaneously via different threads. The effect of the binary log is to serialize these into a linear stream of queries, with the result that when the queries replay back on the slave, they are done so one at a time. (MySQL uses only one slave replication thread.) It's not difficult to see how a single core on the slave could struggle to keep up with the master, and this is another example of how core speed can be just as important as the number of cores. (A slave would likely be better off with 2 × 3 GHz cores than 4 × 2 GHz cores.)

There isn't a great deal you can do about this problem, other than be aware of it. It can help to explain some replication oddities. ("Why is the slave lagging while CPU usage is only moderate?") Slave-side replication filtering can also help here by reducing the number of queries that the slave needs to execute.

The Binary Log

Enabling binary logging (as is required for the master) in MySQL adds a little overhead to the system. But its usefulness in data integrity means that it can often be prudent to enable it on servers that aren't acting as masters, too. The reason binary logging doesn't add much overhead is that MySQL usually leaves it to the operating system to decide when to flush the writes to disk. But this is also rather dangerous because a server crash can cause any log events still in the buffer to be lost.

MySQL provides the sync_binlog variable that can override this behavior. Setting a value of zero disables syncing (MySQL leaves it to the operating system), whereas a positive integer value dictates how regularly the binary log should be synced to disk. A value of 1 means after every transaction, a value of 2 means after every two transactions, and so on.

Naturally, 1 is the safest setting, but it can also be a performance killer. The reason is not data throughput but the seek time involved as the disk moves its head to the end of the binary log each time (assuming other disk I/O causes the head to seek to other locations between writes). With seek times on high-end disks of approximately 3 milliseconds, this limits you to a theoretical maximum of perhaps 300 transaction writes per second — and that's before you even add on other disk activity.

There are various possible workarounds for this problem, of which the following four are the most common:

➤ Disable sync_binlog or set it to a high value (one that balances performance against safety). This risks corruption of the binary log, should the server crash.

➤ Place the binary log on its own hard disk. Providing that nothing else is accessing the disk, this cuts out the seek time involved in syncing the binary log because the disk head is already in the correct position at the end of the binary log.

➤ Many high-end RAID controllers now include a small amount of battery backed-up memory used for buffering disk writes. Writing to this cache is several orders of magnitude faster than writing directly to the disk and has the added benefit that because the memory has a battery back-up, if the server crashes, the data won't be lost.

➤ Use a solid-state device (SSD) such as flash memory. Although seek time is meaningless in this context, there is still an associated access time — but it's usually lower than for a conventional hard disk.

Of these solutions, battery backed-up memory on the disk is by far the best. But using a second disk exclusively for the binary log is a cheaper, workable solution.

BATTERY BACKED-UP MEMORY

Hard disks typically have a small amount of onboard memory that is used to buffer disk writes. In this way, the disk can return an OK to the operating system almost immediately, allowing execution to return to the application that performed the write. Ultimately, the disk's write buffer (not to be confused with write buffering that may occur at the operating system level, in system memory) will be flushed to the disk. But if a power failure occurs before this happens, the data will be lost. This is particularly dangerous because the operating system will be under the impression that the data was written to the physical disk (because the disk controller returned an OK).

One solution is to disable the disk's write buffer, but this tends to cause a significant drop in write performance. Instead, many RAID controllers (and a few disk controllers) use a lithium-ion battery that can supply power to the write cache for a few hours or so if a power failure occurs. When power is restored, the write cache will still be intact and can be flushed to disk by the RAID controller as usual.

These *battery backed-up units* (also referred to as *battery backed-up memory*, *battery backed-up write caches*, and so on) have long been the preferred option for enterprise-level systems, and their relatively modest cost makes them highly wanted additions. However, they are generally found only in RAID controllers, and it can be difficult to find a standard SATA disk with battery backed-up write caches.

Their biggest drawback is the reliability of the battery. Batteries have a nasty habit to gradually discharge over time, and regular checking of the battery is needed — a process that can be physically tricky because it requires the removal of any casing first.

Some battery backed-up units perform their own battery checking, a process that can range from simply checking the battery level and topping it up, to performing a full discharge/recharge cycle (because regularly topping up a rechargeable battery can greatly reduce its capacity). This usually occurs automatically every few months, and while this is happening, the write cache will be disabled, resulting in a significant drop in performance.

Many system administrators have been puzzled by this unexpected drop in disk throughput. The most practical solution is simply to disable auto-learning in the controller and perform it manually at off-peak times via a `cron` job (for example, using the `MegaCli` tool).

Miscellaneous Features of Replication

Before closing the discussion of replication, let's address a couple of miscellaneous points.

Backups

One common use of replication is to set up a slave to be used for the sole purpose to take backups from it. Generating backups from MySQL is a common dilemma. It can be slow, pushing the load up on the server, and causing table or row-level locking, depending on the storage engine used.

With a dedicated backup slave, you can dump data from the databases whenever you like without worrying about locking or load on the master. Although taking a large snapshot of the data will likely cause the slave to lag, this is quite harmless (because nothing else is using the slave), and the slave should soon catch up when the backup finishes.

Using Different Engines and Indexes on Slaves

You've already seen how an intermediate or distribution master typically uses the `Blackhole` engine on tables to cut down on overhead, and there's nothing to stop you from extending this logic and using different engines on the slaves. For example, you might use `InnoDB` for a given table on the master, but use `MyISAM` on the slave because you intend to do lots of lookups on secondary indexes. In this way, you benefit from faster writing on the master, but faster lookups on the slave.

It's usually always a case of wanting to use `InnoDB` on the master but `MyISAM` (or perhaps one of the specialist engines) on the slave — rather than the other way around. One of the most common reasons is to provide full-text search capabilities — something that `InnoDB` lacks. This is by no means the only solution to the full-text issue, though, as you'll see in the "Full-Text Searching" section later in this chapter, when you learn about Sphinx.

Similarly, you can also index different columns on the master than the slave (simply by using `ALTER TABLE` on the slave). Most likely you'd want to index columns only on the master that are used in the `WHERE` clause of `UPDATE` queries, whereas on the slave you could be more relaxed and index more liberally. This would speed up write queries on the master (fewer indexes to update), whereas still offer appropriate indexing for read queries. Remember, though, that more indexes on the slave slows down the execution of replayed events from the master — which is already something of a bottleneck.

As you have seen, replication is not a simple subject, and it can result in quite complex topologies. While it is perhaps the most common way to scale MySQL, it has significant limitations, and there are numerous other ways to scale out. In the next section, you'll meet one of these alternatives — partitioning.

PARTITIONING

In MySQL, *partitioning* has a precise meaning and shouldn't be confused with the more general concept of partitioning seen in strategies such as sharding (which you learn about later in this chapter in the section, "Sharding"). Although the latter is sometimes referred to as "partitioning," you can be pedantic and stick to the precise meaning.

MySQL's implementation of partitioning enables the rows in a table to be transparently split across multiple disk partitions (*horizontal partitioning*). Note the word "transparently." Although the table definition must describe the partitioning that is to be applied, all subsequent queries against the table run as normal. Partitioning is purely a strategy for the physical storage of data, and clients neither know nor care about the underlying way in which the data is stored.

One of the most common reasons for partitioning is to accommodate large datasets, which would not otherwise fit on a single disk. However, there are numerous performance benefits, too. Some of these benefits could also be reaped with the use of RAID, and you'll see a comparison of the pros and cons of partitioning versus RAID later in this section, as well exactly what partitioning can and can't help with.

Creating Partitions

Let's start by reviewing the basics of creating partitions. The syntax is simply as follows:

```
PARTITION BY <partition type> (<partition expression>)
```

This can be appended to CREATE TABLE or ALTER TABLE statements, as shown here:

```
CREATE TABLE test (foo varchar(8)) ENGINE=MyISAM PARTITION BY <type> (<expression>)
```

<type> refers to the partitioning type or the partitioning function used to determine how data should be split across partitions. Four types of partitioning are currently supported:

➤ HASH

➤ KEY

➤ LIST

➤ RANGE

Let's take a closer look at each of these.

HASH

Following is an example of using the HASH type:

```
PARTITION BY HASH (my_column) PARTITIONS 6.
```

With this type, MySQL creates a numeric ID by hashing the given column's value. It then calculates the modulus (note that the number of partitions to use has been specified) to determine which partition to place the row in. For example, a value of 20 would go in partition 2 because mod(20,6) = 2.

A common use of partitioning is to divide rows by date, and you can easily operate on a DATETIME column, as shown here:

```
PARTITION BY HASH ( YEAR(my_dt_column)) PARTITONS 10;
```

Note that the value given to HASH must be a positive integer (be it an unsigned int column, or an expression that returns a positive integer).

One of the most compelling reasons to use the HASH type is that it ensures even distribution of rows over the partitions, and (unlike some of the other types) it is fairly simple to set up and maintain. You simply tell MySQL how many partitions you want, and let MySQL figure out how best to partition each row.

> **NOTE** *As of MYSQL version 5.5*, linear hashing *is also supported. This uses an alternative hashing algorithm based on powers of 2, which is much faster (an effect that is more noticeable with large tables). Unfortunately, this algorithm also causes a much less uniform distribution of rows, and the size of individual partitions will vary considerably.*

KEY

Following is an example of using the KEY type:

```
PARTITION BY KEY (keyname) PARTITIONS 4.
```

Although similar to HASH, KEY has the advantage that the column passed to KEY does not need to be a positive integer. MySQL can use its own internal hashing function, guaranteed to generate a numeric value. This is the primary reason for choosing the KEY type.

LIST

Following is an example of using the LIST type:

```
PARTITION BY LIST (my_column) (
    PARTITION p0 VALUES IN (1,2,5,9),
    PARTITION p1 VALUES IN (3,8,10),
    PARTITION p3 VALUES IN (4,6,7,11)
)
```

With the LIST type, you assign particular column values to each partition. In this example, any row that has a value of 8 for my_column will be placed in partition p1; any row with value 9 will go in partition p0. Note that, as with HASH, values *must* be numeric.

Unlike the previous HASH and KEY types (where MySQL decided in which partitions to place data), LIST gives you the power to specify exactly where you want certain rows to be stored. This can be useful for performance, but with this power comes extra responsibility, too. In this example, if you attempt to write a record with a value of 12 for my_column, MySQL throws an error because you haven't specified in which partition to store such values.

RANGE

Following is an example of using the RANGE type:

```
PARTITION BY RANGE (my_column) (
    PARTITION p0 VALUES LESS THAN (1000),
    PARTITION p1 VALUES LESS THAN (2000),
```

```
        PARTITION p3 VALUES LESS THAN (3000),

        PARTITION p4 VALUES LESS THAN MAXVALUE
    )
```

Here, you specify how to split the data based on ranges. If `my_column` has a value less than `1000`, the row goes in `p0`. For values between `1000` and `1999`, (inclusive) the row goes in `p1`, and so on. Again, only non-negative integers are permitted.

The final partition definition, `p4`, uses `MAXVALUE`. This serves as a catch-all and picks up any values of `3000` or higher.

Deciding How to Partition

With four main partition types, and with each being similar, the question obviously arises as to which is best. As you might expect, there is no simple answer to this, and it largely depends on the type of data — and the ways in which you access the data.

Sometimes the data lends itself well to a particular method — `LIST` for discrete numeric values or `RANGE` for ranges of values. Other times, the choices are already made for you — for strings, `KEY` is the only available type.

Partition Pruning

One of the biggest performance advantages in a partitioned table occurs when MySQL uses *pruning*. Rather than scan every partition to satisfy a query, MySQL can immediately ignore some partitions based on its knowledge of the partition structure.

Pruning typically occurs when you use a `SELECT` with a `WHERE` clause that references the column on which the table is partitioned. Following is an example:

```
PARTITION BY RANGE (my_column) (
    PARTITION p0 VALUES LESS THAN (1000),
    PARTITION p1 VALUES LESS THAN (2000),
    PARTITION p3 VALUES LESS THAN (3000),
    PARTITION p4 VALUES LESS THAN MAXVALUE
)

SELECT * FROM my_table WHERE my_column < 500
```

In a query like this, MySQL looks at the partition structure, realizes that only `p0` contains matches, and doesn't bother to scan the remaining partitions. This performance gain is particularly pronounced when the table's index is too large to fit into memory because it cuts down on costly disk activity.

Of course, this logic works only when you use a `SELECT` against the partitioned column, so deciding which column to partition on often boils down to the question, "Which column will I use most often in `WHERE` clauses?" Through a careful choice of a column, you can maximize the potential for pruning.

Again, `EXPLAIN` is helpful to confirm that queries are executed in the way that you intend them to be. If you query on a column other than the partitioned one, you see that all partitions are scanned, as shown here:

```
mysql> EXPLAIN PARTITIONS SELECT * FROM test WHERE foo=4585\G
*************************** 1. row ***************************
           id: 1
  select_type: SIMPLE
        table: test
   partitions: p0,p1,p3,p4
....
```

However, if you search on the partitioned column, EXPLAIN reflects the pruning that can take place.

```
mysql> EXPLAIN PARTITIONS SELECT * FROM test WHERE my_column=4585\G
*************************** 1. row ***************************
           id: 1
  select_type: SIMPLE
        table: test
   partitions: p4
...
```

Incidentally, when MySQL scans multiple partitions, it still does so linearly. Future versions of MySQL can hopefully implement some degree of parallel scanning, which is a big boost to performance when partitions are stored on different physical disks.

Physical Storage of Partitions

Earlier, you learned that one performance advantage of partitioning is the capability to store different partitions on different disks. However, this is not the default behavior.

With MyISAM tables, each partition will be stored in the data directory using filenames of the structure mytable#P#p0 (where p0 is the partition number). For each MyISAM partition, there will be a .MYD and .MYI file.

With InnoDB, the situation is a little more complicated. Only when innodb_file_per_table is enabled can each partition reside in its own file (using the same naming convention as MyISAM partitions but with the .idb suffix).

Setting the data directory (and in the case of MyISAM, the index directory) for each partition can be achieved like so:

```
PARTITION BY RANGE (my_column) (
    PARTITION p0 VALUES LESS THAN (1000),
        DATA DIRECTORY="/disk1/data/",
        INDEX DIRECTORY="/disk2/index/",
    PARTITION p1 VALUES LESS THAN (2000),
        DATA DIRECTORY="/disk3/data/",
        INDEX DIRECTORY="/disk4/index/",
    PARTITION p3 VALUES LESS THAN (3000),
        DATA DIRECTORY="/disk5/data/",
        INDEX DIRECTORY="/disk6/index/",
    PARTITION p4 VALUES LESS THAN MAXVALUE
        DATA DIRECTORY="/disk7/data/",
        INDEX DIRECTORY="/disk8/index/",
)
```

This snippet sets each file on a different physical disk, but there's no reason why multiple indexes or data files (or a combination of the two) cannot live on the same disk. If increased performance is the goal (as opposed to splitting because of size), and disks are at a premium, it may make sense to group infrequently accessed partitions on the same disk, allowing regularly accessed partitions to reside on their own separate disk. A suitable partitioning expression can help to separate older, less frequently used data into its own partition(s).

Partition Management

This discussion could easily spend many pages examining the processes of removing, merging, and adding partitions, changing partitioning types and expressions, and so on. But such information is readily available online (most notably from MySQL's online docs), so let's concentrate on management directly related to performance.

In Chapter 8, "Tuning MySQL," you learned how repairing and analyzing tables can help to keep MySQL's internal table statistics (which are often used when determining the optimal query execution plan, or QEP) up-to-date — especially important when the table is write-heavy. A slightly different syntax is used when operating on partitioned tables:

```
ALTER TABLE t1 OPTIMIZE PARTITION p0, p1;
ALTER TABLE t1 REPAIR PARTITION p0,p1;
ALTER TABLE t1 CHECK PARTITION p0, p1;
```

In each case, you must specify the partition on which to operate. This can be a single partition, a comma-separated list, or the keyword ALL (for all partitions).

Partitioning is also incompatible with `mysqlcheck` and `myisamchk`, so checking and repairing of tables must be performed via the MySQL CLI.

Pros and Cons of Partitioning

In general, partitioning is an aid to performance, but the extent can vary greatly. Partitioning is particularly suited to large data sets where the index would be too large to fit into memory, and to data access patterns where pruning can be used. If neither of these conditions is present, the main benefit can occur from reduced disk contention by splitting partitions across multiple physical disks. But because you generally want data to be buffered in memory as much as possible, disk activity will already hopefully be low.

Partitioning also introduces some slight overhead. For example, when a row is inserted, MySQL must determine in which partition to store it. Some partitioning types are faster than others (as noted, linear hashing is particularly fast for inserting data) at particular tasks, and the choice of type should, therefore, reflect whether the table is mostly read or mostly write, or a combination of the two.

> **NOTE** *Incidentally, in a master-slave replication setup, it's perfectly acceptable to use different partitioning rules on each server. Thus, you might use* HASH *on the master (faster inserts) but* RANGE *on the slaves (faster lookups).*

Another consideration with partitioning is that if the table has a primary (or unique) key, columns used in the partitioning expression must use this key. For example, the following example is not permitted:

```
CREATE TABLE table1 (
    c1 INT NOT NULL,
    c2 DATE NOT NULL,
    c3 INT NOT NULL,
    c4 INT NOT NULL,
    PRIMARY KEY (c1)
)
PARTITION BY HASH(c4)
PARTITIONS 4;
```

Instead, you would need to use the following:

```
CREATE TABLE table1 (
    c1 INT NOT NULL,
    c2 DATE NOT NULL,
    c3 INT NOT NULL,
    c4 INT NOT NULL,
    PRIMARY KEY (c1,c4)
)
PARTITION BY HASH(c4)
PARTITIONS 4;
```

In some cases, you might need to artificially remove keys or add indexed columns to achieve the wanted partitioning structure.

Partitioning is certainly a useful weapon in any performance-conscious database administrator's arsenal, but it must be used wisely, and big gains can occur only under certain conditions. In the next section you'll meet sharding, a far more powerful method of partitioning data, which solves many of the shortcomings of partitioning.

SHARDING

So far, none of the multiserver MySQL setups examined in this chapter have done much to scale write performance, so, although the techniques discussed thus far are still useful, they are only useful up to a certain point. Depending on the size and estimated growth of your platform, replication and scaling up may be feasible long-term or mid-term solutions. But for large sites, something more is needed.

Sharding is the most common solution to the problem of scaling writes. Sharding is an example of data partitioning and is similar in concept to the MySQL partitioning discussed earlier in this chapter. Just as with partitioning, sharding involves splitting larger tables into smaller parts (called *shards*), but that is where the similarities end. Although partitions are transparent to clients, each shard exists as a separate table and must be referenced as such. Also, the handling of shards is not automatic as it is with partitions.

Although it requires significantly more work to set up, sharding is a better long-term solution than any of the methods mentioned previously. However, there's no point in adding unnecessary complexity for the sake of it, so before embarking on sharding, think carefully about whether you actually do need it.

Let's look at an example. Consider the `posts` table of a busy online forum. The table contains columns for the post text, the date stamp, the user ID for who made the post, the thread that the post belongs to, and the forum in which the thread belongs. Because of the write-heavy nature of this table, contention soon becomes an issue, and you must find a way to scale writes.

Rather than store the posts in a single table, you can split the table into several shards. This process is as simple as creating extra tables, and then manually copying the existing rows across. As with partitioning, you must decide on the criteria for splitting, and, in this example, the forum ID seems like a good candidate. So, you create tables named `posts_1`, `posts_2`, `posts_3`, and so on, and then copy over any rows where the forum ID is 1 into `posts_1`, any rows where the forum ID is 2 into `posts_2`, and so on.

Next, you tell your application that whenever a user creates a post in forum ID x, you write it to the table `posts_x`. Similarly, when you want to view an individual post, a thread, or a list of threads in a given forum, you use the relevant table for that forum.

As you can see, setting up a system like this could require substantial rewriting of the application. However, placing different shards on different servers provides a powerful and flexible way in which to distribute writes across multiple machines.

Lookup Tables

With the possibility that shards may not (and, in fact, almost certainly won't) all exist on the same server, it becomes impractical to hard-code the application to simply look for a table based on a naming convention (for example, `posts_x`). Instead, you also need a way to determine the hostname or IP address of the server on which the shard resides, the login details, and perhaps the name of the database and table.

The usual way to implement this is through a lookup table, which could be either a MySQL table or perhaps a `memcache` object. Table 9-1 shows an example.

TABLE 9-1: Sample Lookup Table

FORUM ID	SERVER IP	SERVER USERNAME	SERVER PASSWORD	SERVER DATABASE
1	192.168.0.1	wwwuser	gDRhux8thu	forum_posts
2	192.168.0.2	wwwuser	94Sa89zvVxj	forum_posts
3	192.168.0.3	web	Fa9q9aLK2a	forum_posts
4	192.168.0.4	forums	bv62RNJuT	forum_posts
5	192.168.0.4	forums	bv62RNJuT	forum_posts
6	192.168.0.4	fourms	bv62RNJuT	forum_posts

In many cases, the login details and database names will be standardized, and you can get away with simply specifying the forum ID and IP/hostname on which the shard resides, thus reducing the size of the table.

The next time the application needs to access a post, it uses the lookup table to determine the MySQL server to connect to on which the required shard is located.

Fixed Sharding

Lookup tables are an example of *dynamic sharding*. The application has no hard-coded knowledge about where and how shards are stored, and must rely on an external map.

You could avoid the need for a lookup table (and, thus, remove some latency and memory requirements, and perhaps a single point of failure) by explicitly telling the application how to handle shards — which is *fixed sharding*. For example, you could use the modulus of the forum ID to divide the data into a predefined number of shards, or you could use hashing.

This method is a lot less flexible. You lose the fine-grained control that a lookup table offers for size and location of shards. For those reasons, dynamic sharding is usually the way to go.

Shard Sizes and Distribution

Although it may be tempting at first to aim for one shard per server, this soon becomes impractical. What happens if the shard becomes too big? (That is, the write traffic for the individual shard becomes too high for the server to cope with.) Conversely, if you have too many shards, the lookup table becomes big, requiring more memory and taking longer to search.

The forum posts example works quite well in this respect. You might expect the number of forums to be in the range of 10 to 100. With 100 shards, you could start by placing them across two servers, each with 50 shards, and then perhaps moving to 25 on each of four servers as the forum grows. This assumes each shard receives the same amount of activity though, which is unlikely to be the case. So, you could just as easily assign a couple of heavily accessed shards to one server and a few dozen infrequently accessed shards to another. With a lookup table, you have a huge amount of flexibility.

Sharding Keys and Accessibility

In sharding parlance, the key is the column on which you split the data. (In the forum example, this was the forum ID column.) Choosing a suitable key is critical for sharding to be a workable solution, and deciding on a key usually starts with an analysis of how the data is typically queried.

In the forum example, the forum ID seems like a sensible choice. The majority of queries fetch lists of threads in a given forum or fetch posts inside an individual thread (which, in turn, belong to a given forum). You can easily determine which shard contains the data and query it.

But what if you want to view all the posts made by a given user? Because you've sharded by forum ID, the user's posts are probably scattered across multiple shards, meaning that you must query each shard one at a time. Because of the linear nature of this, it can be a performance killer.

Of course, you could get around this by sharding on the user ID, allowing you to quickly retrieve all of a user's posts from a single shard. But this would then make life difficult when you want to retrieve all the posts in a given thread, or all the threads in a given forum.

The best compromise here is to shard by the key that is likely to give the most benefit (in this example, you'd anticipate a lot more queries based on the forum ID than on the user ID), and then look for ways to mitigate some of the performance penalties associated with querying multiple shards.

Most of the performance problems (in PHP applications anyway) arise because of the linear nature of querying each shard. Although PHP doesn't actually have the capability to issue multiple database queries in parallel, other languages do (such as C and Java). One solution is a helper application that can issue the queries in parallel, merge the results, and return them to PHP. In the later section, "Full-Text Searching," you learn how Sphinx can be used for this.

Another solution is to implement additional lookup tables. For example, you could map the post ID to the ID of the user who created it and the forum ID that it belongs to. Although such a table could grow big (making it a burden to cache in memory), it would allow you to easily discover which shards contained posts by a given user. This would save you having to query every shard, but you'd still need to query each matching shard one at a time. For a prolific user, you may still need to query a lot of shards.

Rather than face the dilemma of which key to shard on, you could opt to keep two copies of the data, with each copy sharded by a different key. This would allow you to easily perform lookups based on the forum ID or user ID. Unfortunately, it would also double the number of queries associated with writing to the table, so this isn't usually a practical option.

Yet another solution is through the use of *federated tables* (in which a table on a remote MySQL server is represented as a local table). These tend to offer poor performance though, so they aren't recommended.

Aggressive caching is usually the best workaround, falling back on querying multiple shards if the cache does not contain the results. This is far from perfect, though, and it can often feel as if sharding causes more problems than it solves. Despite that, it is still the preferred way to scale writes.

Cross-Shard Joins

One of the most disruptive aspects of sharding is that it severely limits your capability to join across tables. Using the forum posts example, the post shards contain the user ID of each post's author. To display a thread, you probably want to display some basic information alongside each post, such as the user's nickname, avatar, join date, and so on. If the posts' shard sits on a different server than the user table, you can't do a join on the two (at least not without using federated tables, which don't offer good performance).

Again, there's no clean solution, but following are a few possibilities:

➤ Decompose the join, and run the queries separately. That is, fetch the posts from the shard, and then perform a second query to fetch user information for each post author. This hurts performance, but not necessarily drastically.

➤ Denormalize the posts' table. Add additional columns to hold the username, avatar, and so on. This is attractive but could substantially increase the size of the data, wasting precious space in memory and increasing disk I/O. It depends how much extra data you need to add.

➤ Store a copy of the user table on each shard node so that you can still join as normal. You could use replication to ensure that each node has an up-to-date copy of the user table. This is a good solution if the table is relatively small or infrequently updated. (And compared to the posts' table, both would be true.) But this would be impossible if you also decide to shard the user table.

Application Modifications

Sharding can require extensive rewriting of existing applications to make them shard-aware. Using a database abstraction class can help enormously, though, because it provides the opportunity to filter and rewrite queries before they are passed to MySQL.

For example, instead of rewriting every piece of code that queries the posts' table, you can modify the database abstraction class to catch such queries, and rewrite them to use the appropriate shard (or group of shards, if necessary). This is by no means a trivial task, but it's infinitely preferable to auditing every database query in the application.

COMPLEMENTING MYSQL

So far, the multiserver setups examined here have used only MySQL. But there are a number of complementary technologies that can provide useful specialist services such as caching, load balancing, and fail-over. By far, the most popular is MySQL Proxy, and this is what this section focuses on, before briefly reviewing some popular third-party stats/tuning scripts.

MySQL Proxy

MySQL Proxy is an incredibly useful piece of middleware that sits between MySQL servers and clients. Although this introduces a little extra latency into requests (and a single point of failure), it provides the capability to intercept requests (and responses) and to modify or redirect them. The possibilities are endless because of MySQL Proxy's powerful built-in scripting language.

Figure 9-8 shows a basic topology with MySQL Proxy sitting in the middle.

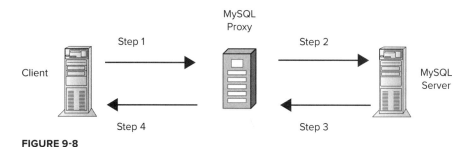

FIGURE 9-8

In step 1, the client connects to the proxy and issues a SQL query. After performing any actions on the request, the query is then forwarded to the MySQL server (step 2), which returns its response to the proxy (step 3). At this point, MySQL Proxy has the opportunity to perform actions on the response before returning it to the client (step 4). The whole process is transparent to the client, which thinks it is connecting to and querying the MySQL server directly.

Common uses for a MySQL Proxy include the load balancing of queries among multiple slaves, logging and generating statistics, splitting reads and writes to separate servers (for replication), implementing sharding, rewriting queries generated by a closed-source application, and filtering queries for security. You can concentrate on the performance-related capabilities.

> **NOTE** *Development of MySQL Proxy is moving rapidly, and it pays to use the latest release. If you use a Linux/UNIX distribution that uses a package repository system, check to see that it carries the latest version. If not, you can download it from MySQL Proxy's Launchpad site (*`https://launchpad.net/mysql-proxy/+download`*).*

Load Balancing

Let's look at a simple example (Figure 9-9) that requires no scripting: basic load balancing between multiple replication slaves. Earlier in this chapter, you learned how load balancing could be achieved by round-robin DNS (or other means by which the client picks a slave at random), with the client (such as a web server) connecting directly to the slave. However, in this example, the client needs no knowledge of the pool of slaves. It simply connects to the proxy and lets it do the legwork. The proxy picks a random slave from a predefined list and sends the query to it.

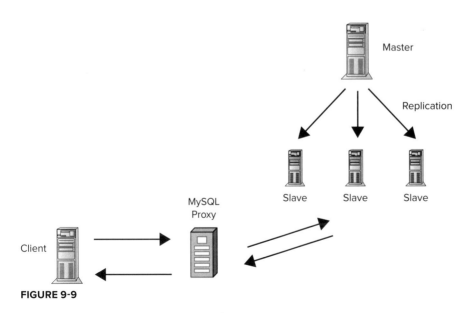

FIGURE 9-9

Setting up this kind of load balancing is trivial with MySQL Proxy. You simply supply a list of `IP:port` combinations at the command line when starting the daemon, as shown here:

```
mysql-proxy --proxy-backend-addresses=serverA:3306 --proxy-backend-
    addresses=serverB:3306 --proxy-backend-addresses=serverC:3306
```

MySQL Proxy listens on TCP/4040 by default. This can easily be changed (for example, to the default MySQL port of TCP/3306) using the `proxy-address` option. (Also you'll probably want to launch the proxy in daemon mode using `daemon`, run it as an unprivileged user with `user`, and set it to restart if it crashes with `keepalive`.)

Alternatively, you can put everything in a configuration file and specify the path to it when starting MySQL Proxy, as shown here:

```
# cat /etc/mysql/mysql-proxy.conf

[mysql-proxy]
proxy-backend-addresses=serverA:3306
proxy-backend-addresses=serverB:3306
proxy-backend-addresses=serverC:3306
keepalive
daemon
user=nobody

# mysql-proxy –defaults-file=/etc/mysql/mysql-proxy.conf
```

Load balancing with MySQL Proxy has another major advantage over methods in which the client itself picks a slave at random (be it via DNS, or from a predefined list of slaves). It can detect if a slave is down and remove it from the pool for a short period of time. This detection is still fairly crude, however, and isn't proactive. The proxy will discover only that a slave is down when it attempts to forward a query to it and is unable to connect. But it will at least forward the query to another slave instead.

Despite these features, MySQL Proxy isn't the perfect solution here. Aside from the latency introduced (the official documentation suggests approximately 400 milliseconds in the proxy, but there will also be network latency to factor in), you also add a single point of failure (SpoF) to the network. If the proxy goes down, all your read queries stop.

Scripting with Lua

MySQL Proxy can be scripted via its Lua support. Lua is a relatively new scripting language, similar to the likes of Perl or C in syntax, and designed to be easy to learn. Certainly, if you're familiar with other scripting languages, you should have no problem picking it up.

A handful of hook points are provided, allowing scripts to execute user-defined functions at key points in the request cycle. For example, you can hook into `connect_server` to modify MySQL Proxy's behavior when a client connects or `read_query_result` to modify a query's results.

With a few dozen lines of Lua, you can write a load balancer. Rudy Rucker has done just this (`http://forge.mysql.com/tools/tool.php?id=259`). Although Rucker's example script offers little more than simply starting the proxy with multiple `proxy-backend-addresses` options, it provides an excellent starting point to create a more advanced load balancer. For example, you could give each back-end server a weight depending on its power, or redirect to different back-end servers based on which table/database is accessed.

A more advanced Lua script could even query multiple shards on different servers and combine the results, effectively hiding from the client that sharding was taking place. The only limit here is your imagination (and time).

Splitting Reads and Writes

A newer feature in MySQL Proxy is the capability to split reads and writes, sending them to different servers. This has the potential to make replication a lot easier for applications to implement because you would no longer have to rewrite code to send writes to the master and reads to the slaves. You simply send the query to a single address (that of MySQL Proxy) and let the proxy figure out where to route the queries.

> **NOTE** *As of this writing, this feature is still in beta and is probably unsuitable for use on production servers. But, hopefully, it will mature as time goes on to become a core part of MySQL Proxy.*

Alternatives

MySQL Proxy is undoubtedly the leader in its class, but there are alternatives (of which Spock Proxy looks the most exciting). It's also worth pausing to think if MySQL Proxy will be necessary in your topology. Rewriting queries and results tends to be a fairly specialist requirement, and the primary use for MySQL Proxy is to load balance across multiple replication slaves. As you have seen, though, balancing across slaves is far from perfect, and often you'll opt for a topology where each slave has a distinct role (to better utilize query caching) or a sharded setup.

Aside from a little extra latency, the main drawback to MySQL Proxy is that it is a single point of failure. If MySQL Proxy goes down, all read queries are affected. Possible ways to mitigate this include running two MySQL Proxy machines and then either balancing traffic across them or using a hot spare that comes online and assumes the primary proxy's IP address if the primary goes offline.

MySQL Tools

A range of useful tools are available for analyzing and monitoring MySQL. This section introduces you to some of the most popular ones. These include tools for monitoring which queries are taking the longest to run, and showing which steps of query execution are taking the longest. The discussion also provides tips on tuning the various buffers and caches.

Monitoring

Mtop (http://mtop.sourceforge.net/) is to MySQL what top is to UNIX — an ncurses-based tool that enables you to see at a glance which queries are taking the most time to run. Mtop also provides detailed statistics and can explain or kill individual queries (or groups of queries), making it as much of a management tools as it is a monitor. Packaged with Mtop is Mkill, a tool for killing long-running queries that come from a particular user or host, or match a given regular expression (regex).

Innotop (http://code.google.com/p/innotop/) is perhaps the best of the top-like MySQL monitoring applications. As its name suggests, it is geared toward InnoDB and offers a huge array of monitoring modes, from replication and transactions, to deadlocks and disk I/O. Innotop takes the pain out of inspecting MySQL and InnoDB stats and is an invaluable tool for any database administrator.

MySQL Query Profiler

New to MySQL 5 is the query profiler, a built-in tool for showing where MySQL spends its time. You already learned about EXPLAIN in Chapter 8, and combined together the two give you a powerful way to debug MySQL performance problems.

The query profiler is enabled on a per-session basis and logs stats for each query subsequently executed. You can then view these stats using the new SHOW PROFILES syntax, as shown here:

```
mysql> SET profiling=1;
Query OK, 0 rows affected (0.00 sec)

mysql> select count(*) from jos_users where username like '%test%';
....

mysql> SHOW PROFILES;
+----------+------------+------------------------------------------------------+
| Query_ID | Duration   | Query                                                |
+----------+------------+------------------------------------------------------+
|        1 | 0.56869400 | select count(*) from jos_users where username like   |
|          |            |                   '%test%'                           |
+----------+------------+------------------------------------------------------+
1 row in set (0.00 sec)
```

By default, the query profiler stores the 15 most recent queries in memory, and you can view the most recent using SHOW PROFILE — or SHOW PROFILE FOR QUERY n for an earlier query (where n is the Query ID):

```
mysql> show profile;
+--------------------------------+----------+
| Status                         | Duration |
+--------------------------------+----------+
| starting                       | 0.000017 |
| checking query cache for query | 0.000046 |
| Opening tables                 | 0.000009 |
| System lock                    | 0.000006 |
| Table lock                     | 0.000019 |
| init                           | 0.000020 |
| optimizing                     | 0.000009 |
| statistics                     | 0.000011 |
| preparing                      | 0.000009 |
| executing                      | 0.000005 |
| Sending data                   | 0.568485 |
| end                            | 0.000010 |
```

```
| query end                       | 0.000003 |
| freeing items                   | 0.000033 |
| storing result in query cache   | 0.000006 |
| logging slow query              | 0.000003 |
| cleaning up                     | 0.000003 |
+---------------------------------+----------+
```

The profiling step names should all be self-explanatory, and they enable you to see where MySQL spends its time. You can determine whether there are issues with locking, or perhaps the table cache is full, and I/O bottlenecks are causing delays in opening the table and reading the data. The `Sending data` step does not refer to the process to transfer data across the wire from server to client, but rather to the whole process to run the query and return the data. Hopefully, future versions of the query profiler will break this step down to provide more useful information.

You can also see the effect of the query cache in action (assuming it is enabled) by immediately re-executing the query and profiling it, as shown here:

```
+---------------------------------+----------+
| Status                          | Duration |
+---------------------------------+----------+
| starting                        | 0.000017 |
| checking query cache for query  | 0.000007 |
| checking privileges on cached   | 0.000004 |
| sending cached result to clien  | 0.000007 |
| logging slow query              | 0.000003 |
| cleaning up                     | 0.000004 |
+---------------------------------+----------+
```

This time, you see fewer steps as a direct result of a hit on the query cache.

You can get more information from the profiler by using the syntax `SHOW PROFILE <type> [for query n]`, where `type` is one of `ALL`, `BLOCK IO`, `CONTEXT SWITCHES`, `CPU`, `IPC`, `MEMORY` (as of version 5.6, not currently implemented), `PAGE FAULTS`, `SOURCE`, or `SWAP`.

Following is a snippet of the profile of the original query using the `ALL` type. For brevity, this just shows one row, and the data has been formatted vertically using the `\G` switch.

```
*************************** 11. row ***************************
             Status: Sending data
           Duration: 0.733316
           CPU_user: 0.304019
         CPU_system: 0.176011
  Context_voluntary: 436
Context_involuntary: 94
       Block_ops_in: 47904
      Block_ops_out: 32
      Messages_sent: 0
  Messages_received: 0
  Page_faults_major*: 0
  Page_faults_minor: 389
              Swaps: 0
    Source_function: unknown function
        Source_file: ../../sql/sql_select
        Source_line: 2317
```

You can see some degree of context switching (but nothing too serious), and some disk activity — mostly reading in from disk (`Block_ops_in`). Presumably, the data is not in memory.

> **NOTE** Page faults *(referred to as* hard faults *in Windows) are not as serious as they sound. Minor faults occur when a page has been loaded in memory but has not been marked as such in the memory management unit (MMU). The kernel remedies this by simply marking the page as loaded in the MMU. By contrast, a major fault occurs when MySQL attempts to access a page that* hasn't *yet been loaded into memory. The kernel remedies this by reading in the page from disk (and, if memory is low, possibly writing out a page to disk to free up some space). This makes major faults much more expensive, but they are still a vital part of memory management.*

Performance

The MySQL Performance Tuning Primer Script (`http://day32.com/MySQL/tuning-primer.sh`) parses MySQL's status counters and generates a report with recommendations for improvement. Following is an example excerpt of a report:

```
KEY BUFFER
Current MyISAM index space = 1 G
Current key_buffer_size = 1000 M
Key cache miss rate is 1 : 310206
Key buffer fill ratio = 44.00 %
Your key_buffer_size seems to be too high.
Perhaps you can use these resources elsewhere

QUERY CACHE
Query cache is enabled
Current query_cache_size = 32 M
Current query_cache_used = 22 M
Current query_cache_limit = 1 M
Current Query cache Memory fill ratio = 71.76 %
Current query_cache_min_res_unit = 4 K
Query Cache is 21 % fragmented
Run "FLUSH QUERY CACHE" periodically to defragment the query cache memory
If you have many small queries lower 'query_cache_min_res_unit' to reduce
    fragmentation.
MySQL won't cache query results that are larger than query_cache_limit in size

SORT OPERATIONS
Current sort_buffer_size = 2 M
Current read_rnd_buffer_size = 256 K
Sort buffer seems to be fine

JOINS
Current join_buffer_size = 132.00 K
You have had 3513200 queries where a join could not use an index properly
You have had 40 joins without keys that check for key usage after each row
```

```
You should enable "log-queries-not-using-indexes"
Then look for non indexed joins in the slow query log.
If you are unable to optimize your queries you may want to increase your
join_buffer_size to accommodate larger joins in one pass.
```

Although all this information can be readily calculated by a savvy database administrator by looking at the output of SHOW STATUS and SHOW VARIABLES, there's no denying that the Tuning Primer Script provides a very useful at-a-glance summary of performance. The suggestions it gives form useful pointers for the less-experienced administrator.

> **NOTE** *Remember that these suggestions are just that and tend to assume that the machine is a dedicated MySQL server.*

If you prefer to view the raw statistics and make your own conclusions, mysqlreport (http://hackmysql.com/mysqlreport) offers an alternative to wading through the output of SHOW STATUS. The output is intentionally minimalistic but provides a wealth of information, as this snippet shows:

```
__ SELECT and Sort _____
Scan            35.17M      3.5/s %SELECT:    9.77
Range           86.37M      8.5/s             23.99
Full join        3.51M      0.3/s              0.98
Range check         40      0.0/s              0.00
Full rng join   12.98k      0.0/s              0.00
Sort scan        4.55M      0.4/s
Sort range      96.97M      9.5/s
Sort mrg pass   35.11k      0.0/s

__ Query Cache _____
Memory usage    23.89M of  32.00M   %Used:   74.66
Block Fragmnt   18.35%
Hits           635.49M      62.4/s
Inserts        347.26M      34.1/s
Insrt:Prune      7.09:1     29.3/s
Hit:Insert       1.83:1

__ Table Locks _____
Waited           1.27M      0.1/s %Total:    0.14
Immediate      932.19M      91.5/s

__ Tables _____
Open            6000 of 6000        %Cache: 100.00
Opened         311.54k      0.0/s
```

Finally, Percona Toolkit (http://www.percona.com/software/percona-toolkit/), which is based on Maatkit, contains many command-line tools for automating various aspects of database monitoring and administration. Inside the kit are tools for killing queries based on regexes, analyzing logs, monitoring and manipulating replication, monitoring disk I/O, and, of course, for generating stats.

Backups

A discussion of MySQL backup strategies could easily fill a whole chapter because not only do you need to consider the creation of the backups themselves, but also the recovery process — for example, determining how quickly they can be reloaded into the system, how easily they can be manipulated if you only need to recover a single table, and so on. The focus here is mostly on performance, and the discussion certainly does not represent a well-rounded, comprehensive backup strategy.

File Backups

The obvious way to create backups of MySQL databases would be to copy the files from the MySQL data directory (for example, `/var/lib/mysql`) — the `frm`, `MYI`, and `MYD` files for MySQL, and the `ib*` files for `InnoDB`. It should be apparent that doing this on a live server is not reliable because it's unlikely that contents of these files will be in sync with the data held in memory.

Shutting down MySQL and then taking a copy of the files is one option, but, of course, this results in the database being down for the duration, making it impractical in many situations. Even if MySQL must be turned off only for a few minutes, it will start back up with empty caches and may take several hours to "warm up" and reach optimal performance.

For `MyISAM` tables, a compromise is to leave MySQL running and execute `FLUSH TABLES WITH READ LOCK` prior to copying the files. This flushes the data to disk and prevents clients from issuing any writes, making it safe to copy the files. After the backup has been taken, the tables can be unlocked with `UNLOCK TABLES`.

This is certainly preferable to shutting down the server, and the caches will still be warm, but it can take some time to flush the tables — especially if there are any long-running queries (it may even be necessary to kill these, simply to minimize the length of time for which the tables are locked) — and tables will be read-only.

This method is unreliable for `InnoDB` tables, however. Because of `InnoDB`'s extensive use of background threads, even flushing the tables does not guarantee that they are completely in sync.

SQL Backups

The alternative to file-based backups is to export the data from MySQL in a format that can be re-imported at a later date. Usually, this means exporting as SQL.

`mysqldump` (shipped with MySQL) is generally used for this and (by default) dumps the schema for each table, along with a series of SQL `INSERT`s to repopulate them. `mysqldump` is flexible and powerful, and is the basis of many MySQL backup scripts. It can back up all databases, individual databases, individual tables, and (because it supports `WHERE`) can be used to back up only selected rows of a table. To restore, the dump file can simply be piped to MySQL.

This has several obvious advantages over backing up raw binary files. The dump file can be manipulated prior to being re-inserted (for example, if you don't want to to-reimport it all), is engine-independent (and, with a little work, MySQL version-independent), is less prone to corruption, and can easily be compared (for example, via `diff`) to previous backups. `mysqldump` is also `InnoDB`-safe.

`mysqdump` isn't without its problems, though. The processes to dump and restore the data are both CPU-intensive and can take a significant amount of time. (When restoring, MySQL must re-execute every statement contained in the dump file.) mysqldump also issues FLUSH TABLES WITH READ LOCK, making it no better than copying raw files. If anything, the locks remain in place longer because dumping is significantly slower.

Also, remember to spend some time thinking about the practicalities of re-importing. Although it's certainly easiest to run mysqldump with the A switch (causing it to dump all databases), a single, huge dump file containing every database is often impractical to work with, and would likely be too big to open in a text editor. Most of the backup tools built around mysqldump can generate a list of databases and tables, and then dump each one to a separate file, making it easy to selectively re-import.

CSV Backups

Although you might automatically associate mysqldump with SQL dumps, it can also be used to create dumps in other formats such as XML or comma-separated value (CSV). Although CSV dumps are no quicker to create, they have a significant advantage over SQL dumps. They can be imported using LOAD DATA INFILE, which is usually a lot faster.

MySQL even ships with a tool, mysqlimport, which provides a command-line interface to LOAD DATA INFILE. Starting with MySQL version 5.1, mysqlimport supports the use of multiple threads (via the use-threads= command-line option), which further improves performance.

To generate CSV dumps, call mysqldump with the tab option. For each table, a schema will also be generated, which must be imported in the usual way.

Incremental Backups

Creating incremental backups is generally thought of as a nonstarter with MySQL, but there are a couple of techniques that can achieve this.

You can use mysqldump's WHERE support, for example, to select rows based on a timestamp column. (Although, for a large table, it might make more sense to archive off older data into a separate table, which could be backed up less often.)

A more complicated method involves backing up the server's binary logs and allowing events to be replayed back to MySQL (in much the same way as a replication slave takes a copy of the master's binary log and replays it). Naturally, it's impractical to keep every binary log, so this technique is most commonly used with full backups generated by another method (for example, mysqldump). In emergencies, you can import the most recent dump and then replay the binary logs from that point.

After taking a copy of the binary logs, you can issue FLUSH LOGS to cause MySQL to start using a new log file. This ensures that the binary logs start and end at points corresponding to when you make the backups. For InnoDB tables, the transaction log may also be backed up and replayed in a similar fashion.

Backing Up from a Slave

Another popular method to create backups is to set up a replication slave specifically for this. (Although, of course, it can double up as a general-purpose slave for read queries.) A slave on its own isn't a backup solution, though. If a DROP or DELETE query were executed on the master, it would propagate instantly to the slave. But a slave does have the advantage that you can usually take it offline (or lock the tables) for a longer period of time. After you unlock the tables, the slave simply catches up with the master in its own time.

This is such a useful method to minimize the downtime associated with backing up that many people choose to run a slave on the same machine as the master, solely for the purpose to take back-ups from it. However, this method isn't without its disadvantages. Because the slave must re-execute every query received from the master, this results in substantially more load on a single-server setup. If you want to use a slave for backups, it's best to run it on another host.

LVM Snapshots

A final method to create MySQL backups (and other types of backups for that matter) is to use the copy-on-write feature of some storage systems, of which Logical Volume Management (LVM) is the most popular under Linux.

LVM acts as a virtualization layer between the physical media and Linux, enabling you to create partitions that can span multiple physical disks and can be extended or reduced relatively easily. The Linux implementation of LVM also supports the concept of *snapshots*, whereby you can create an almost instantaneous copy of a partition (resulting in no downtime) and then archive it at your leisure.

The reason why LVM is so quick to create snapshots is that it doesn't actually make a physical copy of the data elsewhere on the disk. Rather, it implements copy-on-write. Any subsequent writes to the partition you are snapshotting are then made in two places — to the original partition and to a copy-on-write table (which can be thought of as a change log). At any time, LVM can create the illusion of having made a full backup of the partition by overlaying the copy-on-write table with the partition as it currently exists.

This cleverness is also the source of LVM's biggest drawback though (at least from a performance perspective), because the existence of a snapshot results in writing twice as much data to the disk. Not only that, but the copy-on-write table will be located on a different part of the disk, caus-ing lots of disk seeking. Of course, this happens only for the duration of the snapshot's existence, so your aim should still be to create an archive from the snapshot and then remove it as soon as possible.

> **NOTE** *Most of the major operating systems (including the FreeBSD, Windows, OSX, and Solaris) support LVM, but it isn't the only copy-on-write system around. ZFS is a popular choice for Solaris, FreeBSD, OS X, and Linux (via FUSE), whereas BTRFS is another Linux-only option. On Windows, Shadow Copy (which requires NTFS) provides similar features.*

So far, this discussion has concentrated solely on the official MySQL. However, given the permis-sive licensing on MySQL, there's nothing to stop third parties from writing patches or branching off their own versions. Many times, the motivation is to provide better performance, and in the next section, you learn about some of these alternatives.

ALTERNATIVES TO MYSQL

Although MySQL is popular, well regarded, and a cornerstone of many websites, it isn't always the best tool for the job. There's no shortage of competing technologies ranging from performance-enhancing MySQL patches to caching mechanisms to lightweight key/value databases (for situations in which a full relational database is not needed). This section looks at some of the most popular alternatives, along with promising new additions.

MySQL Forks and Branches

It's easy to get caught up in semantics when describing the various MySQL offshoots that exist. Some are little more than a collection of patches compiled into MySQL, whereas others are heavily modified versions incorporating new storage engines. Whether individual projects are best described as forks, branches, patches, or something else is debatable. But the one thing all these have in common is that they are mostly drop-in replacements for the standard MySQL and can be used without the need to drastically (if at all) rewrite existing applications.

Why would you need these offshoots? MySQL is already famed for its performance, but in large applications, it's inevitable that opinions will differ on how best development should proceed. Performance is only one of many factors for the MySQL developers, and the offshoots examined here are mostly geared toward providing better performance (sometimes at the expense of functionality).

MariaDB

With some uncertainty over MySQL's future licensing, the aim of MariaDB (`http://www.mariadb.org`) is to provide a fully compatible general public license (GPL) alternative to MySQL. MariaDB is usually described as a branch and aims to be fully compatible with MySQL — the project is even overseen by the original author of MySQL, Michael Widenius.

Aside from its GPL nature, `MariaDB` includes a host of small performance improvements, including the following:

➤ Changes to `fsync()` behavior on the binary log increase the rate at which changes can be committed (which is often a bottleneck with replication) and lessen the chances of data loss on crashes.

➤ It provides a segmented key cache. By splitting the key cache into pieces (the exact number, if configurable), problems of lock contention are reduced.

➤ It provides progress reports when altering, checking, and repairing tables, and adding/dropping indexes.

➤ It provides better query optimization, in particular for subqueries.

➤ It provides improved thread pooling and handling.

Another main feature of MariaDB is the `Aria` storage engine (but the two are independent of each other, and `Aria` could just as easily be used in MySQL), which aims to be a crash-proof alternative to `MyISAM`. Over time, the goals of `Aria` have widened, and it now supports transactions (to some degree) and is ACID-compliant. Even though these features are still in progress, the crash-proof nature of `Aria` is enough to make it a worthy contender to `MyISAM`.

Drizzle

Although MariaDB is a branch of MySQL that can act as a drop-in replacement, Drizzle (`http://drizzle.org`) is better described as a fork and contains significant recoding. As such, although Drizzle is largely compatible with MySQL, it makes no guarantees of this and will almost certainly continue to diverge from MySQL over time.

Drizzle is built around a microkernel architecture, with most of the noncore functionality (including logging, the query cache, and authentication) supplied by plug-ins. This modular structure results in a slim server. Drizzle is specifically designed for high concurrency and is optimized for multicore machines with large amounts of memory. (Not so long ago, this was an area in which MySQL had problems.)

Following are the main differences between Drizzle and MySQL:

➤ Drizzle supports only `MyISAM` for temporary tables.

➤ Many data types from MySQL are no longer valid. These include `TINYINT`, `SMALLINT`, `MEDIUMINT`, `BIT`, `TIME`, and `YEAR`.

➤ Partitioning is not supported.

➤ Drizzle provides its own replication plug-in, based around Google Protocol Buffers.

It's perhaps best to think of Drizzle as a SQL92-compliant SQL server, rather than as a MySQL fork. This emphasizes that it is mostly in the MySQL-specific extensions that Drizzle differs from MySQL, and helps remind you that MySQL is not the same thing as SQL. Incidentally, if MariaDB's parentage seems hard to beat, it's worth nothing that the likes of Brian Aker, Google, Sun, and Intel have all been involved with Drizzle development.

OurDelta

OurDelta (`http://ourdelta.org`) provides custom builds of MySQL and MariaDB, compiled with a handful of community-contributed patches. These range from Percona's `XtraDB` storage engine (more on this in a minute) to contributions by Facebook and Google. Some patches are performance-oriented, whereas others (perhaps the most useful) provide enhanced logging and diagnostics — for example, millisecond precision in the `processlist`.

OurDelta also provide repositories for Debian, Ubuntu, RHEL, and CentOS, making installation a breeze on such systems.

Percona Server

Percona (`http://www.percona.com/software/percona-server`) describes its server as a drop-in replacement for MySQL, making it much more like MariaDB than Drizzle for compatibility. But whereas MariaDB has a fairly broad scope, Percona Server concentrates on performance and enhanced diagnostics.

For diagnostics and statistics, some of the features of Percona Server include per table/index/user counters, detailed mutex statistics, and enhanced QEP profiling. Performance features include more fine-grained locking, InnoDB buffer pool preloading, better read-ahead support, and special support for solid-state devices such as flash storage.

Percona also develops the XtraDB storage engine (part of Percona Server, but it can also be down-loaded separately and used on MySQL, MariaDB, or Drizzle). This is an InnoDB fork that boasts excellent performance, particularly on busy, high-end systems. Features include better diagnostics (via SHOW ENGINE INNODB STATUS), as well as improved CPU and I/O scaling.

Which to Pick?

With so many MySQL offshoots, which should you choose? Or is it best to stick with the tried-and-tested MySQL? Because performance is of primary interest here, it's almost certainly worth exploring the alternatives.

If you have an application that sticks closely to the SQL92 standards without using any/many MySQL-specific features, Drizzle is probably the most exciting option. It isn't a drop-in replacement for MySQL though, so be prepared to spend some time learning the radical changes that it introduces, and possibly recoding some of your SQL queries.

If you need 100 percent MySQL compatibility, Percona Server, OurDelta, or MariaDB are all excellent options. MariaDB tends to be more focused toward improving MyISAM (via the Aria engine), whereas the Percona team focuses on InnoDB (via XtraDB). Of course, because Aria and XtraDB are not tied in to MariaDB or Percona Server, you're free to mix and match.

Full-Text Searching

Despite InnoDB (and, in particular, XtraDB) having the performance edge in a lot of cases, many users stay with MyISAM because it has a feature not present in other engines: full-text searching.

Just to recap, full-text searching is implemented in MySQL via the FULLTEXT index type. It has numerous performance and accuracy benefits over searching with LIKE or REGEXP, such as boolean searching, ranking of results, and stemming. These features make it highly attractive for use in online searches. But because it is only available in MyISAM, there is a big gap for alternatives that can be used with other engines such as InnoDB.

There are a few options, however. For example, you have already seen how MyISAM can be used on a replication slave, whereas InnoDB is used on the master (and perhaps other slaves, too). If the data to be searched is easily separated from other tables, and is reasonably static in nature, there is also the option to simply leave it as MyISAM — or duplicate the contents of an InnoDB table into a MyISAM table for the purposes of full-text searching. Too often, though, searches run against multiple tables, and keeping them (or copies of them) as MyISAM is impractical.

Full-Text Tuning

Even if using MyISAM is not a problem, full-text searching is far from perfect from a performance perspective. Before delving into alternatives to full-text, let's look at some of the available tuning options.

FULLTEXT indexes can easily grow large — usually they are used on TEXT, MEDIUMTEXT, or LONGTEXT columns. In the interest of accuracy and keeping the index to a reasonable size, MySQL enables the minimum and maximum word lengths to be defined (of these, the minimum is usually the most important) via the cnf settings, ft_min_word_len and ft_max_word_len. Changing the minimum word length can have a dramatic impact on index size. (And as you've seen, keeping indexes small pays off.) So, whenever possible, you should increase this from the default of three characters.

MySQL also uses a list of *stop words* — words to be ignored when creating FULLTEXT indexes. The default list contains the usual filler words, including and, the, this, that, and so on. (For the full list, check storage/myisam/ft_static.c in the MySQL source.) Although the purpose of the stop word list is primarily to improve the relevance of search results, it also helps to keep the index size down. If you plan to use FULLTEXT indexes on text that contains a lot of jargon, foreign language words, or unusual words that appear so often as to be irrelevant in search results, a custom list of stop words can be specified via ft_stopword_file in my.cnf. As with the maximum/minimum word lengths, all FULLTEXT indexes must be rebuilt after any changes are made.

Unfortunately, FULLTEXT indexes are still somewhat slow, even taking into account these tuning opportunities. One problem is that, like any other index, MySQL must update the index whenever data in the table is modified. For large datasets this can be slow, and often it's overkill. Many times, searches just need reasonably up-to-date data, and being a few minutes stale is perfectly acceptable.

Sphinx

Having established that there is a need for a better alternative to FULLTEXT indexes, let's look at the most popular solution to the problem.

Sphinx is a third-party, standalone search engine that works particularly well with MySQL. It's blazingly fast and supports its own subset of SQL (named SphinxQL) — so you can query it directly in much the same way as you would query MySQL. APIs are also available for most of the popular programming languages.

The following sections provide information that you need to know to start with Sphinx, but intentionally speed through much of the basics to spend more time on some of the more advanced features.

Indexes

Querying is always done directly against Sphinx, which maintains its own indexes. Querying Sphinx does not involve MySQL and works even if mysqld is not running. MySQL is often used as a data source, however, and Sphinx can be instructed (often via a cron job) to pull data from a MySQL table and index it — but it can pull data from other databases (or even from XML) equally well.

So, Sphinx maintains its own indexes, and you periodically update these by telling Sphinx to pull data from MySQL. Various types of indexing are possible, but Sphinx goes for a method that maximizes search speed. The downside is that updating such indexes can be painfully slow, so it is impractical to update/rebuild them for data that is regularly updated (for example, on a social networking site, where posts are made almost continually).

Instead, Sphinx supports the use of *delta indexes* — that is, it starts by indexing all the existing data into a master index, and then, for the periodic updates, it writes any new data to a much smaller second index file. This is much faster and enables you to update more frequently (say, every 10 minutes). On a less-frequent basis (say once per day), Sphinx can then merge the delta into the main index, or do a full index rebuild from scratch.

> **NOTE** *Incidentally, Sphinx also supports real-time (RT) indexes that can be updated on-the-fly without the need for periodic* cron *jobs. These have the advantage that new data is immediately available for searching, but they don't offer as good performance as standard indexes. Thus, these are generally not preferred — in most situations, it's acceptable that new data does not appear in searches instantly.*

Data Sources

How do you tell Sphinx from where to pull the data, and, equally important, how do you distinguish "new" data when updating the delta index? The answer lies in the data sources defined in the Sphinx configuration file, which tells it the MySQL connection details (hostname, port, username, and password) and the query to run to retrieve the data. Following is an example:

```
source comments
{
    type             = mysql

    sql_host         = localhost
    sql_user         = sphinxuser
    sql_pass         = dfWH49hs8
    sql_db           = blog
    sql_sock         = /var/run/mysqld/mysqld.sock
    sql_port         = 3306
    sql_query        = SELECT comment_body, comment_title, user_id, \
    comment_date, post_id FROM comments
}

index comments
{
    source           = comments
    path             = /var/data/sphinx/comments
}
```

This defines a source named `comments` and the SQL to execute when retrieving data from this source. In the second section, Sphinx is instructed to also create an index named `comments` based on the `comments` source.

Running this SQL on a large table could potentially cause problems with locking or spikes in resource usage. So, Sphinx also supports the use of ranges where data is fetched chunk by chunk, as shown here:

```
sql_range_step       = 1024
sql_ranged_throttle = 3000
sql_query_range      = SELECT MIN(id), MAX(id) FROM comments
sql_query            = SELECT comment_body, comment_title, user_id, post_id, \
comment_date  FROM comments WHERE id>=$start AND id <= $end
```

Now, when Sphinx builds the index, it first fetches the maximum and minimum values for the id column. It then fetches comments in chunks of 1,024 with a 3,000-millisecond pause in between.

As previously explained, it's undesirable (and often impractical) to rebuild the index from scratch when rows have been added to the database table, and Sphinx supports the use of delta indexes. To define the delta index, you just set up similar index and source declarations in the config file but use a SQL query that returns only recently added data. In many cases, rows have a date stamp column that you can use, or in other situations you can make a note (in another table) of the value of an auto-incrementing column. Following is an example:

```
sql_query            = SELECT comment_body, comment_title, user_id, post_id, \
comment_date  FROM comments WHERE id>= (SELECT cur_id FROM counter)
```

Attributes

Although the previous configuration snippet can be used as the basis for searching comments on a blog, it lacks the flexibility of enabling you to search only on specific fields. To do this, you need *attributes*. By adding the following lines to the configuration (inside the source section), you create attributes on the user_id, post_id, and comment date:

```
sql_attr_uint = user_id
sql_attr_uint = post_id
sql_attr_timestamp = comment_date
```

Shortly, you'll learn how these attributes can then be used for sorting, filtering, and grouping results.

For the physical storage of attributes, Sphinx offers two choices:

➤ They can be stored inline with the indexed data (which resides in a .spd file). This solves the disk-seeking problem (because the attributes will be right next to the index data on disk) but greatly increases the size of the file (because the attribute values will be duplicated for each entry). (There are similarities here with the way MyISAM and InnoDB store indexes.)

➤ They can be stored separately in a .spa file. However, storing in a separate file is something of a performance killer because the disk needs to seek between the .spa and .spd files. For this reason, Sphinx always holds a copy of .spa files in RAM — which may cause problems for large attributes.

All things considered, external attributes are generally the best, unless RAM is at a premium.

Generating Indexes

Creation of index files is done via the indexer binary, part of the standard Sphinx distribution. For example, to index myindex, the syntax is as simple as this:

```
indexer myindex
```

The configuration file may also be specified at the command line using -c, and -all can be used instead of an index name to tell Sphinx to build every index listed in the config file. If you use delta indexes, you must list the index names manually, rather than relying on -all.

A particularly useful option when rebuilding indexes is --rotate, which replaces the old index only after the new one has been rebuilt and sends Sphinx a SIGHUP, causing it to start serving from the new file. Without this option, indexer operates on the live version of the file, causing it to be inaccessible for the entire duration of the re-indexing process.

When using delta indexes, there are two choices:

➤ Merge the delta into the main index on a regular basis because if the delta index grows too large, it defeats the purpose.

➤ Simply rebuild the main index from scratch periodically.

The latter method is preferred because sometimes the nature of the data means that it can be tricky to ensure that all changes are captured when creating the delta. For example, in the blog comments example, it's easy to determine newly added comments to index, but what about edits to existing comments? Rebuilding completely, say, once a day, is a foolproof method to ensure that all changes are indexed.

Still, if you do want to merge indexes, the syntax is as follows:

```
indexer   --merge main delta --rotate
```

Starting Sphinx and Searching

You've now created a configuration file and indexed your data. The next step is to start the Sphinx search daemon, searchd. This can be as simple as executing searchd, which then forks into the background. But following are a few useful command-line options:

➤ --console — This stops Sphinx from forking into the background and causes it to dump its logs to the console.

➤ --iostats — This causes disk activity to be logged on a per-query basis.

➤ --cpustats — CPU usage stats will be logged for each query.

To perform a search, Sphinx offers a choice of two interfaces. As previously mentioned, Sphinx implements basic SQL and can also speak the MySQL protocol — so you can just connect to it (for example, via the MySQL CLI) as if it were a MySQL server. However, first you must add a listener to the configuration file, as shown here:

```
listen = localhost:9306:mysql41
```

Another method is to access Sphinx via its native API, implementations of which exist for all the common languages (including PHP, Java, Perl, Python, Ruby, and C++). Without getting too bogged down in the details of the API (which are well documented on the Sphinx website), a basic PHP snippet might look as follows:

```
require ( "sphinxapi.php" );
$cl = new SphinxClient ();
```

```
$cl->SetMatchMode(SPH_MATCH_ANY);
$res = $cl->Query('linux');
print_r($res);
```

This displays records where any of the fields contain the string `'linux'`. Of course, this isn't flexible. What if you want to just search on a string appearing in the title? Or what if you want to search on a particular user ID? You'd get results if the number appeared in any of the fields. The answer lies in the attributes previously mentioned. With attributes in place, you can further filter results (think of them as similar to an SQL WHERE clause), as shown here:

```
$cl->SetMatchMode(SPH_MATCH_ANY);
$cl->SetFilter('user_id', array(4));
$res = $cl->Query('linux');
print_r($res);
```

This time, you get results only where a field contains `'linux'` and the user_id is 4 (assuming you had previously defined user_id as an attribute in the Sphinx configuration file).

You can also use attributes for sorting and grouping, as shown here:

```
$cl->SetMatchMode(SPH_MATCH_ANY);
$cl->SetFilter('user_id', array(4));
$cl->SetSortMode ( SPH_SORT_ATTR_DESC, "comment_date" );
$res = $cl->Query('linux');
print_r($res);
```

This produces the same results as before, but this time, sorted by comment date (newest first).

It's worth pointing out that Sphinx returns only a list of IDs of matching rows. You still must fetch the row from the MySQL table.

SphinxSE

Recent versions of Sphinx now also support a third way to perform searches. SphinxSE is a storage engine for MySQL that enables the MySQL server to communicate with searchd, issuing queries and receiving results. This has the potential to further blur the distinction in some people's minds between MySQL and Sphinx, so let's clarify that previous sentence. SphinxSE is not a storage engine in the traditional sense — no data is actually stored in tables created with this engine type. It is merely an interface through which to access Sphinx.

Accessing Sphinx in this way has many advantages. For starters, it's a more familiar method for many users. You can send queries and retrieve results in a similar way to other MySQL tables. This removes the need to rewrite queries to use the Sphinx API and makes Sphinx usable in languages where a port of the API doesn't exist. It also enables you to perform joins against other tables.

To create a SphinxSE table, you use the usual ENGINE= syntax. In this case, though, you must include details of the Sphinx back end to connect to and the index name to use, as shown here:

```
CREATE TABLE t1
(
    id          INTEGER UNSIGNED NOT NULL,
    weight      INTEGER NOT NULL,
```

```
    query        VARCHAR(255) NOT NULL,
    INDEX(query)
) ENGINE=SPHINX CONNECTION="sphinx://localhost:9312/comments";
```

Note the column names. The first three columns in the table *must* be of the name and type shown. You can add additional columns for attributes, provided their names match the corresponding attribute names.

Rewriting the earlier search query to use SphinxSE results in the following:

```
SELECT * FROM t1 WHERE query='linux;mode=any';
```

Of course, this just searches for 'linux' in any column. To limit the results to the user_id 4, you add the attribute clause to the query, preceded by a colon, as shown here:

```
SELECT * FROM t1 WHERE query='test it;mode=any:user_id=4';
```

Parallel Querying and Distributed Indexes

One downside of Sphinx (which isn't immediately obvious) is that it utilizes only a single CPU core. All things being equal, running Sphinx on an eight-core machine produces no greater performance than running it on a quad core. However, Sphinx does support distributed indexes, and with a little magic, you can execute queries across multiple cores, or even multiple servers.

A *distributed index* is one in which several sources are defined. The sources will be queries by Sphinx in parallel, and the results merged. The official documentation is currently a little vague on this, so let's look at a skeleton configuration:

```
source src1
{
    sql_query =SELECT comment_body, comment_title, user_id, post_id,
    comment_date  FROM comments WHERE id MOD 4 = 0
}

source src2
{
    sql_query =SELECT comment_body, comment_title, user_id, post_id,
    comment_date FROM comments WHERE id MOD 4 = 1
}

source src3
{
    sql_query =SELECT comment_body, comment_title, user_id, post_id,
    comment_date FROM comments WHERE id MOD 4 = 2
}

source src4
{
sql_query =SELECT comment_body, comment_title, user_id, post_id,
    comment_date FROM comments WHERE id MOD 4 = 3
```

```
}

index dist
{
        type = distributed
        local = src0
        agent = localhost:9312:src1
        agent = localhost:9312:src2
        agent = localhost:9312:src3
}
```

As usual, you define source and index blocks. But notice the use of the modulus of the comment ID in the SQL queries (not dissimilar to the way the modulus is used in MySQL partitioning). This example goes for four sources, so it uses MOD 4 to ensure that each source gets one-quarter of the table rows. The index section then sets the first source as local and adds subsequent sources via the agent option. This example points them at the locally running Sphinx server, but you could just as easily specify a remote host:port

If you now run a query against the dist index, each of these four sources will be searched in parallel and the results aggregated. In this example, each source is local, and Sphinx runs each in a separate thread (on a separate CPU core). The result should be much faster execution of the query, especially with large indexes.

Newer versions of Sphinx now include support for multiple local distributed indexes, meaning that you can simplify (slightly) the index configuration block to the following:

```
index dist
{
        type = distributed
        local = src0
        local = src1
        local = src2
        local = src3
}
```

The advantage here is that you save some overhead on networking (because you now no longer use agent to connect to Sphinx over TCP), but it's a slim savings.

By default, Sphinx still won't search the indexes in parallel. But by using the new dist_threads option, you can control the maximum number of threads (and, therefore, the maximum number of distributed indexes that will be searched in parallel) for a query, as shown here:

```
dist_threads = 4
```

If you use distributed indexes in this way, it generally makes sense to set dist_threads to the number of CPU cores present.

Load Balancing

Setting sources as remote provides the opportunity to load balance Sphinx across several servers, but this isn't a particularly common setup. Sphinx generally forms only a small part of a site (that is, the search feature), and because it offers such good performance, there is usually no need to split load across several servers. Such a setup also causes each node to be a point of failure. If any one of the servers goes down, the whole search is broken.

The situations in which searching across multiple machines in parallel offers a significant performance gain are generally limited to large indexes — halving the execution time of a 1-second query is a lot more beneficial than halving the execution time of a 100-millisecond query. It is more common to require some form of redundancy or load balancing, and you can do this simply by setting up additional Sphinx servers with duplicate content. You can then either put a load-balancing proxy in front of them (for example, HAProxy) or randomly select a server at the application level.

Performance Tuning

Performance tuning tends not to be a big issue with Sphinx in the way that it can be with, say, MySQL. This is partly because Sphinx is already geared toward performance. But with Sphinx tending to play a fairly specialized role in sites, it also tends not to be the focus of attention. There are, however, a number of optimization steps you can take, both in the configuration and implementation of Sphinx.

Stop Words

As with MySQL FULLTEXT indexes, Sphinx supports the use of stop words (that is, commonly used words that should not be indexed because their frequency makes searching for them pointless). Unlike MySQL, though, Sphinx does not have a built-in default word list, so unless this option is specifically set, no stop words are used.

Aside from improving the accuracy of results, use of stop words can greatly reduce index sizes, resulting in less disk I/O, less CPU work, and faster results. The format of the stop words file is simply plain text with one word per line. You can tell Sphinx the location of the file using the following configuration option:

```
stopwords = /usr/local/share/stopwords.txt
```

Partial Matching

Partial word matching is a useful feature. But if you don't need it, leave it disabled — it increases index sizes and is also rather CPU-intensive. If you do need it, Sphinx supports two mutually exclusive types: prefix and infix. *Prefix* only matches at the beginning of words, whereas *infix* matches at any position (including the beginning). Of the two, prefix is less CPU-intensive and doesn't inflate the size of indexes so much.

Sphinx also enables you to configure the minimum string length for matches, rather like ft_min_word_len in MySQL. For the same reasons as with ft_min_word_len in MySQL, it makes sense to set this as high as possible — almost always 3 or higher. The configuration options for partial matching are as follows:

```
min_infix_len = 3
infix_fields = col1, col2
```

Or you can use the following:

```
prefix_fields = col1, col2
min_prefix_len = 3
```

In each case, you supply a comma-separated list of database columns on which to enable partial matching.

On-Disk Dictionaries

The `ondisk_dict` configuration option controls whether each index's dictionary file (`.spi`) is precached in memory or left on disk. The default, `0`, is to cache in memory, and this is usually the optimal setting — it reduces disk I/O and greatly improves access times.

Occasionally, though, it can make sense to enable this option. Typical situations are when memory is scarce, or the dictionary file is particularly large (for example, because prefixes/infixes are enabled). Enabling `ondisk_dict` results in an additional disk read (and seek) for each keyword in a query.

Binary Logging

Generally, real-time (RT) indexes that can updated on-the-fly offer poorer performance, and they are best avoided. But if you do use RT indexes, it's often advisable to enable binary logging. (Updates to RT indexes are stored in RAM, so a crash would result in lost data.)

The `binlog_flush` directive controls how binary log events are flushed to disk and has three possible values:

➤ `0` — Logs are flushed and synced every second.

➤ `1` — Logs are flushed and synced after every transaction.

➤ `2` — (Default) Logs are flushed after every transaction but only synced every second.

As with MySQL, flushing binary logs can cause a significant drop in performance. If you must use RT indexes and need binary logging (sometimes it's acceptable not to), consider battery backed-up RAID memory, as mentioned earlier in this chapter during the discussion of the MySQL binary log.

Pre-Opening Index Files

The `preopen` directive controls whether Sphinx opens all index files at startup:

```
preopen = 1
```

By default, this is zero (disabled), meaning that index files are opened only when a search needs them, resulting in a little extra overhead. Enabling this option removes the overhead, so it's generally worth doing. The only exception is when there are large numbers (thousands) of index files. In this situation, Sphinx may run out of file descriptors if it opens them all at once.

Controlling the Maximum Number of Matches

A query that returns a huge number of results hogs both CPU and RAM, and is usually unwanted. (Most end users care only about the first few pages of results in a search.) `max_matches` controls the maximum number of matches returned and can be set to a modest value (the default is 1,000) to ensure that a single query doesn't put unnecessary strain on the server.

Read Buffers

Sphinx makes use of two read buffers during searches — one for the document list and one for the hit list. read_buffer controls both of these, with higher values hopefully decreasing disk I/O and the expense of RAM. The default is 256 KB.

Multiprocessing Modes

Sphinx supports a number of Multi-Process Modules (MPMs) (via the workers configuration option) that control how it handles concurrent requests. Following are the available methods:

➤ none — Requests will be handled linearly, one by one.

➤ fork — (Default) A child is forked for each request.

➤ prefork — A handful of worker processes are forked at startup.

➤ threads — A new thread is created for each request.

These options will be familiar to anyone who has configured Apache (as discussed in Chapter 7, "Working with Web Servers"), and the pros and cons are broadly the same. Although forking is the default in Sphinx, the act of forking a child uses resources (most noticeably CPU time), and choosing the prefork method is generally the best option, especially when Sphinx will be serving many small queries (which would cause lots of forking).

The threaded MPM is also an option. It offers slightly better performance, but carries the disadvantage that if searchd crashes, all threads will die. (With the other methods, each process is isolated from the others.)

Disk or CPU?

Bottlenecks in Sphinx tend to be caused by either disk I/O or CPU load, and determining which can impact the performance tuning measures that are taken. As previously mentioned, searchd can be started with the --iostats or --cpustats, and these can shed useful light on where Sphinx is struggling. For example, if searches are slow, despite relatively modest disk and CPU usage, you may want to consider distributed indexes. If disk I/O is high, make sure attributes are stored externally — they are held in RAM, which cuts down on disk seeks.

Other Full-Text Engines

Although Sphinx is one of the most popular open source engines for full-text-like search capabilities, it is far from the only one.

Another popular choice is Lucene (http://lucene.apache.org/), a Java search engine from Apache. Lucene is simply a Java library, but there are various full distributions written on top of it. The most popular is Solr, (http://lucene.apache.org/solr/, also written in Java), which is a fully standalone application that uses Lucene at its core. Although Solr tends not to offer such a blistering performance as Sphinx, it does have a number of more advanced features, including replication, automatic warming of caches, and partial index updates. Lucene has a plug-in architecture, making it more extensible than Sphinx.

A newer arrival, elasticsearch (http://www.elasticsearch.org/), is also built on top of Lucene and has succeeded in wooing many users from Solr. The main attraction of elasticsearch is its distributed nature, making it easy to scale out. For example, indexes are automatically sharded across multiple nodes, with management of the shards all taken care of behind the scenes. Replication can also be added painlessly.

Numerous other search engines exist, but they tend to deviate more from the original goal of a simple replacement for MySQL's FULLTEXT indexes.

Other RDBMSs

While MySQL is one of the most popular relational database management systems (RDBMSs), it is by no means the only one. This chapter concludes with a brief look at two of the most relational database management systems (RDBMSs), popular alternatives, both of which are based on SQL, and are sometimes more suitable than MySQL.

SQLite

Through its extensive use in applications on embedded platforms (along with some high-profile desktop applications such as Firefox, Google Chrome, and Skype), SQLite is easily the most widely used SQL engine, far outweighing MySQL. As its name suggests, it is a lightweight SQL implementation (weighing in at a few hundred kilobytes), implemented as a C library that can be linked in to other applications. SQLite represents a radical departure from the standard client-server architecture seen in most other RDBMSs. This makes SQLite easy to deploy, but can it compete with the heavier RDBMSs?

SQLite stores everything in files, so the major bottleneck tends to be when accessing these files — particularly when writing because the file must be locked. As a result, read queries (for example, SELECT) are generally fast, but write queries are handled linearly and can be significantly slower than when using MySQL.

SQLite is often thought of as a SQL engine best used for local development and unfit for use on enterprise web servers. But this is rather unfair. For many websites (where reads generally far outweigh writes), SQLite is a perfectly acceptable solution with a pleasantly low CPU and memory footprint. For write-heavy sites, however, SQLite probably isn't the best tool for the job. In addition, SQLite lacks many of the performance tuning and scaling capabilities offered by the likes of MySQL.

PostgreSQL

MySQL's main competitor in the RDBMS world is PostgreSQL (often referred to simply as Postgres). Like MySQL, it is widely used, has a large support community, and has the stability of a mature, maintained application. In the past, Postgres also had two major advantages over MySQL. It scaled better on mutlicore machines, and it had better support for transactions. Both MySQL and InnoDB have come a long way since those days, however, and these arguments are now redundant.

Still, there are plenty of other arguments in favor of Postgres. It has better support for triggers and user-defined functions, has a more flexible authentication model (based around plug-ins, allowing for authentication against LDAP, Kerberos, PAM, and so on), and has support for parallel querying and multiversioning.

Postgres is highly configurable, and it would be impossible to do justice to a discussion of performance and optimization in less than 100 pages. For that reason, Postgres is not examined in detail here. However, you are encouraged to learn more about Postgres before automatically choosing MySQL as a back end.

Ultimately, the choice between MySQL and Postgres is a personal preference, but MySQL certainly has the edge for performance.

SUMMARY

When your database outgrows a single-server setup, a huge range of options are available for scaling. Replication is one of the most popular, and the topologies available are limited only by your imagination. The overheads of replication (both on the network and each node) can be significant, and care must be taken when using replication.

Partitioning and sharding are alternative approaches to horizontal scaling. MySQL supports partitioning natively, but sharding must be managed manually. Sharding is usually the best option for scaling (with replication, if necessary). However, performing joins becomes problematic, and you'll often find that you must restructure your tables (to reduce normalization) or rewrite code to work with a sharded setup.

The excellent MySQL Proxy is a piece of middleware that you can use to proxy SQL queries and rewrite them on-the-fly. Although it introduces a single point of failure, some situations occur in which MySQL Proxy is invaluable.

A number of forks and branches of MySQL provide additional functionality or enhanced performance. Some (such as Percona) focus on improving InnoDB, whereas others include enhanced MyISAM implementations. If you are a heavy MySQL user, these forks are definitely worth considering.

Full-text searching is a commonly used feature of MySQL but is only available in the MyISAM engine. For those who prefer InnoDB (or find MySQL's full-text searching to be rather resource-intensive), an alternative is needed. Although there are various full-text search engines available, Sphinx is probably the most popular, which can be integrated into MySQL relatively easily. With Sphinx, full-text searching does not need to be the big performance bottleneck that it so often is.

The previous two chapters have revolved around MySQL, which has been something of a cornerstone of web development since the late 1990s. In recent years, however, a new way of thinking has emerged. Rather than big, bulky RDBMSs, many sites (driven by the need to be capable of being easily scaled) are moving away toward lightweight databases that offer higher performance at the expense of simpler relationships between data. In Chapter 10, you learn all about the exciting new world of NoSQL.

10

Utilizing NoSQL Solutions

WHAT'S IN THIS CHAPTER?

➤ Discovering a wealth of high-performance alternatives to heavy database servers

➤ Creating a super-fast distributed key-value store with memcache

➤ Using MongoDB for fast access to more complex data types

➤ Scaling MongoDB across dozens of nodes

In recent years, NoSQL has become a buzzword, and there are dozens of popular projects that fall under this somewhat broad term. Essentially, NoSQL is a covering term for a range of storage solutions that eschew relational models in favor of a more back-to-basics approach. They have been hailed by some as the solution to scalability problems in traditional relational database management systems (RDBMSs).

Although RDBMSs such as MySQL are invaluable in some situations (think of how useful ACID compliance is for handling online financial transactions), in many cases, they are overkill. You don't need the full power of a relational database simply to select, say, a list of configuration options from a single table. NoSQL solutions fill this gap, offering lightweight data storage with a range of features. Some are simple in memory key-value stores, whereas others provide built-in scaling, support for joins, and some degree of ACID compliance.

Unfortunately, NoSQL has been a classic example of the so-called "hype cycle." Early hype around NoSQL promised that it would be a silver bullet for data storage that would spell the end of relational databases. This led to frenzied adoption, even in situations in which it wasn't particularly suited. This, in turn, led to a backlash because NoSQL's weaknesses gradually became apparent. It is only now that the hype has subsided that NoSQL is starting to be re-evaluated as a highly useful tool that can live side-by-side with MySQL.

Because NoSQL is such a broad term, defining exactly what it is can be difficult, but there are a few general features:

➤ Most solutions are nonrelational and do not offer the capability to join tables.

➤ Most solutions offer loose table schema, unlike MySQL, where column names and types must be defined in advance.

➤ A simplified architecture leads to lower latency and higher levels of concurrency.

➤ Solutions are typically easier to scale than with MySQL.

Although it may seem that the lack of join support is a major drawback in migrating from SQL to NoSQL, it's worth remembering that many vertical scaling solutions for MySQL (such as sharding and functional separation) force joins to be forsaken anyway. In these situations, you are losing a lot of the value of using a relational database (but still have the overhead), and NoSQL can be an attractive alternative. Reports of MySQL's death have been greatly exaggerated.

In this chapter, you learn about two of the most popular NoSQL solutions, which occupy opposite ends of the spectrum. At one end is memcache, a lightweight in-memory store. At the other end is MongoDB, a more traditional database system with the power to scale well. This chapter concludes with a round-up of some of the most popular alternatives.

NOSQL FLAVORS

There are three broad classes of NoSQL, each of which has its pros and cons:

➤ Key-value stores

➤ Multidimension stores

➤ Document stores

Let's take a closer look at each.

Key-Value Stores

Key-value stores tend to be the most basic class of NoSQL and are commonly used in web infrastructures for content caching. Examples include memcache/membase, Voldermort, and Redis. They offer fast lookups (usually via a hash table), but the data has no schema, which makes them unsuitable for storing more complex objects or relationships.

Multidimension Stores

Multidimension stores are a step up from the basic key-value stores, offering more complex data relationships. Data is structured and is stored in rows and columns — not unlike traditional relational databases. Such systems tend to be more difficult to implement than key-value stores and are not as fast — but they do offer a lot more flexibility. Examples include Apache Cassandra, Hbase, Google's BigTable, and Amazon Dynamo.

Document Stores

Document databases such as MongoDB and CouchDB offer a semi-structured store, often with support for nested data. Key values are often used to hold data formatted in XML or JavaScript Object Notation (JSON) (which may, in turn, consist of key-value data). These stores are intended more as database replacements than caches and do not offer the blazing performance of key-value stores. (Although performance is still generally good.)

> **NOTE** *Before examining some of the most popular NoSQL solutions, a word of warning is in order. As with sharding, there's the danger of thinking that because the likes of Facebook, Twitter, or Digg use NoSQL, you also must use it. The rationale is that because the big players use a technology, it must be the right thing to do, and you should also do it. Remember, though, that these sites have specific needs — and high levels of traffic. If you have more modest sites, stop and think. Is a full-scale migration away from MySQL to NoSQL necessary, or would NoSQL work better as a means to complement MySQL? MySQL scaling can go a surprisingly long way.*

Now, let's begin wading through the wide range of solutions that fall under the NoSQL banner. Later in this chapter, in the section "MongoDB," you'll meet a popular alternative to MySQL that offers many of the features of a traditional RDBMS, and has been designed from the ground up with performance and scalability in mind. But let's start by looking at memcache, a much simpler in-memory cache that is widely used alongside MySQL as a means of offloading simple queries.

MEMCACHE

memcache was originally developed in 2003 (the same year in which NoSQL frenzy began), and quickly became an important part of many websites. It was never intended to be a replacement for MySQL (unlike some NoSQL applications) but complements it nicely and has found widespread use as a means to reduce load on databases.

memcache is a network-aware cache that stores key-value data in RAM. As such, it isn't persistent storage, and if the machine that it runs on crashes, the data is lost. But this generally isn't a problem because memcache is mostly used for caching data that is also stored in a more permanent location (for example, in a MySQL database).

The typical way to deploy memcache is as a side cache, sitting alongside MySQL rather than in front of it. Clients utilize it like so:

1. The client (for example, some PHP web code) needs to retrieve some data from the database.

2. The client first connects to the memcache server and attempts to retrieve the data.

3. If the data is found in the memcache cache, it is returned to the client.

4. If the data is not found in the cache, the client falls back to querying the database. It then writes the returned data to memcache so that it is available for future queries. Falling back on the database is an essential step because the transient nature of memcache means that you can never be sure a given piece of data will be in the cache.

This is significantly different from the way in which many caches transparently cache data. With memcache, you must explicitly query and populate the cache. Although this means extra client-side coding, it provides the power to decide what to cache and what not to, as well as the caching duration.

Compare this with the MySQL query cache, where even queries that you do not want cached (perhaps because they are rarely executed, or will be invalidated almost immediately) are stored (unless you explicitly override with SQL_NO_CACHE), and invalidation prevents you from storing stale data.

Installing and Running

memcache runs as a daemon (memcached). By default, it listens on ports TCP and UDP 11211, and over a socket on UNIX. It's generally advisable to run it as a nonprivileged user, but remember that any memory limits imposed on this user (check with ulimit under UNIX) also apply to memcache. On 32-bit systems, a single memcached instance won't use more than 4 GB of memory.

Starting memcached is as simple as the following:

```
memcached -u nobody -m 128 -d
```

This launches it as a daemon (-d) running as the user nobody (-u nobody), and sets the maximum cache size to 128 MB (-m 128). This memory won't be allocated immediately, but you should ensure that it is still available — swapping to disk destroys performance.

Among the array of command-line options, a few are worthy of more coverage:

➤ -M — By default, memcache silently removes older items from the cache when it becomes full. With this option, it returns an error instead.

➤ -k — This locks down the paged memory at startup, causing it to be reserved. (The normal behavior is to allocate memory as needed.) This can improve performance a little and prevents other applications from taking the memory.

➤ -c — This is the maximum number of simultaneous connections (default 1,024). This can be raised for extremely busy memcached instances, but remember that this also raises CPU and memory usage.

➤ -b — This is the request backlog size (default 1,024). If the maximum number of connections is reached, new connections will be queued. If the queue becomes full, further connections will be rejected. Although it's tempting to raise this limit to prevent connections from being refused, this will increase request latency. A need to increase the size of the backlog queue is probably a sign that load should be split across multiple memcached servers.

Client APIs

Although memcached speaks a text-based protocol and can be directly communicated with over a socket (be it TCP, UDP, or a UNIX socket), it's more common to access it via one of the many APIs available. APIs exist for C/C++, PHP, Java, Python, and Ruby. In fact, in many cases, several alternative API implementations exist for a given language.

Let's concentrate on the PHP APIs, and perhaps this is a good time to clarify the slightly confusing naming conventions. memcache is the name of the project, and memcached is the name of the memcache daemon (following the standard UNIX naming convention).

PHP offers two implementations: memcache and memcached (both available as PECL extensions). Although this might seem to imply that one is a client and the other a memcache server, this is not the case — both are client APIs. PECL/memcache is the original implementation from 2004, whereas PECL/memcached is a more feature-rich implementation from 2009. You should use PECL/memcached.

Let's look at an example that doesn't use memcache:

```
$r1 = mysql_query("SELECT foo FROM bar WHERE baz=1");
list($foo) = mysql_fetch_row($r1);
print $foo;
```

To lighten load on the database, you can incorporate memcache like so:

```
$cache = new Memcached;
$cache->addServer('192.168.0.1',11211);

if ($foo = $cache->get('baz1')) {
    print "Found in cache: $foo";
} else {
    $r1 = mysql_query("SELECT foo FROM bar WHERE baz=1");
    list($foo) = mysql_fetch_row($r1);
    $cache->put("baz1", $foo, MEMCACHE_COMPRESSED, 180); ## data is compressed
        and expires after 180 seconds
    print " Pulled from database then written to cache";
}
```

Running this code twice should cause the data to be pulled from the database the first time, and then from the cache on subsequent occasions.

> **NOTE** *Although you could use anything for the key name, it makes sense to use a logical naming structure to prevent accidental duplicates. This example uses the column name and value from the MySQL query, and this approach generally works quite well. For example, a common use might be to cache the selection of a user's name, e-mail address, and various preferences from a table based on a numeric user ID. In that case, you might call the key* "userid" *(for example,* "userid1", "userid2", "userid3", *and so on).*

With power, though, comes responsibility, and it generally isn't a good idea to start caching everything in sight. Some data is so dynamic that it simply isn't suitable for caching. (Although, in many cases, you can still see some benefit from using a short caching time.) However, with large datasets, the process of serializing and deserializing the data (memcache stores data serialized) can add significant CPU overhead on the client. Also, remember that the cache is only a finite size, and priority must sometimes be given to smaller, more frequently accessed objects.

The method of querying memcache and then falling back on MySQL also adds latency in situations in which memcache does not hold the data. If you know that memcache is unlikely to hold the result, you may be better off querying MySQL straightaway.

You must also give some thought to the type of query being cached and the reason for caching it. If your MySQL server is ticking along nicely under only modest load, the real benefit comes from caching queries that take a long time to execute. Caching a simple SELECT on an indexed column probably won't speed things up for the end user. (It'll most likely be in the MySQL query cache anyway.) On the other hand, if your MySQL server is under heavy load, and your primary aim is to reduce the number of queries (even light ones), more aggressive caching would certainly help.

memcache versus MySQL Query Cache

Speaking of the MySQL query cache, is memcache more effective than this? If you're talking solely about access times, there isn't much difference between them. Fetching data from memcache isn't usually significantly faster than fetching data that is in the MySQL query cache. But this is missing the point a little because scalability and efficiency are often more pressing concerns.

The big problem with the MySQL query cache is invalidation, or rather the lack of control over it. As previously discussed in Chapter 8, "Tuning MySQL," writing to a table causes all entries in the MySQL query cache that reference that table to be invalidated, even if the actual result in the cache would not have changed. With memcache, you have control over how long data is cached for — if you want to serve stale data, it won't stop you. Also, because memcache doesn't do as much house-keeping as the MySQL query cache (for example, invalidation and checking SQL syntax isn't actu-ally part of the query cache but is still a step when accessing it), there tends to be less locking and overhead, resulting in faster access.

Although the MySQL query cache is limited to caching the results of individual MySQL queries, memcache can be used to cache anything (within reason). In many cases, you can improve performance even more by executing your SQL queries, processing the data, and then storing *this* in memcache.

For example, consider a blog. Typically, there'd be a comments section on each page below the article. Your code for rendering the comments would probably involve fetching all the comments associated with the article ID. Most likely, each comment would have an author ID, so you'd do a JOIN on the users table to fetch the username, user's website URL, and perhaps avatar. You'd then read the database results row by row, substituting the variables into an HTML template fragment.

If you cache the data returned from MySQL as a single object, this isn't a great deal different from the MySQL query cache — although it's still an improvement. But you can go one step further. What if you cache the HTML fragment containing the nicely formatted comments section? The next time you read the data from the cache, you don't need to mess around with reading the template into a variable, replacing placeholders with values for variables, and concatenating each fragment into one — you have the formatted HTML already there. As you can see, with careful thought, memcache can greatly outshine the MySQL query cache.

Finally, the MySQL query cache runs per-MySQL instance. memcache can be accessed globally. The MySQL query cache is by no means useless, but memcache has the upper hand.

memcache versus MySQL MEMORY Engine

The MySQL query cache may be no match for memcache, but what about MySQL's MEMORY storage engine? Recall from the discussion in Chapter 8 that this provides similar in-memory storage. A common use for the MEMORY engine is to hold temporary session data (where it doesn't matter *too* much if the data is lost — users are simply forced to log back in). Would using memcache for session data actually be any better?

As it turns out, the answer is "yes." The MEMORY engine has a number of limitations — only certain data types are supported, scaling is tricky, and only table-level locking is supported — which puts a limit on concurrency. memcache has none of these limitations and is certainly the superior solution for large-scale requirements.

Deploying memcache

Many administrators rush into using memcache without appreciating that it will invariably lead to memory being taken away from other processes. As you know, many operating system kernels like to use free memory as much as possible for buffering and caching disk I/O, so even if user-land applications are not consuming significant memory, you may still be causing degradation of the I/O subsystem.

This effect is at its worst on single-server setups, where Apache, MySQL, and PHP are all competing for RAM. If memcache is used in such a setup, care must be taken not to squander cache memory, but only cache objects where there is a clear overall advantage. Otherwise, you could well be weakening the performance of (particularly) MySQL.

On multiserver setups and when memory isn't in such short supply, you can usually find a machine somewhere on the network that has a few hundred spare megabytes on which to run memcache. Database servers aren't usually a good choice (because they are memory-intensive). Web servers and/or PHP servers are often chosen because they tend to run tasks that are more CPU-intensive than memory-intensive.

Rarely is it necessary to use a dedicated machine for memcache. (Adding an extra memory stick to an existing server usually does the trick.) But if you do, go for a modest CPU with plenty of RAM, situated as few hops as possible from the clients. It would be even better to use a pool of memcache servers.

Multiserver Setups

Because of the temporary nature of data stored in memcache (it would be a mistake to use it for storing anything more critical), the focus in multiserver memcache setups is on distributing load, rather than providing redundancy. A pool of memcache servers works out rather well, enabling you to set up nodes wherever you have a little bit of free memory. But it is fundamentally different from, say, a MySQL replication setup where nodes talk to each other. With memcache, each instance operates independently and has no knowledge of its role in a larger pool.

Instead, distribution of queries across the pool is handled automatically by the memcache client. The client hashes the key, takes the modulus, and uses this to decide which memcache server to send the request to. It's a technique similar to the way in which MySQL decides where to place rows in a partitioned table.

The problem here is that any change to the number of servers causes keys to be mapped to different servers. For example, if your key hashes to a value of 58 and you have four memcache servers in the pool, the query will be sent to server 3 (58 mod 4 = 2). If you add a fifth server, the query ends up going to server 4 (58 mod 5 = 3). All of a sudden, your queries are sent to servers that don't have the answer — or, worse still, have stale data (from an earlier change to the number of servers in the pool).

The answer to this problem lies in consistent hashing. Although the theory of this lies beyond the scope of this book, the effect is to greatly minimize the amount of remapping when servers are added or removed. Because hashing is implemented in the client library, hashing methods can (and do) vary from one API to another. But in PHP, consistent hashing can be enabled by setting the ini directive memcached.hash_strategy="consistent".

Native consistent hashing is a relatively new feature of the PHP memcache/memcached extensions. Prior to that, libketama was the most commonly used library for consistent hashing, and it still has some advantages over the default PHP method:

➤ libketama uses the Message Digest 5 (MD5) algorithm for hashing. Although this isn't ideal, it's an improvement on the Cyclic Redundancy Check 32 (CRC32) algorithm used by PHP, and offers better distribution of keys across servers. PHP now supports the Fowler-Noll-Vo 1a (FNV-1a) algorithm also, which, again, is an improvement on CRC32. The ini directive memcache.hash_function controls which method is used.

➤ In environments in which memcache is accessed through different APIs, using a standard hashing library means that each API can map a given key to the same server, enabling them to read each other's data.

Incidentally, libketama can also work wonders with MySQL slaves. Rather than picking a slave at random to handle a query, you can choose a server based on a hash of the query. Because identical queries always go to the same slave, this increases the chances of a hit from the MySQL query cache and stops the same query from being held in multiple query caches.

Utilizing a pool of memcache servers is as simple as adding them to the client, as shown here:

```
$cache = new Memcached;
$cache->addServer('192.168.0.1',11211);
$cache->addServer('192.168.0.2',11211);
$cache->addServer('192.168.0.3',11211);
```

The hard work of mapping keys to servers is taken care of by the API.

Assigning a weight to a server is an important part of any load-balancing system, and `memcache` supports this concept when adding servers, as shown here:

```
$cache->addServer('192.168.0.1',11211, true, 1);
$cache->addServer('192.168.0.1',11211, true, 3);
```

Another option is to control whether persistent connections are used (the default is `true`), while yet another is to set the number of buckets.

multigets and Parallelization

`memcache` is not MySQL, and you shouldn't use it as such. This may seem obvious, but it's a point worth remembering when storing and retrieving data from it. If rendering a page requires the execution of 10 SQL queries, storing the result of each of these 10 queries separately in `memcache` is usually the wrong thing to do. Instead, you should aggregate the results as much as possible, carry out post-query compiling (such as substituting the data into a template), and then store the results (often HTML fragments) in `memcache`.

However, sometimes the nature of the site means that you can precompile certain sections, but others are too dynamic. Condensing everything into a single `memcache` object isn't desirable, and you need to issue multiple requests.

The obvious way to tackle this would be to issue the requests in a linear fashion, one after the other. Network latencies and TCP overhead soon add up here, though, and `memcache` offers a better solution: using multigets and multisets.

As the names imply, these enable you to get and set multiple objects in a single request. Following is an example:

```
$results_array = $cache->get(array('key1', 'key2', 'key3'));
```

This has a big effect on latency — but there's more. Many of the `memcache` client APIs also support parallelization. If the requested keys are held on different nodes, the requests will be sent in parallel, and the results aggregated by the client. In practice, this doesn't usually have a huge impact on overall performance. `memcache` nodes are typically fast enough that sending 10 queries to a single node is no slower than sending 1 query to 10 nodes, and you should try to keep the number of keys required low anyway. Parallelization is usually only a significant help when large numbers of keys are fetched and set.

Cache Maintenance and MySQL UDFs

When you add an object to `memcache`, there's a certain amount of guesswork involved in setting the expiration time. Imagine your site is raising money for charity, and you want to show the amount raised so far at the top of each page. Clearly, it won't matter much if this data is a little bit stale; so after running some SQL to calculate the total so far, you cache the result in `memcache` with a 10-minute expiration time.

This works fine if you receive a regular stream of donations, but what if donations are more sporadic — say, two or three per day? Recalculating the total money raised every 5 minutes is overkill, but caching the total for, say, 8 hours leads to data being too stale. Wouldn't it be great if MySQL could say to memcache, "I've just added a row to the table listing donations made. Your data will be stale now, so please discard it." Or, better yet, "Your data will be stale now. Here's the new total raised." This way, you have a total that is never stale (even if a little bit of staleness is acceptable, no staleness is still preferable), but that is never dropped from the cache unless it changes.

The good news is that MySQL can, indeed, do this through the use of User Defined Functions (UDFs) and triggers. You set a trigger to run when the table is written to and use a UDF to cause MySQL to issue a set() directly on the memcache server(s).

Do you need this complexity? In the donations example, you could probably just as easily have modified your web code so that when the database table is written to, the memcache object is also updated. This isn't always practical, though. Updates may be coming from multiple sources, some of them perhaps even external, where you have no control over the code. In some situations, updates via MySQL UDFs are the most appropriate solution.

> **NOTE** *The latest UDFs are available from* https://launchpad.net/
> memcached-udfs, *and you can find documentation on installing and setting*
> *up the functions on the MySQL website (*http://dev.mysql.com/doc/
> refman/5.6/en/ha-memcached-interfaces-mysqludf.html*).*

Monitoring Performance

Telling how full the memcache servers are, how many objects have been flushed because of lack of space, the hit ratio, and so on, are invaluable pieces of information.

Each memcache server keeps quite detailed stats, which can be accessed in a number of ways. The simplest is to telnet into the daemon and issue the stats command, as shown here:

```
$ telnet 0 11211
Trying 0.0.0.0...
Connected to 0.
Escape character is '^]'.
stats
STAT pid 9545
STAT uptime 7956383
STAT time 1312417995
STAT version 1.4.5
STAT pointer_size 32
STAT rusage_user 2714.693657
STAT rusage_system 8373.123287
STAT curr_connections 10
STAT total_connections 35934023
STAT connection_structures 190
STAT cmd_get 650171241
STAT cmd_set 69561685
STAT cmd_flush 0
STAT get_hits 649644851
```

```
STAT get_misses 526390
STAT delete_misses 0
STAT delete_hits 0
STAT incr_misses 0
STAT incr_hits 0
STAT decr_misses 0
STAT decr_hits 0
STAT cas_misses 0
STAT cas_hits 0
STAT cas_badval 0
STAT auth_cmds 0
STAT auth_errors 0
STAT bytes_read 30381363330
STAT bytes_written 3607591597981
STAT limit_maxbytes 67108864
STAT accepting_conns 1
STAT listen_disabled_num 0
STAT threads 4
STAT conn_yields 0
STAT bytes 116262
STAT curr_items 36
STAT total_items 691337
STAT evictions 0
STAT reclaimed 0
```

The names of most of these stats should be fairly self-explanatory. Of particular interest in these stats are get_hits, get_misses, and evictions. A high ratio of cache misses to hits may also imply that the cache is full, but remember that this ratio will vary over time. If the memcache server has not been running for long, you would expect a relatively high number of misses. Evictions imply that the cache is full, and older objects are removed to make way for newer ones.

Even more detailed stats are available for each item held in the cache by issuing stats items, stats slab, or stats sizes.

> **NOTE** *Although these stats can also be accessed through the APIs, talking to* memcache *directly over telnet is incredibly useful to perform quick checks, or when you write monitoring scripts. You can find full details of the* memcache *protocol at* http://code.sixapart.com/svn/memcached/trunk/server/doc/protocol.txt.

memcache Performance and Internals

For the most part, memcache performs efficiently, but it's worth looking under the hood to gain a better understanding of how it works, with a goal of troubleshooting problems when they arise.

Threading

At the core of memcache is the hash table containing the cached data. Perhaps surprisingly, managing and setting/getting values from the hash are relatively light on the CPU usage. Most of the CPU cycles actually go on parsing requests and formatting responses.

Global locking is used on the hash table, so this aspect of memcache is single-threaded. (This may change in the future.) However, the rest of memcache is multithreaded, and you can control the number of threads used with the -t command line option to the daemon. The default is 4 threads, but it makes sense to raise this value to the number of CPU cores present on the system. Raising the number of threads higher than this won't produce any benefits but may well cause a degradation in performance (because of increased context switching and lock contention).

Binary Protocol

memcache supports both a binary and an ASCII protocol, and, given that request parsing uses a significant number of CPU cycles, it may be worth switching to the binary protocol (the default is usually ASCII, but this is client API-dependent) on busy servers. Not all client APIs support the binary protocol, but those based on libmemcached do. These include PECL/memcached (but not PECL/memcache), pylibmc (Python), fauna (Ruby), and caffiene (Ruby).

Following is an example of how to enable binary protocol in PECL/memcached:

```
$cache->setOption(Memcached::OPT_BINARY_PROTOCOL,true);
```

UDP Sockets

memcache supports both TCP and User Datagram Protocol (UDP) (as well as UNIX sockets, but this is only applicable if both client and server are on the same machine). Is there any advantage to using UDP to cut down on network overhead and CPU cycles? The answer is surprisingly "not usually" — just the opposite, in fact. Aside from the nonreliable nature of UDP (which may not be a huge concern over an internal network), on lightly busy memcache servers, it will also be more CPU-intensive.

The reason for this is that, with only one UDP socket in existence, all threads must constantly monitor it. When a request comes in, all threads wake up and attempt to read the socket. Only one thread will be successful, and the rest will either go back to sleep, or read any other requests waiting in the socket buffer. This constant waking and sleeping pushes up CPU load, and is really only advantageous if the server is busy enough that there will usually be requests waiting in the buffer. Unless the server is really busy, stick with TCP.

Memory Allocation

Early versions of memcache used malloc() and free() for allocating and freeing memory, but this tends to be inefficient. The result is fragmentation, and finding contingent blocks of memory of the required size ends up taking longer.

Instead, more recent versions of memcache use a built-in slab allocator. This assigns memory in blocks of varying sizes, and these blocks are re-assigned when they become empty. memcache will attempt to use the most appropriately sized slab to hold an object, but this isn't always possible. So, there is more waste than with the malloc/free approach.

Overall, though, slab allocation is the superior method when performance is more important than efficiency of memory management.

membase — memcache with Persistent Storage

One of the most common questions from new memcache users is whether the cache supports persistent storage — and if not, why not? This is missing the point a little. memcache is, by nature, a temporary store and was never designed to be anything else. It was inevitable, though, that hybrid products would be developed in an attempt to merge the high performance of memcache with the persistent, disk-based storage found in databases.

An early implementation was MemcacheDB, but development appears to have been discontinued on that product. The current front-runner is membase. membase is probably best described as a fork of memcache because it is essentially memcache plus persistent storage. As such, it is fully compatible with memcache and can be accessed using the same client APIs. The persistent storage aspect is mostly kept hidden from the client. The client will see it as simply another memcache server — so, there's no need to change any client code.

Persistent Storage

Behind the scenes, though, things are a bit more complicated. When data is added or modified, the in-memory data is updated immediately, and the change is placed in a queue to be written to disk. Control is passed back to the client, and a separate thread periodically processes the queue, writing the changes out to disk. Although this introduces a small chance of inconsistencies (for example, if the client believes the data has been written to persistent storage, but a server crash occurs before the queue can be processed), the queue is processed frequently enough to limit this likelihood. It is still a great performance boost for clients. Incidentally, membase uses SQLite as the back end for storing data.

So far, so good, but what happens when the data set is larger than the available memory? membase uses the same strategy as memcache when new data is added. If the memory cache is full, older (LRU) items are evicted. If a client later requests an object that has been evicted, membase simply reads it back into memory and returns the data to the client.

In fact, membase has two memory thresholds when deciding when the cache is "full": mem_low_wat and mem_high_wat. As the cache fills with data, mem_low_wat is passed, and mem_high_wat eventually is reached. When this happens, a background process begins removing items from the cache (after first ensuring that they are not still waiting to be written to disk) until mem_low_wat is reached. In this way, membase attempts to ensure that there will always be a small amount of free memory for new data.

Writing to disk is naturally a lot slower than writing to memory, and, in theory, you could end up in a situation in which mem_high_wat is reached, and new data is sent to membase faster than it can be written to disk. In these situations, membase returns a temporary error to the client, indicating that it should try again shortly. Lowering mem_low_wat can help prevent this scenario from arising but also results in more disk activity in general. So, this is best avoided unless absolutely necessary.

Buckets and Rebalancing

memcache's hashing function ensures that data is spread evenly over all nodes in multiserver setups. Unfortunately, this fails to take into account that some nodes in the pool may have more memory than others. The usual workaround with memcache is to run multiple nodes on servers with lots of memory. For example, rather than having node A running on server X with a 1 GB cache, and node B running on server Y with a 512 MB cache, you run two 512 MB nodes on server X and one 512 MB node on server Y. Although rather hackish, this results in an efficient use of memory.

membase goes one step better, providing automatic management (including rebalancing) of data across multiple nodes. It does this through the use of *virtual buckets*. Rather than mapping data keys to servers (as memcache does), membase maps them to buckets. A lookup table then tells membase on which node a given bucket currently resides. This introduces an extra step for the client because it must now perform a lookup after hashing the key. Because membase aims to be 100 percent compatible with memcache, this is a problem. But there is a solution.

Moxi

Eventually, bucket-aware client APIs should emerge, but until that time, membase provides an embedded proxy named Moxi. The purpose of Moxi is to reroute lookups to the correct server. The client now does not need to look up the server on which a given bucket resides. It simply sends the lookup to membase, which performs the lookup internally and reroutes the request if the data is not held on the local node.

A result of this is that you need to specify only one membase server in your client code — Moxi handles the rest. This simplifies your web code and means that if membase servers are added or removed, no changes to your code are needed.

Moxi is about more than just rerouting requests, though. It is at the core of the management channel used by membase to communicate between instances. When a node fails, the first Moxi to detect this pushes a message out over the management channel to all other membase instances, informing them of the failure. Moxi also provides a small hot cache for frequently accessed resources (as if membase weren't already fast enough).

Replication and Failover

membase offers peer-to-peer replication (that is, all nodes are equal, and there is not the one-way flow of data seen in master-slave setups) in which buckets are duplicated across multiple nodes. (The number of replicated copies of the data is configurable, up to a limit of three.) This offers some degree of safety against individual nodes failing and is all handled transparently — no need to set up replication users, manually sync data across nodes, or worry about broken replication.

membase Web Console

As a system administrator, you're probably used to configuring and managing services via the console and tend to be a little distrustful of flashy web-based GUIs. After all, aren't those GUIs for inexperienced users who don't like getting their hands dirty? The membase GUI challenges this stereotype, offering a refreshingly easy way to set up and manage a membase cluster, guiding the administrator through the installation (which is painless), and then providing a console for monitoring and managing the live cluster.

Figure 10-1 shows the second step of the installation process.

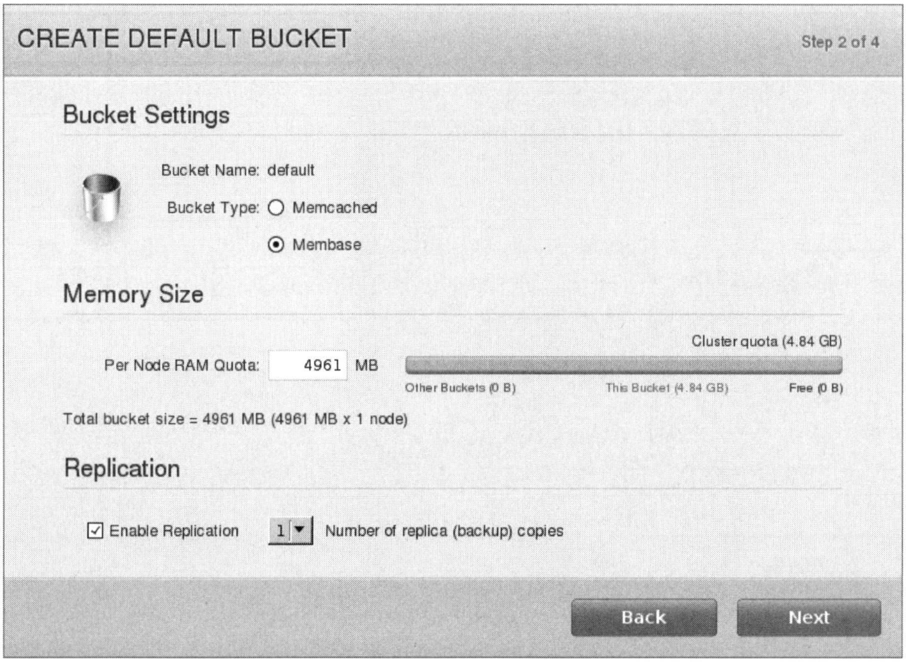

FIGURE 10-1

> **NOTE** membase *also supports* memcache *buckets if you don't want to have replication and redundancy.* memcache *buckets are recommended for when the system will be used for caching database queries.* membase *is recommended for when the system will be used* instead of *a traditional database.*

When installed, you can use the web console to view stats on cache usage and the health of the system, as shown in Figure 10-2. You can even set up e-mail alerts when nodes fail-over, as shown in Figure 10-3.

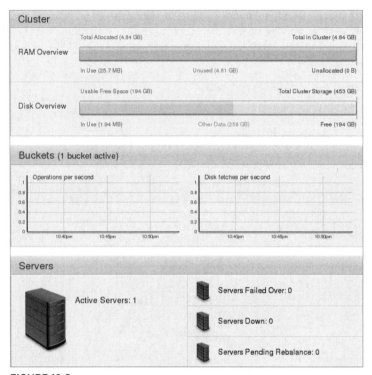

FIGURE 10-2

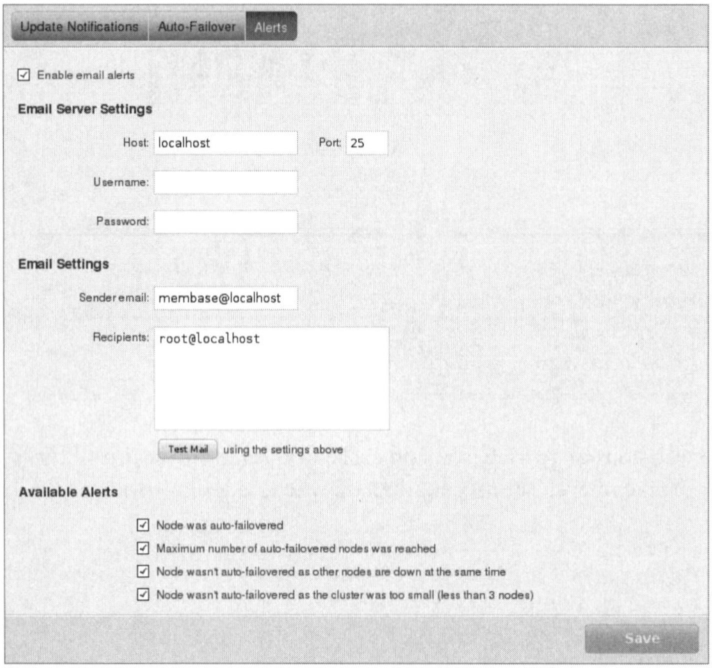

FIGURE 10-3

Remember, though, that membase is a decentralized system with no hierarchy of masters and slaves. The web console is accessible from every membase node, and each is as equally in charge as the others.

memcache is one of the most popular NoSQL solutions, and falls at one extreme of the NoSQL scale — it is a very basic store, with no persistent storage. Although membase addresses some of these limitations, the nature of its key-value store makes it unsuitable for mapping more complex data types. In the following section, you learn about MongoDB, a NoSQL database that offers many of the features of a traditional RDBMS, but was built from the ground up with scalability and performance in mind.

MONGODB

memcache is a lightweight key-value store, a long way removed from MySQL. At the other end of the NoSQL spectrum is MongoDB, a document-oriented database with many features similar to traditional RMDBs. Given MongoDB's size and rich set of features, this discussion won't offer a complete guide to its use. Instead, the discussion begins with a brief overview of MongoDB for new users and then dives straight into a discussion of performance aspects, which will be more suited to intermediate or advanced users.

> **NOTE** *In this discussion, the names MongoDB and Mongo will be used interchangeably. Chapter 9, "MySQL in the Network," provides more detail on many of the concepts used to describe MongoDB, including indexes, locking, sharding, and replication.*

Getting to Know MongoDB

MongoDB uses the familiar client-server model. Mongod is the name of the server, a network-aware daemon that you can connect to over TCP or via a UNIX socket. Mongo ships with its own client, and if you're familiar with the stock MySQL command-line client, you'll feel right at home. Naturally, there are also APIs for all the popular programming languages.

Whereas MySQL uses the concepts of tables, rows, and fields, Mongo revolves around *documents*. A document is composed of fields, not unlike the way in which an RDBMS row consists of columns. These are binary JSON (BSON) objects of arbitrary size, which can be thought of as roughly analogous to rows of an RDBMS table. A group of documents make up a *collection*, and a group of collections make up a *database*.

Table 10-1 illustrates the similarities between MySQL and MongoDB.

TABLE 10-1: Comparing MySQL and MongoDB

MYSQL TERM	MONGODB TERM
Database	Database
Table	Collection
Row	Document
Column	Field
Join	Embedding/linking

Drawing attention to the similarities between MySQL and MongoDB is purely to help you find your footing with Mongo by relating this new terminology to something that you're already familiar with. However, don't be fooled into thinking that Mongo documents are identical to MySQL rows — there are some fundamental differences.

One such difference is that documents do not have a predefined list of fields. When you create a table in MySQL, you define the columns that should exist in it. With Mongo, you can have as many or as few fields as you want. This makes it much easier to model data that does not have consistent fields. Imagine trying to do this in MySQL. (The usefulness of this feature is sometimes over-emphasized, though — in practice, most data consists of consistent fields, and small variations in fields are easy enough to accommodate in traditional RDBMs.) As a result, there's no need to explicitly create databases, collections, or fields — just use them, and they will be created automatically. This is an important concept, so let's reiterate it. In Mongo, fields are a property of the document and are independent of other documents in the collection.

The Mongo Shell

As with MySQL, Mongo ships with its own command-line client; although plenty of other clients are available. The client is named mongo, and executes JavaScript — it's actually based on the SpiderMonkey JavaScript engine used in Firefox. (See Chapter 6, "JavaScript, the Document Object Model, and Ajax," for more details on SpiderMonkey.) By default, the client will attempt to connect to 28017/TCP (mongod's default port) on the localhost, but you can easily override this. Following is an example:

```
$ mongo
MongoDB shell version: 2.0.2
connecting to: test
> db.foo.save( { "name" : "Oscar" , "species" : "hamster", "weight" :
    "154", "fur color" : "charcoal" });
> db.foo.save( { "name" : "Jasper" , "species" : "dwarf hamster",
    "weight" : 47, "fur color" : "white" });
> db.foo.save( { "name" : "Dasiy" , "species" : "cat", "weight" :
    2000, "fur color" : "black" });
> db.foo.save( { "name" : "Stef" , "species" : "human", "height" :
    158, "weight" : 112, "hair color" : "black" });
```

This code connects to the `mongo` shell and issues four `insert` commands. Note that the database or collection hasn't been formally created, nor have any fields been defined. The data is simply added. Also, note the variation in fields. For `human`, an extra column for `"height"` has been added, and `"hair color"` is used rather than `"fur color"`.

With this sample data in place, you can now search it, as shown here:

```
> db.foo.find( {"species" : "dwarf hamster"});
{ "_id" : ObjectId("4f20666b7e657e5d56c29f60"), "name" : "Jasper",
    "species" : "dwarf hamster", "weight" : 47, "fur color" : "white" }
```

Because you didn't specify an index field, Mongo kindly added one for you. This can be thought of as similar to primary keys in MySQL — every collection needs an `_id`, and it must be unique for each document.

One powerful feature of Mongo is its support for nested data structures, and a field can itself be an array. Let's rewrite the original insert queries to list the foods that each animal eats (for clarity, the other fields have been taken out).

```
> db.foo.save( { "name" : Oscar" , "foods : ["carrot", "grape", "apple"] });
> db.foo.save( { "name" : "Jasper" , "foods" :  ["carrot", "grape",
    "human fingers"] });
> db.foo.save( { "name" : "Daisy" , "foods" : ["tuna", "chicken", " mouse"] });
> db.foo.save( { "name" : "Stef" , " foods" : [" salad", " rice pudding",
    "pizza"] });
```

You can now easily search for any animal that likes `"carrot"`:

```
> db.foo.find({foods : "carrot"});
{ "_id" : ObjectId("4f211f1420229f6e98652b15"), "name" : "Oscar",
    "foods" : [ "carrot", "grape", "apple" ] }
{ "_id" : ObjectId("4f211f1420229f6e98652b16"), "name" : "Jasper",
    "foods" : [ "carrot", "grape", "human fingers" ] }
```

> **NOTE** *It's perhaps worth pausing to consider how you would do something similar in MySQL. Although there's nothing to stop you from serializing the array of foods and storing them in a MySQL column, the preferred way would be to normalize the data to some degree. In a second table, you would list the food type along with the ID of the animal that ate it.*

Drivers

To use Mongo in your applications, an API or driver is needed. Although numerous drivers are available for PHP, the standard is called `Mongo`, which is available via PECL. Rewriting the previous search query in the object-oriented syntax of the PHP `Mongo` driver yields the following:

```
$r = new Mongo();
$database = $r->test;
$collection = $database->foo;
```

```
$cursor = $collection->find(array('species' => 'dwarf hamster'));

foreach ($cursor as $row) {
    var_dump($row);
}
```

Naturally, drivers are available for most other popular languages, too, including C/C++, Perl, Python, and Ruby.

MongoDB Performance

The last few pages have served as a brief introduction to MongoDB. If you were unfamiliar with it, hopefully this has whetted your appetite, and provided enough information for you to decide whether Mongo is something you want to explore in more detail. There are plenty of excellent Mongo resources available — in particular, the official website (www.mongodb.org) and the freely available *The Little MongoDB Book* (a free e-book written by Karl Seguin).

The remainder of this section focuses on specific performance aspects of Mongo and assumes that you already have a decent understanding of how to use Mongo in applications. It doesn't assume that you're a wizard, but rather that you're comfortable with the core functionality — adding/removing/searching, as well as the concepts of collections, documents, and fields.

Indexing

Indexes in Mongo work much like they do in MySQL. You can add them to fields, and they improve lookup performance when you search on these fields.

To create an index on the previous animals collection example, use the following:

```
db.foo.ensureIndex({species:1});
```

The 1 here means to create the index in ascending order, whereas -1 would mean descending. For single indexes like this, the direction is unimportant, but after you get to compound indexes, it can matter.

ensureIndex optionally takes the following four additional parameters:

➤ background — Run the index creation in the background (for example, db.foo.ensureIndex({species:1}, {background: true});.).

➤ dropDups — If any documents contain identical values for the index field, drop all but the first occurrence.

➤ unique — Mongo won't allow a document to be inserted if the indexed field matches an existing index. If the document doesn't contain the indexed field, this is treated as a null value. So, with unique indexes, only one document is permitted not to contain the indexed field.

➤ sparse — In situations in which many of the documents do not contain the indexed field, using sparse indexes stops these nonmatching documents from appearing in the index, thus saving space.

From a performance perspective, background creation is perhaps the most interesting operation. Usually, indexes are created in the foreground, but this causes read/write access on the whole database to block for the duration. By telling Mongo to generate an index in the background, you can avoid this locking.

There's no such thing as a free lunch, though. Background indexing takes longer, and may still impact performance to some degree, even if it isn't causing locking. In addition, the algorithm that background indexing uses makes heavy use of RAM. If the newly created index is bigger than the amount of available memory, background creation will be slow.

Compound indexes are also supported with the following syntax:

```
db.foo.ensureIndex({x:1, y:1, z:1});
```

As with MySQL, order is important. In this example, the index will be useable if you are querying on fields x, x and y, or x and y and z — but not y, z, or y and z. Compound indexes are useful, but think carefully about the ordering.

The usual caveats about indexes also apply here. When data is added, deleted, or updated, indexes must be modified. So, on collections that are write-heavy, the overhead of maintaining the indexes may well outweigh the benefits.

Mongo uses B-trees for indexes, too. An interesting side-effect of this is that index values have an impact on performance. If entries are inserted into the B-tree at random locations, this increases disk seeks, and the whole index must be restructured each time. If you simply append entries to the right side of the B-tree each time, no further work must be done. This has an impact when you choose unique IDs. For example, it would be better for performance to choose an ascending numeric value (such as a UNIX timestamp) than, say, a hash of another field.

Blindly adding indexes creates unnecessary overhead, so ensure that an index will actually be useful before adding it. As with MySQL, Mongo works most efficiently when all indexes fit into memory. So, on large collections, it may be necessary to rethink your indexing strategy to keep the size down. The index size for a given collection can be obtained via `db.foo.totalIndexSize()`.

In particular, be aware of indexes that offer low selectivity and do not efficiently narrow down the documents to search. For example, if a field has a binary yes/no state, adding an index would likely still leave a large number of documents to scan. Creating a compound including the field is one possible solution.

Mongo will use only one index on a query. So, if you search on multiple fields, multiple indexes are of no benefit. Either choose the most suitable field to index (think selectivity and field size), or create a compound index.

Explaining Queries

When diagnosing a slow query, the `explain()` method can be invaluable and provides a breakdown of documents scanned, indexes used, and locking. Here's how `explain ()` looks for a query on the sample animals collection with no indexes in place:

```
> db.foo.find( {"species" : "dwarf hamster"}).explain();
{
        "cursor" : "BasicCursor",
        "nscanned" : 4,
```

```
                "nscannedObjects" : 4,
                "n" : 1,
                "millis" : 34,
                "nYields" : 0,
                "nChunkSkips" : 0,
                "isMultiKey" : false,
                "indexOnly" : false,
                "indexBounds" : {

                }
        }
}
```

The meaning of these fields follows:

➤ cursor — This is the cursor used for the scan — BasicCursor when the collection is scanned directly, and BtreeCursor when an index is used.

➤ nscanned — This is the number of items scanned, including indexes and documents.

➤ nscannedObjects — This is the number of documents scanned.

➤ n — This is the number of matching documents.

➤ millis — This tells how many milliseconds the query took to run.

➤ nYields — This is the number of times that the query was interrupted to allow writes to execute.

➤ nChunkSkips — During automatic sharding, skipped chunks indicate that data is actively being moved from one node to another.

➤ isMultiKey — This indicates whether a multikey (that is, compound) index was used.

➤ indexOnly — This will be set to true if a query can be answered simply from the index (that is, a covering index).

➤ indexBounds — If an index is used, this shows the name of the index and the key searched for in it.

Let's add an index to the species field and rerun explain ():

```
> db.foo.ensureIndex({species:1});
> db.foo.find( {"species" : "dwarf hamster"}).explain();
{
        "cursor" : "BtreeCursor species_1",
        "nscanned" : 1,
        "nscannedObjects" : 1,
        "n" : 1,
        "millis" : 0,
        "nYields" : 0,
        "nChunkSkips" : 0,
        "isMultiKey" : false,
        "indexOnly" : false,
        "indexBounds" : {
                "species" : [
```

```
                                  [
                                         "dwarf hamster",
                                         "dwarf hamster"
                                  ]
                            ]
                     }
              }
```

This time, the cursor field tells you that an index was used — an ascending index on the species field (species_1), to be precise. Only one row was scanned this time, and the execution time appears to be lower; although, clearly, zero milliseconds can't be right (most likely it is a result of the time having been rounded down).

Profiling and Slow Queries

Through its profiling system, Mongo enables you to log queries for all operations, or those taking longer than a certain number of milliseconds. This can be enabled via the Mongo shell, as shown here:

```
> db.setProfilingLevel(1,20);
```

Or you can enable this at the command line when launching mongod, as shown here:

```
mongod --profile=1 --slowms=15
```

Three profile levels are supported:

➤ 0 disables logging.

➤ 1 enables logging of slow queries.

➤ 2 enables logging of all queries.

When profile=1 is chosen, the slow query time (in milliseconds) may also be specified. Otherwise, it defaults to 100 milliseconds, which is more than high enough — in practice, though, a lower value is usually desirable.

Log entries are stored in the profile collection (a capped collection) of the system database and can be accessed like so:

```
> db.system.profile.find();
{ "ts" : ISODate("2012-01-31T22:41:57.330Z"), "op" : "insert", "ns" :
    "test.foobar", "millis" : 89, "client" : "127.0.0.1", "user" : "" }
{ "ts" : ISODate("2012-01-31T22:41:57.348Z"), "op" : "insert", "ns" :
    "test.foobar", "millis" : 64, "client" : "127.0.0.1", "user" : "" }
{ "ts" : ISODate("2012-01-31T22:41:57.357Z"), "op" : "insert", "ns" :
    "test.foobar", "millis" : 37, "client" : "127.0.0.1", "user" : "" }
```

Along with a timestamp, you see the operation type (insert), the namespace being operated on (test.foobar), and the time that the query took.

Usually you want to be more specific, though — for example, to show queries on a particular database or collection, or those taking over a certain time to run. The following shows queries taking longer than 10 milliseconds to run:

```
db.system.profile.find( { millis : { $gt : 10 } } );
```

Any queries you run on the profile collection will also be logged. If you inspect the log now, sorted by most recent first, the previous `find` query will now be shown:

```
> db.system.profile.find().sort({$natural:-1});
{ "ts" : ISODate("2012-01-31T22:42:12.229Z"), "op" : "query", "ns" :
    "test.system.profile", "query" : { }, "nscanned" : 40, "nreturned" :
    40, "responseLength" : 3900, "millis" : 23, "client" : "127.0.0.1",
    "user" : "" }
```

In the case of read operations (that is, queries), additional information is shown. `nscanned` shows the number of documents that were scanned, `nreturned` the number that matched (and were returned), whereas `responseLength` is the size (in bytes) of the response. (For brevity only the first line of output is shown, but there were another 19 lines.)

There's a lot that you can learn from the profiler. At its most basic level, it provides an idea of the average query response time, and whether particular queries are problematic. If the `responseLength` is large, this equates to a large amount of data being sent to the client, which will obviously slow things down. If the number of documents scanned is significantly higher than the number returned, this indicates that Mongo must do a lot of searching to return a modest number of matches. This is a strong indication that an index of the searched column would be beneficial.

Locking and Concurrency

In Mongo, locks are implemented globally. Thus, a write lock can cause all databases to be locked — not just the current database or collection. This contrasts with the table- and row-level locking offered by MySQL's `MyISAM` and `InnoDB`. Collection-level locking is currently being worked on, but until then, the only real solution if you are affected by this global locking is to spread out databases across multiple `mongod` instances on the same host.

Despite this, concurrency in Mongo is usually good, partly because Mongo uses a method to periodically yield the locks on slow-running queries so that other queries may run. This makes perfect sense in many cases. You're usually quite happy for a long write query to be interrupted so that (usually) short-running read queries can execute.

Aside from *periodic* yielding of locks, Mongo can also yield when a minor page fault is detected. This effectively interrupts the query because the operating system must read the data into memory from disk, and Mongo uses this time to allow other read queries to run.

The Process List

Just as MySQL gives you the ability to view a list of currently running processes via `show processlist`, Mongo offers `db.currentOp();` for the same purpose:

```
> db.currentOp();
{
        "inprog" : [
                {
                        "opid" : 44024,
                        "active" : true,
                        "lockType" : "write",
                        "waitingForLock" : false,
                        "secs_running" : 0,
                        "op" : "insert",
                        "ns" : "test.foobar",
                        "query" : {

                        },
                        "client" : "127.0.0.1:44084",
                        "desc" : "conn",
                        "threadId" : "0x7fdb6c7f6710",
                        "connectionId" : 2,
                        "numYields" : 0
                }
        ]
}
```

This example shows a single connection from a local client. The client has a write lock (`lockType`) and performs an insert (`op`) on the `foobar` collection in the `test` database (ns, namespace). `active` indicates whether the query is queued, whereas `query` holds the query being executed in the case of reads.

You can also kill queries using `db.killOp(123)`, where `123` is the op ID. A value of `conn` in the `desc` field indicates that the query is a standard client query. Other values indicate system queries (for example, replication, sharding, or indexing), and you probably don't want to kill these.

Data Integrity, Journaling, and Single-Server Durability

One frequent criticism of Mongo is that it does not offer single-server durability — that is, performance is given a higher priority than the integrity of data. This isn't quite true. Mongo does offer some degree of single-server durability. It's just that it isn't the primary focus and must explicitly be enabled. Even then, though, it is not as powerful as, say, the `InnoDB` transaction log.

> **NOTE** *In their defense, the Mongo developers have a number of reasons for this apparent Achilles' heel, which you may read about at* `http://blog.mongodb` `.org/post/381927266/what-about-durability`.

Mongo is designed for scalability, and the expectation is that it will usually run inside a replication cluster. In that situation, the data is stored on multiple nodes, and the failure of one node is not serious. Providing a high degree of data integrity also carries a significant performance price associated with the `InnoDB` transaction log and the use of memory in disk controllers to buffer disk writes. The bottom line is that Mongo would not offer the blazing performance that it does if single-server data integrity were a necessity. There's nothing inherently wrong with this, but you should just be aware of it.

One reason for Mongo's speed when writing data is that it immediately returns control to the client, without waiting until the status of the write can be determined (for example, failure or success). Data is not synced to disk immediately either, and it may be several seconds before the data is finally committed. Both of these factors can make benchmarking somewhat difficult (and other people's benchmarks grossly inaccurate) because data may still be written to disk after the benchmarking finishes. If you call getLastError() after issuing a write, this *will* cause the data to be synced to disk because this is necessary to determine if any errors occurred.

You can control how often Mongo fsyncs to disk using the --syncdelay option when launching mongod. This currently defaults to 60 seconds. But this potentially means up to 60 seconds of data being lost following a crash, and this is too high for many situations. On the other hand, syncing, say, every second, is going to hurt performance and may well be unnecessary the majority of the time. You need to sync only following an important write. On a mostly read setup, using fsync every *x* seconds is an unnecessary overhead.

There is a solution to this problem, however. You can manually ask Mongo to fsync as and when needed. To do this, you would use the following shell commands:

```
use admin
db.runCommand({fsync:1});
```

Naturally, you can also fsync in your web code via the mongo driver. Of course, this could mean substantial rewrites to existing code, but if a database abstraction layer is used, the changes should be minimal.

Syncing isn't the only solution, though. Mongo version 1.7.5 introduced write-ahead journaling; although, it was not enabled by default until version 1.9.2. With journaling, operations are written to the log prior to being executed, and if a crash occurs, the journal can be replayed. In many ways, this is similar to the MySQL binary log. If the server crashes, on restart, Mongo automatically replays the journal prior to accepting client connections.

Journal files are stored under the journal subdirectory of the data directory. In some cases, they will be pre-allocated — so don't be too surprised if a journal file is unexpectedly large.

On 32-bit systems, journaling is disabled by default because of overhead, but on 64-bit architectures, it is now enabled by default.

Backups

Another advantage of journaling is that it makes backing up data easier. On storage systems, such as the Logical Volume Manager (LVM) or the Z filesystem (zfs), all you must do is take a snapshot of everything under the data path. Remember, though, that it's not safe to do this on other filesystems — the data files mostly likely will not be in sync, and corruption will occur.

The other route for backups is via mongodump, a command-line application that generates hot backups of Mongo databases in a binary format. The data can subsequently be imported using mongorestore.

db.serverStatus()

Mongo exposes a wealth of information about the current state of the system via the `db.serverStatus()` command. The full output is too long to show here, but following are some of the most important parts.

Consider the following example:

```
"globalLock" : {
        "totalTime" : 130507162615,
        "lockTime" : 312085,
        "ratio" : 0.0000023913324688597054,
        "currentQueue" : {
                "total" : 0,
                "readers" : 0,
                "writers" : 0
        },
```

Recall that Mongo uses global locking when inserting data (unlike the table- or row-level locking offered by MySQL's `MyISAM` and `InnoDB`). These counters show how long the server has been up, how much of this time has been spent with the global lock in place, and the ratio of these two numbers. Although Mongo's strategy of yielding locks on long-running queries helps to lessen the problems caused by high levels of global locking, a high lock ratio is still a cause for concern and will impact both reads and writes. One of the most common causes is a shortage of RAM, which causes the system to start paging.

The `currentQueue` counters indicate how many operations are queued up waiting for locks (total, read locks, write locks, respectively).

```
"connections" : {
        "current" : 7,
        "available" : 812
},
```

Naturally, if your current number of connections is regularly approaching the available limit, there is the possibility of clients being turned away. Reaching this limit is much less of a problem than it is in MySQL, and you rarely need to increase the limit.

Consider the following example:

```
"indexCounters" : {
        "btree" : {
                "accesses" : 1478,
                "hits" : 1473,
                "misses" : 5,
                "missRatio" : 0
        }
}
```

The first value shown in this example is the number of times that an index has been accessed. Elsewhere in the stats is a section named `opcounters` that shows how many inserts, queries, updates, and deletes have been performed. It can be useful to compare these figures to see how many queries have been hitting indexes. Although there are sometimes valid reasons for not indexing, you'd generally want to see most of your queries utilizing an index.

The hits and misses counters refer to whether the index was found in memory.

As discussed earlier, you can instruct Mongo to `fsync` data to disk every few seconds, or only when instructed. The following counters show the number of flushes, the total time it has taken, the average time, and the most recent time. High times here would indicate either large volumes of data written out or high levels of contention on the disks.

```
"backgroundFlushing" : {
        "flushes" : 2175,
        "total_ms" : 83,
        "average_ms" : 0.03816091954022988,
        "last_ms" : 0,
```

When committing to the journal (if journaling is enabled), operations are written in groups to improve performance. By default, the gap between these commits is 100 milliseconds; although it can be changed at start up (`--journalCommitInterval <time in ms>`). Consider the following example:

```
"dur" : {
        "commits" : 30,
        "journaledMB" : 0,
        "writeToDataFilesMB" : 0,
        "earlyCommits" : 0,
        "timeMs" : {
                "dt" : 3072,
                "prepLogBuffer" : 0,
                "writeToJournal" : 0,
                "writeToDataFiles" : 0,
                "remapPrivateView" : 0
        }
}
```

In this example, `commits` shows the number of commits that were performed in this interval, whereas `journaledMB` shows the number of megabytes of data written again during this interval. Note that although Mongo usually honors `journalCommitInterval`, if a large amount of data must be written, it commits before the interval has passed — this is reflected in an increase in `earlyCommits`, whereas `timeMs.dt` shows the time interval used for the most recent set of stats.

The remaining `timeMs` fields show the time spent preparing to write to the journal (`prepLogBuffer`), writing to the journal (`writeToJournal`), writing to data files after the journaling has completed (`writeToDataFiles`), and remapping any affected memory regions. Again, high values for these first three are a good indication of disk bottlenecks.

mongostat

An alternative tool for gathering statistics is `mongostat`, which produces a `vmstat`-like output, with a new line of output appended every second.

```
$ mongostat
connected to: 127.0.0.1
insert  query update delete getmore command flushes mapped  vsize     res faults
locked % idx miss %    qr|qw   ar|aw  netIn netOut  conn        time
     0       0      0       0       0       1      0   208m   626m     32m       0
         0          0     0|0     0|0    62b     1k      1  19:23:32
     0       0      0       0       0       1      0   208m   626m     32m       0
         0          0     0|0     0|0    62b     1k      1  19:23:33
     0       0      0       0       0       1      0   208m   626m     32m       0
         0          0     0|0     0|0    62b     1k      1  19:23:34
```

> **NOTE** *Although less information is contained in the output, it's easier to read than the output of* db.serverStatus() *and is more suitable for watching a live server.*

The column names should mostly be self-explanatory. The first six columns show counters for the types of query executed, whereas flushes lists how many fsyncs have been performed in the last second (since the previous line of output). mapped, vsize, and res relate to memory usage — the amount of mapped memory, the virtual size of the mongod process, and its residual size.

locked is the percentage of the time that a global lock has been in place (again, over the last second), whereas idx miss gives the percentage of B-tree misses — identical to the missRatio seen in the output of db.serverStatus().

The next two columns give the query backlog for reads and writes, and the number of clients performing reads/writes. This is followed by the volume of network traffic flowing in and out, and the number of client connections. If the server is part of a replication set, an additional two columns show the replica set name and the node's role (for example, master, slave, secondary, and so on).

One useful feature of mongostat is the --autodiscover option, which causes it to search for other nodes in the cluster and query them for stats. Each update of the mongostat output then contains one line for each node discovered.

Schema Design and Joins

In a traditional relational database, the "right" way to organize data is in the third normal form (3NF). This is certainly the most aesthetically pleasing structure, but it typically results in the need to join across many tables, which is something you can't do in Mongo. (You might often deviate from 3NF in traditional databases, too, for performance reasons.) Mongo isn't a traditional RDBMS, though, and you must rethink what you've learned about database structures. Rather than simply looking at the data and deciding how it should be structured, you should look at how the data will be accessed.

In some ways, the lack of support for joins is a good thing. It forces developers to create scalable structures that can later be sharded more easily. If you've ever attempted to shard an existing MySQL-based application, you know that this can involve rewriting lots of code. With Mongo, there isn't the potential to go down this scalability dead end.

Of course, you can still implement joins in a primitive, client-side fashion. Imagine a video-sharing site such as YouTube. In a classic RDBMS, each video would probably exist as a row in a table, with a column for the user ID of the owner, while another table would store the list of categories to which this video belonged. To display a video, you'd link against the user and categories tables so that you could list the owner's username, show his or her location, show the categories to which the video belonged, and so on.

In Mongo, you'd need to break this down into three steps:

1. Send a query to retrieve the required columns from the `videos` collection (owner ID, video duration, video title, and so on).

2. Use the user ID obtained from the first query to fetch the owner's username, location, and so on.

3. Perform a query on the `categories` collection, matching on the video's ID.

Sending these extra queries increases latency a bit, and, in some cases, can cause a substantial increase in network traffic. So, although this method isn't "wrong," it's not optimal either. Using client-side joins in this way also shows that you are still thinking like an RDBMS programmer — it's not the Mongo way to do things.

What if you were to store the owner's username and location as fields in the `videos` collection (as well as in the `users` collection)? Denormalizing tricks like this make updates more difficult. (If a user changes username, you must update entries in the `videos` collection.) However, denormalization removes the need for joins and makes things easier to scale. There's no right or wrong way to do things here, and decisions like this must be made on a per-case basis.

Mongo also offers two features that can reduce the need for joins: *linking* and *embedding*. Linking is achieved using the `DBRef` mechanism in which you store a reference to a document in another collection. This necessitates a follow-up query, and most of the time, `DBRefs` simply aren't needed, because you can simply perform the join manually.

Much more interesting is the capability to embed documents inside others. For example, using the video-sharing example, you could embed each video owner's user document inside a video document. This provides quick access to data relating to the video's owner, at the expense of disk space. Mongo makes it easy to scan and update embedded documents, and this is generally the best option for performance.

Another consideration when designing schema is the way in which documents are physically stored on disk. Imagine a collection containing ten10 documents, each 1 KB in size. Mongo ensures that each document will always be stored sequentially, so the disk will not need to seek multiple times to read a single document. However, reading in all the documents will likely require seeking to te10n different locations (unless two documents just happen to have been placed next to each other on disk).

Data is loaded into memory in 4-KB blocks (the default page size), so if you want to read all te10n documents into memory, each document takes up a 4-KB block, and you end up using 40 KB of memory, not 10 KB. However, if each document was placed sequentially on disk, the 10 KB of data would fit into three pages, and you'd only need 12 KB of memory. Because you've already seen that an individual document will be stored sequentially on disk, you can achieve the wanted effect by embedding the 10 documents inside another document — a process known as *document bundling.* This can significantly cut disk seeks and memory usage under certain circumstances.

Document bundling has the most impact for documents that are small because the minimum unit of currency is a 4-KB page of memory. As the size of the document increases, the percentage gain from using bundling decreases. Also, bundling assumes that you actually want to read all the embedded documents into memory, which isn't always the case. This technique is only helpful if your working set is too large to fit into memory; otherwise, there is nothing to be gained.

Replication

Replication is a big topic in the world of MongoDB, and although it has many similarities with MySQL, it is substantially more involved. Actually, earlier versions of Mongo did use a fairly primitive master-slave replication model, which was similar to MySQL's, but this has been superseded by a more advanced method called *replica sets.*

In Mongo, a replication group is called a replica set, and may contain between 3 and 12 members. At any time, only one node will be the primary, with the others (usually) acting as secondaries and slaving the primary's contents. Reads can go to any node, whereas writes naturally must go to the primary.

Replication Internals and the Oplog

The process to replicate from one node to another is similar to MySQL's use of replay logs. On the primary node, all write events are executed by Mongo, and then written to the oplog, which is a capped collection in the local database. Each secondary node listens to the primary's oplog and copies events over to its own oplog. A separate thread on the secondary then replays events from its own oplog.

As a result of the oplog being a capped collection, only a limited amount of history is stored, and there is always the danger that a secondary node will fall so far behind that the primary has removed entries from the oplog that the secondary has not yet replicated. If this happens, replication to the secondary node stops, and manual intervention is required.

The usual cause of replication lag in Mongo is network latency, but for a particularly write-heavy application, lack of server power can also be an issue. In the former case, you simply must ensure that the oplog is large enough to accommodate this, whereas in the latter, more powerful hardware is the only option.

In addition, it is preferable that the oplog be large enough that you can reboot a secondary server without the current oplog events having been rotated out by the time it comes back online. This way, when you need to carry out operating system or hardware upgrades, the Mongo secondary server can still catch up with its primary server when you bring it back online.

There's no way you can create hard-and-fast rules on how big the oplog collection should be, though, because it depends on how Mongo is used. For a write-heavy application, the oplog may fill up so quickly that you can't tolerate more than 10 seconds of latency — anything more and old log entries will be rotated out before secondary servers have read them. Conversely, a read-heavy application may generate so little write traffic that the `oplog` holds several hours' worth of operations.

In reality, most applications lie somewhere in between and may suffer from occasional spurts of heavy write activity. In this case, the `oplog` would be more than large enough most of the time but could occasionally be too small.

The good news is that a large `oplog` doesn't have a particular impact on performance, so it's safe to err on the size of caution and make it big. For example, the following shows the use of a 10 GB cap:

```
mongod --oplogSize 10240
```

Setting Up Replication

Configuring a replica set in Mongo is relatively simple. First, you start up each `mongod` instance with the `--replSet` option, as shown here:

```
mongod --replSet <setname>
```

In this example, `setname` is an arbitrary name of your choosing for the set. On the first server, you then initiate the set and add the hostnames of other nodes in the set, as shown here:

```
> rs.initiate()
> rs.add("r1.example.com");
> rs.add("r2.example.com");
```

Various configuration options may be passed to `rs.add`, including priority and whether the node is to act as an arbiter (used when a new primary node must be selected) . Following is an example:

```
> rs.add("r1.example.com", arbiterOnly: true);
```

If you start with an empty data set, this is all that needs to be done. For existing data, you must load in a copy of the data into each node using `mongodump` and `mongorestore`.

Using Replication Nodes

In a replication setup, you generally write to the primary node and distribute reads over the secondary nodes. Unless you have a particularly elegant means to provide the information dynamically, this means hard-coding the addresses of the primary and master servers into the application's configuration, and then rewriting certain queries so that they go to a secondary server.

Mongo uses a much more flexible method that enables it to dynamically query nodes for their status, and discover the existence of other nodes in the set. In your code, you supply a list of `host:port` pairs to the driver, which then connects to each (ideally in parallel) and sends an `ismaster()` command. As well as returning the node's status (whether it sees itself as a primary, secondary, or neither), it also returns a list of all other hosts in the replica set. In this way, the Mongo driver can learn the topology of the set without you explicitly listing every member.

This auto-discovery adds some unfortunate latency to the queries, and some drivers implement short-term caching. This in itself can be a source of problems if the primary server goes down and a new one is elected — the last thing you want to do is send write queries to a secondary server. Fortunately, when a new primary is elected, this is usually because the old primary is not responding, so it will not accept any writes anyway. In addition, you can use connection pooling in some drivers (for example, PHP's) to reduce the latency involved in connecting to each node.

After the driver has discovered which node is a primary and which are secondary, you can simply execute your queries, and they will automatically be routed to the primary. Alternatively, you can request that queries go to a slave by setting the `slaveOkay` option. Exact details on how to do this vary from driver to driver. But, in PHP, you can set it on a per-query basis, for a particular database/collection, or for the whole connection. Following is an example:

```
$r->foo->bar->find()->slaveOkay();
```

The PHP driver determines which slave to use based on ping time. A health check is sent every 5 seconds, and the secondary node with the lowest ping time will be the preferred one. Remember that Mongo uses eventual consistency, and if data is written to the primary node, there may be a short delay before it propagates to all slaves. Thus, in some cases, using a secondary node for read queries is not appropriate.

Failover: Elections, Voting, and Arbiters

One of the many great features of replica sets is the support for automatic failover. Each node routinely sends a heartbeat message to the others in the set, and if a secondary node detects that the primary node is down, it forces an *election*. During an election, each node votes on the node it believes should be the new primary. This is mainly based on which server is the most up-to-date with replicating from the primary, but it also takes into account any custom priority you have set on nodes.

One consequence of this democratic approach is that occasionally there will be voting ties. (That is, no node receives a majority vote.) Mongo makes allowances for this through the concept of *arbiters*. These are nodes in the replica set that don't hold any data (that is, don't participate in replication) and are used solely for breaking voting deadlocks. An arbiter is needed only when there are an even number of replication nodes (because an odd number of voters can't result in a tie), and arbiters are light enough that you can run them on the same machine as a replication node. For a given replica set, you generally need only one arbiter (at most), and there is no additional benefit to running multiple arbiters.

To add an arbiter, simply start up a replica set member in the usual way (by starting `mongod` with the `--replicaSet <name>` command-line option), and then tell the primary node to treat it as an arbiter. Following is an example:

```
> rs.addArb("server1.example.com:27017");
```

Priority

Mongo version 2.0 introduced the capability to set priorities on each node in a replica set. If the primary goes down, and a replacement must be found, Mongo favors the most up-to-date server. If several servers are up-to-date, the one with the highest priority will be chosen. A consequence of this is that the primary node may change again at a later date if a server with higher priority subsequently becomes less lagged. For example, you would use the following to change the priority of the first node to 2:

```
> config.members[1].priority = 2;
```

Setting priority has several uses. For example, if you have a set of three replica servers, two in the same data center and one on the other side of the world being used for taking backups, you probably don't want the latter to ever become primary. You can do that by giving it a priority of zero. Similarly, priority can be used to ensure that the most powerful servers are favored as primaries.

Propagation and Eventual Consistency

Recall that write operations in Mongo immediately return control back to the client, without saying anything about whether the write was a success (or had even been attempted yet). In the majority of cases, the write will be successful but will be queued for a short period of time before being committed to disk.

In replication setups, you have additional considerations. The write may have been committed to disk on the primary, but what about secondaries? You know that they will eventually receive and commit the write (depending on any replication lag and use of fsync), but sometimes that isn't good enough.

Earlier in this chapter, you learned that getLastError() forces Mongo to commit a write to disk. (That's the only way it can return whether an error occurred.) The syntax can be extended for replica sets, as shown here:

```
db.runCommand( { getlasterror : 1 , w : 2 } );
```

The w parameter tells Mongo that the operation must have been written to at least two nodes before getLastError will return. One node will be the current one (primary), whereas the other will be a secondary. In the case of sensitive data, this should provide some reassurance that it will not be lost.

As shown here, w also supports the majority keyword, which causes getLastError to return when the majority of secondaries receive the operation:

```
db.runCommand( { getlasterror : 1 , w : "majority" } );
```

This usually provides a satisfactory level of comfort. Ensuring that every node has the data is unnecessary and costly because the speed at which the command returns is effectively governed by the slowest secondary in the set. When all the nodes are in the same data center, this isn't too bad. But for a secondary on another continent, this could cause some annoying latency. Thus, a timeout value is also supported, as shown here:

```
db.runCommand( { getlasterror : 1 , w : "majority", wtimeout : 3000 } );
```

In this example, Mongo waits for the majority of servers to receive the write and returns a timeout if this has not happened within 3 seconds.

Sharding

Given that Mongo was designed from the outset to provide high-performance, multinode data storage, it's not surprising that it features particularly strong support for sharding. With automatic rebalancing, built-in lookup tables and routing, and support for parallel querying, Mongo simplifies many of the obstacles encountered with sharding in MySQL.

The main reason for sharding is to scale write queries (scaling reads is easy), but there are also a number of other (lesser) reasons:

➤ For large amounts of data, it may be that a single server doesn't offer enough disk capacity to hold everything. (Although, given the size of modern hard disks, this isn't going to happen often.)

➤ When searching large collections, sharding can also improve performance by querying each shard in parallel and then aggregating the results.

➤ Sharding increases the overall amount of memory available in the cluster, meaning that more data can be cached in RAM, thus improving read performance.

Chunks and Shards

In MySQL, each range of key values is referred to as a shard and exists on its own separate physical server. Thus, keys a-j might exist on one shard, k-t on another shard, and u-z on another. Each of these ranges directly translates to a particular MySQL server.

With Mongo, the basic unit of currency is the *chunk*. A chunk contains a range of key values (for example, k through t) but is not tied to a particular physical server. Rather, it can be moved across servers (which are referred to as *shards*) as necessary. Chunks are fairly small in size, and each shard usually contains many chunks.

So, in addition to a slight change in nomenclature, Mongo also introduces an extra degree of granularity. This is a significant improvement over MySQL's mode, in which ranges are tied to a physical server.

Choosing a Shard Key

Sharding is performed on a per-collection basis, enabling you to mix and match. Large collections can be sharded, whereas smaller ones continue to operate on a single server.

As always, you should give some thought to the shard key, and you must ensure that it has a high degree of cardinality. For example, there would be no point to shard a user collection based on gender because this would produce only two shards. When your application outgrew two shards, you'd be stuck. Similarly, if you were to shard based on a user's surname, you could end up with quite an uneven distribution of data — there are a lot more Smiths and Joneses in the world than Stallmans or Torvalds. An easy solution is to shard based on two fields — for example, first name and surname. This usually results in a much better distribution of data.

Another consideration is how and where data will be written. Imagine a logging collection. It may seem logical to shard by a timestamp, particularly if you often run queries on this field (for example, generating reports for particular time periods). But this inevitably causes all writes to go to a single shard (containing the chunk covering the current time range). Shards containing older time ranges will not receive any writes.

This is fine if you shard because a single server doesn't have enough disk space, or because you want a subset of the data to be held in memory for performance. But if your aim is to distribute reads and writes, this method fails. The same is true for any ascending key, such as an auto-incrementing counter, where you are always writing to the "end" of the range. Writes end up being concentrated on a single server, resulting in a hotspot.

When choosing a sharding key, you should also give some thought as to how you will be querying the data. If you shard on an e-mail address field, it makes it easy to subsequently pull up the record for a particular user. Mongo knows on which shard this will exist and can send the query to the appropriate server. By contrast, if you then attempt to pull up a list of all users with a particular surname, Mongo would have no choice other than to query each server. Fortunately, this is done in parallel, which eliminates a lot of the performance penalty. But it still results in an increase in network traffic and makes your query as slow as the slowest node.

In many ways, choosing the sharding key is the most difficult part of setting up sharding, and careful thought should be given to the key. It can make a significant difference in how scalable the application will be, and the wrong key can cause serious headaches further down the line. The choice of key is application-specific, but indexed fields are usually the first candidates to consider.

mongos and Configuration Servers

In a MySQL sharding setup, you must add an extra step of logic to your application code. First, you must keep track of which shards reside on which servers. (You can either hard-code this lookup table in your application's configuration file or store it in, say, memcache.) Every time your application performs a query, it must consult this table to determine to which servers to send the query. If you want to query servers in parallel, you often must jump through additional hoops.

In Mongo, all this is taken care of automatically through the use of two additional services: mongos and configuration servers. When the application code issues a query, it sends it to mongos, which then decides which shard nodes to forward the query on to. mongos then returns the result to the application.

If multiple servers must be queried, mongos sends the queries in parallel, collates the results, and then returns them to the application. In this way the application is unaware that sharding is even happening, and thinks it is simply communicating with a single Mongo server. These mongos servers are light enough that they can be run on existing servers. One option is to run a mongos process on each shard server, but you could equally well run then on top of each application server. The latter should result in slightly lower latency.

mongos processes know where to route queries because they pull their logic from the second new addition to the infrastructure — configuration servers. These are similarly lightweight services that contain information on the sharding layout — specifically, which chunks reside on which servers.

For example, all users with e-mail addresses beginning a–h reside in chunk W, which is stored on server X. All users with addresses beginning i–p live in chunk Y on server Z. When a mongos process starts, it pulls this information from the configuration server, and if the mapping subsequently changes (for example, Mongo rebalances a chunk to another node), the configuration server pushes the change to each mongos process.

The configuration servers are kept in sync with each other using replication, but they automatically use their own internal implementation, and you should definitely not set them up as a replica set.

Figure 10-4 shows a minimum setup for sharding. One or more application servers send requests to one or more mongos servers, which, in turn, route the requests on to the appropriate Mongo node. Three configuration servers keep the mongos processes in sync with the location of the shards.

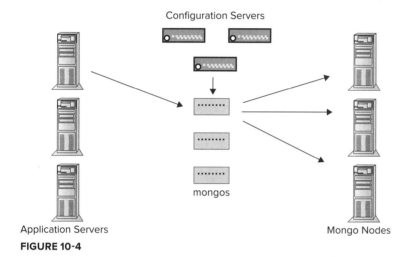

FIGURE 10-4

As already mentioned, though, the configuration and mongos servers are light enough that you'd probably just run them on top of the application servers — one of each on each application server. As shown in Figure 10-5, this simplifies your setup and reduces the number of machines needed.

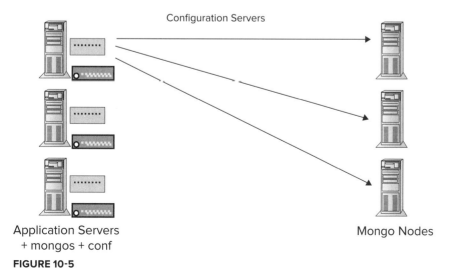

FIGURE 10-5

Setting Up Sharding

Now that you have a topology in mind, you can begin configuring the servers. Let's assume an empty collection because this is simpler than sharding an existing collection.

With each `mongod` server up and running in the usual manner, you can connect to one instance and run the `addShard` command to add the hostname of each shard. (It's preferable to use hostnames rather than IP addresses in case you ever move your `mongod` daemons to different machines.) Following is an example:

```
> db.runCommand( { addshard : "shard1.example.com" } );
> db.runCommand( { addshard : "shard2.example.com" } );
> db.runCommand( { addshard : "shard3.example.com" } );
```

You can confirm that the shards have been added by using `listshards`, as shown here:

```
> db.runCommand( { listshards : 1 } );
```

Next, you must enable sharding for the relevant database and collection, and, in the latter case, also specifying the shard key, as shown here:

```
> db.runCommand( { enablesharding : "foo" } );
> db.runCommand( { shardcollection : "foo.users", key : {username : 1} } )
```

At this point, `mongod` operates in a sharded setup, but you still must set up `mongos` and configuration servers so that clients can access the correct shard.

To start a configuration server, launch `mongod` with the `–configsvr` option, as shown here:

```
mongod -configsvr
```

The MongoDB developers recommend using three configuration servers in a live environment.

For `mongos` servers, pass the `--configdb` command-line option, followed by a comma-separated list of configuration servers, as shown here:

```
mongos --configdb config1.example.com,config2.example.com,config3.example.com
```

At this point, the sharding setup should be fully operational, and clients can be configured to send their queries to any of the running `mongos` daemons.

Chunks and Balancing

You check the status of the sharding setup like so:

```
> db.printShardingStatus();
--- Sharding Status ---
  sharding version: { "_id" : 1, "version" : 3 }
  shards:
        { "_id" : "shard0000",  "host" : "s1.example.com:10000" }
        { "_id" : "shard0001",  "host" : "s2.example.com:10000" }
  databases:
        { "_id" : "admin",  "partitioned" : false,  "primary" : "config" }
```

```
{  "_id" : "foo",  "partitioned" : true,  "primary" : "shard0000" }
        foo.users chunks:
                     shard0000      1
          { "name" : { $minKey : 1 } } -->> { "name" :
               { $maxKey : 1 } } on : shard0000 { "t" : 1000,
               "i" : 0 }
```

From the output, you can see that there are two sharding servers (s1.example.com and s2.example
.com). Of the two databases that exist, admin is not sharded ("partitioned" : false), whereas foo is.

The remainder of the output shows how the chunks have been allocated. At the moment, there's
only one chunk (the collection has little data in it), and it resides on shard0000. The final line shows
the key range contained in this chunk. As you might expect, it contains the full range (minKey to
maxKey). In case you're wondering, the t and i fields are internal versioning fields — t is incremented when a chunk is moved to another shard (this causes i to be reset also), and i is incremented
when a chunk is split.

If you continue adding data to the collection, multiple chunks will eventually be created — by
default, Mongo keeps chunks at approximately 64 MB.

```
    foo.users chunks:
shard0000      6
{ "name" : { $minKey : 1 } } -->> { "name" : "02e74f10" } on : shard0000 {
     "t" : 1000, "i" : 1 }
{ "name" : "02e74f11" } -->> { "name" : "35f4a8d4" } on : shard0000 {
     "t" : 1000, "i" : 9 }
{ "name" : "35f4a8d5" } -->> { "name" : "812b4ba2" } on : shard0000 {
     "t" : 1000, "i" : 10 }
{ "name" : "812b4ba3" } -->> { "name" : "c4ca4238" } on : shard0000 {
     "t" : 1000, "i" : 7 }
{ "name" : "c4ca4239" } -->> { "name" : "fe9fc289" } on : shard0000 {
     "t" : 1000, "i" : 8 }
{ "name" : "fe9fc290" } -->> { "name" : { $maxKey : 1 } } on : shard0000 {
     "t" : 1000, "i" : 4 }
```

At this point, you now have six chunks, but they still all reside on the same shard server. In fact,
Mongo won't start rebalancing until one server has eight more chunks than the other. At that point,
it moves chunks around until the difference between servers is down to two chunks. Let's add some
more data:

```
shard0000      9
{ "name" : { $minKey : 1 } } -->> { "name" : "02e74f10" } on : shard0000 {
     "t" : 1000, "i" : 1 }
{ "name" : "02e74f11" } -->> { "name" : "35f4a8d4" } on : shard0000 {
     "t" : 1000, "i" : 9 }
{ "name" : "35f4a8d5" } -->> { "name" : "642e92ef" } on : shard0000 {
     "t" : 1000, "i" : 15 }
{ "name" : "642e92f0" } -->> { "name" : "812b4ba2" } on : shard0000 {
     "t" : 1000, "i" : 16 }
{ "name" : "812b4ba3" } -->> { "name" : "9bf31c7f" } on : shard0000 {
     "t" : 1000, "i" : 13 }
{ "name" : "9bf31c80" } -->> { "name" : "c4ca4238" } on : shard0000 {
     "t" : 1000, "i" : 14 }
{ "name" : "c4ca4239" } -->> { "name" : "d9d4f495" } on : shard0000 {
```

```
        "t" : 1000, "i" : 11 }
{ "name" : "d9d4f496" } -->> { "name" : "fe9fc289" } on : shard0000 {
        "t" : 1000, "i" : 12 }
{ "name" : "fe9fc290" } -->> { "name" : { $maxKey : 1 } } on : shard0000 {
        "t" : 1000, "i" : 4 }
```

Mongo now begins rebalancing, and if you check back a few moments later, you can see that the first chunk has already been moved. Notice that t has been incremented to reflect this.

```
shard0001        1
shard0000        8
{ "name" : { $minKey : 1 } } -->> { "name" : "02e74f10" } on : shard0001 {
        "t" : 2000, "i" : 0 }
{ "name" : "02e74f10" } -->> { "name" : "35f4a8d4" } on : shard0000 {
        "t" : 2000, "i" : 1 }
{ "name" : "35f4a8d4" } -->> { "name" : "642e92ef" } on : shard0000 {
        "t" : 1000, "i" : 15 }
{ "name" : "642e92ef" } -->> { "name" : "812b4ba2" } on : shard0000 {
        "t" : 1000, "i" : 16 }
{ "name" : "812b4ba2" } -->> { "name" : "9bf31c7f" } on : shard0000 {
        "t" : 1000, "i" : 13 }
{ "name" : "9bf31c7f" } -->> { "name" : "c4ca4238" } on : shard0000 {
        "t" : 1000, "i" : 14 }
{ "name" : "c4ca4238" } -->> { "name" : "d9d4f495" } on : shard0000 {
        "t" : 1000, "i" : 11 }
{ "name" : "d9d4f495" } -->> { "name" : "fe9fc289" } on : shard0000 {
        "t" : 1000, "i" : 1 }
```

Rebalancing isn't an instantaneous process because the 64-MB chunks must be copied across servers. But eventually you reach a situation in which four chunks have been copied over to shard0001, leaving five on shard0000 (again, notice how t and i have changed):

```
shard0001        4
shard0000        5
{ "name" : { $minKey : 1 } } -->> { "name" : "02e74f10" } on : shard0001 {
        "t" : 2000, "i" : 0 }
{ "name" : "02e74f10" } -->> { "name" : "35f4a8d4" } on : shard0000 {
        "t" : 2000, "i" : 0 }
{ "name" : "35f4a8d4" } -->> { "name" : "642e92ef" } on : shard0000 {
        "t" : 2000, "i" : 0 }
{ "name" : "642e92ef" } -->> { "name" : "812b4ba2" } on : shard0000 {
        "t" : 2000, "i" : 0 }
{ "name" : "812b4ba2" } -->> { "name" : "9bf31c7f" } on : shard0000 {
        "t" : 1000, "i" : 13 }
{ "name" : "9bf31c7f" } -->> { "name" : "c4ca4238" } on : shard0000 {
        "t" : 1000, "i" : 14 }
{ "name" : "c4ca4238" } -->> { "name" : "d9d4f495" } on : shard0000 {
        "t" : 1000, "i" : 11 }
{ "name" : "d9d4f495" } -->> { "name" : "fe9fc289" } on : shard0000 {
        "t" : 1000, "i" : 1 }
```

Why 64-MB chunks? This number wasn't chosen at random and has been the source of much debate among Mongo developers. (In fact, earlier versions of Mongo used a much higher chunk size.) On the one hand, you want chunks to be small enough that they can be moved from shard to shard relatively easily without putting too much strain on bandwidth or disk I/O. However, moving chunks also means more work for Mongo — the lookup table held on the configuration servers must be updated and the changes pushed to each mongos server. So, you also want chunks to be large enough that they aren't moved around *too* often.

If wanted, you can change the chunk size like so:

```
> use config
> db.settings.save({_id:"chunksize", value:128});  // 128MB
```

You'd probably want to experiment with this only if huge amounts of data were added, resulting in the default 64-MB chunks being split/moved too often.

If the rebalancing of chunks causes too much of a strain on individual nodes or the network, you can schedule rebalancing only between certain hours — in the following example, between 2 a.m. and 6 a.m.:

```
> use config;
> db.settings.update({ _id : "balancer" }, { $set : { activeWindow :
      { start : "2:00", stop : "6:00" } } }, true );
```

This is handy for stopping rebalancing from potentially impacting traffic during busy times. But you must ensure that the amount of data added is sufficiently low so that the rebalancing can complete within these times. In practice, this is usually only a concern if bandwidth is limited, the time window is too small, or huge amounts of data are written each day.

Replicating Shards

Replication offers you security against nodes failing (and some degree of read scaling), whereas sharding provides write scaling but no redundancy. It seems natural to combine the two together, and, in fact, this is one of the most popular ways for setting up a Mongo cluster. Figure 10-6 shows the topology.

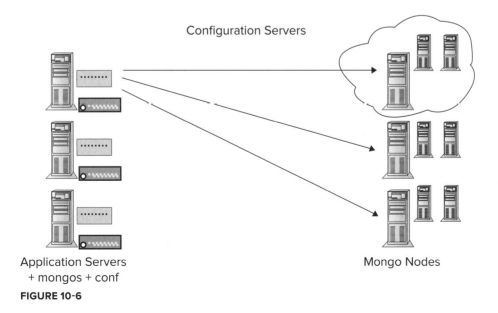

Configuration Servers

Application Servers
+ mongos + conf

Mongo Nodes

FIGURE 10-6

Although this initially looks quite intimidating, it is nothing more than a combination of the two scaling techniques previously described. As before, the application servers connect to mongos processes, which route queries to the appropriate shard. This time, though, each shard is actually a replica set triplet. Again, these replica sets are no different from the examples presented earlier. You can have as many nodes in the set as necessary (although the recommended minimum is three), and you can still direct queries to either a master or a slave to help balance read queries — mongos takes care of ensuring the queries go to the correct shard replica set.

The only difference in the sharding setup with this model is that you can tell Mongo that each shard is a replica set. If the set were named foo, the syntax would now be as follows:

```
> db.runCommand( { addshard : "foo/shard3.example.com" } );
```

This enables the usual auto-discovery and query balancing to take place.

GridFS

Let's move away from sharding and replication, and talk about another feature of Mongo: the Grid Filesystem (GridFS). Storing user-uploaded content (such as avatars) is a common problem on multiserver setups. You can use a network-aware filesystem such as Network File System (NFS) to allow all web servers to access a common area to write uploads to, but NFS is slow. You could use a cron job to periodically rsync files to across to a common area, but this would introduce a delay between the file being uploaded and it being available globally (and could also cause spikes in CPU and bandwidth).

One thing developers are taught to definitely not do is store files in MySQL (for example in a blob column). MySQL is so often the bottleneck in a system that adding extra load to it like this is suicide. It's not what MySQL is designed for either, so access times can be relatively poor, and it can poison your carefully configured caches and buffers. This also greatly increases the size of your tables, making dumping and restoring much slower.

It's perhaps surprising, then, that Mongo actually encourages you to store files in it, and even provides a way to do this via the GridFS. The observations about dumping and restoring slower still stand, but storing files in this way has a number of benefits:

➤   You no longer need to worry about using a shared/network filesystem or syncing files across multiple servers.

➤   If you use replication, you have a backup copy of the files on another server.

➤   You can store meta data (such as an MD5 checksum, date, username, and so on) alongside each file and search on these fields.

GridFS uses its own database, named fs, with two collections: chunks for chunks of the file, and files for meta data associated with each file. Files are stored pretty much as regular documents would be. But because there is a limit of 16 MB on the size of an individual document, in many cases, Mongo would need to split the file into chunks spanning multiple documents. This is actually advantageous. It means that the file is streamed back to the client in chunks, rather than Mongo attempting to buffer the whole file in memory. It also allows you to jump to the midsections of files.

So useful is this that, for GridFS, the chunk size actually defaults to 256 KB, significantly less than the 16 MB maximum.

The `files` collection contains (at a minimum) the following fields:

➤ `_id` — This unique ID for the file will be auto-generated if omitted.

➤ `Length` — This is the size of the file (in bytes).

➤ `chunkSize` — This is how big each chunk should be.

➤ `uploadDate` — This is the date/time when the file was inserted into the database.

➤ `md5` — This is an MD5 checksum of the file.

Additional fields may be added if necessary. For example, it's quite common to include the file's MIME type, a username, and perhaps a title or description.

The `chunks` collection consists of a unique ID field, a field containing the corresponding ID of the file in the `files` collection, the chunk number, and the data. Chunk number is an incrementing value that ensures the chunks of the file are returned in the correct order.

Although you could theoretically handle files as if they were any other kind of data — splitting them into chunks and inserted into the collection — Mongo provides the command-line tool `mongofiles` to take care of these finer points for you.

First, you write a file to GridFS, as shown here:

```
$ mongofiles put twitter.png
connected to: 127.0.0.1
added file: { _id: ObjectId('4f495177bdc23c5be1912771'), filename: "twitter.png",
  chunkSize: 262144, uploadDate: new Date(1330229047751), md5:
  "6ad40e7be284e362fa479eb522241306", length: 3319 }
done!
```

Next, you get a list of existing files:

```
$ mongofiles list
connected to: 127.0.0.1
twitter.png     3319
```

When you're ready, you can fetch the file back, as shown here:

```
$ mongofiles get twitter.png
connected to: 127.0.0.1
done write to: twitter.png
```

Most Mongo drivers also provide methods for interacting with GridFS. For example, in PHP, the following shows the most popular, `MongoGridFS`:

```
$r = new Mongo();
$database = $r->foo;
$grid = $database->getGridFS();
print $grid->storeFile(
```

```
            "/tmp/upload.gif",
            array("metadata" => array(
                "filename" => "upload.gif",
                "mimeType" => "image/gif",
                "uploadedBy" => "pgsmith"
            ),
            "filename" = > "upload.gif"
        )
    );
```

More often than not, you already have the file contents stored in a string and may want to write this to GridFS. In this case, you use `storeBytes` rather than `storeFile` and pass the string as the first parameter (rather than the filename).

GridFS and Nginx

Although GridFS neatly solves the problems of allowing multiple web servers to access contents from a common location, be cautious about viewing it as a new toy and using it for holding all static contents. Although performance is good, it's still generally better to host static resources on a traditional filesystem. (There are a few situations in which GridFS wins over traditional filesystems — for example, there are less restrictions on permitted characters in filenames, and traditional filesystems often struggle when faced with millions of files in the same directory.)

For user-uploaded content, GridFS is great, but having to execute some code to retrieve an image each time is far from ideal. For example, if your users' avatars were stored in GridFS, you might use mark-up like this:

```
<img src="/avatars/pgsmith.gif">
```

You'd then use a `mod_rewrite` rule to catch any requests for resources under /avatars/ and redirect them to a server-side script. This script would pull the appropriate image from GridFS and then echo out the content type and the data.

To the client, it would look like a standard request/response for an image. But behind the scenes, the web server would need to do significantly more work than for a static resource.

The good news is that there exists for Nginx a module that enables it to talk directly to Mongo and pull files from GridFS. This eliminates the overhead involved in executing a scripting language and gives performance closer to the serving of static files. The module is aptly named `nginx-gridfs` and is available from `https://github.com/mdirolf/nginx-gridfs`.

> **NOTE** *Chapter 7, "Working with Web Servers," provides a more complete discussion of Nginx.*

GridFS-fuse

For those not using Nginx, a final method to access GridFS is via the FUSE kernel module, enabling it to be mounted just like a regular filesystem. A GridFS wrapper for FUSE is available from `https://github.com/mikejs/gridfs-fuse`.

Mongo versus MySQL

It's easy to see why some commentators have suggested that Mongo should be the new "M" in LAMP (which currently stands for Linux, Apache, MySQL, PHP). In so many ways Mongo seems to outperform MySQL — whether it be its superior replication and sharding, or its blistering performance — that you might question whether MySQL still has a place in modern web applications.

One of the biggest shortcomings of Mongo at the moment is its reliance on global locking, which can dramatically slow down both reads and writes on write-heavy setups. This level of locking makes even MyISAM's table-level locking seem unobtrusive in comparison. Work is currently underway to implement more granular locking in MongoDB — probably at the collection level — so, hopefully, this will not be an issue for too much longer. In the meantime, both sharding and replication can help alleviate this problem.

Some Mongo advocates also fail to appreciate Mongo's approach to durability. They perform some crude benchmarking that shows how Mongo can make several orders of magnitude more writes per second than MySQL, without realizing that these writes have not necessarily been committed to disk. To achieve a similar level of data security to MySQL, you must enable both journaling and periodic use of fsync, which both impact performance. (Remember that you don't get any feedback on whether the write was successful, unless you specifically ask for it — which, again, impacts performance.) In practice, Mongo still outperforms MySQL, but the gap is now no longer as huge.

That's not to say there's anything wrong with Mongo's approach to data durability, providing that you understand the potentially volatile nature of the data. The biggest problem is not Mongo's behavior, but the users' failure to understand it. Most people are happy with the idea that memcache offers volatile storage, but many simply assume that writes in Mongo will be safe — and without a couple of tweaks, they are not. Even then, if the slight chance of data loss can't be tolerated at all (for example, for financial transactions), Mongo is probably not the best choice.

This raises the next drawback: lack of transactions. Again, in many situations, this is acceptable, and Mongo's model is no worse than, say, MyISAM. But if you deal with money, Mongo isn't the right tool for the job, and you're much better off sticking with InnoDB.

With the exception of global locking (which seems like an issue that should have been addressed much earlier), these points aren't a criticism of MongoDB. It does what it claims to do well and has never been pitched as a complete replacement for MySQL. Consider Mongo as an extra tool in your arsenal, and use it when it makes sense to use it — not because of any NoSQL hype.

The number of new technologies falling under the NoSQL banner is huge. So far, you've seen two of the most important ones. But, in the following section, you learn about some of the many other options.

OTHER NOSQL TECHNOLOGIES

MongoDB and memcache are both at opposite ends of the spectrum, and there are a great number of NoSQL offerings that fall somewhere in the middle. Mongo and memcache are two favorites. (And space does not permit doing justice to all of the others.) But NoSQL is an exciting area, and there are many other technologies that are gaining strong user bases. To round out this discussion of NoSQL, let's look at some of these offerings, and examine the relative pros and cons of each.

Tokyo Cabinet and Tokyo Tyrant

Sponsored by the Japanese social networking site mixi, inc., Tokyo Cabinet is a multithreaded database library (like SQLite) that is both fast and flexible. Tokyo Tyrant is the name given to the accompanying network server that handles client connections and concurrency. Tokyo Tyrant has a reputation for being fast and offers high levels of concurrency via an event-polling model (epoll).

Tokyo Cabinet offers a choice of underlying storage engines, of which the following are the four most common:

➤ **Hash table** — This stores key-value pairs in a traditional hash structure.

➤ **B-tree** — Although this also uses key-value pairs, it allows them to be stored in a user-defined order, making it possible to perform range and prefix matching.

➤ **Fixed length** — This simple array structure is used rather than a hash. Data is accessed by specifying a numeric array key offset. This makes it a truly fast engine; although, it can be somewhat impractical to work with.

➤ **Table** — This behaves like a traditional RDBMS engine with rows and columns. It supports indexing and sorting but is also schema-less (like MongoDB). Locking occurs at the row level.

Tokyo Cabinet has some support for transactions, and ACID compliance with write-ahead logging is available. It also supports replication; although, no built-in sharding support is available. (However, there's nothing to stop you from rolling your own sharding solution.)

Although Tokyo Cabinet is an excellent persistent key-value store, it is not primarily a document database like Mongo, and this is the weakest part of it. For modeling and querying more complex data types, the likes of Mongo or MySQL are still better solutions.

As a key-value store, however, Tokyo Cabinet has numerous benefits over `memcache` and `membase`. It uses a binary protocol for storage (generally more efficient than text-based), supports the compression of data (either via `gzip`, `bzip2`, or a custom implementation), and has support for Lua scripting, making it extensible.

Finally, Tokyo Cabinet also ships with its own full-text search system, Tokyo Distopia. although Tokyo Cabinet is not as well known as `memcache`, it surpasses it in many ways.

CouchDB

CouchDB is another JSON-based document database, similar to Mongo. The most obvious difference on the surface is that CouchDB uses a HTTP REST interface for querying it, and this will always be several times slower than a binary over TCP/IP protocol. In the past, the data querying method has also been rather different, revolving around `MapReduce` and views. In 2011, CouchDB introduced UnQL as a general-purpose NoSQL querying language, providing a more traditional feel to query execution.

CouchDB's attitude to scale is also markedly different, with replication being used as a scaling tool. (In MySQL, replication is seen as a partial solution to scaling, whereas Mongo prefers sharding for scaling and replication for durability.) CouchDB uses master-master replication, and this introduces performance considerations because care must be taken to ensure that data remains in sync. A multiversion concurrency control (MVCC) model is used, which solves many of these problems — and also allows for high levels of simultaneous reads and writes. But this comes at the cost of performance. So, although CouchDB is well suited to write-heavy applications or those that demand data integrity, it doesn't offer the blistering speed seen in its main rival, Mongo.

Project Voldemort

Voldemort is a persistent key-value store developed and used by LinkedIn. It features automatic replication and partitioning (sharding), making it capable of scaling horizontally for both reads and writes.

Voldemort is perhaps most like `membase` in that it combines the in-memory caching of `memcache` with the persistent storage offered by `membase`. It should be remembered that Voldemort isn't intended as a cache, though, and lacks features such as automatic expiration of keys or an LRU retention policy. (If a volatile cache is all that is needed, `memcache` is a better choice.) Rather, Voldemort is a complete storage solution that supports complex objects as keys or values, and versioning of data.

Amazon Dynamo and Google BigTable

Two import products in the NoSQL world are actually proprietary systems developed with only limited availability to the public.

Dynamo is a distributed key-value store, developed by Amazon.com and used by parts of Amazon Web Services (AWS). It is not available to the general public but forms a key part of Amazon's infrastructure. It uses sharding and replication, and puts an emphasis on fault tolerance.

Google's BigTable is a three-dimensional store, with values referenced by a row key, column key, and timestamp triplet — the latter allows for versioning and automatic expiration of data. It runs on top of Google File System (GFS) and uses compression in some situations. It is designed to hold millions of gigabytes of data across thousands of nodes and is a core part of many of Google's services.

Google offers some access to BigTable via its App Engine, and Amazon.com offers DynamoDB (a NoSQL database built on Dynamo) as part of AWS. Other than that, neither of these technologies is available to the public. So, why are they so important in the NoSQL world?

Both are relatively old for NoSQL — BigTable began life in 2004, and Dynamo in 2007 — and both were developed by large companies (that could provide plenty of funding) with high-performance demands. Although neither product is open source, Amazon.com and Google have published plenty of papers on their inner workings, and this has inspired many others to create open source NoSQL applications using similar concepts. As a result, many of the popular open source NoSQL solutions on the market today have their roots indirectly in these two offerings.

Riak

Riak has been designed heavily around Dynamo. Its main selling point is fault tolerance, and it can withstand many nodes going down without any data becoming unavailable. As part of its emphasis on reliability, it has no concept of master and secondary nodes (thus, no single points of failure) and uses consistent hashing to partition data. As with most multidimensional stores, Riak is geared toward storing huge volumes of data.

Cassandra

Developed by Facebook, Cassandra is a multidimensional key-value store inspired by both BigTable and Dynamo and written in Java. It has the unusual characteristic that writes are much faster than reads, making it well suited to write-heavy applications.

As with Riak, Cassandra uses a decentralized network model, with all nodes being equal (no masters and slaves), and data replicated across multiple nodes for fault tolerance. It also supports partitioning and offers two alternative models for distributing the data.

Redis

Another key-value store, Redis, is written in C and sponsored by VMWare. It uses a strategy similar to Mongo for durability and can operate entirely out of memory if performance is more important than data integrity. Alternatively, Redis also supports periodic snapshotting (basically the equivalent to using `fsync` in Mongo) and journaling. The primary selling point of Redis is its speed; although, to achieve such fast read/writes, the working set should be small enough to fit into memory.

HBase

HBase is another BigTable-inspired database, supporting huge volumes of data, and with a particular emphasis on good performance for random read. It offers row-level locking, strong consistency (HBase's obvious main rival, Cassandra, uses eventual consistency), fault tolerance, data locality, and native `MapReduce` support. HBase's approach to scaling out is something of a hybrid method. Although it uses the concept of masters and slaves, it does not depend on masters heavily and can survive even if the master goes down.

SUMMARY

The days when data storage was a choice between flat text files or a bulky RDBMS are long gone, and there is now a wealth of alternative solutions. Although typically grouped together under the name of NoSQL, there is a huge variety in how they work. But one common theme is that they were all designed for scalability in today's modern web world.

`memcache` is one of the most popular NoSQL technologies. It offers a basic key-value store and is perfect for situations in which an RDBMS like MySQL would be overkill. `memcache` is well supported by scripting languages, such as PHP, Python, and Ruby, and can be scaled across multiple nodes.

It should be remembered that data in memcache is volatile and is not stored in persistent storage (such as a hard disk). membase — an off-shoot of memcache — solves this, and introduces a more intelligent way to scale across many nodes.

At the other end of the NoSQL spectrum is Mongo, a document store that offers many of the features seen in traditional databases. Modeling data structures in real-world applications can be tricky in MySQL, and Mongo excels in situations in which the structure of your data is dynamic. It also offers good support for sharding and replication, which are essential when you appreciate Mongo's single-server durability model.

A lot of hype has surrounded NoSQL, with much of the hype claiming it marks the death of the traditional RDBMS. Although it's true that NoSQL has taken over from the likes of MySQL in many environments, MySQL still has its place, and NoSQL should be viewed as another weapon in your arsenal, rather than as a MySQL replacement.

Having spent the past three chapters looking at databases in various shapes and forms, it's time to look at other aspects of back-end performance. Many sites use Secure Sockets Layer (SSL), often without realizing the hit this can have on performance. In Chapter 11, you discover the reasons that SSL can be costly, and what you can do to minimize that cost.

11

Working with Secure Sockets Layer (SSL)

WHAT'S IN THIS CHAPTER?

➤ Caching SSL sessions with session IDs or session tickets

➤ Setting up an SSL endpoint in HAProxy, Nginx, or Apache

➤ Understanding the performance impacts of key and certificate sizes, as well as cipher suites

➤ Looking toward the future

Secure Sockets Layer (SSL) is the encryption method used to securely transmit data over HTTP, where it is often referred to as HTTPS. Widely used for e-commerce and webmail, the extra overhead involved in setting up the secure channel and encrypting/decrypting data can have an impact on performance — both on server load and responsiveness. In this chapter, you learn how to combat this through a variety of techniques.

The discussion here clarifies the distinction between SSL and Transport Layer Security (TLS), and helps you gauge how big of a performance penalty SSL incurs. You also learn about performance-related aspects of SSL, such as key size and intermediate certificates, as well as about enhancements such as session reuse, session tickets, and how these can work in multiserver environments.

> **NOTE** *The terms "SSL" and "TLS" are often used interchangeably, but they are not quite the same thing. The first public release of SSL was version 2.0 in 1995 and, in light of numerous security concerns, this was quickly followed by version 3.0 in 1996. TLS didn't appear until 1999 and was designed as a replacement for SSL. Since then, there have been two revisions to TLS: version 1.1 in 2006 and version 1.2 in 2008. So, although SSL has essentially been replaced by TLS, the discussion in this chapter uses the term "SSL" to mean "SSL/TLS."*

SSL CACHING

The principle advantage of using SSL is session caching, which can significantly reduce CPU usage and lower latency during HTTP requests. But to thoroughly understand session caching, it's important to first take a closer look at the SSL protocol.

Connections, Sessions, and Handshakes

Before HTTP requests can be sent over SSL, a secure channel must first be established. This involves the server sending the certificate (and the browser validating it) an encryption protocol being agreed on and keys being exchanged. Figure 11-1 shows an overview of the process.

Actually, there's more going on here:

1. The initial `hello` from the client includes a random number, as well as a list of encryption methods and SSL/TLS versions that the client supports.

2. The response from the server specifies the encryption method and SSL/TLS version that are to be used (the server having selected from the lists offered in the first step), as well as the certificate.

3. The client verifies the signature on the certificate supplied by the server. It then encrypts the random number with the server's public key and sends this to the server. Optionally, the client may also include a copy of its own certificate, if client authentication is being used.

FIGURE 11-1

4. The server sends back a "finish" message (encrypted with the secret key). The client can now issue HTTP requests.

There's a lot of CPU processing involved here, and the fact that two round trips are needed pushes up latency — for communications across continents, where latency can be more than 100 milliseconds, you spend almost one-half a second simply on the SSL handshake.

Abbreviated Handshakes

To improve this situation, HTTPS allows an abbreviated handshake to be used in certain situations. This eliminates two of the messages (which happen to be the most CPU-intensive two), resulting in a two-step handshake. Figure 11-2 shows the abbreviated form.

To use abbreviated handshakes, one of two competing extensions must be used: session identifiers or session tickets.

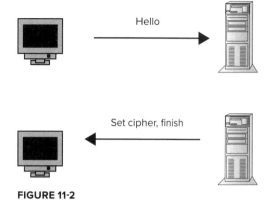

Session Identifiers

Session identifiers (session IDs) have been around since the inception of TLS and are the extension most widely supported by browsers. Under this scheme, the web server may optionally include a session ID in its response to the client's `hello` during step 2 of a full handshake. This ID corresponds to cached session data held locally by the server. The client caches this session ID and sends it in its initial `hello` at the beginning of the subsequent handshakes. If the server finds corresponding session data in its cache for this ID, it proceeds with the abbreviated handshake; otherwise, a full handshake is used.

FIGURE 11-2

In addition to cutting down the number of steps in the handshake, session caching also reduces the size of each step. For example, the server no longer needs to send a copy of its certificate because the client has already accepted it previously. Likewise, the computationally expensive steps of verifying the certificate and encrypting the random number using the server's key are avoided.

Session Caching in Nginx

In Nginx, the settings include options to set the caching type and session lifetime.

```
ssl_session_cache off | none | builtin | shared:name:size
```

`builtin` uses the cache built into OpenSSL, but this means that it isn't shared across worker processes. It is better to use Nginx's cache (`shared`), which is shared across workers. In this case, you must also give the cache a name and a size. The Nginx documentation suggests a 1 MB cache can hold approximately 4,000 sessions. Following is an example set for 5 MB:

```
ssl_session_cache shared:mycache:5M
```

The lifetime for session data in the cache is controlled by `ssl_session_timeout`, as shown here (for 1 hour):

```
ssl_session_timeout 1h
```

With both of these options, it is strongly recommended that you place them in the `http` block of the Nginx configuration file; although, they can also be used in `server` blocks.

Session Caching in Apache

When you use Apache's `mod_ssl`, SSL session caching is disabled by default — which is regrettable because many administrators aren't aware of its existence in order to enable it. The `SSLSessionCache` directive is used to control caching and supports three principle methods: none, disk-based (via a DBM hash file), or in-memory. Naturally the latter is the preferred option because it is implemented in shared memory. This makes the cache accessible globally, rather than being confined to a particular Apache pre-fork process.

For shared memory caching, the syntax is as follows:

```
SSLSessionCache shm:/etc/apache/ssl_cache(1024000)
```

The figure in parentheses is the wanted size of the cache (in bytes).

The lifetime for entries in the cache may also be set. The TLS specifications (RFC 5246) suggest caching for no longer than 24 hours, but values this high may be pointless anyway because most clients won't cache the session ID at their end for this long. (For example, the caching times for Microsoft Windows have varied considerably. Windows 2000 Service Pack 1 cached for 2 minutes, whereas Windows 2000 Service Pack 2 and Windows XP cached for 10 hours.) As shown in the following example, 1 hour (3,600 seconds) is a reasonable option but will naturally require a larger cache size than if you go for a lifetime of a few minutes.

```
SSLSessionCacheTimeout 3600
```

Session Caching in stunnel

stunnel has built-in support for session caching, and it is enabled by default with a session lifetime of 5 minutes. You can override this in the configuration file like so:

```
session = 1800 ## sets a session life of 30 minutes (1800 seconds)
```

The latest versions of stunnel also ships with support for a new feature, sessiond, a shared session cache. The IP:port of the sessiond server can now be specified in the stunnel configuration, as shown here:

```
sessiond = 192.168.10.50:54321
```

This is a big advance for stunnel and helps it to keep up with the shared session caching offered by Apache and Nginx.

Session Caching in stud

stud also offers session caching; although, the option is disabled by default. Use the -C <size> command-line switch to enable the cache and set its size. The cache is shared across all stud worker processes.

Session Tickets

Session identifiers have two fundamental weaknesses because of their reliance on server-side caching:

➤ Caches take up valuable memory, and you can rarely afford to cache sessions for long periods of time. (Instead, you must make a trade-off and lower the session lifetime to keep the cache size down.)

> ➤ Caching is always problematic in a load-balanced setup. For SSL session caching, if you don't use an SSL terminator, each back-end web server maintains its own private session cache. The only way to guarantee that a client will hit the same back-end server each time (and, hence, do an abbreviated handshake) would be to use a session affinity balancing technique.

Session tickets (which are an extension to TLS) solve these shortcomings by storing the session data on the client side. There's now no need for a server-side cache because the client caches instead.

In the first step of the SSL handshake (refer to Figure 11-1), the client advertises its support for session tickets, and in the second step, the server acknowledges support (assuming both client and server support session tickets, of course). In the final step of the full handshake, the server issues a session ticket to the client containing encrypted session information — essentially the same information that is stored server-side with session identifiers. The client stores this ticket locally and presents it to the server during subsequent SSL handshakes. If the server is happy with the integrity of the ticket, the abbreviated handshake is used.

> **NOTE** *Session tickets are still server-specific. A back-end web server will not accept a ticket previously issued by another back-end server in the pool. So, you still need to stick clients to the same back-end server.*

Unfortunately, support for session tickets (both in browsers and web servers) is still poor. So, at the moment, they aren't a viable solution for cutting SSL latency and CPU overheads.

Distributed Session Caching

What if you want to use SSL session caching (via session identifiers), but don't want the potential bottleneck of an SSL terminator sitting in front of your load balancer? You can use source IP-based load-balancing to ensure clients go to the same back-end server each time, but other balancing techniques (such as cookie insertion) can't be used because you're working with encrypted HTTP packets.

The ideal solution would be to use a global cache for the session data, and then, no matter which back-end server the client hit, the session data will be available. In addition, you won't be forced to use source IP-based load-balancing. Happily, both Apache and Nginx support distributed/shared/global (pick whichever name you like) session caching — that is, to some extent.

Nginx

Although Nginx doesn't natively support distributed SSL session caches, a third-party patch is available from `https://github.com/mpalmer/Nginx` to provide shared caching via `memcache`. Unlike modules, patches must be applied to the Nginx source code before compiling, and they are usually version-specific. So, there's no guarantee that this patch will work with the latest version of Nginx.

Also, calls to `memcache` are performed synchronously, which causes a significant performance penalty. There isn't much that can be done about this (it's a weakness in the design of OpenSSL), but it's certainly enough to question whether to implement distributed session caching in Nginx.

Apache and mod_gnutls

Shared session caching has been added to mod_ssl, but, as of this writing, is currently only available in the development branch. If you want to go down this route, you'll either need to build mod_ssl from source, or try an alpha release of Apache version 2.3.

However, the preferred route at the moment is to abandon mod_ssl in favor of mod_gnutls. This alternative SSL module has a number of nice features, including Server Name Indication and session tickets, and also supports distributed session caching via memcache. Because mod_gnutls will be new to many administrators, let's take a brief look at how to install and configure it under Linux.

The first thing to be aware of is that mod_gnutls doesn't use OpenSSL. It uses GnuTLS, so this must be installed first. (Look for libgnutls in your distribution's packages.) After downloading the latest mod_gnutls (from http://www.outoforder.cc/downloads/mod_gnutls/), you should compile it according to the installation file instructions. The resulting module can then be copied to the Apache modules directory, as shown here:

```
cp src/.libs/libmod_gnutls.so /usr/lib/apache2/modules/
```

Two key files have also been created, and these must be copied into Apache's configuration directory, as shown here:

```
cp data/dhfile /etc/apache2/conf/
cp data/rsafile /etc/apache2/conf/
```

Finally, you configure mod_gnutls in Apache, as shown here:

```
LoadModule gnutls_module modules/libmod_gnutls.so
AddType application/x-x509-ca-cert .crt
AddType application/x-pkcs7-crl    .crl
GnuTLSEnable on
GnuTLSCertificateFile /etc/apache2/ssl/mydomain.crt
GnuTLSKeyFile /etc/apache2/ssl/mydomain.key
```

As you can see, configuration of mod_gnutls is similar to mod_ssl, albeit with different directive names. To enable session caching in memcache, you use the following:

```
GnuTLSCache memcache 192.168.5.1:11211
GnuTLSCacheTimeout 3600
```

SSL TERMINATION AND ENDPOINTS

In Chapter 7, "Working with Web Servers," you learned about the use of Nginx and HAProxy as HTTP-aware load balancers. As noted in that discussion, encryption gets in the way because it stops your balancer from inspecting the content of packets, and then balancing based on that content. For example, the load balancer can't see any cookies used for session affinity. You can accept this loss of functionality and fall back on Layer 4 (that is, the transport layer of the OSI reference model) balancing — and then store session data in something like memcache. Or you can make the load balancer one endpoint of an SSL tunnel (the other end being the client, of course).

Figure 11-3 illustrates the topology for a load balancer behind an SSL terminator. In this figure, the SSL terminator is shown as a separate physical machine, but it's perfectly feasible for it to run on the same machine as the load balancer (resources permitting).

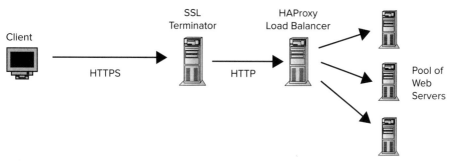

FIGURE 11-3

If you prefer to use HAProxy for load-balancing, you'll soon discover that HAProxy doesn't support SSL termination, and — judging from its author's comments — probably never will.

Willy Tarreau (the author of HAProxy) is very much of the opinion that SSL termination is suicide from a scalability point of view. He certainly has a point. Although it's easy to add cheap back-end servers, a load balancer is an expensive bottleneck, and using it as an SSL endpoint could have a big impact on load. On the other hand, Google's real-life observations (`http://www.imperialviolet .org/2010/06/25/overclocking-ssl.html`) suggest that SSL is no longer a performance killer.

Because HAProxy can't do SSL termination, you must put something in front of it that can. Your choices are web servers such as Nginx and Apache or tunnels/proxies such as `stunnel` and `stud`. Let's take a closer look at these alternatives.

SSL Termination with Nginx

It may seem odd using Nginx as an SSL terminator alongside HAProxy when the former already offers most of the features that you need. The main reasons for doing so are the more advanced load-balancing techniques offered by HAProxy, along with the more sophisticated server health checking. Still, if you need only moderately intelligent load-balancing, Nginx on its own is the preferred solution because it means one less potential point of failure.

In Nginx, you can easily set up SSL termination as an SSL-aware proxy and instruct it to forward the traffic on the backend(s) over HTTP (as opposed to HTTPS). Let's take a look at an example that shows how to enable SSL in Nginx.

The following configuration snippet balances any traffic that Nginx receives over three back-end servers:

```
upstream apachepool  {
   server 192.168.0.100 weight=5;
   server 192.168.0.101 weight=10;
```

```
    server 192.168.0.102 weight=10;
}

server {
  location / {
    proxy_pass  http://apachepool;
  }
}
```

After Nginx has been compiled with SSL support, enabling SSL is as simple as turning it on and setting the path to the certificate and key, as shown here:

```
upstream apachepool  {
  server 192.168.0.100 weight=5;
  server 192.168.0.101 weight=10;
  server 192.168.0.102 weight=10;
}

server {
  listen 443;
  listen 80;
  ssl on;
  ssl_certificate /etc/nginx/ssl/mysite.crt
  ssl_certificate_key /etc/nginx/ssl/mysite.key

  location / {
    proxy_pass  http://apachepool;
  }
}
```

The key here is the `proxy_pass` statement that tells Nginx to proxy to the back-end servers over HTTP. To simply balance the SSL traffic without terminating, you'd use `https://apachepool` (and wouldn't need the earlier SSL statements). For multiple SSL-enabled sites, you simply add additional `server` blocks for each IP address.

SSL Termination with Apache

You can achieve SSL termination with Apache by using its reverse proxy feature. After `mod_proxy` and `mod_ssl` are enabled, the configuration is as follows:

```
SSLEngine On
SSLCertificateFile /etc/apache2/ssl/server.crt
SSLCertificateKeyFile /etc/apache2/ssl/server.key

SSLProxyEngine on
RewriteEngine On
RewriteRule ^/(.*)$ http://localhost:8080/$1 [P]
```

The `[P]` flag to the rewrite rule causes it to proxy to the given URL. In this case, HAProxy listens on port 8080 of the same machine, but, if necessary, the Apache SSL terminator could be on its own box in front of HAProxy.

Despite that Apache offers relatively poor performance, it also offers plenty of scope for SSL performance tuning — in particular, caching.

SSL Termination with stunnel

Whereas Nginx and Apache are full-featured web servers that can be used to provide SSL termination, `stunnel` is specifically an SSL tunneling application. It's highly versatile and can be used to tunnel just about any protocol through a secure, encrypted channel.

Natively, `stunnel` doesn't provide the `X-Forwarded-For` header that is so useful when proxying web traffic. But a patch from the HAProxy website adds this. As such, you need to compile `stunnel` from source.

> **NOTE** *Grab the latest* `stunnel` *source from* `ftp://ftp.stunnel.org/stunnel/` *and the* `X-Forwarded-For` *patch from* `http://haproxy.1wt.eu/download/` `patches/` *for the corresponding version.*

Patching is simply a matter of running the following from *inside* the `stunnel` source directory:

```
patch -p1 < ../stunnel-4.44-xforwarded-for.diff
```

The standard configuration (`make, make install` route) can then be used. The final touches are to create a user for `stunnel` to run as and set appropriate ownerships, as shown here:

```
useradd stunnel
touch /var/log/stunnel.log
chown stunnel:stunnel /var/log/stunnel.log
chown -R stunnel:stunnel /var/run/stunnel
chown -R stunnel:stunnel /usr/local/etc/stunnel
```

Configuring `stunnel` (by default via `/usr/local/etc/stunnel/stunnel.conf`) is straightforward. After a few global options, you create a section for each IP address that you want to act as an SSL endpoint. The following configuration block lists the certificate to use, the `IP:port` to listen on, and the `IP:port` to proxy on to (HAProxy, in this case):

```
cert=/etc/stunnel/stunnel.pem
setuid=stunnel
setgid=stunnel
pid=/var/run/stunnel/stunnel.pid
output = /var/log/stunnel.log

[https]
  cert=/etc/stunnel/server.crt
  key=/etc/stunnel/server.key
  accept=1.2.3.4:443 ## Our external IP address
  connect=127.0.0.1:80  ## Assuming HAProxy listening on 80/TCP on local machine
  xforwardedfor=yes
```

Now, you simply run the stunnel binary. HTTPS traffic hitting port 443/TCP of 1.2.3.4 will be routed to HAProxy listening on port 80 — presumably you also want to listen for client traffic over HTTP and send it straight to HAProxy.

stunnel doesn't have much scope for performance tuning, but you can disable the Nagle algorithm (used for reducing the number of packets needing to be sent) in both directions by adding the following options to the global section:

```
socket=l:TCP_NODELAY=1
socket=r:TCP_NODELAY=1
```

In addition, it makes sense to compile stunnel without tcpwrappers support (./configure-disable-libwrap) because this feature is not needed in this situation.

SSL Termination with stud

stunnel uses a threaded model for handling client connections. Although this is certainly preferable to the one-client-per-process approach, it still isn't optimal. stud (https://github.com/bumptech/stud) is a newer SSL tunneling daemon built around an event-driven model, running one process per CPU core. As such, stud should scale better than stunnel. It even includes support for passing the origin IP address to HAProxy without the need for any third-party patches.

There's no configuration file for stud, so you just launch it with the appropriate command-line options, as shown here:

```
stud --ssl -b 127.0.0.1,80 -f 1.2.3.4,443 -n 4 --write-proxy
```

Here, --ssl enables SSL version 3. -b specifies the back-end server (HAProxy, in this case), and -f specifies the front-end (the public IP address on which to listen). Note that the IP address and port are separated by a comma. The -n option enables you to set the number of worker processes, which should be one per core. So, in this example, you would run on a quad core machine. Finally, the --write-proxy option sends a PROXY header (containing the client IP address) to the back-end server at the beginning of each connection. HAProxy uses this to pass the client's IP address to the back-end web servers.

Options also exist for logging and running as an unprivileged user or inside a chroot jail — see the man pages for full details.

SENDING INTERMEDIATE CERTIFICATES

It isn't just the number of round trips in the handshake that causes a slowdown when using SSL. The amount of data being transferred also has an impact. And it isn't just about bandwidth. The TCP congestion windows mean that, in the early stages of a connection, even small amounts of data can increase latency because of the need for the client to acknowledge (through ACK) the data.

Step 2 of the SSL handshake involves the server sending its certificate to the client. Many certificate issuers use intermediates (that is, the end certificate has been signed against an intermediate certificate, not a root certificate), though, so it may not just be the end certificate that is sent to the client — one or more intermediate certificates may need to be sent, too. Finding an issuer that doesn't use intermediates is probably overkill, but it does make sense to avoid issuers that require more than one intermediate.

What happens if you don't configure the intermediate certificate in the web server? This will cut the amount of data that is sent, and will actually probably still work in many browsers, but it also results in worse performance. In this situation, many browsers have the intelligence to attempt to fetch the intermediate certificate directly (from the issuer's website), but this causes another HTTPS request (and DNS look-up first), so performance is worse overall. It flies in the face of standards, too, and could easily break in future browsers.

DETERMINING KEY SIZES

Closely related to the issue of sending intermediate certificates is the issue of key sizes. These days, most issuers refuse to accept certificate signing requests (CSRs) generated using RSA keys smaller than 1,024 bits — it simply isn't deemed secure enough any longer. So, the usual choices are 2,048 or 4,096. It may seem obvious to go with 4,096 bits — the more security the better, right?

The answer is "yes" and "no." If you're in a line of business that demands the utmost security, a large key size is best. But for the average e-commerce site, 2,048 bits is more than adequate. Current guidelines suggest that computational power won't have advanced enough to make cracking 2,048-bit keys feasible until at least the year 2030. Because most web masters purchase their SSL certificates for 1 or 2 years, this shouldn't be a concern when purchasing a certificate at the moment.

So, the extra security offered by 4,096-bit keys is overkill in most situations. But what a 4,096-bit key does do is increase the size of the SSL certificate sent is step 2 of the SSL handshake, and the keys exchanged in step 3.

Larger keys also mean more work when encrypting and decrypting data (both client- and server-side). Operations using a 4,096-bit key are approximately five times slower than with a 2,048-bit key. And the performance hit isn't just during the handshake. It happens for every HTTPS packet. This may not have much effect client-side, but for a server handling hundreds of SSL requests per second, it can make a huge difference in performance. As you'll see next, the choice of a cipher suite can also have a significant impact on performance.

SELECTING CIPHER SUITES

Unless you're particularly security conscious, the cipher suite's listing of encryption methods supported by a web server may be unfamiliar territory. Cipher suites are about more than just encryption of the data stream. Recall that keys must be exchanged, message digests created, and random (well, pseudo-random) numbers generated during the handshake. A cipher suite defines the algorithms used for all these.

In Apache, `SSLCipherSuite` is used to list (in order of preference) the cipher suites that the web server is willing to speak. When a client connects and advertises its list of support suites, the web server picks the best (highest ranking) match from its list.

Things quickly become complicated because of the sheer number of possible combinations of algorithms. Some combinations are considered insecure, some are only available if OpenSSL has been compiled with particular options, and others are disabled by default because of legal restrictions on strong encryption. To complicate matters further, SSL even allows for renegotiation where initial communications are established via one cipher suite, which is then used to upgrade to a stronger method.

The default cipher string in Apache version 2.2 looks like this:

```
SSLCipherSuite ALL:!ADH:RC4+RSA:+HIGH:+MEDIUM:+LOW:+SSLv2:+EXP
```

In addition to allowing you to explicitly set the algorithms to use, numerous aliases are supported to simplify the string. The example given here starts by enabling all algorithms (ALL), and then excludes Diffie-Helman key exchanges (ADH). Next, the example gives preference to RC4 cipher encoding with RSA authentication and key exchange. What follows are the HIGH, MEDIUM, and LOW aliases, support for SSL version 2, and, finally, all export ciphers (EXP).

In practice, this isn't a great default. SSL version 2 has security flaws, and low-strength ciphers give a false sense of security. The default cipher string on Debian's Apache2 package is as follows:

```
SSLCipherSuite HIGH:MEDIUM:!ADH
```

In other words, it allows any high- or medium-strength cipher, but never allows ADH.

What does this all have to do with performance? As might be expected, there is a significant difference in performance between algorithms.

When using the HIGH alias, the first algorithm in the list is currently AES-256, which is approximately three times slower than RC4. Although AES-256 is certainly more secure, RC4 is still considered "good enough" if implemented correctly. So, for the average e-commerce site, RC4 is still a perfectly acceptable option. Google even uses RC4 plus SHA1 for SSL, and endorsements don't come much bigger than that.

A suitable cipher string to make this the default would be as follows:

```
SSLCipherSuite RC4-SHA:ALL:!ADH:!EXP:!LOW:!MD5:!SSLV2:!NULL
```

> **NOTE** *For security, various weak methods have been explicitly disabled.*

The final thing to do is force your first choice on the client, rather than letting the client choose its preferred method:

```
SSLHonorCipherOrder on
```

With this directive enabled, the server's preferences are given priority over the client's.

Having looked in detail at configuration options that can affect performance, let's take a brief look at hardware considerations

INVESTING IN HARDWARE ACCELERATION

Dedicated SSL-processing hardware is available, usually in the form of a PCI card. However, because of the price, it's often just as economical to invest in more CPU power.

In recent years, both Intel and AMD have started producing chips that support Advanced Encryption Standard (AES) instructions (AES-NI), with the aim to make AES encryption/decryption significantly faster. As of this writing, this feature is limited to the AMD Bulldozer, as well as the Intel Westmere and Sandy Bridge processors. It should be stressed that only some members of these families support AES-NI.

Of course, to use these new AES instructions, software must be aware of their existence. The latest versions of OpenSSL support AES-NI, and patches are available for some earlier versions.

If you have a CPU that supports AES-NI, RC4-SHA may not be the fastest option after all. AES-256 is probably still overkill, though, and a good trade-off is to use AES-128, giving the benefit of AES-NI without the expense of 256-bit keys.

```
SSLCipherSuite AES-128:RC4-SHA:ALL:!ADH:!EXP:!LOW:!MD5:!SSLV2:!NULL
```

THE FUTURE OF SSL

A number of SSL-related technologies and extensions are currently in the development pipeline. Some have been around for a few years now and are gradually gaining popularity. Others are still experimental but will likely become important within the new few years.

Part of the reason for slow adoption of these extensions is that many require changes in both the client and server. So, although it's easy to hack your web server to support the latest extension, it's not much use if you need to wait a few years for web browsers to start implementing the extensions.

The following technologies are still new enough not to have widespread support yet, but are also mature enough for you to be confident that they aren't just a flash in the pan. In years to come, they will likely become important parts of SSL setups, so it's certainly worth becoming acquainted with them now.

OCSP Stapling

When a browser connects to a website over SSL, there is usually a need to check that the certificate has not been revoked. The standard way to do this is via the Online Certificate Status Protocol (OCSP), in which the client issues an OCSP request to the certificate issuers. Of course, this necessitates that the client perform an additional DNS lookup and send a query to the issuer, so performance suffers.

With OCSP stapling, the web server provides an OCSP response guaranteeing the validity of the certificate. The response is included with the certificate in step 2 of the SSL handshake. Although it may seem insecure allowing the server to guarantee its own certificate, the OCSP response is signed by the issuer, offering the assurance that it has not been tampered with.

There are advantages and disadvantages to OCSP stapling. It saves the client the expense to send an additional query to the issuer (which would probably involve a DNS look-up, too). It also improves client privacy — with the traditional method, the issuer could learn the client's browsing habits by tracking for which certificates a status request is being made.

The downside of stapling is that it increases the amount of data sent during the SSL handshake. You've already learned about certificate sizes and intermediate certificates, and how they affect the TCP congestion window. The presence of an OCSP response is likely to exacerbate this. It's worth noting, too, that stapling has no benefit server-side. It's only a performance boost for the client.

As of this writing, Apache version 2.3 supports stapling, but Nginx does not.

False Start

Developed by Google for its Chrome browser, False Start is a client-side modification that speeds up the SSL handshake.

Recall the final two steps of the full SSL handshake — the client sends its key along with a finish message (step 3), and then waits for the server to acknowledge this with its own "finish" message (step 4). Only then does the client send its HTTP request.

False Start recognizes that it is largely unnecessary for the client to wait for the server's "finish" message before sending a request. Instead, the client can send a request after step 3 — in this way, you eliminate the latency of one trip.

According to Google's figures (`http://blog.chromium.org/2011/05/ssl-falsestart-performance-results.html`), less than one-half a percent of web servers have trouble handling False Start, and Google maintains a blacklist of affected sites. The blacklist is publically available and used by Firefox's implementation of False Start (although it is disabled by default).

SUMMARY

SSL inevitably has a performance impact on both client and server. There is a lot that can be done to improve performance, however, and it doesn't need to be a serious drain on resources.

On multiserver setups, using an SSL endpoint in front of the load balancer is popular for two reasons:

➤ It lets the load balancer to work with unencrypted HTTP traffic, allowing for balancing based on packet contents.

➤ It provides the most efficient option for caching SSL sessions.

The downside to using an endpoint is that it can easily become a bottleneck. Think carefully before introducing what could become a serious barrier to scalability.

The alternative is to allow each back-end server to handle SSL, but this makes caching of sessions more tricky. Apache, Nginx, and `stunnel` support distributed caching via `memcache`, but this can reduce performance, too, because of the nonasynchronous nature of the `memcache` `GETs`/`SETs`.

Some CPUs support AES-NI instructions, which provide a significant boost for AES encryption. If you use such CPUs, consider AES-128 over AES-256 — it's secure enough and a lot faster. For CPUs that don't support AES-NI, RC4 is a lot faster than AES.

In Chapter 12, you learn about how to optimize PHP to enhance performance.

12

Optimizing PHP

WHAT'S IN THIS CHAPTER?

➤ Using opcode caching to speed up execution

➤ Handling PHP sessions

➤ Profiling bottlenecks with xhprof

➤ Optimizing your PHP code

With so many different programming languages and development frameworks in use on the modern web, it would be impossible to even attempt to do them justice trying to completely cover them in a single book. Since PHP has easily become the most popular web scripting language in UNIX/Linux environments, it's worth delving a bit deeper into how the language affects performance.

The downside to the popularity of back-end scripting is, of course, higher performance over-heads. Although PHP scripts are typically fairly lightweight, they are still a lot slower to serve up than static HTML documents. In the case of heavier scripts, there can be a significant performance hit — both for the client (in the form of higher latency in requests), and for the server (in the form of higher resource usage, and a lower limit on the number of concurrent requests). In this chapter, you learn about a variety of ways in which PHP performance can be improved, both in how the operating system executes it, and in the language itself.

This chapter starts with a look at PHP modules and extensions — how too many extensions can adversely affect performance, as well as situations in which it can be worth writing your own. After that, you learn about opcode caching, a powerful technique that can overcome many of the limitations of an interpreted language. You also learn about why Alternative PHP Cache (APC) is rapidly becoming the standard in this field.

Sessions are widely used in PHP, but introduce their own performance considerations — particularly in load-balanced environments, where a means to share session data across back-end servers is sometimes needed. In this chapter, you discover various solutions to these problems, including the use of `memcache` to store session data.

The remainder of the chapter examines considerations of the language itself (regular expressions, loops, including files, and so on), and how to profile your code to discover where the bottlenecks are occurring.

EXTENSIONS AND COMPILING

With many applications, there is significant scope for optimization at the installation stage when decisions are made on which modules to compile in or enable. PHP is no different, and in this section, you learn how PHP handles extensions, and the effect that they can have on performance.

Removing Unneeded Extensions

The PHP source code comes bundled with more than 80 extensions that provide additional functionality, ranging from image manipulation to XML parsing to database interaction. When compiling PHP, you have the option of building extensions statically into the PHP binary, or as shared modules that can be loaded at run time.

From a performance point of view, the primary advantage of using shared extensions is that only one instance of the module must be loaded into memory, and can be shared across multiple PHP instances. This can cut memory usage substantially. Aside from that, shared extensions are also more convenient, because they can easily be loaded or unloaded via `php.ini`. Static extensions must be built into PHP at compile time, making it more awkward to change which extensions are enabled.

The one disadvantage to compiling in extensions is that there is a little extra overhead involved in dynamically loading shared extensions. Generally, though, the advantages of shared extensions (on memory usage) far outweigh this.

People often give the vague reason that removing unrequired extensions is to reduce bloat. But what precisely does this mean? In Chapter 7, "Working with Web Servers," you learned about Apache's prefork Multi-Process Module (MPM) and how the worker MPM isn't suitable for use with PHP. You also learned how the memory footprint of each Apache thread has a direct influence on the maximum concurrency you can support. Thus, your goal is to keep the Resident Set Size (RSS) usage as low as possible for each Apache thread.

Running the PHP Apache module has a significant impact on memory usage. Although each thread in a PHP-free Apache setup may have a typical RSS of 4 MB or 5 MB, enabling `libphp5.so` with most of the bundled extensions can easily shoot this up to more than 50 MB. In some ways, this is a worst-case scenario, but there are plenty of system administrators who use `apt-get` or `yum install` for every available PHP package, simply to avoid the inconvenience of PHP moaning at a later date that a particular extension isn't installed. So, there's potentially a lot to be gained from keeping PHP lean, and you should disable any modules that you don't currently need.

Table 12-1 shows the size of some of the most common modules in a PHP version 5.3 installation.

TABLE 12-1: PHP Module Sizes

EXTENSION	SIZE (KB)
apc.so	655
curl.so	62
ffmpeg.so	35
gd.so	94
imagick.so	328
imap.so	86
mysqli.so	107
mysql.so	42
sasl.so	15
tidy.so	42

As you can see, there's quite a difference in sizes, with the heaviest taking up more than one-half a megabyte. This isn't the full story, though, because these modules are invariably linked to other libraries. As an example, consider `curl`:

```
$ ldd curl.so
        linux-gate.so.1 =>  (0xffffe000)
        libcurl.so.4 => /usr/lib/libcurl.so.4 (0xb7f75000)
        libc.so.6 => /lib/i686/cmov/libc.so.6 (0xb7e2f000)
        libidn.so.11 => /usr/lib/libidn.so.11 (0xb7dfd000)
        libssh2.so.1 => /usr/lib/libssh2.so.1 (0xb7ddc000)
        liblber-2.4.so.2 => /usr/lib/liblber-2.4.so.2 (0xb7dd0000)
        libldap_r-2.4.so.2 => /usr/lib/libldap_r-2.4.so.2 (0xb7d8b000)
        librt.so.1 => /lib/i686/cmov/librt.so.1 (0xb7d82000)
        libgssapi_krb5.so.2 => /usr/lib/libgssapi_krb5.so.2 (0xb7d52000)
        libssl.so.0.9.8 => /usr/lib/i686/cmov/libssl.so.0.9.8 (0xb7d08000)
        libcrypto.so.0.9.8 => /usr/lib/i686/cmov/libcrypto.so.0.9.8 (0xb7bb0000)
        libz.so.1 -> /usr/lib/libz.so.1 (0xb7b9c000)
        /lib/ld-linux.so.2 (0x80000000)
        libgcrypt.so.11 => /usr/lib/libgcrypt.so.11 (0xb7b28000)
        libresolv.so.2 => /lib/i686/cmov/libresolv.so.2 (0xb7b13000)
        libsasl2.so.2 => /usr/lib/libsasl2.so.2 (0xb7afc000)
        libgnutls.so.26 => /usr/lib/libgnutls.so.26 (0xb7a64000)
        libpthread.so.0 => /lib/i686/cmov/libpthread.so.0 (0xb7a4b000)
        libkrb5.so.3 => /usr/lib/libkrb5.so.3 (0xb7999000)
        libk5crypto.so.3 => /usr/lib/libk5crypto.so.3 (0xb7975000)
        libcom_err.so.2 => /lib/libcom_err.so.2 (0xb7972000)
        libkrb5support.so.0 => /usr/lib/libkrb5support.so.0 (0xb796b000)
        libdl.so.2 => /lib/i686/cmov/libdl.so.2 (0xb7967000)
        libkeyutils.so.1 => /lib/libkeyutils.so.1 (0xb7964000)
        libgpg-error.so.0 => /usr/lib/libgpg-error.so.0 (0xb795f000)
        libtasn1.so.3 => /usr/lib/libtasn1.so.3 (0xb794f000)
```

On Linux, the `ldd` command displays a list of shared libraries linked in to a binary. So, in addition to the memory footprint of `curl.so`, there is the footprint of each of these libraries to consider. (For example, `libcurl.so.4` is 359 KB on this particular machine.)

Things aren't as simple as just adding up the size of each of these libraries, however. The whole point of a shared library is that only one instance must be loaded into memory because it can be shared across multiple processes. So, in this example, the additional footprint of `curl.so` might be zero if each of these shared libraries has already been loaded into memory by another process (be it another PHP process, or a completely unrelated application).

Common libraries such as `libcrypto` and `libssl` will almost certainly already be in memory, whereas more esoteric ones such as `libXdmcp.so` (which provides interaction with the X Display Manager and is linked in to `gd.so` on Linux) probably won't be. All this means that determining the memory footprint of a particular PHP extension is no simple matter. Actually, it's somewhat ambiguous as to how you even define the memory footprint.

Unless you are overly obsessive about memory usage, avoid the headache of attempting to calculate a module's memory usage, and go down the simple route of just disabling modules that you don't need.

One source of frustration is that some extensions may be needed only occasionally, and, yet, by enabling them, they will be running for every Apache thread. A classic example would be a CAPTCHA image on a contact form. You might not need `gd.so` at all on the rest of the site, yet you need to enable it so that you can generate some unreadable text on a patterned background for a contact form.

PHP used to allow you to load extensions at run time via the `dl()` function. However, for stability reasons, as of PHP version 5.3, this has been disabled in the Common Gateway Interface (CGI) and Apache scheduling application programming interfaces (SAPIs). (It will still work via the command-line client.) Hopefully, this feature will return in the future.

If you use a version of PHP supplied with your distribution, chances are that, although most of the extensions have been compiled as shared modules, some have not. Thus, for full control, it is necessary to compile PHP from source.

Writing Your Own PHP Extensions

PHP extensions have all the usual benefits of being written in a compiled language (C) — they are faster to execute and have a lower memory footprint; and there is a much lower delay before they begin executing. That's why extra features like GD or MySQL support are built as extensions rather than PHP libraries.

Given the advantage of an extension over a script, there's something to be said for recoding all or parts of your PHP application as a PHP extension in C. At first, this seems to defeat the whole point of using a high-level language like PHP (flexibility, ease of use, and rapid development). Why not just write the application completely in C, and run it as a CGI, without the need for PHP?

In practice, a happy ground exists somewhere in the middle. Certain intensive functions could be moved into an extension (because these will have the greatest potential for gain), keeping the majority of the application as PHP code.

This argument about the performance of compiled versus interpreted languages isn't entirely accurate, though. As you'll see later in this chapter, a popular method to boost the performance of PHP scripts is through an opcode cache — basically, it stores the PHP script in a semi-compiled form, reducing the performance hit of interpreting the script. Because of this, the performance of PHP scripts can be much closer to that of a compiled language such as C, and the benefits of moving code into a PHP extension aren't so clear-cut. Actually, it may not prove to be worth your time and money to do this, especially because the gains may be quite modest.

Custom PHP extensions are by no means pointless, but they are definitely something to consider only after you have exhausted the possibilities described in this chapter.

Compiling

Aside from giving you complete control over installed modules, compiling PHP from the source also enables you to implement the usual compile-time performance options (such as CPU-specific features and higher levels of optimization). For example, with GCC under Linux, the -O3 switch is commonly used to produce a higher level of optimization.

A particularly useful configuration flag is `--disable-all`, which disables the extensions that are usually enabled by default. You can selectively re-enable them later in the list of `./configure` options. Remember that, for Apache, you must compile `--with-apxs`, whereas for FastCGI (for example, when using PHP with Nginx) you must build in CGI support (enabled by default).

Following are two particularly useful options:

➤ `--enable-inline-optimiziation` — This causes the C compiler (for example, GCC under Linux) to use function inlining when compiling the PHP binary. Note that this applies only to PHP — it emphatically does not cause function inlining to be used when your PHP scripts are parsed and compiled.

➤ `--disable-debug` — This causes PHP to be built without debugging symbols. Actually, the default these days is not to compile in debugging symbols anyway (rather, you must explicitly enable them using `--enable-debug`), so this option is redundant.

INLINING

Inlining, a technique familiar to C programmers, is a compile-time strategy that involves replacing function calls with the body of the function. Consider the following code:

```
for ($x=0; $x<=100; $x++) {
    $sqr = getsquare($x);
}

function getsquare($x) {
    return ($x * $x);
}
```

continues

continued

Each time `getsquare` is called, there is overhead involved. Variables are pushed and popped from the stack, execution jumps to a different region of memory, the function's return value is passed back to the caller via the stack, and so on. With inlining, the compiler removes this overhead by rewriting the code to something like this:

```
for ($x=0; $x<=100; $x++) {
    $sqr = ($x * $x);
}
```

In this example, inlining actually reduces the size of the code, but in most situations, there will be an increase — imagine if the `getsquare` function was much larger and called from dozens of different points in the code.

So, the downside is extra work for the compiler and an increase in the code size. The benefit is faster execution of the resulting code.

COMPILER FLAGS

As with any other C application, compiler flags (`CFLAGS`) can often be used to improve performance. On x86 UNIX/Linux, setting the `-prefer-non-pic` flag causes non-position-independent code to be built, which produces a noticeable increase in performance. Position-independent code (PIC) refers to code that can be executed, regardless of its absolute address in memory. It is commonly used for shared libraries, but is slower than non-PIC code. Similarly, the `-march` flag can be used to specify your CPU architecture, allowing additional processor-specific optimizations to take place.

As usual, it's also standard to compile with the `-O3` level of optimization, which can potentially improve performance. The overall build process on Linux may look something like this:

```
$ export CFLAGS="-march=opteron -prefer-non-pic -O3"
$ ./configure --enable-inline-optimization
$ make
$ sudo make install
$ sudo strip /usr/lib/apache2/modules/libphp5.so
```

The final step strips any additional debugging symbols from `libphp5.so`, resulting in a smaller binary. (Just don't hope to diagnose any crashes with `gdb`.)

By now, you should have a good idea of how best to install and configure PHP on your system. In the next section, you discover perhaps the single most effective means of boosting PHP performance — opcode caching.

OPCODE CACHING

Scripted languages such as PHP, Python, and Perl are easy to deploy. You simply write and run. This is in contrast to languages like C, where you must go through the additional step of compiling your code before you can run it. This convenience comes at a cost, though, and interpreted languages are never as fast as compiled ones.

In PHP, execution happens in two steps:

1. The lexical parser compiles the script into opcode (sometimes also referred to as *bytecode*).

2. The Zend engine at the heart of PHP executes the opcode.

This happens every time the script is executed. Recompiling code like this is rather wasteful of resources, and one of the most popular and efficient methods to improve PHP performance is through the use of opcode caches.

In addition to caching the compiled opcode for future use, these caches often also perform optimization of the PHP code prior to compiling. Although, on its own, optimization would hurt performance overall (what you gain through optimized code, you lose in the overhead involved in performing the optimization), when coupled with opcode caching, this provides an additional performance boost.

Variations of Opcode Caches

Unfortunately, opcode caches have historically been the subject of much bigotry, and the Internet is full of users who insist that cache X is several orders of magnitude better than cache Y. Often, these claims are backed up by half-baked statistics, and it doesn't take long to find an alternative benchmark that shows cache Y is, actually, several orders of magnitude better than cache X. This is one area in which benchmarks are even less meaningful than normal.

The opcode landscape has changed quite a bit in the last few years, though. So, rather than being too preoccupied with benchmarks, it may be better to think in terms of which opcode caches are actually still maintained.

For a long time, the big three were XCache (written by the author of lighttpd), Turck MMCache, and eAccelerator (itself a fork of MMCache). eAccelerator has been a personal favorite of the author, but neither it nor MMCache are maintained any longer. In addition, there is a new rival in town in the shape of Alternative PHP Cache (APC). Although APC is not quite as fast as the competition (yet), it has the weight of the PHP team behind it and is set to become the primary opcode cache for PHP. Thus, this is the recommended cache,, so let's take a closer look at it.

Getting to Know APC

In the near future, APC will be bundled with PHP as an extension. But until that time, the standard way to install it is via PECL (`pecl install apc`). Alternatively, your distribution may provide a `php-pecl` package, but, as previously noted, it's much better to compile PHP from source.

Depending on how you install, entries may be added to `php.ini` to load and configure APC, or a separate configuration file may be created (most likely under `/etc/php5/conf.d/`). Or you may need to do it yourself.

A minimum configuration such as the following would simply load the APC extension:

```
extension=apc.so
```

However, you will almost certainly want to set some of the many options available.

Memory Management

The first decision is whether to use shared memory (`shm`) or mapped memory (`mmap`), and likely this decision has already been made for you. If PECL has compiled APC with `--enable-mmap`, your system supports `mmap`, and this is the method that will be used. If not, the older `shm` method will be used. There isn't a huge difference in performance between the two. `shm` is more portable, but `mmap` is slightly more efficient with memory management.

Regardless of the memory method used, `apc.shm_size` controls the size of the each memory segment, whereas `apc.shm_segments` controls the number of segments. With `mmap` (the default under Linux), `apc.shm_segments` has no effect. The default cache size is 32 MB, which is a reasonable default for the moment. If you're using `shm`, larger values may require first raising the shared memory size, as shown here:

```
# cat /proc/sys/kernel/shmmax
33554432    ## 32 MB
# sysctl -w kernel.shmmax=67108864
```

Optimization

As previously mentioned, some opcodes also support optimization of the code prior to compiling and caching. APC is one of these, but optimization is still marked as "experimental" and may not produce significant speed increases. This option was removed in APC version 3 but may return in the future.

Time-To-Live (TTL)

Left to its own accord, APC will happily continue to add entries to the cache until it becomes full. At that point, no new entries will be added, but potentially stale content will remain. Like all good caches of a finite size, APC utilizes a Time-To-Live (TTL) to set the maximum lifetime for cache entries. When this limit is reached, expired entries will be purged from the cache if space is needed for new entries. This option is controlled by `apc.ttl` and defaults to zero. If a TTL of zero is set, the whole cache will be purged if it becomes full.

An hour or two is a reasonable default for the TTL, but a lot depends on available system memory and the number of scripts that may potentially be cached. For example, with a large number of scripts, it may be impractical to set aside enough memory to cache them all, and a lower TTL may be needed to keep the cache size down. In most cases, though, it's better to increase the size of the cache to hold as much as is reasonably possible.

The other issue with cache TTL is that entries can become stale — even if your script is edited, PHP will still continue to use the cached version. APC gets around this by issuing a `stat()` on the file and checking the `mtime` each time it is about to request the compiled version from the cache. If the file on the filesystem is more recent than the timestamp on the compiled version, the cache entry is expired.

The first problem here is that the `mtime` isn't always a reliable indication that the file has changed. Tools such as `rsync` and `svn` may modify a file's `mtime`, even if the content hasn't changed. Thus, you end up purging entries from the cache when it was unnecessary.

APC can be configured to also check a file's `ctime`, as shown here:

```
apc.stat =1  ## standard mtime check
apc.stat_ctime = 1 ## also check ctime
```

This isn't ideal either, but for a different reason. Running `stat()` on every PHP script prior to executing is a drag on disk performance, especially when the vast majority of the time, the script won't have been changed. You can set both of these `stat` settings to zero to disable `stat()` checks, but if you subsequently alter a file, you must clear the entire cache (at present there's no way to delete a single entry) — either by executing `apc_clear_cache` or restarting Apache. Despite this, disabling `stat()` is still definitely the preferred option on production servers.

Locking

APC supports the following four locking methods:

➤ **File locks** — These are the most stable but offer poor performance.

➤ **IPC semaphores** — These are faster than file locks and well supported.

➤ **Pthread mutex** — These are only available in Linux version 2.6 onward but offer a much greater performance gain.

➤ **Spin locks** — These offer the best performance of all but are still considered experimental.

If you feel brave, spin locks can be enabled when configuring APC with `--enable-apc-spinlocks`. In most cases, pthread mutexes are best, though, which are the default when building APC through PECL on Linux version 2.6.

One situation in which locking comes into play (and in which lock performance can have a big impact) is when there is a flood of requests for an uncached resource — perhaps because the server has just come online, or the resource has been modified and purged from the cache. Either way, you encounter a situation in which multiple PHP processes simultaneously compile the script and then attempt to insert it into the cache — a process known as *slamming*.

Earlier versions of APC dealt with slamming via the `apc.slam_defense` setting. This value told PHP not to bother caching a script that it had just compiled (but was not in the cache) a certain percentage of the time. The rationale here was that it was likely that other PHP processes could also be attempting to insert the opcode into the cache. By setting a value of, say, 80 percent, only one in five processes would attempt to insert into the cache, reducing the severity of the slamming.

Of course, if the server isn't busy, the likelihood of two processes compiling the same script at the same time is low, and this defense simply delays the caching, so it isn't an ideal solution. Instead, the preferred solution now is by enabling `apc.write_lock`. This causes the first PHP process to handle an uncached script to set a lock, preventing other processes from caching it.

Sample apc.ini

Now that you are familiar with the most important runtime configuration options for APC, let's look at a configuration file that should serve as a good starting point in the majority of cases:

```
extension=apc.so
apc.enabled = 1
apc.stat = 0
apc.stat_ctime = 0
apc.slam_defense = 0
apc.write_lock = 1
apc.ttl = 7200
apc.optimization = 0
```

APC Caching Strategies

Memory is always a scarce resource, and, invariably, you discover that there isn't enough room to cache as much as you would like. You've already learned about the TTL setting (which is used to control the size of the cache by automatically expiring items), but there are other considerations, too.

As shown in Figure 12-1, fragmentation occurs when items are removed from the middle of the cache, leaving a gap that is either not big enough to hold another item, or that holds an item but leaves a small gap.

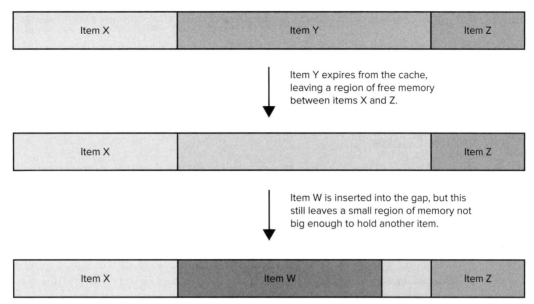

FIGURE 12-1

The more frequently you expire items from the cache (that is, the lower the TTL), the more likely fragmentation is to occur.

The solution to this problem is simply to increase the size of the cache, such that even when fragmentation does occur, there is still plenty of room. It may not be an elegant solution, but it is the only one that you have.

With the knowledge that the cache is only a finite size, it might be worth thinking about *what* you cache. APC caches everything by default, but it may be worth concentrating on only the most frequently used code. After all, there is little to be gained from caching an admin-only script that may be run only once or twice a day.

APC has two settings that provide control over exactly what is cached:

➤ `apc.cache_by_default` — This controls whether to cache by default.

➤ `apc.filters` — This lets you supply a comma-separated list of regexes to control what is cached and what isn't.

If `cached_by_default` is set to zero, the regexes in `apc.filters` can be prepended with a +, indicating that any file matching the pattern should be cached. Conversely, if `cache_by_default` is set to one, the regexes can be prepended with a -, telling APC not to cache any matches.

So, if you want to cache everything except the contents of the `/admin` directory and a particularly large script, you could use the following:

```
apc.cache_by_default = 1
apc.filters = "-/var/www/html/largescript.php, -/var/www/html/admin/.*"
```

Or if you want to cache only the contents of a particular directory, you could use the following:

```
apc.cache_by_default = 0
apc.filters = "+/var/www/html/some_dir/.*"
```

Remember, though, that the filter will match the exact filename passed to include or require, which may be a relative path.

Monitoring the Cache

APC comes bundled with a PHP script, apc.php, which provides a web interface for monitoring and administration of the cache. If you have the PHP GD module enabled, you'll also get some nice pie charts showing cache usage and the hit-to-miss ratio.

The control panel also provides a complete list of every script in the cache, along with its size, the number of hits it has received, and the access and creation times. This information can be invaluable when deciding whether to exclude certain files or directories from the cache to save space.

An option to clear the cache is also provided, but this should be used as a last resort because there will be a significant spike in CPU usage.

Using APC as a Generic Cache

APC can also be used as a generic in-memory cache, much like memcache. Using APC in this way has the benefit of no latency being incurred when connecting to memcache (which may be running on a different machine) and simplified server administration because there is one less service to manage.

The APC documentation (http://www.php.net/manual/en/book.apc.php) lists several functions that you can use in your PHP code to set and fetch arbitrary data from APC. Naturally, this data will persist across requests, which can make it a great way to avoid repeated database calls. The following code writes a variable called foo (with a value of bar) to the cache and sets the TTL to 1 hour (3,600 seconds):

```
apc_add("foo", "bar", 3600);
```

You can later retrieve the value of foo like so:

```
$foo = apc_fetch("foo");
print $foo;
```

Similar functions exist for deleting stored data, checking if a key exists, and incrementing/decrementing a value.

Does this mean that memcache is redundant? Certainly, APC is faster than memcache, but it cannot be used in a distributed environment like memcache and can't be used for permanent storage (like membase). Remember that, in an Apache setup with libphp, restarting Apache will cause the cache to be purged, so the data in APC can be more volatile than memcache. Thus, memcache certainly isn't redundant, but one option would be to use a two-tier caching system with APC as a smaller, local cache, which is certainly worth exploring.

Warming the Cache

Whether you choose to use APC as an opcode cache, or as a generic memory cache (or both), it can be useful to preload data into the cache to avoid the heavy CPU usage incurred by a high ratio of cache misses. On a busy site, bringing a server back into the pool with an empty cache can often bring it to its knees.

If you're using HAProxy, ramping can be used to gradually bring the server back into the pool, slowly increasing the weight so that it is not swamped with connections until the cache has had a chance to warm up. Alternatively, APC has a couple of tricks of its own.

You can use `apc_compile_file()` to ask APC to parse and compile a file and store the opcode in the cache. In this way, you could write a priming script that calls `apc_compile_file()` for your most accessed PHP scripts. By running the script before you bring the server back into the pool, you can be confident that your cache is suitably primed. As an alternative, you could write a simple `wget` or `curl` script to request certain pages over HTTP, thus also priming the cache.

APC also includes functions that allow you to read and write the entire contents of the cache, making it possible to dump the cache to disk and then subsequently re-importing it. This might be useful if you must restart Apache but don't want to lose the contents of the cache. Following is an example:

```
apc_bin_dumpfile(null, null,"/tmp/apcdump.data");
```

The first two arguments to `apc_bin_dumpfile` are an array of files and user variables to dump. (You can leave these blank to dump all of them.) The final argument is the filename to write to.

Importing this binary data back in is as simple as the following:

```
apc_bin_loadfile("/tmp/apcdump.data");
```

You could even incorporate this call into the Apache `init` script so that issuing an Apache restart will cause APC to dump to disk before then importing after Apache has restarted.

Using APC with FastCGI

So far, this discussion has assumed that PHP is being run on top of Apache via `mod_php` (`libphp5`), but this is far from the most optimal method for performance. Rather, many administrators choose to run a lightweight web server such as Nginx with PHP requests being passed to a pool of FastCGI daemons.

Over the years, PHP has supported several methods of running as a CGI, including `fcgi` and FastCGI, and these methods have not worked well with APC. Rather than sharing the cache memory between all processes, each PHP process would have its own private cache. With each process being long-lived, there is still ample opportunity for caching, but if new processes are spawned (to cope with an increase in load), they will start with an empty cache. The whole arrangement isn't memory-efficient anyway.

The good news is that the default FastCGI implementation in PHP is now PHP-FPM (FastCGI Process Manager) which *does* allow the APC cache to be shared across all PHP processes.

Of course, one fundamental restriction on PHP's efficiency is because it is an interpreted language. However, in the next section, you learn how work by Facebook and others has brought the possibility of compiling PHP one step closer.

COMPILING PHP

Given that interpreted languages are inherently slower than compiled ones, the thought of compiling PHP into an executable format is a tempting one. To some extent, this is what opcode caching does — it stores your PHP code after it has been compiled into bytecode and allows this to be reused. Bytecode still isn't as fast as native machine code, though (because it must still be interpreted). A true compiled program would offer significant advantages.

Despite the potential gains, PHP compilation isn't an area that has gained widespread interest. Over the years, there have been numerous attempts to create a PHP compiler, and although some have been reasonably successful, none have gone on to widespread usage.

phc

One of the most interesting entries into this compiler arena was phc, a well thought-out compiler, which sadly appears to have fizzled out. A lot of work went into making phc compatible with dynamic constructs (such as eval() statements, variables with dynamic names, and so on) — a particular source of problems for any PHP compiler. Extensive testing was carried out on existing PHP extensions and third-party code. So, although phc no longer appears to be in active development, it is well worth a look, as long as you appreciate the fact that you may be investing time in a project that has no future.

Phalanger

For Windows users, the Phalanger compiler offers PHP compilation, in some sense of the word. Phalanger does not generate native (machine) code. Rather, it compiles the PHP into common intermediate language (CIL) bytecode, which can then be just in time (JIT) compiled by the .NET framework. This probably isn't quite what you'd expect from a PHP compiler, and little is done in the way of optimization. Obviously, it's also only suitable for .NET developers on Windows, so this discussion won't go into further detail.

HipHop

HipHop is Facebook's (open source) answer to this problem — a compiler that takes a PHP script, converts it to C++, and then compiles this into an executable — either with or without its own built-in web server. Thus, HipHop can act as a complete replacement for the traditional setup of a web server and PHP. In this topology, Nginx is often used as a front-end load balancer, providing some of the features missing from HipHop's fairly basic HTTP features.

How fast is HipHop? Facebook reported a 50 percent drop in CPU usage, which is a significant starting point, which will doubtlessly improve even more in the future. Although human-written C++ has the potential to be much faster than this, it should be remembered that automatically translating PHP to C++ can be a tricky business, particularly because of PHP's weak typecasting of variables. This is still one of those situations in which human judgment can win over a computer.

Getting existing code to compile in HipHop is not a trivial matter either and often requires some degree of rewriting. For example, HipHop has no support for PHP's `eval()` or the `mysqli` extension. These limitations mean that HipHop is currently only suitable for large sites that can justify investing the time needed to make it work. For smaller sites, techniques such as opcode caching (and caching in general) can produce greater gains and should be the first line of attack.

As you have seen, opcode caching is a very powerful means of boosting the performance of PHP, and the APC extension is rapidly becoming the default choice. There are still plenty of other things that can aid performance, however, and in the next section, you learn about the negative effects of sessions, and how they can be reduced.

SESSIONS

Sessions tend to be used extensively in PHP as a means of keeping state, but they can be a source of performance issues — particularly when multiple web servers are involved. In Chapter 7, you learned about the issue of session affinity and the various solutions that exist. Let's recap briefly.

Storing Sessions

By default, PHP stores session data in files (usually somewhere like /tmp or /var/lib/php/). Although not perfect, this offers acceptable performance on moderately busy sites. The problems start when you run a pool of web servers behind a load-balancing proxy. With file-based sessions, you must ensure that each request from a particular client always goes to the same back-end server — if the requests hit a different server, the session file won't be there.

The solution to this is to use sticky sessions (also known as session affinity). Here, the load balancer will use various techniques (looking at the client's IP address, setting a cookie, and so on) to ensure that the client always goes to the same back-end server. This isn't perfect either, though. It's more work for the load balancer and stops you from using other balancing algorithms to ensure an even distribution of load across the back-end servers.

At this stage, some administrators look into using network filesystem (NFS) to provide a centralized filesystem to hold the session files. However, NFS performance is poor, and this route is something of a dead-end.

As a result, it's usually best to move away from storing session data in the filesystem. MySQL is often the next choice, and, at first, it seems to be an attractive alternative. Chances are that you're already running MySQL, and PHP can easily be configured to use it for holding sessions. Again, it works reasonably well, but performance suffers on busy sites, and with MySQL so often being a bottleneck, you don't want to be burdening it with a large number of additional queries.

Storing Sessions in memcache/membase

A favorite solution is to use `memcache` as a decentralized session store. Again, PHP has built-in support for this, and using `memcache` is as simple as setting the following options in `php.ini`:

```
session.save_handler = memcache
session.save_path = "tcp://192.168.0.100:11211"
```

> **NOTE** *Incidentally, if you're thinking that MySQL's* MEMORY *engine would be just as good, you may want to refer back to the discussion in the section, "memcache versus MySQL MEMORY Engine," in Chapter 10, "Utilizing NoSQL Solutions."*

The main drawback to using `memcache` is that you don't have persistence. If `memcache` goes down, you lose your session data. Sometimes this is a minor inconvenience to your users and just requires them to log back in. But on an e-commerce site, it may result in customers losing the content of their shopping carts, which will not endear them to shopping with you in future.

Using Shared Memory or tmpfs

If only one web server is used (or, at least, just one web server that needs access to session data — there could be another web server handling static content), you can store session data in memory. This speeds up access and cuts down on disk I/O.

One option is to use PHP's built-in shared memory-based session storage module, MM. Alternatively you can continue to store session data in files but write them to a RAM disk.

In `/etc/fstab`, add the following:

```
tmpfs /var/lib/php5 tmpfs size=128M,atime 0 0
```

Then, issue the following:

```
mount /var/lib/php5
```

For a single web server, this makes more sense than using `memcache` (be it locally or over the network). Even with multiple web servers, you can still use this technique with sticky sessions to eliminate a global `memcache` instance from being a single point of failure.

There are two downsides to this method:

➤ It's not persistent. It's nice to have web servers that you can swap out at your leisure (for example, to reboot or perform upgrades on), but if you do this, you lose the session data.

➤ It's eating up precious memory, and depending on your session length and the amount of data stored, this could be significant.

Overall, the memcache/membase solution is preferred because it removes the need for session affinity, offers persistence, and allows less-frequently accessed session data to be pushed out to disk. There's no point in holding session data in memory for a few hours if the user is long gone.

Session AutoStart

PHP offers the option (via session.auto_start) to automatically start sessions on each page, saving you from manually calling session_start(). While this might seem like rather a useful feature, it's usually better not to enable it. As you've seen, there is a performance penalty associated with starting or resuming a session, and there are often instances where you need sessions on some pages, but not all. By only calling session_start() on pages where it is really needed, you can minimize this performance hit.

Sessions and Caching

If a session is running, PHP may automatically add headers to prevent caching. These comprise a Expires header dated in the past, Cache-Control: no-cache, and Pragma: no-cache. In otherwise static pages, where session data is not used, this is somewhat inconvenient.

This caching behavior can be controlled via the session.cache_limiter and session.cache_expire settings, which control which cache control headers are sent, and when they expire.

Table 12-2 shows the four possible values for session.cache_limiter, along with the HTTP headers that they cause to be sent (where xxx represents the value set in session.cache_expire).

TABLE 12-2: Values for session.cache_limiter and HTTP Headers

VALUE	HTTP HEADERS
public	Expires: xxx Cache-Control: public, max-age=xxx Last-Modified: <date when session was last saved>
private_no_expires	Cache-Control: private, max-age=xxx, pre-check=xxx Last-Modified: <date when session was last saved>
private	Expires: Thu, 19 Nov 1981 08:52:00 GMT Cache-Control: private, max-age=xxx, pre-check=xxx Last-Modified: <date when session was last saved>
nocache	Expires: Thu, 19 Nov 1981 08:52:00 GMT Cache-Control: no-store, no-cache, must-revalidate, post-check=0, pre-check=0 Pragma: no-cache

While session performance is not as big an issue as many of the other topics covered in this chapter, you have still seen several ways in which there is scope for optimizations to be made.

So far, the focus of this chapter has primarily been on optimizing PHP as an application — best practices for installing and configuring how it interacts with the operating system. But this is only half the story, and in the following section, you learn how careful programming of the language itself also plays its part in performance.

EFFICIENT PHP PROGRAMMING

Thus far in this chapter, you have learned about server-level aspects of PHP performance — extensions, compiling, and caching. Let's now take a look at the language itself and ways in which you can write more streamlined code.

Minor Optimizations

There are dozens of small ways in which you can make your PHP code more efficient. But the gains can be so small as to make them virtually insignificant, and the danger is that you end up focusing on these trivial things rather than seeing the bigger picture.

For example, using single quotes is generally faster than using double quotes — the reason being that variables inside double-quoted strings are expanded, so there is extra work involved in parsing a double-quoted string. The gain is tiny, though — less than 1 percent.

Another trivial tip is that `echo "foo", $bar, "baz"` is faster than `echo "foo" . $bar . "baz"`. Again, the gain is less than 1 percent, making it almost pointless.

In some situations, `echo` is faster than `print`, but the gain is approximately 0.1 percent, and this rule doesn't even always hold true.

Major Optimizations

That's not to say that all code optimization is pointless. There are plenty of things you can do that make a significant difference in speed, particularly when dealing with loops, because changes here can have an impact on the speed of every iteration of the loops.

Loops

Following is a classic example seen a lot in the wild:

```
for ($i = 0; $i < count($x); $i++) {
    ## do something
}
```

The problem here is that `count()` is called for every iteration, and although the cost of an individual `count()` is tiny, it can build up into something significant for large arrays.

The solution is to call `count` before the loop, as shown here:

```
$y = count($x);
for ($i = 0; $i < $y; $i++) {
   ## do something
}
```

No doubt, the reason for the popularity of the first method is that it looks cleaner and more concise. (And it eliminates the need to create a new variable.) But the second method is actually the most efficient.

> **NOTE** *Incidentally,* while *and* do-while *loops are a little faster than* for *loops (approximately 25 percent faster, if benchmarks are to be believed).*

Regular Expressions

Regular expressions (regexes) are costly, so it makes sense to avoid using them whenever possible. For example, in many situations, str_replace is just as suitable as preg_replace. (Incidentally, the PCRE regex functions — those beginning preg_* — are faster than the default POSIX regexes.) Regexes are often used for input validation, too (for example, to filter out any nonalphanumerics from a string). But PHP already has some useful functions for doing this — ctype_alnum, ctype_alpha and so on — and these are much more efficient.

When you do need to use a regex, care must be taken. Although a little contrived, it's not too difficult to come up with expressions that use exponentially more CPU time for each additional character in the matching string. Although regexes that take minutes or hours to run are extreme, it's quite easy to lose one-half a second or so on a complex regex simply through not writing it efficiently.

Including Files

It's common to see include files in PHP like so:

```
include "file.php";
```

However, this is not optimal for performance because it causes PHP to search the current directory and each include path until file.php is found. Running strace shows what is going on:

```
# cd /var/www/html
# strace php -r 'include "foo.php";'
...
lstat("/var/www/html/./foo.php", 0x7fff7d2b7680) = -1 ENOENT
(No such file or directory)
lstat("/usr/share/php/foo.php", 0x7fff7d2b7680) = -1 ENOENT
(No such file or directory)
lstat("/usr/share/pear/foo.php", {st_mode=S_IFREG|0644, st_size=4, ...}) = 0
```

First, PHP looks in the current working directory, and then it searches the include paths. On the third attempt, it finds foo.php under /usr/share/pear/.

These extra `lstats` aren't usually a killer, but they are unwanted (especially because disk I/O is usually a bottleneck), and will grow in number for every extra path in `include_path`. The solution is to include path info in the `include()`. Even a relative path will work (useful for including files that exist in the same directory), as shown here:

```
include "/usr/share/pear/foo.php";
include "./foo.php";
```

realpath

PHP 5.1 introduced the caching of paths in an attempt to alleviate this problem. The `realpath` cache is a per-thread cache that stores the location in which an `include` file was found when absolute paths are not given.

Thus, in the first `include()` example, when PHP finds `foo.php` in `/usr/share/pear/foo.php`, it caches this information. Subsequent attempts to `include "foo.php"` will then automatically use `/usr/share/pear/foo.php`, rather than causing PHP to search each directory listed in `include_path`

> **NOTE** *However, the cache is not used if PHP is running in safe mode, or with* `open_basedir` *restrictions.*

The cache is stored in memory and is only a finite size — by default, 16 KB. This is usually too small for large amounts of code, but it can easily be changed via the `realpath_cache_size` ini setting, as shown here:

```
realpath_cache_size=64K
```

To best judge how big the cache should be, PHP provides two functions that allow you to view the size and contents of the cache:

```
var_dump( realpath_cache_size() );
var_dump( realpath_cache_get() );
```

Note that because the cache is held in memory, it isn't persistent across PHP processes. If you run PHP as an Apache module, each Apache thread has its own private `realpath` cache, which persists for the lifetime of the thread (as defined through `MaxRequestsPerChild`, unless there are too many spare child processes). If you run PHP as FastCGI, the cache is again private to each PHP thread. Naturally, this weakens the effectiveness of the `realpath` cache, but it is still a welcome addition to PHP.

If the cache is close to being full, you should probably look at increasing it. But keep in mind that when PHP runs as an Apache module, there could be several hundred instances of the cache, which could potentially add up to a lot of memory.

Another trick you can use to increase the efficiency of the cache is to raise the TTL on entries. By default, this is 120 seconds, which is low for a production server, where paths will rarely be changing. Consider raising this to at least an hour in `php.ini`, as shown here:

```
realpath_cache_ttl=3600
```

Again, depending on how PHP runs, individual threads may not typically last long enough for there to be any gain in raising the TTL further.

The drawback of the `realpath` cache (and of using a high TTL) is that PHP won't see any changes on the filesystem immediately. For example, if you move one of your `include` files to a new location, PHP still looks for it in the old place and throws an error. This doesn't tend to happen much on production servers, and restarting Apache or the FastCGI PHP threads can solve it. Alternatively, you can call `clearstatcache()` to purge the cache — but remember, it clears only the cache of the PHP thread on which it runs.

include versus require

A related subject is whether to use `include()` or `require()`, or even `include_once()` or `require_once()`. The main differences are that `require()` throws a fatal error if the file cannot be found (while `include()` just generates a warning). `include_once()` and `require_once()` stop you from accidentally including a file multiple times.

In terms of performance, there is no clear winner, and different benchmarks have shown contradictory results; although, you should expect the `*_once` functions to be a little slower. Certainly, any real gain is tiny, and your choice should instead be governed by other factors (such as the way they handle files that don't exist).

Garbage Collection

In Chapter 6, "JavaScript, the Document Object Model, and Ajax," you saw how JavaScript uses garbage collection to reclaim unused memory. As with JavaScript, circular references can occur in PHP, too, and PHP uses a very similar garbage collection method to combat the problem.

In PHP version 5.3 onward, by default, garbage collection only kicks in when the root table (basically a list of all variables in existence) reaches a certain level — the default being 10,000 entries. (This threshold can be altered by modifying `gc_root_buffer_max_entries` in `zend/zend_gc.c` in the PHP source code, and then recompiling.) For small scripts, this means that garbage collection may not run at all. But you can trigger it manually if you want by calling `gc_collect_cycles()`. In the case of small scripts, this usually simply isn't necessary. For long-running (but small) scripts, there may be some benefit.

The downside to garbage collection is the additional CPU work involved. If garbage collection leads to significant freeing of memory, this overhead is worth it. But for smaller scripts, the memory gains will be slim, and the extra CPU work often produces no overall benefit.

Autoloading Classes

PHP version 5 introduced *autoloading* of classes, a feature whereby classes can be automatically loaded as needed. The obvious benefit is that it saves you from manually including each class at the top of your code. For example, consider the following:

```
require_once("lib/foo.php");
require_once("lib/bar.php");
require_once("lib/baz.php");
```

Rather that using this code, you can create an `autoload` function to carry out the leg work, as shown here:

```
function __autoload($class) {
    require_once("lib/" . $class . ".php");
}
```

Now, when you come to use the class, PHP will automatically load it (if it has not already been loaded).

```
$x = new foo();
```

Is there any performance benefit to using this method? Potentially, there is. By only loading classes at the point at which a new instance is created, you save the overhead of loading classes that potentially aren't used in your code. Many developers are guilty of simply copying and pasting in a block of `include`/`require` statements, without stopping to think if each class is actually needed in this particular script.

Persistent MySQL Connections

The various PHP MySQL extensions offer the capability to create persistent connections to the database server. With persistent connections, when a script finishes executing, the connection to the database is not automatically closed, but remains open in a pool. Subsequent processes can then reuse these already open connections.

In theory, this sounds great, because it should eliminate the overhead and latency involved in opening and closing connections. In practice, however, the gains are actually rather slim.

When connecting to a MySQL instance running on the same machine as the web server, a UNIX socket is normally used rather than a TCP connection. In this situation, the overhead is tiny anyway, and the benefit of persistent connections is negligible.

With a preforking Apache server, the pool of persistent connections is local to each process. If a new process is forked, it starts with an empty pool. Thus, in many cases, the benefits of persistent connections cannot be realized.

Finally, using persistent connections involves extra self-discipline. You must remember to remove any temporary tables, unlock any locked tables, unset session variables, and so on — activities that would normally be handled automatically when the connection was closed.

Overall, there tends to be little practical advantage to using persistent connections.

Caching HTML Output

There are many ways to perform caching of content — through HTTP headers, reverse proxies, or caching modules in the web server. Yet another option is to perform caching of dynamically generated content by using PHP.

This method isn't as efficient as, say, one of Apache's caching modules (which can serve up a resource directly from the cache, without the need to evoke PHP). But it is a lot more flexible. You can cache whole pages or just fragments, set different cache periods on different resources, and so on.

Let's look at a quick example that illustrates how you might implement your basic caching mechanism:

```php
print "<h2>Users Currently Online</h2>";
$r1 = mysql_query("SELECT username, id FROM users where online=1");
while ($res = mysql_fetch_array($r1)) {
    print "<a href='/profiles.php?uid=" . $res['id'] . "'>";
    print $res['username'];
    print "</a><br />";
}
```

This code simply pulls a list of online users from the database and prints them in a list (along with a link to each user's profile).

Does this information need to be generated on each page load? It probably does not. In many cases, it is quite acceptable for it to be a few minutes stale. So, you can generate the list, cache it, and then (for the next few minutes anyway) serve subsequent requests from the cache, as shown here:

```php
print "<h2>Users Currently Online</h2>";

$maxage = 300; ## Cache for 5 minutes

if (filemtime("./cache/online.txt") < (time() - $maxage)) {

$r1 = mysql_query("SELECT username, id FROM users where online=1");
while ($res = mysql_fetch_array($r1)) {
    $users_html .= "<a href='/profiles.php?uid=" . $res['id'] . "'>";
    $users_html .= $res['username'];
    $users_html .= "</a><br />";
}
file_put_contents("./cache/online.txt", $users_html);

} else {
    $users_html = file_get_contents("./cache/online.txt");
}
```

In this example, the cached HTML fragment is stored in ./cache/online.txt. First, you check the last modified time of the file. If it is longer than 5 minutes ago, you query MySQL and then write the data to the file. Otherwise, you load the contents of the file directly into the $users_htm l string.

There are a few problems with this method. Although you've eliminated the MySQL query (and a little bit of work concatenating strings), you now must read and write a file, and query its last modified time. With a relatively lightweight SQL query, the benefits will probably be slim (especially if the nature of the query means that it will likely be served from the MySQL query cache). But for heavy SQL queries — or computationally expensive PHP code — the benefits are greater, and increasingly outweigh the overhead of the file operations.

Of course, you can also do some of this work outside of PHP via a `cron` job. For example, you could use a stand-alone PHP script that fetches the list of online users every 5 minutes and then writes it to a file. The PHP code in the web page can then just read the contents of this file, without needing to check its `mtime`, saving a little bit of overhead.

As you've already seen, APC allows the programmer to cache variables, so another option is to store your HTML fragments in APC, cutting out the need to read from a file on disk. This method isn't practical for large fragments, however.

Another downside to the example previously given is that it doesn't perform any sort of file locking. If one PHP process attempts to read the file as another is writing to it, or two processes attempt to write at the same time, things will get messy. Things are starting to get more complicated, but rather than re-inventing the wheel, there are a number of PEAR and PECL modules for performing such caching.

A favorite is `Cache_Lite` (available through PEAR) designed to be small and fast, and to handle high levels of concurrency (via file locking). The result is a module that is easy to use and takes the pain out of manually implementing caching. Check out the PEAR website for more details.

Even armed with a handful of tips on which features of the PHP language have the potential to be inefficient, your code can still sometimes run surprisingly slow. A crude way to diagnose such problems is by scattering your code with calls to `microtime()` to determine which blocks are taking the longest to run. Fortunately, there are much more powerful means of finding bottlenecks. In the following section, you learn about `xhprof`, a popular profiling tool that can show exactly where your code is spending its time.

PROFILING WITH XHPROF

`xhprof` is a function-level profiler developed by Facebook and available through PECL. It provides a detailed breakdown of the memory usage and CPU times for each function call, allowing you to see where your code is spending most of its time. This section briefly describes installation and then shows `xhprof` in action.

Installing

As of this writing, automatic installation via `pecl` was broken, but installation is still easy enough:

```
pecl download channel://pecl.php.net/xhprof-0.9.2
tar -zxvf xhprof-0.9.2.tgz
cd xhprof-0.9.2/extension
phpize
```

```
./configure
make
make install
```

You can then load the `xhprof.so` extension in the usual way. The `xhprof` package also contains two directories: `xhprof_lib` and `xhprof_html`. Place these in your web root.

A Simple Example

Earlier in this chapter, you learned how inefficient the following is because it causes `count()` to be called for each iteration of the loop:

```
for ($i = 0; $i < count($x); $i++) {
```

Let's use `xhprof` to confirm this.

```php
<?php
$x = array();
for ($i = 0; $i < 100000; $i++) {  $x[$i] = $i;  }
xhprof_enable(XHPROF_FLAGS_CPU + XHPROF_FLAGS_MEMORY);

$y = 0;
for ($i = 0; $i <= count($x); $i++) {
    $y++;
}

$xhprof_data = xhprof_disable();

$XHPROF_ROOT = "/var/www/xhprof";
include_once $XHPROF_ROOT . "/xhprof_lib/utils/xhprof_lib.php";
include_once $XHPROF_ROOT . "/xhprof_lib/utils/xhprof_runs.php";

$xhprof_runs = new XHProfRuns_Default();
$run_id = $xhprof_runs->save_run($xhprof_data, "xhprof_testing");
echo "Done, go here: /xhprof/xhprof_html/index.php?run={$run_id}"
. "&source=xhprof_testing\n";
?>
```

In this example, you create an array with 100,000 items. Then you enable `xhprof` and ask it to track CPU and memory usage. Next, you include the code you want to profile, iterating through the array. Finally, you disable `xhprof` (you're finished with profiling), and save the details.

Heading over to the URL outputted, you can view the report, as shown in Figure 12-2. The table confirms the suspicions — 100,003 calls were made to `count()`, and the whole block of code took 136 microseconds to run.

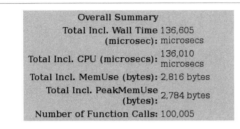

Overall Summary		
Total Incl. Wall Time (microsec):	136,605 microsecs	
Total Incl. CPU (microsecs):	136,010 microsecs	
Total Incl. MemUse (bytes):	2,816 bytes	
Total Incl. PeakMemUse (bytes):	2,784 bytes	
Number of Function Calls:	100,005	

Function Name	Calls	Calls%	Incl. Wall Time (microsec)	IWall%	Excl. Wall Time (microsec)	EWall%	Incl. CPU (microsecs)
main()	1	0.0%	136,605	100.0%	136,046	99.6%	136,010
count	100,003	100.0%	558	0.4%	558	0.4%	64,005
xhprof_disable	1	0.0%	1	0.0%	1	0.0%	0

FIGURE 12-2

Let's try rewriting the loop:

```
$count = count($x);
for ($i = 0; $i <= $count; $i++) {
}
```

Figure 12-3 shows the output.

Overall Summary		
Total Incl. Wall Time (microsec):	4,687 microsecs	
Total Incl. CPU (microsecs):	4,001 microsecs	
Total Incl. MemUse (bytes):	2,960 bytes	
Total Incl. PeakMemUse (bytes):	2,928 bytes	
Number of Function Calls:	3	

Function Name	Calls	Calls%	Incl. Wall Time (microsec)	IWall%	Excl. Wall Time (microsec)	EWall%	Incl. CPU (microsecs)
main()	1	33.3%	4,687	100.0%	4,669	99.6%	4,001
count	1	33.3%	17	0.4%	17	0.4%	0
xhprof_disable	1	33.3%	1	0.0%	1	0.0%	0

FIGURE 12-3

Although memory usage is pretty much the same, the number of function calls has dropped (as you would expect), and overall execution time is down to approximately 4 microseconds — a significant improvement. Of course, it's not often you need to iterate through an array of 100,000 elements, so this is a somewhat artificial example. But it illustrates how useful xhprof can be in diagnosing these sorts of problems.

Don't Use PHP

One of the best ways to improve the performance of PHP is not to use it. Even a lean, highly optimized PHP page takes more memory and CPU, and takes longer to serve than a static HTML file. Creating a new page and automatically giving it the `.php` extension is something that many developers are guilty of, but it's worth taking a step back and thinking whether `.html` might not be more appropriate. Will you actually be using any PHP scripting in the page?

Even for pages that do need PHP, the content is still often fairly static. You might use it to include a common footer, header, and navigation menu, or to pull some paragraphs of text from the database. In these situations, the content is the same each time (except for when you manually update the `include` files or database), and having PHP execute the same code on each page load is unnecessary.

Pages with only modest PHP usually can benefit a lot by being generated offline as pure HTML documents. Consider a site that uses PHP solely to include a common header and footer. Rather than publish these PHP files, you can execute them at the command line, piping the output to an `.html` file. Providing you take care to ensure that the links use the correct extensions, the static version of the site functions identically to the PHP version, but is faster. Of course, if you edit your header/footer templates, you must rebuild these static pages. But if the whole process is scripted, then this is a minor inconvenience.

With a bit of thought, you can extend this logic to more complicated sites. Given how popular it is to offer personalized content to logged-in users, the opportunities to pregenerate the whole page are becoming increasingly rare. But you can still often pregenerate parts.

For example, if the homepage of a site shows a list of currently logged-in users, this information rarely needs to be 100 percent accurate. You can cut out some PHP and database work by using a `cron` to execute the code for fetching the list of logged-in users, dumping it to a file, and then including this via PHP (or writing it directly to your homepage template). The possibilities here are endless.

SUMMARY

Server-side, an opcode cache, is virtually essential and is usually the single most important thing that can be done to improve PHP performance. Sessions can also hurt performance and should be used only when necessary.

Removing unnecessary modules from PHP can dramatically reduce its memory footprint, allowing greater levels of concurrency, whereas compiling PHP from a source can also reap many rewards — not least of which is the ability to compile specifically for your processor type.

It's easy to get bogged down in debates on whether `echo()` is faster than `print()`, but, in practice, many "tips" like this have only a tiny effect on speed. Instead, you should concentrate on areas in which the biggest gains are to be made. Regular expressions are a common problem, as are loops (because any inefficiency inside the loop is multiplied by the number of iterations of the loop). Profiling with a tool like `xhprof` can be an excellent way to discover where the bottlenecks are in a script.

No matter how efficient your PHP code, it will always be several orders of magnitude more expensive than serving up static HTML documents. Many simple sites can be built as static HTML documents, using a scripting language like PHP to construct the pages in advance.

PART III
Appendixes

▶ **APPENDIX A:** TCP Performance

▶ **APPENDIX B:** Designing for Mobile Platforms

▶ **APPENDIX C:** Compression

A

TCP Performance

A good knowledge of the TCP/IP protocol suite is essential to gain full understanding of network performance. Although a full examination of this suite is a bit outside the scope of this book, this appendix briefly reviews the transmission control protocol (TCP) from the perspective of the three-way handshake, interpreting the output of `netstat`, and a couple of techniques that you can use to improve TCP performance.

This is not a definitive guide — whole books have been written on the subject — but it should hopefully serve as a starting point for those wanting to learn more.

THE THREE-WAY HANDSHAKE

When reviewing waterfall views of web browsers that are loading sites, you can see how, for many resources, there is a delay during which the client establishes a TCP connection to the web server. (This doesn't happen for all resource requests because connections that are already open are reused if both sides support `KeepAlive`.) Figure A-1 shows this region indicated by an arrow on the first request for `google.com`.

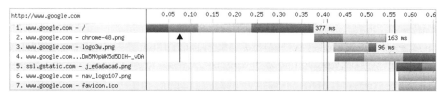

FIGURE A-1

So, what exactly is going on in this time frame? TCP is a reliable, connection-based protocol, and before data can flow, a connection must be established. This is done by means of the *three-way handshake*.

A lot happens during this handshake — for example, timestamps and sequence numbers are set (so that if packets arrive in the wrong order, they can be re-assembled correctly). However, all you actually need to know is that this is a three-step process, as shown in Figure A-2:

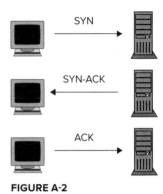

1. The client sends a packet with the synchronization (SYN) flag set.

2. The server responds with a synchronization acknowledgment (SYN-ACK).

3. The client responds by sending its own acknowledgment (ACK).

FIGURE A-2

The connection is now established, and data can flow. For HTTP, this means a request can be issued.

On the Internet (which uses the Internet Protocol, or IP, as the underlying delivery method), each packet has a 40-byte overhead — 20 bytes for IP (at least for IPv4 — eventually the Internet will switch to the new IPv6) and 20 bytes for TCP. The packets have no payload, so their size is small. As such, bandwidth isn't usually a factor in the time it takes to perform the handshake.

However, latency is a factor. If the latency between the client and server is one-half a second, it will be 1.5 seconds before the connection has been established and a HTTP request can be issued. If the HTTP resource requested is small, the overhead of opening the TCP connection can easily be greater than the time spent requesting and receiving the resource (especially if a DNS lookup must be performed). For that reason, it isn't always wise to trick the browser into opening up lots of connections (for example, by hosting resources on multiple subdomains).

Aside from network latency, another consideration is the time it takes the operating system on both the client and server to process and respond to the packets in the three-way handshake. Almost always, any delays occur on the server side. The reason is that the server is typically processing a high volume of packets (possibly hundreds per second), and each of these requires a little bit of RAM and CPU time.

To avoid swamping the network with connection requests, the network stack of the operating system typically queues requests. When viewing waterfall graphs for your site, if you see large delays in connections established (and also the time to first byte, or TTFB), check your server's network latency (using a tool like ping). Also, if it is swamped with connections, the netstat tool is useful for checking latency.

Some operating systems, such as Linux, are highly configurable in how the network stack behaves. But the defaults are usually good, and you need to exercise care if you decide to adjust them — it could make matters a lot worse.

The following is a section of the output of netstat running on a busy Linux web server:

```
tcp    0    0 192.168.0.1:80       10.4.3.2:2417        SYN_RECV
tcp    0    0 192.168.0.1:80       10.4.3.2:2424        SYN_RECV
tcp    0    0 192.168.0.1:80       10.4.3.2:2425        SYN_RECV
tcp    0    0 192.168.0.1:80       10.4.3.2:2421        SYN_RECV
```

```
tcp    0    0 192.168.0.1:80       10.4.3.2:2422          SYN_RECV
tcp    0    0 192.168.0.1:80       10.55.2.145:53922      SYN_RECV
tcp    0    0 192.168.0.1:80       10.4.3.2:2419          SYN_RECV
tcp    0    0 192.168.0.1:80       10.55.2.145:53923      SYN_RECV
tcp    0    0 192.168.0.1:80       10.4.3.2:2423          SYN_RECV
tcp    0    0 192.168.0.1:80       10.4.3.2:2426          SYN_RECV
tcp    0    0 192.168.0.1:80       10.4.3.2:2420          SYN_RECV
tcp    0    0 192.168.0.1:80       10.4.3.2:2418          SYN_RECV
tcp    0    0 127.0.0.1:46948      127.0.0.1:11211        TIME_WAIT
tcp    0    0 192.168.0.2:80       10.143.231.33:42890    FIN_WAIT2
tcp    0    0 192.168.0.2:80       10.4.3.2:2413          FIN_WAIT2
tcp    0    0 192.168.0.1:80       10.19.4.2:2475         TIME_WAIT
tcp    0    0 192.168.0.1:80       10.244.200.74:3675     TIME_WAIT
tcp    0    0 192.168.0.1:80       10.0.4.181:25617       FIN_WAIT2
tcp    0    0 192.168.0.1:80       10.8.144.134:51776     FIN_WAIT2
tcp    0    0 127.0.0.1:47155      127.0.0.1:11211        TIME_WAIT
tcp    0    0 192.168.0.1:80       10.143.231.33:38277    TIME_WAIT
tcp    0    0 127.0.0.1:47041      127.0.0.1:11211        TIME_WAIT
tcp    0    0 192.168.0.2:80       10.99.43.2:39957       TIME_WAIT
tcp    0    0 127.0.0.1:46951      127.0.0.1:11211        TIME_WAIT
tcp    0    0 127.0.0.1:47030      127.0.0.1:11211        TIME_WAIT
tcp    0    0 192.168.0.1:80       10.99.5.5:52704        ESTABLISHED
tcp    0    0 127.0.0.1:47055      127.0.0.1:11211        TIME_WAIT
tcp    0    0 192.168.0.1:80       10.122.4.1:2151        FIN_WAIT2
tcp    0    0 192.168.0.1:80       10.23.5.204:50740      TIME_WAIT
tcp    0    0 192.168.0.2:80       10.1.142.194:2692      ESTABLISHED
tcp    0    0 192.168.0.2:80       10.0.44.29:43449       ESTABLISHED
```

Here, you can see the status for each connection. For example, SYN_RECV indicates that a SYN has been received as part of the three-way handshake. TIME_WAIT indicates a connection is in the process of being shut down. Consult the netstat man pages for a complete list of socket status.

When a TCP connection has been established, ACK flags are still used — this time to acknowledge receipt of packets from the other party. For example, if a web server returns a resource to a client, the resource will likely be split across several packets. (The maximum size of a TCP packet is 64 KB, but the underlying layers also impose restrictions — Ethernet, for example, sets a maximum size of 1,500 bytes.)

For each packet that the client receives, it sends an acknowledgment (ACK) back to the server. This is part of what makes TCP a reliable protocol. If an ACK isn't received within a certain amount of time, the sender assumes that the packet is lost and resends it.

If the sender waited for each packet to be acknowledged before it sent the next one, things would move slowly. Instead, *sending windows* are used. These define the maximum amount of data that the sender is willing to send without receiving an ACK from the recipient. When this limit is reached, the sender will hold off sending any more until some of the data has been acknowledged.

This is great for overcoming the effects of latency. In many cases, the sender can just keep pumping out data, knowing (at least hoping) that the recipient will eventually acknowledge. This does cause problems on unreliable networks, though, because there's a greater chance of packet loss, and a greater chance that the sender must retransmit some (or all) of the data.

The network stack of the operating system defines a default size for this sending window, but it can also be renegotiated during the TCP session. For example, if the server sends out data faster than the client can acknowledge it, the client can ask for the window to be reduced.

TCP PERFORMANCE

You can improve TCP performance in many ways. Let's take a quick look at a couple of the most common.

Nagle's Algorithm

As mentioned, each TCP packet (flowing over an IP network) has a 40-byte header. If the payload of the packet is small, this overhead can be significant. The classic example is a telnet session. Each time the user presses a key, a packet is sent to the server. The payload of the packet is tiny, but it still has the 40-byte overhead. Now, imagine that the user can type five characters per second. That's 200 bytes per second of overhead, and just a few bytes per second of actual data.

In the 1980s, John Nagle was the first person to document this problem, and his solution was that the sender should wait for the other party to acknowledge the data before it sent any more. In effect, this gives the sender a chance to buffer data first, resulting in a larger payload and a lower percentage of overhead. Using Nagle's algorithm, if there are no packets waiting to be acknowledged, new data will be sent immediately. If there are packets waiting to be acknowledged, new data will be buffered by the sender until either earlier data has been acknowledged, or the maximum packet size is reached.

This is great for saving bandwidth, but it increases latency. It is actually counter-productive to overall performance on web servers. Some web servers provide a means to alleviate this performance problem. For example, Nginx provides an option (`tcp_nodelay`) you can use to disable the Nagle algorithm if wanted.

TCP_NOPUSH and TCP_CORK

On Linux, the `TCP_CORK` option achieves a similar result as the Nagle algorithm. It buffers partial frames (for up to a maximum of 200 milliseconds) before sending them out, giving the operating system a chance to group them together. Again, this cuts down on bandwidth (because of less header overhead), at the expense of an increase in latency. FreeBSD offers a similar option, `TCP_NOPUSH`, but this has been plagued by bugs in the past.

You'll sometimes encounter server applications that allow `TCP_NOPUSH`/`TCP_CORK` to be enabled or disabled. `tcp_nopush` in Nginx is a prime example. With Nginx, the effect will be to attempt to send the entire HTTP response inside a single packet if this is enabled.

In general, `TCP_NOPUSH`/`TCP_CORK` should not be enabled if your want to reduce latency as much as possible.

B

Designing for Mobile Platforms

For a long time, desktop PCs accounted for the vast majority of the traffic that a typical website was likely to receive. It was relatively safe to simply ignore mobile users — they made up a tiny percentage of the market and accepted that most sites would not display correctly on their devices. All this is changing, though, and the mobile users currently make up approximately 8 percent of the market — a figure that is rising every year. The days when mobile users were a minority who could be ignored are long gone.

In this appendix, you learn about a variety of methods for detecting mobile devices and serving up custom content to them. In this way, you can ensure that users on devices with lower bandwidth or smaller screens still experience a fast, usable interface.

UNDERSTANDING MOBILE PLATFORMS

It's worth defining exactly what is meant by *mobile platforms*. Once upon a time, it was easy to distinguish these platforms. Cell phones had a screen of approximately 2 inches, whereas PCs had a screen of approximately 15 or 17 inches. However, today, a huge range of devices fall somewhere in between — laptops, netbooks, tablets, smartphones, PDAs — all with varying screen sizes, and (perhaps just as important) different resolutions. Simply designing a mobile version of your site for users who have a cell phone with a 2-inch display fails to accommodate those with, say, a netbook with a 7-inch display.

Table B-1 shows some of the most common mobile platforms, along with their screen sizes and display resolution(s).

TABLE B-1: Common Mobile Platforms

PLATFORM	SCREEN DIMENSIONS (INCHES)	RESOLUTION (PIXELS)
Netbook	5–12	varies
iPad (first and second generation)	9.7	1024 × 768
iPad (third generation)	9.7	2048 × 1536
iPhone (first three generations) 3.5	Varies	320 × 480
iPhone (fourth generation)	3.5	640 × 960
iPhone (fifth generation)	4.0	640 × 1136
BlackBerry Bold 9000	2.8	480 × 320
Samsung Galaxy Tab 10.1	10.1	1280 × 800
Nokia N810	4.1	800 × 480

A less-appreciated consideration when designing a website for mobile devices is bandwidth. These devices are often connected over higher-latency networks, and many service providers charge by the gigabyte. Not only should you accommodate lower screen resolutions, but you should also aim to reduce the size of resources. For example, this means that simply scaling down an image via the width and height img attributes to fit mobile devices isn't a good idea — opt instead to serve a low-resolution version of the image.

In the next section, learn about a variety of methods to achieve this, including the use of JavaScript, server-side detection, and CSS3.

RESPONSIVE CONTENT

Responsive content (of which *responsive images* are a subset) is a somewhat fancy term for a technique that you may already use to some degree — delivering different content to different users based on characteristics of their display capabilities. Technically, this could probably apply to things like gzip content compression (because it is based on whether the client advertises support), but it almost always refers to differentiating mobile users from desktop users, and feeding them appropriate content.

A number of techniques have been developed for this, but not all are completely satisfactory. Usually, a combination of techniques produces the best results. Let's take a look at some of the most popular.

Getting Browser Display Capabilities with JavaScript

Using JavaScript, you can obtain the browser's resolution and color depth — a good starting point to decide on the image dimensions/resolutions to use. You can then use this information to rewrite the URLs in image tags.

In the following code, if the screen resolution is 400 pixels or less in either direction, you iterate through each image tag and prepend /small/ to the beginning of the URL. Then you simply must make smaller versions of each image and place them in the /small directory. The technique could be expanded to give more fine-grained control than simply using normal or small — perhaps one set of images for smartphones and another for tablets.

```
if ((screen.width<=400) || (screen.height<=400)) {
    var images = document.getElementsByTagName('img');
    for (var i=0;i<images.length;i++){
        images[i].src = '/small/' . images[i].src;
    }
}
```

This code must be executed before the browser begins downloading images from the page, so it must go in the document head, and be executed when a DOM ready event fires. Even then, modern browsers are now so aggressive at fetching content (which is usually a good thing) that you can't guarantee that this code will execute before images start being requested. In a worst-case scenario, the browser might end up requesting both the small and normal copies of an image, which defeats the purpose to reduce data transfer. Of course, this technique also relies on the browser supporting JavaScript.

In this example, the normal-sized images are used by default (in the img tags). What if you start by assuming small and then upgrading to large if the screen resolution is above a certain size? This way, mobile browsers still get the smaller images even if they don't support JavaScript. You still inconvenience desktop users who have no JavaScript support. (They'll just see the small images.) But the percentage of desktop PC browsers not supporting JavaScript (or with JavaScript disabled) should be a lot lower than the percentage of mobile devices with no JavaScript.

Finally, it would be only desktop PC users who were affected by the possibility of two copies of the image being requested — and generally they are on faster connections.

Server-Side Detection of Capabilities

Rather than relying on JavaScript, you could also attempt to perform client detection on the server — for example, by looking at the UserAgent string in requests. You might reference your image like so:

```
<img src="/images/logo.php">
```

Then, in logo.php, you can add some logic to read the UserAgent and send the appropriate image. You could either maintain several copies of the image at different dimensions/resolutions, or resize the image on-the-fly (for example, via GD).

Both methods have their pros and cons. It's tedious to generate and maintain multiple copies of an image, but this method does provide the best control. For example, you may decide that a combination of cropping and resizing works best on small screens. Resizing on-the-fly is the easiest solution but is much more CPU-intensive.

Either way, there are two additional downsides to this method:

➤ Using PHP introduces additional overhead. Usually, you'd want to serve images from a lightweight, static file server.

➤ Returning different content from an identical URL could potentially cause serious caching problems. Imagine two clients on the same Internet Service Provider (ISP), behind a transparent, caching proxy provided by the ISP. Client A, which uses a smartphone, requests an image. Your code spots the smartphone and returns a low-resolution version of the image. The response is cached by the ISP's proxy. When Client B, a regular user of a desktop PC, later requests the image, the ISP's proxy sees that it already has the resource cached, and returns this instead. The desktop user sees an image intended only for smartphones. This all happens because the two URLs are identical.

Sending a 3xx redirect error to the appropriate resource is one way to combat the second problem. But be careful of browsers caching the redirect, and remember that this will incur the penalty of an extra HTTP request.

Server-side detection also has the drawback of being less reliable than client-side detection. Using JavaScript, you can accurately obtain the user's display resolution. With a server-side solution, you must make assumptions based on the UserAgent. To do this, you must build a basic database that maps UserAgent to the appropriate capabilities — not a particularly appealing task, given the range of devices out there.

Luckily, help is at hand. WURFL (http://wurfl.sourceforge.net) is an AGPL-licensed XML file containing the UserAgents and capabilities of thousands of mobile devices. Using the PHP API supplied with it, you can easily query the screen resolution of a given client, as shown here:

```
include_once './inc/wurfl_config_standard.php';
$requestingDevice = $wurflManager->getDeviceForHttpRequest($_SERVER);
Resolution Width: <?php echo $requestingDevice->getCapability
    ('resolution_width'); ?> <br />
Resolution Height: <?php echo $requestingDevice->getCapability
    ('resolution_height'); ?><br />
```

A Combined Approach

Neither the client-side nor server-side approach is perfect. The client-side approach relies on JavaScript being present and causes potential race conditions. (Can JavaScript update the path in the img tags before the browser begins fetching them?) The server-side approach interferes with caching, is less reliable, and causes higher server load.

However, you can combine the two approaches to create an effective compromise. The logic goes like this:

1. On the initial page request, JavaScript is used on the client side to set a cookie containing the client's screen resolution.

2. Because this cookie will be sent only for subsequent requests, you use WURFL (or similar) to perform server-side detection if the cookie isn't present. This detection could be carried out in either your PHP code or via mod_rewrite.

3. If the cookie is present, you send out an HTML document containing appropriate image tags (for example, src="/images/tablet/logo.png").

With this approach, you use only server-side detection for the initial page request, before the JavaScript has had a chance to return a (hopefully) more accurate response. And because you rewrite the image tags in the back-end scripting language before sending the HTML document to the client, you don't need to worry about caching problems.

CSS3 Media Queries

Most front-end developers are familiar with the CSS2 feature that allows different style sheets to be used for different media types (for example, one style sheet to use when displaying the document in a browser, and another to use when printing the document). CSS3 takes this one step further with the introduction of media queries — individual rules (or groups of rules) that only take effect under particular conditions. In the following example, the font size will be set at 80% if the display is 600px or less in width:

```
@media screen and (max-width: 600px) {
  .myclass {
    font-size:80%;
  }
}
```

Of course, this is only the tip of the iceberg, and a lot more is possible with more complex CSS rules. A common use for media queries is to hide side bars or extra columns for low-resolution displays. You can even use media queries inside `<link>` tags to selectively load entire style sheets.

In following example, a different style sheet is used, depending on whether the display is aligned in portrait or landscape mode, something that can easily be changed on many mobile devices:

```
<link rel="stylesheet" media="all and (orientation:portrait)"
    href="portrait.css">
<link rel="stylesheet" media="all and (orientation:landscape)"
    href="landscape.css">
```

Determining Connection Speed

Screen size is only one factor in the equation, and it could be argued that connection speed is equally important. This applies to users of desktop PCs with dial-up connections, too. But how do you determine the user's connection speed? You could look for strings like `ppp` or `dialup` in the client's hostname — these are usually reliable indicators of a client on a dial-up modem. But then it's not safe to assume that the lack of such strings in the hostname means that the client has a fast connection — even broadband users can be hampered by high latency and low bandwidth.

The most reliable way to determine the client's latency and bandwidth is to measure it directly — by timing how long it takes the client to retrieve a file — and even this is far from perfect. If the file is too big, you waste the user's bandwidth. If the file is too small, the results can be inaccurate.

This is also one of those techniques that is not good for the initial page request. A bandwidth test like this would need to run in the background after the initial page had been loaded. By that stage, most of the static resources should already be in the browser's cache, making the results of the test pointless. So, although serving different content for those on a slow connection is an admirable goal, it's not a realistic one at the moment.

JAVASCRIPT AND CSS COMPATIBILITY

It's tempting to think that mobile browsers are divided into two categories: those that support JavaScript, and those that don't. The truth is less appealing. Most mobile browsers do support JavaScript, but to varying degrees. Inconsistencies can even be present between identical browsers on different platforms (in the same way that Internet Explorer on a Mac can behave differently than Internet Explorer on a Windows machine).

The same is also true of CSS. For example, Opera Mobile on a Nokia E66 supports `font-size: 150%`. Opera Mobile on an HTC Touch Diamond doesn't. It's a compatibility minefield and is reminiscent of the state of desktop web browsers in the late 1990s. The best advice is to keep things as simple as possible.

The ever-useful `quirksmode.org` has a compatibility table (`http://www.quirksmode.org/m/table.html`) for both JavaScript and CSS, illustrating some of the differences. Be aware, though, that this page dates from 2010, and the landscape is changing fast. At the least it illustrates how subtle the differences between devices can be.

CACHING IN MOBILE DEVICES

The topic of how mobile browsers cache content is a minefield. Not only does it vary from browser to browser, it can also change significantly between the same browser running on different platforms, and even different versions of the same platform.

It has been widely documented that Safari on early versions of the iPhone would not cache individual resources bigger than 25 KB and had an overall cache size of approximately 500 KB to 1,000 KB. That was in 2008, and things have changed since then. However, the overall message is still the same. You can't rely on a mobile browser to cache large resources, and the cache is only a finite size. This is something often forgotten when working with desktop browsers, which generally have large caches. (Internet Explorer 9, for example, uses a maximum cache size of 250 MB.) With a cache size measured in kilobytes, there's a good chance that your resources will have been kicked out to make way for fresher content.

The situation is better in the iPhone 4, which now has a 100 MB browser cache (much bigger than other mobile devices, incidentally). There's a "but," though. This is an in-memory cache, so it does not persist across device reboots, or even browser restarts. This isn't quite as bad as it sounds. Although it's common for desktop users to close their browsers when they've finished, the behavior on iPhone tends to be to keep the browser process running in the background, but minimized. So, browser restarts on an iPhone don't happen as frequently as you might first think.

The same lack of persistence is present in iPads too, but the situation is better in Android (both smartphone and tablet) and Blackberry devices. They generally have a persistent cache equal to the size of the memory cache.

Although mobile devices are often guilty of not caching enough, the opposite appears to be true for the iPhone 5, with developers finding that POST requests are often being cached by default. (They should not be cached, unless explicitly permitted via an Expires or Cache-Control header.)

What is the lesson you learn from all this? Don't rely on a mobile device to perform caching. If you have a bulky website but shrug your shoulders and think it doesn't matter because your far-future Expires headers will mean there is only a performance hit on the first page load, think again. You should probably design the mobile version of your site under the assumption that no caching will take place (and that any caching that does occur is a bonus).

Compression

Compression has been a recurring theme in this book, for image formats (such as GIF and PNG), command-line compression tools (such as bzip2 and gzip), and HTTP compression through gzip and deflate. Despite this diversity in how compression is used, the majority of implementations actually employ the same underlying algorithms. This appendix provides a brief examination of the most common compression methods.

THE LZW FAMILY

The origins of the widely used LZW family of compression algorithms have their roots in two papers written by Abraham Lempel and Jacob Ziv in 1977 and 1978. These papers defined the LZ77 and LZ78 algorithms, two contrasting approaches to achieve compression by spotting repeating patterns.

LZ77

LZ77 looks for patterns of repeating data in previously seen input and replaces the data with a reference to the first instance of the pattern. The reference takes the form of a length-offset pair, indicating the length of the pattern, and it's offset (from the current position). Consider the following stream of data:

    ABCDEFXYZABCD

The second instance of ABCD can be replaced with a length-offset pair, like so:

    ABCDEFXYZ(4,9)

Here, the number 4 indicates the length of the pattern, and the number 9 indicates the offset (nine characters back from the current position).

Sliding Window

In many cases, it would be impractical for LZ77 to search the whole stream of previous data for matches. It could potentially be hundreds of megabytes, and the CPU and memory overhead would be huge.

Instead, a sliding window is used, with LZ77 searching only the most recently seen data. The size of this window varies from implementation to implementation, but is generally measured in kilobytes — deflate, for example, uses a 32 KB window. A larger window means a greater opportunity for LZ77 to find matches in previously seen data. However, it also increases the CPU and memory usage — and, hence, also the time — for compressing and uncompressing.

Performance

Although LZ77 is easy to implement, the compression levels achieved are generally rather mediocre — partly because of the limited size of the sliding history window. You can sometimes take advantage of the knowledge that LZ77 will search back only so far for matches. For example, in some situations, you can re-arrange data in your CSS or JavaScript files so that similar strings of text appear close together. Even so, LZ77 compression isn't brilliant, and it is most often combined with entropy encoding algorithms such as Huffman (which you will learn more about later in this appendix).

LZ78

LZ78 works in a similar way to LZ77, replacing multiple occurrences of patterns. However, whereas LZ77 uses a length-offset pair, LZ78 uses a dictionary. The dictionary is dynamically created based on the input data.

For example, consider the following example data:

```
ABCDEFXYZABCD
```

Table C-1 shows what a basic dictionary might look like. (Dictionary entries are stored in reverse order, but this has been ignored here for simplicity.)

TABLE C-1: Sample Dictionary

INDEX	DICTIONARY ENTRY
0	A
1	B
2	C
3	D
4	E
5	F
6	X

7	Y
8	Z
9	AB
10	BC
11	CD
12	DE
13	EF
14	FX
15	XY
16	ZA
17	ABC
18	BCD

Repeating strings are replaced with a two-part codeword giving the index of the matching string and the first nonmatching symbol to occur after the string. Thus, the example string could be converted to the following:

```
(24,E)(20,Z)(17,D)
```

This is somewhat of an oversimplification because a complete dictionary hasn't been constructed, but it shows the general principles involved. The main performance concern with LZ78 is the size of the dictionary because it could potentially grow to take up all available memory. (Even for this small test string, the number of ways in which it can be tokenized is large.)

All LZ78 implementations limit the size of the dictionary in some way — either by freezing it when it reaches a certain size, removing the least recently used entries, or even erasing it completely. The UNIX tool compress adopts the latter approach and erases the dictionary if it detects that the compression level has dropped below a certain ratio. (The assumption is that the dictionary entries must be poor.) Also, because longer tokens (which are the most wanted) appear later in the dictionary, they are more likely to have been excluded because of lack of space.

Doesn't a large dictionary vastly increase the size of the compressed data, eliminating any saving from the compression? Actually, it does not. One of the cool features of LZ78 is that the dictionary does not need to be sent in the header of the compressed data — the dictionary can be reconstructed simply by analyzing the compressed stream.

LZW

In 1984, Terry Welch published a paper describing an enhanced version of the LZ78 algorithm named LZW. Among the changes, LZW uses a more rigid dictionary format. The first 256 entries are used for the standard ASCII table, with the remaining entries populated dynamically with strings appearing in the data. LZW uses 12-bit codes, giving a maximum of 4,096 dictionary entries. As with LZ77, because the dictionary is (mostly) populated dynamically, the compression ratio tends to start off poorly, but increases as more and more data is compressed, with typical compression levels for text of approximately 50 percent.

LZW was the first LZ-derivative to be widely used. (The UNIX compress tool is a notable example.) But it also became famous for less positive reasons, including its licensing restrictions.

Although LZ77 and LZ88 were license-free, LZW had been patented in 1983 (the holding company eventually becoming Unisys), a fact unknown to CompuServ when it created the GIF image format (which is built around LZW) in 1987. Unisys became aware of this patent infringement in 1993 and began negotiations for licensing. In fairness, the licensing fees were modes, and only applied to big companies — end web developers were not affected. But there was a huge public outcry, and the search was on for a license-free alternative. The result was PNG.

Although the patents on LZW expired several years ago, the likes of LZ77 plus Huffman encoding (which you will learn more about shortly) provide better levels of compression. As a result, there is little impetus to use LZW any longer.

> **NOTE** *Incidentally, the US patent on GIF expired in 2003 (in other countries it was 2004), so the GIF format is now completely free to use.*

LZ Derivatives

Various other dictionary-based encoding schemes exist, based on the original LZ77 and LZ88 papers. Although none of these are as omnipresent as LZW, let's take a brief look at a few of them.

Lempel-Ziv-Markov Chain Algorithm (LZMA)

Based on LZ77, LZMA uses a much bigger dictionary (up to 4 GB), along with a range encoder to keep its size down, and generally offers good compression levels. It is used in 7-Zip (7z).

Statistical LZ

Statistical LZ is based on LZ78 but uses statistical analysis to determine the most appropriate (that is, most frequently occurring) data to store in the dictionary. This keeps the size of the dictionary down, resulting in faster decompression with lower CPU and memory usage. The flip side is that compression takes longer. But this often isn't a concern, and the overall compression ratio is generally better than other LZ derivatives.

Statistical LZ has found a use in compressing ringtones on cell phones — a situation in which compression speed is not important, but compression ratio and decompression speed are.

Lempel-Ziv Ross Williams (LZRW)

The LZRW subfamily of LZ77 variants focuses on increasing compression speed by placing tokens in a hash table. Referencing this table is faster than specifying a length-offset pair. The LZRW families were published during the early 1990s — a time when memory and CPU were a fraction of what is standard today — and LZRW concentrates on efficient use of resources, rather than optimal compression.

These days, the situation has reversed. Memory and CPU are generally plentiful, and higher compression is wanted. As a result, the LZRW family is no longer in common usage, except in specialist, low-resource situations.

Although the LZ family offers reasonable levels of compression, the most popular implementations combine it with some form of entropy encoding (that is, assigning codes to symbols) to further increase the compression ratio. As you learn in the next section, the most commonly used is Huffman encoding, which traces its roots back to a paper published in 1952 by David Huffman.

HUFFMAN ENCODING

The basic idea behind Huffman encoding is to encode the input data, replacing it with a series of symbols. At first, this may sound rather like LZ88, but the implementation is quite different. Rather than using a dictionary, Huffman encoding uses a binary tree that is constructed by analyzing the input data. The tree is arranged so that more frequently used characters are higher up the tree, and, hence, can be referenced by a shorter symbol.

The first step, therefore, is to order the characters in the input by frequency. Consider the following example stream:

    ABCDEFXYZABABCABDECA

The frequency of each character is as shown in Table C-2.

TABLE C-2: Character Frequency

CHARACTER	FREQUENCY
A	5
B	4
C	3
D	2
E	2
F	1
X	1
Y	1
Z	1

A priority queue is then created, with the least frequently occurring characters placed first, as shown in Figure C-1. For clarity, the frequency is shown above each character.

1	1	1	1	2	2	3	4	5
Z	Y	X	F	E	D	C	B	A

FIGURE C-1

To see how the binary tree is constructed, you start at the left and create two child nodes from the first two characters in the queue, as shown in Figure C-2. In the parent node (which would otherwise be empty), you see the new priority.

This tree fragment is then reinserted into the queue. Its priority is the sum of the priority (frequency) of the two characters that it comprises, as shown in Figure C-3.

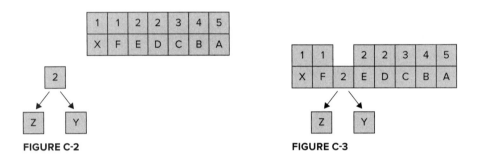

FIGURE C-2   **FIGURE C-3**

The process is then repeated for the next two leftmost elements, resulting in the structure shown in Figure C-4.

These two nodes are joined together (their parent now having a priority of 4), and are re-inserted into the queue, as shown in Figure C-5.

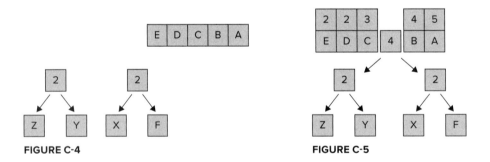

FIGURE C-4   **FIGURE C-5**

The process continues until the final two items in the queue have been joined, at which point you end up with a complete tree, as shown in Figure C-6.

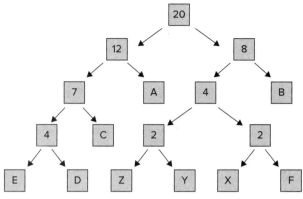

FIGURE C-6

Because each node of the tree has at most two descendants, you can reference any node of the tree as a series of zeros and ones, describing the path that must be taken (starting from the top of the tree) to reach the desired nodes. Figure C-7 illustrates this (with the frequency counts removed because they don't play a final part in the tree).

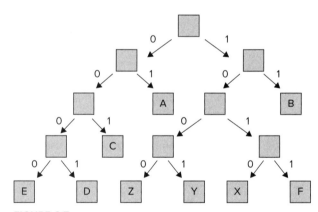

FIGURE C-7

By convention, 0 means follow the branch to the left, and 1 means follow the branch to the right. Thus, the character "E" could be represented by the sequence 0000 and the character "A" by the sequence 01. The original string could thus be encoded as follows:

```
0111001000100001011101010011000011101110010111000100000101
```

Although this seems a lot longer than the original string, remember that you're dealing with binary data here. Although this example has used characters of the alphabet for simplicity, the binary representation of the unencoded string would actually be longer. With 8 bits used for a single character, it would be 160 bits long. Compared with the 49 bits for the encoded version, this is a significant savings.

This savings occurs for two reasons:

➤ The tree is structured so that more frequently occurring characters can be referenced by a shorter path (at the expense of less frequently accessed characters represented by a longer path).

➤ In this example, the entropy is fairly low — only eight unique characters occur in the input data.

If the input data contained all the characters of the ASCII set (256), using a fixed (or randomly generated) binary tree to represent the data wouldn't offer any savings. The real power occurs because the tree is optimized and contains characters that actually appear only in the input stream.

Incidentally, you may be wondering how a decoder knows that (in this example) 01 represents "A"? Couldn't 01 be the start of the path for another character? In this binary stream, how does the decoder know where one path sequence ends and another starts?

As it turns out, another property of the binary tree is that such ambiguities simply can't occur. In Figure C-7, you can see that no other path begins 01. The same is true for every other sequence. Each character occurs at the end of a branch and has no children below it.

Decoding, therefore, is simple and just involves walking the tree. Unlike LZ78 (where the dictionary structure can be deduced from the compressed data), the binary tree cannot be dynamically constructed by the decoder and must be included in the header of the compressed data. This adds some slight overhead, but unless the encoded data is small, it is minimal enough not to be a problem.

COMPRESSION IMPLEMENTATIONS

Huffman encoding and the LZ family are by far the most popular compression methods in use. (Of course, this discussion does not address lossy compression methods such as JPEG because they constitute a whole different story.) To conclude this discussion, let's look at some of the most commonly used Huffman and LZ implementations. Knowing the underlying compression methods used by these implementations is helpful to understand how best to optimize them.

deflate was originally created for PKZIP but is now a staple of the open source world. It uses LZ77 (with a 32 KB sliding window) followed by Huffman encoding, supporting either static or dynamically created Huffman binary trees. Details of which tree method to use are stored in a header block.

PKZIP also introduced an enhanced version, deflate64, which uses a 64 KB sliding window. This leads to slightly higher levels of compression but is not in widespread use because of its proprietary nature. The main implementations are PKZIP and 7-Zip (which is part of the reason why 7-Zip generally offers slightly better compression than its competitors).

You'll most commonly encounter the standard (32 KB window) deflate in gzip, zlib, PKZIP, and 7-Zip.

deflate is an algorithm. zlib is a commonly used C library that implements this algorithm. gzip is an end application that uses zlib. So, gzip implements deflate compression via the zlib library. It's also worth noting that data compressed with deflate will not be identical to data compressed with `gzip`. The `gzip` format defines a header (consisting of a timestamp, version number, and other optional fields) and a footer (containing a CRC32 checksum and the length of the original, uncompressed data) sandwiching the `deflated` body. Thus, `gzip` can simply be thought of as "`deflate` with headers and checksums."

Confusion between the differences of `deflate` and `gzip` is one of the reasons why some web browsers had trouble coping with compressed HTTP content in the past — they either expected `gzip` headers in a `deflate` stream or failed to realize headers would exist in a `gzip` stream. Naturally, purely `deflated` content results in the smallest overall size, but the headers added by `gzip` are still fairly modest and can be useful for integrity checking.

As previously mentioned, the `zlib` library is ubiquitous and forms the heart of PNG compression, via `libpng`. `zlib` also crops up in `rsync`, OpenSSH, and even the Linux kernel.

> **NOTE** *In case you're wondering,* `bzip2` *("the other" UNIX compression tool) uses the Burrows-Wheeler Transform (BWT), which is a different technique but does generally offer better compression than* `gzip`/`zlib`/`deflate`.

INDEX

Symbols and Numbers

"" (quotation marks), HTML attributes, 64–65
? (question mark), placeholders, 253
^ (carrot), regular expressions, 126
$ (dollar sign), regular expressions, 126
3xx, 412
301, 33–34
302 Found, 34
303 See Other, 34

A

Accept-Encoding, 41, 42, 44, 45
access logs, 146
ACK, 368, 407
ACLs. *See* Access Control Lists
active-passive master-master, 269–270
ActiveX, 4
adaptive flushing, 221
adaptive hashing, 217, 221
Adobe Photoshop, 82
Advanced Encryption Standard (AES), 371
advpng, 84
AGAINST, 239
AIO. *See* Asynchronous I/O
AJAX, 136–138, 326
ALL, 237
-all, 300
Allow From, 148
AllowOverride None, 149
alpha transparency, 78
alt, 66

ALTER TABLE, 247, 273
Alternative PHP Cache (APC), 375, 381–388
Amazon, 47, 117, 310, 355
ANALYZE TABLE, 247
Animated Portable Network Graphics (APNG), 109
Antelope, 218, 223
antivirus software, 44
any, 166
aol.com, 4, 21
Apache, 141–158
    cache, 150–155, 361–362
    Cache-Control: max-age, 29
    concurrency, 145–146
    content, 155–158
    DirectoryIndex, 149
    DNS lookups, 148
    dynamic shared object (DSO), 142
    Expires, 29
    FastCGI (fcgi), 167–168
    .htaccess, 149
    init, 387
    logging, 146–148
    MaxClients, 137, 143, 144, 145–146
    mod_cache, 150
    mod_deflate, 46, 155–157
    mod_disk_cache, 150
    mod_fcgid, 167–168
    mod_file_cache, 153
    mod_gnutls, 364
    mod_gzip, 46
    mod_mem-cache, 152
    mod_memcache_cache, 153

    mod_php, 167
    mod_qos, 137
    mod_rewrite, 157
    mod_status, 153–155
    modules, 142
    Multi-Purpose Models (MPMs), 142–144
    multiserver setups, 169–172
    Nginx, 172
    NoSQL, 310
    parallel downloads, 18–19
    performance, 148–150
    PHP, 144, 164–168, 376
    proxies, 170–172
    Redirect, 33
    scheduling application programming interfaces (SCIs), 378
    Secure Sockets Layer (SSL), 155, 366–367
    SendBufferSize, 149–150
    SSLCipherSuite, 369–370
    symlinks, 149
apachepool, 177
APC. *See* Alternative PHP Cache
apc_bin_dumpfile, 387
apc.cache_by_default, 385
apc_compile_file(), 387
apc.filters, 385
apc.slam.defense, 384
apc.write_lock, 384
APNG. *See* Animated Portable Network Graphics
+append, 99
-append, 99
Application Layer, 6
appsession, 185–186
apt-get, 376

arbiters, 341
ARCHIVE, 198
<area>, 90
Aria, 294–295
async, 128
Asynchronous I/O (AIO), 161–162
attributes
    Boolean, 66
    HTMl minification, 64–65
    Sphinx, 299
autoloading classes, 396
Average, 79

B

<b>, HTML minification, 65
-b, memcache, 312
background, 106, 328
background threads, 221
background-image, 91–92
background-position, 91–92
backups, 273, 291–293, 334
balance, 187
bandwidth, 221, 270, 349
$bar, 392
Barracuda, 218, 223
baseline, JPEG, 75
battery backed-up memory, 272
baz, 392
BigTable, 310, 355
Bina, Eric, 4
binary JSON (BSON), 325
binary logs, 271–272, 292, 305
binary protocol, memcache, 320
binary transparency, 78
binlog*db, 264
binlog_flush, 305
BIT, 295
bKGD, 77
Blackhole, 268, 273
block, 93
Boolean attributes, HTML
    minification, 66
boolean innodb_adaptive_
    flushing ini, 221
border-level cache proxies, 25
box shadows, 106–107
BSON. See binary JSON

B-tree, 198, 218, 329, 354
buffer. See also cache
    insert, 216–217
    output, 49–50
    per-session, 204–205
    pools, 214–216
    read, 306
bulk writes, 249–250
bulk_insert_buffer_size, 250
Burrows-Wheeler Transform (BWT),
    425
bzip2, 47

C

-c, 300, 312
cache, 23–37. See also Alternative
    PHP Cache; memcache
    Apache, 150–155, 361–362
    cold, 209
    covering indexes, 246
    FastCGI (fcgi), 166–167
    hot, 209
    HTTP, 9–10, 32–34
    InnoDB, 212–217
    key, 205–210
    Least Recently Used (LRU), 199
    mobile platforms, 414–415
    MySQL, 198–204
        queries, 194, 225–234
    Nginx, 180, 361
    PHP, 381–388, 391–392,
        397–398
    reverse proxies, 397
    Secure Sockets Layer (SSL),
        360–364
    stale content, 30–31
    types, 23–25
    warm, 209, 387
    web browsers, 23–25
CACHE INDEX, 209
Cache-Control, 9, 31–32
Cache-Control:max-age, 28, 29
Cache-Control:max-
    age=<seconds>, 31
Cache-Control:
    must-revalidate, 32
Cache-Control:no-cache, 32

Cache-Control:no-store, 32
Cache-Control:private, 31
Cache-Control:
    proxy-revalidate, 32
Cache-Control:s-maxage=
    <seconds>, 31
CacheIgnoreQueryString On, 152
Cache_Lite, 398
Canonical Name (CNAME), 30
cascading style sheets (CSS), 4,
    91–93
    background, 106
    box shadows, 106–107
    cache, 30
    data URIs, 104
    default values, 104
    expressions, 101–102
    external files, 100
    @font-face, 107
    <head>, 100
    Internet Explorer (IE), 5
    @import, 100
    inheritance, 104
    inlining, 65, 100
    linear gradients, 108
    <link>, 100
    minification, 59–63
    minifiers, 60–62
    mobile platforms, 413, 414
    mouse-over techniques, 104
    performance, 99–110
    PHP, 51
    properties, 102–103
    rounded corners, 105
    selectors, 100–101
    sprites, 91–99
    text shadows, 106
    transformations, 108–109
Cassandra, 310, 356
Cello, 3
certificates
    intermediate, 368–369
    Online Certificate Status
        Protocol (OCSP), 371–372
certificate signing requests (CSRs),
    369
CFLAGS. See compiler flags
CGI. See Common Gateway
    Interface

check, 190
cHRM, 77
Chrome, 36, 44, 109, 114
chunks, 343, 346–349
Chunked Transfer Encoding
  (CTE), 49
chunkSize, 310
CIL. *See* common intermediate
  language
cipher suites, 369–371
circular references, 121–122
class, 93
classes, autoloading, 396
clearstatcache(), 395
CLI. *See* command-line interface
closing tags, 66
Closure Compiler, 56–58
CNAME. *See* Canonical Name
cold cache, 209
collections, 325
color, 78, 81, 97
columns, 240–242, 273
command-line interface (CLI), 67,
  195, 258
comma-separated value (CSV), 249,
  292, 305
comments, 54, 64
comments, 298
commits, 336
Common Gateway Interface (CGI),
  163, 378
common intermediate language
  (CIL), 388
compiler flags (CFLAGS), 380
compiler, PHP, 379–381,
  388–389
composite indexes, 243–244
compress, 42
compression, 417–425. *See also*
  content compression
  GIF, 72
  HTTP, 425
  InnoDB, 223–225
  JPEG, 80–84
  lossless, 72, 80
  lossy, 72
  MySQL, network performance,
    271
  Nginx, 162–163

Shared Directory Compression
  for HTTP (SDCH), 47–48
  zone, 82–84
compress_ops, 224–225
compress_ops_ok, 224–225
compress_time, 224
com_select, 230
concurrency, 145–146, 160–161, 332
  MVCC, 355
concurrent_insert, MyISAM, 210
conditional logging, 147
--configdb, 346
configuration servers, MongoDB
  sharding,
  344–345
connection handling layer, MySQL,
  194
connection speed, mobile platforms,
  413
connect_server, 285
--console, 300
const, 236
content
  negotiation, Apache, 157–158
  stale, 30–31
  web browsers, 10–21
content compression, 39–52
  Apache, 155–158
  CSS minification, 62–63
  disadvantages, 45
  how it works, 41–49
  methods, 42–48
  PHP, 49–51
  Transfer Encoding (TE), 48–49
  users, 39–41
  web browsers, 43–44
Content Encoding, 48
Content-Encoding, 41
Content-Length, 42, 48–49
Content-Type, 8, 156
cookies, 45, 185–186, 412
CouchDB, 354–355
count(), 392
covering indexes, 246
--cpustats, 300, 306
cron, 99, 298
cross-shard joins, 282–283
CSRs. *See* certificate signing requests
CSS. *See* cascading style sheets

CSS Sprite Generator, 98
CSSMin, 63
CSSTidy, 61
CSV. *See* comma-separated value
CTE. *See* Chunked Transfer
  Encoding
ctype_alnum, 393
ctype_alpha, 393
cursor, 330
Cyclic Redundancy Check 32
  (CRC32), 316

D

Data Link layer, 6
data URIs, 85, 104
db.currentOp(), 332–333
db.serverStatus(), 335–336
DCT. *See* Discrete Cosine Transform
default values, CSS, 104
defaults, 184–187
defer, 128
deflate, 42, 43–44, 73, 79, 80,
  424–425
deflate64, 424
DeflateBufferSize <bytes>, 156
DeflateCompressionLevel, 156
DeflateMemLevel <int>, 156
DeflateWindowSize <int>, 156
delay_key_write, 211
DELETE, 195, 230, 246, 249
  concurrent_insert, 210
  TRUNCATE, 252
denial-of-service (DoS), 20, 185
Deny From, 148
DEPENDENT SUBQUERY, 235
DEPENDENT UNION, 235
DERIVED, 235
diff, 291
DirectoryIndex, 149
--disable-debug, 379
Discrete Cosine Transform
  (DCT), 81
distributed indexes, 302–303
distribution master, 268
div, 92, 102
<div>, 102
do while, 393

doctype. *See* Document Type
 Declaration
documents
  HTML, 11
  MongoDB, 325
Document Object Model (DOM),
 115–122
  CSS selectors, 102
  Google Closure, 57
  JavaScript, 111, 115
  mobile platforms, 411
  MongoDB, 326
  rendering, 111
  web workers, 136
document stores, 311
Document Type Declaration (DTD,
 doctype), 64
domain name service (DNS), 34–37
  kernel.org, 10
  lookups, 11, 36
   Apache, 148
   MySQL, 252–253
   Online Certificate Status
    Protocol (OCSP),
    371–372
   parallel downloads, 18
   TCP, 406
   Time-To-Live (TTL), 269
DoS. *See* denial-of-service
downloads, 10–21, 128–130
Drizzle, 295
dropDups, 328
DTD. *See* Document Type
 Declaration
dynamic sharding, 281
dynamic shared object (DSO), 142
Dynamo, 310, 355

E

eAccelerator, 381
eBay, 117
echo "foo", 392
ECMAScript, 112
elasticsearch, 307
elections, 341
<em>, 65
--enable-apc-spinlocks,
 383–384

--enable-inline-optimization,
 379
endpoints, 364–368
env, 34
error logs, 146
ErrorLog, 148
errors, SQL, 260–261
Erwise, 3
European Computer Manufacturers
 Association (ECMA), 112
eval, 58
eval(), 125, 388
Evans, Jason, 219
event bubbling, 119
event delegation, 119–120
evictions, 319
exec(), 127
execution engine, MySQL, 194
EXI, 48
expiration policies, cache, 30
Expires, 28, 29, 87
ExpiresByType, 30
EXPLAIN, 234–237, 276
explain(), 329–331
expressions. *See also* regular
 expressions
  CSS, 101–102
ExtendedStatus On, 155
Extra, 235, 237

F

failover, 322, 341
fail_timeout, 178
fall, 190
False Start, 372
FastCGI (fcgi), 164–168, 387–388
fastcgi_buffers, 166
fastcgi_max_temp_file_size,
 166
favicon.ico, 85–87
fdatasynd(), 217
federated tables, 282
feedback, JavaScript, 129–130
file backups, MySQL, 291
file descriptors, 201–202
file locks, 383–384
file systems

Grid Filesystem (GridFS),
 350–352
Network File System (NFS),
 350, 389
Z filesystem (zfs), 334
File Transport Protocol (FTP), 6
filters, 78–79, 263–264
Firefox, 4–5, 7, 43, 107, 113–114
  DNS, 35, 36
  MongoDB, 326
Fireworks, 82
fixed sharding, 282
Flash, 30
flash memory, 272
FLUSH TABLES, 199
FLUSH TABLES WITH READ LOCK,
 291
flushing, adaptive, 221
@font-face, 107
foo, 34
for, 393
fork, 306
Fowler-Noll-Vo 1a (FNV-1a), 316
fragmentation, 231–232
free(), 320
fsync, 334, 342
fsync(), 217, 294
FTP. *See* File Transport Protocol
FUL, 239
FULLTEXT, 296–297
full_text, 236
full-text searching, 296–307
  Sphinx, 297–306
  tuning, 296–297
FUSE, 352

G

garbage collection, 121, 395
gc_collect_cycles(), 395
gc_root_buffer_max_entries,
 395
Gecko, 109
GET, 25–28, 136, 167
get_hits, 319
getLastError(), 342
get_misses, 319
gettimeofday(), 155

GIF. *See* Graphics Interchange
   Format
GIFSicle, 85
glibc, 219
global, 183–184
@@GLOBAL, 208
global variables, 56, 124–125
GNU Image Manipulation Program
   (GIMP), 74, 82
Google, 37, 94, 117, 219. *See also*
   Chrome
      BigTable, 310, 355
      Closure Compiler, 56–58
graphics. *See also* images; *specific
   formats*
      waterfall, 10
graphical user interface (GUI), 3,
   322–325
Graphics Interchange Format (GIF),
   71, 72,
   80, 96, 109
      favicon.ico, 86
      progressive rendering, 76
Grid Filesystem (GridFS), 350–352
GROUP BY, 204, 237, 240
gzip, 45, 46–47, 424–425
   LZ77, 42
   minification, 53, 59
   Nginx, 160, 162–163
   web browsers, 43–44

H

H.245, 6
handshakes, 360–364, 405–408
HAProxy
   defaults, 184–187
   global, 183–184
   listen, 187–191
   Nginx, 181–191
hardware acceleration, 371
hardware load balancers, 173
HASH, 274–275, 278
hashing, 174, 354
   adaptive, 217, 221
   indexes, MEMORY, 198
   memcache, 322
   PHP, 316
   Upstream Hash, 179

HBase, 310, 356
hdr(name), 188
HEAD, 167
<head>, 100
HEAP tables, 241
height, 88–89
HipHop, 388–389
HIST, 77
Holds Adaptive Hash Latch,
   217
horizontal CSS sprites, 95
horizontal partitions, 274
HostnameLookups, 148
hot cache, 209
hotspots, <area>, 90
.htaccess, 149
htcacheclean, 152
HTML, 11, 63–68, 99
   cache, 30
   DNS prefetching, 36
   meta tags, 31
   PHP cache, 397–398
   test.html, 8
   web pages, 10
htmlcompressor, 67–68
HTMLMinifier, 67–68
HTTP Live Headers, 7, 156
HTTP REST, 354
HTTPS, 176, 359, 360–364
Huffman encoding, 79, 421–424
hype cycle, 309
HyperText Transfer Protocol
   (HTTP), 5–10, 20–21, 359, 406
   cache, 9–10, 32–34
   Cache-Control: max-age, 28
   compression, 42, 47–48, 425
   Chunked Transfer Encoding
      (CTE), 49
   Expires, 28
   requests, 86–87, 88, 96, 137,
      185
   Shared Directory Compression
      for HTTP (SDCH), 47–48
   transparent proxies, 25

I

<i>, 65
ICO, 86

ICT. *See* Information
   Communication Technology
id, 152, 235
_id, 310
identity, 42
IDS. *See* Intrusion Detection System
IE. *See* Internet Explorer
if/else, 56
If-Modified-Since, 25, 28
iframes, 129
ignore_persist, 186
images, 71–110. *See also specific
   formats*
   conditional logging, 147
   CSS sprites, 91–99
   data URIs, 85
   favicon.ico, 85–87
   formats, 71–74
   height, 88–89
   interlacing, 75–77
   lazy loading, 87–88
   maps, 89–91, 93
   optimization, 74–91
   progressive rendering, 75–77
   repeating, 94–99
   src, 88–89
   width, 88–89
image/gif, 8
images/gif, 29
<img>, 88, 93
@import, 100
include, 393–394
include(), 395
incremental backups, 292
index, 236
indexes
   columns, 240–242, 273
   composite, 243–244
   covering, 246
   distributed, 302–303
   hashing, 198
   InnoDB, 247
   Key, 239
   management, 247
   MongoDB, 328–329
   MyISAM, 247
   MySQL, 239–247
   partial, 244

indexes *(continued)*
  prefix, 244–246
  preloading, 207
  replication, 273
  SELECT, 239
  Sphinx, 297–301
  tables, 242
indexBounds, 330
index_merge, 236
indexOnly, 330
index_subquery, 236
infix, 304
Information Communication
  Technology (ICT), 112
information_schema, 224
inheritance, CSS, 104
ini_set(), 50
init, 195, 387
inlining, 56, 65, 100, 134,
  379–380
InnoDB
  adaptive hashing, 217
  backups, 291
  buffer pool, 214–216
  cache, 212–217
  compression, 223–225
  data structure, 218
  file formats, 218
  full-text searching, 296
  indexes, 247
  insert buffer, 216–217
  I/O, 219–222
  memory, 218–219
  monitoring, 211–212
  mutex, 222–223
  partition storage, 277
  replication, 273
  spin locks, 222–223
  tablespaces, 217–218
  threading, 291
  transactions, 196–197
  tuning, 211–225
innodb_buffer_pool_instances,
  216
innodb_buffer_pool_size, 212,
  216
innodb_change_buffering, 216
INNODB_CMP, 224

innodb_file_format ini, 218
innodb_file_per_table, 217
innodb_flush_method, 213
innodb_io_capacity, 221
innodb_max_dirty_pages_pct,
  221
innodb_old_blocks_pct, 214
innodb_old_blocks_time, 220
innodb_purge_threads, 221–222
innodb_read_ahead_threshold,
  220
innodb_spin_wait_delay, 223
innodb_thread_concurrency,
  217, 291
innodb_use_sys_malloc, 218
innodb_write_io_threads, 222
Innotop, 287
INSERT, 230, 246, 291
  bulk writes, 249, 250
  MyISAM, 195, 196
insert buffer, 216–217
inter, 190
interframe transparency, 80
interlacing, images, 75–77
intermediate cache, 24–25, 31–32
intermediate certificates, 368–369
intermediate masters, 268
Internet Explorer (IE), 4, 16, 35, 85,
  107, 112
  content compression, 43
  CSS, 5
  favicon.ico, 87
  just in time (JIT), 114
  PNG, 73
  Scalable Vector Graphics
    (SVG), 74
Internet Protocol (IP), 5, 10, 164,
  171, 269
  Apache, 148
  load-balancing, 174–175
  parallel downloads, 18
Internet Service Providers (ISPs), 23,
  24–25, 35, 412
Intrusion Detection System (IDS), 20
I/O, 217, 246, 306
  asynchronous I/O (AIO),
    161–162
  InnoDB, 219–222, 223

MongoDB sharding, 349
Nginx, 161–162
IonMonkey, 114, 300, 306
isMultiKey, 330

J

JägerMonkey, 113
Java, 4, 67
JavaScript, 111–115
  AJAX, 137
  async, 128
  cache, 30
  defer, 128
  downloads, 128–130
  eval(), 125
  event bubbling, 119
  feedback, 129–130
  garbage collection, 121
  global variables, 124–125
  gzip, 45
  iframes, 129
  inlining, 65, 134
  loading, 127–128
  local variables, 124–125
  loops, 122–124
  merging, 130–133
  minification, 54–59
  mobile platforms, 411, 414
  mod_deflate, 155–156
  MongoDB, 326
  Node.js, 169
  optimizing, 122–136
  PHP, 51
  regular expressions, 126–127
  script, 129
  splitting, 133–134
  unobtrusive, 120–121
  web workers, 134–136
JavaScript Object Notation (JSON),
  311, 354
  binary JSON (BSON), 325
JEMalloc, 219
JIT. *See* just in time
join, 240
joins, 251–252, 282–283,
  337–339
join_buffer_size, 204–205

Joint Photographic Experts Group (JPEG), 71, 72, 75–76, 80–84, 86
journaledMB, 336
journaling, 333–334
JPEG. *See* Joint Photographic Experts Group
JPEG 2000, 110
JPEGTran, 85
JQuery, 138
JScript, 112
JSON. *See* JavaScript Object Notation
just in time (JIT), 114, 115, 388

K

-k, memcache, 312
Keep-Alive, 13–14, 20, 48, 186–187
kernel.org, 10
KEY, 275
Key, 239
key, 235
key cache, 205–210
KEY_BLOCK_SIZE, 224, 225
key_buffer_size, 205
key_cache_age_threshold, 210
key_cache_block_size, 207–208
key_cache_division_limit, 210
key_len, 235
Key_read_requests, 206
Key_reads, 206
key-value stores, 310, 311

L

LAN. *See* local area network
Last-Modified, 25–26, 28
Last_SQL_Errno, 260
Last_SQL_Error, 260
lazy loading, 87–88
ldd, 378
Least Recently Used (LRU), 24, 199, 210
leastconn, 187
Lempel-Ziv Ross Williams (LZRW), 420–421

Lempel-Ziv Welch (LZW), 42, 62–63, 71, 72, 80
    compression, 417–421
    horizontal, 95
Lempel-Ziv-Markov algorithm (LZMA), 420
Length, 310
lexical parser, 381
libcrypto, 378
libketama, 316
libpng.zlib, 425
libssl, 378
lighttpd, 168–169
LIKE, 296
LIMIT, 204
linear gradients, CSS, 108
<link>, 100
Linux, 183, 219, 375, 378, 425
LIST, 275
listen, 187–191
ListenBacklog, 146
LiveScript, 112
LOAD DATA FROM MASTER, 258
load balancing
    MongoDB sharding, 346–349
    MySQL Proxy, 284–285
    Nginx, 163, 173–191
    Sphinx, 303–304
    SSL, 364–368
local area network (LAN), 25, 185
local variables, 56, 124–125
localhost, 147
Location, 171
locks, 222–223, 332, 383–384
logging
    Apache, 146–148
    binary logs, 271–272, 292, 305
    slow query log, 237–238, 331–332
Logical Volume Management (LVM), 293, 334
logresolve, 148
LONGTEXT, 297
lookup. *See also* domain name service
    tables, 280–281
loops, 122–124, 392–393
lossless compression, 72, 80

lossy compression, 72
low_priority_updates, 211
LRU. *See* Least Recently Used
Lua, 285–286
Lucene, 306
Lynx, 3, 44
LZ77, 42, 79, 417–418
LZ78, 418–419
LZMA. *See* Lempel-Ziv-Markov algorithm
LZRW. *See* Lempel-Ziv Ross Williams
LZW. *See* Lempel-Ziv Welch

M

-M, memcache, 312
malloc, 219
malloc(), 204, 320
mapped memory (mmap), 204, 382
MariaDB, 294–295
master, 256–257, 262, 268, 273
master-master, 268–270
MATCH, 239
MAX(), 240
MaxClients, 137, 143, 144, 145–146
maxconn, 183
max_fails, 178
max_heap_table_size, 197
max_matches, 305
maxqueue, 189
MaxRequestsPerChild, 143, 152, 394
MaxSpareServers, 143
MD5. *See* Message Digest 5
md5, 310
Media Access Control (MAC), 6
MEDIUMINT, 295
MEDIUMTEXT, 297
membase, 310, 321–325, 390
memcache, 310
    Alternative PHP Cache (APC), 386
    binary protocol, 320
    client APIs, 313–314
    deploying, 315
    hashing, 322
    key-value stores, 311

memcache *(continued)*
    membase, 321–325
    memory, 320
    multigets, 316
    multiserver setups, 315–317
    multisets, 316
    MySQL, 314–315
    Nginx, 363
    NoSQL, 311–325
    parallelization, 316
    performance, 318–320
    persistent storage, 321
    PHP, 390
    threading, 319–320
    User-Defined Functions (UDFs), 317–318
    User Datagram Protocol (UDP), 320
    virtual buckets, 322
-memlock, 214
memory
    Alternative PHP Cache (APC), 382
    battery backed-up memory, 272
    Document Object Model (DOM), 121–122
    flash, 272
    InnoDB, 218–219
    memcache, 320
    mmap, 382
    Non-Uniform Memory Access (NUMA), 213
    out of memory (OOM), 214
    pages, 163
    shm, 382, 390–391
    Uniform Memory Access (UMA), 213
MEMORY, 197–198, 315
Message Digest 5 (MD5), 316
meta tags, 31
microtime(), 398
MidasWWW, 3
Midpoint Insertion Strategy (MIS), 210
millis, 330
MIME. *See* Multipurpose Internet Mail Extension
MIN(), 240

minification, 53–69
    CSS, 59–63
    HTML, 63–68
    JavaScript, 54–59
minifiers, 53, 58, 60–62
MinSpareServers, 143
Mkill, 287
mlockall, 214
mmap. *See* mapped memory
MNG. *See* Multiple-Image Network Graphics
mobile platforms, 409–415
    cache, 414–415
    cookies, 412
    CSS, 413, 414
    Document Object Model (DOM), 411
    Internet Service Providers (ISPs), 412
    JavaScript, 411, 414
    PHP, 412
mod_cache, 150
mod_deflate, 46, 155–157
mod_disk_cache, 150
mod_expires, 28–30
mod_fcgid, 167–168
mod_file_cache, 153
mod_gnutls, 364
mod_gzip, 46, 51
modifiers, regular expressions, 126
mod_mem_cache, 152
mod_memcache_cache, 153
mod_php, 144, 167
mod_qos, 137
mod_rewrite, 33–34, 157, 412
mod_status, 153–155
modules
    Apache, 142
    Nginx, 163–164
    PHP, 377
MongoDB
    arbiters, 341
    backups, 334
    concurrency, 332
    data integrity, 333–334
    db.serverStatus(), 335–336
    drivers, 327–328
    elections, 341

    explain(), 329–331
    failover, 341
    indexes, 328–329
    joins, 337–339
    journaling, 333–334
    locks, 332
    MySQL, 326, 353
    NoSQL, 325–353
    performance, 328–339
    priorities, 341–342
    processlist, 332–333
    profiling, 331–332
    queries, 329–332
    replication, 339–342, 349–350
    schema, 337–339
    sharding, 343–353
    shell, 326–327
    single-server durability, 333–334
    slow query log, 331–332
    voting, 341
mongodump, 334
mongorestore, 334
mongostat, 336–337
monitoring lag, 261–262
Mosaic, 4
mouse-over techniques, 104
Moved Permanently. *See* 301
Moxi, 322
-moz-box-shadow, 107
Mozilla Foundation, 4
Mtop, 286–287
multidimension stores, 310
multigets, 316
MULTIPLE, 244
Multiple-Image Network Graphics (MNG), 109
Multi-Process Models (MPMs), 142–144, 306, 376
Multipurpose Internet Mail Extension (MIME), 8, 29, 30, 155, 351
multisets, 316
multiversion concurrency control (MVCC), 355
mutual exclusion (mutex), 222–223
my.cnf, 253, 261, 264

my_column, 275–276
MyISAM, 195–196, 205–211
    bulk_insert_buffer_size,
        250
    FLUSH TABLES WITH READ
        LOCK, 291
    full-text searching, 296
    indexes, 247
    partition storage, 277
    replication, 273
myisampack, 196
mysqdump, 291–292
MySQL
    alternatives, 294–307
    ARCHIVE, 198
    backups, 291–293
        comma-separated value
            (CSV), 292
        file, 291
        incremental, 292
    bulk writes, 249–250
    command-line interface (CLI),
        195, 258
    complements, 283–293
    connection handling layer, 194
    DNS lookups, 252–253
    execution engine, 194
    EXPLAIN, 234–237
    FULLTEXT, 296–297
    indexes, 239–247
    init, 195
    joins, 251–252
    Logical Volume Management
        (LVM), snapshots, 293
    MEMORY, 197–198, 315
    MongoDB, 326, 353
    monitoring, 286–287
    networks, 255–308
        compression, 271
        replication, 256–273
        SQL errors, 260–261
    normalization, 250–251
    optimizer, 194
    parser, 194
    partitions, 273–279
    performance, 289–290
    per-session buffers, 204–205
    possible_keys, 242

prepared statements, 253–254
query cache, 194, 225–234,
    314–315
query cost, 248–249
query optimization, 247–248
query profiler, 287–289
SELECT *, 252
sharding, 279–283
slave backups, 292–293
slow query log, 237–238
SQL backups, 291–292
stop words, 297
storage engines, 195–197
table cache, 198–202
thread cache, 202–204
tokens, 248
tools, 286–293
tuning, 193–254
User-Defined Functions (UDFs),
    317–318
MySQL Proxy, 283–286
mysqld_safe, 214
mysqldumpslow, 238
mysqlimport, 292

N

Nagle's algorithm, 408
nbproc, 183
nChunkSkips, 330
Nedmalloc, 219
NetBios, 6
Netscape Navigator, 4, 43, 112, 156
netstat, 407
networks. See MySQL
Network Address Translation
    (NAT), 173
Network File System (NFS), 350,
    389
network interface card (NIC), 270
Network Layer, 6
Nginx, 158–191
    Apache, 172
    cache, 361
    CGI, 163
    compression, 162–163
    concurrency, 160–161
    configuration, 159–160

gzip, 160, 162–163
HAProxy, 181–191
I/O, 161–162
Internet Protocol (IP), 164
load balancing, 163, 173–191
memcache, 363
modules, 163–164
multiserver setups, 169–172
PHP, 164–168
processor affinity, 160
proxies, 170–172
sendfile, 161
server-side includes (SSIs), 163
Secure Sockets Layer (SSL),
    160, 164, 175–176, 365–366
Stub Status, 164
tcp_nodelay, 161
tcp_nopush, 161
worker_connections,
    160–161
worker_processes, 160
NIC. See network interface card
Nitro Extreme. See SquirrelFish
nobody, 312
nocache, 391
Node.js, 169
nondeterministic queries, 233–234
Non-Uniform Memory Access
    (NUMA), 213
non-youngs/s, 215–216
normalization, MySQL, 250–251
NoSQL, 309–357
    Amazon Dynamo, 310, 355
    Cassandra, 310, 356
    CouchDB, 354–355
    document stores, 311
    Google BigTable, 310, 355
    HBase, 310, 356
    key-value stores, 310
    memcache, 311–325
    MongoDB, 325–353
    multidimension stores, 310
    Redis, 356
    Riak, 356
    Tokyo Cabinet, 354
    Tokyo Tyrant, 354
    Voldemort, 310, 355
nreturned, 332

nscanned, 330
nscannedObjects, 330
nYields, 330

O

ob_gzhandler, 50–51
observe, 191
O_DIRECT, 161, 213
Old database pages, 215
ondisk_dict, 305
Online Certificate Status Protocol (OCSP), 371–372
opcode, PHP, 381–388
Open Systems Interconnection (OSI), 6
open_files_limit, 201–202
OpenSSH, 425
OpenSSL, 361
Opera, 35, 44, 109, 114–115
oplog, 339–340
OPTIMIZE TABLE, 247
option forceclose, 187
option httpclose, 187
option http-pretend-keepalive, 187
ORDER BY, 204, 237, 240
OurDelta, 295
out of memory (OOM), 214
output buffering, 49–50
output_compression, 50

P

<p>, 102
Paeth Predictor, 79
pages, 10, 163
Pages made not young, 215
Pages made young, 215
palette, 72
parallel downloads, 14–21
parallel queries, 302–303
parallelization, 316
parse trees, 248
parsers, 194, 381
partial indexes, 244
partial matching, Sphinx, 304–305
partitions, 273–279

Drizzle, 295
PHP Extension Community Library (PECL), 313, 327, 382
peerdist, 48
Percona, 290, 295–296
performance
    Apache, 148–150
    CSS, 99–110
    DNS lookups, 36
    gzip, 46–47
    LZ77, 418
    memcache, 318–320
    MongoDB, 328–339
    MySQL, 289–290
    networks, 270–271
    replication, 270–272
    slaves, 271
    Sphinx, 304–306
    TCP, 405–408
Performance Tuning Primary Script, 289
periodic yielding, 332
per-session buffers, 204–205
persistent connections, 13–14, 396–398
persistent storage, 321
Phalanger, 388
phc, 388
PHP
    Apache, 144, 164–168, 376
    autoloading classes, 396
    cache, 391–392
        HTML, 397–398
        opcode, 381–388
    Common Gateway Interface (CGI), 378
    compiler, 379–381, 388–389
    content compression, 49–51
    efficient programming, 392–394
    extensions, 376–379
    FastCGI (fcgi), 165–166, 387–388
    garbage collection, 395
    hashing, 316
    include, 393–394
    include(), 395
    inlining, 379–380

loops, 392–393
membase, 390
memcache, 313, 390
mobile platforms, 412
modules, 377
MongoDB, 327
Multi-Purpose Models (MMPs), 376
Network File System (NFS), 389
Nginx, 164–168
non-use of, 401
optimization, 375–401
parser, 381
persistent connections, 396–398
prepared statements, 254
realpath, 394–395
regular expressions, 393
require(), 395
sessions, 389–392
session.auto_start, 391
sharding, 282
T9, 48
xhprof, 398–400
PHP_FCGI_CHILDREN, 165
pHYs, 77
Physical layer, 6
ping, 406
piping logs, 147–148
PKZIP, 424
PNG. See Portable Network Graphics
pngcrush, 84
PNGOUT, 84
Portable Network Graphics (PNG), 72, 77–80
    CSS sprites, 96
    deflate, 73, 79
    favicon.ico, 86
    interlacing, 76
    MNG, 109
position-independent code (PIC), 380
possible_keys, 235, 242
POST, 136, 167
PostgreSQL, 307–308
<pre>, 64
preemptive loading, 138
prefetching, 36–37
prefix indexes, 244–246

prefix, partial matching, 304
prefork, 143–144, 306
preopen, 305
prepared statements, 253–254
prepLogBuffer, 336
Presentation Layer, 6
PRIMARY, 235
privacy, 24
private, 391
private_no_expires, 391
processlist, 332–333
processor affinity, 160
profiling, MongoDB, 331–332
progressive rendering, 75–77
properties
    CSS, 102–103
    re-ordering, 63
Prototype, 138
proxies. *See also* HAProxy; MySQL
    Proxy;
    reverse proxies
    Apache, 170–172
    Internet Protocol (IP), 171
    Nginx, 170–172, 177–180
    parallel downloads, 20
    transparent, 23, 25
proxy_redirect, 171
pruning, partitions, 276–277
public, 391

Q

Qcache_free_blocks, 229
Qcache_free_memory, 229, 232
Qcache_hits, 229
Qcache_inserts, 229
Qcache_lowmen_prune, 229
Qcache_not_cached, 229
Qcache_queries_in_cache, 229
Qcache_total_blocks, 229
QEP. *See* Query Execution Path
queries
    MongoDB, 329–332
    MySQL
        cache, 194, 225–234,
            314–315
        cost, 248–249
        optimization, 247–248

profiler, 287–289
    nondeterministic, 233–234
    parallel, 302–303
    slow query log, 237–238,
        331–332
    strings, intermediate cache, 31
Query Execution Path (QEP), 248,
    296
query_cache_limit, 228, 233
query_cache_min_res_unit, 228,
    231–232
query_cache_size, 227, 232
query_cache_type, 227, 228, 233
query_cache_wlock_invalidate,
    228
query_cache_write_lock, 231
queue, Document Object Model
    (DOM), 119
q-values, 42

R

RAID, 272, 274
RANGE, 275–276, 278
range, 236
RBR. *See* row-based replication
RDBMS. *See* relational database
    management system
RDP. *See* Remote Desktop Protocol
rdp-cookie, 188
read buffers, 306
read-ahead, 220
read_buffer_size, 204
read_query_result, 285
read_rnd_buffer_size, 204
realpath, 394–395
real-time (RT), 298, 305
Redirect, 33
Redis, 310, 356
redundant headers, 77
ref, 235, 236
reflow, 117–119
ref_or_null, 236
REGEXP, 296
RegExp, 126
regional compression. *See* zone
    compression
regular expressions, 126–127, 393

relational database management
    system (RDBMS), 193,
    326
Remote Desktop Protocol (RDP),
    188
remoteapache, 148
render tree, 117–118
rendering, 11–12, 111
repaint, 117–119
replicatedo-db, 264
replicate-ignore-db, 264
replication
    active-passive master-master,
        269–270
    backups, 273
    Drizzle, 295
    filters, 263–264
    lag, 259
    master-master, 268–269
    membase, 322
    MongoDB, 339–342, 349–350
    monitoring and maintenance,
        259–260
    monitoring lag, 261–262
    MySQL networks, 256–273
    partitions, 278
    performance, 270–272
    single master, multiple slaves,
        262
    types, 262–263
--replSet, 340
request latency, 144
request-learn, 186
require(), 395
responseLength, 332
responsive content, 410–413
reverse proxies, 142, 170–171, 177,
    366
    cache, 397
    web servers, 23, 25
RGB, 73, 80
RGBA, 73
Riak, 356
RIOT, 84
rise, 191
--rotate, 300
rounded corners, 105
roundrobin, 187

round-robin algorithm, 174
row-based replication (RBR), 262–263, 270
ROW_FORMAT, 218
rows, 235
rpaf, 172
rsync, 425
RT. *See* real-time

S

Safari, 44, 115
sBIT, 77
SBR. *See* statement-based replication
Scalable Vector Graphics (SVG), 73–74
SCGI. *See* Simple CGI
scheduling application programming interfaces (SAPIs), 378
schema, MongoDB, 337–339
script, 129
SDCH. *See* Shared Dictionary Compression for HTTP
searchd, 300
Seconds_Behind_Master, 260
Secure Shell (SSH), 6, 271
    OpenSSH, 425
Secure Sockets Layer (SSL), 359–373
    acceleration, 175–176
    Apache, 155, 366–367
    cache, 360–364
    cipher suites, 369–371
    endpoints, 364–368
    False Start, 372
    future, 371
    handshakes, 360–364
    hardware acceleration, 371
    HTTP, 359
    intermediate certificates, 368–369
    key size, 369
    load-balancing, 364–368
    Nginx, 160, 164, 175–176, 365–366
    Online Certification Status Protocol (OCSP), 371–372
    OpenSSL, 361
    session identifiers, 361–362
    session tickets, 362–363

termination, 175–176, 364–368
SELECT, 195, 240, 243, 246
    com_select, 230
    concurrent_insert, 210
    indexes, 239
    MySQL query cache, 225–226, 230, 232
SELECT *, 252
selectors, CSS, 60, 100–101
select_type, 235
semaphores, 383–384
SendBufferSize, 149–150
sendfile, 161
sending windows, 407
server-side includes (SSIs), 163
sessions, 389–392
    sticky, 174, 179
session affinity, 174, 179, 185–186
session identifiers, 361–362
Session Layer, 6
session tickets, 362–363
session.auto_start, 391
session.cache_expire, 391
session.cache_limiter, 391
sessionid, 152
SET SESSION, 204
7-Zip, 46–47
SFX. *See* SquirrelFish
sharding
    MongoDB, 343–353
    MySQL, 279–283
Shared Dictionary Compression for HTTP (SDCH), 47–48
shared memory (shm), 382, 390–391
SHOW ENGINE INNODB MUTEX, 222, 223
show engine innodb status, 215
SHOW PROFILE, 287–288
SHOW SLAVE STATUS, 259–260, 262
SHOW STATUS, 290
SHOW VARIABLES, 290
showalert, 57
showalert(), 57
Simple CGI (SCGI), 163
Simple Message Transport Protocol (SMTP), 6
Simple Network Management Protocol (SNMP), 174

Sina.com, 117
single master, multiple slaves, 262, 264–267
single-server durability, 333–334
skip-name-resolve, 253
skip-slave-start, 261
slamming, 384
slaves, 273
    backups, MySQL, 292–293
    network performance, 270
    single master, multiple slaves, 262
    SQL networks, 256–257
slave_compressed_protocol, 270
Slave_IO_State, 260
slaveOkay, 341
sliding window, LZ77, 418
slow query log, 237–238, 331–332
slow starts, 187
slowstart, 191
SMALLINT, 295
SMP. *See* symmetric multiprocessing
SMTP. *See* Simple Message Transport Protocol
snapshots, LVM, 293
SNMP. *See* Simple Network Management Protocol
SOCKS, 6
software load balancers, 173
solid-state device (SSD), 272
sort_buffer_size, 204
source, 187
Sparse, 328
spatial compression. *See* zone compression
Sphinx
    attributes, 299
    binary logs, 305
    cron, 298
    data sources, 298–299
    distributed indexes, 302–303
    full-text searching, 297–306
    indexes, 297–301
    I/O, 306
    load-balancing, 303–304
    max_matches, 305
    Multi-Purpose Models (MMPs), 306
    ondisk_dict, 305

parallel queries, 302–303
partial matching, 304–305
performance, 304–306
preopen, 305
read buffers, 306
real time (RT), 298, 305
stop words, 304
SphinxSE, 301–302
spin locks, 222–223, 383–384
splicing, TCP, Linux kernel, 183
sPLT, 77
Spock Proxy, 286
Spreadsheet Syndrome, 251
sprites. See cascading style sheets
SpriteMe, 98
SQL
backups, 291–292
errors, 260–261
SQL injection attacks, 254
SQL_BIG_RESULT, 253
SQL_CACHE, 234
SQLite, 307
SQL_NO_CACHE, 233, 234
SQL_SMALL_RESULT, 253
SquirrelFish, 115
src, 88–89
SSD. See solid-state device
SSH. See Secure Shell
SSIs. See server-side includes
SSL. See Secure Sockets Layer
SSLCipherSuite, 369–370
stale content, 30–31
StartServers, 143, 144
statement-based replication (SBR),
262–263,
270
static file server, 180
static-rr, 187
statistical LZ, 420
stats, 318–319
sticky sessions, 174, 179
stop words, 297, 304
storage engines, MySQL, 195–197
storeBytes, 352
storeFile, 352
<strong>, 65
str_replace, 393
Stub Status, 164
stud, 362, 368

stunnel, 362, 367–368
style sheets, 11. See also cascading
style sheets
Sub, 79
SUBQUERY, 235
SVG. See Scalable Vector Graphics
swappiness, 214
symlinks, 149
symmetric multiprocessing (SMP),
213
SYN flood, 20
sync_binlog, 271
--syncdelay, 334
SYN_RECV, 407
syslog, 148
syslog-ng, 148
system, 236

T

table, 235
tables
cache, MySQL, 198–202
federated, 282
HEAP, 241
Huffman encoding, 79
indexes, 242
lookup, 280–281
management, 247
Tokyo Cabinet, 354
table_definition_cache,
200–201
table_open_cache, 199–200
tablespaces, 217–218
Tagged Image File Format (TIFF), 72
TCMalloc, 219
TCP. See transmission control
protocol
TCP_CORK, 408
TCP_NODELAY, 161
tcp_nodelay, 161
TCP_NOPUSH, 161, 408
tcp_nopush, 161
TE. See Transfer Encoding
termination, SSL, 175–176, 364–368
test(), 127
test.html, 8
TEXT, 297
text shadows, 106

third normal form (3NF), 337
thread_cache_size, 203
threading
background, 221
cache, MySQL, 202–204
InnoDB, 291
memcache, 319–320
threads, 306
Threads_cached, 203
Threads_connected, 203
Threads_running, 203
3NF. See third normal form
three-way handshake, 405–408
TIFF. See Tagged Image File
Format
TIME, 295
tIME, 77
timeMs, 336
timeout check, 185
timeout client, 185
timeout connect, 185
timeout http-keep-alive,
185
timeout http-request, 185
timeout queue, 185
timeout server, 185
timeouts, HAProxy defaults,
184–185
Time-To-Live (TTL), 35, 36, 269,
382–383
Tiny HTTPD (thttpd), 169
TINYINT, 295
title, 66
TLS. See Transport Layer Security
tne.rcvbuf.client, 184
tokens, MySQL, 248
Tokyo Cabinet, 354
Tokyo Tyrant, 354
TraceMonkey, 113
traffic shaping, 176
transactions, 196–197
Transfer Encoding (TE), 48–49
transformations, 108–109
transmission control protocol (TCP),
5, 10,
405–408
memcache, 312
splicing, Linux kernel, 183
transparency, 78, 80

transparent proxies, 23, 25
Transport Layer, 6
Transport Layer Security (TLS), 359
TRUNCATE, 252
TTFB, 406
TTL. *See* Time-To-Live
tune, 184
tune.bufsize, 183
tune.chksize, 183
tune.maxaccept, 184
tune.maxpollevents, 184
tune.maxrewrite, 184
tune.rcvbuf.server, 184
tune.sndbuf.client, 184
Turck MMCache, 381
type, 235, 236–237

U

-u nobody, 312
UDFs. *See* User Defined Functions
UDP. *See* User Datagram Protocol
UNCACHEABLE SUBQUERY, 235
uncompress_ops, 224
uncompress_time, 224
UNI, 239
Uniform Memory Access (UMA), 213
UNION, 235
UNION RESULT, 235
UNIQUE, 244
unique, 328
unique_subquery, 236
UNIV_DEBUG, 222
UNIX, 42, 54, 99, 375
UNLOCK TABLES, 291
unobtrusive JavaScript, 120–121
UnQL, 354
Up, 79
UPDATE, 246, 249, 273
    concurrent_insert, 210
    MyISAM, 195
    MySQL query cache, 230
uploadDate, 310
upstream, 177
Upstream Hash, 179
upstream_fair, 179
uri, 188

URIs, data, 85, 104
url_param, 188
UseCanonicalNames, 152
User Datagram Protocol (UDP), 6, 36, 312, 320
User Defined Functions (UDFs), 317–318
UserAgent, 411, 412
Using filesort, 237
Using index, 237
Using temporary, 237
Using where, 237
us.png, 11

V

var, 56
varchar, 218
variables, 56, 124–125
Vary, 9
vertical CSS sprites, 95
virtual buckets, 322
virtual hosting, 9
Voldemort, 310, 355
voting, MongoDB, 341

W

w, MongoDB, 342
W3C. *See* World Wide Web Consortium
Waiting for master to send event, 260
warm cache, 209, 387
waterfall graphics, 10
web browsers, 3–21. *See also specific browsers*
    Accept-Encoding, 45
    cache, 23–25
        DNS, 35
    content, 10–21
        compression, 43–44
    deflate, 43–44
    downloads, 10–21
    favicon.ico, 86
    gzip, 43–44
    history of, 3–5

HTTP, 5–10
JavaScript, 112–115
Keep-Alive, 13–14
linear gradients, 108
Nginx, 158–191
parallel downloads, 14–21
persistent connections, 13–14
queue, Document Object Model (DOM), 119
rendering, 11–12
Scalable Vector Graphics (SVG), 74
web console, 322–325
web pages, 10
web servers, 141–192. *See also* Apache
    AJAX, 137
    lighttpd, 168–169
    Node.js, 169
    reverse proxies, 23, 25
    thttpd, 169
web workers, JavaScript, 134–136
-webkit-box-shadow, 107
-webkit-gradient, 108
weight, 189
weighted compression. *See* zone compression
what-you-see-is-what-you-get (WYSIWYG), 133
WHERE, 237, 273, 276, 291
while, 393
whitespace, 54, 55–56, 61, 64
white-space, 64
width, 88–89
Wikipedia, 21
Wordpress.com, 117
worker_connections, 160–161
worker_processes, 160
World Wide Web Consortium (W3C), 48, 72
writeToDataFiles, 336
writeToJournal, 336
WURFL, 412
WYSIWYG. *See* what-you-see-is-what-you-get

X

XCache, 381
XCF, 82
xhprof, 398–400
XHTML, 63
XML, 48, 73–74, 311
XMLHttpRequest, 136–137
XtraDB, 296

 Y

Yahoo, 55–56
YCbCr, 80
YEAR, 295
youngs/s, 215–216
YUI Compressor, 55–56
yum install, 376

Z

Z filesystem (zfs), 334
Zend, 381
zlib, 50–51, 79, 156, 223, 424
zone compression, 82–84